Pro-Poor Macroeconomics

Social Policy in a Development Context

General Editors: **Thandika Mkandawire and Huck-Ju Kwon**, both at UNRISD

Social Policy in a Development Context is a new series which places social policy at the centre of research while maintaining the United Nations Research Institute for Social Development (UNRISD)'s unified approach to social development. The series provides a new and exciting contribution to the literature in economic development and social policy. In economic development, social policy has been recognized as an integral part of development, but the literature often falls short of elaborating social policy for a unified approach to economic and social development. In social policy, analysis has concentrated mainly on European and North American countries, and studies on developing countries often lack comparative rigour. The bridge between economic development and social policy will not only contribute to the academic research but also inform the policy debate at the international and national levels.

Titles include:

Giovanni Andrea Cornia (*editor*)
PRO-POOR MACROECONOMICS
Potential and Limitations

Olli Kangas and Joakim Palm (*editors*)
SOCIAL POLICY AND ECONOMIC DEVELOPMENT IN THE NORDIC COUNTRIES

Massoud Karshenas and Valentine M. Moghadam (*editors*)
SOCIAL POLICY IN THE MIDDLE EAST
Economic, Political and Gender Dynamics

Huck-Ju Kwon (*editor*)
THE DEVELOPMENTAL WELFARE STATE AND POLICY REFORMS IN EAST ASIA

Maureen Mackintosh and Meri Koivusalo (*editors*)
COMMERCIALIZATION OF HEALTH CARE
Global and Local Dynamics and Policy Responses

Thandika Mkandawire (*editor*)
SOCIAL POLICY IN A DEVELOPMENT CONTEXT

Shahra Razavi and Shireen Hassim (*editors*)
GENDER AND SOCIAL POLICY IN A GLOBAL CONTEXT
Uncovering the Gendered Structure of 'the Social'

Social Policy in a Development Context
Series Standing Order ISBN 1–4039–4295–1 (hardback) 1–4039–4296–X (paperback)
(*outside North America only*)

You can receive future titles in this series as they are published by placing a standing order. Please contact your bookseller or, in case of difficulty, write to us at the address below with your name and address, the title of the series and the ISBN quoted above.

Customer Services Department, Macmillan Distribution Ltd, Houndmills, Basingstoke, Hampshire RG21 6XS, England

Pro-Poor Macroeconomics
Potential and Limitations

Edited by

Giovanni Andrea Cornia

© UNRISD 2006

All rights reserved. No reproduction, copy or transmission of this publication may be made without written permission.

No paragraph of this publication may be reproduced, copied or transmitted save with written permission or in accordance with the provisions of the Copyright, Designs and Patents Act 1988, or under the terms of any licence permitting limited copying issued by the Copyright Licensing Agency, 90 Tottenham Court Road, London W1T 4LP.

Any person who does any unauthorized act in relation to this publication may be liable to criminal prosecution and civil claims for damages.

The authors have asserted their rights to be identified as the authors of this work in accordance with the Copyright, Designs and Patents Act 1988.

First published in 2006 by
PALGRAVE MACMILLAN
Houndmills, Basingstoke, Hampshire RG21 6XS and
175 Fifth Avenue, New York, N.Y. 10010
Companies and representatives throughout the world

PALGRAVE MACMILLAN is the global academic imprint of the Palgrave Macmillan division of St. Martin's Press, LLC and of Palgrave Macmillan Ltd. Macmillan® is a registered trademark in the United States, United Kingdom and other countries. Palgrave is a registered trademark in the European Union and other countries.

ISBN-13: 978–0–230–00488–7 hardback
ISBN-10: 0–230–00488–1 hardback

This book is printed on paper suitable for recycling and made from fully managed and sustained forest sources.

A catalogue record for this book is available from the British Library.

Library of Congress Cataloging-in-Publication Data

    Pro-poor macroeconomics : potential and limitations / edited by Giovanni Andrea Cornia.
      p. cm. – (Social policy in a development context)
    Includes bibliographical references and index.
    ISBN 0–230–00488–1 (cloth)
      1. Economic policy – Case studies. 2. Poor – Case studies. 3. Macroeconomics. I. Cornia, Giovanni Andrea. II. Series.

HD87. P755 2006
339—dc22   2006043353

10 9 8 7 6 5 4 3 2 1
15 14 13 12 11 10 09 08 07 06

Printed and bound in Great Britain by
Antony Rowe Ltd, Chippenham and Eastbourne

Contents

List of Figures	vii
List of Tables	viii
Notes on the Contributors	xii
Foreword	xv
Acknowledgements	xvii
List of Acronyms	xviii

Part I Overview and Poverty Impact of Main Macroeconomic Policies

1. Potential and Limitations of Pro-Poor Macroeconomics: An Overview — *Giovanni Andrea Cornia* — 3
2. Pro-Poor Fiscal Policy in the Globalized Economy — *Raghbendra Jha* — 27
3. Can Monetary Approaches to Stabilization Be Pro-Poor? — *Sheetal K. Chand* — 49
4. Exchange Rate Regimes for Development and Poverty Alleviation — *Giovanni Andrea Cornia* — 75
5. Portfolio Flows, Macroeconomic Policy and Global Poverty — *Christian E. Weller and Radha Chaurushiya* — 97
6. The Effects of FDI on Growth and Inequality — *Chiara Bonassi, Giorgia Giovannetti and Giorgio Ricchiuti* — 119
7. Safety Nets for the Poor: A Missing International Dimension? — *Sanjay G. Reddy* — 144

Part II Country Case Studies

8. Financial and Trade Reforms and Impact on Poverty and Income Inequality: The Case of Mauritius — *Sunil Kumar Bundoo* — 169
9. Macroeconomic Policy, Growth, Redistribution and Poverty Reduction: the Case of Malaysia — *Wee Chong Hui and Jomo K. S.* — 193

10 The Search for Macroeconomic Stability and Growth under
    Persistent Inequality: The Case of Chile   217
    Andrés Solimano and Molly Pollack

11 Macroeconomic Policy, Inequality and Poverty Reduction
    in Fast-Growing India and China   248
    C. P. Chandrasekhar and Jayati Ghosh

12 Heterodox Macroeconomic Policies, Inequality and
    Poverty in Uzbekistan   282
    Giovanni Andrea Cornia

13 Macroeconomic Policy and Pro-Poor Growth in a Dualistic
    Economy: The Case of Bolivia   305
    Stephan Klasen

14 Has Macroeconomic Policy Been Pro-Poor in Brazil?   326
    Jorge Saba Arbache

Index   349

List of Figures

3.1	Projected and actual current account balance in GRA-supported programmes (in percentage of GDP)	63
3.2	Gross domestic investment in first programme year (in percentage of GDP)	64
5.1	Net capital flows to emerging market and developing countries	98
5.2	Net portfolio flows to select regions	99
5.3	Total capital inflows and foreign exchange reserves: India	107
5.4	Portfolio inflows and size of domestic credit market	112
7.1	Effect of uncertain access to resources on survival	146
10.1	Chile: GDP and GDP per capita levels, 1960–2004 (Index 100 = 1960)	221
10.2	Chile: inflation rate, 1960–2004 (percentage per year)	222
10.3	Chile: exchange rate regimes – Floating band and flexible exchange rate systems periods, 1984–2005	225
10.4	Chile: real exchange rate, 1977–2004 (Index 100 = 1986)	225
10.5	Chile: inflation rate, 1990–2004 (percentage per year)	226
10.6	Chile: terms of trade, 1990–2004 (January 1977 = 100)	227
10.7	Chile: rate of growth of GDP, 1990–2004 (percentage per year)	229
11.1	Terms of trade (by GDP price deflators)	253
11.2	Total government expenditure as a percentage of GDP	254
11.3	Total taxes–GDP ratios	255
11.4	Investment as percentage of GDP	256
11.5	Indices of real per capita income by fractile groups	258
11.6	Budget surplus/deficit to GDP ratio	263
11.7	Trend rates of growth of GDP: sub-periods	265
11.8	Investment rate and rate of growth of GDP	266
11.9	Investment rate and inflation rate	267
11.10	Trend rates of growth of GDP: sub-periods	267
11.11	Annual rates of GDP growth and inflation	268
11.12	Poverty in rural China	279
12.1	Impact of uncontrolled shocks on aggregate supply and demand	290
12.2	Percentage changes in the Gini coefficient and the PHR	298
13.1	Growth incidence curve for Bolivia, 1989–2002	311
14.1	Per capita output growth rate	342
14.2	Ln per capita output	343
14.3	Population under poverty line and GDP	343

List of Tables

2.1	Tax revenue as percentage of GDP	32
2.2	Summary of tax reforms and their impact on the poor	34
2.3	Public expenditure as a percentage of GDP	36
2.4	Successful stabilization funds in developing countries	41
2.5	Tax buoyancy in select low-income countries, 1975–1998	44
3.1	Eastern Europe: IMF programmes and outcomes	62
3.2	Projected and actual current account adjustment in capital account crisis programmes	62
4.1	Countries accepting the obligations of Article VIII of the IMF agreement on the liberalization of the current account	76
4.2	Index of controls on capital account transactions	76
4.3	De jure classification of exchange rate regimes, 1970–1999 (percentages of total observations from 167 countries)	77
4.4	Distribution of de jure and de facto classification in the 1990s	78
4.5	Economic performance under different exchange rate arrangements, 1970–2001	84
4.6	Hypothetical poverty impact matrix of the effects of a real devaluation	93
5.1	Select measures of economic performance in relation to portfolio investment inflows	102
5.2	Relative size of extra tax revenue under the US tax model	114
6.1	Average values of cross-border M&A sales and greenfield investments inflows (as a percentage of GDP)	128
6.2	Sectoral composition of US FDI in selected regions, 1995	129
6.3	Sectoral composition of US FDI in selected regions, 2001	130
6.4	Income inequality changes in sample (27) countries from the 1960s to the 1990s	133
6.5	Income inequalities and poverty	133
6.6	Estimation results of foreign investments in the manufacturing, services and mining sectors (dependent variable: growth)	135
6.A1	Short summary of the literature on FDI and growth	138
6.A2	Short summary of the literature on FDI and inequality	139
8.1	Main economic indicators	173
8.2	Movements in social indicators	173
8.3	House ownership	175
8.4	Share in total tax revenue (per cent)	177
8.5	Current account balance and net reserves	179
8.6	Trends in inflation and interest rates	180
8.7	Productivity indicators: annual average growth rate (1995–99)	180

8.8	Hourly labour cost in US$ terms in the textile industry in 1998	180
8.9	FDI inflows (US$ milion)	181
8.10	Trends in economic indicators	182
8.11	Movements in social indicators	182
8.12	Government expenditure on community and social services	183
8.13	Number of firms and employment in the EPZ sector	184
8.14	Economic indicators	187
8.15	Movements in social indicators	187
8.16	Dependent variable: one-third mean income (relative poverty measure)	189
9.1	Malaysia: incidence of poverty, 1970–2002 (percentage)	194
9.2	Malaysia: federal government finance, 1963–2004 (nominal value in RM million)	198
9.3	Malaysia: federal government expenditure by functional classification, 1963–2000 (percentage)	198
9.4	Malaysia: development and poverty eradication expenditure, 1971–2005	200
9.5	Malaysia: changes in total government expenditure and expenditure on social services, 1973–1989 (percentage of nominal value per annum)	200
9.6	Malaysia: long-term economic track record, 1971–2003	200
9.7	Malaysia: savings, investment and FDI, 1970–2003 (percentage of GNP)	201
9.8	Malaysia: mean monthly household incomes by ethnic group and stratum, 1970–1999	202
9.9	Malaysia: sources of federal government revenue, 1963–2000 (percentage)	203
9.10	Malaysia: distribution of bank credit for select purposes, 1970–2004 (percentages share)	205
9.11	Malaysia: external debt service ratio, 1970–2003 (percentage)	205
9.12	Malaysia: net services balance, 1965–1999 (RM million)	206
9.13	Malaysia: merchandise account, 1970–2003 (percentage of GNP)	207
9.14	Malaysia: annual capital inflows by major category, 1989–2002 (percentage of GDP)	209
9.15	Malaysia: changes in total government expenditure and expenditure on social services, 1996–2003 (percentage of nominal value per annum)	211
10.1	Chile: selected macroeconomic indicators, 1960–2004	220
10.2	Chile: ratio of total external debt to GDP (percentage)	228
10.3	Chile: GDP growth rates of selected countries, 1990–2004	229
10.4	Chile: economic performance by administration, 1990–2004	231
10.4a	Chile: macroeconomic policy matrix by administration, 1990–2004	231
10.4b	Chile: economic behaviour matrix and social policy/public policy by administration, 1990–2004	233

10.5	Chile: households and population below the poverty and indigence line (percentage)	234
10.6	Chile: sociodemographic profile and labour market indicators by poverty strata, 2000 (average)	235
10.7	Chile: population working in the informal sector by income level, 2000 (percentage)	236
10.8	Chile: urban population employed in low-productivity sectors of the labour market, 1990–2003 (percentage of employed urban population)	237
10.9	Chile: household total income distribution, 1990–2003 (percentage)	238
10.10	Chile: income distribution considering pre-transfers per capita income from households by deciles, 1990–2000	239
10.11	Chile: income distribution considering total per capita income from households by deciles, 1990–2000	239
10.12	Chile: distribution of monetary household subsidies by autonomous per capita income (percentage)	240
10.13	Chile: structure of total income households by quintile, 2003 (percentage)	240
10.14	Chile: social expenditures, 1990–2000 (percentage)	241
11.1	Annual rates of growth of national income (percentage)	250
11.2	Structural change in the Indian economy (percentage of GDP)	251
11.3	Growth rates of employment (percentage change per annum)	251
11.4	Trends in poverty (percentage of population below poverty line)	260
11.5	Investment in capital construction by source of funds and administrative relationship (percentage)	264
11.6	Composition of fixed assets formation	271
11.7	Sources of finance for fixed asset formation	272
11.8	Estimates of inequality, 1984–2000	274
12.1	GDP index (1989 = 100) in the Central Asian transitional economies, 1990–2004	283
12.2	Government expenditure, revenue and budget balance (percentage of GDP)	284
12.3	Money and interest rates	285
12.4	International transactions of Uzbekistan (US$ millions)	286
12.5	Exchange rates of the soum	286
12.6	Energy balance of Uzbekistan (thousand tons)	287
12.7	Growth rates of GDP and its components (average annual % rate of change)	288
12.8	Implicit taxes and subsidies on foreign trade due to multiple exchange rate regime (in percentage of GDP, unless otherwise stated)	294
12.9	Percentage structure of the monetary income of the population, 1991–2004	296
12.10	Changes in the distribution of money wages, 1989–2001	297

12.11	Incidence of poverty by location, employment status and level of education, 2001	299
12.12	Employment and incomes of the poor and non-poor	300
13.1	Macroeconomic policies to promote PPG: research findings, consensus policies and remaining debates	307
13.2	Basic economic indicators for Bolivia	309
13.3	Poverty and inequality trends using the moderate poverty line	310
13.4	Annual growth rates per capita	312
13.5	The impact of shocks and policies on growth and poverty	317
14.1	Per capita output growth and social indicators – Brazil	327
14.2	Brazil's economic and social indicators, 1980–2004	329

Notes on the Contributors

Jorge Saba Arbache is Senior Economist in the Office of the Chief Economist, Africa Region, World Bank. Prior to this he was Professor of Economics at the University of Brasilia, Brazil. His research has focused on the impact of trade liberalization and structural reforms on employment, poverty and inequality, as well as on the determinants of performance and competitiveness of firms, FDI and regional integration.

Chiara Bonassi is a research fellow at the Italian Institute for Foreign Trade (ICE) in Rome, Italy. She holds a PhD in International Economics and Law from Bocconi University, Milan. Her work has focused on FDI and outsourcing, with particular reference to the transition countries of Eastern and Central Europe.

Sunil Kumar Bundoo is Senior Lecturer at the University of Mauritius, where he teaches, *inter alia*, Financial Economics, Microeconomics and Macroeconomics. He has worked for WIDER and other institutions on financial liberalization and macroeconomic issues in developing countries.

Sheetal K. Chand is currently Visiting Researcher in the Department of Economics at the University of Oslo, Norway, and worked previously for several years at the IMF. His recent papers include 'Macroeconomics: Which Way Now? Old versus New Styles' and 'Stabilizing Poverty in the Context of the IMF's Monetary Model'.

C.P. Chandrasekhar is Professor at the Centre for Economic Studies and Planning at Jawaharlal Nehru University in New Delhi, India. He has published widely on macroeconomic and political economic issues in South and East Asia.

Radha Chaurushiya is an economic policy analyst at the Center for American Progress in Washington, DC. She worked previously on economic and financial markets research for the Federal Reserve Board of Governors, where she studied the Board's past experiences targeting long-term interest rates.

Wee Chong Hui is Lecturer in Economics at Universiti Teknologi MARA (UiTM) in Sarawak, Malaysia. She has conducted studies on the equity aspects of public finance, fiscal federalism, the Sarawak economy and poverty.

Giovanni Andrea Cornia is Professor of Economics at the University of Florence, Italy and has lectured at several European universities. He was previously Director of WIDER in Helsinki, Finland and has held research positions at Fiat, UNCTAD, UNECE and UNICEF. He has authored or co-authored 11 books and many journal articles on inequality, macroeconomics, poverty and human capital in developing and transition countries.

Giorgia Giovanetti is Professor of Economics at the University of Florence, Italy and Head of Research at the Italian Institute for Foreign Trade (ICE). She is the coauthor of 'Trade Links with the SEECs: Trade Specialization and Industrial Structure' and 'A Tale of Parallel (Non-)integration Processes: A Gravity Analysis of EU Trade with Mediterranean and Central and Eastern European Countries'.

Jayati Ghosh is Professor and, currently, Chair of the Centre for Economic Studies and Planning, Jawaharlal Nehru University in New Delhi, India. She is also Executive Secretary of IDEAs, a South-based network of heterodox development economists. She has authored and edited several books and written numerous articles in development economics, and writes columns for newspapers and journals.

Raghbendra Jha is Rajiv Gandhi Professor of South Asian Economics at the Australia South Asia Research Centre in Canberra. His research focuses on macroeconomics, optimal tax and price policy, and poverty, undernutrition and financial reforms in India. His latest publications include *Economic Growth, Economic Performance and Welfare in South Asia* and *Macroeconomics for Developing Countries*.

Stephan Klasen is Professor of Development Economics at the University of Göttingen, Germany. He holds a PhD from Harvard University and has held positions at the World Bank, King's College (Cambridge, UK) and the University of Munich, Germany. His research focuses on issues of poverty and gender inequality in developing countries.

Jomo K.S is Assistant Secretary-General for Economic Development at the United Nations in New York, and holds visiting professorships at the University of Singapore and the University of Malaya in Kuala Lumpur, Malaysia. He has authored over 35 monographs and edited over 50 books. His recent books include *The New Development Economics*, *The Origins of Development Economics* and *Pioneers of Development Economics*.

Molly Pollack is an independent consultant to international agencies and governments in matters dealing with labour markets, social policies, poverty and competitiveness. Her recently co-published papers include 'International Mobility of the Highly Skilled: The Case Between Europe and Latin America' and 'Urban Poverty and the Labour Market: Access to Jobs and Incomes in Asian and Latin American Cities'.

Sanjay G. Reddy is Assistant Professor of Economics at Barnard College, Columbia University, New York, where he also teaches in the School of International and Public Affairs. He holds a PhD from Harvard University. His research areas focus on development economics, international economics, and economics and philosophy.

Giorgio Ricchiuti is a researcher at the University of Florence, Italy, where he obtained his PhD in Development Economics. He was previously a research consultant for UNICEF. His research focuses on macroeconomics in developing countries, currency crises, and the effects of FDI in both developed and developing countries.

Andrés Solimano is Regional Advisor at UN-ECLAC in Santiago, Chile. He was formerly Country Director at the World Bank and Executive Director at the

Inter-American Development Bank in Washington, DC. He has edited several books on growth, inequality and development as well as a book on political economy.

Christian E. Weller is Senior Economist at the Center for American Progress, Washington, DC, where he specializes in social security and retirement income, macroeconomics, the Federal Reserve and international finance.

Foreword

Modern macroeconomics was cast in the crucible of the Great Depression and for many years was driven by the social objectives of full employment and the social welfare regimes associated with it. Its policy instruments were also constrained by these social objectives. In its developmental form macroeconomics paid special attention to economic growth and structural changes as instruments for the social objective of eradicating poverty and improving social welfare. In the 1980s, macroeconomics was detached from these social moorings, becoming increasingly socially blind. Economic policies and the instruments chosen to implement them were no longer constrained social objectives, such as protecting people's incomes or eradicating poverty. Instead they were almost exclusively assigned the tasks of reducing the twin deficits, containing public debt and inflation, liberalizing product and factor markets, privatizing state assets, and liberalizing external trade and capital flows. Their main function was to re-establish the preconditions for growth; growth itself and safety nets were to take care of poverty. While some of these objectives have been achieved, as in the field of inflation control and trade liberalization, the impact on growth and poverty alleviation has been unsatisfactory in most cases.

It was against this backdrop that calls for macroeconomics 'with a human face' arose. During the 1990s poverty was brought back onto the agenda, culminating in the adoption in September 2000 of the Millennium Development Goals by the United Nations General Assembly in which poverty reduction has become the centrepiece of international development debates. Among the MDGs, that of halving the proportion of people living in extreme poverty by 2015 has attracted perhaps the greatest interest. Yet the achievement of this objective is proving elusive for the majority of countries in Latin America and sub-Saharan Africa, for parts of South Asia, the Middle East and North Africa and, until the late 1990s, for most transition economies. In light of this experience, one would have expected an interrogation of the macroeconomic policies that formed the basis of the 'Washington Consensus'. Instead, one has witnessed a process whereby poverty has been added on to the policy objectives without any fundamental re-examination of the core macroeconomic problems. Tellingly, the countries that have achieved rapid poverty reduction and are poised to reach the MDG of halving extreme poverty – China, India, Viet Nam and a few others – mostly adopted macroeconomic policies that differed markedly, or at least in part, from those promoted by the neoliberal approach. Indeed, while fully adhering to the general principles of secure property rights, market-based competition and microeconomic efficiency, these countries adopted policies in consonance with their local structures and institutions.

The ability to achieve rapid poverty reduction depends critically, *inter alia*, on the nature of the development, the social and macroeconomic policies adopted to promote rapid growth and the extent of equitable income distribution. While scholars and policy makers of different economic persuasions generally agree on the broad lines of suitable pro-poor development and social policies, a similar convergence is nowhere in sight for macroeconomic policies. The nature of macroeconomic policies consistent with poverty reduction remains controversial, and the discord has intensified with the liberalization of international capital movements. Indeed, the economic debate seems to be affected by a growing schizophrenia, with important efforts to explicitly link social and development policies to poverty reduction, and simultaneous promotion of a uniform macro-liberalization package in countries characterized by very different institutional and structural conditions. Disagreements in this area have been exacerbated by rising financial instability and a long series of banking and currency crises with a negative impact on poverty, as well as by growing macroeconomic imbalance in some industrialized countries, huge fluctuations among the main currencies, and the rapid development of difficult-to-regulate international financial markets that have drastically narrowed the policy space of domestic policy makers.

As part of its project, *Social Policy in a Development Context*, UNRISD commissioned research to examine macroeconomic policies in the context of a number of social policy concerns, including poverty reduction and development. The result is this volume, one of the first attempts to articulate a set of principles to inspire the formulation of macroeconomic policies that – together with supportive development and social policies – will facilitate the achievement of the goal of reducing poverty in the years ahead. The collection of studies, assembled by Professor Giovanni Andrea Cornia of the University of Florence and former Director of WIDER, reviews the respective problems of different approaches to macroeconomic policy, and proposes some broad principles that should characterize a pro-poor macroeconomic policy that – after adaptation to the local circumstances of each country – can help to promote growth and poverty alleviation in a macroeconomically sustainable way. The collection represents a unique combination. It discusses the potential and limitations of, as well as agreement and disagreement about, fiscal, monetary, exchange rate and FDI policies, controls on portfolio flows and international safety nets. And this is merged with analysis of the approaches to macro policy formulation in eight countries. Chile, China, India, Malaysia and Mauritius succeeded in rapidly reducing poverty, including by adopting macro policies in tune with local conditions and institutions; in the three other countries – Bolivia, Brazil and Uzbekistan – the results were less satisfactory, because of inappropriate macroeconomic choices or the limitations faced by these policies in countries with a large subsistence sector.

UNRISD is grateful to the Swedish International Development Cooperation Agency (Sida) and the United Kingdom Department for International Development (DFID) for their financial support for the research on which this volume is based. I would also like to take this opportunity to express our gratitude to the governments of Denmark, Finland, Mexico, Norway, Sweden, Switzerland and the United Kingdom for their contributions to our core budget, without which work on individual projects would not be possible.

THANDIKA MKANDAWIRE
Director, UNRISD
December 2005

Acknowledgements

This volume would not have seen the light of day without the collective effort of many people working together in myriad ways. To start with, my sincere thanks go to Thandika Mkandawire, Director of UNRISD, for enthusiastically accepting my proposal to launch a research project in this area. Warm thanks also go to the contributors for their precious time and scholarly application, their original analyses, and their patience in revising their papers (often several times). My gratitude goes to participants in the ACDC workshop held in Antigua, Guatemala, in September 2003 for comments on the interaction between macroeconomic and social policy; to the external co-ordinators of UNRISD research on Social Policy in a Development Context who met in Geneva in April 2002, and whose comments helped focus on some of the poverty issues related to global economic policies; and to contributors to this volume who attended the project workshop at the University of Florence in February 2005. The frank comments and useful discussions at that meeting have helped in revising, often radically, the initial drafts of the chapters included in this volume.

Throughout its life, the general articulation of the project benefited substantially from the keen insights of economists and social scientists from different academic and research institutions, including Yilmaz Akyuz, Yusuf Bangura, Ha-Joon Chang, Gerry Helleiner, Terry McKinley, Thandika Mkandawire and José Antonio Ocampo.

At the University of Florence, particular thanks go to Simone Bertoli, Marco Dardi, Vinicio Guidi and Pan Yotopoulos for their comments on papers presented at the workshop, and to Simone Bertoli and Luca Tiberti for their cheerful support in the workshop organization. At UNRISD, Josephine Grin-Yates, Angela Meijer and Wendy Salvo provided enthusiastic, efficient and patient support in administering the project and organizing the Florence meeting; and AvisAnne Julien, Maria V. Aviles Blanco and Jenifer Freedman ensured the English editing of the manuscript and its formatting, and helped keep contact with the publisher. To all of them goes my gratitude for their patience, for accepting with a smile the numerous changes and revisions and, more generally, for excellent professional support.

GIOVANNI ANDREA CORNIA
University of Florence
December 2005

List of Acronyms

ACP	Africa, Caribbean and Pacific
AFL-CIO	American Federation of Labor and Congress of Industrial Organizations
AFTA	ASEAN Free Trade Area
AGOA	Africa Growth and Opportunity Act
ANDE	A Nou Diboute Ensam
APEC	Asia Pacific Economic Cooperation
ASEAN	Association of South East Asian Nations
BBC	basket, band and crawl
BOI	Board of Investment
BOM	Bank of Mauritius
BOP	Balance of payments
BWIs	Bretton Woods Institutions
CAR	Central Asian Republic
CAAS	Chinese Academy of Social Sciences
CB	Central Bank
CEEC	Central and Eastern European countries
CEEP	Centre for Effective Economic Policy
CFF	Compensatory Financing Facility
CGE	Computable General Equilibrium
CPI	Commodity Price Insurance
DC	developed countries
EBRD	European Bank for Construction and Development
ECLAC	Economic Commission for Latin America and the Caribbean
EIU	Economist Intelligence Unit
EPZ	Export Processing Zone
EU	European Union
FDI	Foreign Direct Investment
FII	Foreign Institutional Investor
FL	Financial Liberalization
FLEX	European Union Instrument for Compensation of Loss of Export Earnings
FP	Financial Programming
GATT	General Agreement on Tariffs and Trade
GCI	Global Commodity Insurer
GDP	Gross Domestic Product
GNP	Gross National Product
HBS	Household Budget Survey
HDI	Human Development Index
HIPC	heavily indebted poor countries
ICT	Information and Communication Technology
IFAD	International Fund for Agricultural Diversification
IMF	International Monetary Fund
ISI	import substitution strategy

List of Acronyms xix

ITC	Investment Tax Credit
KLCI	Kuala Lumpur Composite Index
LDC	least developed countries
M&A	mergers and acquisitions
MFA	Multi-Fibre Agreement
MNB	Multinational bank
NBU	National Bank of Uzbekistan
NHDC	National Housing Development Corporation
NEP	New Economic Policy
NPL	non-performing loans
NSF	National Solidarity Fund
OECD	Organisation for Economic Co-operation and Development
OLS	ordinary least squares
PAYE	Pay As You Earn
PBC	People's Bank of China
PHR	poverty headcount ratio
PPG	pro-poor growth
PPM	pro-poor macroeconomics
PRGF	Poverty Reduction and Growth Facility
PRSP	Poverty Reduction Strategy Papers
R&D	research and development
RM	Ringitt Malaysia
SDR	Special Drawing Rights
SOE	state-owned enterprises
SMEs	small and medium-sized enterprises
SSSP	Sugar Sector Strategic Plan
STABEX	Stabilization of Export Earnings of Agricultural Commodities
SYSMIN	System for Mining Assistance
TFP	total factor productivity
TFSIVG	Trust Fund for the Social Integration of Vulnerable Groups
TVEs	Township and Villages Enterprises
UNCTAD	United Nations Conference on Trade and Development
UNDP	United Nations Development Programme
UNICEF	United Nations Children's Fund
UNU	United Nations University
UNRISD	United Nations Research Institute for Social Development
US	United States
VAT	value added tax
VRS	Voluntary Retirement Scheme
WB	World Bank
WDI	World Development Indicators
WIDER	World Institute for Development Economics Research
WTO	World Trade Organization

Part I

Overview and Poverty Impact of Main Macroeconomic Policies

1
Potential and Limitations of Pro-Poor Macroeconomics: An Overview

Giovanni Andrea Cornia[1]

Introduction

Since the mid-1990s, poverty reduction and the achievement of better living conditions in poor countries have slowly gained a place on the national policy agenda of developing countries, while, following the adoption of the Millennium Development Goals, the achievement of quantitative targets in these areas has become the main goal of international development.

The ability to achieve such goals, and in particular the goal of halving the incidence of income poverty by 2015, critically depends on how much pro-poor growth (PPG) will be realized. In this regard, a huge literature has developed on the factors that lead to PPG, including initial conditions, factors endowment, comparative advantages, exogenous shocks, external financing and public policies. Simplifying a little, the latter can be divided into macroeconomic, development and social policies. A key issue of PPG is the extent to which these three sets of policies accelerate growth and improve the distribution of income. In this regard, the theoretical debate of the last two decades has led to an important convergence among different schools of thought about the development and social policies that reduce poverty.[2]

A similar convergence has not yet been reached for macroeconomic policies. While there is also agreement in this area about the need for avoiding the excesses of macroeconomic populism, viewpoints still differ on how ambitious stabilization targets should be, the choice of the exchange rate, the effectiveness of devaluation, the appropriate level of taxation, the extent of deregulation, the opening of the capital account, the effectiveness of capital controls, the speed of adjustment to shocks, and so on. This disagreement has become even more acute in the wake of a string of macroeconomic crises and of the growing need to orient public policy toward poverty reduction.

In the past, macroeconomic policies were traditionally assigned the tasks of reducing the twin deficits, containing public debt and inflation, liberalizing product and factors markets, privatizing state assets and liberalizing external trade and capital flows. Their success or failure was assessed in terms of the extent of reforms implementation in these areas and not of their poverty impact, as it was felt that their main task was to re-establish the preconditions for growth, and that growth itself, along with safety nets, would have taken care of poverty. In most developing and transitional countries, the implementation of such an approach has reduced inflation and, to a lesser extent, current account deficits. Yet, the growth performance and poverty reduction were unsatisfactory. With rare exceptions, in the 1980s and 1990s, growth remained elusive in Latin America, sub-Saharan Africa, the Middle East and North Africa and, until the late 1990s, in most transition economies. In these regions, between 1987 and 2000, poverty declined less rapidly than required to halve poverty by 2015. Where growth accelerated and poverty declined, as in China, India and Viet Nam (see Chapter 11), macroeconomic and development policies differed markedly from those promoted by the liberal approach. While the above disappointing outcomes might have been caused by inappropriate development and social policies, unexpected shocks or unfavourable initial conditions, this volume argues that they were due to an important extent to unexpected problems caused by liberal macroeconomic policies.

Thus, the nature of a pro-poor macroeconomic (PPM) policy remains controversial, and the controversy has intensified with the liberalization of the capital account and rapid all around liberalization. In this regard, this volume briefly reviews the problems of unsustainable packages, macroeconomic populism and liberal policies, and then proposes the elements of an intermediate approach that – after adaptation to local circumstances – can achieve the objective of promoting growth and poverty alleviation in a sustainable way. The search for an innovative PPM is made even more pressing because of two considerations. First, several macroeconomic problems, such as high levels of inflation, that led to the implementation of stringent fiscal and monetary policies are no longer present. The main macro imbalances are caused now by the policies followed in the major industrialized countries, the United States *in primis*, and the development of international financial markets that have drastically narrowed the policy space of national governments. Between 1992 and 2001, the daily turnover in the foreign exchange market increased from a daily average of $0.7 trillion to $1.2 trillion, which is more than 50 times the daily trade in goods and services and 10 times that in securities. As a result, the combined official reserves of all central banks have fallen from about 15 days of private turnover in the foreign exchange market in 1977 to about one day in 1995 (Bhaduri 2005). Because of these trends, national governments are now compelled to follow policies aligned to the expectations of financial markets.

Unsustainable, populist and intermediate macroeconomic regimes

Unsustainable and populist macroeconomic policy regimes

There are many examples of unsustainable macroeconomic policies that are sanctioned by the International Monetary Fund (IMF). These policies are only briefly mentioned here, as their problems are well understood; rather, the main focus of this volume is on the limitations of liberal macroeconomics and the search for a PPM.

While the research evidence shows that budgetary stability is a necessary – though not sufficient – precondition for PPG (Klasen 2004), several countries are characterized by a weak fiscal policy. This is most often due to the inability or unwillingness to raise an adequate amount of tax revenue – as often observed in highly informal or unequal economies – with the result that even moderate levels of public expenditures lead to persistent deficits that are financed with monetary emissions, state bonds carrying high interest rates or external borrowing. While there is nothing wrong with budget deficits per se if they are financed with domestic bonds, the level of debt is non-explosive, the level of output is well within the production possibility frontier and public expenditure creates productive infrastructure, this is not so when the deficit is financed with excessive seignorage or foreign borrowing contracted under a fixed peg. The Russian Federation in 1996–1998 and Argentina in 1996–2001 are just two examples of how a weak fiscal policy leads to crises and poverty rises.

A second unsustainable policy concerns the adoption of a fixed nominal exchange rate. Such a regime is unable to cope with external shocks, is prone to speculative attacks and unavoidably leads to an appreciation of the real exchange rate. In turn, this provokes balance-of-payments difficulties, large sudden devaluations and growing dollarization that, as shown in Chapter 13 on Bolivia, significantly limits the possibility of conducting an independent monetary and exchange rate policy. A third, related, unsustainable policy concerns the adoption of multiple exchange rates. As noted in Chapter 4, if applied temporarily and with reduced spreads in countries where the poor are employed in the non-traded sector, then such a policy might serve some purpose, though it leads to a misallocation of resources and a fall in exports over the medium term. The impact is much worse if most of the poor work in the export sector. As shown in Chapter 12 of this volume, in 1999, the application of such a policy in Uzbekistan transferred 16 per cent of gross domestic product (GDP) from agriculture to the manufacturing sector, massively raising in this way rural poverty and overall inequality.

Fourthly, financial repression – entailing the administrative setting of interest rates and credit allocation, public control of the main banks and the ability of the government to unload on the commercial banks and the central bank the budget deficit – is another example of unsustainable policy that favours state parastatals and penalizes small and medium-sized enterprises (SMEs). It also causes financial disintermediation and – if real interest rates are negative – transfers large amounts of resources from depositors to borrowers. Fifthly, for some economies in transition, price liberalization remains incomplete and relative prices distorted. While countries can deliberately distort relative prices for social purposes, as lump sum taxes and subsidies might not be technically feasible, a generalized policy of this type generates a contraction in aggregate supply and can be practised only in countries – such as Turkmenistan – where the government can count on the distribution of mineral rents. Finally, illiberal policy regimes tend to feature also excessive trade protection and, especially, a considerable anti-export bias taking the form of low procurement prices paid by state marketing boards, export taxes and overvalued exchange rates.

More nuanced is the evaluation of those policy regimes that Dornbusch and Edwards (1991) labelled 'macroeconomic populism', that is, policy regimes that emphasize economic reactivation in depressed economies with large unused capacity, and pay less attention to the problems posed by inflation, deficit finance and the reaction of economic agents to administrative interventions. In this approach, the inflationary and balance-of-payments pressures that might have otherwise resulted from this fiscal stimulus are restricted by a drop in average and marginal cost of production induced by the output expansion and the drop in profit rate per unit of value added. Inflation reduction might be possible because of the excess capacity available in the economy and the concurrent freeze of prices, tariffs and wages, the stability of the nominal exchange rate, a swift reduction in interest rates and high initial currency reserves. Though this approach emphasizes little direct redistribution, the poor ought to benefit from lower inflation and the jobs, higher wages and greater demand for goods produced in the informal sector or by small farmers induced by the reactivation of the economy.

While the Keynesian and structuralist theories supporting such an approach indicate that it works only under specific conditions, the policies followed in practice often deviated from the theory and, for instance, adopted an expansionary stance even when the level of output had neared full capacity and inflation, supply and balance-of-payments problems had started to emerge. However, such choices were the result of political economic considerations, such as imminent elections or the search for short-term consensus, rather than of any theoretical recommendation. The evidence on the impact of heterodox adjustment shows positive initial results followed by a macro crisis in some cases, while in others the short-term gains were permanent but did not improve long-term performance. The Austral, Cruzado and Inti Plans introduced in 1985–1986 in Argentina, Brazil and Peru led to an improvement in growth, inflation and poverty performance over the first two years, but to a worsening situation over the medium term. Perhaps the most serious criticism concerns the fleeting nature of the redistributive gains in favour of the poor. While increases in wages and agricultural prices boosted real incomes among the low- and middle-income groups over the short run, a weak fiscal and monetary policy massively eroded the real value of wages, incomes and social expenditures over the medium run.

Intermediate macroeconomic regimes

Intermediate macroeconomic regimes accept the broad logic that guides the liberal approach, but apply it selectively and after adaptation to local institutions and conditions. As noted by Rodrik (2003), while some basic principles – such as protection of property rights, contract enforcement, market-based competition, appropriate incentives, responsible monetary and fiscal policy and debt sustainability – are universally valid, they do not map into unique policy packages and need to be applied in different ways under different institutions and conditions. Thus, reformers have substantial 'policy space' to transform some general principles into concrete packages sensitive to local conditions. From the perspective of this volume, successful countries are those that have effectively exploited this 'policy space' for growth and poverty alleviation purposes.

A first group of positive experiences in this camp refers to several cases of successful unorthodox stabilization programmes. Two famous cases in the 1980s are Israel and Turkey. Unorthodox stabilization was also pursued with success in Uzbekistan in 1991–1995 (see Chapter 12), thanks to the gradual liberalization of prices, the maintenance of industrial subsidies, trade and foreign exchange controls and the launch of a successful import-substitution programme for oil and wheat. The adoption of these 'best second-best policies' allowed the containment of the transitional recession in relation to the Central Asian Republics that followed a liberal approach.

A second group of intermediate regimes concerns countries that followed a different approach to macroeconomics. As noted by Chandrasekhar and Ghosh in Chapter 11, though it broadly and gradually adhered to the principles of protection of property rights, market competition, sound money and so on, macroeconomic policy in China followed a trial-and-error reform path in consonance with local conditions that differed drastically from the liberal approach. China liberalized prices in steps using a dual-track pricing system, redistributed commune land without granting the right to sell it due to the incompleteness of credit markets, created township and village enterprises owned by local authorities, used public banks to foster capital accumulation, controlled the capital account and managed the exchange rate. In addition, macroeconomic stabilization was based on administrative measures that restrained investments by regional governments and public corporations. In turn, a large share of foreign trade remained under administrative control, either through quotas and fairly high tariffs or because state-owned enterprises accounted for more than half of all trade.

A third group of countries liberalized according to the liberal wish list, but did so gradually, often following a two-track system including a liberalized sector and a protected sector, and after having strengthened their domestic institutions and creating greater regulatory capacity to withstand the shocks caused by the external liberalization. As noted by Bundoo in Chapter 8, what initially put Mauritius on a successful track was the creation in 1970 of an export processing zone that generated a boom in garment exports. However, while export processing zone firms were granted tax holidays, free repatriation of profits and finance at preferential interest rates, the traditional sectors remained protected until the mid-1980s. Imports were fully liberalized and restrictions on current payments were removed only in the early 1990s when the foreign exchange reserves had reached a safe level. Similarly, minimum interest rates on deposits and the ceiling on bank credit to priority sectors were abolished in steps, and the financial sector was liberalized only after strong regulatory institutions were developed. In general terms, the state strongly guided the restructuring of the economy that gradually evolved from sugar, to textile and tourism, and then to financial, transport and information and telecommunication technology services.

A fourth group of countries followed a basically orthodox approach, but adopted – if at times temporarily – policies that deviated from the standard blueprint. In

Chile, for instance, from 1992 to 1999, measures were introduced to discourage short-term portfolio inflows, while the exchange rate was managed (see Chapter 4). In a different way, Malaysia successfully managed its macroeconomy from the real side. In Chapter 9, Jomo and Wee note that the main macroeconomic objective was sustained growth of the tradable sector, rather than price stability or external balance. This was achieved by raising the rate of investment financed by high public and private savings and foreign direct investment (FDI) attracted by generous incentives and guarantees and a liberal trading and capital account regime. Monetary policy was accommodating and allowed for some inflation, while fiscal policy was used to influence the level and allocation of public investment. Problems of overheating were treated as structural problems requiring long-term measures to raise supply rather than short-term demand management measures.

Liberal macroeconomics and its problems

As noted in the introduction, during the last 20 years, liberal policies succeeded in opening up the economy, devaluing the real exchange rate and achieving greater commercial and financial integration. Even in the difficult context of sub-Saharan Africa, real exchange rates fell on average by 30 per cent in the period 1980–1998, inflation declined and the trade/GDP ratio rose from 51 per cent to 62 per cent (Kayizzi-Mugerwa 2000). In Latin America, such reforms were implemented to an even greater extent, as confirmed in Chapters 10, 13 and 14. However, the growth, inequality and poverty alleviation results were disappointing in most cases because of the problems discussed hereafter.

Stabilization overkill

As noted by Chand in Chapter 3, the standard monetarist approach to stabilization typically leads to larger-than-expected improvements in the balance of payments and inflation and greater-than-expected declines in GDP, investment and employment. A possible explanation of this 'overkill' is that expenditure-reducing monetary and fiscal policies take effect more quickly and generate a bigger depressive effect than the supposedly expansionary exchange rate policies. Second, large and rapid deficit reductions entail a fall in revenue that requires more fiscal cuts. Third, capital markets tend to exacerbate the problem as they behave pro-cyclically due to the 'flight to security' and falling 'appetite for risk'. Fourth, improvements in the external balance and inflation do not, by themselves, restore credibility and trigger a recovery of domestic and foreign investments in severely depressed economies with sky-high interest rates. Finally, and most importantly, credit restraint results in reductions in expenditure, especially for private investment, far greater than projected by the IMF's financial programming model.

IMF-type stabilization induces recessions that affect long-term growth and poverty alleviation. As just noted, investment demand falls two to three times faster than GDP due to steep rises in interest rates, the working of the flexible accelerator mechanism, the worsening of expectations and greater risk aversion in periods of mounting uncertainty. Secondly, recessions may cause a fall in enrolments as children are pulled out of school, with the effect of abandoning for good the educational system (World Bank 2000). Thirdly, in poor countries, inequality worsens during recessionary periods as flexible labour markets allow enterprises to shed labour and cut wages, while weak safety nets do not compensate for the loss of labour income. If the deterioration in inequality is large, then incentive problems may arise. Finally, severe cuts in public expenditure may affect the functioning of essential state services, raising in this way inefficiency over the long term. In brief, the view that the orthodox approach causes 'short-term pain but long-term gains' is misplaced. A botched stabilization can – and indeed often does – affect growth and poverty for several years.

Sequencing problems

Domestic financial liberalization in the presence of large deficits tends to generate sharp rises in interest rates, as governments can no longer force the central bank or the commercial banks to buy government debt at artificially low interest rates. To finance their deficit, they are obliged to create domestic bond markets in order to sell large amounts of treasury bills. Because of a lack of credibility and the size of the bonds issue, governments have to raise interest rates on their bonds. Such a rise spreads quickly to the banks' lending rates, causing a contraction in credit demand and levels of activity and attracting speculative capital, the inflow of which raises the real exchange rate, and thereby shifts relative prices against the traded sector, with possible destabilizing effects on the current account balance. In Chapter 14, Arbache illustrates other examples of sequencing mistakes characteristic of the liberal approach.

Liberalization with incomplete institutions

Domestic financial liberalization was expected to lead to financial deepening, greater competition in banking, private credit expansion and the creation of bonds and stocks markets. In other words, measures that, by increasing financial intermediation, were expected to raise the saving, investment and employment rates and to reduce poverty incidence. However, the empirical evidence points to disappointing results in many cases. With financial de-repression, the banking sector was often transformed from a public into a private oligopoly, as signalled by sharp rises in real interest rates and spreads. Even the entry of foreign banks did not raise competition, as these concentrated on a small number of low-risk customers. As a result, the credit expansion was lower than expected, market competition did not improve and the poor continued to be excluded from formal credit. In addition, financial liberalization was not preceded by a prior strengthening of the regulatory capacity of the central banks. In sum, financial deregulation in the absence of institutions ensuring market competition and prudential regulation led, in most cases, to oligopolistic markets characterized by little competition and high instability, as signalled by the recent rise in the frequency and severity of banking crises.

Loss of domestic policy making in economies with an open capital account

Capital account liberalization imposes severe restrictions on monetary, exchange rate and fiscal policies. Much depends, of course, on the extent of liberalization and the composition of the inflows. As noted in Chapter 6 by Bonassi *et al.*, FDI in labour-intensive manufacturing can generate favourable effects by transferring capital, technology and managerial skills to the host country, though, as mentioned in Chapter 14, the level of FDI depends to a considerable extent on privatization policies. In Brazil, for instance, privatization generated revenues equal to 25 per cent of the current account deficit in 1997–2000, but once most assets were sold, the country had to rely on less stable portfolio flows.

Likewise, if accompanied by the ability to impose controls on inflows and outflows and restrictions on bank lending to the non-tradable sector, the selective opening of capital inflows can secure precious resources for the tradable sector without causing instability. According to the 'impossible trinity debate', in the absence of interventions by the central bank, a country that opens up its capital account loses its monetary independence but enjoys considerable benefits, including lower domestic interest rates. Yet the literature shows that domestic interest rates seldom converge towards the US rate as a result of several factors that are ignored by standard analysis (Ticci 2004). In addition, the opening of the capital account prevents the adoption of policies of 'financial restraint'[3] that would lead to an outflow of domestic capitals. Finally, in some countries – Brazil being one of them – domestic interest rates are indexed to the nominal exchange rate and thus move upwards any time the exchange rate falls.

Secondly, the opening of the capital account narrows the range of exchange rate choices. As noted in Chapter 4, intermediate exchange rate regimes are difficult to implement in the presence of an open capital account. Under these circumstances, a country is unable to target a competitive exchange rate, as this can easily become the target of speculative attacks. Even assuming a country has the ability to do so, strong financial integration may lead to large dollar-denominated indebtedness that discourages the recourse to devaluation. Third, in a world of mobile capital and immobile labour, globalization can make the conduit of an independent fiscal policy and tax-financed redistribution problematic. Developing countries aiming to attract FDI and other foreign capital are under pressure to reduce the rates of corporate income tax and to grant tax holidays and industrial subsidies that – altogether – reduce the level of public revenue. Finally, as noted by Klasen in Chapter 13, the opening of the capital account can increase the dollarization of the economy, thus preventing the introduction of an active monetary and exchange rate policy and the recourse to devaluation to kick-start export-based growth. Therefore, a complete opening of the capital account may lead to a 'worst-case' policy scenario characterized by high interest rates, a high exchange rate and low tax revenue, that is, macro signals that impede long-term development and poverty alleviation (Taylor 2004).

Perverse interactions between policy instruments and policy reversals

Trade liberalization entailing sharp cuts in import duties worsens the fiscal deficit, as the decline in easy-to-collect trade taxes is not offset by a revenue rise from other taxes. The ensuing rise in the budget deficit may call for deflationary policies.

Secondly, in most of the countries that have received large amounts of portfolio flows, overall savings and capital accumulation have not generally increased or have even fallen, as domestic savings decline or stagnate, giving rise in this way to a kind of investment substitution. Indeed, domestic savers seize the opportunity offered by financial opening to diversify their portfolios by investing abroad, institutions lessen their effort at mobilizing domestic resources and public savings fall in an attempt to achieve the lower budget deficit required to attract foreign funds, while the capital inflows may be used to finance current consumption rather than investment. A third perverse interaction is observed on the occasion of import liberalization intended to expose domestic producers to foreign competition and induce gains in microeconomic efficiency. However, a simultaneous liberalization of the capital account can offset the intended effects of this measure, as the appreciation of the real exchange rate leads to import booms and a deterioration of the current account, as frequently observed in Latin America during the 1990s.

Asymmetric distribution of the benefits and costs of trade and financial globalization

Capital account liberalization could benefit the poor, because of the increase in output and employment that it makes possible. Such effects, however, are not automatic. Greenfield FDI in manufacturing favourably affects employment and wages, but the impact of mergers and acquisitions is mixed. And finally, as shown by Bonassi *et al.* in Chapter 6, greenfield FDI can generate positive growth and distributive effects if they are directed to labour-intensive manufacturing, but are less successful in this respect when they are directed to capital- and skill-intensive mining.

Even when the poor benefit from greater employment opportunities linked to capital inflows, they are unlikely to benefit from them directly, as capital inflows generally fund an expansion of consumer credit of the middle-upper class or are invested in high-return and high-risk short-term activities in finance, insurance and real estate that employ few unskilled workers. In turn, any expansion in bank credit is unlikely to benefit SMEs, as a lack of collateral and high transaction costs reduce their access to formal credit. For these reasons, foreign resources are channelled to clients who were already well served, such as multinational corporations and high net worth individuals. As small firms are more labour intensive than big firms, a continued segmentation of the credit market in spite of a credit expansion has a high social opportunity cost. Finally, purchases of shares in the domestic stock market benefit the large quoted companies, but not the SMEs and small rural and informal sector producers with high rates of return.

Employment may also fall due to the appreciation of the real exchange rate that accompanies a surge in inflows. Indeed, while the credit boom induced by the capital inflows increases demand, the appreciation of the exchange rate increases the share of the latter satisfied with imports. Meanwhile, the loss of a competitive hedge by traded sector firms, following the appreciation of the real exchange rate, pushes domestic enterprises to restructure, adopt more flexible contracts or subcontract work to informal sector firms. While raising labour productivity, such measures swell informal employment and cut wages even during growth spells. In

Brazil, for example, informal employment rose from 37 per cent to 50 per cent of the total between 1990 and 2002.

Financial liberalization and antirural bias

As noted by Klasen (2004), any kind of growth – whether labour intensive or not – could be made pro-poor if it involved a policy of progressive taxation and transfers. However, much more preferable is a growth that occurs in sectors where most of the poor are employed and that makes use of the factors of production that they own. In most developing countries, the majority of the poor are employed in agriculture and SMEs, and PPG ought to be focused on these sectors. As noted by Chandrasekhar and Ghosh in Chapter 11, the poverty alleviation elasticity of agricultural growth is, in fact, higher than that of non-agricultural growth.[4] This confirms findings by Ravallion and Datt (2000), who showed that rural growth reduces poverty faster than urban growth and that it also diminishes poverty in urban areas, as an increase in agricultural wages raises the reservation wage of unskilled workers in cities. Similar consideration can be made for SMEs and labour-intensive manufacturing. Their growth improves the situation of the urban poor and migrating rural poor and – via remittances and rises in rural wages – that of the rural poor left behind.

Given all this, macroeconomic policy must avoid an antirural bias and stimulate economic activity in labour-intensive agriculture, SMEs and the informal sector. In this regard, a main problem of the dominant approach is that it tends to distort the macroeconomic signals against the traded sector, and agriculture in particular. Fixed pegs tend to appreciate the real exchange rate, discourage exports and facilitate the imports of agricultural and manufactured goods. The liberalization of the capital inflows generates similar effects. In addition, financial liberalization tends to reduce access to credit for the small-scale agricultural, manufacturing and services sector due to problems of asymmetric information, collateralization and high transaction costs and also because of the removal of directed credit allocation to these sectors (see Chapter 11 on India), while the additional credit booms favours the non-poor and sectors where production is little labour intensive.

Growth and consumption instability

Since the mid-1980s, growth instability has increased perceptibly in many developing countries in parallel with a greater international integration (Caprio and Klingebiel 1996). Focusing on the industrialized countries, Lucas argued that what matters for welfare is mean income growth over a given period and not its variance around the mean, as credit markets can move resources backwards and forward. But, where credit markets are incomplete, the time horizon short and information problems severe, higher growth volatility raises uncertainty, lowers investment and, if income per capita is close to subsistence level, augments transitory and permanent poverty. In addition, as noted by Prasad *et al.* (2003), greater financial integration has also led to increasing consumption volatility, as highly financially integrated countries followed a cycle of consumption boom–panic–crisis–collapse. A main factor behind this trend is the pro-cyclical nature of interest rates and spreads that reduces the ability to borrow abroad in crisis periods.

More frequent crises with real effects

In an increasingly integrated world economy, emerging economies directly affected by sudden shifts in capital flows as well as those 'innocent bystanders' with connections to them are more easily hit by financial, banking and currency crises and new forms of contagion than in the pre-globalized world. Such crises have long-lasting real effects. Stiglitz (1998) shows that countries that suffered banking and financial crises in 1975–94 saw their GDP growth decline on average by 1.3 per cent over the subsequent five years compared to countries that did not experience such crises. The impact of such crises is also asymmetric, particularly in countries with weak labour institutions and safety nets. Székely (2003), for instance, found that the liberalization of the capital account in Latin America generated a strong rise in wage inequality. In turn, the World Bank (2000) showed that poverty rises due to financial liberalization persisted after returning to full-capacity growth, as large income falls forced the poor to adopt unsustainable survival strategies.

Elements of pro-poor macroeconomics

It is difficult to determine *ex ante* which macroeconomic policies are most suitable for the poor or for society as a whole, as these will depend on a long list of local conditions, including whether the poor work in the traded or non-traded sector, the country has a rigid or elastic supply of wage goods, the government plays an important role in the economy, the size of the foreign debt, the nature of domestic institutions, the efficiency of markets, and so on. Thus, the best solutions can only be country specific. Yet some broad principles apply fairly generally. At a general level, a PPM policy is characterized by policies of crisis avoidance and maintenance of a reasonable macroeconomic balance. However, macro stability appears increasingly insufficient to ensure long-term growth, let alone long-term PPG. The experience of the 1990s shows that growth will not materialize if macro stability is not accompanied by: (i) a competitive and stable real exchange rate encouraging investments in the labour-intensive tradable sector; (ii) low-to-moderate real interest rates; (iii) strong institutions for the regulation of the financial and banking sector; (iv) measures to speed up the accumulation of capital by linking, as in Malaysia, the macroeconomic policy to development policy; (v) trade liberalization that avoids a collapse of the import-competing sectors, while quickly removing any anti-export sector bias; and (vi) preservation of adequate pro-poor and pro-growth public expenditure during stabilization.

Measures to prevent macroeconomic crises

In an increasingly unstable world economy, the first task of PPM is to adopt measures that reduce the risk of macro shocks. Key choices in this regard include the following measures.

Limit foreign indebtedness and mobilize domestic savings

The liberalization of the current account offers an opportunity to access a global pool of savings. However, as noted earlier, this entails several risks. Thus, the recourse to foreign resources should be selective – for example, for the traded sector – while countries with large foreign debt should aim at gradually reducing it, as done for instance in Chile, where the stock of foreign public debt fell from 39 per cent to 13 per cent of GDP between 1990 and 2004 (see Chapter 10).

In Chapter 5, Weller argues that capital accumulation should be funded through a mobilization of domestic resources to be achieved through the strengthening of indigenous financial institutions. This can be achieved by providing them with infrastructural support, tax-free status and public guarantees for loans, or by relying on existing postal office networks. Or, as argued in Chapter 9 by Jomo and Wee in the case of Malaysia, by ensuring a low level of inflation, imposing mandatory savings through the Employee Provident Fund and tightening consumption credit. Following a mixture of such policies, China was able to raise its investment rate to 32–44 per cent of GDP, with FDI accounting for only 5 per cent and domestic savings for the rest. In recent years, Chile was also able to increase its national savings and investment rate (see Chapter 10). In the same vein, the empirical evidence shows that open economies with larger domestic banking systems have smaller portfolio inflows than those with smaller domestic banking systems. A policy of moderate financial restraint (see above) could also be used to raise domestic savings. And, finally, public savings can be raised to finance infrastructural development and safety nets by increasing tax pressure as done in China in 2000–04, where revenue rose from 15 per cent to 20 per cent of GDP. This approach is recommended in particular in the 60 or so developing countries with tax/GDP ratios below 10–12 per cent.

Controlling capital inflows and harnessing their sectoral allocation

PPM should delay capital account liberalization in countries with large budget deficits and weak regulatory capacity. Once these conditions are met, the policy maker ought to treat different types of inflows differently. In countries with a large labour supply, an opening to FDI in manufacturing is likely to be favourable to the poor. In Malaysia, for instance, the government succeeded in attracting FDI to priority manufacturing sectors, while, as argued by Bundoo in Chapter 8, Mauritius attracted significant levels of FDI to the export processing zone, a sector that became critical in terms of employment and export earnings. The benefits to the host country increase further if national regulations make the FDI inflow conditional to the establishment of joint ventures that facilitate technology transfers, require the hiring of national engineers and managers and require a minimum local content of intermediate inputs.

Even when stable macroeconomic conditions and appropriate regulatory institutions are in place, a country should be free to impose controls on capital flows if they become a danger to economic stability. As noted by Weller in Chapter 5, countries can impose minimum stay requirements or impose international capital transactions taxes on inflows varying with the asset maturity, as was done in Chile between June 1991 and March 2000. In turn, the central bank can limit the foreign exchange exposure of domestic banks, forbid them to borrow internationally to extend loans to the non-tradable sector and introduce temporary or permanent administrative controls on inflows and outflows, as done in Colombia, India, Malaysia, Singapore and Taiwan. As noted by Jomo and Wee in Chapter 9, between January and August 1994, the Malaysian authorities subjected bank funds to stricter reserve and liquidity requirements, imposed limits on non-trade-related foreign indebtedness of domestic banks and restricted the sale of short-term monetary instruments to non-residents. In turn, following the exodus of funds during the East Asian financial crisis, strict controls were imposed on short-term outflows by banning offshore ringgit trading, restricting ringgit exports and imports, limiting ringgit loans to non-residents and compelling non-residents to retain their investments in Malaysia for at least 12 months.

A key issue in this regard is the duration of the controls. The IMF supports the introduction of temporary controls during crisis periods, but countries may consider extending such measures as long as they are needed, as in the case of China. The example of India also illustrates the possibility for an emerging economy to attract foreign capital amid continued, if slowly declining, capital controls, without being subject to sharp and potentially destabilizing capital inflows.

Capital controls are not easily implemented, especially in countries with limited administrative capacity. Helleiner (1997) and Chapter 5 of this volume suggest that their effectiveness is influenced by the administrative capacity of the country, that controls cannot replace sound macroeconomic policies, that no single measure can be effective everywhere, that controls slow down the flow of capitals but do not eliminate it completely and that controls can be circumvented. Others underscore that countries that adopted controls, such as Chile and India, abandoned them at a later stage. Altogether, it would appear that while capital controls are unable to stop all inflows and outflows, they could – in conjunction with other measures – constitute a deterrent against massive shifts in financial assets. A related key issue is to understand what domestic institutions and regulations permit channelling financial flows to the traded sector. The experience of Malaysia and Mauritius shows that appropriate incentives can attract FDI toward labour-intensive manufacturing. In turn, the central bank can forbid domestic banks to borrow abroad to invest in the non-traded sector, limit foreign ownership in sectors such as real estate, require commercial banks to allocate a share of their lending to the agricultural sector and SMEs (see Chapters 9 and 11) and set up loan guarantees to these sectors.

Policy makers can also apply measures to offset the monetary effects of the inflows. Such measures include asking state-controlled financial institutions to switch their deposits from the commercial banks to the central bank, sterilizing the capital inflows, increasing the reserve ratio of commercial banks with large foreign deposits, substituting foreign with domestic borrowing whenever the interest differential is not excessive and encouraging domestic institutions such as pension funds to invest part of their assets abroad.

Choosing a pro-poor exchange rate regime

Such a regime should minimize the risk of currency crises, and at the same time provide adequate incentives to the expansion of the traded sector where the majority of the poor is often employed. This means rejecting the view about the superiority of two 'corner solutions' over intermediate regimes. Indeed, in theory and practice, neither of these two approaches performs better in terms of growth and crises avoidance than the intermediate regimes. Though it is difficult to generalize, particularly in developing countries that need to grow to reduce poverty but can count only on narrow domestic markets to sell their output, an intermediate regime aiming at credibly stabilizing the real exchange rate and its expectations is the best option. For example, it is possible to adopt an intermediate exchange rate of the BBC (basket, band and crawl) type, fix its central parity at a competitive level – equal, say, to 70 per cent of the purchasing power parity exchange rate – allow it to fluctuate within a given band to neutralize small shocks and devalue the central parity in case of large inflation differentials with the basket reference countries, so as to leave the real exchange rate unaltered. Empirical research has shown that a competitive exchange rate has been a key factor to kick-start growth (Rodrik 2003) and improve long-term performance.

However, this approach leads to a slower decline of inflation, and needs to be supported by moderately expansionary fiscal and monetary policies and measures that limit capital inflows. In addition, this approach may not fit the needs of countries where the poor are located in the non-traded sector, where the traded sector is skilled labour intensive – as in most mining economies and industrialized countries – or where the poor are located in the traded sector, but structural factors reduce the pass-through of the benefits of devaluation. Also, in very small economies with highly volatile terms of trade and difficulties in diversifying their exports, dollarization may be an option. Finally, in large developing economies with comparatively low trade/GDP ratios, a competitive exchange rate is less important for growth and poverty alleviation. These objectives can be better pursued through an expansion of the domestic components of aggregate demand driven by fiscal policy (Bhaduri 2005).

Stabilization funds and contingency rules

In many developing countries, government revenues oscillate widely because of large fluctuations in the demand and prices of the commodities they export and climatic shocks. Capital markets behave pro-cyclically and so reduce the possibility of stabilizing consumption in bad years. All this leads to large public expenditure cuts that exacerbate the impact of the shocks on poverty, investments and growth through Keynesian multiplier effects.

In this type of country, PPM can try to limit the impact of shocks by creating stabilization funds that set aside resources during periods of high demand and prices of the exported commodities and release them in crisis years. During the boom years, such a policy helps to reduce the inflationary pressures arising from the non-traded sector, while in case of crisis the release of funds to the state budget sustains aggregate consumption. As discussed in Chapters 2 and 10, stabilization funds have helped to smooth public expenditure fluctuations in Chile, Norway and Venezuela.

An essential requirement for the smooth functioning of stabilization funds is that the rules that regulate their functioning – how much and when it needs to be set aside, in which assets to invest the fund's resources, under what circumstances to release such funds, and so on – are set *ex ante* by law and are not left to the discretionary decisions of policy makers. A second requirement is that the price of the commodity does not follow a random walk without mean reversion, as this would exhaust the fund resources in just a few years. Thirdly, to have an impact, the funds must count on large endowments generated by a commodity for which there is substantial demand in world markets during normal times, as in the case of copper and petroleum. For developing countries that export less valuable commodities, stabilization funds are out of reach. Fourthly, the rainy days must come late and not early. Finally, as argued by Reddy in Chapter 7, in order for stabilization funds to be protected from risks and be readily available for use they have to be kept in a safe and liquid form, yielding in this way limited returns. For this reason, a diversion of resources from the satisfaction of present needs to the fund is likely to be suboptimal in poor countries with a high social discount rate.

Another solution to the problems posed by the instability of public revenue is the adoption *ex ante* of contingency rules that establish, in case of unanticipated shocks, that governments are not bound by the usual fiscal targets and are free to increase public expenditure, raise taxes or allow for a widening of the deficit. Such measures provide credibility and transparency to an expansionary fiscal stance in countries where automatic stabilizers are weak and discretionary anti-cyclical fiscal policies are often looked upon with suspicion by the markets and the IMF.

International safety nets

As noted by Reddy in Chapter 7, in recent decades, a few international mechanisms were created to deal with exogenous shocks affecting developing countries. The IMF used the Compensatory Financing Facility to offer financing in case of declines in export earnings or rises in cereal import costs. This facility was replaced at a later stage by the Poverty Reduction and Growth Facility (IMF 2003). A second market-based approach, which was later abandoned, was based on international buffer stocks aiming at stabilizing commodity prices. In addition, the Lome Convention established aid-based mechanisms, including the STABEX and FLEX funds, to stabilize the export earnings for certain commodities and countries. Yet these mechanisms offer limited protection against global shocks and are mostly loan based.

New approaches to be explored by PPM include insurance-based, aid-based and international tax-based global mechanisms. Included among the first group are catastrophe bonds, weather derivatives, commodity-indexed bonds or other derivatives contracts that transfer a given risk to others in exchange for an initial payment. In principle, these contracts could be extended to cover the risk of financial shocks. Yet such contracts are costly, carry a high default risk and create moral hazard in case of external shock due to the improper behaviour of international economic agents. Yet in Chapter 7 Reddy notes that this problem could be solved if an international public intermediary financed the derivative contracts covering against the risk of external shocks.

A second approach emphasizes the possibility that insurance against global risks is built into systems of aid provision that explicitly counteract adverse cyclical shocks of international origin. One example could be a global contingency fund, financed in advance by donors, providing additional resources to countries affected by severe shocks. Present proposals in this area cover natural disasters, but could be extended to macro shocks. A third mechanism could be based on the institution of earmarked international taxes on activities that cause global negative externalities, such as short-term portfolio flows and carbon emissions. Such taxes would generate the double benefit of reducing the activities that cause the externalities, while at the same time making resources available to deal with their consequences (Atkinson 2005). Such an approach has the advantage of recognizing the causal role played by countries in creating adverse shocks that are experienced by other countries.

Managing macroeconomic crises in a pro-poor mode

If successfully implemented, the measures discussed above should reduce the frequency of macroeconomic crises, but will not be able to eliminate them entirely. Thus, PPM must also develop broad principles to manage crises in ways that control macro imbalances, while avoiding surges in poverty. A first step in this regard is to formally introduce a poverty target into macroeconomic stabilization models along the lines suggested by Chand in Chapter 3. Setting an explicit poverty target helps identify trade-offs between stabilization and poverty targets, measure the 'sacrifice ratio' of alternative approaches and determine the amount of international assistance or the nature of alternative policies that could ensure consistency between stabilization and poverty objectives.

Exchange rate-based versus money-based adjustment

This choice depends on a host of factors, and clearly there is no 'one-size-fits-all' solution. However, as argued in Chapter 4, in economies with a price-elastic supply of tradable goods, a moderate foreign debt and rigid wages and utility rates, a controlled devaluation of the exchange rate, accompanied by fiscal expansion, low interest rates, a rapid reorganization of banks in the wake of the shock and, if needed, capital and import controls may help re-establish balance-of-payments equilibrium more quickly and with smaller output and employment losses than following a monetarist approach that causes a contraction in the domestic components of aggregate demand, while being unable to raise exports. As noted by Jomo and Wee in Chapter 9, Malaysia initially responded to the financial crisis of 1997–1998 by adopting a contractionary approach, but then opted to increase spending and pegged its devalued currency to the US dollar, containing in this way the rise of unemployment and poverty. However, conscious of the possible short-term contractionary and inflationary effects of devaluation, governments ought to set up employment-based safety nets and subsidize key consumption items.

Such an approach may be less likely to succeed in economies where the traditional export is capital intensive and the new exports are more land intensive than labour intensive, or where labour demand is biased towards skilled labour. Problems can also arise in countries with an inelastic supply of exports, a high share of imports on exports and rigidities that make devaluation contractionary

(Krugman and Taylor 1978). Devaluation may also be resisted in countries where banks, firms and governments have large unhedged short-term foreign currency exposures.

It is also likely that the devaluation raises inflation-induced poverty, especially among the low-income net food buyers in the urban and rural sector. This conclusion, however, needs to be juxtaposed with the costs of an output contraction induced by the monetarist approach. While devaluation-induced inflation affects the poor disproportionately, they might be hit even harder by a fall in GDP and employment induced by the adoption of a monetarist adjustment. In both approaches, the rise in poverty will also depend on the safety nets in place. Their extent may be more limited, however, in the case of the fiscal retrenchment typical of the monetary approach.

Fiscal policy, deficit size and pace of deficit reduction

As noted by Jha in Chapter 2, in many developing countries, budget deficits result not so much from excessive expenditures, as from extremely low and falling tax/GDP ratios.[5] In such countries, a strengthening of the tax/GDP ratios and the retrenchment of non-productive expenditures during normal times would widen the scope for conducting a counter-cyclical fiscal policy in crisis years.

During crisis periods, the fiscal policy of industrialized countries allows an expansion of the deficit. This occurs automatically owing to the working of the automatic stabilizers and through a discretionary fiscal expansion. In developing countries, the widening of the deficit is not generally due to an increase of public expenditure – as automatic stabilizers are weak or non-existent – but to sharp falls in revenue due to high tax buoyancy.[6] Countries endowed with stabilization funds can moderate this impact but, as noted, this option is not available to all. Under such circumstances, a temporary rise in the deficit maintains aggregate demand at an acceptable level and limits the impact of shocks on output and poverty. However, until recently, the IMF has demanded crisis-affected countries to quickly reduce the deficit, with yearly cuts of 3–4 per cent of GDP. Such a policy generates several negative effects. The most obvious is a fall in aggregate demand, output and employment and a rise in poverty and inequality. In addition, large cuts affect the deficit itself, as tax revenue is endogenously determined by the level of output. Hence, an attempt at rapidly reducing the budget deficit could lead to its increase, demanding in this way the imposition of further restrictive measures. This partly explains the disappointing performance of IMF programmes in reducing fiscal deficits and the persistence of fiscal stress in countries undergoing adjustment.

As mentioned, contingency rules can establish that, in the case of external shocks, governments are not bound by the usual fiscal targets and are free to sustain spending levels, increase taxes or allow a widening of the deficit. A key issue is the choice of a sustainable deficit under crisis situations and of its subsequent pace of reduction. In this regard, the IMF argues that an optimal fiscal deficit should be sustainable over the next five to 10 years, but in determining this it assumes the rate of growth, fiscal revenue and interest rates as exogenous, while – as shown above – such variables and the deficit are jointly determined. Nor can the case for quick deficit reductions be argued on the basis that temporary deficits are costly, as there is no convincing evidence in this regard (see above). In contrast, there is evidence that large and rapid fiscal cuts reduce growth over the short and long term and can cause irreversible declines in the well-being of the poor. So, while large deficits certainly need to be reduced over time, this should be done gradually. As suggested by Adam and Bevan (2001), deficit reductions of up to 1.5 per cent of GDP per year help to re-establish fiscal balance with a minimal impact on growth, but larger reductions actually hurt growth.

How to achieve a given target deficit?

Relation (1.1) below suggests that there are several strategies to reduce the budget deficit (*BD*) as a percentage of GDP (*Y*). It is possible to act alternatively on the primary public expenditure (*PPE*), taxes (*T*), non-tax revenue (*NTR*), foreign aid (*FA*), interest rate on the domestic debt (*r*) and foreign debt (*r'*), national and foreign public debt (*NPD* and *FPD*), exchange rate (*E*) and expansion of the monetary base (ΔH). Each of these strategies affects the deficit and poverty both directly and indirectly via the relations linking the variables on the right hand side of equation (1.1)

$$BD_t/Y_t = PPE_t/Y_t - (T_t + NTR_t + FA_t)/Y_t + (r - g)NPD_{t-1}/Y_t + (r' - g)E_t FPD_{t-1}/Y_t$$
$$- \Delta H/P_t Y_t \qquad (1.1)$$

In Chapter 2 Jha notes that the IMF deficit reduction strategies generally focus on reducing *PPE*. While cutting unproductive expenditures is certainly desirable, if the cuts are marked, aggregate demand and GDP will fall, and public opposition may derail the entire stabilization effort. Secondly, if the cuts affect pro-growth expenditure, *g* (the growth rate of GDP) may fall and the long-term deficit rise. Thirdly, given the asymmetric distribution of lobbying power, large spending cuts hurt the poor more than the rich.

The fiscal deficit can also be reduced by raising *T* and *NTR*, a policy seldom implemented in IMF-supported programmes, even in countries with low initial tax/GDP ratios. The macroeconomic impact of rising taxation is less contractionary than that of cutting public expenditure, as governments have a lower propensity to save than households or enterprises. Taxation may also help redistribution, especially in countries with low tax/GDP ratios. Foreign aid (*FA*) in the form of international safety nets, such as those discussed above, can also help stabilize the budget and the balance of payments and, if well targeted on pro-poor programmes, reduce the social impact of the initial shock. Yet, so far donors' discretion continues to dominate aid granting. Perhaps greater trade and financial liberalization – a frequent source of exogenous shocks – should be made conditional on the creation of international safety nets.

In addition to stimulating growth, a lowering of the domestic interest rate (*r*) would also diminish the cost of servicing the public debt, thus reducing the need to cut pro-poor and pro-growth expenditures. In view of the high level of nominal and real interest rates in many countries (see, for instance, Chapter 14 on Brazil), such a measure would generate considerable 'fiscal space'. Yet to be effective, such a measure needs to be accompanied by the imposition of controls on capital outflows as, in the absence of such a measure, the domestic asset holders might move their funds abroad, thus weakening the exchange rate (E) and so raising the international interest rates (r') with the result of raising the domestic currency cost of servicing the foreign debt (FPD).

A controlled expansion of the monetary base (ΔH), leading to a less than proportional increase in prices (P), can also create fiscal space and help reduce the deficit, though this is more likely to occur if a country has considerable unutilized capacity. As argued in Agénor and Montiel (1999), resources equal to 2–3 per cent of GDP were created in this way in countries with moderate initial inflation and a controlled monetary expansion. Finally, in crisis situations, countries may be unable to service their debt. This is particularly the case for countries hit by large external shocks or facing enduring crises such as the heavily indebted poor countries. Thus, a given target deficit might be achieved through measures that reduce the stock of domestic debt (NPD) or foreign debt (FPD). Measures here could reduce or cancel part of the interest payment on the foreign debt ($r'FPD$) or the stock of debt itself (FPD) – along the lines of the measures cited in Chapter 7 – or introduce costless debt standstills by which the payment of principal and interests is suspended in cases of *force majeure*.

Which route to take to reach a given target deficit depends upon the initial conditions and thus varies from country to country, but there are certainly options available other than cutting public expenditure. With a low tax/GDP ratio, Bolivia and India (see Chapters 13 and 11 respectively) should raise more tax revenue. Chile, on the other hand, already has a high tax/GDP and expenditure/GDP ratio and adjustments might concentrate on the expenditure side or the lowering of interest rates.

Composition of expenditure cuts and domestic safety nets
PPM requires that under crisis situations, pro-poor and pro-growth public spending on health, education, public works, basic income support, infrastructure and key productive investments be protected or even expanded. The impact on the poor can be reduced further by focusing a growing share of public expenditure within each of the above sectors on programmes with low administrative costs and high intrinsic efficiency, such as child immunization, elementary education and the rehabilitation of transport infrastructure. In the budget process, such objectives can be promoted by earmarking the revenue of certain taxes to essential programmes or by establishing by law transparent priorities. Such an approach has been applied in 1990–1992 in Chile when an expansion of social programmes focused almost exclusively on services for the poor. In addition, as argued by Solimano and Pollack in Chapter 10, monetary transfers targeted at the bottom 40 per cent of the Chilean population dampened the effects of crises on the poor, as their share in total transfers rose from 56 per cent to 73 per cent between 1987 and 2000. The cost of such safety nets need not be large. For instance, the Mexican programme *Progresa*, which

targets a whole range of interventions and benefits to about two million households, costs only 0.2 per cent of GDP and one per cent of the federal budget.

A particularly effective way to focus public subsidies on the poor are conditional transfers – that is, transfers that affect poor families if their children attend school regularly or are taken for periodic checkups at health centres. This approach provides an incentive to the poor to uptake essential services, while improving their consumption capacity. Another specific measure needed to contain the rise in poverty during crisis and adjustment periods consists of ensuring that food prices, which constitute the main component of the poverty line, do not rise unduly. This objective can be achieved by setting up public distribution networks, adopting anti-speculation measures or introducing food subsidies financed by taxing windfall earnings on foreign exchange assets during adjustment periods.

Pace of stabilization and optimal adjustment path of the poor

The case for adopting a gradual adjustment programme and/or instituting compensatory safety nets for the poor acquires particular relevance when taking into account the differences in social discount rates of the main social groups. Indeed, the poor have a higher social discount rate than the middle class or the rich, and therefore prefer an adjustment path that scatters the adjustment burden over a longer period of time, even if this entails greater inter-temporal welfare costs both for themselves and for society as a whole. For them, an approach – such as that entailed by a successful hard peg – that entails a less pronounced initial contraction and larger distant losses, to which they attach lower values due to their higher discount rate, may be preferable to the smaller but frontloaded losses associated to real devaluation (Lustig 2000).[7] Thus, a more gradual approach maximizes the net present value of the income streams of the poor over the entire adjustment period, making use of their specific social discount rate. A PPM would thus choose a slower approach, even if this is suboptimal from an aggregate perspective. The best solution, however, consists of adopting the overall optimal adjustment path, while compensating the poor with transfers equal to the drop in their income caused by the choice of a devaluation-based adjustment approach.

Inflation targeting and monetary policy

The orthodox view is that inflation is costly as it changes relative prices – and so reduces the informational power of the price system, erodes profits and wages, raises uncertainty and discourages investments, and has the greatest impact on the poor. Secondly, high inflation can have perverse monetary effects: it reduces real money supply and raises the interest rate, induces a contraction of output and a fall in tax revenue and, in extreme cases, leads to currency substitution and dollarization. Thirdly, if the capital account is open, even comparatively small inflation differentials may cause capital flights. For all of these reasons, the standard prescription is to aim at single-digit rates of inflation through raises in interest rates and credit restrictions.

Yet a PPM focusing on reducing inflation must also take into account other considerations. To start with, Bruno and Easterly (1998) and Stiglitz (1998) show that driving inflation below 40 per cent per year produces no discernible economic benefits, though it might affect poverty favourably. Secondly, as argued above, a rapid reduction of inflation is likely to cause a contraction in GDP and – because of the endogeneity of tax revenue to GDP – a widening of the fiscal deficit. In addition, as noted in Chapter 10 on Chile, a policy of high interest rates increases the concentration of financial wealth in the hands of the holders of financial assets. Furthermore, given the limited internal cashflow of firms in developing countries, the low elasticity of their demand for money in relation to the interest rate and the mark-up price formation mechanism dominant in these countries, a rise in interest rates has the effect of raising production costs and prices. Thirdly, reducing inflation to single digits requires sharp recessions that disproportionately affect the poor. These points are now recognized by the IMF Institute, which argues that while the optimal inflation is 2 per cent to 3 per cent per year in industrialized countries, it is 10 per cent to 15 per cent in developing countries.

A PPM will thus adopt less ambitious inflation targets, and aim at their gradual reduction over time. This means that while real interest rates will aim at the 3 to 5 per cent range, the nominal rates ought to increase less markedly than in the standard approach. This policy should help to contain cost-push inflation, and at the same time avoid a contraction in investment and growth that would negatively affect employment and poverty. While the money supply compatible with this approach needs to be accommodating, the policy maker should simultaneously introduce microeconomic reforms to reduce other components of cost-push inflation. Finally, credit policy should aim at eliminating the segmentation of the credit market that reduces access to credit by SMEs.

Conclusions and limitations of pro-poor macroeconomics

A first finding of this study is that the World Bank (1990) poverty alleviation strategy based on growth, investments in the human capital of the poor and safety nets for those left behind has failed to ensure a rapid decline in poverty. As noted in the case studies on Bolivia, Chile and India, this approach did not explicitly promote the productive activities of the poor or address the large inequality problems permeating these countries at the beginning of the reforms. For instance, the *Concertación* governments in power in Chile since 1990 focused on poverty reduction, but did not set any target for the redistribution of income and assets, despite a wealth of evidence that high levels of inequality negatively affects growth and poverty alleviation. The neglect of high levels of inequality possibly explains the suboptimal results obtained in this country in terms of poverty alleviation and worsening of the distribution of market income during the 1990s. In contrast, the highly egalitarian conditions prevailing at the beginning of the reforms in China facilitated growth and poverty reduction.

A second finding is that while some basic economic principles – incentives, certainty of property rights, reasonable macro balances, and so on – were followed in all successful countries analysed in this volume, the way these objectives were pursued by national macroeconomic policies varied substantially depending on the structural and institutional conditions of each country. In China and Malaysia, for instance, rapid poverty alleviation, moderate inequality, market competition and secure property rights were achieved under conditions of strong state presence in manufacturing, state control over financial institutions, a managed exchange rate and a controlled capital account.

Thirdly, this volume shows that several obstacles to PPG cannot be removed by macroeconomic policy. To start with, PPM cannot produce all of its beneficial effects if deep-seated inequalities in the distribution of asset, credit, opportunities and human capital are not removed or, as argued in Chapter 12 on Uzbekistan, if inequality rises because of the development approach that is followed. Chapter 14 shows that in highly unequal Brazil, poverty is more responsive to a fall in inequality than to an acceleration in growth induced by good macroeconomic policies, as the poverty reduction effect of growth is much lower when the initial inequality is high. Thus, PPM cannot wait for poverty to be reduced by the positive distributional consequences of better macro policies that might take time to materialize.

The impact of PPM is also limited in economies with a large subsistence and informal sector that is only loosely integrated in the economic mainstream and is located in rural and mountainous areas, marginal urban areas, small towns and remote regions. In Brazil and Chile, the main problems faced by the poor in the informal sector are a lack of education and poor integration with modern sector activities; in Bolivia, geographical isolation is an additional factor. Indeed, such a subsistence or informal sector is weakly influenced by changes in macro signals. There is a need, therefore, to better integrate such sectors into the overall economy, while avoiding the instability that could be associated with growing economic integration. Public expenditure policies can do a lot to achieve this goal by developing public infrastructure in the fields of transport, communications and energy, although this effort will take several years and considerable resources to bear fruit. A proactive tax and incentive policy is obviously needed to improve such integration and – as in the case of Malaysia and Mauritius – to mobilize investments for absorbing the migrants from the subsistence sector to the modern sector.

PPM is also much more difficult to implement in small, dependent and undifferentiated developing economies with exogenous terms of trade and a high reliance on the exports of few primary commodities. As seen in Chapter 13 on Bolivia, such structural weaknesses and the limited scope for diversifying the export basket severely limit the scope for conducting PPM. To become more effective, PPM requires microeconomic changes in the goods, labour, credit and insurance markets that permit a diversification of the production structure, as observed in Mauritius. In economies with deeply segmented credit and goods markets, for instance, the poor do not benefit from lowering interest rates or devaluation to start new activities. Under such circumstances, sound macroeconomic policies alone are not enough. A promising approach – which could not be explored in detail in this volume – would be co-ordinating macro with micro policies that simultaneously attack the structural determinants of poverty, combining, for instance, a removal of market imperfections with pro-poor macro policies such as those illustrated above. Finally, PPM would benefit from strengthening institutions, governance and administrative capacity. Problems in these areas often reduce the impact of potentially useful pro-poor policies aiming at the mobilization of domestic resources, capital controls, decentralization, and so on.

Notes

1 The author would like to thank Yilmaz Akyuz, Stephan Klasen, Gerry Helleiner and José Antonio Ocampo for discussions and comments on earlier drafts of this chapter. The usual disclaimers apply.
2 There is broad agreement that investments in health, education, child nutrition, gender balance and empowerment of the poor improve well-being, generate high returns, reduce inequality and contribute to macroeconomic stability. The main elements of pro-poor structural policies such as human and physical capital accumulation, technology transfer, land reform, agricultural growth, microcredit and insurance are also agreed by scholars of different schools of thought. Thus, *ex ante* interventions that improve the functioning of markets and public institutions are likely to enhance the poverty impact of macro policies. For instance, devaluation has a greater impact on poverty in a country with more egalitarian agrarian structures and flexible labour markets than in the case of *latifundia* and rigid labour markets. Differences persist in other areas – such as the extent of industrial policy – and, within some of these areas, on the way in which the agreed policy objectives should be pursued. For instance, some authors suggest that the threat of expropriation is an unavoidable component of a land reform, while others favour an approach based on the willing-buyer–willing-seller basis. For a review of the main areas of agreement and disagreement, see Klasen (2004).
3 Where asymmetric information prevails and the level of domestic savings is suboptimal – as in many developing countries – maintaining real interest rates on deposits at positive but below the market-clearing level and limiting entry by the domestic and foreign banks generates a moderate amount of rents for banks that are encouraged to expand efforts at mobilizing deposits and monitoring their borrowers. Such a policy was widely pursued in East Asian countries in the earlier phase of their development.
4 All countries that achieved rapid growth and poverty reduction over the long term experienced an increase in land yields, agricultural growth and farm and rural non-farm incomes during the take-off phase of their growth. The experience of China in 1978–84 and India in the 1980s confirms this rule, which was verified in the East Asian Tigers and elsewhere.
5 Chapter 2 demonstrates that unweighted average tax/GDP ratios of 13 emerging economies shows a downward trend between 1985 and 1999, while a recent panel study by Chu *et al.* (2004) points to an average drop of one percentage point in the tax/GDP ratio during the 1980s–1990s period, as opposed to a rise of 1.6 points between the 1970s and 1980s.
6 Lustig (2000) indicates that a one per cent drop in GDP causes a revenue decline of 1.8 per cent in the Organization for Economic Co-operation and Development countries, but of 5.8 per cent in Latin American countries.
7 This conclusion may change, however, if the discount rate is lowered by the development of credit and insurance markets, which allow them to sustain their consumption during a sharp adjustment spell.

References

Adam, C. and D. Bevan. 2001. *Non-linear Effects of Fiscal Deficits on Growth in Developing Countries*. Working Paper, Department of Economics, Oxford University, Oxford.

Agénor, P.R. and P. Montiel. 1999. *Development Macroeconomics*. Princeton, NJ: Princeton University Press.

Atkinson, A. 2005. *New Forms of International Taxation*. Oxford: Oxford University Press.

Bhaduri, A. 2005. *Macroeconomic Policies for Higher Employment in the Era of Globalisation*. Employment Strategy Papers No. 2005/11, Employment Analysis Unit, Employment Strategy Department. Geneva: International Labour Organization.

Bruno, M. and W. Easterly. 1998. 'Inflation Crises and Long-Term Growth'. *Journal of Monetary Economics*, 41(1), 3–26.

Caprio, G. and D. Klingebiel. 1996. *Bank Insolvencies: Cross-Country Experience*. Policy Research Working Papers No. 1620. Washington, DC: World Bank.

Chu K.Y., H. Davoodi and S. Gupta. 2004. 'Income Distribution and Tax and Government Social Spending Policies in Developing Countries'. In G.A. Cornia (ed.), *Inequality, Growth and Poverty in an Era of Liberalisation and Globalisation*. Oxford: Oxford University Press.

Dornbusch, R. and S. Edwards (eds). 1991. *The Macroeconomics of Populism in Latin America*. Chicago and London: University of Chicago Press.

Helleiner, G.K. 1997. 'Capital Account Regimes and the Developing Countries'. In *International Monetary and Financial Issues for the 1990s, Vol. VIII*. New York and Geneva: UNCTAD.

International Monetary Fund. 2003. *Fund Assistance for Countries Facing Exogenous Shocks*. www.imf.org/external/np/pdr/sustain/2003/080803.pdf, accessed on 12 August 2005.

Kayizzi-Mugerwa, S. 2000. *Globalisation, Growth and Income Inequality: A Review of the African Experience*. Paper presented at the Conference on Poverty and Inequality in Developing Countries: A Policy Dialogue on the Effects of Globalisation, OECD Development Centre, Paris, 30 November–1 December.

Klasen, S. 2004. 'In Search of the Holy Grail: How to Achieve Pro-Poor Growth'. In B. Tungodden, N. Stern and I. Kolstad (eds), *Towards Pro-poor Policies: Aid, Institutions, and Globalization*. Oxford: Oxford University Press.

Krugman, P. and L. Taylor. 1978. 'Contractionary Effects of Devaluation'. *Journal of International Economics*, 8(3), 445–56.

Lustig, N. 2000. 'Crises and the Poor: Socially Responsible Macroeconomics'. *Economia*, 1(1), 1–19.

Prasad, E., K. Rogoff, S.J. Wei and M.A. Kose. 2003. *Effects of Financial Globalisation on Developing Countries: Some Empirical Evidence*. Working Papers, IMF, Washington, DC.

Ravallion, M. and G. Datt. 2000. *When is Growth Pro-Poor?* Mimeo. Washington, DC: World Bank.

Rodrik, D. 2003. *Growth Strategies*. Working Paper No. 10050. Cambridge, MA: National Bureau of Economic Research.

Stiglitz, J. 1998. *Broader Goals and More Instruments: Towards a Post-Washington Consensus*. Annual Lecture No. 2. Helsinki: WIDER.

Székely, M. 2003. 'The 1990s in Latin America: Another Decade of Persistent Inequality but with Somewhat Lower Poverty'. *Journal of Applied Economics*, 6(2), 317–39.

Taylor, L. 2004. 'External Liberalisation, Economic Performance and Distribution in Latin America and Elsewhere'. In G.A. Cornia (ed.), *Inequality, Growth and Poverty in an Era of Liberalisation and Globalisation*. Oxford: Oxford University Press.

Ticci, E. 2004. *Does the Liberalization of the Capital Account Impact the Distribution of Income in Emerging Economies?* Mimeo (Italian), University of Florence, Florence. December.

World Bank. 2000. *World Development Report*. Washington, DC: World Bank.

World Bank. 1990. *World Development Report*. Washington, DC: World Bank.

2
Pro-Poor Fiscal Policy in the Globalized Economy

Raghbendra Jha[1]

Introduction

The current phase of globalization has been characterized by increasing frequency of economic crises/downturns for developing countries. Several reasons can be advanced for this, including severe drought in agriculture-dependent economies, such as Zimbabwe, or a secular decline in the terms of trade for primary exporting countries, such as Zambia. However, the most important reason has been the inexorable march of the developing world to currency boards or dollarization – with consequent surrender of any semblance of an independent monetary policy – or, more likely, to flexible exchange rates preceded by long maintenance of unsustainable pegs.

Economic crises have serious impacts upon the poor. Lustig (2002) argues that except for wars, macroeconomic crises have been the single most important cause of large increases in income (or consumption) poverty. Crises are frequently accompanied by rising income inequality, as well as deterioration in social indicators such as infant mortality rates and average years of schooling. Even macroeconomic downturns and poverty are strongly linked. Fields (1991) estimated that for every percentage point decline in growth, poverty rises on average by nearly 2 per cent. Lustig (2002) argues that had Latin America reached the levels of macroeconomic stability achieved by industrial economies, roughly 25 per cent of poor people in the region would have been lifted out of poverty. Furthermore, even after the macroeconomic parameters of the economy have recovered after a crisis, there are strong hysteresis effects on the poor (Lokshin and Ravallion 2000). Expenditure cuts during downturns that are not fully blown crises impact differentially on the poor and the non-poor with the former being disadvantaged (Ravallion 2002).

Macroeconomic/fiscal adjustments affect the poor through two broad channels. First, there are direct effects including public sector lay-offs, freezes on the wage bill and cuts in government expenditures on transfers and subsidies and increases in public sector prices. Secondly, there are indirect effects such as a drop in aggregate demand and, hence, increased unemployment and poverty. If public and private capital expenditure are complementary, then a drop in public investment may lead to a drop in private investment as well. This effect could be tempered on two counts: (i) incomplete Ricardian equivalence, typically the case in developing countries, implies that the drop in public investment need not lead to an equivalent drop in private investment; and (ii) furthermore, if the drop in public investment leads to a fall in interest rates, this could stimulate private investment. However, an increase in taxes, in order to lower the fiscal deficit, and restrictive monetary policy would raise interest rates and dampen aggregate private demand, thereby reducing employment and raising poverty.

It becomes imperative then to design a programme for recovery from crises with an eye to its implications for the poor. This chapter articulates a rationale and a structure for such pro-poor adjustment policies and is organized around two principal themes: (i) policy design in the intermediate run, that is, in the steady state bereft of crises; and (ii) the elements of a response to a crisis. The chapter is organized as follows. I initially discuss the background to a pro-poor adjustment policy framework, followed by a discussion of the measurement of the fiscal deficit and the need to check high deficits. The next section addresses policy options in the steady state in order to reduce the risk of crises, followed by a discussion of some elements of a pro-poor fiscal adjustment policy. I conclude with some final thoughts.

The background of a pro-poor adjustment policy framework

A pro-poor stance to fiscal adjustment in developing countries is desirable not only to insulate the poor from the worst effects of a crisis, but also to create a climate for economic reforms. If the poor regard macroeconomic adjustment as pain without much subsequent gain, political support for economic reforms will wane. Because of the weakness of institutions to mobilize and direct savings, the role of fiscal policy is crucial in harnessing resources for development. Since the regulatory apparatus is weak and market signals imperfect, the state has an important role to play in allocating investment funds.

Concurrently, and for some of these same reasons, fiscal policy in developing countries is handicapped in its ability to play an activist role. First, the state is a weaker entity politically than in most developed countries with little consensus on the contours of a tax and expenditure programme (Heady 2004). Secondly, the resources available with the government are meagre since tax bases are small and tax administration weak, with much of the tax revenue coming from inefficient taxes such as excise duties and international trade taxes. Even so, expenditures routinely, and even increasingly, outpace revenues. With poor credit and bond markets and fiscal expenditures that are inflexible in the downward direction, some of the financing of the resultant deficit spills over onto the external sector and the central bank.

With rapidly diminishing official aid and poor private equity flows, external financing of the fiscal deficit in the poorest countries has to rely increasingly on private loans. These are available at increasingly difficult terms since the domestic resource cost – often underestimated – of servicing these goes up with additional borrowing. In addition, as UNCTAD (2000) estimates, the deleterious effects of external shocks in the average least developed country are twice as severe as in the average developing country. External finance is the obvious way to get around this sharp resource crunch. However, such supplies are meagre. Large, stable market economies such as India and South Africa attract considerable capital inflows, whereas for most poor economies of the sub-Saharan region both foreign direct investment (FDI) and portfolio flows are inadequate, with FDI flows being concentrated largely in resource extraction.

Another important factor influencing the vulnerability of developing economies to crises is their inadequate financial depth. Pre-Maastricht developed countries such as Belgium and Italy could run up large deficits without encountering any crisis, whereas Argentina, with a much lower deficit, faced severe crises. Caballero and Krishnamurthy (2004) argue that an important determinant of whether an economy will experience crisis following an episode of high fiscal deficit is the extent of financial depth – as measured by the ratio of credit to the private sector to gross domestic product (GDP) of the country. In developing and transition economies, limited funding constrains the use of fiscal policy during crises. With low financial depth, any increase in public expenditure during a crisis has a more pronounced crowding-out effect on private investment than during normal times.

Low-income countries differ sharply with regard to the depths of their financial markets and continuity and stability of policy regimes. The costs of borrowing abroad are higher for countries with frequent reversals of policy stance since risks associated with lending rise sharply.

Reining in the fiscal deficit

The conventional measure of the fiscal deficit as the difference between total government expenditure and current government revenue while being clear, as an accounting concept, is not above controversy as an economic entity. The associated conceptual and procedural ambiguities include asymmetric effects of tax and expenditure categories in economies with high and variable inflation, strong mutual endogeneity between tax and expenditure categories and, with underdeveloped financial markets and vulnerable external accounts, limited availability of tools for financing deficits (Hermes and Lensink 2004).

Other problems in measuring the deficit include accounting for arrears. Does the deficit go down if interest payments on foreign debt are rescheduled? If the government delays some payments – for example, the public wage bill – but takes in all of its revenues, does fiscal deficit go down? These questions become particularly relevant during high inflation since delaying payments denominated in nominal terms would significantly lower the real value of such payments. How should contingent liabilities be treated?

In federal countries, the fiscal deficits of all levels of government should be included. The deficits of central banks as well as those of accounts such as India's 'oil pool' – which records excesses of payments for petroleum imports over what is collected from consumers – should be included.

Thus, conventional measures of the fiscal deficit in many developing countries are typically underestimates. Nevertheless, a straightforward application of tests of fiscal sustainability to such reported data revealed that in the case of many developing countries either fiscal deficit sustainability or current account sustainability or both are violated (Jha 2004).

Persistently large fiscal deficits pose real threats to the stability and growth of the economy. Budget deficits from the national income identity detract from domestic savings and reduce resources available for investment and growth, assuming that foreign savings are neither plentiful nor imprudent to rely upon – in view of crises – or both. If there is substantial debt overhang, the ability of the government to conduct counter-cyclical public expenditure policy is compromised. During an expansion tax revenues rise and so can public expenditure, whereas during a recession tax revenues drop and, with large debt-servicing charges, little is left for (even essential) public expenditure. Thus, fiscal policy ceases to be stabilizing. Any monetization of the deficit makes monetary policy dependent upon budgetary policy and its stabilization potential is compromised. Excessive budget deficits could lead to a combination of inflation, exchange rate crises, external debt crises and high real interest rates. A high fiscal deficit leads to increasing monetization, which then leads to high inflation although this positive relationship is not easily detectable in the data because of the complex short-run dynamics of high inflationary processes. But Catão and Terrones (2001) argue that once these empirical problems are accounted for there is a strong positive relation between deficits and inflation in developing, particularly, emerging market countries. In that case, sustained fiscal deficits will lead to higher inflation. Since the inflation tax is particularly regressive, this provides a further reason to curb the fiscal deficit, and once a default-type situation occurs – most likely on external debt – it becomes even more difficult to establish credibility in capital markets and borrowing must necessarily occur on increasingly difficult terms.[2]

If the public debt could be lowered directly – say, through a programme of privatization – there would be less need to reduce public expenditures or raise taxes, *ceteris paribus*. However, with underdeveloped capital markets and general non-marketability of public sector assets, privatization is, at best, slow and faltering. Thus, a critical question is how to dovetail sensitivity about poverty reduction in a credible programme of deficit reduction.

Reforms to insulate the poor from crises

Efforts to insulate the poor from the worst effects of a crisis and the ensuing necessary macroeconomic/fiscal adjustment must occur before the crisis sets in. A crisis is, by definition, an emergent situation where harsh decisions have to be taken, and when the crisis is gone there is little incentive to reform. Developing countries can do a considerable amount to plan for a crisis, particularly to reduce its impact on the poor in normal times. Such measures include: (i) capital controls – discussed in Chapters 4 and 5 in this volume; (ii) pro-poor tax policy;

(iii) pro-poor expenditure policy; (iv) social funds; (v) pro-poor institutional reform of fiscal policy; and (vi) measures to insulate the assets of the poor from the effects of crises.

Tax policy to improve fiscal balance in developing countries

Although fiscal deficits are high and often unsustainable, expenditure–GDP ratios in many developing countries are 5 per cent to 10 per cent below Organization for Economic Co-operation and Development (OECD) levels, thus tax reform is a matter of pressing concern. Table 2.1 reports some evidence on tax–GDP ratios in select developing countries.

During 1985–1999, Chile, Egypt, Malaysia and South Africa were able to maintain tax–GDP ratios at OECD levels. During 1999–2002, South Africa was able to maintain this momentum, whereas tax–GDP ratios in Chile and Egypt started slipping. Sri Lanka has experienced a sharp reduction in the tax–GDP ratio since the mid-1980s and India a less severe one. Thailand's tax–GDP performance improved until the 1997 crisis and then suffered a considerable setback, but its tax–GDP ratio was still better than India's. The unweighted average of the tax–GDP ratios for these countries shows a downward trend between 1985 and 1999. There is considerable scope for improvement of the tax–GDP ratio in the countries with low values and/or declining trends.

A panel fixed effects regression of the log of the tax–GDP ratio against the log of per capita real income, a time trend and a constant for these countries during the period 1985–1998 is revealing.

$$\ln(\text{tax/GDP}) = 0.978 - 0.01064 * \text{time trend} + 0.263401 * \ln \text{PC real income}$$
$$(1.85) \quad (-4.19) \quad\quad\quad\quad (3.83)$$

The t-statistics are in parenthesis. The constant is significant at 6.6 per cent and the time trend and per capita real income at one per cent. The F-statistic is highly significant. There is a declining trend in the response of tax collection. The elasticity of the tax–GDP ratio with respect to per capita real income is significant and has the right sign, but is small in magnitude though larger than the coefficient on the time trend.

The agenda for tax reform in developing countries has been widely discussed in the literature (World Bank 1991). Fine-tuning the tax structure to make it progressive should be looked upon as a component of an overall programme of such tax reform. Existing patterns of taxation in developing countries are not only insufficiently progressive, but also create distortions reducing potential economic growth, thereby stifling already scarce funds for poverty alleviation. In many developing countries there is a persistent gap between public expenditure and tax revenue, with most tax revenues being collected from distortionary and regressive taxation such as excise and import tariffs. Income taxes have small bases and direct taxes get skewed in favour of corporate taxation, creating an avenue for inter-tax arbitrage and evasion. High and arbitrary import tariffs have unintended consequences for effective rates of protection and industrial growth. One of the

Table 2.1 Tax revenue as percentage of GDP

	1985	1988	1991	1994	1997	1998	1999	2000	2001	2002
Argentina	15.62	9.26	11.19	14.88	13.60	13.82	NA	17.30[a]	16.90[a]	16.10[a]
Cameroon[b]	22.73	17.69	16.88	10.19	NA	15.39	15.70	18.80	20.60	18.50
Chile[c]	28.36	22.55	22.34	22.57	23.34	22.99	22.51	19.69	20.15	20.06
Colombia[d]	12.02	12.85	14.10	11.40	12.56	11.74	12.34	15.39	15.58	16.04
Dominican Republic[e]	11.01	14.66	11.39	16.40	17.10	16.92	NA	NA	16.93	NA
Egypt[f]	37.12	33.22	34.40	40.37	28.95	NA	22.20	21.20	20.70	21.10
India[g]	13.96	14.23	14.62	12.81	12.37	12.11	14.20	14.50	14.40	15.80
Indonesia[h]	20.05	15.35	16.44	17.35	16.12	16.28	NA	21.24	NA	NA
Malaysia	30.15	25.72	28.78	29.26	25.43	NA	NA	NA	NA	NA
South Africa[i]	26.15	25.77	26.88	26.34	25.96	26.93	25.00	24.60	25.90	25.30
Sri Lanka[j]	24.36	21.78	22.65	20.43	19.36	17.90	18.25	14.50	14.60	13.99
Thailand[k]	16.05	17.21	20.00	19.43	18.68	16.22	15.98	15.15	16.14	17.05
Zimbabwe[l]	29.61	28.82	26.50	27.88	NA	NA	29.20	28.10	26.60	28.00
Unweighted average for these countries	22.09	19.93	20.47	20.71	18.80	17.03	17.26	NA	NA	NA

NA = not available.

Notes:

[a] Source: Central bank of Argentina Web site, www.bcra.gov.ar/.

[b] Data for 1999 onward refer to financial years 1998/99, 1999/2000 and 2000/01 and total revenue and grants. Source: African Development Bank Website, www.afdb.org/.

[c] Figures for 2000, 2001 and 2002 computed from data available on the central bank of Chile. Website: www.bcentral.cl/ (reference only to the central government).

[d] Data for 2001–2002 from International Financial Statistics, IMF.

[e] Data for 2001 from International Financial Statistics, IMF.

[f] Data for 1999 onward refer to financial years 1999/2000, 2000/01, 2001/02 and 2002/03.

Source: African Development Bank Website, www.afdb.org/.

[g] Last four data points for India refer to financial years 1999/2000, 2000/01, 2001/02 and 2002/03. Source: Economic Survey, Government of India, 2002–2003.

[h] Data for 2000 from International Financial Statistics, IMF.

[i] Data from 1999 onward refer to financial years 1999/2000, 2000/01, 2001/02 and 2002/03., Source: IMF and Reserve Bank of South Africa.

[j] Source: Central Bank of Sri Lanka Website, www.lanka.net/centralbank/.

[k] Data for 2000, 2001 and 2002 from International Financial Statistics, IMF.

[l] Source: IMF and other projections as reported by the OECD at http://www.oecd.org/dataoecd/45/43/32411615.pdf.

Source: World Bank Global Development Network Database, unless otherwise stated.

most regressive and distortionary taxes is the inflation tax, which countries in crisis routinely face during phases. Furthermore, tax structures in developing countries are complex with a multiplicity of taxes, rates and exemptions, complicating tax administration.

The literature advocates increasing the emphasis of the tax structure on direct taxation – enlarging the income tax base, reducing the number of rates and substantially cutting the top marginal rates with a flat corporation tax rate that is harmonized with the highest income tax rate. Special tax preferences should be scrutinized since using the system to provide tax incentives usually causes a serious drain on the national exchequer by conferring windfall gains on existing activities or by shifting resources to tax-preferred activities. A uniform broad-based consumption tax, such as a value added tax (VAT), with few exemptions – for example, for goods and services consumed in disproportionately large amounts by the poor – and harmonized across levels of government in federal countries and with few rates is advocated. These could be supplemented with excise duties on environmental detriments or 'luxuries'. Peak tariff duties and effective rates of protection should be reduced gradually. Such tax reforms could improve the allocation of resources and be administratively simpler. If the tax base admits few exemptions and there are fewer rates, costs of compliance and monitoring will fall. A significant exception to this is the VAT, which requires sophisticated account keeping to net out input costs and exempt exports. Such expertise may be lacking in many developing countries. The credibility of the tax regime is also important and tax reforms should aim for a stable tax environment. Tax reform should be well coordinated. Tariff cuts should be accompanied by an upward revision of VAT rates to compensate for tax revenue. The welfare effects of such tax reforms are ambiguous. Warr (2003) advocates increasing the direct tax component, paid largely by the rich and hence progressive, of the total tax burden at the extent of indirect taxes, paid by the poor as well as the rich and hence regressive. His simulations for Thailand indicate that this policy would reduce poverty as well as inequality. On the structure of indirect taxes – particularly the VAT – there is little room for optimism. Emran and Stiglitz (2003a, 2003b) show that the standard prescription of reducing trade taxes with a revenue-compensating upward revision of the rate of a broad-based VAT is welfare improving only in an economy with no informal sector with all production and exchange activity in the tax net – conditions typically not satisfied in developing countries. CSO (2000) notes that in 1999–2000, as much as 60 per cent of India's GDP came from the unorganized sector, and this sector employed 92 per cent of the labour force! When only the formal sector can be taxed, the introduction of a VAT – or a hike in its rate – far from removing distortions across goods and services, ends up creating a distortion between the formal and the informal sectors and may reduce welfare under plausible conditions. Even broadening the VAT base to include more of the informal sector may reduce welfare (Piggott and Whalley 2001).

How successful have these tax reforms been in raising revenue? Given the high tax buoyancy and elasticity of tax structures in many developing countries (see Table 2.5), it can be expected that tax reforms that raise the rate of growth of the economy will, in general, lead to substantial incremental revenues. Estimated buoyancies of the overall tax system, income tax, sales tax and import tax were all higher than their respective elasticities, indicating that tax reform had played a significant role in tax revenue growth. In particular, the expansion of trade following devaluation and tariff reforms appear to have contributed significantly to revenue growth. Munoz and Cho (2003) argue that the introduction of a comprehensive VAT in Ethiopia has not had an adverse impact on the poor, is progressive in its incidence and has raised public sector revenue over the medium term, but not in the short run. Ebrill et al. (2001), however, find that the introduction of the VAT has lowered tax revenues. Direct tax reform – about the beneficial effects of which there seems to be the most consensus – is harder to pursue than indirect tax reforms. These arguments reinforce the case for including exemptions for purposes of VAT goods consumed in disproportionately large amounts by the poor (see Table 2.2).

Table 2.2 Summary of tax reforms and their impact on the poor

Author(s) and countries studied	Principal results
Chen et al. (2001), Uganda	The authors conduct a welfare dominance analysis of tax incidence in Uganda. They discover that the tax structure was progressive before the reforms and remained so after the reforms. Export taxes on coffee, one of Uganda's main exports, remained highly regressive, as the burden of the tax is shifted to relatively poorer rural farmers. The pay-as-you-earn tax remains the most progressive tax, as it is applied to the formal sector, where the non-poor are employed. Substituting VAT for sales taxes does not necessarily worsen the welfare of the poor, since most goods consumed by the poor were zero rated.
Younger et al. (1999), Madagascar	Most taxes are progressive, with the exception of kerosene taxes and export duties on vanilla. A movement away from trade taxes and towards broadly-based value-added or income taxes would be both more equitable and efficient, since these would apply to the formal sector where the non-poor are employed. Furthermore, taxes on petroleum – except those on kerosene, which is heavily used by the poor – are highly progressive and also provide a good tax handle for the government.
Younger (1993), Ghana	The author uses Ghana's 1988 Living Standard Survey and discovers that broad-based taxes are either proportional (sales taxes) or progressive (income and property taxes). A greater reliance on broad- based taxes will improve both equity and efficiency. Petroleum taxes are proportional or slightly progressive, even after taking into account the intermediate effects such as the cost of public transportation.
Gibson (1998), Papua New Guinea	The author discusses the case for introducing a VAT. Instead of removing existing distortions by virtue of being a uniform consumption tax, VAT will introduce new distortions through the proposed 'merit good' exemptions on financial services, health and

Continued

Table 2.2 (Continued)

Author(s) and countries studied	Principal results
	educational services and public road transport. Exemptions from VAT should be on items consumed more heavily by the poor. These include axes, bush knives and garden tools, school fees and children's clothing, pots and pans, salt, rice and tinned fish.
Alderman and del Ninno (1999), South Africa	The authors use the World Bank's 1993 Living Standard Development Survey and assess VAT exemptions and their targeting of the poor. They estimate a welfare cost to revenue benefit ratio, which gives a cost–benefit ratio to assess commodity-specific exemptions. They find that maize is the best choice for low rates from the standpoints of equity, efficiency and the impact on the nutritional value of the poor. Low tax rates on beans, sugar and kerosene are beneficial from the viewpoint of equity. Lower tax rates on fluid milk and meat are not good instruments for achieving equity or nutritional objectives.
Ahmad and Stern (1984) use 1979–1980 data, India and Pakistan	The authors discover that taxes on cereals, fuel and light are less socially desirable relative to a tax on clothing for social welfare functions that are averse to inequality.
Ahmad and Stern (1987, 1991), India and Pakistan	The authors examine the impact of replacing a number of direct and indirect taxes on consumption by a simple proportional VAT. Using 1979–1980 data they find that switching to a VAT would be equivalent to reducing the real expenditures of the poorest rural households by 6.8 per cent and increasing those of the richest rural households by more than 3 per cent. In the case of India at higher levels of inequality aversion, import duties are the most attractive form of indirect tax revenue. In the case of Pakistan for higher levels of inequality aversion, wheat and pulses are not desirable candidates for sources of additional tax revenue, whereas housing, fuel and light are. A less desirable commodity for a tax increase is one whose consumption is concentrated among the poor, has a low shadow price and is less responsive in terms of revenue increase, ceteris paribus. A single rate VAT seems inappropriate for developing countries since a number of agricultural sectors cannot be covered under a uniform VAT. They discuss the introduction of a tiered-VAT system with zero rating for exports, exemptions for the agricultural sector, a standard rate of 10 per cent and a luxury rate of 20 per cent, together with excises. Such a VAT could be revenue-neutral without having a progressive impact on income distribution.

Making tax reforms in developing countries more pro-poor

There is some consensus in the literature that tax structures in developing countries are not particularly progressive. Chu *et al.* (2004) find that: (i) only 13 of the 36 overall tax systems surveyed by them are progressive, seven are proportional, seven are regressive and the rest neutral or insignificant; and (ii) income taxes are progressive in 12 of the 14 cases studied, whereas indirect taxes are broadly regressive; the progressivity of direct taxes declined over time in eight cases.

A brief taxonomy of the extant literature's view on how to fine-tune tax reforms to make them pro-poor is presented in Table 2.2. Although many results are context specific, a general result is that items that are consumed in disproportionately large amounts by the poor and exportables should be taxed at lower rates – or exempted from taxation – including any VAT.

Public expenditure reform in developing countries

Table 2.3 indicates that public expenditure in developing countries – even those with low tax–GDP ratios – has not been excessive. If one nets out debt-servicing charges, expenditure–GDP ratios are likely to be even lower.

Table 2.3 Public expenditure as a percentage of GDP

	1985	1988	1991	1994	1997	1998	1999	2000	2001	2002	2003
Argentina[a]	17.68	10.81	11.41	15.21	15.26	15.41	NA	18.60	18.20	16.90	NA
Cameroon[b]	20.89	17.43	22.17	12.77	NA	13.88	18.90	17.40	18.30	NA	NA
Chile[c]	30.40	23.17	21.01	20.95	21.21	22.53	23.93	26.70	27.10	26.9	NA
Colombia[d]	14.06	13.70	11.53	12.58	16.09	16.62	18.76	19.60	20.6	20.7	20.6
Dominican Republic[e]	12.55	16.34	11.08	17.08	16.68	16.29	NA	NA	NA	17.00	NA
Egypt[f]	39.91	36.60	31.92	37.36	30.64	NA	26.10	26.80	26.50	27.40	NA
India[g]	16.42	17.56	17.03	15.26	15.21	14.95	17.70	18.00	18.50	20.00	NA
Indonesia[h]	20.47	18.28	16.01	15.46	15.98	17.82	NA	NA	24.70	NA	NA
Malaysia	29.04	27.94	29.24	24.52	NA	NA	NA	NA	NA	NA	NA
South Africa[i]	29.24	30.60	30.62	32.27	29.40	29.83	27.00	26.60	27.40	26.60	26.70
Sri Lanka[j]	33.36	31.08	29.29	27.19	25.69	24.93	24.06	26.65	27.41	25.39	NA
Thailand[k]	20.87	15.80	15.01	17.12	20.48	22.51	24.92	17.35	17.73	17.60	16.70
Zimbabwe[l]	33.62	33.72	31.88	29.59	NA	NA	38.70	48.80	34.70	38.20	NA
Unweighted average for these countries	24.5	22.54	21.4	21.33	20.66	19.47	21.87	NA	NA	NA	NA

Notes:
NA = not available.

[a] Figures for 2000–2002 computed from data available on the Central Bank of Argentina website, www.bcra.gov.ar/. Variable defined as national primary spending.

[b] Data for 1999 onward refer to financial years 1998/99, 1999/2000 and 2000/01.
  Source: African Development Bank website, www.afdb.org/.

[c] Figures for 2000–2002 computed from data available on the central bank of Chile Website, www.bcentral.cl/.

[d] Last four data points from International Financial Statistics, IMF.

[e] Data for 2002 from International Financial Statistics, IMF.

[f] Data for 1999 onward refer to financial years 1999/2000, 2000/01, 2001/02 and 2002/03.
  Source: African Development Bank Website, www.afdb.org/.

[g] Last four data points for India refer to financial years 1999/2000, 2000/01, 2001/02 and 2002/03 and refer to revenue expenditure.
  Source: Economic Survey, Government of India, 2002–2003.

[h] Data for 2001 from International Financial Statistics, IMF.

[i] Data from 1999 onward refer to financial years 1999/2000, 2000/01, 2001/02 and 2002/03.
  Sources: IMF and Reserve Bank of South Africa.
  Data for 2003 from International Financial Statistics, IMF.

[j] Data from the Central Bank of Sri Lanka website, www.lanka.net/centralbank/.

[k] Last four data points from International Financial Statistics, IMF.

[l] *Source*: IMF and other projections as reported by the OECD at http://www.oecd.org/dataoecd/45/43/32411615.pdf.

  Source: World Bank Global Development Network Database, unless otherwise stated.

Results of a panel fixed effects regression of ln (exp/GDP) against ln (per capita real income) and a time trend using annual data for the period 1980–1998 are as follows:

ln (exp/GDP) = 3.55 − 0.00635 * time trend − 0.05965 * ln (pc real income)
   (6.504) (−2.888)   (−0.837)

The t-statistics are in parentheses below the respective coefficients. The time trend and the constant are strongly significant. The coefficient on per capita real income is insignificant. The F-statistic is strongly significant.

With growth of per capita income tax–GDP ratios tend to increase, whereas there is no significant change in the expenditure–GDP ratio. Over time, both tax–GDP and expenditure–GDP ratios fall. Over the medium term, as globalization proceeds demands for public expenditure are likely to rise (Rodrik 1998).

Pro-poor expenditure reform in developing countries

Pro-poor tax reforms should be complemented with appropriate adjustment of government expenditures. The impact of public expenditure is usually ascertained through an *ex post* incidence analysis. The questions typically asked, given some tax or public expenditure, are: Who pays or receives the benefits of public spending?

How much does everyone receive in accounting terms? How much does everyone receive when taking into account behavioural responses to taxes or the free delivery of public services? What are the indirect effects of the programme? Such analyses enable the researcher to ascertain the actual distribution of the amount budgeted as a tax receipt or a public expenditure and helps decide whether public expenditures are worth their cost.

A problem with this methodology is that only existing taxes or public programmes may be analysed. We must evaluate not what does exist, but what might exist. This is the theme of benefit incidence analysis.[3] The questions asked are: What if some features of the tax system or public spending were modified? How different would it be for individual households from the initial situation or the status quo? Such analysis is both marginal – because it should capture differences from the status quo – and behavioural – because of the need to generate counter-factuals.

Addressing behavioural issues – especially labour supply and income generation – is important. But such modelling is difficult in the case of developing countries because direct transfers to households, whether positive or negative, are limited. Furthermore, the distinction between formal and informal labour markets is critical with jobs in the former being subject to some form of rationing.

Delineating expenditure adjustments according to their effects on the poor in developing countries cannot await the development of *ex ante* analysis. A good rule of thumb would be to delay/reduce the cuts in public expenditure on goods and services that are directly or indirectly of high importance in the budget of the poor, for example, coarser types of food, fuel and agricultural subsidies.

An example of a successful programme comes from Chile (Schkolnik 1992). During the period 1990–92, there was a sharp drop in government expenditure and Chile adopted the neoliberal doctrine of development in a rather pure form, cutting back on many social programmes. However, social programmes, to the extent they were retained, focused exclusively on the services of the poor.

Even within the broad category of basic services, however, the selection of programmes needs to be sensitive to the type and severity of deprivation. A programme of subsidized nutritional supplements would be more effective than an elementary education scheme for widespread malnutrition. Rudra (2004) establishes that only the education component of public expenditure encourages a more favourable distribution of income in the face of globalization. Thus, when high inequality is a concern expenditure on education should not be cut; but the decision on what expenditure items are pro-poor is country specific (Van de Walle 1995).

Problems of targeting

Some economists argue that as long as targeting is effective, a general rule like directing public expenditure towards basic services need not be followed. However, there is no guarantee that targeting will be effective – the poor may be excluded or there may be leakages to the non-poor and costs of targeting may be high. These include the initial screening costs and the costs of delivery to the poor to the exclusion of the non-targeted group and the incentive effects of targeted programmes, as the targeted groups alter their labour supply and private transfers to them may be reduced. Some targeted programmes have been known to be effective. For instance, poor workers have self-selected themselves into employment guarantee schemes like the Employment Guarantee Scheme in Maharashtra, India. But programmes targeted towards the poor could become 'poor programmes', political support for which may falter. Hence, targeting may be politically unsustainable in such cases.

When pruning public expenditures there is naturally an inclination to avoid cuts in public subsidies geared towards the poor. During crises, both consumption and production get hit. However, there is some controversy about the impact of targeted subsides (Cornia and Stewart 1995). Food subsidies have some degree of targeting built into them depending on which food items are subsidized and the consumption pattern of the poor. However, the costs of a targeted programme, including the costs of verification as well as administration, may be high. Cornia and Stewart (1995) consider the two errors of targeting – one of including the non-poor (E) and the other of excluding the poor (F). If the intent of the food subsidy is to improve food access for the poor, in the case of universal subsidies, F mistakes are generally low, if access to the subsidy is rationed and widely accessible. However, universal schemes involve considerable E mistakes. With low incomes the incidence of the E errors is likely to be small. Furthermore, if 'poor people's grains' can be identified and the subsidy is on such grains, then an implicit subsidy to the poor exists with further reduction in E errors. The broader the definition of the target group, the lower the incidence of E errors.

Universal schemes save on verification and monitoring costs but err because they include the non-poor. A move from a universal to a targeted scheme could lead to a major increase in *F* errors, while reducing *E* errors. In Sri Lanka, the value of this subsidy has actually fallen over time, indicating lower political support for a targeted as opposed to a universal subsidy programme. Since the political clout of the poor does not rise during a crisis, it might be worth designing a more defensible intervention that is universal but focused on food items consumed in disproportionately large amounts by the poor.

Thus, a good public expenditure design would incorporate elements of both universal as well as targeted programmes with the optimal combination depending on a number of factors, including characteristics of the poor – Can the poor be easily identified? How many poor are there and why are they poor? – and on country-specific and context-specific circumstances. There needs to be broad political consensus to protect the most important elements of this programme in case of a general reduction in public expenditure mandated by a structural adjustment programme.

Broader issues in subsidy reform

There are many issues in subsidy reform that go beyond their impact effect on the poor, for example, general equilibrium effects with both efficiency and equity implications. A comprehensive study of such implications is beyond the scope of this chapter and only a few illustrative examples are provided. In the case of the food subsidy in India, the base from which this subsidy is calculated is inflated because of the high procurement prices paid to farmers – mostly from the richer states of Andhra Pradesh, Haryana and Punjab. Since 2001, this subsidy has discriminated between consumers above and below the poverty line, but verification and administrative costs have been high and targeting has been poor, with only 3.7 per cent of the food subsidy actually going to those below the poverty line (Panagariya 2002).

A production subsidy – for example, the fertilizer subsidy in India – has other problems. In the interest of establishing a domestic fertilizer industry – behind high tariff walls – the government provides support through a retention price mechanism assuring fertilizer plants a minimum guaranteed rate of return on their cost and eliminating all incentive to minimize costs. A subsidy is added to lower the price paid by farmers, making them a captive market for these inefficient fertilizer plants. Ghosh (2003) shows that in India small farmers are inclined towards fertilizer use and that the fertilizer subsidy does not appear to be unduly regressive.

However, in Africa there is an urgent need to increase phosphorus use in an area covering about 530 million hectares. Africa also needs a combination of inorganic fertilizer, biological fixation technologies, biomass transfer of organic matter into fields and animal manure/compost. However, fertilizer use has been hampered by sharp rises in price following adjustment programmes.

A pro-poor policy approach in such cases would combine macroeconomic stabilization, thereby obviating the need to cut subsidies drastically, with more market/regulatory related reforms such as reduction in export taxes, which limit the access of many African farmers to the international market, a better distribution network for fertilizers – preferably through the private sector – and rationalization of the subsidy structure to ensure that the fertilizer mix suits soil conditions.

A distinction needs to be drawn between policies towards the alleviation of chronic as opposed to temporary (rises in) poverty following a programme of structural adjustment, although with hysteresis effects such temporary rises in poverty could become chronic. Social funds have often been the preferred policy response to the problem of short-run increases in poverty. They are social safety nets designed to mitigate the impact on the poor of structural adjustment, premature financial liberalization and unguided globalization and are used for short-term purposes to address employment, infrastructure and community development, social services and decentralization. Social funds involve lower transactions costs, and greater accountability, flexibility and transparency than regular public sector antipoverty programmes; they are demand-driven and since they directly provide services to target populations – the most deprived – they could aid in the decentralization process. Cornia and Reddy (2004) show that allocations under social funds are inadequate, unpredictable, and not well targeted and that allotments often come at the expense of longer-standing antipoverty programmes. Furthermore, since social funds provide short-term relief, they fail to build institutional capacity for sustained poverty reduction.

Stabilization funds

Given the uncertainty in the revenue response of tax reforms, a case can be made for creating a fund that might help to maintain public expenditure in key areas at reasonable levels without running high public debt. Some countries, particularly those that are dependent on revenues from resource exports, have established stabilization funds. This type of fund is augmented during periods of resource price booms and accumulated funds are used for stabilizing state spending during years of recession or unfavourable conditions for resource exports. Table 2.4 summarizes the principal characteristics of stabilization funds in the two developing countries where they have been successful.

Stabilization funds have helped Chile to smooth out the fluctuations in public expenditure following changes in copper prices. Venezuela's fund has helped to stabilize state finances. However, those developing countries that have been able to successfully create such stabilization funds are the ones with large endowments of one or more natural resource for which there is substantial demand in international markets during normal times – for example, copper in Chile and petroleum in Venezuela. For most developing countries, stabilization funds are out of reach. Nevertheless, some earmarking of budgetary surpluses, as they occur, as well as international donations can help create stabilization funds that could arrest the slide in pro-poor public expenditures during downturns.

Pro-poor institutional reform of fiscal policy

A growing body of literature has recently argued that the institutional context within which fiscal policy is made could be reformed to make such policy pro-poor. Brautigam (2004) cites several examples of such pro-poor budgeting, which essentially involves three components: (i) participation; (ii) transparency; and (iii) accountability. These principles have been included as core elements of Ethiopia's Poverty Reduction Strategy Programme and in some other cases in successful gender budgeting in nearly 40 countries worldwide. There is evidence to

Table 2.4 Successful stabilization funds in developing countries

Fund	Copper Stabilization Fund of Chile	Macroeconomic Stabilization Fund of Venezuela
Year of creation	1985 (no receipts before 1987)	1998
Purpose	Stabilization of the real exchange rate and state budget revenues in face of fluctuations in world copper prices	Protection of state budget and economy against oil price fluctuations
Formation	Under conditions of central government budget surplus	From central government budget, regional government budget and oil companies
Size	$1.7 billion by January 2000	Special Framework of Assistance, $27.1 billion (1999) Constitutional Budget Reserve Fund, $6.1 billion (1999)
Utilization	Government can withdraw funds when copper prices are below long-run levels; at the end of the 1980s the fund was used to repay government debt of the Bank of Chile and to subsidize domestic gasoline prices	Only in the short run to be repaid at times of budget surplus; all three levels of government have the right to access it
Management	Government of Chile	Utilization of funds by permission of the government of Venezuela, management by the central bank
Specific Features	Government operates according to a permanent rule, defined by law	Being reformed to permit use in the medium term

Source: Adapted from Zolotareva et al. (2002).

suggest that pro-poor budgeting has helped improve outcomes for the poor in many of these countries during normal times as well as in responding to macroeconomic downturns.

Towards a pro-poor deficit finance policy for developing countries

During a downturn are there automatic stabilizers at work that can mitigate its effects? As the economy slides into a recession, incomes fall, hence collected taxes fall, imports fall, and therefore import duties fall. As unemployment rises, payment of unemployment benefits rise. Subsequently, the fiscal deficit starts to rise; during a boom the reverse process takes place.

Discretionary fiscal policy and structural changes – for example, demographic changes – in the economy also affect fiscal balances. Typically, these are long-term changes that do not concern us when discussing stabilization policy. The sensitivity of the fiscal balance to the economic cycle depends upon:

- the size of the government sector – the larger the revenue–GDP and expenditure–GDP ratios, the more sensitive the fiscal balance will be to fluctuations in GDP;
- the progressivity of taxes and the generosity of unemployment benefits – the more progressive the rate structure of the tax, the more sensitive it will be to fluctuations in income; and
- the tax structure – the larger the share of progressive or cycle-sensitive taxes in total revenue, the more sensitive total tax revenue will be. In developed countries the role of automatic stabilizers is very important but far less important in developing countries because the revenue–GDP and expenditure–GDP ratios are far smaller and the share of income-elastic taxes is small.

An excess of public expenditure can be financed in four ways: (i) printing money; (ii) running down foreign exchange reserves; (iii) borrowing abroad; and (iv) borrowing domestically. However, these measures could lead to potentially serious problems. Printing money can lead to high inflation and the rise in prices of essential commodities can be regressive and raise poverty. Drawing upon foreign exchange reserves excessively can lead to a balance-of-payments crisis and, due to contagion effects, to a full-blown currency crisis. The policy of borrowing abroad excessively – either by the public sector (Brazil) or by the private sector (Thailand) – can lead to currency crises. In such cases, financing the deficit can be worse than the deficit itself. Internal borrowings can lead to pressures on interest rates. Most developing countries use a combination of these measures and rely significantly on non-bond (monetary) financing of the deficit, which compromises the independence of monetary from fiscal policy.

Thus, cutting spending or increasing revenue through additional and/or more streamlined taxation remain the most important methods to reduce the deficit. The conceptually correct way to choose between the two is to compare the marginal cost of raising a dollar of revenue with the marginal benefit of expenditure. From the viewpoint of designing a pro-poor stabilization policy these gains/losses should be distributionally weighted, with gains/losses to consumers at the lower end of the income distribution being given greater weight than those for consumers at the upper end of the income distribution. The specification of these weights depends upon the welfare function used; for example, we could multiply gains/losses to different income classes by the reciprocals of their incomes. Whereas income/consumption for different income groups typically exist in practice, there might be problems in obtaining reliable estimates for either the cost of mobilizing extra tax revenue or the benefit of marginal public spending, especially if these have to be weighted to reflect distributional concerns.

Which route – increasing taxation or lowering public expenditure – is to be given greater weight in a programme of adjustment could depend upon initial conditions and thus vary across countries. With a low tax–GDP ratio India should raise more tax revenue, but with a low expenditure–GDP ratio it needs to switch rather than reduce public expenditure. Chile, on the other hand, already has a high tax–GDP ratio as well as a high expenditure–GDP ratio and adjustments should concentrate on the expenditure side. This recommendation is at variance with the findings in World Bank (1992), which makes the case for generalized expenditure cuts unless, for political or other reasons, public expenditures are inflexible in the downward direction.

All arguments to cut public expenditure or raise taxes to reduce the budget deficit must recognize that both are endogenous to GDP. Thus, if GDP declines during a recession, tax revenue would go down. The response of tax revenues to base changes is often measured through measures such as tax buoyancy and tax elasticity. Elasticity of a tax system is defined as ε, where:

$$\varepsilon = \frac{\text{Percentage change in tax revenue (with unchanged tax system)}}{\text{Percentage change in tax base (GDP)}}$$

Whereas tax buoyancy is defined as:

$$\theta = \frac{\text{Percentage change in tax revenue}}{\text{Percentage change in tax base}}$$

The only difference between the two is that tax elasticity is computed without any change in the tax structure. Both are computed in real terms (Haughton 1998) and both use GDP as the tax base. For 1999–2000, Muganyizi (2002) computes the buoyancy and elasticity of Tanzanian tax revenues to be 1.1 and 0.7 respectively.

Teera (2002) estimates tax buoyancy for a number of developing countries during the period 1975–1998 to be quite high (see Table 2.5). The unweighted average of tax buoyancy for the 40 countries is 1.045.

Although parallel concepts could be defined for public expenditure, the pertinent point is that during an adjustment-induced downturn in most cases public expenditures would be reduced only marginally, whereas with high tax buoyancy and elasticity tax revenues could fall substantially. Hence, the net impact effect of this adjustment policy could be to raise the fiscal deficit. The revival in public finances would depend largely upon the rise in tax revenue as a condequence of any subsequent economic growth. This partly explains the inadequate performance of International Monetary Fund (IMF) adjustment programmes in reducing the fiscal deficit over a reasonable time horizon, and the persistence of fiscal stress in many countries with such programmes.

The stance of discretionary fiscal policy depends upon the targeted fiscal deficit. Some IMF economists have argued that a general rule of thumb for determining the optimal fiscal deficit should be that the gross fiscal deficit is sustainable in the medium term – say, 10 to 15 years. However, tests for sustainability usually treat

Table 2.5 Tax buoyancy in select low-income countries, 1975–1998

Country	ε	Country	ε	Country	ε
Bangladesh	2.26	Guinea-Bissau	0.43	Nigeria	0.15
Bhutan	1.61	Haiti	0.94	Pakistan	1.16
Burkina Faso	1.08	India	0.95	Rwanda	1.20
Burundi	1.46	Indonesia	0.99	Senegal	1.25
Cameroon	0.69	Kenya	1.45	Sierra Leone	0.73
Chad	0.48	Lesotho	1.95	Solomon Islands	1.38
Comoros	0.33	Liberia	1.22	Togo	0.91
Congo(DRC)	0.52	Madagascar	0.56	Uganda	0.72
Congo	0.23	Malawi	1.48	Viet Nam	0.67
Côte d'Ivoire	0.98	Mali	1.47	Yemen	1.45
Ethiopia	0.18	Mauritania	1.07	Zambia	0.59
Gambia	1.55	Myanmar	0.55	Zimbabwe	1.612
Ghana	0.96	Nepal	1.76	Unweighted average for these countries	1.045
Guinea	0.82	Nicaragua	1.99		

Note: DRC = The Democratic Republic of the Congo.
Source: Teera (2002).

the rate of economic growth and, sometimes, the rate of interest paid on the debt as exogenous. A current macroeconomic adjustment by reducing the short-run rate of economic growth may lower the *ex post* tax revenue and chances of fiscal adjustment. However, deficit reduction should not become an end in itself – even if we discount the effects of such adjustments on the poor. Adam and Bevan (2001) argue that if the intention is to minimize the impact of the fiscal deficit on growth, deficit reduction is useful only up to a limit – 1.5 per cent of GDP – with further reductions actually hurting growth.

The optimal size of the budget deficit, particularly from the vantage point of the poor in developing countries, depends upon factors such as the levels of internal and external debt and the level and future path of the current account deficit since these will determine how the fiscal deficit spills over onto the external account. With high monetization, further deficits will add to inflation. The overall policy regime is also a key determinant. Under an open capital account, the appropriate level of sustainable fiscal deficit and of sustainable government debt should be significantly reduced. A lower long-run fiscal deficit will help to avoid frequent and large fiscal adjustments as capital flows turn around and reduce risk of capital outflows. A large fiscal deficit and high government debt will make the country more vulnerable to shifts in market sentiment, increase the risk premium that accompanies high levels of debt and increase contingent liabilities. The government may carry hidden liabilities, for example, guaranteed borrowing by state-owned enterprises. Capital inflows are generally associated with sharp increases in domestic credit. Sudden outflow of funds can affect the health of the financial institutions and government support will be necessary, for instance, as was the case during the Asian financial crisis. Developing countries should, in principle, be wary of lifting capital controls too soon and certainly not before banking and financial sector reforms have been put firmly in place. Those that have even partially lifted capital controls should consider re-imposing capital controls.

During the period of reduction of the fiscal deficit, the path followed by adjustment can be made pro-poor. Lustig (2002) views this adjustment as having three essential components: (i) avoiding excessive adjustment (overkill); (ii) avoiding postponing adjustment (underkill); and (iii) protection, to the extent of programmes benefiting the poor. Excessive adjustment can lead to or prolong a sharp recession. If there are hysteresis effects in this recession the downturn may last for an unnecessarily long period and cause substantial loss of output. However, neither inadequate adjustment nor postponing adjustment are options – particularly in these days of contagion effects. If markets perceive that there is an inadequate response to financial sector weakness, or fiscal or current account deficits, there will be strong repercussions and what was a situation merely requiring adjustment may degenerate into a crisis.

However, within these two limits there is room for a pro-poor response to the crisis, although this is complicated by the fact that different types of poor – for example, the rural poor versus the urban poor – may be affected differently by crisis. Lustig (2002) advocates, at the margin, the general approach of development of safety nets for the poor – as opposed to sector-specific approaches – especially since some of the spending targeted to the poor is distinctly pro-cyclical. Non-governmental organizations and international donors should be involved in deciding the design of safety nets and supplementing funds for these safety nets. Expenditure reduction should be prioritized so that those with the greatest relevance to the poor are cut last and the least. The cost of safety nets need not be large. The Mexican programme *Progresa* targets a whole range of development indicators and benefits about two million households, but costs only 0.2 per cent of Mexican GDP and one per cent of the total federal budget.

> Had Progresa existed when the 1995 crisis hit Mexico, the rural poverty gap and the square poverty gap ... would have declined by 17 percent and 25 percent respectively, in the year after the crisis. (Lustig 2002: 17)

Maintaining Nicaragua's social safety net programme, even with the least rationalization of existing taxes and expenditure programmes, would have raised the fiscal deficit by only about 2 per cent (Arcia 2002).

This leads to the broader point that contingency plans for addressing a crisis must be instituted before any crisis takes place and not improvised in an ad hoc manner during a crisis. For this, one needs a data base on consumption patterns of the poor and a structure of programmes that are of greatest benefits to them – these would include targeted human development programmes and workfare or public works programmes – and contingency plans for funding of the most effective programmes or subsidies, either through budgetary switching or through contributions from international donor agencies. Since the crowding-out effect of public investment on private investment is aggravated by lack of financial depth, such deepening should occur during normal times.

Conclusion

Macroeconomic adjustment in developing countries has strong distributional consequences, particularly for the poor. Such adjustment, while effecting a revival in macroeconomic parameters, may have hysteresis effects such that the attendant rise in poverty may become chronic. Furthermore, there is a risk that if this rise in poverty is long enough or the benefits of any ensuing revival do not sufficiently favour the poor, a reform programme for economic revival may lose the support of the poor and become unviable. Thus, from both an efficiency point of view – maintaining political support for an economic reform programme promising rapid economic growth – and an equity viewpoint – shielding the poor from the worst effects of a downturn – it is important to append a pro-poor fiscal policy to an economic stabilization programme.

This chapter outlines the basic contours of such a strategy. It argues that although the fiscal deficit in many developing countries appears to be unsustainable, a policy package involving tax and expenditure reforms when the economy is not in crisis can help to reduce the risk from high fiscal deficits. Furthermore, such tax and expenditure reforms can also be finetuned to help the poor. This chapter also discusses measures to shield the poor in anticipation of a downturn and the contours of a pro-poor fiscal adjustment once this becomes necessary. Given the wide heterogeneity among developing countries, the conclusion is that policy prescriptions are both context- and country-specific.

Notes

1 I am grateful to Giovanni Andrea Cornia for helpful comments on earlier versions of this chapter and to Anurag Sharma for research assistance. Helpful comments from the Milan conference participants are also acknowledged. All opinions and any errors are mine alone.
2 Lustig (2002) argues that the effects of inflation are asymmetric across groups of poor. Market-integrated groups are adversely affected, but non-market groups are not. Bruno and Easterley (1995) argue that the link between growth and inflation is fragile, however inflation crises are associated with low growth.
3 See Demery (2002). Younger (2003) argues that the standard method gives a good first-order approximation to the marginal approach in most, but not all, cases.

References

Adam, C. and D. Bevan. 2001. *Non-Linear Effects of Fiscal Deficits on Growth in Developing Countries*. Working Paper, Department of Economics, Oxford University, Oxford.

Ahmad, E. and N. Stern. 1984. 'The Theory of Reform and Indian Indirect Taxes'. *Journal of Public Economics*, 25(3), 259–98.

Ahmad, E. and N. Stern, 1987. 'Alternative Sources of Government Revenue: Illustrations from India, 1979–80'. In D. Newbery and N. Stern (eds), *The Theory of Taxation for Developing Countries*. Oxford: Oxford University Press.

Ahmad, E. and N. Stern. 1991. *The Theory and Practice of Tax Reform in Developing Countries*. Cambridge: Cambridge University Press.

Alderman, H. and C. del Ninno. 1999. 'Poverty Issues for Zero Rating VAT in South Africa'. *Journal of African Economies*, 8(2), 182–208.

Arcia, G. 2002. *Briefing Note for Consulting Assistance on Economic Reform II*. Discussion Paper No. 82. www.cid.harvard.edu/caer2/htm/content/papers/bns/dp82bn.htm, accessed on 13 May 2004.

Brautigam, D. 2004. *The People's Budget? Politics, Power, Popular Participation and Pro-poor Economic Policy*. Brighton: Institute of Development Studies.

Bruno, M. and W. Easterley. 1995. *Inflation Crises and Long-Run Growth*, Working Paper 5209. Cambridge, MA: National Bureau of Economic Research.

Caballero, R. and A. Krishnamurthy. 2004. *Fiscal Policy and Financial Depth*. Working Paper. Cambridge, MA: Massachusetts Institute of Technology.

Catão, P. and M. Terrones. 2001. *Fiscal Deficits and Inflation: A New Look at the Emerging Market Evidence*. Working Paper WP/01/74. Washington, DC: International Monetary Fund.

Central Statistical Organization (CSO). 2000. *National Sample Survey, 55th Round, 1999–2000*. New Delhi: CSO.

Chen, D., J. Matovu and R. Reinikka. 2001. 'A Quest for Revenue and Tax Incidence'. In R. Reinikka and P. Collier (eds), *Uganda's Recovery: The Role of Farms, Firms and Government*. Washington, DC: World Bank.

Chu, K., H. Davoodi and S. Gupta. 2004. 'Income Distribution and Tax and Government Social Spending Policies in Developing Countries'. In A. Cornia (ed.), *Inequality, Growth, and Poverty in an Era of Liberalization and Globalization*. New York: Oxford University Press.

Cornia, G.A. and S. Reddy. 2004. 'The Impact of Adjustment Related Social Funds on Income Distribution and Poverty'. In A. Cornia (ed.), *Inequality, Growth, and Poverty in an Era of Liberalization and Globalization*. New York: Oxford University Press.

Cornia, G.A. and F. Stewart. 1995. 'Two Errors of Targeting'. In D. Van de Walle and K. Nead (eds), *Public Spending and the Poor: Theory and Evidence*. Baltimore, MD: John Hopkins University Press for the World Bank.

Demery, L. 2002. 'Benefit Incidence Analysis'. *Poverty Analysis Tool Kit*. Washington, DC: The World Bank.

Ebrill, L., M. Keen, J. Bodin, J. and V. Summers. 2001. *The Modern VAT*. Washington, DC: International Monetary Fund.

Emran, M. and J. Stiglitz. 2003a. *On Selective Indirect Tax Reform in Developing Countries*. Mimeo, Columbia University, New York.

Emran, M. and J. Stiglitz. 2003b. *Price-Neutral Tax Reform with an Informal Economy*. Mimeo, Columbia University, New York.

Fields, G. 1991. 'Growth and Income Distribution.' In G. Psacharopoulos (ed.), *Essays on Poverty, Equity and Growth*. Oxford: Pergamon Press.

Ghosh, N. 2003. *Fertilizer Use Strategy in the Emerging Era of Liberalisation and Class Equity*. Mimeo, Institute of Economic Growth, New Delhi.

Gibson, J. 1998. 'Indirect Tax Reform and the Poor in Papua New Guinea'. *Pacific Economic Bulletin*, 13(2), 29–39.

Haughton, J. 1998. *Estimating, Tax Buoyancy, Elasticity and Stability*. African Economic Policy Paper, Discussion Paper No. 11. Cambridge, MA: Harvard Institute for International Development.

Heady, C. 2004. 'Taxation Policy in Low-Income Countries'. In Addison and Roe (eds), *Fiscal Policies for Development*. Basingstoke and New York: Palgrave Macmillan.

Hermes, N. and R. Lensink. 2004. 'Fiscal Policy and Private Investment in Less Developed Countries'. In Addison and Roe (eds), *Fiscal Policies for Development*. Basingstoke and New York: Palgrave Macmillan.

Jha, R. 2004. 'Macroeconomics of Fiscal Policy in Developing Countries'. In Addison and Roe (eds), *Fiscal Policies for Development*. Basingstoke and New York: Palgrave Macmillan.

Lokshin, M. and M. Ravallion. 2000. *Short-Lived Shocks with Long-Lived Impacts? Household Income Dynamics in a Transition Economy*. Working Paper. Washington, DC: World Bank.

Lustig, N. 2002. 'Crises and the Poor: Socially Responsible Macroeconomics'. *Economia 2000*, 1(1) (Fall), 1–19.

Muganyizi, T. 2002. *Fiscal Policy and Monitoring: The Tax Revenue Side in Tanzania*. Mimeo, World Bank, Washington, DC.

Munoz, S. and S. Cho. 2003. *Social Impact of a Tax Reform: The Case of Ethiopia*, Working Paper WP/03/22. Washington, DC: International Monetary Fund.

Panagariya, A. 2002. 'Stamping in Nutrition'. *Economic Times*, 24 April, p. 3.

Piggott, J. and J. Whalley. 2001. 'VAT Base Broadening, Self Supply, and the Informal Sector'. *American Economic Review*, 91, 1084–94.

Ravallion, M. 2002. *Who is Protected? On the Incidence of Fiscal Adjustment*. Mimeo, World Bank, Washington, DC.

Rodrik, D. 1998. 'Why do More Open Economies have Bigger Governments?' *Journal of Political Economy*, 106(5), 997–1032.

Rudra, N. 2004. 'Openness, Welfare Spending and Inequality in the Developing World'. *International Studies Quarterly*, 48, 683–709.

Schkolnik, M. 1992. *The Distributive Impact of Fiscal and Labour Market Policies: Chile's 1990–1991 Reforms*. Innocenti Occasional Papers, Economic Policy Series, Number 33. Florence: UNICEF.

Teera, J. 2002. *Tax Performance: A Comparative Study*. Working Paper No. 01/2002, Department of Economics, University of Bath, UK.

United Nations Conference on Trade and Development (UNCTAD). 2000. *The Least Developed Countries 2000 Report*. Geneva: UNCTAD.

Van de Walle, D. 1995. 'Incidence and Targeting: An Overview of Implications for Research and Policy'. In Van de Walle and Nead (eds), *Public Spending and the Poor: Theory and Evidence*. Baltimore, MD: John Hopkins University Press for the World, Bank.

Warr, P. 2003. 'Fiscal Policies and Poverty Incidence: The Case of Thailand'. *Asian Economic Journal*, 17(1), 27–44.

World Bank. 1991. *Lessons of Tax Reform*. Washington, DC: World Bank.

World Bank. 1992. 'Structural Adjustment and the Level and Composition of Public Expenditures'. In Policy and Research Series 22, *Adjustment Lending and Mobilization of Private and Public Resources for Growth*. Washington, DC: World Bank.

Younger, S. 1993. *Estimating Tax Incidence in Ghana: An Exercise Using Household Data*. Working Paper 48, Cornell Food and Nutrition Policy Program, Cornell University, Ithaca, NY.

Younger, S. 2003. 'Benefit on the Margin: Observations on Marginal Benefit Incidence'. *World Bank Economic Review*, 17(1), 89–106.

Younger, S., D. Sahn, S. Haggblade and P. Dorosh. 1999. 'Tax Incidence in Madagascar: An Analysis using Household Data'. *World Bank Economic Review*, 13, 303–31.

Zolotareva, A., S. Drobyshevskil and P. Kadochnikov. 2002. 'A Stabilization Fund for Russia: Problems and Prospects'. *Problems of Economic Transition*, 45(2), 5–85.

3
Can Monetary Approaches to Stabilization Be Pro-Poor?

Sheetal K. Chand[1]

Introduction

Developing countries are frequently exposed to shocks that generate balance-of-payments problems, trigger bouts of inflation and disrupt incomes. These can cause the poverty ratio to rise, which is often further aggravated by inappropriate stabilization policies. A case in point is Indonesia, whose headcount ratio, i.e. the proportion of the population falling below the national poverty line, jumped from eight to 19 percentage points during the recent East Asian crisis. Another example is Mexico, for whom the poverty ratio rose from 15 to 21 percentage points at the time of its 1994/5 currency crisis. Similar episodes are to be found in many other countries.

Even though reversals in the poverty ratio may eventually occur, the experience is painful. It would therefore be helpful if solutions could be found that would dampen fluctuations in the poverty ratio. Surprisingly, despite the effort devoted by the international financial institutions to ameliorating the incidence of poverty in developing countries, there has been little attempt to integrate that objective analytically in the stabilization programmes that they support.[2] Most adjustment strategies are worked out in the context of IMF programmes, which are based on monetarist underpinnings, but the issue of how to control macroeconomic-induced jumps in the poverty ratio does not feature prominently in these programmes.

This chapter examines how a poverty ratio objective can be introduced into macroeconomic models, and especially monetarist models of stabilization. Having the poverty ratio as an explicit policy objective in a stabilization framework is important because it helps identify possible trade-offs with other stabilization objectives such as the balance of payments. This has at least two advantages. First, it places a potential brake on excessively ambitious balance of payments and other targets that may generate unnecessary increases in the poverty ratio. Secondly, for example where an ambitious balance-of-payments target is unavoidable, a signal is provided of how adverse the poverty implications are likely to be. This is important since it generates the basis for a better-founded appeal for international assistance: a country may eschew the conventional approach to stabilization if the

50 *Overview and Impact of Macroeconomic Policies*

poverty consequences are dire unless adequate international assistance is available, while the international community has to decide how strongly to support the conventional approach.

The plan here is as follows: In the next section, a poverty ratio-based indicator is derived that is suitable for macroeconomic applications. Then, it is applied to Polak's (1957) version of the IMF's monetary model, and the trade-offs that emerge with respect to its stabilization objectives are examined. A key finding is that the more ambitious the balance-of-payments target, the worse the poverty ratio outcome. However, applying the indicator to the financial programming variant of the IMF's monetary model that is widely used in its operations does not result in any trade-offs. This is also the case with a recently proposed Bank–Fund hybrid model. Such outcomes are attributed to the simplifying assumptions employed in the variants, which will need to be removed if these approaches are to be useful in addressing macroeconomic-induced fluctuations in the poverty ratio. The chapter then reviews some evidence that IMF-supported programmes often result in balance-of-payments over-kill, which could worsen the poverty ratio. It is argued that the monetarist underpinnings of the stabilization framework, which enjoins a tight causal link between credit creation and expenditure, could generate this outcome if expenditure falls by more than the link provides. The concluding section of the chapter examines the scope for overcoming this limitation of monetarism, which is needed to impart a pro-poor orientation to monetary approaches to stabilization. Finally, there are some concluding observations.

A poverty measure for macroeconomic analysis

Shocks and adjustment measures influence the poverty ratio through several channels such as jobs, wages, earnings, prices for essentials, taxes, debt interest payments, and the availability of in-kind budgetary and other benefits (see, for instance, Chapters 13 and 14). If we had detailed information on how the factors impact at the individual level, the change in the poverty ratio could be established from simple aggregation. Since we would also know who is being impacted, interventions can be tailored to individual needs. But such detailed information is not usually available, and approximations have to be employed.

The individual impacts that carry through to the headcount ratio can be classified into three categories: (i) those that affect the overall growth in incomes; (ii) those that involve changes in the relative distribution of incomes; and (iii) those that concern the poverty line. Knowing how these factors impact will help explain changes in the overall headcount ratio, and of particular interest is the extent to which they are attributable to common macro forces. An indicator is needed to capture such effects.[3] The formulation here is based on the headcount ratio H and its underlying determinants.

The headcount ratio

In its income version this ratio indicates the proportion of individuals whose incomes fall below a designated poverty line z. This threshold is determined by the cost of a minimal consumption basket, which for developing countries is dominated by food staples.[4]

Formally, the headcount or poverty ratio is defined as

$$H = \frac{N_p}{N} \qquad (3.1)$$

where N_p represents the number of individuals whose incomes fall below the poverty line z, and N is the total number of persons.

The issue of how to incorporate the headcount ratio in a macroeconomic analysis is not trivial. One approach would be to treat the headcount ratio analogous to the unemployment ratio. If there is a robust empirical relationship, say, similar to Okun's well-known link between the rate of economic growth and the unemployment ratio that also applied to the poverty ratio, the treatment would be straightforward.[5]

However, the several attempts that have been made to estimate empirical relationships between changes in the headcount ratio and real output growth have been unsatisfactory. As is explained later in this section this may be due to an omitted variable and nonlinear specification biases. An alternative to the heuristic approach is to employ the threefold classification set out above and to focus on underlying determinants such as income fluctuations and changes in the valuation of the poverty line.

Classifying sources of change in the headcount ratio

Suppose the N individuals in the economy can be arranged in ascending order of nominal income x. Let incomes be distributed according to some continuous density function $f(x)$. Its cumulative density function $F(z)$ denotes the proportion of the population whose income does not exceed the value of the poverty line z

$$F(z) = \int_0^z f(x)dx \qquad (3.2)$$

The headcount ratio defined in (3.1) can also be stated as

$$H \equiv \frac{N_p}{N} \equiv F(z) = \int_0^N f(x)dx \qquad (3.3)$$

Drawing on the earlier threefold classification, note that shifts in the headcount ratio can result from movements in the valuation z of the commodity basket that defines the poverty line, changes in the absolute levels of incomes and shifts in the relative distribution of incomes. On normalizing incomes x and the poverty line z by mean income μ, the following identity can be set up to explain the change in the headcount ratio.[6]

$$\Delta H = F_{t^1}(\frac{z^1}{\mu_{t^1}}) - F_t(\frac{z}{\mu_t})$$

$$= \underbrace{\left[F_{t^1}(\frac{z^1}{\mu_{t^1}}) - F_{t^1}(\frac{z}{\mu_{t^1}})\right]}_{\text{poverty line}} + \underbrace{\left[F_t(\frac{z}{\mu_{t^1}}) - F_t(\frac{z}{\mu_t})\right]}_{\text{mean income}} + \underbrace{\left[F_{t^1}(\frac{z}{\mu_{t^1}}) - F_t(\frac{z}{\mu_t^1})\right]}_{\text{distributional}} \quad (3.4)$$

The superscript[1] in the above equation refers to a subsequent time period. The first term in square brackets indicates the effect of a change in the cost z of the basket that defines the poverty line – an increase implies a higher poverty ratio; the second term represents the effect of a change in mean income – an increase shifts the distribution further to the right of the (normalized) poverty line, thereby reducing the headcount ratio; and the last term focuses on changes in the relative income distribution or the F function – a worsening causing a higher poverty ratio.

In general, all of the preceding three effects can be operative. Mean income is affected by macroeconomic forces that influence income growth. The cost of the basket defining the poverty line could reflect a variety of factors, including macroeconomic ones that impact on the prices of food staples. Distributional effects can also be generated by macro developments. Since people can and do react to such changes, establishing the full effects can be quite complex. For example, an exchange rate depreciation could result in those whose consumption baskets are more import-intensive suffering proportionately more than others. If they now become poor the poverty ratio will rise, but they may decide to change their consumption pattern and avoid becoming poor. Comprehensive modelling such as that involved in dynamic computable general equilibrium models is needed to establish the extended effects.

Since identifying each of the various sources of change in the poverty ratio can be difficult, simplifying hypotheses are employed. A frequently used hypothesis is to abstract from distributional and poverty line effects and relate fluctuations in the headcount ratio solely to real per capita income growth.[7] This hypothesis implies that if real per capita income growth is negative the headcount ratio will rise. But this is valid only if we rule out possible offsetting effects from a lowering in the costs of the poverty line basket or favourable changes in the distribution of income. Since the hypothesis has not performed well empirically, it would seem best to follow the threefold division between poverty line, income, and distributional effects and seek a compact formulation to represent them.

In principle, the first two effects on the poverty ratio indicated in (3.4) should be relatively easy to establish, but determining the third factor concerning distributional effects is more difficult. It would be facilitated if the income distribution can be represented by a well-defined functional form such as Pareto or log-normal that relies on only a few parameters and whose evolution over time is somehow known. Otherwise it might be necessary as a first approximation to assume that distributional effects are neutral as suggested by Bourguignon et al. (2002).[8]

Poverty line, and mean income i.e. 'net income' effects

To derive an analytical expression for the change in the poverty ratio as a result of the first two effects in (3.4), which we label 'net income' effects, consider the underlying income distribution's Lorenz curve. The mean income of the poor is

$$\frac{X(H)}{N_p} \int_0^z xf(x)dx \tag{3.5}$$

Expressing this subtotal as a proportion of the population's mean income μ generates the Lorenz curve for the distribution

$$L(H) = \frac{\int_0^z xf(x)dx}{\mu}, \quad L(0) = 0, L(1) = 1 \tag{3.6}$$

The first derivative of $L(H)$ is found on applying the chain rule to (3.6) and (3.3).[9]

$$L'(H) = \frac{dL}{dz}\frac{dz}{dH} = \frac{z}{\mu} \tag{3.7}$$

On differentiating (3.7) the second derivative results

$$L'(H) = \frac{1}{\mu f(z)} > 0 \tag{3.8}$$

The expression in (3.7) indicates that when the proportion of the poor increases, the share of income accruing to the poor also increases and equals the ratio of the poverty line to mean income.

To find how the headcount ratio varies when both mean income and the poverty line are varying, totally differentiate the logarithm of equation (3.7) with respect to time. This yields, after some arrangement, the following convenient representation for the rate of change in the headcount ratio

$$\frac{\dot{H}}{H} = \eta_{H,z}\left[\frac{\dot{z}}{z} - \frac{\dot{\mu}}{\mu}\right] \tag{3.9}$$

where the dot over a variable refers to its time derivative. According to (3.9), the headcount ratio rises with the poverty line, but falls when the nominal income growth rate increases, with the strength of the relationship depending on the elasticity of the headcount ratio with respect to the poverty line

$$\eta_{H,z} \equiv \frac{\partial H}{\partial z}\frac{z}{H} = \frac{zf(z)}{H} > 0, \quad \begin{array}{l}\eta_{H,z} = \infty : H = 0 \\ \eta_{H,z} = zf(z) : H = 1.\end{array}$$

This elasticity is not constant but varies inversely with the size of the headcount ratio, exhibiting high values when H is low and vice-versa.

Distributional effects

The effects of changes in income distribution on the headcount ratio can be readily found if the form of the income distribution is known and can be summarized by a few parameters. For example, the Pareto income distribution, as is shown in Appendix A3.1, enables an especially convenient parametric representation of the effects of distributional changes on H. The distributional effects modify the net income effects additively.

$$\frac{\dot{H}}{H} = \eta_{H,z}\left[\frac{\dot{z}}{z} - \frac{\dot{\mu}}{\mu} + \ln\left(\frac{b}{z}\right)\frac{\dot{a}}{a}\right] \tag{3.10}$$

An increase in the parameter a indicates a worsening income distribution that raises the headcount ratio. Here b is a parameter that indicates the lower bound of the distribution, which can be interpreted as representing subsistence income (see Appendix A3.1). If the poverty line is set at this level, distributional effects disappear from the relationship. For very poor countries, whose poverty line is close to the subsistence level, net income rather than distribution effects may account for much of the change in the headcount ratio.

Attending to the poverty line

Both the poverty lines for the very poor, usually defined by reference to a commodity basket yielding some minimum calorie level, and for the less poor, where the basket is supplemented with other essential needs, are likely to behave differently from the overall GDP deflator. This is because of the different commodity compositions and weights that enter in the respective definitions. The prices entering the poverty line will also be affected by subsidies, which could further reduce the correlation between movements in the aggregate price indices and the poverty line.[10] It is therefore not generally valid to assume that these two are identical, as is done (implicitly) when the poverty growth equation is specified in real terms from the outset. To see this add and subtract the rate of change in the GDP deflator π from the poverty line and income variables in equation (3.9).

$$\frac{\dot{H}}{H} = \eta_{H,z}\left(\frac{\dot{z}}{z} - \pi - \frac{\dot{\mu}}{\mu} + \pi\right) \tag{3.11}$$

The expression in parenthesis reduces to the real rate of income growth only when the π and z deflators are identical

$$\frac{\dot{H}}{H} = -\eta_{H,z}\left(\frac{\dot{\mu}}{\mu} - \pi\right) \tag{3.12}$$

Equation (3.12) is usually estimated in linear form with fixed intercept and slope coefficients (see, for example, World Bank 2000).[11] However, as the derivation of (3.9) demonstrates, such a specification is not likely to be valid. First, there is a misspecification from imposing a fixed coefficient in place of the nonlinear elasticity η. Second, there is an omitted variable problem from ignoring differences between changes in the valuation of the poverty line and those of the GDP deflator. Failure to take these aspects into account would seem to account for the poor empirical results obtained.

Equation (3.12) indicates that the poverty ratio could be stabilized when $(\frac{\dot{\mu}}{\mu} - \pi) = 0$, i.e. real per capita income growth is kept equal to zero. In a typical shock cum stabilization episode this could be difficult to ensure as real per capita income growth could be negative. However, according to (3.11) there is an added degree of freedom involving the term $(\frac{\dot{z}}{z} - \pi)$. Changing the valuation of the poverty line, for example by manipulating food prices, could be a potentially important instrument for influencing the aggregate poverty outcome.

Incorporating the poverty indicator in IMF monetary model variants

The poverty indicator (3.9), together with any extensions to include distributional effects in (3.10), is now in a form that can be embedded in a macroeconomic model. It will be incorporated here in two variants of the IMF monetary model, referred to respectively as the Polak model and the financial programming or 'basic' version. The section concludes with an examination of a recent IMF–World Bank hybrid model – the so-called 123PSRP model.

The Polak version of the IMF's monetary model

The official claimant to this title is the model associated with Polak (1957, 1998). Its remarkable longevity, it is now some fifty years old, testifies to the power of its basic insight. While the Polak model provides the conceptual underpinnings, the IMF staff employs a simpler version for daily use – the so-called financial programming approach (see IMF 1987, 2004b; and Chand 1989). The latter version also underlies the 123PSRP framework that is discussed below.

The underlying rationale of the two variants is that a balance-of-payments deficit (specifically the current account) results from residents spending more than their income. This can only persist if they have access to financing, and both versions require that access to financing be curtailed in order to bring the balance of payments under control. In keeping with typical country circumstances they assign a key role to domestic bank credit as the principal source of financing. Specific formulas are then derived for calculating the rates of domestic credit expansion that are consistent with designated balance-of-payments targets.

The Polak model extends the classical quantity theory of money to the open economy. There are two endogenous variables – GDP and the balance of payments – but only one instrument to address them both, namely the rate of credit expansion, the implications of which are noted subsequently.

The model is predicated on a stable demand for money function, with the economy in equilibrium when money supply growth equals the rate of growth in the demand for money. There are two sources of monetary creation – domestic bank credit and the monetization of foreign exchange inflows. Given the demand for money, restraining the domestic source component of the money supply forces an increase in the external source component so as to meet money demand. This induces an improvement in international reserve holdings, which explains the IMF's preferred strategy for relying on domestic credit control to improve the external accounts. In the Polak model, domestic money supply restraint reduces the growth in income, which leads to import compression.[12] This improves the balance of payments and provides the external, offsetting, source for cash replenishment.

Formally, the model comprises the following equations (Polak, 1998):

$$Mo = \frac{1}{v}Y \tag{3.13}$$

$$M = mY \tag{3.14}$$

$$\Delta Mo \equiv \Delta D + B \tag{3.15}$$

$$B \equiv X - M + K \tag{3.16}$$

where Mo is the Money stock, v the velocity of circulation of money, M is imports, m is the propensity to import, B is the local currency value of the change in international reserve holdings, identified with the balance of payments, D is the stock of net domestic assets of the banking system, X represents exports, K denotes net capital inflow, and Δ is the first difference operator. The model refers to an interval in time t, with all variables in nominal local currency values unless otherwise specified.

Equation (3.13) is a demand for money function; equation (3.14) is an import function; equation (3.15) is an identity relating money supply to two sources of monetary expansion, domestic and external; and equation (3.16) defines the balance of payments. Net capital inflows and exports are exogenously determined, as are the parameters v and m. To simplify the exposition Polak assumes constant parameter values, which will also be assumed here. Exchange rate adjustments in the model are treated as exogenous, with their effects captured in the values inserted for exports, capital inflows, and the import coefficient.

The solutions of interest are obtained on equating the incremental flow supply of money given in (3.15) to its incremental demand, which on taking first differences of (3.13) yields

$$\frac{1}{v}\Delta Y = B + \Delta D \tag{3.17}$$

To solve for nominal income, apply in (3.17) the definition of B from (3.16), the import demand function (3.14), and use the property $Y = \Delta Y + Y_{-1}$. All variables on the right-hand side (RHS) of the resulting equation are stated here as growth rates of the domestic money stock so as to bring out explicitly their roles in the money supply process.

$$\frac{\Delta Y}{Y_{-1}} = \frac{1}{(1+mv)}\left\{\left(\frac{\Delta(K+X)}{Mo_{-1}}\right) + \left(\frac{B_{-1}}{Mo_{-1}}\right)\right\} + \frac{1}{(1+mv)}\left(\frac{\Delta D}{Mo_{-1}}\right) \tag{3.18}$$

The rate of growth in nominal GDP is a function of two components: an exogenous component shown as the first bracketed term, and the domestic bank credit control variable, which is the last term. The exogenous component comprises changes in net capital inflows and export earnings. It is readily seen from equation (3.18) that net increases in foreign exchange inflows, whether from net capital inflows or exports, stimulate GDP growth, as do increases in domestic bank credit. However, a higher import propensity m reduces it.

To obtain a solution for the balance of payments apply (3.18) to (3.17)

$$\frac{B}{Mo_{-1}} = \frac{1}{(1+mv)}\left(\frac{\Delta(K+X)}{Mo_{-1}} + \frac{B_{-1}}{Mo_{-1}}\right) - \frac{mv}{(1+mv)}\left(\frac{\Delta D}{Mo_{-1}}\right) \quad (3.19)$$

Increases in net capital inflows and exports improve the balance of payments, while more domestic bank credit worsens it.

Specifying a balance of payments target B^*, the amount of domestic credit expansion that will ensure the target is found from (3.19) as

$$\frac{\Delta \tilde{D}}{Mo_{-1}} = \frac{1}{mv}\left[\frac{\Delta(K+X) + B_{-1}}{Mo_{-1}}\right] - \frac{1+mv}{mv}\left(\frac{B^*}{Mo_{-1}}\right) \quad (3.20)$$

Here a tilde ~ indicates a solution value. The domestic bank credit solution depends positively on the expected change in exports and net capital inflows, and negatively on the balance-of-payments target.

Suppose the solution for the credit instrument stated in (3.20) is implemented for a given bop target. Inserting that solution into (3.18) shows what nominal income growth will be for the assumed values of the exogenous and target variables.

$$\frac{\Delta \tilde{Y}}{Y_{-1}} = \frac{1}{mv}\left(\frac{\Delta(K+X)}{Mo_{-1}}\right) - \frac{1}{mv}\left(\frac{\Delta B^*}{Mo_{-1}}\right) \quad (3.21)$$

According to equation (3.21), the more ambitious the balance-of-payments target the smaller is the implied growth in nominal GNP. This is because the domestic allocation of credit has to be curtailed further, which reduces the growth in income and hence imports causing the balance of payments to improve.

The solution obtained for nominal income growth can now be introduced into the formula for the change in the headcount ratio in (3.9), but since income growth in (3.9) is per capita, the population growth rate has to be subtracted from it.

$$\frac{\Delta H}{H_{-1}} = \eta_{H,z}\left(\frac{\Delta z}{z_{-1}} + n - \frac{\Delta \tilde{Y}}{Y_{-1}}\right) \quad (3.22)$$

Inserting equation (3.21)'s solution for nominal income growth into (3.22) indicates the direct nature of the dependence between changes in the headcount ratio and the balance-of-payments target.

$$\frac{\Delta \tilde{H}}{H_{-1}} = \eta_{H,z}\left[\frac{\Delta z}{z_{-1}} + n - \frac{1}{mv}\left\{\frac{\Delta(K+X)}{Mo_{-1}}\right\} + \frac{1}{mv}\left(\frac{\Delta B^*}{Mo_{-1}}\right)\right] \qquad (3.23)$$

The following proposition can now be stated

Proposition 1: *In the Polak model, the more ambitious the balance of payments target, the greater the deterioration in the head-count ratio.*[13]

The main instrument that the model relies upon is the rate of domestic credit expansion. If this is directed primarily at the balance-of-payments target, the system is one instrument short with respect to objectives involving the growth rate of income. Potentially, exchange rate depreciations, which frequently accompany adjustment programs, could play a role. To consider their poverty effects differentiate equation (3.23) with respect to the exchange rate e. The latter could affect the poverty line, the import propensity m, and the responsiveness and valuation of exports and net capital inflows.

$$\frac{\partial}{\partial e}\left(\frac{\Delta \tilde{H}}{H_{-1}}\right) = \eta_{H,z}\left\{\frac{\partial}{\partial e}\left(\frac{\Delta z}{z_{-1}}\right) + \frac{\frac{\partial}{\partial e}(m)}{vm^2}\left[\frac{\Delta(K+X)}{Mo_{-1}} - \frac{\Delta B^*}{Mo_{-1}}\right] - \frac{1}{vm}\left[\frac{\partial}{\partial e}\left(\frac{\Delta(K+X)}{Mo_{-1}}\right)\right]\right\} \stackrel{\leq}{>} 0$$

(3.24)

The direct effect on the valuation of the poverty line, shown as the first term on the right-hand side, is positive given some exchange rate pass-through effect. This raises the headcount ratio. In a textbook devaluation the import propensity declines and domestic production and exports are stimulated, which would raise domestic incomes and help improve H. However, valuation effects are also important, especially since the exercise is conducted in nominal terms as here. In local currency terms import propensities could rise, and if the local value of the improvement sought in the balance of payments exceeds that of the increase in exports and capital inflows (second term on the RHS), domestic incomes would decline. The net effect could be to worsen the headcount ratio.[14] The conditions for there to be an unambiguous improvement in the headcount ratio through the use of the exchange rate instrument are thus stringent.

The financial programming (FP) approach

There are at least three troubling features with the Polak model, even assuming monetarist causality: first, how reliable are the solutions for Y and B and their implied time-paths; second, how should we deal with two potential targets involving Y and B, when we have only one readily available credit instrument; and, third, even if interest focused solely on B, restraining credit will cause Y and the associated incremental demand for money to decline, and how acceptable then is the requirement that there be an even bigger degree of credit restraint to achieve the balance-of-payments target? The FP approach (see IMF 1987, 2004b) circumvents these potential problems by reducing the behavioural content of the model, and emphasizing instead the use of monetary identities so as to ensure consistency between the assumptions made for different components.[15]

In particular, the GDP growth rate is rendered exogenous, i.e. orthogonal to the credit instrument, by making it a projected magnitude. As is noted in IMF (2004a), and using the terminology in this report, 'Real output growth is projected, $\Delta y = \Delta \bar{y}$, the inflation target is given, $\pi = \bar{\pi}$, and velocity, v, is predictable, therefore money demand is predictable'. This gets rid of the insufficient instrument problem, and also the need to solve for realistic time paths of Y, since this is now a targeted magnitude. It also deals with the third potential problem noted above of requiring that the credit expansion solution take account of feedbacks on the solution for Y. Unspecified policies underlie the projected nominal GDP growth rate: the projection for real output growth in the next year or so, the usual horizon for a FP exercise, would be based on various sources such as the likely harvest, etc., while the inflation target would be set at a 'reasonable' level. With the incremental demand for money given in this manner, a one-to-one relationship is enjoined between the credit instrument and the balance of payments.

Working out details of the 'permissible amount' of credit and its phasing over time is central to IMF supported programs.[16] Its division between the private sector and the government is based on out-of-model considerations as to the appropriate balance, since the models do not generate internal criteria for the distribution. In addition to the overall credit ceilings, specific ceilings are applied to public external borrowing and domestic government non-bank borrowing, the last so as to prevent crowding out of the private sector. The size of the overall government deficit can thus be effectively controlled from the financing side. This ensures that the sub-ceiling on credit to government will bite, which provides an important lever for monitoring and encouraging the agreed fiscal actions.

Using the terminology and identities from the Polak model set out earlier, the relations of the basic model underlying the FP exercise are interpretable as follows:

$$Mo = \frac{1}{v}Y \tag{3.13}$$
$$M = M(\Delta D) \tag{3.14a}$$
$$\Delta Mo^s \equiv \Delta D + B \tag{3.15}$$
$$B \equiv K + X - M \tag{3.16}$$

Aside from the exogeneity of Y, the principal difference from the Polak model is in the specification of the import function (3.14a). This must now be a function of expenditure, which in turn is influenced by the change in domestic credit, given that income is exogenously determined.[17]

The incremental demand for money is determined from (3.13) as

$$\Delta Mo^d = \frac{\Delta \bar{Y}}{Y_{-1}} Mo_{-1} \tag{3.25}$$

where the hat '-' refers to a given value. To solve for the permissible amount of credit expansion (3.25) is equated to the incremental supply of money given by (3.15).

$$\Delta \tilde{D} = \frac{\Delta \overline{Y}}{Y_{-1}} Mo_{-1} - B^* \qquad (3.26)$$

Equation (3.26) indicates a one-to-one relationship between the credit instrument and the balance-of-payments target. Unlike with the Polak model, where monetary equilibration occurred through Y adjusting, here the equilibration involves only the balance of payments. Reducing credit improves B directly, and since exports and net capital inflows are assumed to be exogenous, the improvement can only come about through imports contracting by the amount of credit reduction. As long as projected growth of Y is not affected then irrespective of the balance of payments target and credit instrument setting there can be no macroeconomic effect on the incidence of poverty. Equation (3.23) reduces to

$$\frac{\Delta \tilde{H}}{H_{-1}} = \eta_{H,z} \left[\frac{\Delta z}{z_{-1}} + n - \frac{\Delta \overline{Y}}{Y_{-1}} \right]$$

The following proposition can now be stated:

Proposition 2: *Varying the balance-of-payments target in the financial programming (FP) version of the IMF's monetary approach has no within model effect on the poverty ratio.*

The FP approach pays a high price for the convenience of being able to disregard some of the consequences of having GDP endogenously determined as in Polak's model.

The '123PRSP Model'

This is an umbrella model of recent vintage (Devarajan and Go 2002) that employs a modular design to combine several models (see also Ames *et al.* 2001). The '123' in its title refers to its application to a single country, with two sectors (domestic and export), and three goods (exports, imports and domestic use). The acronym 'PRSP' denotes Poverty Reduction Strategy Paper, which refers to the model's use in assessing the impact on poverty of macroeconomic policies formulated in connection with the poverty reduction strategy embraced by the BWIs in 1999. Its modular design is intended as a source of strength, since it confers flexibility. However, this could also be a potential source of weakness since it does not fully incorporate sub-model inter-linkages, especially feedbacks.

The scope of the model is best described by considering its sub-models and their intended use. The starting point for *123PRSP* is the financial programming (FP) model of the IMF. Macroeconomic policy measures such as the degree of credit restraint are determined at this stage and then fed into two separate sub-models that focus respectively on growth effects and on price distributional effects (relative prices, factor prices). Two alternatives are presented for the growth sub-model, a shorter-run version (up to five years) referred to as the 'Trivariate VAR' and a longer-run variant, labeled the 'Get Real' model. The price distributional sub-model is referred to as the 1-2-3 Model. The extended output and price implications of the macro adjustment measures are identified through the use of the sub-models. The findings at this stage are then linked in the last stage to household survey data on incomes and expenditures to establish who will be impacted and how adversely.

The question arises as to the purposes of the 'Trivariate Var' and 'Get-Real' components in the 123PRSP framework. The latter is intended to identify the longer-term (beyond five years) growth implications of the macroeconomic strategy contained in the FP module, and can be disregarded in a stabilization context. The 'Trivariate Var' component examines growth implications during the first five years of a programme, especially with respect to government expenditure. However, there is no iterative interaction specified between the sub-models that would systematically change the growth assumptions at the FP stage. Since this hybrid approach does not rectify the FP model's core assumption that nominal GDP growth is an exogenous projection, it cannot generate a macroeconomic balance of payments–poverty trade-off function, and proposition 2 applies.

Is there overkill bias in monetarist models?

The IMF's monetary approach as embodied in FP is widely used in developing country stabilization, so there is considerable experience available regarding its performance. A persistent finding is that of over-performance on the current account of the balance of payments (see, most recently, IMF 2004a). Since export over-performance is not usually the case, the explanation has to be one of excessive import compression. How and why does this occur? Unfortunately individual country data comparing program targets and outcomes do not appear to be readily accessible, but some insights can be obtained from partial country detail provided in Bruno (1994) and IMF (2004b).

Bruno (1994) provides a useful comparison for five eastern European countries with IMF supported programmes (see Table 3.1). The last column of Table 3.1 shows systematic over-performance on the balance of payments (current account). Data on export performance and other more detailed statistics (see Bruno 1994) indicate that this occurred primarily because of import compression. Since the economies underwent considerable external sector liberalization during this period, imports should have increased much more than was observed. The fact that they fell instead, points to the strength of contractionary effects. This is confirmed by the data in the first column of the table, which shows systematic underperformance in GDP growth.

Table 3.2 reproduces a table from IMF (2004a) on the projected and actual current account adjustment in countries such as the recent Asian crisis countries, and Argentina, Russia and Turkey. The average projected current account adjustment

Table 3.1 Eastern Europe: IMF programmes and outcomes

Programme/actual	GDP (% change)	Consumer prices (year-end % change)	National wage (year-end % change)	Convertible Current account (US dollars)
Hungary				
1991 Program	−3	31	0	−1.2
1991 Actual	−8	32	20	0.3
Poland				
1990 Program	−5	94	0	−3.0
1990 Actual	−12	249	160	0.7
1991 Program	3	36	0	−2.7
1991 Actual	−8	60	54	−2.2
Czechoslovakia				
1991 Program	−5	30	17	−2.5
1991 Actual	−16	54	14	0.2
Bulgaria				
1991 Program	−11	234	146	−2.0
1991 Actual	−23	339	142	−0.9
Romania				
1991 Program	0	104	0	−1.7
1991 Estimate	−12	223	124	−1.3

Source: Extracted from Bruno (1994).

Table 3.2 Projected and actual current account adjustment in capital account crisis programmes

	Approval year	Crisis year	Current account adjustment	
			Projected	Actual
Argentina	2000	2002	0.1	12.0
Brazil	1998	1999	0.6	−0.6
Indonesia	1997	1998	0.5	6.0
Korea	1997	1998	2.5	14.4
Mexico	1995	1995	3.7	6.5
Russia	1996	1999	0.0	12.1
Thailand	1997	1998	2.0	14.8
Turkey	1999	2001	0.3	7.2
Uruguay	2000	2002	0.2	4.4
Average			1.1	8.5

Source: IMF (2004a, 10).

was for an improvement of 1.1 per cent of GDP. Instead, the actual improvement that occurred amounted to 8.5 per cent of GDP, which represents an extraordinary degree of overkill. The IMF report states 'Although these programs, are at one level, little different from more traditional programs – typically targeting some external adjustment – their salient feature is the large and sudden capital outflows that

force much larger-than-envisaged adjustments of the current account balance ...'
(IMF 2004: 9). The essential point to note is that the over-performance on the current account of the balance of payments represents a massive increase in savings and shortfalls in investment that were accompanied by huge reductions in imports. That this should occur during the program, contrary to intentions and projections, points to some major limitations of the adopted policy programming approaches.[18]

Figure 3.1 compares the outcome and projection of the current accounts of the balance of payments of IMF-supported programmes for countries that were financed through the normal lending facility of the Fund over the period 1995–2000. If the outcomes and projections are close, the points would cluster on the 45-degree line. The chart appears to indicate that many, if not most of the points are above the line, indicating some over-performance. Figure 3.2 exhibits data on actual and projected investment outturns. The vast majority of points appear to lie below the 45-degree line indicating investment shortfalls from projected levels.

The bits and pieces of evidence assembled here suggest a systematic contractionary bias, and a linkage between the findings portrayed in Figures 3.1 and 3.2. If expenditures, for example, private investment, are below projected levels, the balance of payments will tend to overshoot. Could balance of payments over-performance be a consequence of the monetary approach to stabilization?

Consider FP's basic monetary identity, stated here as a variant of (3.15):

$$\Delta \overline{Mo}^d - \Delta \tilde{D} = B^* \tag{3.27}$$

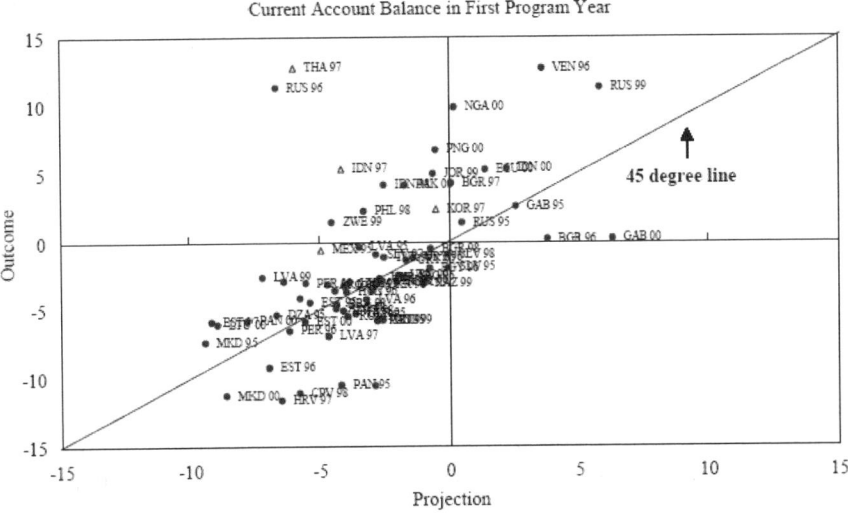

Figure 3.1 Projected and actual current account balance in GRA-supported programmes (in percentage of GDP)

Source: IMF (2004b, p. 28).

64 Overview and Impact of Macroeconomic Policies

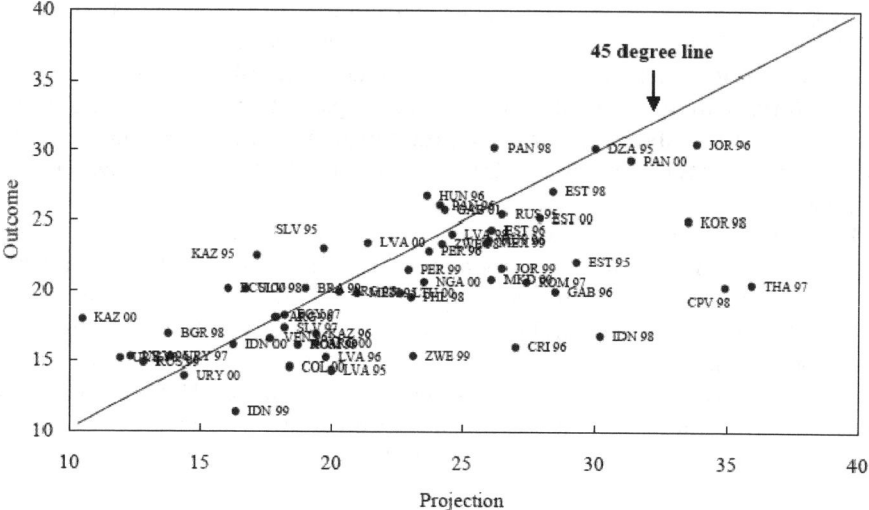

Figure 3.2 Gross domestic investment in first programme year (in percentage of GDP)
Source: IMF (2004b, p. 29).

An outcome where the actual balance-of-payments outcome B exceeds the targeted level B^* could be the result of either the actual demand for money being greater than targeted, $\Delta Mo^d > \Delta \overline{Mo}^d$, or the actual utilization of credit being less than provided, $\Delta D < \Delta \tilde{D}$, or both.

It could be that the demand for money has been underestimated. For example, people in a crisis may want to hold more cash for precautionary reasons as they view the contractionary effects of the stabilization programme. If so they would curtail their expenditures and hoard more, thereby reducing velocity. Turning to the credit channel, credit tightening could result in expenditures falling by an even greater amount. This not only drags both income growth and imports below projected levels, but also leads to underutilization of credit.

It is interesting to ask which expenditures are likely to be affected by credit restraint. Since private consumption exhibits some smoothing over the cycle, as does government consumption expenditure, the most likely candidate is domestic investment (see Figure 3.2). The experience of declining sales could trigger accelerator-type considerations that cause investment demand to fall below projected levels, while interest rate increases and adverse net worth effects could result in greater credit rationing by banks.[19]

More empirical work is needed to properly establish the hypothesis of systematic overkill in the IMF's monetary based programs. Nonetheless, the tentative findings presented here conform to the criticism of monetarist models that it may be difficult to impose a tight relationship between credit allocations and the willingness to spend – 'you cannot push on a loose string'. Such a bias may be further compounded by an institutional preference to promote balance of payments adjustment that originates from the IMF's mandate. The greater the balance of payments adjustment, even if unintended, the more successful will the achievement be regarded.[20]

Focusing on expenditure

This section considers whether, operating within the basic monetary framework, it is possible to obtain more acceptable expenditure and balance-of-payments outcomes.

Monetarist models focus on the elimination of an excess demand for money, and do not elaborate on the expenditure implications. Nonetheless, for there to be an excess demand for monetary flows, there must be an excess supply of at least one other good, which we shall treat here as the aggregate good. By Walras's law the two market conditions – goods or monetary flows – are interchangeable, and equilibration could be undertaken in either market. However, the assumptions made with regard to the behaviour of the underlying aggregates do make a difference, since they determine the market in which equilibration takes place. In monetary models the monetary sector 'controls' the credit variable to which private agents and the government are assumed to adjust their behaviour. The analysis for the determination of income is then properly conducted in the market for money, since both the demand and supply of the domestic component of money are independent. But under the alternative assumption, where private agents or the government insist on their expenditure plans, it is the goods market that forces the equilibration.[21]

The above point is readily made in a bare bones closed economy model of national income determination, comprising only the private sector and the monetary sector.[22]

$$Y + \Delta D = C + I + \Delta Mo^d$$
$$C = cY$$
$$\Delta Mo^d = \frac{1}{v} \Delta Y \quad (3.28)$$

The first equation in (3.28) is the aggregate budget restraint, where sources of financing, i.e. national income and credit flows, are shown on the LHS, and their uses for consumption, investment and accumulation of cash shown on the RHS. Consumption is a linear function of income, and the standard demand for money function is assumed. The aggregate budget restraint can be rearranged to show the two markets present, with the goods market on the LHS and that for monetary flows on the RHS:

$$Y - C - I = \Delta Mo^d - \Delta D \quad (3.29)$$

The two model alternatives are:

A. Monetarist: $\Delta D = \overline{\Delta D}$ (3.30)

Here credit expansion is the discretionary control variable and feeding this assumption into (3.29) shows that it is the LHS that will have to give way to the RHS, given the demand for money. Y is then determined from the monetary flow equilibrium condition, with investment falling out residually as $I = Y - C - (\Delta Mo^d - \Delta D)$. The solution for Y, obtained on setting the RHS in (3.29) equal to zero, is

$$Y = v\overline{\Delta D} + Y_{-1} \qquad (3.31)$$

B. Goods Market: $\quad I = \bar{I} \qquad (3.32)$

Here investment is exogenously determined, and inserting this assumption into (3.29) shows that the goods market dominates in the determination of Y, given the consumption and hence saving function. Credit expansion is now the residual variable and is determined as $\Delta D = \Delta Mo^d - (Y - C - I)$. The solution for Y is

$$Y = \frac{1}{1-c}\Delta I + Y_{-1} \qquad (3.33)$$

On the face of it, (3.31) and (3.33) show two fundamentally different solutions for Y, with one a function of the change in the stock of credit, while the other is in terms of the increment in investment flows.[23] However, they are really two sides of the same face: one implies the other by Walras's law. The point is that had we started with the instrument ΔD we may not have attained a target Y^* but a smaller Y, owing to a greater than projected fall in I. The actual determinant of Y is then I even though the fall in I was triggered by credit restraint. Since I falls excessively it is no longer liquidity-constrained, and we would observe some slack in the credit and monetary variables. The money stock would then exceed its programmed level, while credit would fall below.

Going beyond the simple example introduced above, distinguish next between the monetary, external and rest of the economy sectors, with the last broken down into its private and government components. This imposes a corresponding distinction in bank credit allocations and net capital inflows: $\Delta D = \Delta D_p + \Delta D_g$; $K = K_p + K_g$ where the subscripts refer to private and government respectively.

The private sector restraint condition, showing sources of funds on the LHS and their uses on the RHS, is $(Y - T) + K + \Delta D = C + I + \Delta Mo^d$ where T refers to tax revenue. The corresponding government sector restraint is $T + K_g + \Delta D_g = G$ where G denotes government outlays.

On consolidating the private and governmental sectoral restraints

$$(Y - T) + K + \Delta D = C + I + (G - T) + \Delta Mo^d \qquad (3.34)$$

If credit accommodates expenditure, it is residually determined from (3.34)

$$\Delta D = C + I + G + \Delta Mo^d - Y - K \qquad (3.35)$$

Using (3.35) to substitute for the credit term in the condition for monetary flow equilibrium in (3.17) generates the familiar goods market equilibrium condition

$$(I - S) + (G - T) + (X - M) = 0 \qquad (3.36)$$

Both government expenditure and private investment are assumed to be exogenous discretionary variables. The import function in the monetary model (3.14) is retained, and linear consumption and tax functions introduced. The consumption function is

$$C = c(1 - t)Y \qquad (3.37)$$

where small letters indicate the average propensities to consume and to pay tax, respectively.

On substituting these into (3.36) the familiar textbook result obtains

$$Y = a[X + I + G]$$
$$\text{where } a = \frac{1}{1 + m - c(1 - t)} \qquad (3.38)$$

is the Keynesian multiplier. In difference terms, and for a constant multiplier,

$$\Delta Y = a\Delta[X + I + G] \qquad (3.39)$$

Introducing a balance-of-payments target into (3.16), and using (3.38) and the import function to make the relevant substitutions generates

$$B^* = \Delta(X + K) + B_{-1} - ma\Delta(X + I + G) \qquad (3.40)$$

The solution for G as instrument follows

$$\Delta \tilde{G} = \frac{1}{ma}\Delta K + \frac{1 - ma}{ma}\Delta X - \Delta I - \frac{1}{ma}\Delta B^* \qquad (3.41)$$

Focusing on the goods market shows that if the investment decline overshoots, government outlays should be increased, or taxes cut, to prevent the balance of payments target from being overshot.

Pro-poor stabilization: some policy options

Given the focus of this chapter on avoiding an unnecessary worsening of the poverty ratio, fiscal variables and in particular government expenditure, the solution for which was provided in equation (3.41), would be preferred instruments for attaining the balance-of-payments target as a consequence of the problems associated with the credit instrument. For some effective tax rate t and nominal GDP solution, the fiscal deficit is determined as

$$\tilde{G} - t\tilde{Y} = \Delta D_g + \Delta B_g + \Delta K_g \qquad (3.42)$$

This leaves open the question of its financing (RHS of (3.42)). Depending on the available amounts of foreign financing and domestic non-bank financing, the residual will be the amount of credit accommodation to be sought from the domestic banking system. Since the equilibrium solution for nominal GDP has already been found (e.g. as in (3.38)), the demand for money will also be determined. Subtracting from the last the amount of money to be supplied through the balance-of-payments determines the overall level of credit expansion. Taking note of the credit allocation to the budget, the allocation to the private sector is then found. If this is inadequate, the financing exercise is repeated. Here causal sequencing proceeds from the fiscal solution to the credit allocation, which is the reverse of monetarism.

Under the suggested approach, if actual private investment is going to be lower than projected, government expenditure from equation (3.41) could be raised, or taxes cut, so as to ensure attainment of the balance-of-payments target. The additional financing needed would come from domestic bank credit, but this is not an inflationary development since it merely reallocates credit that would was intended to finance private investment.

Once the overall macroeconomic profile is correctly aligned with the balance-of-payments target, equation (3.23) will indicate the implied change in the poverty ratio from the net income effects. To this a term representing distribution effects will need to be added, provided of course the required information is available.[24] The resulting poverty ratio, while no longer reflecting balance of payments overkill, may still not be acceptable, and other options will have to be considered.

A fix is needed on the appropriate target poverty ratio, and a convenient starting point is that of stabilizing the headcount ratio at the pre-stabilization level. From equation (3.23), the maximum permissible improvement in the balance of payments, indicated by two asterisks, that is compatible with poverty ratio stabilization is

$$\Delta B^{**} = \Delta(K + X) - mY_{-1}(\frac{\Delta z}{z_{-1}} + n) \qquad (3.43)$$

If this is smaller than what the international community would prefer, various alternatives will need to be examined: (i) is the sought after balance-of-payments target too ambitious? (ii) Is it possible to reduce the amount of GDP adjustment that is needed to attain a given balance-of-payments target? (iii) Could there be a change in the valuation adjustment of the poverty line, and (iv) what about specific pro-poor measures?

If the balance-of-payments target cannot be lowered further, consideration might be given to raising additional foreign assistance.[25] If the problem is one of large adverse capital movements, some controls could be beneficial, which might even involve a stay on external debt repayments (Krueger, 2002). Should highly depreciated exchange rates be unavoidable, steps to cushion the impact of the latter on the valuation of the poverty line may be advisable.

In general, could more be done to ensure that food prices do not rise unduly? Several policy actions may be available, ranging from anti-speculation measures to food subsidies. Food costs for the poor are often prone to increases – for example, when export restraints on staples are removed. An overly depreciated exchange rate that contributes to higher food prices is especially damaging to the poverty ratio. It might then be necessary to subsidize or otherwise restrain the rise food prices.[26]

An additional option for cushioning the adverse impact on the poor of typical stabilization episodes is to engage in more income redistribution. However, the political economy of implementing it, difficult under normal times, could be even more problematic in a period of negative or declining income growth. A related option would be to provide adequate relief to the poor through higher pro-poor budget outlays. However, this can be very costly and most likely infeasible when account is taken of the need for fiscal restraint during stabilization. The best strategy would appear to be that of attending to the initial design of the adjustment program so as to avoid the need for such difficult options.

Conclusion

The objective here has been to examine the extent to which stabilization programmes, especially those based on a monetarist approach, could be rendered pro-poor. A particular concern was that of how to avoid large jumps in the poverty ratio during crises episodes. As a step in this direction, an indicator was derived that could indicate the consequences for the poverty ratio of different stabilization approaches.

In particular, the indicator was incorporated in the Polak version of the IMF's monetary model, where it was shown that there is a systematic inverse trade-off between the headcount ratio and the balance-of-payments target. However, in the standard financial programming or 'basic' version of the monetary model that is routinely employed by the IMF in its operations the indicator did not indicate any trade-offs, since this version of the monetary model does not articulate the effects of stabilization policies on GDP. This limitation also applies to the proposed '123PSRP' hybrid Bank–Fund model. The limitation will need to be lifted if these approaches are to be useful in addressing macroeconomic-induced fluctuations in the poverty ratio.

To bring out the policy trade-offs, the poverty indicator requires at a minimum that GDP be endogenously determined. This can be readily handled in properly articulated monetarist models, but their assumption that there is a tight relationship between credit policy and expenditures can be problematic. Credit restraint could result in a greater than projected reduction in expenditure, especially private investment. This would appear to account for the frequently observed balance of payments overshooting and investment undershooting.

Nonetheless, it is still possible to operate within the monetary framework, while reversing the causal chain so as to cope with the 'you cannot push on a string' phenomenon. This will require dealing explicitly with the expenditure side.

Insofar as the adverse poverty effects of stabilization episodes are associated with under-performing expenditures, an approach that focuses on influencing such expenditures through fiscal or other means rather than sweeping them behind a monetary veil is likely to be more successful.

Appendix A3.1 Growth and distributional effects for a Pareto income distribution

The Pareto income distribution takes the form

$$f(x) = ab^a x^{-a-1} \quad a > 1. \tag{A3.1}$$

Here b represents the lower income bound of the distribution. It can be interpreted as demarcating the subsistence level of income, with the poverty line z lying above it. The distribution assumes a uniform rate of decline in the proportion of the population above subsistence that earns higher levels of income. This rate of decline is measured by the power parameter a.

Some key expressions are derived next for the Pareto distribution. The headcount ratio is

$$H \equiv \frac{N_p}{N} \equiv F(z) = \int_b^z ab^a x^{-a-1} dx = 1 - \left(\frac{b}{z}\right)^a \tag{A3.2}$$

where $z > b$

The mean of the distribution is

$$\mu = \int_b^\infty x ab^a x^{-a-1} dx = \frac{ab}{a-1} \tag{A3.3}$$

The Lorenz curve of this distribution is

$$L(H) = \frac{1}{\mu} \int_b^z ab^a x^{-a} dx = 1 - (1-H)^{\frac{(a-1)}{a}} \tag{A3.4}$$

The elasticity of the headcount ratio with respect to the poverty line is

$$\eta_{H,z} \equiv \frac{L'(H)}{L''(H)} \frac{1}{H} = \frac{a(1-H)}{H} \tag{A3.5}$$

From the logarithmic time differentiation of A3.2, and using A3.5, the proportionate growth in the headcount ratio for the Pareto distribution is

$$\frac{\dot{H}}{H} = \eta_{H,z} \left(\frac{\dot{z}}{z} - \frac{\dot{b}}{b}\right) \tag{A3.6}$$

This relationship is similar in form to (3.9), except that it involves a term in b, the subsistence level, rather than mean income.

For an unchanged income distribution a is constant, implying

$$\frac{\dot{b}}{b} = \frac{\dot{\mu}}{\mu} \tag{A3.7}$$

which can be inserted in (3.56), to generate the same formula stated in (3.9).

The headcount elasticity expression can be expressed alternatively in a manner that overcomes the need for a direct estimate of a, provided estimates of the Gini coefficient G are available. From the definition of the Gini inequality coefficient (as the difference in the area between the line of equality and the Lorenz curve), manipulation of (3.14) yields the following relation between G and the power coefficient a.

$$G \equiv 1 - 2\int_0^1 L(p)dp = \frac{1}{2a-1} \qquad \text{A3.8}$$

The headcount elasticity in A3.5 can now be redefined as

$$\eta_{H,z} = \frac{1}{2}\left(\frac{1+G}{G}\right)\left(\frac{1-H}{H}\right) \qquad \text{A3.5a}$$

To determine the effects of a changing income distribution differentiate A3.2 with respect to the parameter a.

$$\frac{\dot{H}}{H} = -\eta_{H,a}\frac{\dot{a}}{a} \quad \text{where} \quad \eta_{H,a} \equiv \frac{a}{H}(H-1)\ln\left(\frac{b}{z}\right) > 0 \qquad \text{A3.9}$$

An increase in a indicates an improvement in the income distribution i.e. a reduction in G. Note from the definition of $\eta_{H,z}$ in A3.5 that

$$\eta_{H,a} \equiv -\eta_{H,z}\ln\frac{b}{z} \qquad \text{A3.10}$$

Combining the growth effects and the distributional effects on the poverty ratio

$$\frac{\dot{H}}{H} = \eta_{H,z}\left(\frac{\dot{z}}{z} - \frac{\dot{b}}{b} + \ln\left(\frac{b}{z}\right)\frac{\dot{a}}{a}\right) \qquad \text{A3.11}$$

To give some orders of magnitude, suppose a Gini of 0.5 and a headcount ratio of 0.15. The elasticity of the headcount ratio with respect to the poverty line is then 8. A Gini of 0.5 implies a value of $a = \frac{3}{2}$ from (3.14a). To determine $\ln\left(\frac{b}{z}\right)$, it suffices to use μ and an estimate of z.

Operationally, one could identify b with the poverty line for the very poor and z with the poverty line for the poor. Using the World Bank's criteria of $1 to demarcate the very poor and $2 for the poor, gives the fixed value $\ln\frac{b}{z} = -0.3$. Inserting the appropriate values in A3.11 enables the distributional effects of changes in a to be evaluated.

Notes

1 The author is especially grateful for comments received from Giovanni Andrea Cornia and Marco Dardi, who are not responsible for any remaining errors.
2 See, for example, the latest comprehensive review of the design of programmes (IMF 2004a,b). In particular, there is a dearth of models that address the issue of fluctuations in the poverty ratio from a short-run macroeconomic perspective: see the surveys in

Lipton and Ravallion (1995) and World Bank (2000). Chand and Shome (1997) approached the problem through the heuristic incorporation of Sen's well-known poverty index in the IMF's financial programming model. However, this index is quite complex as it integrates different dimensions of poverty such as its incidence, intensity, and the distribution of income among the poor. The present chapter focuses solely on the poverty ratio so as facilitate the needed analytical integration.

3 Answering such questions is different from that of identifying who the poor are, which requires a micro-oriented analysis.
4 For cross-country comparisons standard practice is to use the $1-a-day criterion recommended by the World Bank, adjusted for purchasing power differences. This corresponds to the minimal food dominated consumption basket used for demarcating the very poor. A $2-a-day criterion is used to identify the poor.
5 Dollar and Kray (2002) argue for a similar heuristic relationship.
6 The intervening terms in (3.4) cancel out. Bourguignon et al. (2002) provide a breakdown of the change in the headcount ratio with respect to the last two terms of (3.4), but not for valuation changes in the poverty line. However, the latter is required whenever the price index relevant for the poverty line diverges from that applying to total income, which is generally the case. There may also be some interactions between the three terms, but these are ignored here.
7 See Dollar and Kray (2002).
8 The implied assumption that distributional changes may not be pronounced is belied by the data. See, for example, Cornia and Kiiski (2001).
9 See Kakwani (1993). $\frac{dH}{dz}$ is determined from (3.3) and inverted.
10 Note, however, the widespread practice of defining a poverty line by reference to the food requirements of a minimum calorie level, but then subsequently updating it using a general consumer price index. This results in understating the numbers of the poor when food prices rise more than the consumer price index. Pogge and Reddy (2003) provide a telling critique of these procedures.
11 This is usually estimated as $\Delta \ln H = a_0 + a_1 \ln Y$ where Y is real GDP and a_1 is constant value elasticity. Bourguignon (2002) refers to this model as the naïve model.
12 There is a conceptual problem with the Polak model, which breaks down if the small country assumption is maintained and nominal income is fixed. This is because the transmission mechanism for adjusting to shifts in credit and money supply relies on changes in nominal income to induce changes in imports. The problem is avoided if imports are made a function of domestic expenditure instead (Chand, 1989).
13 The outcome could be worse than indicated insofar as the macro restraint induces adverse distributional effects.
14 See also Krugman and Taylor (1978) on the contractionary effects of devaluation.
15 Easterly (2004) provides a detailed and valuable assessment of the use of identities in the FP approach. He concludes that simply ensuring consistency between aggregates does not guarantee outcomes.
16 Since the concern here is with the conceptual use of the model, no specifications are provided of definitions, stock and flow valuations, and other aspects needed for empirical applications. These are to be found in numerous IMF documents explaining the technique of financial programming (for example, IMF 1987, 2004b). As a set of accounting relations with minimal behavioural specifications, it confers a high degree of flexibility for informed guesswork in a consistent framework. In light of the poor data and uncertainty concerning behaviour in the typical program country, such flexibility confers an advantage over more structured models. On this point see Polak (1998) and Mussa and Savastano (1999).
17 This can only be valid if the economy is small, completely open, and the law of one price prevails internationally, so that any domestic surplus is readily disposed off abroad.
18 The report refers to the Heisenberg uncertainty principle in physics to assert that 'there may be inherent limits to whether the effect of policies on macroeconomic targets can

be knowable in crisis situations ...' (p. 10, fn. 13, op. cit.). This proposition is certainly of major methodological interest, which raises fundamental questions about the role of IMF policy prescriptions in crisis situations.
19 This is consistent with the frequent observation that the banking sector becomes more liquid during the stabilization phase despite a tighter monetary policy. It is also common for budget tightening to fall heavily on government investment.
20 Baqir *et al.* (2003, p. 10) ask (their italics) 'How did Fund programs perform with respect to their original intent "*to shorten the duration and lessen the degree of disequilibrium in the international balance of payments?*" The answer is a resounding success – the improvement in the current account was more than programmed and the reserve target met with a high degree of precision – quite amazing the latter, given that we are talking about several programs in 18 countries.'
21 The situation could have started off as liquidity-constrained (where agent behaviour is tightly controlled by the availability of credit), but if reducing credit causes expenditure to decline sufficiently, a non-liquidity-constrained one results.
22 The treatment here is in terms of the more general monetary model, which allows for nominal GDP adjustment. This contrasts with the FP approach, where the assumptions made force equilibration entirely through the current account of the balance of payments.
23 There was considerable debate in the 1960s as to which, velocity in (3.31) or the Keynesian income multiplier in (3.33), was more stable as a means to establishing the more valid theory. Those tests were on the whole inconclusive.
24 This would be additive if the income distribution is Pareto. As shown in Appendix A3.1, the additional term to be added is $\frac{\Delta H}{H_{-1}} = \eta_{H,z}(-0.3\frac{\Delta a}{a_{-1}})$.
25 There is also the alternative of reducing the import ratio, for example through selective and temporary import protection. Although not efficient for inelastic imports such as energy, food and semi-processed goods for which domestic substitutes may not be available, it could be feasible for non-basic consumer goods.
26 A means for paying for it, without violating the fiscal adjustment needed for balance-of-payments stabilization, is to tax windfall earnings on foreign exchange inflows or holdings of foreign assets. This can be justified on equity grounds. Furthermore, a credible windfall tax, in place before a crisis hits, might even contribute towards restraining the initial speculative excesses that resulted in exchange rate overshooting.

References

Ames, B., W. Brown, S. Devarajan, and A. Izquierdo. 2001. 'Macroeconomic Policy and Poverty Reduction'. In *PRSP Sourcebook*. Washington DC: IMF.
Baqir R., R. Ramcharan, and R. Sahay. 2003. *IMF Program Design and Growth: What is the Link?*, manuscript. Washington DC.
Bourguignon, F. 2002. *The Growth Elasticity of Poverty Reduction: Explaining Heterogeneity Across Countries and Time Periods,* Working paper No. 2002-03. Paris: Delta.
Bourguignon, F., L. Pereira da Silva, and N. Stern. 2002. *Evaluating the Poverty Impact of Economic Policies: Some Analytical Challenges*. Mimeo, The World Bank.
Bruno, M. 1994. 'Stabilization and Reform in Eastern Europe: A Preliminary Evaluation'. In O.J. Blanchard, K.A. Froot and J.D. Sachs (eds), *The Transition in Eastern Europe, Vol. 1.* Cambridge, MA: NBER-PR.
Chand, S.K. 1989. 'Towards a Growth-Oriented Model of Financial Programming'. *World Development*, 17(4), 567–98.
Chand, S.K., and P. Shome. 1997. 'Integrating Poverty Alleviation into the Fund's Financial Programming Framework'. In Mario Blejer and Teresa Ter-Minassian (eds), *Fiscal Policy and Economic Reform*. New York and London: Routledge.

Cornia G.A. with S. Kiiski. 2001. *Trends in Income Distribution in the Post World War 11 Period: Evidence and Interpretation.* UNU/WIDER Discussion Papers 2001/89. Helsinki: WIDER.

Devarajan, S. and D.S. Go. 2002. *A Macroeconomic Framework for Poverty Reduction Strategy Papers, With an Application to Zambia.* African Region Working Paper Series No. 38. Washington DC: World Bank.

Dollar, D. and A. Kraay. 2002. 'Growth is Good for the Poor'. *Journal of Economic Growth*, 7(3), 195–225.

Easterly, W. 2004. *An Identity Crisis? Examining IMF Financial Programming.* Mimeo, New York.

IMF. 1987. *Theoretical Aspects of the Design of Fund-Supported Adjustment Programs.* IMF Occasional Paper No. 55. Washington DC: IMF.

IMF. 2004a. *Fund Supported Programs – Objectives and Outcomes.* SM/04/404. Washington DC: IMF.

IMF. 2004b. *Policy Formulation, Analytical Framework, and Program Design.* SM/04/405. Washington DC: IMF.

Kakwani, N. 1993. 'Poverty and Economic Growth with Application to Côte d'Ivoire'. *Review of Income and Wealth*, Vol. 39, pp. 121–39.

Krueger, A. 2002. *Crisis Prevention and Resolution: The Role of Sovereign Debt Renegotiation*, http://www.imf.org/external/np/speeches/2002/100702a.htm, accessed on 17 October 2002.

Krugman, P. and L. Taylor. 1978. 'Contractionary Effects of Devaluation'. *Journal of International Economics*, 8(3), 445–56.

Lipton, M. and M. Ravallion. 1995. 'Poverty and Policy'. In Jere Behrman and T.N. Srinivasan (eds), *Handbook of Development Economics*. Amsterdam: Elsevier, vol. 3B, Ch. 41.

Mussa, M. and M. Savastano. 1999. *The IMF Approach to Economic Stabilization.* IMF WP/99/104.

Pogge, T.W. and S.G. Reddy. 2003. *Unknown: The Extent, Distribution, and Trend of Global Income Poverty*, manuscript.

Polak, J.J. 1998. 'The IMF Monetary Model at Forty.' *Economic Modelling*, 15, 395–410.

Polak, J.J. 1957. *Monetary Analysis of Income Formation and Payments Problems.* IMF Staff Papers, 6, pp. 1–50.

World Bank. 2000. *Attacking Poverty. World Development Report 2000/2001.* Oxford: Oxford University Press.

WDI. 2002. *World Development Indicators.* Washington DC: World Bank.

4
Exchange Rate Regimes for Development and Poverty Alleviation

Giovanni Andrea Cornia[1]

Introduction

In the early twenty-first century the background against which policy makers have to choose an exchange rate regime is characterized by global financial integration, the dominance of capital account over current account transactions, large unhedged foreign currency liabilities, unpredictable fluctuations between the three main currencies and frequent financial crises linked to financial reforms and volatile portfolio flows. Given all of this, the mainstream advice to developing countries has been to adopt one of the two 'corner solutions' – that is, a hard peg or a pure float. However, whether this suggestion is good for growth and poverty alleviation is not at all clear. In this regard, this chapter reviews the evolution of the exchange rate regimes, examines the impact of alternative exchange rate regimes on growth, inflation and the balance of payments and discusses the choice of the exchange rate regime that minimizes poverty under normal conditions and crisis periods.

Post-1991 de jure and de facto exchange rate regimes

Exchange rate regimes have evolved substantially over the last 50 years. When the Bretton Woods system of fixed exchange rates was abandoned in 1971, countries opted for a variety of regimes ranging from fixed pegs to floating rates, with most developing countries opting for some kind of fixed peg in relation to one of the main currencies.

During the post-1971 period, the choice of the exchange rate regime has been strongly influenced by changes in the openness of the current and capital account of the balance of payments. Until about 1990, the capital account of most countries, and particularly of the developing ones, was almost completely closed, convertibility for current account transactions was limited (see Table 4.1) and the exchange rate was determined mainly by import and export flows.

Since then, the capital account has been increasingly liberalized, either because capital controls were relaxed, or because greater current account convertibility entailed some de facto liberalization of capital movements or because constraints

Table 4.1 Countries accepting the obligations of Article VIII of the IMF agreement on the liberalization of the current account

	1975	1980	1985	1990	1995	2000	2005
IMF reporting countries	129	140	148	153	182	183	184
% accepting the obligations of Article VIII							
% of all countries	34.1	37.9	40.5	43.8	62.1	81.4	87.5
% of developed countries	66.7	70.8	79.2	87.5	100.0	100.0	100.0
% of developing countries	27.2	31.6	33.9	37.4	59.7	80.0	85.5
% of transition economies	0.0	0.0	0.0	0.0	37.0	70.4	85.2

Source: Author's compilation on IMF data.

Table 4.2 Index[a] of controls on capital account transactions

	1995	1996	1997	1998	1999	2000	2001	2002	2003
IMF reporting countries	112	130	142	158	161	164	167	169	170
Average value of the index									
All countries	2.57	2.62	2.64	2.68	2.57	2.58	2.58	2.54	2.49
Developed countries	1.88	1.80	2.04	1.81	1.62	1.69	1.73	1.58	1.54
Developing countries	2.70	2.76	2.71	2.80	2.73	2.75	2.74	2.72	2.72
Transition economies	3.15	3.05	3.00	3.04	2.88	2.73	2.74	2.68	2.43

Note:
[a] Sum of (0,1) dummy variables measuring 'restrictions on the purchase of capital market securities', 'restrictions on the purchase money market instruments', 'controls on derivatives' and 'controls on foreign direct investment'. The index ranges between 0 (no controls) and 4 (complete controls).

Source: Author's compilation on the basis of data provided by Gian Maria Milesi-Ferretti of the IMF.

on most currency transactions were lifted. Under these new circumstances, capital movements increasingly determine the exchange rate. As International Monetary Fund (IMF) data show, between 1966 and 1990 the share of countries with restrictions on narrowly-defined capital account transactions remained at around 80 per cent, dropping to 70 per cent in 1995. Since then, however a more diversified trend has emerged (see Table 4.2). While the developed and transition economies gradually reduced capital controls – except for the crisis years 1997–1998 – in the developing countries this trend seems to have come to a complete halt.

All of this explains in part the shift of the last three decades in de jure exchange rate arrangements. In fact, Table 4.3 shows that the number of single-currency pegs fell drastically, currency boards and monetary unions rose steadily – in part due to the creation of the European Union – intermediate regimes, especially floats with discretionary interventions, increased and free floats rose sharply from a low

Table 4.3 De jure classification of exchange rate regimes, 1970–1999 (percentages of total observations from 167 countries)

Exchange rate regime	1970–1979	1980–1989	1990–1999
A. Pegged regimes	84.8	68.4	46.6
(1) Hard pegs	10.0	13.8	15.4
Dollarization	0.5	0.7	0.6
Currency Board	4.6	4.7	6.1
Monetary Union	4.9	8.4	8.7
(2) Single currency pegs	61.2	27.4	13.9
(3) Basket pegs	13.6	27.1	17.2
Published basket pegs	7.3	13.9	8.1
Undisclosed basket pegs	6.2	13.3	9.1
B. Intermediate regimes	11.0	22.5	26.4
(4) Floats with rule-based interventions	5.9	9.5	9.6
Cooperative regimes – crawling pegs	3.8	5.7	6.0
Targets zones and bands	1.1	1.3	1.9
Unclassified rule-based systems	0.5	0.8	0.9
(5) Floats with discretionary interventions	5.1	13.0	16.8
Managed floats with heavy interventions	0.5	3.2	0.6
Unclassified managed floats	0.8	6.1	16.1
Other floats	3.8	3.7	0.1
C. Free floating	4.3	9.1	27.0
(6) Floats	4.3	9.1	27.0
Floating with light interventions	1.1	2.6	0.8
Floating with no interventions	3.2	6.5	26.2

Source: Ghosh *et al.* (2004) on official IMF data.

level. However, most economists consider the analyses of exchange rate regimes based on the de jure IMF classification of little analytical use. Indeed, countries are allowed to declare to be pegged to an undisclosed basket of currencies, but it is not possible to verify if exchange rate changes reflect changes in the basket currencies or discretionary interventions, and analyses of changes in interest rates and international reserves show that in many cases the exchange rate was managed. Likewise, many floating rates are in reality fixed to an anchor currency.

For all of these reasons, the recent research draws a distinction between the 'official' (or de jure) classification and the 'effective' (or de facto) classification of exchange rate regimes, with the latter being consistent with the observed variations in interest rates and currency reserves. For instance, while the number of free floaters increased markedly between the 1970s and 1990s (see Table 4.3), in the 1990s, only 40 per cent of them effectively allowed the fluctuation of the exchange rate, while in many others it was actively managed (see Table 4.4). Misclassifications were almost as common in the case of floating regimes and, to a lesser extent, pegged regimes. Thus, shifting from the de jure to the de facto classification permits us to reach more realistic conclusions about the growth, inflation and trade effects of alternative exchange rate regimes.

Table 4.4 Distribution of de jure and de facto classification in the 1990s

	de facto classification		
de jure classification	Pegged regimes	Intermediate regimes	Floating regimes
Pegged regimes	2265	378	178
Intermediate regimes	432	270	179
Floating regimes	124	233	254
Total observations	2821	881	611

Source: Ghosh *et al*. (2004); Reinhart and Rogoff (2003).

Advantages and disadvantages of the main foreign exchange regimes

Pegged regimes

With the dollarization, the dollar, euro, etc., acts as the only legal tender and the monetary policy passively follows that of the anchor country. This regime has the advantage of eliminating the volatility of the exchange rate as well as the exchange risk in international transactions. Because of this, several small economies with unstable external terms of trade, such as Panama, have dollarized, while others allow substantial dollar-denominated bank deposits and are de facto semi-dollarized (see Chapter 13 on Bolivia).

The main problem of this approach is that the loss of control of the interest and exchange rate policies remove a country's ability to jump start its economy (Rodrik 2003), to respond to external shocks by devaluing its currency (see Chapter 13) or to change its interest rate to affect levels of economic activity. Thus, poverty may rise if the anchor country raises its interest rate to control overheating, while the dollarized country needs to reduce it to combat recession. In all of these cases, the only way to absorb a shock and restore competitiveness is to cut nominal wages, corporate taxes and utility rates. However, these changes are slow in producing their effects and might meet insurmountable political resistance. Also, with the policy of dollarization, the central bank can no longer act as a lender of last resort, and such a function must be shifted to the fiscal authority.

In the case of currency boards, the domestic currency is fixed by law in relation to an anchor currency at a given unchangeable rate, and the domestic monetary base must be backed by a high proportion or an equivalent amount of the anchor currency. Supporters of such a regime stress that it provides credibility, transparency, low inflation and low interest rates. Indeed, such a regime helped to rapidly reduce inflation, as, for instance, in Argentina in the early 1990s.

But currency boards also have drawbacks. They require the costly immobilization of huge reserves at the central bank, while external shocks cannot be compensated by changes in the exchange rate and interest rate and the role of lender of last resort of the central bank is severely limited. In addition, the system works poorly in the presence of 'mistakes' in other policy areas, in particular, in the case of insufficient fiscal discipline – as in the case of Argentina in the late 1990s – or of an initial overvaluation of the real effective exchange rate. In this regard, Williamson (2003) notes that the success of the Southern Cone countries in reducing inflation consistently entailed an initial appreciation of the real exchange rate as, after fixing the parity, inflation remained for some time above that of the anchor country. Currency boards may also cause disincentives to save due to heavy liquidity requirements imposed on the banking system, and require considerable wage flexibility to accommodate shocks without large increases in the rate of unemployment. In addition, the lack of synchronization of the business cycle with that of the anchor country is a problem in this case.

In turn, traditional pegs fix the nominal value of the domestic currency in relation to a currency or basket of currencies. Such an approach reduces exchange rate volatility, while leaving control of fiscal, monetary and exchange rate policy in domestic hands. Unlike the previous two policies, this regime imposes no automatic restrictions on fiscal and monetary policy and its credibility thus depends upon the measures adopted in this area. In addition, while reducing volatility, the fixed peg may be affected by persistent misalignment. It is also doubtful whether such a regime can be sustained in a world of high capital mobility, as the fixed peg can easily become the target of speculative attacks.

Intermediate regimes

These regimes include crawling peg, target bands and managed floats. In the first case, the exchange rate 'crawls' in relation to the anchor currency – or basket of currencies – according to a pre-established rule such as the inflation differential with the anchor country. If successful, this approach leaves the real exchange rate broadly unchanged, and it is thus used by countries aiming to gradually reduce inflation without letting the real exchange rate appreciate, a fact that would penalize the traded sector. In a world of free capital movements, however, a crawling peg can become the target of speculative attacks. And also in this case, the credibility of this regime depends on the accompanying policies in the fiscal, monetary and capital controls areas.

With the target band approach, the exchange rate is free to vary within a pre-set band of a width varying between plus or minus 2.5 per cent and 10 per cent. When the rate reaches the upper or lower limit of the band, it is defended through open market interventions, but intra-band fluctuations are not intervened upon. This regime too can become subject to speculative attacks and by itself does not constrain fiscal and monetary policy. Its credibility depends, therefore, on policies in these areas. For instance, Chile managed to grow impressively for more than a decade, while keeping a policy of exchange rate bands that afforded its currency some flexibility (see Chapter 10). Finally, in the case of managed floats with discretionary interventions, the exchange rate is fixed in the currency market, but authorities can and do intervene to influence its level without being bound to any predetermined rule. The system does not by itself constrain monetary and fiscal policy that can thus be used to target inflation.

Free floats

A pure float is the regime most often adopted by strong currencies. It allows a country to respond to shocks through exchange rate adjustments determined by the market and eliminates, therefore, the need to hold large reserves. However, such a regime does not provide an expectation anchor, increases the exchange risk and may thus discourage international trade and domestic investments. It can also be subject to costly currency misalignments and overshootings that fuel imported inflation and recession. Indeed, in 12.5 per cent of the countries studied by Reinhart and Rogoff (2003) a 'free float' turned into a 'free fall'. In addition, with expansionary fiscal and monetary policies, free floats may lead to a surge in imported inflation that fuels the inflation–devaluation spiral, while for countries exporting the same goods, a free float is an inherently unstable regime that sets incentives for 'beggar-thy-neighbour' competitive devaluations and non-cooperative strategies.

Among the various domestic and external shocks that can affect the nominal and real exchange rate there are changes in income inequality. The basic argument (Min 2002) is that the demand elasticity of non-tradables – for example, real estate, communication and insurance services – is higher among the rich than the poor, while its supply is basically inelastic, due to a lack of competition and various kinds of rigidities. Under these circumstances, a rise in the demand of non-tradables, triggered by an increase in income inequality, increases inflation, appreciates the real exchange rate, worsens the exports and balance-of-payments accounts and – *ceteris paribus* – leads to slower growth and poverty reduction. The cross-country evidence provided in this regard is quite robust (Min 2002). In turn, a fall in income inequality would shift aggregate demand toward the tradables and cause a depreciation of the real exchange rate.

Choice of a pro-poor exchange rate regime under normal conditions

What are the long-term objectives that must be pursued by the exchange rate policy? What exchange rate regime promotes long-term development and poverty alleviation in a world of high capital mobility? Discussion in these areas is dominated by the 'impossible trinity' debate according to which a country must abandon one of the following three policy goals: exchange rate stability, monetary independence or financial market integration (Braga *et al*. 2001). How true is this view? How unavoidable are its implications? To answer these questions it is necessary to discuss the three main approaches to the choice of the exchange rate regime (Williamson 2003).

The nominal anchor approach

In this approach, the main policy objective is price stability and the tool of choice is the hard peg. Given the constraints they impose on monetary policy, hard pegs permit pursuing a policy of financial integration combined with exchange rate stability, though this precludes the possibility of influencing the level of domestic activity through the interest rate. In fact, with perfect capital mobility, the no-arbitrage condition ensures that

$$i = i^* + de \qquad (4.1)$$

where i is the nominal domestic interest rate, i^* is the world interest rate, and de the expected percentage change in the nominal exchange rate. With a credible hard peg, de is equal to zero and the domestic interest rate equals the world interest rate. In case of international financial integration, hard pegs are also supposed to help re-establishing balance-of-payments equilibrium and the control of inflation when the economy is hit by external shocks. The balance-of-payments deficit, in fact, causes a fall in money supply, a rise in the interest rate and a slowdown in inflation. In turn, the rise in the interest rate attracts capitals from abroad that helps re-establish the equilibrium of the balance of payments. Considering then that the equilibrium in the money market is guaranteed by

$$M = P\, m(i,Y) \qquad (4.2)$$

where M is the monetary base, P the domestic price level, i the domestic interest rate and Y the domestic output. As in small open economies $P = eP^*$, which means that domestic inflation P is determined by the global inflation P^*, to maintain equilibrium M must follow changes in P and Y. An expansion of M in excess of the changes in these two variables would result in monetary imbalances, capital outflows, loss of credibility of the peg and, possibly, speculative attacks.

As noted earlier, this approach has been shown to reduce inflation over the short term, while in some cases it stimulated a surge in capital flows, though these were often short term and speculative in nature. However, greater price stability has to be weighed against the initial or subsequent appreciation of the real exchange rate that may lead finally to a collapse of the peg, as well as to slow growth due to the immobilization of huge reserves, disincentives to save, the need to unload asymmetric shocks on the labour market and a lack of synchronization of the business cycle with that of the anchor country.

The real targets approach

As noted by Williamson (2003), in this approach the floating of the exchange rate has the objective of re-equilibrating the balance of payments, while the monetary and fiscal policy are used to target the internal balance. Therefore, a floating rate permits the achievement of two of the three objectives of the 'impossible trinity', that is, financial integration and an independent monetary policy, as the effects of decisions concerning M and i, as well as changes in Y, are unloaded on e. The adjustment of e should be accompanied by limited variations in the level of reserves, since authorities refrain from intervening in currency markets, and in interest rates. But the evidence produced by Calvo and Reinhart (reported in Branson 2001) shows that reserves and interest rates were more volatile among the floaters than the peggers, indicating that monetary policy was actively used to stabilize the exchange rate, pointing in this way to a 'fear of floating' possibly induced by the effects of devaluation on dollar-denominated liabilities.

Full floats should also allow interest rates to differ from the US rate. But, with the exception of a few large industrialized countries able to pursue an independent monetary policy, the interest rates of most countries correlate closely with the US rate regardless of the exchange rate regime adopted, thus underscoring the inability to pursue a supposedly independent monetary policy.

Exchange rate stability and the development strategy approach

This approach emphasizes that the instability of exchange rates cannot be easily rationalized on the basis of changes in fundamentals and is mainly explained by expectations about their future values. For this reason, a free float is likely to overshoot, thus generating harmful effects on growth, employment and poverty. While the exchange rate could also be stabilized by increasing the interest rate, this policy generally depresses the level of economic activity. To avoid this, the policy maker should, therefore, credibly stabilize the real exchange rate as well as its expectations.

One way to do this consists in the adoption of a basket, band and crawl (BBC) approach proposed by Williamson (2003). In this approach, which belongs to the group of 'intermediate regimes' in Table 4.3, the country fixes the nominal exchange rate in relation to a basket of currencies, allows it to fluctuate within a given band so as to neutralize small shocks and raises the central parity in case of large shocks that by raising domestic inflation could lead to an appreciation of the real exchange rate, with long-term negative effects on the tradable sector, growth and poverty rates.

Maintaining a competitive real exchange rate is thus a key component of the development strategy of a country, particularly if it is small – as in the case of many developing nations – and can therefore count on only a small domestic market to sell its production. As noted by Balassa (quoted in Williamson 2003), a competitive exchange rate would encourage the entrepreneurs of a country to try to sell on the world market goods other than their traditional exports, invest in new plants and hire new workers. This view is supported by the evidence provided by Rodrik (2003), who identifies a competitive exchange rate as being among the key factors triggering growth spurts.

The case for maintaining a competitive exchange rate is particularly compelling in poor developing countries that need to grow to reduce poverty, control large fluctuations in their net foreign exchange earnings to avoid a devastating overshooting of floating rates, face little demand for their domestic currency assets and do not, therefore, benefit from the 'credibility' and 'disciplining effect' supposedly associated with fixed nominal pegs. It is increasingly accepted, therefore, that the optimal exchange rate policy for a developing country consists of stabilizing the real effective exchange rate at a competitive level against a basket of currencies (Branson and Katseli 1980; Frenkel and Taylor 2005).

Maintaining a competitive exchange rate is, therefore, one essential component of a development policy focusing on exports, domestic investment and growth. In principle, capital inflows can contribute to this goal by increasing domestic investment. But this is not guaranteed. By reducing interest rates, capital inflows encourage both consumption and investment in tradables and non-tradables. Consumption and investments in non-tradables financed by foreign borrowing are, however, questionable as they increase future debt-servicing obligations without increasing the capacity to earn foreign exchange. In addition, capital inflows raise the exchange rate as – with an open capital account – this is increasingly determined on the market for financial assets.

What policies can prevent this from happening? Does a country have to abandon financial integration or control over the real exchange rate, as suggested by the 'impossible trinity' theorem? This is not necessarily true as, even with an open capital account, the central bank can introduce a series of measures that either limit some capital inflows or offset their effects on the expansion of the monetary mass (Williamson 2003; Frenkel and Taylor 2005). Among the first group of measures, it is possible to include the Chilean-style obligation to deposit a certain proportion of the non-equity capital inflow for a year on a non-interest bearing account at the central bank, irrespective of the maturity of the asset being purchased with the inflow; to limit the extent of the foreign exchange exposure of domestic banks, or forbid them to borrow internationally to extend loans to the non-tradable sector; and to drop tax holidays and other incentives addressed to foreign investors. The second group of measures entails asking state-controlled financial institutions such as the postal savings scheme to switch their deposits from the commercial to the central bank, as has happened in the past in Singapore; sterilizing the capital inflows by issuing domestic bonds, though this measure may be costly; increasing the reserve ratio of commercial banks hosting foreign deposits; substituting foreign with domestic borrowing whenever the interest differential is not excessive; and liberalizing capital outflows or encouraging domestic financial institutions such as national pension funds to invest part of their assets abroad (see Chapters 9 and 10 on Malaysia and Chile).

The empirical evidence supports the preference for a regime that targets the stability of the real exchange rate. A study of alternative exchange rate regimes from 1970 to 2001 shows (see Table 4.5) that when countries are grouped according to the official (de jure) classification, the limited flexibility regimes – that is, rule-based crawling pegs and bands – perform the best in all areas. Yet, Ghosh *et al.* (2004) suggest instead that pegged regimes exhibit lower inflation rates, due to lower money growth (the discipline effect) and greater confidence in the currency (the credibility effect). Shifting to the de facto classification somewhat affects the results. Indeed, once the free falling cases are removed from the free floating category, the differences in performance narrow down, while their ranking changes somewhat (see Table 4.5). However, the limited flexibility category continues to exhibit the best performance in all areas, if by a narrower margin.

Table 4.5 Economic performance under different exchange rate arrangements, 1970–2001[4]

Classification of exchange rate regimes	Fixed pegs	Limited flexibility	Managed floating	Free floating	Free falling
Average annual inflation rate					
IMF de jure classification	38.8 (2)[a]	5.3 (1)	74.8 (3)	173.9 (4)	NA
de facto classification	15.9 (3)	10.1 (2)	16.5 (4)	9.4 (1)	443.3 (5)
Average annual GDP growth					
IMF de jure classification	1.4 (3)	2.2 (1)	1.9 (2)	0.5 (4)	NA
de facto classification	1.9 (3)	2.4 (1)	1.6 (4)	2.3 (2)	−2.5 (5)
Exports plus imports in percentage of GDP					
IMF de jure classification	69.9 (2)	81.0 (1)	65.8 (3)	60.6 (4)	NA
de facto classification	78.7 (2)	80.3 (1)	61.2 (3)	44.9 (5)	57.1 (4)
Overall score[b]					
IMF de jure classification	7 (2)	3 (1)	8 (3)	12 (4)	NA
de facto classification	8 (2)	4 (1)	11 (4)	8 (2)	14

Notes:
NA = not applicable.
[a] numbers in parenthesis indicate the performance rank.
[b] the overall score is the sum of the performance rank in the field of inflation, growth and foreign trade.
Source: Reinhart and Rogoff (2003).

Choice of a pro-poor exchange rate regime during crisis situations

Intermediate exchange rates and devaluation

The argument in favour of an exchange rate of the BBC type is that adjustment to external shocks takes place more rapidly and with smaller losses of output and employment than under fixed pegs, especially when nominal wages and utility rates are rigid downward. By swiftly depressing wages, devaluation allows competitiveness to recover rapidly, with minimal losses of output and employment. In addition, according to the standard view focusing on the current account effects, if there is unused capacity, devaluation is expansionary because it increases the demand for tradables due to the switch away from imports – and the greater incentives to increase the supply of exports due to the rise in their domestic currency supply price. In contrast, if all resources are fully employed, devaluation can be expected to raise prices. Yet even countries with unused capacity resist devaluation. Some of the explanations of this stance are illustrated below.

Devaluation, inflation and poverty

One of the negative effects of devaluation is that inflation might accelerate, possibly affecting the poor unduly, especially the urban poor. Much of the literature

(Easterly 2001 and the authors mentioned therein) confirms that inflation disproportionately affects the poor who are less able to protect their assets against inflation, depend more than the rich on non-indexable social transfers such as pensions and poor relief and assign a high share of their income to the consumption of tradable 'wage goods' such as food that are likely to be affected by price rises. In addition, Easterly (2001) showed on a poll of 32,000 citizens from 38 countries that people with low income, education and skills are more likely than other groups to mention inflation as their top concern.

Yet there are other effects that need to be accounted for. For instance, inflation may not significantly affect the already poor in rural areas, as their shares of monetary income and cash holdings are negligible. Furthermore, the poor may be less affected by the fiscal drag induced by inflation. In addition, the nexus between inflation and poverty is mediated by the concave relation existing between inflation and growth, so that a moderate increase in unanticipated inflation is likely to lead to an expansion of output and employment. Indeed, earlier findings show that inflation rates of up to 40 per cent do not affect output and employment (Bruno and Easterly 1998), while policies aiming at quickly reducing inflation to a single digit do affect them.

Devaluation, structural effects, growth and poverty

Earlier research has focused on the effectiveness of devaluation in strengthening the current account. In many cases, the import and export elasticities were found to be sufficiently large, so that devaluation improved the current account. However, these conclusions have not been verified in countries where the import and export elasticities are low due to all kinds of rigidities. Under such circumstances, devaluation does not significantly increase the supply of tradables and the current balance can be improved only by rationing of imports of essential production inputs, with the effect of causing an output contraction. As for the poverty impact, incomes were found to rise in the export sector (see above), while employment and incomes fell in the import-dependent domestic sector and non-tradable sector due to the hike in tradable prices.

The structuralists (Krugman and Taylor 1978) have argued that – even when the Marshall–Lerner conditions apply – devaluation in developing countries can be contractionary as well as inflationary. They indicate four main channels through which this can happen. To start with, devaluation is contractionary if it occurs in a situation of trade deficit as, given the low value of the import elasticity, the rise in the domestic price of imported goods absorbs an amount of domestic income greater than the income rise recorded in the export sector, with the effect of reducing real incomes aty home and depressing aggregate demand. Secondly, even when foreign trade is balanced, devaluation leads to an immediate increase in prices, while it takes time for nominal wages or the money supply to catch up, so that real wages and real balances decline temporarily and so reduce aggregate demand. Thirdly, in large firms, devaluation might shift the distribution of income towards profits as prices in the traded sector rise, while real wages are eroded by the price rise due to devaluation. If the propensity of profit earners to save is higher than that of workers, output will contract. Finally, if there exist ad valorem taxes on imports and exports, devaluation redistributes income from the private sector to the government. As government has a unity propensity to save in the short run, this too will reduce aggregate demand.

Other effects concern the monetary aggregates. Devaluation-induced inflation will – *ceteris paribus* – reduce real money supply and so raise interest rates with contractionary effects. In addition, the rise of the domestic interest rate will raise the cost of production of firms that depend on bank credit. All of this may shift the aggregate supply curve to the left. Thus, if the above analysis is true, and it must be emphasized that it relies on some restrictive assumptions, the policy maker would be confronted with a trade-off between an improvement in the current account and stagflation.

Thus, while not denying the role of devaluation in rectifying balance-of-payments disequilibria over the medium term, Krugman and Taylor (1978) conclude that devaluation-based short-term adjustments may be costly, and that governments can instead borrow to cover the short-term deficit, while improving exports' performance over the medium term by removing the structural rigidities that block their expansion through subsidies, preferential credit and investments in infrastructure.

Evidence of the impact of devaluation on growth

The evidence about the impact of devaluation (see the literature reviewed in Kamin and Klau 1997) is inconclusive but points to the existence of widespread J-curve effects. The main findings are that devaluation is not expansionary, or may even be contractionary, over the short term but is neutral over the long term. In particular, in Latin America, real devaluation curtailed real output during 28 adjustment spells but raised growth after two or more years.

According to Kamin and Klau (1997), most of the analyses in this field are subject to methodological problems as they do not distinguish between short- and long-term effects, do not control for shocks that may simultaneously induce a contraction and a devaluation, do not emphasize regional differences and do not consider reverse causation between growth and devaluation. To solve these problems, they run a panel regression with controls for different regions and separate out the short-term from the long-term effects. They find that devaluation can be contractionary over the short term but not over the long term, so that the balance of payments can be improved over the medium term without losing output and employment, and that devaluation seems to be more contractionary in Latin America than in East Asia or the industrialized countries.

Devaluation, capital account effects and poverty

The growing importance of capital account transactions in many countries has made these analyses look increasingly incomplete – as the focus on the current account effects of devaluation needs to be complemented by analyses of its effects on the capital account. Indeed, where it serves to restore confidence as part of a credible macroeconomic strategy comprising an appropriate anti-inflationary fiscal and monetary policy, a devaluation of the exchange rate at a level perceived to be close to what the markets see as an equilibrium rate has an expansionary impact, as it stimulates capital inflows. However, if it is perceived as a panic measure unable to restore confidence, devaluation triggers an outflow of capital and further self-fulfilling devaluations. In addition, in countries adopting a hard peg, devaluation entails a loss of credibility for the monetary authorities, loss of confidence by foreign investors and a reversal of capital flows.

Secondly, in countries where the banks, firms, government and households have large unhedged short-term exposures in foreign currency, devaluation increases the domestic cost of servicing the foreign debt, implying a squeeze of other sources of public and private expenditure that produces a deflationary effect, and an anti-poor effect in case the public expenditure cuts affect pro-poor transfers and services. In the corporate sector, devaluation can have devastating balance sheet effects leading to default or losses that curtail private and public demand. In addition, the liquidity shortage experienced by banks following devaluation prevents traded sector firms from increasing exports in the wake of a devaluation. As in the case of the Indonesian crisis, this may lead to an overshooting of the exchange rate with large negative real effects (Bird and Rajan 2000).

All of this de facto limits the choices of policy makers who fear that devaluation would cause devastating balance sheet effects. Instead of adjusting by devaluing the exchange rate, many countries choose to raise interest rates or to dollarize – a decision that likely leads to higher unemployment and poverty than in the case of devaluation.

The defence of the nominal exchange rate

Such a policy requires large – if allegedly temporary – rises in interest rates and considerable public expenditure cuts. These measures are intended to avoid inflationary pressures, strengthen credibility, reinforce the exchange rate and attract new capital inflows to offset the current account deficit. However, as argued by Stiglitz (2002), it is unclear how a temporary increase in interest rates can lead to a permanent strengthening of the currency, restoration of confidence and the return of foreign capital.

As a result, the firms directly affected by the shock that are unable to recover competitiveness by cutting labour and utility costs, either go bankrupt or reduce their level of activity. The impact upon employment obviously depends upon whether the sector affected is labour or capital intensive and the breadth of its backward linkages to other labour-intensive sectors. In addition, even if not directly affected, heavily indebted firms may be forced into bankruptcy by the interest rate hike or see their return fall, thus possibly triggering a capital outflow in search of better risk-adjusted returns. All of this has a contractional effect on output, and causes unemployment, poverty and inequality to rise faster than under a managed exchange rate regime, in which case the adjustment burden falls on wages rather than unemployment. In turn, heavily indebted governments experience a worsening of their fiscal position and – *ceteris paribus* – either cut expenditures or raise taxes, with the net effect of exacerbating the downturn.

Thirdly, higher interest rates characteristically lead to lower asset prices that, in turn, discourage firms from investing and hiring new workers, leading in this way to a simultaneous drop in aggregate demand and supply (Stiglitz 2002). Fourthly, as firms go bankrupt and default on their loans, banks may become increasingly unwilling to lend, especially if the government chooses to enforce risk-adjusted capital adequacy standards that entail that the banks put more money into loan loss provision accounts and reduce lending. As a result, lending rates may rise and credit may be rationed, and even firms that are not directly affected by the crisis, may not be able to continue producing and exporting as they cannot borrow working capital.

Thus, the defence of the exchange rate through interest rate hikes and fiscal contraction causes a large number of domestic bankruptcies, a credit contraction and an output downturn without increasing the supply of exports. Of course, the intensity of these effects will vary from place to place. For instance, it will be less pronounced in countries where the public debt/gross domestic product (GDP) ratio is low, where firms mainly finance themselves out of their cash flow and where export performance can be reinvigorated by a drop in nominal wages, taxes and utility rates.

Trade-offs and the search for the least costly exchange rate and adjustment approach

The choice of the best adjustment and exchange rate policy during crisis periods must be guided by the least costly approach principle. Such a choice boils down to comparing the respective costs and benefits of the monetarist and Keynesian approach in the following areas.

Extent of output contraction and its poverty impact

Output retrenchment and the rise in poverty are likely to be more pronounced if the monetarist cum fixed peg approach is followed. Such an approach causes a contraction in the domestic component of aggregate demand, while being unable to raise exports. The Keynesian cum managed rate approach also causes output to fall as devaluation raises the domestic currency cost of servicing the foreign debt, affecting in this way the balance sheets of households, government and firms. In some cases, however, such as for dollar-indebted exporters or already bankrupt firms in the non-traded sector, devaluation does not generate a contraction (Stiglitz 2002). Furthermore, if banks are helped to quickly reorganize in order to finance the expansion of exports made possible by devaluation, the foreign component of aggregate demand can rebound in a year or so, though this is less likely in economies with an inelastic export supply or a high share of imports on exports.

Inflation and poverty

It is likely that the Keynesian approach raises inflation-induced poverty more than the monetarist approach. This conclusion needs to be weighted, however, against the greater output contraction induced by the latter. Thus, there is a trade-off between the Keynesian cum intermediate exchange rate regimes approach (which leads to lower output losses but higher inflation) and the monetarist cum fixed exchange rate regime approach (which generates less inflation but greater output losses). While, as noted, inflation disproportionately affects the poor, there is evidence that the poor are even more deeply affected by a fall in GDP (Stewart 1995; Stiglitz 2002). In both approaches, the rise in poverty will also depend on the safety nets in place. Their scope may be more limited, however, in the context of the fiscal retrenchment typical of the monetary approach.

Exports, balance of payments and poverty

The balance-of-payments effects are not easy to compare as they depend, inter alia, on the adjustments that take place in the banking-financial sector. If successful, the monetarist approach should improve the capital account balance, owing to the return of foreign capital, but not the current account balance, upon which the long-term external sustainability of an economy depends. Indeed, in the monetarist approach the tradable sector does not expand. In turn, the expansion of exports under the Keynesian approach depends on structural factors, the quick elimination of collapsed firms and banks and external conditions. But, at least in semi-industrialized countries, such an approach has a chance of raising exports and improving the current account balance.

Bankruptcies, asset losses and moral hazard

The rise in interest rates inherent in the monetarist approach leads to a surge in bankruptcies among domestic firms while foreign creditors are bailed out with international loans, thus creating a moral hazard problem. In contrast, if the emphasis is placed on devaluation, the domestic borrowers of dollar-denominated loans may go bankrupt and the number of defaults on international loans rises, thus shifting the capital loss from the domestic sector to the foreign lenders who should have used greater diligence in granting large amounts of short-term dollar-denominated loans. The moral hazard problem is thus contained.

Credibility and exclusion from financial markets

The increasing number of defaults on foreign loans alluded to above is likely to cut off the country concerned from international lending. Yet the benefits of international capital flows remain elusive, and their decline may not cause growth losses over the long term (Stiglitz 2003). Indeed, as noted by Prasad *et al.* (2003), with the exception of foreign direct investment improving access to technology, management skills and new markets (see Chapter 6), there is no evidence that international capital accelerates the rate of growth of recipient countries, while there is clear evidence that it can raise the levels of both economic instability and poverty. Indeed, capital account liberalization may have become a lazy way of mobilizing financing over the short term, while potentially generating considerable long-term costs.

In conclusion, while there is no 'one-size-fits-all' solution, weighing up all of the above effects, it seems that – except in specific circumstances, some of which were mentioned above – the Keynesian cum intermediate exchange rate approach might be, on balance, the best choice.³

Exchange rate regimes, income distribution and poverty

This section reviews the poverty impact of alternative exchange rates regimes via changes in the distribution of income and assets. Chapter 12 on Uzbekistan shows, for instance, that the dual exchange rate adopted therein in the second half of the 1990s entailed the redistribution of up to 16 per cent of GDP from the export to the import substitution sector, with a huge negative effect on poverty. Thus, what is the distributive and poverty impact of hard pegs, managed BBC rates and free floats?

A standard way to approach this problem is to break down the economy into traded and non-traded sectors. Within this framework, hard pegs that lead to an appreciation of the real exchange rate raise real income in the non-traded sector – which includes construction, real estate, domestic finance and insurance, utilities, import sector, government and most informal sectors – while reducing it in the traded sector – that is, most of agriculture, all manufacturing and internationally tradable services. The opposite occurs if nominal devaluation succeeds in raising the price of tradables in relation to that of non-tradables, quite independently from the expansionary effect this change may have on output. However, whether these exchange rate changes actually reduce or augment poverty depends on the factors discussed below.

The initial distribution of the poor between the traded and non-traded sector

If the majority of the poor and low-income households are located in the traded sector – for example, in export-oriented agriculture, as is the case in Ghana – a real appreciation of the exchange rate will increase the overall poverty rate, the poverty gap and the share of poor people in the traded sector. The opposite occurs, for instance, in the case of highly urbanized Peru, where a large share of the poor is engaged in the informal non-traded sector. In this case, a real devaluation would, *ceteris paribus*, increase poverty overall and in the non-traded sector in particular, though it should reduce it in export-oriented agriculture. In practice, a real devaluation reduces overall poverty if its initial incidence in the tradable sector exceeds that in the non-tradable sector. All of this holds under restrictive conditions about competition in factors and products markets, but is also true to some extent in case of non-perfectly competitive markets.

Factors intensity of production in the tradable and non-tradable sectors

If the production of tradables is intensive in natural resources such as land, capital equipment and skilled labour, the poverty reduction effect of a real devaluation will be small as the output increase will be realized by making use of resources owned by the non-poor, the additional demand for unskilled labour being modest and the effect on the wage rate negligible. Poverty will fall, in contrast, if an expansion of tradables entails a greater demand for unskilled labour, as happened in the East Asian fast exporters of manufactures. Real devaluation also raises the domestic price of tradables. The impact on the incomes and poverty risk of the workers in the non-tradable sector is negative, but depends on their initial income level. If the sector employs mainly high-wage skilled workers, poverty will only rise slightly as the fall in their real incomes will not be large enough to push them below the poverty line. The same cannot be said if the non-tradable sector includes many informal workers – street vendors, domestics and day labourers – with incomes near the poverty line. In turn, an appreciation of the real exchange rate will worsen poverty in the tradable sector if exports are labour-intensive, but less so if they are land- or mineral-intensive. The poverty impact in the non-tradable sector is likely to vary considerably. In middle-income economies, such a sector is heterogeneous, as a large skill- and capital-intensive sector coexists with a low-skill informal sector.

Labour market and poverty

The poverty impact also depends upon whether wages are upward and downward flexible or depend on a rigid social norm. If wages are rigid, the entrepreneurs in the non-traded sector facing an output contraction will adjust their output downward, and unemployment will rise. In the absence of social safety nets, this is more likely to increase poverty than in the case of flexible wages, in which case the output contraction will be absorbed in part by a decline in the wage rate. Likewise, if traded sector wages are rigid, the benefits of devaluation will be mainly appropriated by the landlords and capitalists, as wages will not rise, though employment will rise in line with the output increase and the labour intensity of production.

Prices of consumer goods

The poverty impact of exchange rate changes will also depend upon whether the 'wage goods' consumed by the poor are produced in the traded or non-traded sector. The best situation is observed when the poor are employed in the traded sector, benefit from devaluation – as they own some of the sector's production factors – and allocate a large part of their consumption expenditure to non-tradable goods and services, such as locally produced foods not traded on the world market. However, working in the tradable sector is no guarantee of a lower poverty risk. If the tradable sector workers do not own the goods they produce, as in the case of agricultural labourers, devaluation leads to greater poverty as money wages stagnate, while the price of the tradables they produce – for example, food – rises, as observed in India in the wake of the 1991 devaluation (see Chapter 11). A similar trap is faced by workers in the non-tradable sector who, after devaluation, are caught between lower labour demand and wages and rising tradable prices.

Changes in the value of financial assets and liabilities and access to credit

The poverty impact of alternative exchange rate regimes is also influenced by the distribution of foreign assets and liabilities among local residents, the risk of financial crises associated with fixed pegs and changes in access to credit following the liberalization of capital flows. As noted earlier, an appreciation reduces the domestic currency cost of debt servicing, while a devaluation increases it – asset prices rise in the first case and fall in the second. The beneficiaries of the appreciation can be the government (as in Brazil) and traded and non-traded sector firms with a large foreign debt. But an appreciation reduces the domestic currency returns on foreign assets held by nationals (as in China), while depreciation raises it.

Poverty may also be affected by changes in credit availability associated with exchange rate regimes that facilitate capital mobility such as hard pegs. Capital inflows do not directly benefit the poor, as employment and wages tend to rise in high-skilled sectors such as banking and construction, and the credit booms they triggered do not reduce the market segmentation that prevents the poor from accessing formal credit and interest rates often rise in the wake of the capital inflows (Taylor 2004). During financial crises, credit allocation becomes particularly skewed as decapitalized banks reduce their lending and restrict its allocation to all but preferential borrowers such as large firms (Oxfam America 2002). Finally, exchange rate regimes that attract volatile capitals can contribute to long-term poverty due to the long-term costs borne by governments for resolving financial crises associated to fixed pegs. In five Latin American countries such costs included the recapitalization of bankrupt banks, bailouts of influential depositors and debt relief for borrowers, and entailed a redistribution of income from poor non-participants to the financial sector to large participants and in the 1990s averaged 14.7 per cent of their GDP (Halac and Schmuckler 2003).

Conclusions on the distributive effects of exchange rate policies

As noted by Kanbur (1998), it is difficult to determine *ex ante* the poverty and distributive effects of alternative exchange rate policies, as these depend on the country circumstances discussed in the previous section. For instance, it is likely that a real devaluation will reduce poverty in countries where many poor are employed in the labour-intensive tradable sector, land and capital is fairly equitably distributed, the labour market is flexible, wage goods are mostly produced in the non-traded sector and external indebtedness is limited or concentrated in the export sector or the already bankrupt sectors. Devaluation might, in contrast, be more costly when most of these conditions are not met. Table 4.6 illustrates the poverty effects of a real devaluation on the main social groups. The decision of whether to devalue or not ought to be taken country by country after having compared the relative weight of the groups that would be affected.

Likewise, if the level of reserves permits it, the defence of a hard peg may be conceivable in semi-industrialized and highly urbanized countries, like those of the Middle East and Latin America, if most of the poor are employed in the non-traded sector (informal services, non-traded agriculture), labour markets are rigid, factor mobility is low, wage goods are imported and many agents have large dollar-denominated short-term liabilities, while the firms and employees of the traded sector are comparatively better off and can adjust to the real appreciation by

Table 4.6 Hypothetical poverty impact matrix of the effects of a real devaluation

Before devaluation \ After devaluation	Poor	Non-poor
Poor	(i) unaffected structural poor lacking • human capital • land and credit • access to market • public services (ii) poor getting poorer • urban poor in the NT sector hit by terms of trade changes between T and NT • landless rural workers and food deficient farmers affected by rising prices of food	(iv) former poor exiting poverty • small-scale producers of tradable (if T/NT total are effectively modified) • newly employed workers in T sector • T workers benefiting from higher wages
Non-poor	(iii) non-poor getting poor • low-income workers in the NT sector (hit by T-NT terms of trade changes) • low-income employees in the T sector if wage/employment increases is smaller than the rise in the price of traded wage goods • people surviving on non-indexed transfers • households with $ denominated debt	(v) non-poor getting richer • medium- and large-scale entrepreneurs of T goods • people with scarce human capital • domestic creditors of $ denominated loans (vi) non-poor getting impoverished but not poor • upper layers of the bureaucracy • high-income people in the NT sector • enterprises with $ denominated debt • foreign lenders suffering a default by domestic borrowers

Note: T and NT refer to the traded and non-traded sectors of the economy.
Source: Author's compilation.

reducing the domestic costs of production and through innovation, and short-term macroeconomic balance can be achieved by means of temporary controls on imports and capital outflows.

Tentative conclusions

The 'two corners' approach to the management of the exchange rate has come under increasing attack in recent years, as evidence mounts that neither of these two solutions represent a 'first best', and as their effects on poverty are likely to be negative in most cases because of the output contraction and adverse poverty effects they frequently engender.

While prescriptions always have to be country-specific, this chapter has argued that in low- and middle-income countries the development approach to the exchange rate is the best choice from both a poverty and growth perspective. Such an approach preserves competitiveness in tradables by means of a BBC-type crawling peg with target bands. After fixing the nominal exchange rate at a competitive level, the real exchange rate is allowed to float within a narrow band. Bigger inflationary shocks that cause a real appreciation are dealt with by depreciating the central parity in proportion to the inflation differential with the main trading partners. In a world of mobile capital and speculative attacks, such an approach needs to be accompanied by reasonable monetary and fiscal policies and measures to limit short-term portfolio inflows and to sterilize their effects so as to avoid possible currency crises. From 1978 to 1996, fiscally disciplined Southeast Asia succeeded in reconciling stable real exchange rates, low inflation and large capital inflows. Exchange rates target zones with little intra-marginal interventions were also pursued in Chile, Colombia and Israel in the early 1990s, despite considerable financial openness, and permitted achieving a balance between the conflicting objectives of reducing imported inflation and maintaining export growth.

The choice of an appropriate exchange rate under conditions of turmoil is less easy and depends on a host of factors affecting the size and distribution of the costs and benefits of alternative exchange rate regimes. However, in the midst of a crisis it is unlikely that a devaluation can be entirely avoided. Indeed, a controlled devaluation accompanied by fiscal expansion, low interest rates and, when needed, temporary capital and import controls may help to rapidly re-establish equilibrium in the balance of payments and – under certain conditions – exert an expansionary effect over the medium term, especially if the country concerned has a limited foreign debt. However, conscious of the short-term contractionary effects of devaluation, the policy maker ought to introduce adequate employment-based safety nets and supportive measures in the macroeconomic area, while working at removing the rigidities that prevent devaluation from being expansionary.

Notes

1. The author would like to thank Leonardo Menchini for his help in compiling the data for Tables 4.1 and 4.2 and for useful bibliographical indications, as well as Gian Maria Milesi-Ferretti of the IMF for sharing his dataset on capital account liberalization and for providing the 2000–2003 data on capital account restrictions.
2. These results, however, may not be conclusive as they refer to heterogeneous countries and averages over long periods of time characterized by widely different degrees of capital mobility.
3. A formal presentation of the problem could take the following form. Assume with FitzGerald (2001) an aggregate model of a dependent open economy where the real exchange rate e is defined as the ratio of traded and non-traded prices P_t/P_{nt}, traded prices are the product of the nominal exchange rate E and world prices p so that $e = P_t/P_{nt} = E.p/P_{nt}$. Real exports X are a function of e ($X = x_0 + x_1.e$), and imports are a function of e and domestic activity Y ($M = m_0 + m_1.e + m_2Y$). Given the capital inflows F, the authorities' task is to ensure balance-of-payment equilibrium ($X-M = F$). With appropriate substitutions one can express the level of domestic activity Y, employment L (assumed to depend linearly on output) and poverty PHR (assumed to depend more on employment than wages), in terms of e and F:

$$Y = 1/m_2 [F + e(x_1 - m_1) + x_0 - m_0] \quad (4.3)$$

$$L = \lambda Y = \tilde{\lambda} \{1/m_2[F + e(x_1 - m_1) + x_0 - m_0]\} \quad \Box a$$

$$PHR = f(-L, -w) \quad (4.3b)$$

If F fall due to a financial crisis, then either Y must decline to restore equilibrium, for example, through a raise in the interest rates, or e must be raised. Now, remember that $e = P_t/P_{nt}$, that prices in the traded sector P_t are exogenous and that prices in the non-traded sector are set by a markup r on the cost of labour inputs u at the nominal wage rate W and imported inputs m ($P_{nt} = (1 + r)[u.W + mP_t]$) Rearranging, one obtains a relationship between the real wage w and e:

$$w = 1/u[1/(1 + r) - m.e] \quad (3.4)$$

which shows that the higher (more depreciated) is e, the lower will be w. In conclusion, when faced with a decline in F, the government faces an adjustment trade-off. To re-establish equilibrium in (4.3), it can choose to adjust Y and L downward by tightening monetary policy. Alternatively it can raise e though, as shown in (4.4) this will cause a fall in the real wage rate that – if (4.3b) is correctly specified – will have a lesser impact on poverty than in case of money-based adjustment.

Yet this conclusion crucially depends on the value of x_1 (that is, the export elasticity of devaluation), the omission from the export function of structuralist effects and the correct specification of (4.3a) and (4.3b). Lastly, following a fall in F, equilibrium in (4.3) could also be restored by reducing m_2 (the import elasticity of output) through the imposition of import restrictions on non-essential goods and goods that can be substituted domestically, and by raising x_1 through export promotion measures such as the reimbursement of VAT and export subsidies.

4. These results, however, may not be conclusive as they refer to heterogeneous countries and averages over long periods of time characterized by widely different degrees of capital mobility.

References

Bird, G. and R.S. Rajan. 2000. *Recovery or Recession? Post-Devaluation Output Performance: The Thai Experience*. Discussion Paper No. 0043, Centre for International Economic Studies, Adelaide University, Adelaide.

Braga de Macedo, J., D. Cohen and H. Reisen (eds). 2001. *Don't Fix, Don't Float*. Development Studies Centre. Paris: OECD.

Branson, W.H. 2001. 'Intermediate Exchange Rate Regimes for Groups of Developing Countries'. In J. Braga de Macedo, D. Cohen and H. Reisen (eds), *Don't Fix, Don't Float*.

Branson, W.H. and L.T. Katseli. 1980. 'Income Instability, Terms of Trade, and the Choice of the Exchange Rate Regime'. *Journal of Development Economics*, March, 49–69.

Bruno, M. and W. Easterly. 1998. 'Inflation Crises and Long-term Growth'. *Journal of Monetary Economics*, 41(1), 3–26.

Easterly, W. 2001. 'Inflation and the Poor'. *Journal of Money, Credit and Banking*, 33(2), 160–78.

FitzGerald, V. 2001. 'Financial Globalisation and Child Well-Being'. In G.A. Cornia (ed.), *Harnessing Globalisation for Children*. Florence: Innocenti Research Centre, www.uniceficdc.org/research, accessed on 10 June 2005.

Frenkel, R. and L. Taylor. 2005. *Real Exchange Rate, Monetary Policy and Employment: Economic Development in a Garden of Forking Paths*. Paper presented at a High-Level United Nations Development Conference, New York, 14–15 March.

Ghosh, A., A.M. Gulde and H. Wolf. 2004. *Exchange Rate Regimes: Classifications and Consequences*. Cambridge, MA: MIT Press.

Halac, M. and S. Schmuckler. 2003. *Distributional Effects of Crises: The Role of Financial Transfers*. Mimeo, Washington, DC: World Bank.

Kamin, S.B. and M. Klau. 1997. *Some Multi-country Evidence on the Effects of Real Exchange Rate on Output*. Working Paper No. 48. Basle: Bank for International Settlements.

Kanbur, R. 1998. 'The Implications of Adjustment Programs for Poverty: Conceptual Issues and Analytical Framework'. In Ke-young Chu and Sanjeev Gupta (eds), *Social Safety Nets: Issues and Experiences*. Washington, DC: IMF.

Krugman, P. and L. Taylor. 1978. 'Contractionary Effects of Devaluation'. *Journal of International Economics*, 8(3), 445–56.

Min, Hing-Ghi. 2002. *Inequality, the Price of Nontradeables and the Real Exchange Rate: Theory and Cross-Country Evidence*. www.worldbank.org, accessed on 10 February 2005.

Oxfam America. 2002. *Global Finance Hurts the Poor*. Boston, MA: Oxfam America.

Prasad, E., K. Rogoff, S.J. Wei and M.A. Kose. 2003. *Effects of Financial Globalisation on Developing Countries: Some Empirical Evidence*. Occasional Paper No. 220. Washington, DC: IMF.

Reinhart, C. and K. Rogoff. 2003. *A Modern History of Exchange Rate Arrangements: A Reinterpretation*. Mimeo, Washington, DC: IMF, March.

Rodrik, D. 2003. *Growth Strategies*. Working Paper 2003-17, Department of Economics. Linz: Johannes Kepler University,

Stewart, F. 1995. *Adjustment and Poverty: Options and Choices*. London and New York: Routledge.

Stiglitz, J. 2003. *Alternative Approaches to Stabilization Policies: An Overview*. Preliminary draft of a paper prepared for the Initiative for Policy Dialogue Task Force on Macroeconomics, Barcelona, 2–3 June.

Stiglitz, J. 2002. *Macro-Policy Issue: Dealing with an Economic Downturn*. New York: Initiative for Policy Dialogue, Columbia University.

Taylor, L. 2004. 'External Liberalization, Economic Performance, and Distribution in Latin America and Elsewhere'. In G.A. Cornia (ed.), *Inequality, Growth and Poverty in an Era of Liberalisation and Globalisation*. Oxford: Oxford University Press.

Williamson, J. 2003. *Exchange Rate Policy and Development*. Working Paper. New York: Initiative for Policy Dialogue, Columbia University.

5
Portfolio Flows, Macroeconomic Policy and Global Poverty

Christian E. Weller and Radha Chaurushiya

Introduction

Globalization has been one of the most pertinent and also most controversial economic forces of recent decades. Often referring to the opening of countries to more capital and trade flows, globalization has been praised as a crucial vehicle for faster growth and rising living standards in developing economies, but also criticized for increasing financial instability in emerging economies.

The challenge today is formidable as billions of people live in abject poverty. Poverty is widespread and poverty reduction has been isolated to only a few, albeit large, countries such as China. Even where poverty has been reduced, levels of inequality have often risen.

The rationale for fewer restrictions on trade flows has been that more trade would foster economic growth through specialization and through technological enhancements following specialization and more competition.

In the same vein, more capital flows presumably benefit the financial sector directly through more competition and innovation, lowering the costs of capital and facilitating investment. This would supposedly benefit the non-financial sector as well. Since all of this should contribute to faster growth and since the incomes of the poor tend to rise with growth, proponents of liberalization concluded that it would help alleviate poverty if more trade and capital flows resulted in faster growth.

Following capital market deregulation, capital flows to and from emerging countries grew rapidly, especially in the form of *short-term portfolio flows*. While this tended to result in faster growth in the short term, it frequently proved to have a destabilizing effect in the medium term. Moreover, the benefits of more capital mobility are often unevenly distributed. Subsequently, poverty reduction has often been hampered with unequal growth and growing instabilities.

A number of countries have notably escaped the fate of rising instability. For instance, Central and Eastern European economies were spared from the fall-out of the Asian and Russian financial crises in the late 1990s. Also, China and India have seen prolonged periods of strong growth without a rise in instability (see Chapter 11 of this volume). What have distinguished many of these countries are numerous forms of restrictions on capital flows. However, these experiences show the dilemma that many emerging economies face. More capital controls allow for more control over one's destiny, but they can also lower technology and capital transfers into economies that are often woefully short on both.

A series of economic institutions can be identified that foster more stable growth and that help to lower capital constraints in developing economies. These institutions include better civil liberties, public support for indigenous banking systems and progressive taxation coupled with effective tax collection among others.

Trends in portfolio flows

Since the early 1990s, emerging economies have made great strides towards liberalizing their capital accounts in order to foster faster growth and to combat poverty. These investments can take several distinct forms: foreign direct investment (FDI), portfolio flows (both equity and bond) and bank lending. FDI is a long-term, fixed investment in specific projects, which often include technology transfers. Portfolio flows are short-term investments in bonds and stocks.

Following the spurt of capital account liberalizations, net private capital flows into emerging economies boomed (see Figure 5.1). In 1990, capital movements into these countries netted about $29 billion, which quickly ballooned to a peak

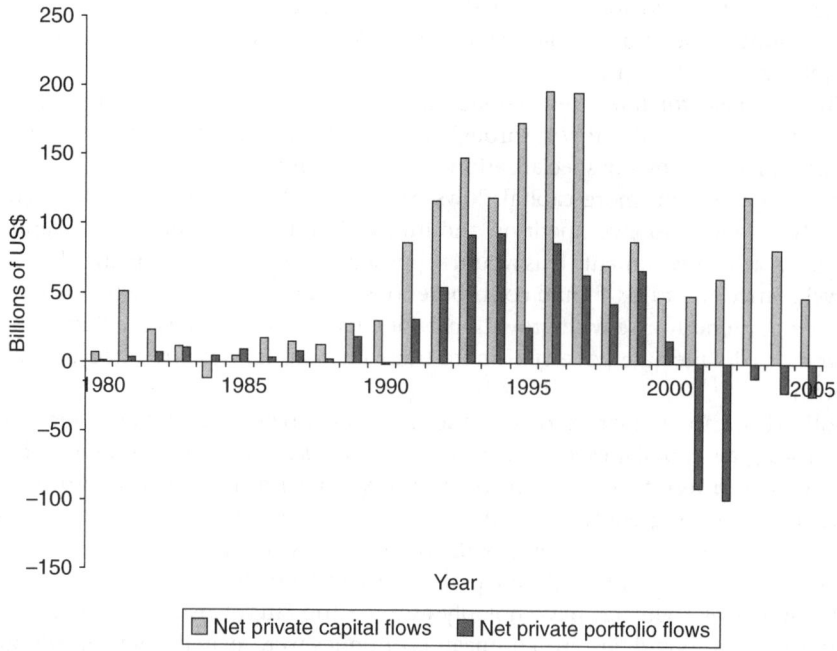

Figure 5.1 Net capital flows to emerging market and developing countries
Note: Data for 2005 are projections.
Source: IMF (2004).

of $197 billion in 1996. Net private portfolio flows accounted for much of this increase. Portfolio flows turned from a net outflow of $1.8 billion in 1990 to a net inflow of $86 billion in 1996 (IMF 2004). After the mid-1990s, however, capital flows to developing economies and particularly portfolio flows began to taper due to a spate of financial crises in Mexico (1995), Asia (1997) and Russia (1998). Although portfolio flows to developing countries rose again towards the end of the 1990s, they have remained negative in net terms since 2001. Continuing this trend, the International Monetary Fund's (IMF) World Economic Outlook projections showed an estimated net outflow of $23 billion in 2005 (IMF 2004).

The largest recipients of FDI over the last 30 years have been Asian economies, while Latin American countries have depended more heavily upon portfolio flows (see Figure 5.2) (IMF 2001).

To some degree, the changes in portfolio flows reflect changes in government finances. For instance, the IMF (2001) attributed the difference in the composition of capital flows to Asia and Latin America to larger fiscal deficits in Latin American countries, which have relied on international portfolio inflows to finance their deficits. Similarly, the reversal of capital flows between developing and developed economies after 2000 reflected, to some degree, the reversal in the US fiscal balance. Asian countries, especially China, have been heavily purchasing the increasing issues of US treasuries, resulting in an outflow of capital from developing countries to the United States. Since March 2001 through the middle of 2004, foreign investors purchased on average 80 per cent of new US government debt issues (Weller 2004).

In addition, current account deficits also appear to be a systematic determinant of short-term capital flows. Rath and Dasgupta (1999) found that increases in current

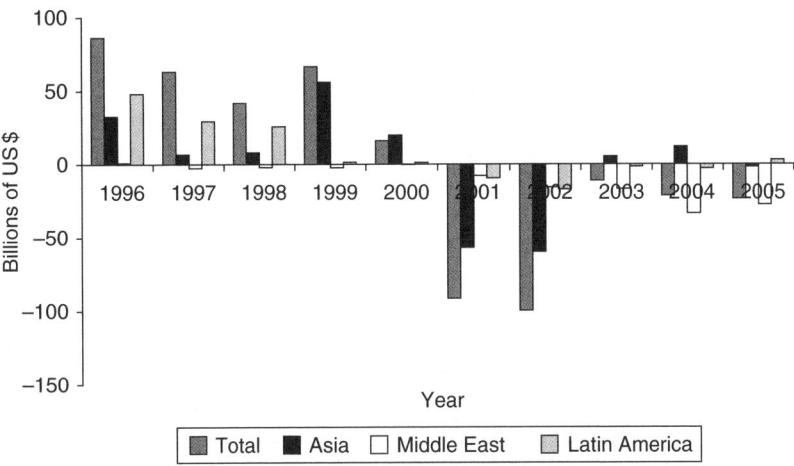

Figure 5.2 Net portfolio flows to select regions
Note: Data for 2005 are projections.
Source: IMF (2004).

account deficits are followed by a rise in portfolio capital flows. Other factors, such as per capita income and a rise in FDI, also play important roles, whereas country-specific factors, such as location, appear to have no influence (see Figure 5.2) (Rath and Dasgupta 1999).

Portfolio flows as a means to combat poverty

The link between portfolio flows and poverty reduction is largely an indirect one. Portfolio flows can arguably lead to faster economic growth. In turn, economic growth is seen as a necessary – although insufficient – condition for poverty reduction.

Portfolio flows and economic growth

Emerging and industrialized economies can theoretically benefit from more liberal capital movements. Financial markets should be able to allocate liquid capital to the most efficient uses. Because of large capital constraints, the marginal rate of return to new investments in emerging economies should be greater than in countries with less capital rationing, all else being equal. Thus, by allowing capital to flow more freely, economic growth should receive a boost. Due to trade linkages, this faster growth should also spill over into faster growth in industrialized trading partner countries.

This is an extension of the original financial liberalization (FL) argument (Fry 1995; McKinnon 1973; Shaw 1973). FL comprises both the elimination of regulations on domestic financial markets and external liberalization through capital account opening. The rationale for FL is that 'financially repressed' economies suffer from suboptimal financial intermediation and from an inefficient allocation of financial capital. By eliminating interest rate ceilings and entry restrictions, financial intermediaries will collect more funds and provide more loanable funds. The elimination of lending requirements allows financial intermediaries to allocate funds to their best uses, thereby raising the average productivity of capital, and ultimately the economic performance of an economy. Externally, the liberalization of capital flows raises the potential for more short-term capital mobility and more FDI flows. Finally, asset markets should become more efficient thanks to greater liquidity and, due to foreign participation, to more transparency and better investor protections (Litan *et al.* 2001). All of these factors should work to reduce capital constraints for domestic borrowers and ease investments, presumably laying the groundwork for faster growth and less poverty.

An important aspect of this argument is that international lenders are looking for a comparatively high-risk adjusted rate of return. Traditionally, it is assumed that good macro policies and high-quality economic governance can reduce inherent macroeconomic risks and thereby raise the risk-adjusted rate of return. Poor macroeconomic management can lead to high inflation and high interest rates, while low-quality governance can raise economic uncertainties for investors and thus keep investments below optimal levels. Thus, capital flows may encourage good macroeconomic policies in the countries that are looking to receive foreign capital, as investors are supposedly favouring countries with good governance, fair and enforced regulations and attractive investment climates (Chakraborty and Rawlins 2004). However, this can prove to be a double-edged sword since this disciplining device also constrains government's ability to conduct counter-cyclical policies (Blecker 1999; Grabel 1996).

There is some support for the notion that portfolio flows may be positively related to growth. For instance, Levine (1997) shows that increased cross-border portfolio flows in emerging economies help to build capital markets. Levine (1997, 2001) also links capital market developments to economic growth. Furthermore, the IMF (2001) concludes that more capital flows can raise investment possibilities, create technology spillovers and deepen domestic capital markets. Ignoring the potential costs associated with increased capital account liberalization, the IMF (2001) estimates that greater liberalization is associated with economic growth that is 0.5 percentage points higher annually. However, Kose *et al.* (2004) conclude, in a comprehensive review of the empirical literature, that it is difficult to establish a causality between financial integration and growth.

The link between capital markets and growth is generally made over long periods of time and tends to ignore increasing macroeconomic fluctuations that can occur in the mean time. For instance, Grabel (1995a) and Singh and Weisse (1998) linked portfolio flows to rising stock market volatility and Weller (2001b) established a systematic connection between increased portfolio flows and the incidence of financial crises. The different perspective on the timing of the effects of portfolio investment on growth – long-term versus short-term – may explain the divergence in the observed results (Durham 2003).

Economic growth and poverty

If successful, greater capital account openness can foster faster growth. Over the long term, studies have suggested that faster economic growth should benefit all groups equally, including the poor (Dollar and Kraay 2001a, 2001b; Weller and Hersh 2004).

Also, if greater capital mobility can promote better macroeconomic management and governance, emerging economies should become more stable. Since the poor have less insurance than the rich against the fall-out from crises, more stability should disproportionately benefit the poor. Specifically, poor and lower-income families typically have no savings and are thus immediately vulnerable to economic shocks. This is particularly important in countries where social safety nets are underdeveloped, or available only to parts of the working population, for example, restrictions on unemployment insurance to the formal labour market. Greater stability as a result of better macroeconomic management could help to ensure that growth effects are distributed more equally among all income groups, all else being equal.

Arguments against portfolio flows as an anti-poverty tool

History has shown, however, that capital account liberalization also comes at a cost (see Table 5.1). In all areas, private sector investment is relative to the gross

Table 5.1 Select measures of economic performance in relation to portfolio investment inflows

	Total	Latin America	Middle East	Asia	Transition economies	Africa
PI[a] inflows/GDP	1.1	1.1	1.2	1.0	0.6	−0.3
Investment/GDP						
Total	22.4	18.4	25.4	20.7	26.2	10.7
Above median PI flows	22.4	20.2	23.9	28.1	29.6	20.8
Below median PI flows	19.2	18.7	22.1	25.9	29.0	18.1
Credit						
Total	68.5	63.4	100.6	39.4	65.4	20.7
Above median PI flows	103.7	97.7	115.3	58.6	74.6	35.5
Below median PI flows	37.0	28.3	155.3	49.7	76.2	30.4
Reserves/GDP						
Total	5.7	6.1	10.7	7.3	1.4	6.6
Above median PI flows	9.7	8.4	10.6	13.2	10.9	10.2
Below median PI flows	6.3	5.8	15.1	12.4	8.1	6.0
Income share of bottom 20%						
Total	6.3	3.3	5.5	6.6	10.0	5.9
Above median PI flows	3.8	3.0	5.7	6.4	8.0	3.3
Below median PI flows	4.8	4.4	6.6	6.2	7.8	3.9

[a] private sector investment.

Notes: All figures are in percentages. All figures are weighted averages with the real dollar GDP for each region as the respective weight. Calculations for totals include all available observations for emerging economies. For comparative analysis, only observations are considered when portfolio inflows are present. Median portfolio flows relative to GDP are calculated only for emerging economies on a real GDP weighted basis. Authors' calculations are based on the IMF, International Financial Statistics and the UNU/WIDER World Income Inequality Database. Where observations are missing, the share of income for the bottom 20 per cent are calculated based on the methodology described in Dollar and Kraay (2001a).

domestic product (GDP), and is higher with larger portfolio inflows. This is commensurate with greater credit markets relative to GDP. Simultaneously, in all regions, except the Middle East, countries are amassing increasing amounts of reserves as a protection against rising instabilities. Finally, in Africa, Latin America and the Middle East the income share of the bottom 20 per cent falls as portfolio investment inflows increase. Thus, greater portfolio flows may result in more private sector investments, but the distribution of the gains from more investments may remain unchanged or worsen, while emerging economies are simultaneously preparing themselves for a greater degree of economic and financial instability.

Portfolio flows and income inequality

Portfolio flows can be direct investments in bonds and stocks, short-term international bank loans to domestic borrowers and transfers to multinational banks (MNBs) in emerging economies. Typically, only a small section of the credit market will gain access to the additional liquidity. For instance, only large domestic corporations and the government will have access to the local capital markets. Similarly, international bank credit will likely only be extended to large borrowers that meet specific criteria, for example, minimum size. However, if reductions in financial constraints are limited to specific sectors, greater capital mobility will contribute to income inequality.

This leaves access to MNB credit. The often-expressed hope has been that increased MNB presence would result in fewer financial constraints for everybody due to the greater capital base and advanced technology that MNBs bring with them (Litan *et al.* 2001). However, greater MNB presence in emerging economies tends to increase financial constraints for some market segments and thus contributes to rising income inequality. Specifically, MNBs tend to concentrate their activities on specific market segments, such as large domestic corporations, multinational corporations, the central government and high net worth individuals (Weller 2000; Weller and Scher 2001). By creating more competition in these comparatively low-cost, low-risk market segments, though, the overall calculation changes for domestic banks. Cross-subsidization of higher cost market segments, such as start-ups, small and medium-sized enterprises (SMEs), middle-class borrowers and rural producers becomes harder. Domestic banks often reduce their credit exposure to these market segments in a reaction to greater competition from MNBs (Weller 2001a, 2005). As credit market segments experience rising financial constraints, income inequality will likely be exacerbated because investment and economic growth are unequally distributed as a result of the changed institutional credit market structure.

Portfolio flows, financial crises and poverty reduction

Portfolio flows can be withdrawn quickly from emerging economies when investors become jittery about the prospects of those countries, leading to financial crises. There is substantial evidence that links growing financial instability to financial deregulation. Furthermore, financial crises affect the poor more than the rich.

Deregulation of capital markets often means that greater liquidity is used increasingly for unsustainable, speculative expansions. For instance, Chang *et al.* (1998) argue that the cause of the Korean crisis had been FL, which allowed large short-term capital inflows to be used for excessive investments. While each episode of financial crisis has its own unique characteristics, there are some general trends evident in all of them that point an accusing finger at capital account liberalization.

Short-term portfolio investments are attracted by and fuel asset price speculations (Weller and Morzuch 2000; Grabel 1993, 1998). Financial crises that result from such investments are preceded by a widening gap between financial market trends and real economic outcomes. As investors recognize that their investments are unlikely to yield the expected returns, they withdraw their short-term portfolio funds, precipitating a crisis (Grabel 1993, 1998; Weller 2001b).

Previously credit-constrained sectors receive financing after FL because interest rate constraints are reduced and more capital is available due to higher deposit rates, increased capital inflows, or both. More capital might increase investment, expanding the real and the financial sectors, which may result in the generation of additional funds through more deposits and more capital inflows. Capital inflows in turn lead to an appreciating currency, thereby attracting again more capital, but hampering the real sector through worsening terms of trade (see, for example, Chapter 14 on Brazil).

Investors seek new investment opportunities with these additional funds, which become increasingly available in domestic equity markets (Arestis and Demetriades 1999; Weller 2001b); faster stock market growth and enhanced stock market liquidity attract more speculative equity market investments. At the same time, credit rises since higher interest rates and asset prices offer banks incentives to expand their lending (Grabel 1993, 1995b; Weller 2001b). Both asset market investments and increased credit expansion are made in anticipation of increasing short-term rates of return. Although increased liquidity may help to bolster productive investments, short-term financial rates of return tend to outgrow rates of return for productive investments due to deteriorating terms of trade and deregulation euphoria, thus leading to further diversion of funds into financial market investments, fuelling an asset market boom (Demetriades 1999). With a growing diversion of funds into speculative investments, less financing is available for productive investments. Thus, asset market speculation fosters the divergence of rates of return on short-term speculative financial investments and productive investments.

Three factors influence this divergence. First, due to large capital inflows, the terms of trade tend to worsen, weakening the current account balance and slowing the real sector slows. Secondly, lenders become less willing to extend credit to the real sector where expected rates of return are below those generated in speculative asset markets. Thirdly, asset market speculation is also fuelled by deregulation euphoria. Specifically, rising asset prices inflate the collateral of borrowers, which in turn increases the amount of credit available in an economy; however, increasing prices also raises the expectations of lenders in terms of their anticipated rates of return. Simultaneously, rising wealth raises domestic consumption through the wealth effect. As, at least temporarily, above average rates of return on financial investments are sustained, investors are likely to underestimate their risks. Financial market competition can quickly created a 'too big to fail' problem due to herd behaviour, thus perpetuating the speculative boom.

Policy makers are caught in a bind since stabilizing measures for the exchange rate fuel investors' expectations of a slowdown, such as higher interest rates, or they are limited in scope, such as the selling of reserves. Thus, speculative booms tend to end in a financial crisis as expected and realized rates of return eventually diverge. Subsequently, investors may withdraw their funds to seek more lucrative investments elsewhere, resulting in rapidly falling exchange rates, rising borrower default, bank failures, declining growth and increasing unemployment (Alba *et al.* 1999; Demetriades 1999).

A number of studies have argued that stronger institutional settings could improve the chances to reap the full benefits of greater capital mobility (Arestis and Demetriades 1999; Chang *et al.* 1998; IMF 2001; Kose *et al.* 2004, Litan *et al.* 2001; McLean and Shrestha 2002). Weak institutional environments include, among other factors, inadequate capital standards for banks, lax regulatory standards for bank management and loan officers, loose licensing practices and insufficient transparency of capital markets as well as weak investor protection. Other important institutional weaknesses can include poor macroeconomic management, especially reflected in inconsistent and potentially politically-motivated monetary policies as well as large fiscal imbalances.

In contrast, a number of researchers have concluded that, while strong institutions can mitigate rising instability following FL, they cannot fully eliminate it. Arestis and Demetriades (1999) find that even where the necessary preconditions exist, such as effective supervision or macroeconomic stability, a strong link between FL and increased financial instability can be found. In addition, already existing structural weaknesses are likely to become even more severe in a deregulated environment. Alba *et al.* (1999) conclude that the crisis in Thailand can be traced back to FL that was introduced in a weak institutional environment. Similarly, Demetriades and Fattouh (1999) find that premature FL had caused the Korean crisis before existing weaknesses in the financial system could be addressed. This is not to say that institutional or macroeconomic weaknesses may not raise the likelihood of crises, but that they are unlikely to completely disappear.

This reflects the finding of several studies that the rise in crises was associated with more FL. Demirgüç-Kunt and Detragiache (1999) find, based on a study of 53 countries covering the period 1980–95, that the chance of a banking crisis increases after FL. Similar results are found by Kaminsky and Reinhart (1999) and Weller (2001b).

Greater economic instability tends to weaken the link between growth and poverty reduction. Lustig (2000), for example, finds that frequent crises are the single most important cause of rapid increases in poverty in Latin America. There have been more incidences of crises since 1980, when the wave of capital account liberalization began, which have cost countries up to 40 per cent of their GDP to resolve (Honohan and Kligebiel 2000). Although high-income earners are most likely to hold financial assets and thus feel the brunt of declining asset prices during a crisis, studies have also found that the economic burdens of a financial crisis are disproportionately borne by a country's poor, who are more likely to be affected by declining demand as unemployment rises (Eichengreen *et al.* 1995). Weller and Hersh (2004) also show that it was macroeconomic volatility that adversely affected the incomes of the poor during crises and not financial instability per se.

At the same time that the need for social safety nets grows, capital flows limit governments' ability to help the poor. Capital flows tend to punish governments for rising deficits (Blecker 1999). Investors tend to withdraw their funds following increasing government expenditures, and when the IMF is called upon to help bail out the country, it often requires that the government reduce its spending in order to receive a loan. Subsequently, counter-cyclical macroeconomic policies are harder to enact by countries in a crisis. If they choose to pursue a counter-cyclical, expansionary path during an economic crisis, the costs of capital can rise sharply, thereby reducing the effects of the expansionary policy. Moreover, poor people, who are the most vulnerable in a crisis, are more likely to depend on the expansion of social safety nets. However, the expansion of social safety nets is automatically made more costly for emerging economies because of greater capital mobility. Thus, the fall-out from economic crises for the poor are larger, *ceteris paribus*, in more open economies than in more closed ones (Weller and Hersh 2004).

The case of India

To understand the interactions between portfolio flows, other macroeconomic factors, capital controls and poverty and inequality, it is useful to consider the example of a particular country, such as India (see also in this regard Chapter 11). It has moved very slowly towards capital account liberalization. As a result, it has received much less foreign investment than other countries, but managed to avoid the fall-out from the Asian financial crisis. At the same time, however, increased liberalization has led to a build-up of foreign reserves as a means of protection against greater instability, which appears to hamper poverty reduction.

From September 1992, India began allowing foreign institutional investors (FIIs) to invest in Indian stock markets. Unlike many other countries in the region that quickly loosened capital controls, India's liberalization was intended to be gradual. Its portfolio flows have not been as volatile as those of many other emerging market countries and its portfolio flows on net have remained positive save for one year, 1998. In particular, India was one of the few Asian countries relatively unaffected by the 1997–1998 Asian financial crisis.

India has a variety of capital controls in place that, while less strict than in the past, are still used to manage its capital account. In terms of foreign portfolio inflows, India has a web of regulations that control who can invest in Indian companies and place limits on the level of investment. Only FIIs are allowed to invest in India's markets and they must register with the Securities Exchange Board of India (SEBI) before investing. Limits were placed on how much a single FII could invest in a company and how much of a company can be owned by FIIs. India continues to loosen these regulations with the eventual goal of complete liberalization. For instance, the amount that FIIs could invest in a company has been raised from 24 per cent at the outset in 1992 to 49 per cent – although requiring approval from the company's board and directors for any amount larger than 24 per cent.

Research has found that portfolio flows into India have been largely driven by returns on Indian stock markets (Chakrabarti 2001). Yet foreign investors also appear to care about macro policies, and both domestic (stock market returns and credit ratings) and external (London Interbank offered rate/LIBOR and emerging stock market returns) are found to be about equally important in determining portfolio flows to India (Gordon and Gupta 2003). Thus, by improving the fundamentals of its economy, India does have some control over portfolio flows into the country, despite continued capital controls.

As India moves towards further liberalization, it will inevitably focus on creating an economic environment that can harvest benefits of portfolio flows while attempting to mitigate, to the extent possible, the risks of a financial crisis. India has identified low inflation, fiscal consolidation, comfortable foreign exchange reserves and a strong financial system as conditions necessary to achieve both of these ends. On several of these fronts, India has made good progress – inflation has remained at less than 5 per cent, and foreign exchange reserves currently stand around $140 billion, about half of which was accumulated in 2003 and 2004. Yet, the government's fiscal deficits remain high compared to its target of 3.5 per cent of GDP. In addition, the financial system is still plagued by a relatively large amount of non-performing assets (Jadhav 2003).

This approach has not been without its drawbacks. Specifically, the build-up of massive reserves has given rise to a debate over the use of the excess capital as means of furthering investment or protection from the fall-out of greater capital mobility. Indeed, the rapid accumulation of reserves is a common feature of many developing countries that have opened up their capital accounts, especially in Asia. These reserves, although a necessary precaution to warding off financial crises, are also a drag on economic growth. Foreign capital that could be used to finance crucial investments are instead locked up and invested in the safest asset there is – low-yielding US Treasury bills (see Figure 5.3).

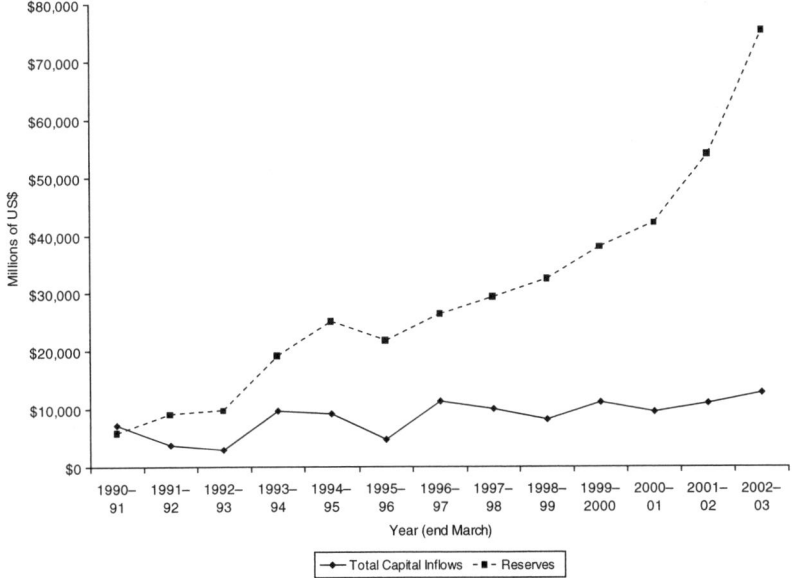

Figure 5.3 Total capital inflows and foreign exchange reserves: India
Source: Jadhav (2003).

As India pursues the continued opening up of its capital account, its focus also remains on prudent macroeconomic management as a means of attracting foreign capital. The results of this gradual policy approach appear to be reflected in a comparatively low likelihood of financial crises. At the same time, income inequality remained low in comparison with other developing countries (WIDER 2005). Yet problem spots are becoming apparent. Although private investment has grown in India, this has largely come as a replacement of public investment (Chandrashekar and Ghosh 2005). Furthermore, even though officially reported levels of inequality are low, they mask rising inequality due to measurement problems. Consequently, the lack of a serious acceleration in investment and rising inequality, among other factors may prove a serious impediment to successful poverty reduction (Chandrashekar and Ghosh 2005).

Policy options

The literature shows that portfolio flows may have beneficial effects on poverty reduction in rather indirect and ambiguous ways. More portfolio capital inflows reduce capital constraints and they seem to foster financial market developments (Durham 2003; Levine 1997; Litan et al. 2001). Fewer financial constraints help to foster increased investments (Calvo and Coricelli 1993; Cornelli et al. 1996; Dixit and Pindyck 1994; Fazzari et al. 1988; Weller 2001b) and thus can result in faster growth. There is also some evidence that improved financial market developments may foster economic growth over the long run (Levine 1997). However, this comes at the price of systematically increasing instability (Arestis and Demetriades 1999; Grabel 1998; Weller 2001a). To some degree, high-quality institutions can mitigate the rising chance of financial crises (Alba et al. 1999; Arestis and Demetriades 1999; Demetriades and Fattouh 1999), but residual risks remain.

Consequently, policy makers and researchers have to consider two alternative venues. One would be to limit capital flows through capital controls. The other would be the development of strong domestic institutions to manage portfolio flows adequately and reduce the need for more capital inflows through greater domestic resource mobilization.

A country's ability to use public policies to stabilize its financial market is limited by a lack of capital controls. At the same time, liquidity constraints may exist that provide countries with incentives to attract portfolio capital. The public policy issue is then to determine which capital flows are desirable and which ones are not. Specifically, is there a way to reduce portfolio flows and increase more long-term financial flows?

Capital controls

It is recognized, especially in light of the Asian financial crisis, that a country should have the right to control capital flows if they become a danger to its economic stability. The unilateral imposition of strict capital controls by Malaysia in the autumn of 1998 has served as a case study for the use of capital controls during currency crises (Ariyoshi *et al.* 2000). The case of India also highlights the possibility for an emerging economy to attract foreign capital amid continued capital controls.

Countries can implement capital controls through a variety of mechanisms. For one, countries can impose minimum stay requirements. International investors would be prohibited from withdrawing their funds prior to a pre-set time limit; capital could only be withdrawn gradually, thereby helping to avoid a financial panic. Another approach is international capital transactions taxes, which would levy a penalty on short-term capital withdrawal, while impacting long-term capital to a lesser degree. Chile's unremunerated reserve requirement (URR), in effect between June 1991 and September 1998, constituted an 'asymmetric Tobin tax' that was levied only on capital inflows. The URR was designed to make international loans with maturities of less than 90 days more expensive than loans with a greater maturity. Similar controls existed in Colombia with some effectiveness (Cardenas and Barrera 1997). Thirdly, countries could also impose outright prohibitions of certain types of capital movements. For instance, countries could require that profits earned on FDI be reinvested in the host economy.

Evaluations of the effectiveness of capital controls are rare. In a collection of 14 country studies, Ariyoshi *et al.* (2000) provided a preliminary evaluation of the effectiveness of capital controls in terms of stabilizing emerging economies. They found that: (i) capital controls cannot substitute for sound macroeconomic policies; (ii) no single measure can always be effective everywhere; (iii) targeted controls leave sufficient room to be circumvented, and hence are likely to be less effective than comprehensive controls; and (iv) the choice of controls is determined by the administrative capacity of a country.

However, the research did not consider the potential trade-off between greater stability and slower growth following the lack of capital. Klein and Olivei (1999) find that developed countries with open capital accounts were also more likely to grow faster from 1986 to 1995 than countries with closed capital accounts. Although their results did not find a link for developing economies, these findings may be subject to revisions as more and better data become available. Edison *et al.* (2002) concluded that greater financial integration, including fewer capital controls, might be associated with faster growth. Considering the aforementioned drawbacks, though, it is possible that faster growth in the short run will come at the expense of greater macroeconomic instability. In sum, this may prove an impediment to poverty reduction since the poor are more vulnerable to the fall-out from macroeconomic crises than other groups.

Besides controlling short-term capital, policy makers have also focused on attracting FDI (see Chapter 6). Some FDI includes the physical relocation of technology. But how much of this technology will benefit the host economy depends on national regulations. Wholly owned subsidiaries, for instance, are likely to guard their technological advantages very closely so as not to nurture competitors. In the case of joint ventures between foreign and local partners, such proprietary control is less likely. Public policies can encourage technology transfers, for example by requiring that foreign investors partner with local businesses by setting limits on the share of a local business that foreign residents can own. Similarly, host economies can prohibit foreigners from owning real estate.

Although there are clear economic advantages on a theoretical level to implementing or maintaining capital controls in emerging economies, there are often drawbacks to their implementation (Gros 1987; Cardenas and Barrera 1997; Kitano 2004; Ariyoshi *et al.* 2000). For one, countries often need additional financial capital to finance investment. Also, once rules for capital inflows are loosened, it is difficult to reinstate controls on some form of capital flows and not on others. Countries that typically have had some form of capital controls, such as Chile or India, have gradually eliminated these, either because the remaining capital controls have been circumvented or because of a greater need for more foreign capital. Also, some capital controls are meant to slow down the flow of capital, not to eliminate it altogether, such as Tobin taxes. The expected rates of return from short-term investments in emerging economies are often a multitude larger than the speculation taxes imposed on short-term capital flows. Consequently, the effective use of capital controls requires supporting policies, for example, efforts at greater domestic resource mobilization.

Institutional improvements to stabilize emerging economies

Policies to stabilize portfolio flows could also focus on improving domestic institutions. Strong domestic institutions can at least mitigate, if not fully eliminate, the adverse effects of greater portfolio flows. Specifically, effective bank-level management and sound official supervision should strengthen the stability of emerging financial sectors and market discipline (McNaughton *et al.* 1992; Caprio and Honohan 1999; Barth *et al.* 2002; Goldstein and Turner 1996). Also, sound financial regulation that would result in more asset diversification, more balanced financial structures – for example, between debt and equity – and better enforcement of contracts and regulations can help to raise the stability of local banking systems as risk exposures of individual institutions are limited. Finally, greater market discipline appears to work well if banks are forced to disclose accurate information and if private market participants have incentives to monitor financial institutions.

Another stabilizing institution in developing economies is increased civil liberties. Civil liberties in general and workers' rights in particular can create a macroeconomic environment that is less conducive to speculative investments. Improved workers' rights result in higher productivity growth in the formal economic sector, thus leading to faster economic growth. Improved workers' rights and, more broadly, better civil liberties tend to result in a better distribution of income, both among workers and between workers and firms. These benefits tend to be spread beyond the formal labour market just as civil liberties tend to give rise to more redistributive policies and more public investment, for example, in education. In other words, better civil liberties lead to larger overall output that gets more evenly distributed. As the benefits of faster growth are more evenly distributed, local demand is stronger and more stable. Because the liberalized pre-crisis environment is typically characterized by more credit and more investments, stronger demand as a result of better civil liberties means that supply and growth increase in tandem, rather than supply outpacing demand. Default risk falls and the chance of a crisis is diminished.

The bulk of the research on workers' rights and civil liberties shows that they are associated with significant increases in economic growth in the nations that have implemented and enforced them. In particular, child labour, forced labour, labour market discrimination and legislation barring unionization or collective bargaining all inhibit productivity growth (Maskus 1997; Acemoglu and Shimer 1999; Palley 2000, 2001; Buchele and Christensen 2000, 2003; Aidt and Tzannatos 2003).

The evidence on the effect of workers' rights and civil liberties on income distribution is even more powerful. Besides making the economic pie larger, adopting labour standards also increases how equally the pieces of this pie are cut (Rodrik 1999; Palley 2000; Aidt and Tzannatos 2003). Additionally, Alesina and Rodrik (1994) pointed out that more equal income distribution is, in and of itself, correlated strongly with improved economic performance. Workers' rights, then, help bring about a virtuous circle of equality and economic growth. Buchele and Christiansen (2003) found a similarly striking correlation between an index of workers' rights and income equality in a sample of Organization for Economic Co-operation and Development (OECD) nations.

As a result, financial stability increases. Weller and Singleton (2004) showed that political freedom – including labour standards – is an important determinant of financial stability. The evidence also shows that the severity of crises, if they occurred, was muted in countries with better workers' rights and civil liberties. After the Asian currency crisis of 1997–1998, South Korea fared relatively well in its recovery, while Indonesia fared particularly poorly. Rodrik (1999) found that institutions promoting democratic rights, rule of law and social safety nets are an important factor in enabling nations to rebound more quickly from economic shocks. Lustig (2000) similarly argued that the existence of decent social safety nets is one of the most important crisis-recovery policies a nation can adopt. Finally, Chakraborty and Rawlins (2004) showed that countries with more political freedoms were better able to take advantage of increased capital flows.

Institutional improvements to mobilize additional saving

Improved institutions may only reduce, rather than eliminate financial instability. Consequently, proposals also focus on raising funds domestically – for example, through the developments of indigenous banking systems and the introduction of tax reform.

To improve the collection of funds domestically, indigenous financial institutions could be strengthened. Many policy makers in emerging economies have pinned their hopes on foreign participation to improve local financial markets. Although emerging financial systems have seen the market share of foreign institutions rise quite rapidly, most of the benefits from this development have been concentrated among clients, such as multinational corporations, large domestic corporations and high net worth individuals, who were already well served. At the same time, financial constraints for other markets may actually increase, as previously discussed.

112 *Overview and Impact of Macroeconomic Policies*

To counter this trend, public support could be granted to local banks, where banking services are currently scarce. Public support can come in the form of tax-free status, for example, credit unions in the USA; public ownership and thus public guarantees for loans, for example, public savings banks in Germany; or office space for postal savings unions, for example, postal savings unions in Japan (see also in this regard Chapter 9 on Malaysia).

Among open countries, those with larger domestic banking systems have smaller portfolio capital inflows than those with smaller domestic banking systems and vice versa. The differences are quite sizeable. Among all open emerging economies, those with domestic banking systems that are larger than the median size for all emerging economies, portfolio inflows totalled 0.4 per cent of GDP. In those with domestic banking systems below the median size for open emerging economies, portfolio flows totalled 1.3 per cent of GDP (see Figure 5.4). Broken down by region, we see that there is little difference for Africa and Latin America, but that the size of portfolio capital inflows varies sharply in line with the size of the domestic banking sector in Asia, the Middle East and the transition economies of Central Asia and Central Europe.

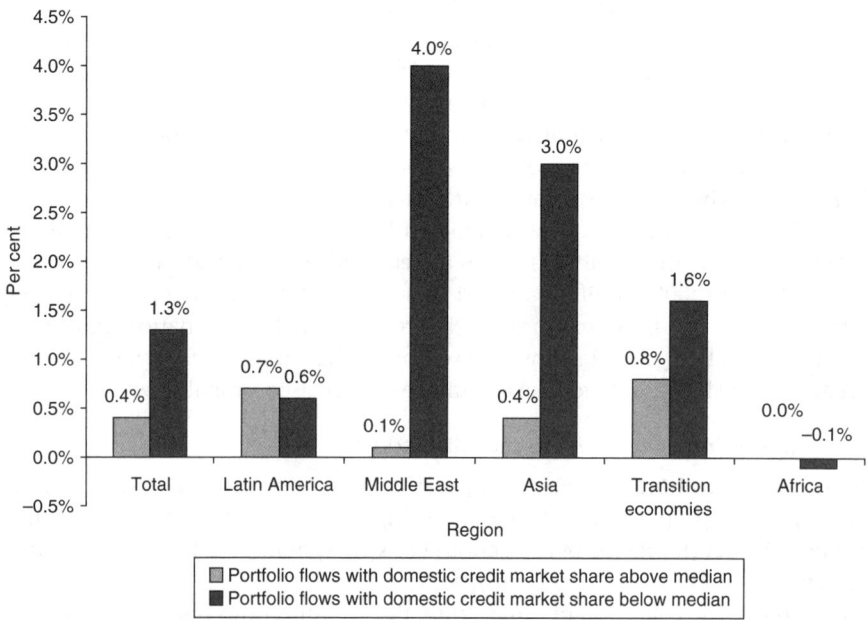

Figure 5.4 Portfolio inflows and size of domestic credit market

Notes: Authors' calculations based on data from the IMF, International Financial Statistics; IMF, Exchange Rate Arrangements and Restrictions; and the Bank for International Settlements, International Financial Statistics. Domestic credit is defined as total credit minus MNB credit relative to total credit. The median size of the domestic credit market is determined for all open emerging economies. An emerging economy is classified as open following the IMF's classification until 1995. Since 1995, a country has been classified as open if the IMF indicates that it has more capital mobility categories without restrictions than with restrictions.

Among the most important publicly supported financial institutions are postal savings banks (Scher 2001). Much of the public subsidy comes in the form of subsidized office space for these financial institutions since they are housed within the post office. Another subsidy results from tax exemption, for example in China, India and Viet Nam. Because of the relatively small cost, postal savings institutions can be effective in garnering money in underbanked populations. Postal savings institutions tend to be particularly successful for the savings mobilization among rural populations and for the provision of financial services to low-income populations and women (Scher 2001).

Focusing on expanding domestic financial institutions may offer two advantages. First, it may reduce the probability of financial crises, which tend to harm the poor disproportionately. Second, it may disproportionately benefit populations that are already likely to face greater financial constraints than others, helping to counter the direct adverse inequality effects of portfolio inflows.

In addition, the efficiency and progressivity of the tax system could be enhanced (Schmitt 2003). If a government can raise more revenues and do so in a more progressive manner, it has more resources available for public infrastructure investments and for a bigger social safety net, without restricting demand unnecessarily in the short run and building a foundation for faster growth in the future, for example, by investing in health and education (Schmitt 2003).

To improve the tax system, though, requires two separate policy moves. First, the efficiency of tax collection has to be raised. Developing economies tend to collect comparatively smaller shares than industrialized economies (Tanzi and Zee 2000). This can be improved through the use of modern information technology systems in conjunction with a reorganization of local tax collection authorities, and through the implementation of effective self-assessment by implementing credible deterrents for tax evasion and effective internal supervision of staff (Baer *et al.* 2002; McCarten 2004)

One proposal suggests the establishment of large taxpayer units with the tax administration. These units would be 'focusing on the few largest taxpayers with a highly trained and closely monitored small team of elite tax administrators' (McCarten 2004, 13). The goal is to reduce tax negotiation with the largest taxpayers. This should increase the efficiency of tax collection and reduce the uncertainty about tax liabilities for investors. Empirical evidence suggests that such narrowly focused institutional changes can be successful (Baer *et al.* 2002; McCarten 2004).

At the same time that tax collection is improved, the tax structure could be made more progressive. Many tax systems in industrializing countries are substantially less progressive than those in industrialized countries (Schmitt 2003). Both changes could help to mobilize large amounts of money, which often would exceed other sources of income for emerging economies, such as foreign aid (see Table 5.2). Also, the additional revenues that could be raised could surpass developing countries' expenditures on health and education. With investments in a better tax collection and a more progressive tax structure, developing economies may be able to finance large-scale improvements without depending on foreign capital.

Table 5.2 Relative size of extra tax revenue under the US tax model

	Comparisons (1995–2000 average)						
	Current revenue	Extra revenue	Public spending		Surplus or deficit	Interest on foreign	foreign aid received
			Education	Health			
Argentina	22.9	8.0	3.7	1.0	−1.9	3.4	0.0
Bolivia	22.9	7.8	5.3	3.7	−2.5	3.1	8.5
Brazil	38.1	−5.7	4.8	2.9	−7.5	1.7	0.0
Chile	22.7	9.2	3.4	3.8	1.0	2.1	0.2
Colombia	12.4	19.6	3.3	4.5	−4.4	3.0	0.2
Costa Rica	19.9	10.9	4.5	5.0	−1.8	3.3	0.1
Dom. Republic	16.4	14.6	2.0	1.8	0.2	2.1	0.1
Ecuador	15.7	14.8	3.2	2.4	NA	NA	1.0
El Salvador	11.0	20.5	2.3	2.8	−0.6	1.9	2.2
Guatemala	10.3	21.5	1.8	1.7	NA	NA	1.4
Honduras	19.6	12.3	3.8	3.7	NA	NA	9.0
Mexico	17.4	14.2	NA	2.4	−1.0	4.8	0.0
Nicaragua	30.5	1.9	3.5	8.7	−2.5	9.5	31.2
Panama	27.6	3.4	5.0	5.3	0.4	5.8	0.4
Paraguay	14.1	18.0	4.0	1.6	NA	NA	1.1
Peru	17.7	13.2	3.2	2.4	−0.3	3.0	0.7
Uruguay	28.3	2.1	2.7	2.3	−2.0	3.5	0.2
Venezuela	17.2	14.0	NA	2.4	−1.3	3.7	0.0

Notes:
NA = not available.
All figures are in percentage of GDP.

Source: Schmitt (2003).

Conclusion

Developing economies have, for the most part, taken to the idea that opening their countries to trade and international capital helps them to grow faster, and in turn to reduce poverty in their countries. With regard to liberalized capital flows, the record has been clear in showing that although there are indeed benefits to having access to foreign capital, there are also great costs. These costs are most acute when considering short-term portfolio flows, which can quickly be pulled out by foreign investors when they become sceptical about their investments in emerging markets, causing financial crises, crippling economic growth and hindering poverty reduction.

Some economies have played with the idea of returning to some form of capital controls to maintain greater stability in their financial systems. These have been successful to some extent in certain cases, such as that of Malaysia following the Asian financial crisis. For long-term uses, the need for short-term stability may conflict with the more long-term need for additional capital. To address these potentially conflicting goals, policy makers should not consider capital controls in isolation. Instead, the use of capital controls should be considered carefully in conjunction with other policies to stabilize emerging economies and to mobilize additional savings.

Serious policy options should consider institutional improvements as a way to lower the chance of financial crisis. Although some research indicates that institutional improvements cannot prevent a financial crisis, they can at least lower the probability of such an occurrence. Institutional reforms can focus on raising more domestic capital and ensuring more efficient allocation of it. Improved bank management and official supervision, sound financial regulation that encourages financial diversification and implementation of stronger political freedoms, including workers' rights, could help allocate capital to more productive uses and distribute income more equitably. At the same time, improved tax collection and the development of indigenous banking systems can help economies raise capital domestically, so that they do not have to depend to the same extent on foreign capital to make necessary investments. By promoting economic growth through implementing such policies, developing countries could accelerate their poverty reduction efforts.

References

Acemoglu, D. and R. Shimer. 1999. 'Productivity Gains from Unemployment Insurance'. *European Economic Review*, 44, 1195–1224.

Aidt, T. and Z. Tzannatos. 2003. *Unions and Collective Bargaining*. Washington, DC: World Bank.

Alba, P., L. Hernandez and D. Klingebiel. 1999. *Financial Liberalization and the Capital Account: Thailand 1988–1997*. Policy Research Working Paper No. 2188. Washington, DC: World Bank.

Alesina, A. and D. Rodrik. 1994. 'Distributive Politics and Economic Growth'. *Quarterly Journal of Economics*, 109(2), 465–90.

Arestis, P. and P. Demetriades. 1999. 'Financial Liberalization: The Experience of Developing Countries'. *Eastern Economic Journal*, 25(4) (Fall), 441–57.

Ariyoshi, A., K. Habermeier, B. Laurens, I. Otker-Robe, I. Canales-Kriljenko and A. Kirilenko. 2000. *Country Experiences with the Use and Liberalization of Capital Controls*. Occasional Paper No. 190, Washington, DC: International Monetary Fund.

Baer, K., O. Benon and J. Toro Rivera. 2002. *Improving Large Taxpayers' Compliance: A Review of Country Experience*. Occasional Paper No. 215. Washington, DC: International Monetary Fund.

Barth, J., G. Caprio and R. Levine. 2002. *Bank Regulation and Supervision: What Works Best?* Paper presented at the conference Basel II: An Economic Assessment. Basel: Bank for International Settlements, 17 May.

Blecker, R. 1999. *Taming Global Finance: A Better Architecture for Growth and Equity*. Washingston, DC: Economic Policy Institute.

Buchele, R. and J. Christensen. 2000. *Worker Rights and Socio-Economic Performance in the OECD*. Paper presented at the annual meeting of the International Working Party on Labour Market Segmentation (IWPLMS), Manchester, UK, 10 August.

Buchele, R. and J. Christensen. 2003. *Worker Rights and Socio-Economic Performance in Advanced Capitalist Economies*. Paper presented at the Annual Meeting of the Union for Radical Political Economics (URPE), Washington, DC, 3–5 January.

Calvo, G. and F. Coricelli. 1993. 'Output Collapse in Eastern Europe'. *IMF Staff Papers*, 40(1) (March), 32–52.

Caprio, G. and P. Honohan. 1999. *Beyond Capital Ideas: Restoring Banking Stability*. Working Paper No. 2235. Washington, DC: World Bank.

Cardenas, M. and F. Barrera. 1997. 'On the Effectiveness of Capital Controls: The Experience of Colombia During the 1990s'. *Journal of Development Economics*, 54(1), 27–57.

Chakrabarti, R. 2001. 'FII Flows to India: Nature and Causes'. *Money and Finance*, 2(7) (October–December).

Chakraborty, C. and G. Rawlins. 2004. 'Financial Resource Flows, Macro Policy Response, and the Socio-Economic Environment: The Experience of Latin America and East Asia'. *Journal of Socio-Economics*, 33(4), 469–89.

Chandrashekar, C.P. and J. Ghosh. 2005. *Macroeconomic Policy, Inequality and Poverty Reduction in India and China*. Paper presented at the UNRISD workshop on Pro-Poor Macroeconomics, University of Florence, Italy, 24–5 February.

Chang, H., H. Park and C. Yoo. 1998. 'Interpreting the Korean Crisis: Financial Liberalisation, Industrial Policy and Corporate Governance'. *Cambridge Journal of Economics*, 22(6) (November), 735–46.

Cornelli, F., R. Portes and M.E. Schaffer. 1996. *The Capital Structure of Firms in Central and Eastern Europe*, Discussion Paper No. 1392. London: Centre for Economic Policy Research.

Demetriades, P. 1999. *Financial Liberalization and Credit-Asset Booms and Busts in East Asia*. Paper prepared for the conference The Credit Crunch in East Asia: What Do We Know? What Do We Need To Know? Washington, DC: World Bank, 30 November–1 December.

Demetriades, P. and B.A. Fattouh. 1999. 'South Korea's Financial Liberalization: An Experiment in Faith'. *International Affairs*, 75(4), 779–92.

Demirgüç-Kunt, A. and E. Detragiache. 1999. 'Financial Liberalization and Financial Fragility'. In B. Pleskovic and J. Stiglitz (eds), *Annual World Bank Conference on Development Economics 1998*. Washington, DC: World Bank.

Dixit, A. and R.S. Pindyck. 1994. *Investment Under Uncertainty*. Princeton: Princeton University Press.

Dollar, D. and A. Kraay. 2001a. *Growth is Good for the Poor*. World Bank Development Research Group Working Paper No. 2587. Washington, DC: World Bank.

Dollar, D. and A. Kraay. 2001b. *Trade, Growth, and Poverty*. World Bank Development Research Group Working Paper No. 2615. Washington, DC: World Bank.

Durham, J. 2003. *Foreign Portfolio Investment, Foreign Bank Lending, and Economic Growth*. International Finance Discussion Papers, Board of Governors of the Federal Reserve System, Washington, DC.

Edison, H., M. Klein and L. Ricci. 2002. *Capital Account Liberalization and Economic Performance: Survey and Synthesis*. Working Paper No. 9100. Cambridge, MA: National Bureau of Economic Research.

Eichengreen, B., A.K. Rose and C. Wyplosz. 1995. 'Exchange Market Mayhem: The Antecedents and Aftermath of Speculative Attacks'. *Economic Policy*, 21, 251–312.

Fazzari, S.M., R.G. Hubbard and B.C. Petersen. 1988. 'Financing Constraints and Corporate Investment'. *Brookings Papers on Economic Activity* 1, 141–95.

Fry, M.J. 1995. *Money, Interest, and Banking in Economic Development*, 2nd edition. Baltimore, MD: The Johns Hopkins University Press.

Goldstein, M. and P. Turner. 1996. *Banking Crises in Emerging Economies: Origins and Policy Options*. Economics Paper No. 46. Basel: Bank for International Settlements. Switzerland.

Gordon, J. and P. Gupta. 2003. *Portfolio Flows into India: Do Domestic Fundamentals Matter?* Working Paper WP/03/20. Washington, DC: International Monetary Fund, January.

Grabel, I. 1993. 'Fast Money, "Noisy Growth": A Noise-Led Theory of Development'. *Review of Radical Political Economics*, 25(3), 1–8.

Grabel, I. 1995a. 'Assessing the Impact of Financial Liberalisation on Stock Market Volatility in Selected Developing Countries'. *Journal of Development Studies*, 31(6), 903–17.

Grabel, I. 1995b. 'Speculation-Led Economic Development: A Post-Kynesian Interpretation of Financial Liberalization Programmes in the Third World'. *International Review of Applied Economics*, 9(2), 127–49.

Grabel, I. 1996. 'Marketing the World: The Contradictions of Portfolio Investment in the Global Economy'. *World Development*, 24(11), 1761–76.

Grabel, I. 1998. 'Rejecting Exceptionalism: Reinterpreting the Asian Financial Crises'. In J. Michie and J. Grieve Smith (eds), *Global Instability and World Economic Governance*. Oxford: Routledge.

Gros, D. 1987. 'The Effectiveness of Capital Controls: Implications for Monetary Autonomy in the Presence of Incomplete Market Separation'. *IMF Staff Papers*, 34(4), 621–42.

Honohan, P. and D. Klingebiel. 2000. *Controlling the Fiscal Costs of Banking Crises*. Working Paper No. 2441.Washington, DC: World Bank.

International Monetary Fund (IMF). 2004. *World Economic Outlook*. Washington, DC: IMF.

International Monerary Fund (IMF). 2001. *World Economic Outlook*. Washington, DC: IMF.

Jadhav, N. 2003. *Capital Account Liberalization: The Indian Experience*. Paper presented at IMF seminar A Tale of Two Giants: India's and China's Experience with Reform and Growth, New Delhi, 14–16 November.

Kaminsky, G. and C. Reinhart. 1999. 'The Twin Crises: The Causes of Banking and Balance-of-Payment Problems'. *American Economic Review*, 89(3), 473–500.

Kitano, S. 2004. 'Macroeconomic Effect of Capital Controls as a Safeguard Against the Capital Inflow Problem'. *Journal of International Trade and Economic Development*, 13(3), 233–63.

Klein, M. and G. Olivei. 1999. *Capital Account Liberalization, Financial Depth, and Economic Growth*, Working Paper No. 7384. Cambridge, MA: National Bureau of Economic Research.

Kose, A., P. Eswar, K. Rogoff and S. Wei. 2004. *Financial Globalization, Growth and Volatility in Developing Countries*, Working Paper No. 10942. Cambridge, MA: National Bureau of Economic Research.

Levine, R. 2001. 'International Financial Liberalization and Economic Growth'. *Review of International Economics*, 9(4), 688–702.

Levine, R. 1997. 'Financial Development and Economic Growth: Views and Agenda'. *Journal of Economic Literature*, 35(2), 688–727.

Litan, R., P. Masson and M. Pomerleano. 2001. *Open Doors: Foreign Participation in Financial Systems in Developing Countries*. Washington, DC: Brooking Institution Press.

Lustig, N. 2000. *Crises and the Poor: Socially Responsible Macroeconomics*. Sustainable Development Department Technical Paper Series No. POV-108. Washington, DC: Inter-American Development Bank.

Maskus, K. 1997. *Should Core Labor Standards Be Imposed Through International Trade Policy?* Working Paper No. 1817. Washington, DC: International Monetary Fund.

McCarten, W. 2004. *Focusing on the Few: The Role of Large Taxpayer Units in the Revenue Strategies of Developing Countries*. Paper presented at the Andrew Young School's Fourth Annual Conference on Public Finance Issues in an International Perspective: The Challenges of Tax Reform in a Global Economy, Georgia State University, Atlanta, 24–5 May.

McKinnon, R.I. 1973. *Money and Capital in Economic Development*. Washington, DC: The Brookings Institution.

McLean, B. and S. Shrestha. 2002. *International Financial Liberalization and Economic Growth*. Discussion Paper No. 2002–03. Sydney, Australia: Reserve Bank of Australia.

McNaughton, D., D. Carlson and C. Dietz. 1992. *Banking Institutions in Developing Markets, Volume 2: Building Strong Management and Responding to Change*. Washington, DC: World Bank.

Palley, T.I. 2000. *The Impact of Labor Standards on Economic Governance, and Income Distribution: Some Cross-Country Evidence*. Public Policy Department Technical Paper 029, AFL-CIO, Washington, DC.

Palley, T.I. 2001. *Is There a Relationship between the Quality of Governance and Financial Crises? Evidence from the Crises of 1997*. Unpublished manuscript, AFL–CIO, Washington, DC.

Rath, D. and D. Dasgupta. 1999. *What Factors Appear to Drive Private Capital Flows to Developing Countries? And How Does Official Lending Respond?* Policy Research Paper Working Paper Series No. 2392. Washington, DC: World Bank.

Rodrik, D. 1999. 'Democracies pay Higher Wages'. *The Quarterly Journal of Economics*, 114(3), 707–38.

Scher, M. 2001. *Postal Savings and the Provision of Financial Services: Policy Issues and Asian Experiences in the Use of the Postal Infrastructure for Savings Mobilization*, Discussion Paper

No. 22. New York: United Nations Department of Economic and Social Affairs, United Nations.
Schmitt, J. 2003. *Is it Time to Export the U.S. Tax Model to Latin America?* Briefing Paper. Washington, DC: Center for Economic and Policy Research.
Shaw, E. 1973. *Financial Deepening in Economic Development.* New York: Oxford University Press.
Singh, A. and B.A. Weisse. 1998. *Emerging Stock Markets, Portfolio Capital Flows and Long-Term Economic Growth: Micro and Macroeconomic Perspectives.* Accounting Working Paper, Department of Applied Economics, University of Cambridge, Cambridge.
Tanzi, V. and H. Zee. 2000. *Tax Policy for Emerging Markets: Developing Countries.* Working Paper WP/00/35. Washington, DC: International Monetary Fund.
Weller, C. 2005. *The Presence of Multinational Banks and the Supply and Quality of Credit in Emerging Economies.* Unpublished manuscript, Center for American Progress, Washington, DC.
Weller, C. 2004. *The Dollar's Decline in Perspective.* Economic Policy Column, 23 November, Center for American Progress, Washington, DC.
Weller, C. 2001a. *The Supply of Credit by Multinational Banks in Developing and Transition Economies: Determinants and Effects*, Discussion Paper No. 16, United Nations Department of Economic and Social Affairs. New York: United Nations.
Weller, C. 2001b. 'Financial Crises After Financial Liberalization: Exceptional Circumstances or Structural Weakness?' *The Journal of Development Studies*, 38(1), 98–127.
Weller, C. 2000. 'Financial Liberalization, Multinational Banks and Declining Real Credit: The Case of Poland'. *International Review of Applied Economics*, 14(2), 193–213.
Weller, C. and A. Hersh. 2004. 'The Long and Short of It: Global Liberalization and the Incomes of the Poor'. *Journal of Post-Keynesian Economics*, 26(3), 471–504.
Weller, C. and B. Morzuch. 2000. 'International Financial Contagion: Why are Eastern Europe's Banks not Failing, When Everybody Else's Are?' *Economics of Transition* 8(3), 639–63.
Weller, C. and M. Scher. 2001. 'Multinational Bank Credit in Less Industrialized Economies'. *Journal of International Business Studies*, 32(4), 833–51.
Weller, C. and L. Singleton. 2004. 'Political Freedom, External Liberalization, and Financial Stability'. *International Review of Applied Economics*, 18(1), 43–61.
World Institute for Development and Economic Research (WIDER). 2005. World Income Inequality Database (WIID) WIID2beta. Helsinki: UNU/WIDER.

6
The Effects of FDI on Growth and Inequality

Chiara Bonassi, Giorgia Giovannetti and Giorgio Ricchiuti

Introduction

North–South capital flows are likely to allow countries in the South to grow independently from their (low) domestic saving rate, thereby reducing possible financial constraints to growth. They allow the financing of balance-of-payments deficits in the early stages of development, so that a country can import intermediate and capital-intensive goods, which are essential for productive capacity. They improve the allocation of domestic and foreign capital and facilitate the transfer of technology and know-how. Hence, private capital flows have the potential to boost growth and to contribute to improvements in the standard of living in developing countries. This potential does not seem to have been fully exploited yet, especially in African countries.[1]

At the same time, capital inflows affect income distribution though the direction of causality is not always clear. According to Oxfam (2002, 3), over the last 30 years or so the flows seem to have generated a redistribution of income from 'the poor to the wealthy in a magnitude such that it has probably more than cancelled out any positive impact they may have on growth, even in the long term'. This redistribution has been both between countries – from the South to the North, especially in terms of repatriation of profits and as a consequence of financial instability – and within countries – from unskilled to skilled workers and/or from workers to rent seekers and entrepreneurs.

Against this background, foreign direct investment (FDI) offers a number of advantages with respect to other types of private capital inflows, making it, in the term coined by Loungani and Razin (2001), 'the private capital inflow of choice' for many developing countries. With respect to portfolio flows, FDI – that is, 'the category of international investment in which an enterprise resident in one country (the direct investor) acquires at least 10 per cent in an enterprise resident in another country (the direct investment enterprise)[2] – are more stable, do not show a pro-cyclical pattern and have been resilient during the recent financial crisis. The relatively low volatility of FDI is likely to depend upon the presence of an element of irreversibility in the decision-making process: investors, when deciding about an FDI, take a long-term view of the market; furthermore, it is more difficult to liquidate assets, at least in the case of greenfield investments. Because of these characteristics, greenfield FDI, which make up more than half of the private flows to developing countries, are considered the most important for boosting growth[3] (in this regard see Chapters 8 and 9 on Mauritius and Malaysia). But, if there are no major changes in income distribution, faster growth rates are likely to lead to higher rates of poverty reduction (Dollar and Kraay 2002); on the other hand, inward FDI increases wages in leading sectors and may negatively affect income distribution and therefore has a perverse effect on poverty. Furthermore, the effect of FDI on growth, income distribution and poverty in developing countries depends to a large extent on their composition – for example, mergers and acquisitions (M&A) are more likely to be temporary than greenfield investments – and on the sectors where capital is allocated; the level of labour intensity affects the distribution of wages, profits and rents and the share of skilled versus unskilled workers affects the relative wages.

In this chapter, we analyse the effects of (the new patterns of) FDI on growth and inequality on a sample of 27 countries located in different regions of the world,[4] with the aim of assessing whether they can play a role in poverty reduction. The chapter begins with a (brief) selective review of the current literature of why capital inflows can be beneficial and/or harm long-term growth and affect income distribution. We make separate analyses of the links between FDI and growth[5] and those between FDI and inequality,[6] identifying the channels of transmissions.

This is followed by a brief sketch of the main characteristics of capital inflows, their sectoral distribution and the trend in income inequality and poverty. In various respects, the countries in our sample are very different from one another as far as the capacity to attract funds, the endowment of resources, the stage of industrialization and, therefore, the sectoral composition of inflows. Next, we test the presumption that FDI in different sectors activates growth in different ways: with FDI in the highly labour-intensive (low skilled) manufacturing sector more likely to increase gross domestic product (GDP) than FDI in mining, energy or construction, which are more capital-intensive and characterized by a higher share of skilled workers and high rents.

We conclude by drawing some policy implications, discussing whether it is worthwhile for countries that do not have 'good initial conditions' to initiate FDI and whether incentives for FDI could be allowed under the current rules of the World Trade Organization and, finally, addressing the issue of how the credibility of institutions, in a broad sense, may affect the relationship between FDI, growth and income distribution.

Review of the literature

This section, after a brief introduction on FDI motivations, sketches the channels through which FDI can boost growth in developing countries and those through which it affects income distribution.[7] It also analyses the indirect effects: FDI feeds growth and in turn growth alleviates poverty and affects distribution.

The theoretical literature: motivation and channels of transmissions

FDI tends to follow an 'industrial logic'[8] and can be:

- *resource seeking*: firms invest in countries with (abundant) cheap production factors – while in the past there were only (cheap) natural resources to trigger FDI, more recently skilled inexpensive labour has also become an important motivation;
- *market seeking*: access to host countries' markets for processed goods is crucial in a global world, hence, transport costs, differences in consumer tastes and the magnitude of host economies are important;
- *efficiency seeking*: the efficient use of resources can depend on the degree of openness to trade; and
- *strategic asset seeking*: for instance, through the internationalization of research and development (R&D) activities.

However, the impact of FDI and, in particular, the benefits that a country may receive, depends upon a number of macroeconomic factors, such as the saving–investment balance in the country and the degree of international integration with trade partners. FDI generally occurs together with greater trade integration, which may reflect increasing vertical integration trade linkages.[9] More precisely, the relationship between FDI and foreign trade at the company or industry level depends upon whether FDI is aimed at 'substituting' or 'complementing' the export activity and this, in turn, depends upon where funds are channelled. In general, in services trade and FDI can be expected to be largely complementary because establishing a commercial presence abroad generally brings stronger services trade.[10] In manufacturing, vertical – that is, for specialized products that are at different stages of the production process – and horizontal – for differentiated products – FDI coexist. As pointed out by Markusen (2002) among others, in fact, the interdependence of trade and FDI derive from the fact that the decision to export or invest abroad in local production is increasingly made by the same groups. The objective of vertical investment is to take advantage of cross-country absolute and comparative advantage patterns by locating plants in different countries that specialize in different stages of production. In this case, trade and vertical FDI are complementary activities: firms will typically export components to foreign affiliates and re-export to the home (or other) markets the goods produced abroad. The objective of horizontal investment, on the other hand, is often to enter a large market and, in this case, FDI and export tend to be substitutes. For developing countries, a vertical strategy dominates, in which production is fragmented into stages in order to exploit cross-country comparative advantages.

Institutions and other factors

Domestic institutions can also play an important role in attracting FDI and, at the same time, affect their possible impact on growth, income distribution and the poverty level. The existing literature has focused on the level of democracy, transparency and good governance, property rights, tax systems and economic freedom to explain differences in capital inflows to different countries, on the grounds that capital tends to flow into countries with higher (better) investor protection.[11] In contrast, natural resources and market size are investment conditions that can be changed by the domestic government – they are not exogenous but endogenously determined.

There is some agreement that politically stable countries attract more FDI than countries characterized by systems where property rights are not ensured or consolidated, since participation in international markets has obvious risks to investors, most notably the risk of direct or indirect expropriation.[12] Furthermore, corruption and a high level of bureaucratic practices may also deter foreign investors.[13] Apart from raising the cost of undertaking business, corruption slows down the process of obtaining permits necessary to operate in a country.

For developing countries, however, schools and other institutions developing human capital may be the most crucial factor, since they allow the bypassing of possible bottlenecks in the supply of labour. A critical level of education may exist below which it is not likely to attract capital.[14]

Furthermore, financial markets often do not work properly (efficiently); improving their functioning can help channel the funds, which is particularly important for M&A. The legal and regulatory environment within a country is often not clear, thus differences in laws, regulations and enforcement between countries might increase transaction costs and asymmetries of information.[15] The efficiency of firms is in turn affected by differences in the investor protection and corporate governance practices. The level of protection is higher in developing than in developed countries. However, this can be both a deterrent and a stimulus to FDI since firms producing in a country are not subject to restrictions – for instance, in exporting. Furthermore, it may be that the level of protection itself may not be significant, but could become so when combined with effective institutions. In addition, developing countries often lack good physical infrastructures. In short, all of these factors may define the 'business environment', which is a policy variable.

The channels through which FDI affects growth

While the traditional literature has focused on the exogenous growth model where the direction of causation between FDI and GDP growth was well determined, more recently causality has become an issue in the framework of endogenous growth models.[16]

To the extent that FDI adds to existing capital stock, it is likely to have a 'direct' effect on growth – similar to that of domestic investments (see Zhang 1999) – and to allow for the transfer of technology, particularly in the form of a new variety of capital inputs; this channel may be crucial for developing countries, even if it can take time to be able to produce the imported technology independently. In addition, FDI can have a positive 'indirect' effect on growth through its impact on human capital. In developing countries, the spillovers due to training workers and managers by foreign multinationals in host countries could turn out to be even more important than the direct effect on growth. Finally, the presence of foreign investors increases competition by overcoming entry barriers and reducing the market power of existing firms. Thus, FDI can enhance long-term growth in the South through capital accumulation, knowledge transfer – labour training and skill acquisition and diffusion – and positive externalities of various types. FDI is likely to increase productivity of domestic firms by exerting competitive pressure on local firms and forcing them to be more productive (Blomström and Kokko 1998). However, the existence of a positive correlation between the presence of FDI and higher productivity, as found in some studies, does not necessarily imply the existence of spillovers from foreign to domestic firms.[17]

A number of mechanisms also exist through which foreign investment can generate negative externalities: foreign investors may increase the demand for scarce resources such as skilled labour and domestic credit and, therefore, raise production costs. Against this background, it is particularly relevant to assess the role of human capital and the interaction between FDI and human capital. It is the level of human capital that determines the ability to adopt foreign technology so that a larger endowment of human capital can induce higher growth. Also, a minimum threshold stock of human capital is likely necessary for FDI to have beneficial effects on growth.

The composition of capital inflows also affects their impact on growth. Since M&A consist of a transfer of property of existing capital, such investments in domestic investment are far less likely than greenfield investment – creating new capital – and have, therefore, a lower impact on growth. Furthermore, the advantages of FDI in terms of growth and income distribution, as mentioned above, are more likely to be observed in labour-intensive manufacturing and not in mining, where the peculiar composition between skilled and unskilled workers and between workers and rent seekers 'reduces demand for unskilled labour and discourages investment in education' (Cornia 2004, 196).

To sum up, the growth effects of FDI are complicated; however, for labour-intensive manufacturing sectors such as textiles, shoes, food processing and furniture (see Cornia 2004), they are in principle similar to those of international trade. When they are set in motion, they can, under specific circumstances, speed up convergence with a country entering a virtuous cycle of M&A followed by new greenfield investments to exploit the gains of efficiency.

The channels through which FDI affects inequality

In addition, the links between FDI and income inequality are complex and, in contrast to traditional trade and FDI theories that predict by allowing developing countries to specialize in less skill-intensive activities FDI reduces wage inequality in developing countries, hint that FDI is likely to perpetuate inequalities.

There are several channels at work described in the (scant) literature; see for instance, te Velde (2003). First of all, foreign firms tend to produce in skill-intensive sectors. If FDI then causes a relative expansion of skill-intensive sectors, this will improve the relative position of skilled workers and raise wage inequality (Feenstra and Hanson 1995).

Skilled workers are likely to be in a stronger bargaining position than less-skilled workers and this can increase the levels of income inequality. FDI may also affect the supply of skills through firm-specific and general training and through contributions to general education. FDI is also likely to induce a faster productivity growth of labour in both foreign (technology transfer) and domestic firms (spillover effects). If such productivity growth is skill-biased, FDI may increase skill-biased technological change (Berman and Machin 2000).

FDI can also affect non-wage income. For instance, FDI may increase profits and the return to capital, relative to other types of income such as that of the self-employed and employees. Finally, other effects on income inequality could be indirect – for example, through the effects on fiscal revenues and expenditures.[18]

We believe that to better understand the impact of FDI on inequality (both functional and personal), a 'sectoral' approach has to be followed. Again, as with growth, the channels by which FDI affects inequality are likely to be different in different sectors. Mining, for example, is a capital-intensive sector where workers are highly skilled and rents tend to be high. FDI in the mining sector is likely to raise the wages of high-skilled workers, widening the income gap. Moreover, once the rents are created, they can be shared in various ways, affecting the distribution of the gains. For instance, the government can extract rents by taxation and then redistribute it to poor people, thereby decreasing income inequality. However, this is not likely to be the case for most developing countries: a foreign firm may find it more convenient to pay high wages and 'commissions' in order to create strong local support for the firm, both between politicians and workers.

Conversely, manufacturing is a labour-intensive sector, and foreign firms investing in this sector in developing countries, seek low-paid, unskilled workers to reduce their costs. On the one hand, this raises the employment rate but, on the other hand, it reduces income inequalities between skilled and unskilled workers by increasing the demand for the latter.

Finally, services are not clearly labour or capital intensive. Hence, to analyse the impact of capital inflows in this sector on inequality we may need to look at the subsectors. For instance, telecommunications is capital intensive and uses skilled workers; in contrast, hotels and restaurants are more labour intensive and use unskilled labour forces. In this way, we can expect that capital going to the former affects inequality in a manner similar to that observed in the mining sector, while capital going to the latter affects inequality similar to manufacturing.

The empirical literature

FDI and growth

Many empirical contributions have tried to explain the relationship between FDI and growth;[19] some have also considered how the credibility of institutions affects the FDI–growth nexus. Different studies, of course, use different explanatory variables and different methods to assess the FDI–growth–income distribution issue; however, there seems to be a consensus on using market size (often measured by the size of the population) and development level (measured by per capita GDP) of the host country as major determinants of FDI.[20] An issue that is difficult to solve empirically is the mutually reinforcing relationship between FDI and growth: FDI is reactive to domestic conditions in the sense that foreign investors are able to exploit favourable host country conditions – investment may lag rather than lead growth (see OECD 2001).

To by-pass the issue of causality, several recent empirical contributions have emphasized the use of gravity-style models, which incorporate both macroeconomic and geographical factors. In particular, beyond the market size and development level of the host country, FDI flows are assumed to depend upon the geographical distance between the home and host country. Distance is generally used to proxy not only transport, but also information costs since familiarity with the investment opportunities in the recipient country tends to decrease with distance. The role of transport and information costs, however, is likely to decrease with improvement in the transport systems and with increasing access to information typical of the current phase of globalization. Hence, the state of physical infrastructures becomes a relevant issue. To account for the observed geographical concentration of FDI, other control variables are often considered, such as dummy variables signalling whether the host and the source country share a common border or language or whether both are in the same trade agreement or currency union. As we have stated, FDI generates (positive or negative) spillovers through: (i) informal contacts and turnover of workers that can enhance productivity, but this channel only works if the host country is capable of absorbing the available knowledge (positive); or (ii) competition for scarce resources, therefore increasing production costs (negative). Using cross-sectional regressions, Caves (1996) finds that an increase in FDI – measured by the percentage of sales from foreign-owned firms – tends to lower domestic firms' profitability and suggests that the absorptive capacity of the host country may not be appropriate. Haddad and Harrison (1993), in an early study on firm-level data for Morocco, claim that FDI hurts local firms, at least in the short term, because larger foreign firms compete with domestic ones (smaller) that lose market share and left with excess capacity, experience a decline in the productive use of their resources. However, several studies – for example, Globerman (1979) and Blomström and Persson (1983) – have observed a positive relationship between FDI and labour productivity. The rise in capital accumulation, knowledge and competition following an upsurge of FDI inflows can also improve the export performance of recipient countries. This occurred, for instance, in Southeast Asia.

As for the role of financial markets, Alfaro *et al.* (2004: 92) point out that

> well-functioning stock markets, by increasing the spectrum of sources of finance for entrepreneurs, play an important role in creating linkages between domestic and foreign investors [...] determining whether foreign firms operate in isolated enclaves with no links whatsoever with the domestic economy.

Hence, countries with more developed markets can exploit FDI more efficiently.

FDI and inequality

As far as the nexus between FDI and inequality is concerned, the literature is limited. There are two main reasons for this: the absence of a commonly accepted theoretical framework and difficulties in comparing data. Furthermore, the results of the tests depend crucially on the proxy used – that is, FDI stock rather than FDI flow or income rather than wage inequality. Moreover, some empirical studies have used FDI just as an indicator for globalization (see Table 6.A2).

Tsai (1995), using an ordinary least squares (OLS) analysis, finds that there is a positive relationship between FDI and income inequality in the least developed countries (LDC); however, adding geographical dummies, he finds that the positive relationship may capture more differences in inequality between countries than the role of the FDI. In a recent paper, Basu and Guariglia (2004), using panel analysis both to estimate a fixed effect and a GMM first-difference model on the data of 199 countries, find that FDI induces growth, but also inequality. In terms of elasticity, they find that a 10 per cent rise in FDI increases the income inequality by 0.28 per cent.

Te Velde (2003, 21) confines the analysis on the impact of FDI on (wage) inequality to Latin America, claiming that even if 'the results are tentative and the regressions on annual time series need to be extended to other LA countries', FDI does not reduce income inequality. The effect of FDI on inequality strictly depends upon the initial conditions, the policies implemented and on the sectoral distribution of inflows. Using data from surveys for the period 1985–98, Milanovic (2002) studied the impact of globalization on relative income shares of low and high deciles. Defining globalization both as openness of the economy (using imports plus exports over GDP) and as FDI inflows (as share of GDP), he found that, at very low average income those with the highest income benefit from open trade. In countries with higher income levels the situation changes: the lowest and the middle class income increases more than the highest class. However, these results are not confirmed once FDI is taken into account, even when controlling for country-specific effects. Along the same lines, Ali (2003) uses the Gini coefficient to measure income inequality and the World Bank's measures of globalization – that is, the rate of increase of the trade intensity ratio, the stock of FDI as a percentage of GDP and the log of average annual number of immigrants to the United States – as explanatory variables. While the growth rate of trade and the annual immigrants to the United States are negatively correlated with income (or consumption) inequalities, FDI has a positive impact. However, even if FDI explains 15 per cent of the variation in inequality and the effect is statistically significant, its magnitude is small. A percentage point increase in the variable increases the Gini index by only 0.01 per cent.

In a recent paper, Benassy-Queré and Salins (2005) claim, on the basis of both panel regressions (on 11 countries) and cross-section (on 42 developing countries), that openness to FDI tends to favour the wealthiest quintile of the population to the expenses of the others. However, FDI tends to reduce income differences between rural and urban areas, since although jobs for more educated workers are concentrated in cities, recently immigrated workers send money home (to the countryside).

This (scant) literature fails to catch an important aspect – that is, the sectoral composition of FDI. If, indeed, foreign investments are addressed toward the labour-intensive manufacturing sector, the demand for unskilled workers and their wage rate is likely to increase (see Chapter 8 on Mauritius). On the contrary,

FDI inflows to capital-intensive manufacturing reduce demand for unskilled workers and hence their wage rate, as production requires a lot of capital relative to unskilled labour. Furthermore, as Cornia *et al.* (2003) point out, high volatility in commodity prices lowers incentives to invest in education and, as a consequence, worsens the long-term distribution of income. In addition, especially in the mining sector, FDI exacerbates inequalities as ownership of natural resources is concentrated in a few hands and the resulting rents are collected by the elites, whereas the distributive impact of FDI in the utilities sector depends upon the privatization process that has been carried out in the recipient countries. Indeed, such as in Latin America, the (often rising) prices of the services supplied by the privatized foreign-controlled companies and the employment impact on industrial restructuring did not contribute to reduce income inequalities.

Another important issue refers to the type of foreign investments: acquisition of domestic companies is expected to increase foreign exchange, but not the capital stock, employment and consumer welfare as greenfield FDI could do. To our knowledge, no empirical test addresses this issue.

Empirical evidence: data and trends

FDI in developed and developing countries: some stylized facts

In the last two decades foreign investments grew rapidly – from $55 billion in 1990 to almost $1.4 trillion in 2000 – and more countries as well as sectors have been involved in the internationalization process. However, FDI inflows experienced an abrupt halt in 2001, declining to $735 billion, less than half of the 2000 figure. In 2003, global inflows of foreign investments shrank for the third year in a row – to $560 billion – and an uneven pattern of regional trends emerged. While the worldwide downward trend was prompted by a plunge in FDI flows to developed countries, developing countries as a whole experienced a recovery. However, within this group the pattern was mixed; whereas FDI to Latin America and Central and Eastern Europe countries (CEEC) decreased, Africa and Asia benefited from an increase of foreign investments' inflows. Preliminary data for 2004 (see UNCTAD 2005) seem to confirm this trend, even though Latin America becomes attractive again and services – especially in tourism, telecommunications and information technology – continue to attract relatively more funds than manufacturing.

The shift of FDI towards services is the result of a process started in the 1990s, initially in developed countries and more recently, although to a lesser extent, in developing countries and economies in transition. This shift is in line with the growing importance of services in GDP and with the limited tradability of many services. Most services are non-storable and hence need to be produced when and where they are consumed. Furthermore, the only way of serving foreign markets is by setting up local operations through FDI or by using non-equity arrangements, such as licensing.[21] As a consequence, the world's inward stock of services FDI quadrupled between 1990 and 2002, from an estimated $950 billion to more than $4 trillion – based on a survey of 61 countries accounting for more than four-fifths of the world's stock of FDI, extrapolated to the world.

These developments point to a change in the channels by which capital inflows affect growth, poverty and income distribution in a developing economy. However, the net sum is unclear, since both positive and negative forces are at work. Services are in general less labour-intensive than manufacturing, have a different ratio of skilled to unskilled workers and tend to have higher rents. On the other hand, FDI could induce productivity gains to sectors where productivity was traditionally low and where the gap between developed and developing countries' efficiency levels is larger.

In order to better understand the channels through which foreign capital can impact economic growth, Table 6.1 provides an overview of the weight of different types of FDI relative to GDP.

Table 6.1 Average values of cross-border M&A sales and greenfield investments inflows (as a percentage of GDP)

Countries	1995–1997		1998–2000		2001–2003	
	M&A	Greenfield	M&A	Greenfield	M&A	Greenfield
Argentina	1.31	1.50	4.24	0.86	1.70	−0.73
Brazil	2.63	1.49	5.66	3.35	1.24	4.01
Bulgaria	0.08	0.01	4.46	0.08	0.97	0.34
Chile	0.67	1.01	5.31	0.87	3.34	0.31
Croatia	0.03	−0.01	2.22	0.16	3.12	0.29
Czech Republic	0.46	0.23	2.55	1.33	4.08	1.00
Estonia	0.01	0.07	1.50	0.11	0.61	0.21
France	5.02	3.87	3.62	5.56	1.39	10.89
Germany	4.04	−0.90	7.49	−3.42	2.00	−6.51
Hungary	0.52	0.14	1.25	0.49	1.98	0.71
Indonesia	0.22	0.35	0.55	−1.17	1.69	−1.52
Italy	1.32	1.59	1.48	−0.03	0.95	1.27
Republic of Korea	NA	0.87	NA	3.36	NA	0.36
Latvia	0.02	0.00	1.57	0.05	0.21	0.11
Lithuania	0.00	0.05	1.90	0.07	1.31	0.10
Malaysia	0.16	0.59	0.80	0.64	0.75	0.54
Mexico	1.30	3.06	0.67	4.41	1.34	3.49
Morocco	0.12	0.16	0.18	0.18	3.46	0.22
Poland	0.36	1.33	2.85	1.05	1.30	0.86
Romania	0.09	−0.04	1.07	−0.02	0.43	0.41
Slovakia	0.02	0.04	3.12	0.11	6.69	0.20
Slovenia	0.02	0.05	0.07	0.10	2.91	0.04
Spain	0.88	1.64	2.38	3.73	1.15	8.63
Thailand	0.13	0.13	1.66	0.21	0.35	0.70
Tunisia	NA	0.12	0.58	0.14	0.57	0.21
Turkey	0.09	0.25	0.05	0.31	0.35	0.41
United Kingdom	13.87	−5.02	18.96	−16.87	3.31	−7.49

Note:
NA = not available.

Source: Authors' analysis from UNCTAD data on FDI flows and cross-border M&A.

Data on M&A operations are from the United Nations Conference on Trade and Development's (UNCTAD) *World Investment Reports* for various years and, in line with Calderón *et al.* (2004), we construct greenfield FDI by subtracting cross-border M&A from FDI inflows. In developing economies, over time the M&A have substantially increased and now tend to prevail on greenfield investments. According to Calderón *et al.* (2004), much of this M&A increase is probably due to privatization of public assets (roughly one third).

To shed some light on the impact of FDI on growth and income inequalities, we need to take into account where the capital goes. Since disaggregated data are not readily available, we use a 'shortcut', drawing on the detailed online database provided for US FDI by the Bureau of Economic Analysis of the US Department of Commerce. Comparable data are not available for other home countries, and even though it cannot be ruled out that FDI from other countries can have different motivations and therefore a different impact on growth and inequality, it should be noted that the United States is one of the most important foreign investors and account for more than a quarter of worldwide outward FDI stocks (UNCTAD 2004).

Let us split up the value of US FDI (at historical cost basis) by industry, as in Tables 6.2 and 6.3, in 1995 and 2001 respectively.

Note that the system for classifying data on US affiliates by industry has changed between 1995 and 2001, making it sometimes difficult to compare data and calling for the exercise of particular caution.[22] In 1995, resource-seeking FDI in the 'petroleum' sector accounted for almost 50 per cent of total US foreign investments in

Table 6.2 Sectoral composition of US FDI in selected regions, 1995

	Total industries	Petroleum	Manufacturing	Wholesale trade	Depository institutions	Finance and insurance	Services	Other industries
DC[a]	211,884	15,712	84,275	17,796	8,795	63,850	11,544	9,911
(%)	7.42	39.77	8.04	4.15	30.13	5.45	4.68	
LA[b]	55,751	1,860	31,846	5,337	2,585	7,294	1,117	3,147
(%)	3.34	57.12	9.57	4.64	13.08	2.00	5.64	
Africa and Turkey[c]	6,990	3,317	1,724	382	357	692	217	302
(%)	47.45	24.66	5.46	5.11	9.90	3.10	4.32	
ASIA[d]	25,990	7,019	8,442	1,394	2,009	2,001	444	497
(%)	27.01	32.48	5.36	7.73	7.70	1.71	1.91	
CEEC[c]	5,136	557	1,925	100	NA	1,086	44	NA
(%)	10.85	37.48	1.95		21.14	0.86		

Notes:
NA = not available.
[a]France, Germany, Spain and the United Kingdom.
[b]Argentina, Brazil, Chile and Mexico.
[c]Given the lack of disaggregated data by country, the region as a whole is taken into account.
[d]Indonesia, Malaysia, the Republic of Korea and Thailand.
Source: Author's calculations based on Bureau of Economic Analysis, US Department of Commerce.

Table 6.3 Sectoral composition of US FDI in selected regions, 2001

	Total industries	Mining	Utilities	Manufacturing	Wholesale trade	Information	Depository institutions	Finance and insurance	Professional scientific and technical services	Other industries
DC[a]	382,808	8,345	7,474	95,731	29,685	12,878	22,404	58,769	14,694	130,554
(%)	2.18	1.95	25.01	7.75	3.36	5.85	15.35	3.84	34.10	
LA[b]	110,632	3891	5,124	35,887	5,748	3,264	4,648	12,686	1,056	12,578
(%)	3.52	4.63	32.44	5.20	2.95	4.20	11.47	0.95	11.37	
Africa and Turkey[c]	17,215	10,720	269	1,794	1,195	743	754	643	131	907
(%)	62.27	1.56	10.42	6.94	4.32	4.38	3.74	0.76	5.27	
Asia[d]	34,153	8,867	0	13,821	1,795	157	2,540	1,210	1,373	1,862
(%)	25.96	0.00	40.47	5.26	0.46	7.44	3.54	4.02	5.45	
CEEC[c]	16,945	3,737	512	5,847	502	603	2,010	897	195	2,641
(%)	22.05	3.02	34.51	2.96	3.56	11.86	5.29	1.15	15.59	

Note:
[a]France, Germany, Spain and the United Kingdom.
[b]Argentina, Brazil, Chile and Mexico.
[c]Given the lack of disaggregated data by country, the region as a whole is taken into account.
[d]Indonesia, Malaysia, the Republic of Korea and Thailand.

Source: Author's calculations based on Bureau of Economic Analysis, US Department of Commerce.

Africa and Turkey, but a lower proportion in developed countries.[23] This pattern is even clearer in 2001, when US FDI in the mining sector, a proxy of this type of FDI, accounted for more than 60 per cent in Africa and Turkey, compared to 2.2 per cent in developed countries. Mining is capital intensive and, given the high costs required to enter the market, is monopolized by large multinationals, whose foreign investments tend to be in economic enclaves with few linkages to the local product and labour markets. Rather than spurring economic growth of poor host countries, they tend to be rent seeking and might cause 'Dutch disease' effects.

In 1995, the structure of US FDI in the tertiary sectors also differed significantly between developed and developing countries. In the former, investments are mostly concentrated in finance and insurance – except for the CEEC, but in 2001, US FDI shows approximately the same weight among developed countries and some emerging economies. FDI in these sectors can have an important impact on both the efficiency and stability of the banking system through increased competition and access to global financial markets. Hence, if FDI in the sector provides an efficiency upgrading of the domestic credit market, the whole economy is likely to be positively affected.

Skill-intensive services – professional, scientific and technical services – cover 4 per cent of total US FDI to Asia, the highest relative contribution. Even excluding India, where recently trends of international de-localization of services have been detected, foreign investments go to Asia thanks to the endowment of human capital. What we expect is a positive correlation between FDI in these sectors and income inequalities: a higher demand of skilled workers triggered by foreign firms should determine an increasing gap between wages of skilled and unskilled workers.

US foreign investments in manufacturing are evenly distributed across all areas: they account for almost 60 per cent in Latin America and, in 1995, were widespread in all countries except in Africa and Turkey. However, in 2001 their weight dropped heavily in some regions (excluding Asia) and there was a surge of 'other industries', with such construction and transportation having a likely detrimental effect on domestic growth. Without an appropriate and stable regulatory system, foreign investors could have a superior market power causing a sort of, 'crowding-out' effect towards domestic firms. FDI to manufacturing sectors is likely to have a much larger effect on recipient economies, as the linkages to the host country are better defined; however, different peculiarities have to be taken into account.

US FDI in food products shrinks in all areas, while their share in chemicals and transport equipment – that is, medium-high technology industries, according to the Organization for Economic Co-operation and Development (OECD) classification based on technology – generally increases. On the one hand, a higher technological nature of industries such as chemicals is likely to increase the probability of technology transfer and know-how spillovers from foreign to domestic firms. On the other hand, the larger amount of physical and human capital used could spur income inequalities.

Effects of sectoral composition of FDI are presumably different across regions. During the time period considered, US foreign affiliates operating in electrical equipment weight heavily in Asia and in developed countries, while they play a marginal role in other areas. By contrast, in the CEEC foreign investments in (unskilled) labour intensive industries can be detected.[24]

An uneven pattern across regions also emerges regarding the distribution of 'other manufacturing' industries, which denotes prominently medium-low sectors.[25] In 1995, FDI in these sectors is substantial in all areas considered. However, while in most LDC economies they represent the bulk of foreign investments, in Asia and in developed countries they are less than US FDI in high- and medium-high-tech industries such as chemicals, machinery and electrical equipment. While in 1995 R&D activities were largely concentrated in developed countries and Latin America, in 2001 it seems that, probably also as a result of the economic crises in South America, they have been partially shifted to developed countries and Asia. In other regions, scarce R&D investments may have not contributed to the generation of technological spillovers, which have probably constrained growth in host economies. On the other hand, R&D expenditure, which is in general positively correlated with skilled workers, has prevented widening income inequalities. Furthermore, it is worth noting that, notwithstanding a decline in 2001, US foreign affiliates employ a larger share of workers in developing countries. Again, this can suggest that FDI tends to be more labour intensive in developing countries, and, as a consequence, more likely to increase the labour share and incomes of the bottom quintiles of population.

Income inequality and poverty: some stylized facts

Cornia *et al.* (2003) point out that within-country inequality rose during the 1980s and 1990s. Analysing 73 countries that account for 80 per cent of the world's population and 91 per cent of GDP, they show that after a general decline from the 1950s to the 1970s[26] income inequality started to rise again in 66 per cent of the countries analysed. In roughly two-thirds of the sample – that is, 59 per cent of world population and 71 per cent of world's GDP – the levels of inequality increased.

In particular, 40 per cent of countries with rising inequality show either a continuous or stable increase in inequality, whereas the remaining 60 per cent show a U-shaped trend. The turnaround started at a different point for each country: in the 1970s in Sri Lanka, Thailand and the early OECD liberalizers and from 1989 to 1992 in the transition economies. By contrast, there was a decline in inequality in only 12 per cent of the sample but, apart from France and some East Asian tigers (Malaysia, the Philippines and the Republic of Korea), these are small countries (the Bahamas, Honduras and Jamaica). Finally, in 22 per cent of the sample the trend is unclear.

In an attempt to explain this trend in income inequality, Cornia and Court (2001) claim that 'traditional causes' of inequality – that is, land concentration or urban bias – offer little help. Looking at changes in the world economic system, they detect 'new causes' – that is, capital account and trade liberalization – that are linked to liberalization policy carried out in the last three decades and to the development of structural programmes proposed by international organizations.

In Table 6.4, we report the inequality trend from the analysis by Cornia and Court (2001) for the 27 countries included in our sample. Roughly 70 per cent of the countries show a rising trend in inequality and, in particular, all economies in transition. Among the developing countries, however, only those from Southeast Asia show a constant or declining trend.

Inequality and growth are strictly correlated to poverty reduction. The debate on whether the poor benefit from economic growth is also relevant in this context as we claim that FDI affects growth and, hence, indirectly inequality and poverty. It is interesting to analyse how poverty reduction is affected by variation in both inequality and growth. Table 6.5 reports data on income inequality and poverty based on Ravallion (2001).

Table 6.4 Income inequality changes in sample (27) countries from the 1960s to the 1990s

Inequality	Developed countries	Developing countries	Transitional countries	Total
Rising	Italy, Slovenia,[a] Spain, United Kingdom, Germany	Argentina, Chile, Mexico, Morocco,[a] Thailand	Bulgaria, Croatia,[a] Czech Republic, Estonia, Hungary, Latvia, Lithuania, Poland, Romania, Slovakia	19
Constant		Brazil, Indonesia Turkey		4
Declining	France	Malaysia, Republic of Korea, Tunisia		4
All	6	11	10	27

Note:
[a] Croatia, Morocco and Slovenia were not included in Cornia *et al.* (2003).

Source: Cornia *et al.* (2003).

Table 6.5 Income inequalities and poverty

		Average household income per capita	
		Falling	Rising
Income inequality	Rising	(17% of cases) poverty rising at 14.3% per year	(30% of cases) poverty falling at 1.3% per year
	Falling	(26% of cases) poverty rising at 1.7% per year	(27% of cases) poverty falling at 9.6% per year

Source: Ravallion (2001).

According to Table 6.5, even if the impact of FDI on growth is positive, its effects on poverty depend upon income inequality. A rising level of income inequality reduces the effect that growth has on poverty: the proportion of the population living under the poverty line declines by just 1.3 per cent per year, despite a 9.6 per cent decline if growth is rising but inequality is decreasing. On the other hand, a decrease in inequality may reduce the impact on poverty during a recession: poverty rises by only 1.7 per cent if both growth and inequality decline. Otherwise, a growing inequality during a recession may push the median rate of increase of 14.3 per cent per year in the proportion of the population living under the poverty line. Poverty tends to be even more widespread because of falling average income per capita and worsening inequality.

Does FDI affect growth and income inequality? A sectoral analysis

The purpose of our empirical analysis is to understand the different impacts on growth and inequality of FDI in manufacturing, services and mining. In other words, we claim that there is a potential important impact of sectoral composition of foreign capital flows.

The analysis is carried out for the period 1990–2001 with a sample of 27 countries selected from developed, transitional and emerging countries. We have not included low- and medium-low-income countries, where institutional weakness is particularly pronounced and the misallocation of FDI could have an even more distorted effect on growth and distribution. We run panel data models with random effects and the estimation results are reported in Table 6.6.

In columns (1), (2) and (3), we control for the impact of foreign investments in manufacturing, services and mining sectors respectively. In order to address the issue of causality, we enter lagged (one period) FDI. Since the Hausman test does not allow us to reject the null that the difference of coefficients is not systematic, we only report results obtained with fixed effects, which are more consistent[27] than random effects in this case. From the results in column (1) we see that FDI in manufacturing has an overall positive and significant impact on the annual economic growth rate of the recipient countries. We expect this result since, as pointed out above, manufacturing investments by nature tend to create more backward and forward linkages in the local economy. However, the interaction variables denote that this effect is not the same for all geographical areas. Indeed, the interaction term is negative and so is the overall numerical value in developing countries, both CEEC and LDC in other regions. This could be due to the fact that in these countries foreign capital inflows could be characterized by higher volatility. Secondly, the effect is likely to depend on the specific industries within manufacturing. CEEC and other LDC receive less FDI in high-tech sectors, that is, in those industries that contribute mostly to host countries' economic growth given their R&D intensity.

The overall impact of services is higher than that of manufacturing, as shown in column (2). But also in this case, we find that the geographical distribution of FDI

Table 6.6 Estimation results of foreign investments in the manufacturing, services and mining sectors (dependent variable: growth)

Dep. Var: growth	(1)	(2)	(3)	(4)
Initial GDP per capital	−0.12[b]	−0.16[c]	−0.15[c]	−0.16[c]
	(0.05)	(0.04)	(0.05)	(0.04)
Credit development	0.15[c]	0.16[c]	0.17[c]	0.12[c]
	(0.04)	(0.03)	(0.04)	(0.03)
R&D	0.21	0.32[c]	0.23[b]	0.47[c]
	(0.13)	(0.10)	(0.11)	(0.10)
Schooling	0.42[c]	0.38[c]	0.43[c]	0.38[c]
	(0.04)	(0.03)	(0.03)	(0.03)
Institutional index	0.12	0.19[a]	0.08	0.14
	(0.11)	(0.09)	(0.11)	(0.09)
K	0.07	0.09[a]	0.10	0.04
	(0.06)	(0.05)	(0.06)	(0.05)
FDImanuflag1	3.03[a]	—	—	1.86
	(1.74)			(1.71)
(ceecs = = 1)*FDImanuflag1	−3.20[a]	—	—	−1.55
	(1.75)			(1.76)
(other ldc = = 1)*FDImanuflag1	−3.03[a]	—	—	−2.25
	(1.76)			(1.73)
ServicesFDIlag1	—	−4.27[c]	—	−3.49[b]
		(1.18)		(1.34)
(cees = = 1)*ServicesFDIlag1	—	−4.31[c]	—	−2.80[a]
		(1.18)		(1.40)
(other ldc = = 1)*ServicesFDIlag1	—	−3.33[b]		−2.78[a]
		(1.42)	(1.55)	
MiningFDIlag1	—	—	−1.34	−51.52[a]
			(6.44)	(29.63)
(cees = = 1)*MiningFDIlag1	—	—	−0.46	14.82
			(6.68)	(35.20)
(other ldc = = 1)*MiningFDIlag1	—	—	4.45	53.60[a]
			(6.54)	(29.64)
Constant	4.02[c]	3.30[c]	4.30[a]	22.61[b]
	(0.93)	(0.82)	(2.55)	(8.71)
Observations	74	76	75	64
R-squared (within)	0.81	0.86	0.85	0.93

Notes:
[a] significant at 10%
[b] significant at 5%
[c] significant at 1%

Description of variables:
Growth: (log of) annual GDP per capita growtwh rate (at 1995 prices).
FDI, sectoral: the main source is UNCTAD (2004) for different countries, except for Czech Republic, France, Hungary, Mexico, Poland and the Republic of Korea for which the OECD data was used for the FDI. The variables regarding the FDI in manufacturing, services and mining (lagged by one period) are ratios between the value of sectoral FDI inflows and the gross value added of each industry, data drawn from the World Bank's 2003 World Development Indicators.
Schooling: a (log of) school enrolment in tertiary education as a percentage of gross school enrolment, data drawn from the World Bank's 2003 World Development Indicators.
Credit development: (log of) domestic credit provided by the banking sector, as a percentage of GDP, data drawn from the World Bank's 2003 World Development Indicators.
R&D: (log of) R&D expenditure as percentage of GDP, data drawn from the World Bank's 2003 World Development Indicators.
Initial GDP per capita: (log of) one time lag of annual GDP per capita (at 1995 prices), data drawn from the World Bank's 2003 World Development Indicators.
K: (log of) Gross Fixed Capital Formation, data drawn from the World Bank's 2003 World Development Indicators.
Institutional variable: a composite index that ranks countries according to the institutional strength of the economy, data from www.icrgonline.com/.

matters. Again, it depends pretty much on what kind of services attracts the foreign capital. Particularly relevant has been the privatization of state-owned utilities in Latin America, Mediterranean countries and in the CEEC. At the very beginning of the privatization process foreign companies can benefit from a quasi-monopolistic power, which can have a detrimental effect on local economic growth. In addition, these economies have recently liberalized their FDI regimes in industries (services) previously closed to foreign entry, and a 'crowding-out' effect of domestic firms could prevail in this case. Finally, we expect the negative impact of FDI in mining especially in some developing countries, given their rent-seeking nature.

Other co-variates have the expected sign: R&D expenditure has a positive impact on local growth, as well as our index of human capital – that is, the share of people enrolled in tertiary education. Also, the development of financial markets – proxied by domestic credit provided by the banking sector – contributes, in accordance with the main conclusion of the theoretical and empirical literature.[28]

Instead, initial level of GDP per capita negatively affects economic growth. The same results have been achieved when FDI in all sectors are analysed together (Table 6.6, column 4).

We also run a panel analysis of the effect of sectoral FDI on inequality. Possibly due to the limited amount of data points available, the econometric evidence did not show a significant effect.

Conclusion

During the surge of capital flows in the 1990s, FDI was the main source of capital flows to developing countries. Contrary to other capital flows, FDI is less volatile and does not show a pro-cyclical behaviour. It has, therefore, become the 'favourite capital inflow' for developing countries.

In general, FDI is associated with increases in productivity and, therefore, growth. Furthermore, for developing countries, FDI is an important vehicle for technology transfer and a stimulus to innovate and enhance competitiveness. So, theoretically, FDI has a positive effect on the growth rate of countries even though, at the empirical level, the results are not always clear-cut. As for the impact on inequality, neither theory nor empirical analyses have clear-cut implications.

Our aim was to confront the literature by analysing the relationship between FDI, growth and income distribution in a sample including developed and developing countries. The contribution of this chapter is empirical. We use data over the last decade. Our data support the prevalence of new patterns, both in terms of increasing M&A in developing countries and in terms of a shift towards services to the expenses of manufacturing, which have had an important impact on growth and, especially, on distribution. M&A are less 'stable' than greenfield investments and lack the inner element of irreversibility. However, for some developing countries, domestic residents probably would not have had sufficient financial resources and/or management experience to operate large-scale firms, thus potential gains may have resulted from the foreign purchase of state-owned assets.

The sectoral analysis, though limited for lack of data, offers additional hints: results confirm that FDI in low-tech manufacturing and services transfers more effectively to growth than it does in energy or mining. This also supports the claim that the interaction term is significant and differs between areas.

Also, for the distributive impact of FDI, the division between greenfield investments and M&A is relevant. While greenfield investments, especially in low-tech manufacturing, stimulate growth via capital accumulation and demand induces an increase in wages of unskilled workers, M&A may have a perverse effect on wages and employment because multinationals may want to be more efficient and may lay off workers employed in previously owned domestic firms. The sectoral distribution is relevant, too, since manufacturing in developing countries tends to be highly labour intensive, while mining is highly capital intensive.

To sum up: most developing countries do not seem to have the appropriate 'domestic condition' to attract capital flows. However, some are rich in natural resources; if the hypothesis that FDI for mining does not stimulate much growth because of a low multiplier, is it worth doing something to attract foreign capital if, for instance, this allows the host country to avoid the balance-of payments constraint? Cannot the consequences be better than what we expect on the basis of our analysis? Does it make sense for a developing country to do something in order to attract FDI? And, if so, do the international rules allow doing something? Do all of the results depend on how efficiently resources are used? The answers to these questions are topics for further research.

Some policy recommendations can be sketched even at this stage:

- Since some developing countries are still characterized by heavy reliance on oil and gas, high population growth rates, the prominent role of the state, the low level of integration with the rest of the world and within the area, underdeveloped capital and financial markets, unstable institutions, and low rates of return on human capital, a viable option for them is to become an export platform for low- to medium-technology goods. More specifically, some measures could be implemented without major disruption and with possibly great results. As we mentioned, the 'business environment' can be changed, contrary to other FDI determinants. School- and firm-based training schemes aimed at reducing skilled supply bottlenecks, profit repatriation regimes for FDI and improvement of legal infrastructures and property rights regimes can be implemented and improve the likelihood of obtaining capital inflows.
- The reduction of trade barriers and opening of economies can stimulate capital inflows.
- A solid set of fundamentals is important.
- Especially for newcomers to capital markets, it is crucial to have credible institutions, well-developed financial markets as well as a stable macroeconomic framework.

Appendix 6.A Analysis of the literature

Table 6.A1 Short summary of the literature on FDI and growth

Authors	Sample	Period	Methodology	Impact on growth	Interaction between FDI and other factors
Alfaro et al. (2004)	Net FDI flows, different samples: 39/mixed, 41/ primarily DC, 49/ primarily LDC	1981–1997	Cross-country OLS and IV	FDI contributes to growth	Development of local financial markets is crucial for positive effects of FDI on growth
De Mello (1999)	Net FDI inflows from 16 OECD and 17 non-OECD	1970–1990	Stationarity and cointegration; dynamic panel	Not strong: if positive depends on country-specific factors	Impact tends to be lower in technological leaders and higher in laggards
Hermes and Lensink (2003)	WB data on FDI as % of GDP	Average of 1975–1995	Cross-country OLS	FDI contributes to growth	Result holds only if a threshold of human capital and financial market development is reached
Reisen and Soto (2001)	WB data on net FDI on 44 non-OECD	1986–1997	Dynamic panel data	Positive and significant	
Morrisey and Lensink (2001)	WB data on FDI/GDP, 115 countries	1975–1998	OLS and IV for cross-section; fixed effect panel using three 10-year periods	Robust and positive	Volatility of FDI has negative impact (can capture the political uncertainty
UNCTAD (2000)	UNCTAD data on FDI inflows for more than 100 LDC	1970–1995	Granger causation and OLS	Positive	Lagged FDI is significant only if interacted with schooling FDI is correlated with past trade
Nair-Reichert and Weinhold (2001)	WB data on net FDI inflows as % of GDP, 24 developing countries	1971–1995	First differenced instrumental panel and mixed effects model	Significant and positive	

Table 6.A2 Short summary of the literature on FDI and inequality

	Sample	Methodology	Interaction of FDI
Tsai (1995)	LDC	OLS	There is a positive relationship between FDI and inequality
Basu and Guariglia (2004)	119 developing countries	Panel analysis, fixed effect	FDI induces both growth and inequality
Benassy-Quéré and Salins (2005)	42 developing countries	Panel analysis and cross-section	FDI tends to favour the wealthiest quintile of the population, but reduces differences between rural and urban areas
te Velde (2003)	Latin American countries	OLS	FDI does not reduce income inequality; the effect of FDI on inequality strictly depends on the initial conditions, the policies implemented and on the sectoral distribution of inflows
Milanovic (2002)	88 countries	Pooled cross-section	The effect of FDI on inequality is not statistically significant
Ali (2003)	7 Arab countries	OLS	FDI has a positive impact on inequality

Notes

1. According to Oxfam (2002, 7), 'capital flows have been useful in some cases and harmful in others, depending on an array of factors including national development strategies, the strength of the domestic private sector, and the type of capital flows'. Conversely, Giovannetti et al. (1993), using a theoretical model and correlation analysis, claim that capital inflows could lose financial constraints and have a positive effect on the growth of developing countries.
2. From the definition in Eurostat, Statistics in Focus, theme 2, December 2004.
3. According to Oxfam in 2002, it is the volatility of portfolio flows that transmits instability through the economy and has a detrimental effect on growth.
4. Our sample includes Argentina, Brazil, Bulgaria, Chile, Croatia, Czech Republic, Estonia, France, Germany, Hungary, Indonesia, Italy, Latvia, Lithuania, Malaysia, Mexico, Morocco, Poland, the Republic of Korea, Romania, Slovakia, Slovenia, Spain, Thailand, Tunisia, Turkey and the United Kingdom.
5. There is some evidence of a positive link for developed countries, but the evidence on the size of the specific benefits for developing countries is mixed and limited to countries that have attracted large amounts of capital relative to their size. The effect of the FDI on economic growth is only supported for LDC in the aggregate data. Hence, the pooling of countries carried out in most studies biases the results.
6. For instance, Feenstra and Hanson (1995) in a seminal paper on outsourcing – the transfer of production from developed to developing countries – suggest that the wage gap between skilled and unskilled workers increases, pointing to an increase of inequality, which contrast with the standard Heckscher–Ohlin prediction that the price of the abundant factor increases – unskilled labour in developing countries – with a decrease of inequality.

7. See OECD (2001) for a recent and exhaustive survey of the FDI in developing countries.
8. Note that the recent shift to the M&A may change this perspective, since the M&A is not a part of long-term industrial strategies and are not illiquid, and hence are more similar to portfolio flows.
9. The correlation between various measures of foreign trade and FDI flows and positions is significantly positive (Nicoletti and Scarpetta 2003).
10. Foreign commercial presence tends to increase bilateral trade in transport services (for example, supplying goods to foreign affiliates in the distribution sector), communications (for example, data transactions with foreign affiliates in the financial, telecommunications or tourism sectors), and the like.
11. The issue here is fairly complex and deals with different aspects. Mody (2004) claims that investment treaties – bilateral and multilateral under the World Trade Organization – are a way to supplement or substitute weak domestic institutions. There is, however, no unanimous empirical support for this claim. For instance, Hallward-Driemeier (2003) claims that bilateral investment treaties have no influence on increasing FDI flows between the signatory parties and that they are not substitutes for domestic laws protecting property rights.
12. Indirect expropriation could be due to levying high unexpected profit taxes, ex post imposition of capital restrictions and devaluation of local currency. In the empirical literature stability tends to be linked to democracy, but empirically in developing countries this may not be the case.
13. Some empirical studies (see, for example, Mauro 1995) have confirmed that corruption adversely affects economic growth. However, the evidence of the effect of corruption on the FDI is somewhat inconclusive: Heinsz (2000) finds a positive correlation, whereas Wheeler and Mody (1992) fail to find a negative relationship. Furthermore, according to Smarzynska and Wei (2000), corruption affects the ownership structure of foreign investments – joint ventures versus subsidiaries wholly owned by foreign firms.
14. While it is true that part of FDI to LDCs is motivated by cheap labour and a reduction in production costs, some firms producing differentiated goods look for quality labour. The empirical evidence on the effect of wage costs is somehow mixed, while there is some evidence of a positive effect of education on the FDI.
15. There is research dealing with this issue emphasizing different mechanisms – for instance, see Rossi and Volpin (2003) and Dyck and Zingales (2004).
16. While in exogenous growth models the FDI induces growth, in an endogenous theoretical framework the FDI stimulates growth. However, it also goes to fast-growing countries and the direction of causation is difficult to detect.
17. Interestingly enough, the empirical support for this claim seems significantly stronger for the period ending in 1995 (see Murshid and Mody 2005). The marginal impact of the FDI flows declined in the second part of the 1990s, possibly due to the increase of the M&A with respect to greenfield investments.
18. The FDI contributes to increased tax revenues in host countries – again, a sensitive issue in developing countries where the tax base is in general lower than in industrial countries.
19. Appendix 6.A, Table 6.A1 summarizes the results of this review with no attempt at being exhaustive given the huge number of studies.
20. Wheeler and Mody (1992) have tried to determine the relative importance of these two explanatory variables and found that market size is more important for developed countries, while per capita GDP is more important for developing countries.
21. This may change as more services and service components become tradable via computer communication links but, so far, these services account for only a small part of the services sector.
22. For instance, the 'information sector' recorded in 2001 includes industry groups formerly included either in the manufacturing industry or in the services sector. Specifically, the information sector includes publishing, which was included in 'other manufacturing', 'motion picture and sound recording industry' and 'information and

data processing services', which were included in services, and 'broadcasting and communications', which was included in the transports, communication and public utilities division.
23 Note that in the tables 'DC' denotes those developed countries in our sample: France, Germany, Italy, Spain and the United Kingdom; and 'ASIA' comprises Indonesia, Malaysia, the Republic of Korea and Thailand; 'LA' considers Argentina, Brazil, Chile and Mexico. Due to the lack of country data, the labels 'Africa and Turkey' and 'CEEC' denote the entire groups of countries in those geographical areas.
24 In our analysis we have identified a residual category labelled 'other manufacturing and electric equipment'. However, we believe that, according to the pattern of specialization displayed by these countries, the bulk of foreign investments is in textile and clothing (included in 'other manufacturing' industries).
25 Tobacco, textile and leather products, furniture, pulp and paper products, printing and publishing, rubber, glass and non-metallic mineral products.
26 Exceptions can be found in sub-Saharan countries and Latin America.
27 Estimation results with random effects are available from the authors upon request.
28 See, for instance, Alfaro *et al.* (2004).

References

L. Alfaro, A. Chanda, S. Kalemli-Ozcan and S. Sayek. 2004. 'FDI and Economic Growth: The Role of Local Financial Markets'. *Journal of International Economics*, 64(1), 89–112.
Ali, A.G. 2003. *Globalization and Inequality in the Arab Region*, Working Paper No. 0307. Kuwait: Arab Planning Institute, Information Center.
Basu, P. and A. Guariglia. 2004. *FDI, Inequality and Growth*, Working Paper No. 04/01. Durham, UK: Economics and Finance, University of Durham.
Benassy-Queré, A. and V. Salins. 2005. *Impact de l'ouverture Financière sur les Inégalités internes dans les Pays Emergents*. Working Paper No. 11/05, Centre d'études prospectives et d'informations internationales, Paris, July.
Berman, E. and S. Machin. 2000. *Skilled-Biased Technology Transfer: Evidence of Factor-Biased Technological Change in Developing Countries*. Mimeo, Department of Economics, Boston University.
Blomström, M. and A. Kokko. 1998. 'Multinational Corporations and Spillovers'. *Journal of Economic Surveys*, 12(3), 247–77.
Blomström, M. and H. Persson. 1983. 'Foreign Investment and Spillover Efficiency in an Underdeveloped Economy: Evidence from the Mexican Manufacturing Industry'. *World Development*, 11(6), 493–502.
Calderón, C., N. Loayza and L. Servén. 2004. *Greenfield and Foreign Direct Investment and Mergers and Acquisitions: Feedback and Macroeconomic Effects*, Policy Research Working Paper No. 3192. Washington, DC: World Bank.
Caves, R.E. 1996. *Multinational Enterprise and Economic Analysis*, 2nd edition. Cambridge: Cambridge University Press.
Cornia, G.A. 2004. 'Trade Liberalization, Foreign Direct Investment and Income Inequality'. In E. Lee and M. Vivarelli (eds), *Understanding Globalization, Employment and Poverty Reduction*. Basingstoke: Palgrave Macmillan.
Cornia, G.A., T. Addison and K. Sampsa. 2003. *Income Distribution Changes and their Impact in the Post-World War II Period*. Discussion Paper No. 2003/28. Helsinki: UNU/ WIDER.
Cornia, G.A. and J. Court. 2001. *Inequality, Growth and Poverty in the Era of Liberalization and Globalization*, Policy Brief No. 4. Helsinki: UNU/WIDER.
De Mello, L.R. 1999. 'Foreign Direct Investment-Led Growth. Evidence from Time Series and Panel Data'. *Oxford Economic Papers*, 51, 133–51.
Dollar, D. and A. Kraay. 2002. 'Growth is Good for the Poor'. *Journal of Economic Growth*, 7(3), 195–225.

Dyck, A. and L. Zingales. 2004. 'Private Benefits of Control: An International Comparison'. *Journal of Finance*, 59, 537–601.
Feenstra, R. and G.H. Hanson. 1995. 'Foreign Direct Investment and Relative Wages: Evidence From Mexico's Maquiladoras'. *Journal of International Economics*, 42, 371–93.
Giovannetti, G., A. Marcet and R. Marimon. 1993. 'Growth, Capital Flows and Enforcement Constraints'. *European Economic Review*, 37, 418–25.
Globerman, S. 1979. 'Foreign Direct Investment and Spillover Efficiency Benefits in Canadian Manufacturing Industries'. *Canadian Journal of Economics*, 12(1), 42–56.
Haddad, M. and A. Harrison. 1993. 'Are There Positive Spillovers From Direct Foreign Investment? Evidence from Panel Data for Morocco'. *Journal of Development Economics*, 42, 51–74.
Hallward-Driemeier, M. 2003. *Do Bilateral Investment Treaties Attract Foreign Direct Investment? Only a Bit ... and They Could Bite*, Policy Research Working Paper No. 3121. Washington, DC: World Bank.
Hermes, N. and R. Lensink. 2003. 'FDI, Financial Development And Economic Growth'. *The Journal of Development Studies*, 40(1), 142–63.
Heinsz, W. 2000. 'The Institutional Environment for Multinational Investment'. *Journal of Law and Economics and Organization*, 16, 334–64.
Loungani, P. and A. Razin. 2001. 'How Beneficial is FDI for Developing Countries?' *Finance and Development*, 38(2), 231–49.
Markusen, J.R. 2002. *Multinational Firms and the Theory of International Trade*. Cambridge, MA: MIT Press.
Mauro, P. 1995. 'Corruption and Growth'. *Quarterly Journal of Economics*, 110, 681–712.
Milanovic, B. 2002. *Can We Discern the Effect of Globalisation on Income Distribution?*, Policy Research Working Paper No. 2876. Washington DC: World Bank.
Mody, A. 2004. 'Is FDI Integrating the World Economy?' *The World Economy*, 27(8), 1195–1222.
Morrisey, O. and R. Lensink. 2001. *Foreign Direct Investment: Flows, Volatility and the Impact on Growth in Developing Countries*. CREDIT Research Paper No. 01/06, School of Economics, University of Nottingham.
Murshid, A.P. and A. Mody. 2005. 'Growing up with Capital Flows'. *Journal of International Economics*, 65(1), 249–66.
Nair-Reichert, U. and D. Weinhold. 2001. 'Causality Tests For Cross Country Panels: New Look at FDI and Economic Growth in Developing Countries'. *Oxford Bulletin of Economics and Statistics*, 2, 153–72.
Nicoletti, G. and S. Scarpetta. 2003. 'Regulation, Productivity and Growth: OECD Evidence'. *Economic Policy*, 18(36), 9–72.
Organization for Economic Co-operation and Development (OECD). 2001. *Foreign Direct Investment for Development: Maximizing Benefits, Minimising Costs*. Paris: OECD.
Oxfam. 2002. *Global Finance Hurts the Poor: Analysis of the Impact of North–South Private Capital Flows on Growth, Inequality and Poverty*, Oxfam America Report. Oxford: Oxfam.
Ravallion, M. 2001. 'Growth, Inequality and Poverty: Looking Beyond Averages'. *World Development*, 29(11), 1803–15.
Reisen, H. and M. Soto. 2001. 'Which Types of Capital Inflows Foster Developing Countries?'. *Journal of International Finance*, 4(1), 1–14.
Rossi, S. and P. Volpin. 2003. *Cross-Country Determinants of Mergers and Acquisitions*, Working Paper No. 3889. London: Centre for Economic Policy Research.
Smarzynska, B. and S. Wei. 2000. *Corruption and Composition of Foreign Direct Investment: Firm-level Evidence*, Working Paper No. 7969. Cambridge, MA: National Bureau of Economic Research.
te Velde, W.D. 2003. *Foreign Direct Investment and Income Inequality in Latin America*, Mimeo. London: Overseas Development Institute.
Tsai, P.L. 1995. 'Foreign Direct Investment and Income Inequality: Further Evidence'. *World Development*, 23(3), 469–83.

United Nations Conference on Trade and Development (UNCTAD). 2000. *The Competitiveness Challenge: Transnational Corporations and Industrial Restructuring in Developing Countries*. Geneva and New York: UNCTAD.

United Nations Conference on Trade and Development (UNCTAD). 2004. *World Investment Report*. Geneva and New York: UNCTAD.

United Nations Conference on Trade and Development (UNCTAD). 2005. *World Investment Report*. Geneva and New York: UNCTAD.

Wheeler, D. and A. Mody. 1992. 'International Investment Location Decisions: The Case of US Firms'. *Journal of International Economics*, 33, 57–76.

Zhang, J. 1999. 'How Does FDI Interact with Economic Growth in a Large Developing Country? The Case of China'. *Economic Systems*, 21(4), 291–303.

7
Safety Nets for the Poor: A Missing International Dimension?

Sanjay G. Reddy[1]

The problem

Considerable attention has been given to the appropriate extent and form of safety nets for the poor in developing countries (see Chapter 3 of this volume). However, the literature on this subject has focused almost exclusively on domestic institutional arrangements which may protect the poor from adverse shocks. A question that has received insufficient consideration is whether international institutions and instruments can play a useful role in helping poor countries (and poor persons in poor countries) cope better with the shocks that they experience. That is the question addressed in this chapter.

We should distinguish the origination (national or international) of the shocks faced by poor people in poor countries from the appropriate level of remediation (national or international) for these shocks. For example, some shocks may be largely national in origin, but it might be quite appropriate to create insurance arrangements which ensure that their impact is spread across countries. Conversely, some shocks may be significantly international in origin, but the appropriate response to these shocks may be to design national institutions that can cope well with them and defuse their effects. The question explored below is whether there are shocks (whether or not international in origin) whose appropriate level of remediation is at least in part international and, if so, what form the arrangements governing such remediation should take.

Why poor countries and poor people in poor countries may experience more shocks and suffer more from the shocks that they experience

There is an extensive and burgeoning literature on the volatility of incomes of poor countries and on the volatility of incomes of low-income people within these countries. Inter alia, this literature establishes that the incomes of poor countries, and of poor people in poor countries are both volatile.[2]

The literature emphasizes that aggregate incomes of poor countries are volatile for a variety of reasons. One of the most important of these is the fact that a large number of these countries rely substantially for their export earnings on sales of a very small number of primary commodities, the world prices of which market are quite unstable.[3] The substantial dependence of many poor countries on agriculture (and especially of rain-fed agriculture) is another reason for volatility in aggregate incomes, since changes in natural conditions can have a large impact on agricultural incomes from year to year. Fluctuations in exchange rates, to which poor countries are especially prone because of their limited capacity to intervene in financial markets and their weak monetary and fiscal institutions, can also give rise to large fluctuations in national income (see Chapter 4). Unstable world interest rates may also substantially influence countries' real income, especially if they are highly indebted and must refinance debts at current interest rates. Unreliable external assistance is another possible reason for fluctuations in national income and in government expenditures. There is also evidence that very low income countries are more likely to suffer from natural disasters.[4] Another reason that poor countries have high volatility of aggregate income is that their production may not be very sectorally diversified. An economy with a small number of sectors of production, each of which employs a small number of inputs, is likely to be one in which aggregate incomes are greatly sensitive to variation in costs of individual factors of production, prices of individual outputs and production conditions. Large countries (in particular, continental-sized countries such as India, China and Brazil) may be able to insure themselves against the effects of shocks as many shocks that they experience are likely to have an impact that is sub-national rather than national. This option may not be available to smaller countries.

Fluctuations in aggregate incomes are likely to be experienced differently by different groups within a poor country. Who bears the brunt of adverse shocks depends upon specific circumstances and is difficult to characterize in general. However, in many countries poor persons are more likely to be exposed to aggregate fluctuations because of their heavy dependence on a single source of income (very often related to agriculture) and their inability to protect themselves from aggregate fluctuations, due to insurance mechanisms that are either inadequate or entirely absent. Such protection may be costly and therefore unavailable to the poor. In countries in which the price of necessities is greatly influenced by world prices, the cost of living of the poor may be greatly influenced by (fluctuating) world prices.[5] The poor may also rely on government services. As a result, they may be harmed by decreases in government expenditure that follow adverse aggregate shocks.[6]

There are a number of reasons why adverse shocks may have more long-lasting deleterious effects in poor countries than in rich ones. One of the most important reasons for this is that the very survival of individuals may be jeopardized by adverse shocks. Adverse shocks may severely decrease the ability of persons to survive. There is empirical evidence that adverse shocks have an impact on survival even in rich countries.[7] The relationship between resources and survival is sometimes summarized by a 'survival function' which describes the probability of survival

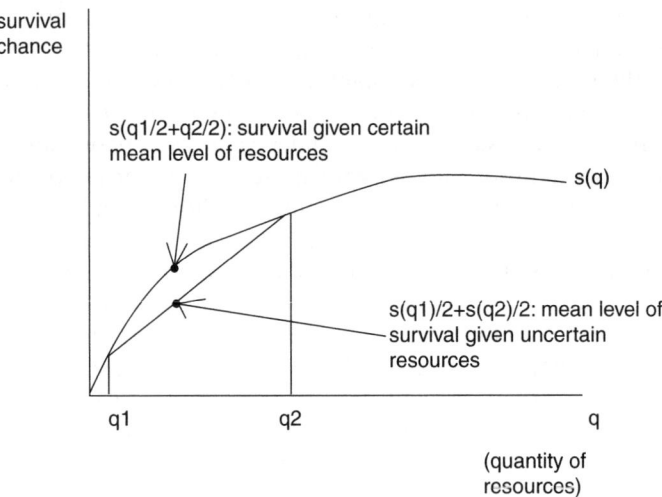

Figure 7.1 Effect of uncertain access to resources on survival

given a specific level of consumption of resources. It is frequently assumed that the incremental impact of additional resources consumed on survival is greater when a person is poorer, in which case the survival function is concave. In this case, greater variability in consumption will be associated with decreased survival (see Figure 7.1).[8]

More generally, asset holdings, health, nutrition and schooling can be harmed by adverse shocks, which may have effects that are long lasting and difficult to reverse. Damaging hysteresis effects of this kind can help to cement poverty traps. Long-lasting 'dynastic effects' can arise which, in the absence of further intervention, may last over long periods and perhaps even generations.[9]

Adequacy and risk

The premise of this chapter is that it is morally desirable that individuals attain a minimally adequate level of 'advantage' as assessed in *some* space. The space in which advantage is assessed can be defined in various ways (for example, in terms of money, an index of command over resources or 'primary goods', utility or capabilities) so as to reflect the normative priorities and practical judgments of an evaluator. Once the focal space is specified, the level of advantage deemed minimally adequate in this space must also be specified. We choose to refer to advantage and the minimally adequate level of advantage rather than to any specific conception of advantage or minimally adequate level thereof in order to develop a very general framework.

We suppose that objective to be pursued is adequacy of individual advantage. This objective can give rise to a *derivative* concern about volatility: even where a minimally adequate level is *often* achieved, due to volatility the minimally adequate level may *sometimes* fail to be achieved. A person whose level of advantage is below the minimally adequate level will be referred to as poor, and a person whose level of advantage is not presently below the minimally adequate level but whose level of advantage could come to be below the minimally adequate level due to adverse shocks will be referred to as potentially poor.

Let us explore the problem in a more formal framework. Consider the following simple model. Assume that there is a well-defined metric of individual advantage, and that the level of attainment of individual advantage can be indicated by a real number. $a \in R$. Now, suppose that each individual, i, has a level of advantage at a moment in time, t, described by a stochastic process (possibly differing from individual to individual) which possesses the following form:

$$a_t = a_t + \varepsilon_t \qquad (7.1)$$

where $a_t \in R$, and ε_t is a random variable with mean zero. An interpretation of ε_t is that it describes the shocks experienced around a baseline level of advantage a_t. We may refer to (7.1) as the advantage generation process. This formulation is rather general in that both ε_t and a_t are permitted to vary with time and perhaps also to be influenced by prior history. Now, represent the level of advantage deemed minimally adequate for an individual by z. In that case, we are concerned with whether the following inequality (let us call it the adequacy condition) is satisfied:

$$a_t \geq z \qquad (7.2)$$

We may consider different ways of modifying (7.1). For example, we may consider:

$$a_t = a'_t + \varepsilon'_t + \tau_t \qquad (7.3)$$

where $a'_t = a_t + \Delta a_t$, $\varepsilon'_t = \varepsilon_t + \Delta \varepsilon_t$ is a random variable with mean zero, and τ_t a non-trivial (i.e., non-constant) deterministic function of ε_t with mean zero over possible states of the world (i.e. $\int_{-\infty}^{\infty} \tau_t(\varepsilon'_t) d\varepsilon'_t = 0$) and the property that $\tau_t(\varepsilon'_t) \leq 0$ when $\varepsilon'_t \geq 0$ and $\tau_t(\varepsilon'_t) \geq 0$ when $\varepsilon'_t \leq 0$ (i.e. $\tau_t(\varepsilon'_t)\varepsilon'_t \leq 0$).

We may distinguish different means of changing the advantage generation process (7.1). A 'risk modification mechanism' is any action taken before time period t which causes the replacement of ε_t (in (7.1)) by $\varepsilon'_t = \varepsilon_t + \Delta \varepsilon_t$ (as in (7.3)). An 'insurance mechanism' is a function $\tau_t(\varepsilon_t)$, which provides compensatory transfers that increase the level of advantage experienced in some states of the world in which adverse shocks (i.e. negative realizations of ε_t) have arisen and requires the payment of 'premiums' which diminish the level of advantage experienced in some other states of the world in which positive shocks (i.e. positive realizations of ε_t) have arisen. Insurance mechanisms compensate for the occurrence of adverse shocks but do not directly diminish them. A 'baseline modification mechanism' is any action taken before time t which causes the replacement of a_t (in (3.1)) by $a'_t = a_t + \Delta a_t$ (as in (7.3)).

An unconditional social transfer (in which resources transferred to an individual are independent of the realization of ε_t) is an example of a baseline modification mechanism. Economic growth (which influences individual private income and thereby changes a_t) is another example of a baseline modification mechanism. Many actions that we may find of interest in practice may fall into more than one of these categories.

Consider equation (7.1) more closely. Since ε_t is a random variable there are three possibilities:

1. The adequacy condition is always satisfied.
2. The adequacy condition is never satisfied.
3. There are some states of the world in which the adequacy condition is satisfied and some states of the world in which it is not.

Now, in the first case, we have no reason for concern, at least if our sole objective is to achieve minimal adequacy. In the second case, we have great reason for concern. Since by definition τ_t and ε_t have mean zero, no risk modification or insurance mechanism (or combination of such mechanisms) can ensure that the adequacy condition is always satisfied, although they may ensure that the adequacy condition is sometimes satisfied (at the cost of ensuring that shortfalls from adequacy are even more severe than they would otherwise be at other times). Furthermore, if we treat each additional unit of shortfall from adequacy as being increasingly disvaluable, then risk modification and insurance mechanisms which ensure that the adequacy condition is sometimes satisfied will be undesirable ex ante since they will have the effect of causing shortfalls from adequacy for the corresponding increases in other states of the world. Therefore, only a baseline modification mechanism offers a potentially desirable approach to ensuring that the adequacy condition is attained in at least some states of the world. When the adequacy condition is never satisfied, it is appropriate to think of shortfalls from minimal adequacy as arising from endemic structural causes such as poverty (expressed by a_t) rather than from adverse shocks or vulnerabilities (as expressed by ε_t). For that reason, although it is of great practical importance, this case will not be studied further in this chapter.

The third case is that which is of interest to us in this chapter. In this case, both risk modification or insurance mechanisms and baseline modification mechanisms can influence how often the adequacy condition is met, and if it is not met, then to what extent it fails to be met. It is obvious that policies that raise a_t and those that decrease the net effect ($\varepsilon'_t + \tau_t$) on individual advantage of negative shocks can each increase the frequency with which the adequacy condition is met, and diminish the extent of shortfalls from the adequacy condition when such shortfalls arise.

Our premise is that it is desired to identify institutional arrangements and policies (i.e. baseline modification mechanisms, risk modification mechanisms, and insurance mechanisms) that will enable as many persons as possible to attain the adequacy condition (7.2) as frequently as possible, given that the process initially underlying the determination of individual advantage is described by the advantage generation process (7.1). We ignore other objectives here in order to simplify the choice problem, although these will, of course, have to be considered in public policy analysis more generally. In order to identify 'optimal' institutions and policies, it will be necessary to employ evaluative judgements with which to determine how good or bad are alternative states of the world as well as how good or bad are actions that influence the likelihoods of these alternative states of the world arising. There are many plausible ways of forming such evaluative judgements and associated aggregation structures, each of which may induce distinct conclusions concerning optimal policies. For purposes of exposition, we may consider a simple example of the optimal policy choice problem. Let the shortfall of each person, i, from minimum adequacy, z, in discrete time period t be represented by $s_{it} = (z - a'_{it} + \varepsilon'_{it} + \tau_{it})$. We assume z to be the same across all individuals and time periods for expositional simplicity. Each individual's shortfall from minimum adequacy in a given time period is an element in a matrix, S, of the shortfalls experienced by all individuals in all time periods during the planning horizon. The values of the matrix, S, depend on the realizations of the random variable ε'_{it}. If we define Ω as the matrix consisting of elements ε'_{it} then we may express this dependence in the form $S = S(\Omega)$. A particular choice of policies affects both Ω and the effect of Ω on S.

We may define, on the basis of appropriate evaluative judgements, some aggregate over all persons (for example $\varphi_t = \sum_{i=1}^{n} s_{it}^{\alpha}$ where $\alpha \in R$ is a measure of aversion to increased shortfalls) of the shortfalls experienced in each time period. In effect, this is a means of aggregating the information in a given column of S. We may define further, on the basis of appropriate evaluative judgements, an aggregate over time periods of the aggregate shortfalls experienced in each timeperiod (for example, $\Phi = \sum_{t=1}^{m} \varphi_t$, where it is assumed that the planning horizon consists of m time periods and no discounting is applied). In effect, Φ is a means of aggregating all of the information contained in each possible realization of the matrix S and assigning a disvaluation to this realization. Since there is uncertainty about the value of S, the choice of optimal policies must reflect an approach to decision-making under uncertainty. Specifically, such an approach must recognize that each combination of policies influences the possible states of the world, their associated likelihoods and the individual shortfalls experienced in each state of the world. The value attached to a specific combination of policies derives from aggregating the valuations associated with the alternative states of the world that can arise as a result of these policies, given the associated likelihoods of each of these states arising under this combination of policies. There are plausible means of undertaking such aggregation. One possible, and well-known, means of undertaking such aggregation is the expectation operator. Without further effort at justification, we adopt it here so as to provide an example of the steps involved in defining fully the problem of optimal policy selection. Let A, N and T respectively represent the set of feasible baseline modification, risk reduction and insurance policies. Then, the problem of optimal policy selection is:

min $E(\Phi)$ subject to $a'_{it} \in A$, $\varepsilon'_{it} \in N$ and $\tau_{it} \in T$

More generally, one may wish also to impose the constraint that the cost, c, of implementing a combination of policies is less than some maximum (e.g., $c(a'_{it}, \varepsilon'_{it}, \tau'_{it}) \leq \bar{c}$, where $c(a'_{it}, \varepsilon'_{it}, \tau'_{it})$ is a cost function representing the cost of implementing a specific combination of policies). Under suitable technical assumptions this problem is well defined and possesses a solution.

A typology of policy options and their international dimensions

In the framework of analysis introduced above, it is clear that public policies to protect poor or potentially poor people from the impact of adverse shocks can take three forms: those that increase the baseline level of advantage (which can be modelled by the effect of the policies on a_t), those that diminish the occurrence of adverse risks (as modelled by the effect of the policies on ε_t), and those that diminish the ultimate disadvantages experienced as a result of the occurrence of adverse outcomes (which can be modelled by the effect of the policies on τ_t). We have referred to these policies respectively under the headings of development, risk reduction, and insurance. A specific policy option may, of course, fall into more than one of these categories.

Let us characterize each of these approaches in general terms, and attempt specifically to understand the role of *international* policies of each of these kinds in influencing the exposure of persons to disadvantage.

Development policies

Development policies increase the baseline level of advantage of individuals (modelled as an increase in a_t). Development is by itself a means of protecting poor or potentially poor people from the impact of adverse shocks, as it diminishes the likelihood that adverse shocks will cause their level of advantage to fall beneath a given threshold of adequacy. National and international policies which promote development are therefore valuable not only in raising absolute levels of advantage, but also in reducing vulnerability to the occurrence of serious disadvantages. If the source of potential adverse shocks that may be experienced by the poor or potentially poor is international, and if these adverse shocks cannot directly be diminished, then a moral as well as practical case for international assistance to promote development may arise: Steps to enhance the baseline level of advantage of poor or potentially poor people help to protect them from shocks of international origin.

Risk reduction policies

Risk reduction policies diminish the occurrence of adverse risks (modelled by an effect on ε_t). Actions on the part of countries which influence the extent to which adverse risks are created or transmitted to poor countries (and poor people within them) qualify as risk-reducing. For example, policies which stabilize the world prices of essential commodities consumed by poor people or of the commodities exported by poor countries, policies which stabilize interest and exchange rates and more generally which stabilize world financial markets, and policies which diminish climatological and other environmental risks may all be classified as risk-reducing. Fluctuations in interest rates and other key features of the world market economy have in the past adversely affected developing countries (and, in particular, the poor within them). The developing world debt crisis of the early 1980s, triggered by sharp increases in world interest rates, is one example. The international origins of these risks may gave rise to a moral as well as practical case for international policies aimed at risk reduction.

Insurance policies

Insurance policies diminish the disadvantages experienced as a result of the occurrence of adverse outcomes (modelled by an effect on τ_t). We will consider three types of insurance policies by way of example. Each has been widely discussed in the literature: self-insurance through stabilization and reserve funds, mutual insurance through formal insurance contracts or risk-sharing institutional arrangements, and insurance equivalence through the use of market-based instruments. In principle, these can each be implemented through contractual or institutional arrangements at sub-national, national, or international levels.

Insurance mechanisms can take diverse forms which should be separately considered. We focus especially on measures to reduce aggregate income fluctuations, recognizing that the level of advantage of individual poor persons is likely to be influenced by such aggregate fluctuations but also by independent factors.

(i) Self-insurance through stabilization and reserve funds

This approach to insurance has a lengthy history in both developing and in developed countries. In particular, many natural resource exporting countries have established 'rainy day' funds as a means of providing self-insurance (see Chapter 10 on Chile). There are at least four obstacles to such self-insurance by countries. First, a supposition of self-insurance is that the rainy day comes late and not early. Without this supposition being satisfied, it may not be possible to accumulate adequate self-insurance funds. Countries that have access to credit may in principle be able to borrow against a future reserve fund. However, countries may be constrained from additional borrowing due to a variety of reasons. In the presence of credit constraints, the initial 'seeding' of a self-insurance fund through international assistance, which would be augmented by subsequent payments into the fund of 'insurance premia', could be one mechanism through which poor countries could begin self-insurance.

Secondly, for self-insurance funds both to be protected from risks and to be readily available for use they may have to be kept in a fairly safe and liquid form, as a result of which these funds may be unavailable for investment in domestic productive opportunities. These funds may therefore be viewed as 'sterile'. Self-insurance can only provide fully for potential losses if it diverts substantial resources from present productive investment and consumption. Diversion of resources from other present needs to a large extent is likely to be sub-optimal.[10] This is an important reason why self-insurance may be unattractive, especially in poor countries.

Thirdly, self-insurance funds provide a tempting resource which invites 'raiding' by unprincipled or undisciplined political authorities. Self-insurance funds must be readily available for use if they are to provide an effective insurance mechanism. However, as a consequence they are potentially depletable.

Fourthly, self-insurance by countries leaves unused opportunities to insure against risks that are uncorrelated across countries. As a result, it is a comparatively costly form of insurance. Self-insurance has a place in the panoply of insurance instruments but is unlikely to be the most attractive of mechanisms for these reasons.

In addition to self-insurance by individual countries, the possibility of self-insurance by groups of countries which possess common characteristics (for example, that are exporters of a certain commodity) must also be considered. Programmes of this type attempt to provide collective self-insurance for member countries against aggregate level fluctuations (for example, in export prices). The history of such programmes is extensive and varied.

(ii) Mutual insurance through formal insurance contracts or risk-sharing, institutional arrangements

Mutual insurance can take diverse forms. One form is a formal insurance contract which takes advantage of the fact that the parties to the contract face at least partially independently determined risks in order to diminish the extent to which the effects of adverse occurrences are experienced by each individual party. Another form that it can take is an informal insurance contract embodied in redistributive institutions. For example, federal governments often implement some form of resource redistribution between their constituent entities which is contingent on actual occurrences (or states of the world).

Major obstacles to the existence of mutual insurance schemes can include (i) a lack of verifiability of the outcomes being insured, (ii) difficulty in identifying the risks associated with a particular outcome, (iii) the potential that an insurance scheme may create 'moral hazard' problems in which the incentive to avoid the risks being insured against is diminished, and (iv) the potential that an insurance scheme may face 'adverse selection' problems in which it is only joined by those parties which face the highest unobserved risks. Insurance schemes can become unviable for any of these reasons. For all of these reasons, formal insurance contracts rarely insure against risks to incomes themselves, but rather may insure against adverse fluctuations in the determinants of income (such as costs and prices). There are few examples at the international level of informal insurance contracts embodied in redistributive institutions. A notable exception is the European Union, which effectively offers insurance to its member countries against medium and long-term fluctuations in relative income, through measures such as its structural funds and other income-sensitive tax and transfer policies.[11]

Arguably, to the limited extent that the international aid regime is responsive to the relative prosperity of countries, as well as to the occurrence of adverse occurrences such as natural disasters, it provides another such example. There are also a few examples of insurance schemes at the international level focused on commodity prices, as will be discussed further below.

It may be difficult to characterize the risks associated with aggregate income fluctuations in developing countries, because of the changing and complex causal structure underlying incomes, and the frequent occurrence of unpredicted and perhaps unpredictable 'small sample' events, which may make it extremely difficult to understand the risks associated with specific outcomes and bedevil any effort to bring into being functioning insurance schemes.

(iii) Insurance equivalence through the use of market-based instruments

An alternative means of insuring against adverse occurrences is to make use of appropriate market-based instruments, if they exist. In particular, options, futures and other derivatives instruments can potentially be used in a manner that reduces countries' risks. The appropriate use of options and futures markets, if they exist, can ensure that adverse risks to aggregate income are avoided. Indeed, from the standpoint of an agent seeking to reduce the impact of adverse occurrences, there is a functional equivalence between derivatives appropriately used and insurance contracts.[12] There are, however, a number of issues to be faced in this regard. First, whereas derivatives markets for some of the important determinants of aggregate income – such as commodities prices, interest rates and even weather – often already exist, derivatives markets for a number of the other aggregate risks faced by countries – such as fluctuations in local agricultural output – do not exist. The problems identified above as obstacles to the existence of straightforward insurance contracts are also potential obstacles to the creation of derivatives markets. Shiller (1993, 2003) emphasizes that these problems can potentially be overcome in relation to aggregate incomes, since their aggregative feature diminishes the moral hazard problems present in relation to individual agents and since credible index numbers for aggregate incomes already exist or can potentially be created.[13] There are, however, some dangers associated with the creation of additional derivatives markets which can be used by poor countries to hedge against risks. One concern is that the existence of these markets can provide incentives for destabilizing speculation. The impetus to undertake speculative attacks may be enhanced if doing so can give rise to profits. In particular, the ability to influence the prices of the underlying assets in relation to which derivatives are defined while undertaking derivatives trades typically provides profit-making opportunities. There is a danger that efforts to shift such prices will emerge purely for this reason. The possibility that the role played by derivatives will be market destabilizing and risk increasing rather than market stabilizing and risk decreasing is real.[14]

Moral reasoning and minimal adequacy

The achievement of minimal adequacy is by definition an end of special moral concern.

There are special reasons to disvalue shortfalls from minimal adequacy, which go beyond the reasons that there may be to disvalue disadvantage as such, whether relative or absolute in nature. The existence of such shortfalls may demand special moral attention, and induce strong obligations to remedy such shortfalls on the part of agents who do not suffer these shortfalls, whether or not they can be deemed causally responsible for the existence of the deprivations.[15]

Such obligations may be more intense still if there is reason on the part of an agent to think that she has contributed to the existence of shortfalls from minimal adequacy. The special moral opprobrium that is to be attached to such contributions to others' severe disadvantages gives rise to strong moral obligations to perform remedial actions. Indeed, it may not even be necessary to demonstrate such contributions with certainty. If it cannot be significantly discounted that the past actions of an agent have causally contributed to present disadvantages, this may give rise to moral obligations to undertake remedial actions.[16]

There is therefore special moral reason for rich countries that cannot adequately discount the possibility that they were involved in the production of international shocks which have had adverse impact on the poor to take steps to reduce severe deprivation. These steps could take the form of development-oriented policies which help to enhance the baseline level of advantage of poor and potentially poor people, changes in policies and actions which reduce the extent to which risks arise in the first instance, and the creation and subsidization of insurance mechanisms so as to diminish the ultimate impact on poor persons of adverse shocks which do take place.

Although the requirement to promote minimally adequate levels of advantage for human beings generates especially strong moral obligations, there are other moral arguments for reducing the creation of systemic risk-creating activity. Foremost among these is that such risk-creating activity can be viewed as imposing upon others negative externalities to which they have not consented. The moral and legal arguments that typically apply in such cases pertain here.

The political economy of volatility and insurance

In order to understand what policy options are likely to be feasible or infeasible, it is essential to take note of the political economy underlying volatility and insurance.

It is interesting to note that uncertainty can theoretically be in the interest of firms, especially those that lack price-setting power in product or factor markets.[17] This result, which may at first appear surprising, is a consequence of the convexity of such a firm's profit function (defined in relation to output prices and input costs). If firms can make flexible input and output decisions then their average profits may be higher in a volatile environment. Empirical evidence concerning the effects of uncertainty on investment and profits is mixed, and does not therefore permit a clear rejection of this possibility. In contrast, as we have noted, volatility of prices is not in the interests of consumers in general, and in particular of poor ones. These background facts give rise to the possibility of a conflict of interest between producers and consumers, whether they are respectively within the same country or in different countries. Similarly, government decision makers may have less incentive to reduce exposure to risk than do individual persons, especially if decision makers respond to the interests of small constituencies who are relatively insulated from such risks. We may imagine, for instance, the existence of an inner belt of constituents who enjoy government influence and are well protected from variations in government expenditure and an outer belt of constituents which enjoy little government influence and bear the brunt of such variations. A government 'captured' by privileged interests in this way may have little incentive to reduce aggregate-level fluctuations.

Many social insurance schemes contain an implicit transfer component in addition to their risk-sharing component. When risks are not fully understood it may be difficult to identify the extent of the transfer element in a social insurance scheme. Unsurprisingly, such schemes may be opposed by those groups which provide a net contribution to the transfer component of the scheme. Efforts to reduce systemic volatility (and even more so volatility experienced by disadvantaged or vulnerable groups) may not be met with strong support from all quarters if it is perceived that they are likely to include a transfer component.

We have noted that at present few formal insurance schemes exist at the international level. There is a reason, however, that explicit ex-ante insurance schemes may be preferable to ad-hoc ex-post compensation schemes (i.e. those that compensate countries ex-post for the occurrence of an adverse event); whereas net beneficiaries and net payers into a scheme are necessarily known in *ex-post* compensation schemes, they are not known in ex-ante insurance schemes, which increases the likelihood that membership in such schemes will appear comparatively attractive to countries, even if membership requires financial contributions. As a result, the level of compensation likely to be provided to eventual beneficiaries under such schemes may be higher than under the ex-post alternative. Presently, ad-hoc ex-post compensation schemes, which are often under-financed, are the norm.

Past international-level risk-reduction and insurance mechanisms

A number of risk-reduction and insurance arrangements which seek to diminish shocks of international origin faced by developing countries or to protect them partially from the impact of aggregate shocks to national income and to foreign exchange earnings have arisen in recent decades. Some of these continue to exist whereas others are defunct. These arrangements can be separated into two kinds. The first are *ad hoc* schemes which protect countries against the impact of aggregate shocks on an *ad hoc* or discretionary and *ex post* basis. For example, donors have sometimes provided additional aid to countries that have experienced negative shocks to aggregate income or foreign exchange earnings, especially as a result of natural disasters. This aid practice can be viewed as providing a degree of *de facto* insurance to countries. The financing offered by international financial institutions to countries suffering exchange rate imbalances might also be viewed as providing a degree of *de facto* insurance. Although the conditioning of such financing on having experienced adverse shocks is typically informal, this is not always so.[18] A crucial distinction, however, is that international financial institutions typically provide opportunities to borrow rather than grant assistance. From this point of view, their activities are not insurance providing in the traditional sense.[19]

The second type of scheme seeks to diminish risks faced by countries or to insure them against the impact of adverse occurrences through institutional and *ex ante* mechanisms.

For example, an interesting (and unique) example of explicit insurance against natural disasters is that of the Commonwealth and Small States Disaster Management Scheme (CDMS), launched jointly by the Commonwealth and Lloyd's Syndicates. Under the scheme, countries with small populations can negotiate insurance which provides partial repayment of debts in the event of natural disasters. However, to date the premiums involved appear to have been too high to generate widespread interest.

There is a long history of the use of international buffer stocks as a means of attempting to stabilize the prices of commodities and, thereby, of national real incomes. Famously, John Maynard Keynes forcefully advocated national and international efforts to achieve commodity price stability through the use of buffer stocks and envisioned that they would play an important role in the postwar international economic system.[20] The use of international buffer stocks to stabilize specific commodity prices became prevalent in the 1960s and 1970s as part of international commodity agreements. In the 1970s, it was sought unsuccessfully to expand these within the context of an 'Integrated Programme for Commodities'. Most such schemes have ceased to exist, in some instances after enjoying brief successes. Failed agreements to manage such schemes have existed under the International Sugar Agreement (scheme ended in 1984), the International Tin Agreement (scheme ended in 1985), the International Cocoa Agreement (scheme ended in 1998), the International Coffee Agreement (scheme ended in 1989), and the International Natural Rubber Agreement (scheme ended in 1999).[21] Of course, there are some examples of enduring and successful stabilization schemes.[22] Reasons for the termination of such agreements are complex, but appear to include differences in opinion regarding the price objective to be sought between importing and exporting country members,[23] difficulty in determining what constitutes a long-run equilibrium price, difficulty in making predictions as to the duration of negative shocks, openness to speculative attack if target prices are perceived as lacking credibility, difficulties in policing the behaviour of member countries, and the interest and carrying costs of buffer stocks.[24] The long run of low prices experienced in the 1980s appears to have been a decisive factor in the collapse of a number of such schemes.[25] A central difficulty of buffer stocks schemes is the exhaustion of available funds due to unexpectedly long periods of low prices. Moreover, buffer stocks are difficult to begin because of the cost of their initial financing. There is a strong case to be made that most buffer stock agreements were bound to fail because of the low level at which they were financed. As a result, it cannot be concluded on the basis of past experience alone that such schemes are infeasible.[26]

There have also been efforts to stabilize export earnings of countries without stabilizing prices of exported commodities. The European Union's STABEX fund attempted to stabilize export earnings related to specific commodities for ACP (African, Caribbean and Pacific) countries under the Lome Convention between

1975 and 2000. The fund provided transfers to countries based on reductions in export-earnings relative to a previous multi-year average. However, only certain commodities were covered, and a small number of countries were overwhelmingly the beneficiaries of the fund.[27] Moreover, for many years it required that gains from the fund should be reinvested in the specific sector covered by the fund, limiting its ability to cushion the impact in other sectors of the economy of export-earning induced variations in government revenue, demand and employment. The fund was moreover perceived as having a slow rate of disbursement (up to 12 months after the decline in export-earnings was registered). Another fund established under the Lome Convention, SYSMIN, provided similar stabilization of export-earnings arising from minerals exports (other than oil, gas, and precious metals) of ACP countries. This fund has ceased operation in 2000 as a result of the expiry of the Convention. Since then, under the successor convention (the Cotonou Agreement) a system of financial support 'to mitigate the adverse effects of any instability in export earnings' known as FLEX has been in operation. The eligibility criterion is an adequately sizable loss of export earnings as compared with average earnings in preceding years. Support is limited to four successive years. Unlike STABEX and SYSMIN, FLEX does not focus narrowly on specific export commodities and does not presently require that funds transferred under the scheme be spent on specific purposes. Disbursements under FLEX have thus far been relatively modest (€36.5 million in 2000–2002).[28]

Practical proposals

The reduction of the creation of risks that are international in origin is a worthy end. A number of sources of such risks are presently discernible. Institutional mechanisms at the international level (such as the so-called Tobin tax on currency transactions) may play an important role in diminishing creation of risks of this kind.

There is no single best option for developing countries to reduce their exposure to risks. The use of a broad portfolio of strategies to reduce risks will be appropriate for most countries. However, here we would like specifically to consider the question of how countries can best reduce the likelihood that their poorest citizens will suffer adverse shocks, as well as the impact of such shocks, should they be suffered.

A number of means have been proposed to address aggregate income shocks faced by developing countries. Past and present schemes of this kind, aiming at the reduction of export price and income volatility, were surveyed in the preceding section. Instruments of this kind (discussed in the previous section) have played an important role in reducing the fluctuations in export income faced by some (especially smaller poor countries). As noted above, in practice relatively few countries and commodities have been covered by these schemes, and their importance has diminished over time (or they have even ceased to exist over time) because of difficulties in managing and financing them.

Recently, interest has grown substantially in the use of market-based instruments to provide insurance to countries against aggregate fluctuations, although there are as yet few, if any instances of countries systematically using these instruments to provide such insurance. Dodd (2004), Pollner (2001), Freeman *et al.* (2003b) and IMF (2003) contain a useful catalogue of such instruments that are presently traded, and the suggestion that they may be fruitfully employed by developing countries to diminish vulnerability to aggregate fluctuations. These instruments include catastrophe bonds, contingent surplus notes, exchange traded catastrophe options, catastrophe equity puts, catastrophe swaps, weather derivatives, commodity-indexed bonds, and commodity-linked bonds. Market-based instruments of these kinds can potentially be applied to limit the risk faced by individual countries. Their essence is to transfer risk to others in exchange for a payment. For example, catastrophe bonds are bonds which are subject to default by the issuer in the event that a defined catastrophe takes place. A contingent surplus note gives the issuer a right to sell debt at a specific price to the buyer of the note in the event of a defined catastrophe. Exchange-traded catastrophe bonds entitle the buyer of the option to payment in the event that total insurance claims of a specified type exceed a defined level. Catastrophe swaps guarantee that an investor assumes an insurer's liabilities in the event of a defined catastrophe, in return for specified payments to an investor. Weather derivatives guarantee payments in the event that a specific weather event takes place. These market-based instruments are at the time of writing almost exclusively traded in, and defined in relation to, events in developed countries. Moreover, their use has been limited even in developed countries, although it is growing.[29]

There is a widespread and growing view that market-based instruments of these kinds offer better options for diminishing the risks to foreign exchange earnings and aggregate income faced by many developing countries than the traditional mechanisms such as commodity price stabilization through buffer stocks.[30] Indeed, in principle the two approaches can deliver equivalent results.[31] However, at present the belief in their potential is largely speculative, and is likely driven by private as well as public interests. It must be remembered that the use of derivatives contracts can also carry significant costs, in the form of margin requirements. Costly or inadequate access to credit can make it especially difficult to meet these requirements.[32] Moreover, in the absence of adequate international regulation, it is not obvious that such contracts will be adequately reliable. The default risk associated with derivatives contracts is inherent. It may be addressed through an adequate public role in securities markets (presently lacking at the international level) and through the development of private systems for identifying default risks.

Perhaps unsurprisingly some recent proposals for mechanisms that reduce aggregate income instability faced by developing countries have emphasized the need for an international public intermediary to play a role in financing, creating, monitoring or issuing the derivative contracts that may be employed by countries.

Bower and Kamel (2003) call, in a detailed and well-argued proposal, for the creation of an international agency (to be called the Global Commodity Insurer or GCI) 'that would operate an international Commodity Price Insurance (CPI) scheme with the objective of protecting national government revenues, spending and investment against the adverse impact of short-term deviations in commodity prices, and especially oil prices, from their long-term equilibrium level'. The GCI 'would take advantage of the rapid growth of trading in derivative securities in the global capital market since the 1980s by selling CPI insurance contracts tailored to the specific commodity price exposure faced by national government, and offsetting the resulting price risk with a portfolio of derivative contracts of five-year or longer maturities, supplied by banks, insurers, reinsurers, investment institutions, and commodity trading companies, with investment grade credit ratings'. Similarly, Sarris (n.d.) calls for the developed countries to establish a fund which acts as an international financial intermediary that would make available to low-income commodity- or food-dependent countries single year or multi-year 'put and call like options' for commodity exports and cereal imports and would 'reinsure its own risk exposure with commercial options or swaps, etc.' The fund would potentially offer subsidies to individual countries. Although there are certainly technical and practical problems involved in implementing schemes of this kind, the logic underlying them seems highly plausible.

Other recent proposals (e.g. Loser (2004), Martin and Bargawi (2004), and Guillaumon, Guillaumont Jeanneney, Jacquet, Chauvet and Savoye (2003)) have emphasized the possibility that the provision of insurance may become a goal that is built into systems of aid provision, so as to provide aid to individual countries in a manner that explicitly counteracts adverse 'cyclical' economic shocks (especially those of international origin, such as commodity price variations).

Another possibility is to create a global contingency fund that would provide additional resources to countries facing severe negative shocks. The fund could be financed in advance and could rapidly disburse resources to countries that suffer adverse shocks of specific kind (for example, due to natural disasters), after an appropriate international assessment (for example, by a standing 'peer and partner review committee' which includes representatives from other countries).[33] Recent proposals for a standing United Nations fund for providing rapid disbursements to countries affected by emergencies are along these lines.

Schemes of the kind described above are designed to protect countries against shocks to aggregate income (or, more specifically, to foreign exchange and government revenues). As instruments to address adverse shocks experienced by the poor, they suffer possible disadvantages. First, as they are often designed to insure against variations in aggregate income arising from a specific source (for example, commodity prices) they cannot adequately insure countries against variations in aggregate incomes from other sources (for example, adverse climatic events, or sudden decreases in remittances) which may have an important impact on the poor. Secondly, they cannot directly insure the poor against adverse shocks to their level of advantage. For example, the level of advantage of the poor (or potentially poor) may be influenced by the distribution of aggregate income (as distinguished from the level of aggregate income) and by the level and nature of public expenditures which advance their interests. For this reason, although aggregate stabilization schemes are potentially helpful, they do not offer a fully adequate means of diminishing the volatility of incomes (or, more generally, levels of advantage) experienced by the actually or potentially poor. The extent to which stabilization of aggregate incomes helps to achieve that end will depend upon the extent of correlation between incomes of the poor or potentially poor and aggregate incomes (or, more specifically, the insured components of aggregate income such as foreign exchange and government revenues). There is reason to think that in practice the link between aggregate export incomes and the advantages experienced by the poor may sometimes be weak. Variations in aggregate export earnings may not be translated directly into variations in wages and employment within the export sector (especially in the case of capital-intensive resource-extracting industries). The poor may work in production of non-tradable or import-competing items and the effects of fluctuations in the export sector on their wages and employment may accordingly be limited.[34] The extent and pattern of public expenditures from which the poor benefit may fluctuate for reasons other than that there are variations in aggregate income.[35]

In principle, insurance schemes that insure the poor or potentially poor against fluctuations in *their* levels of advantage are needed. The informational barriers and transactions costs involved in establishing such schemes directly (i.e. with individual persons as parties to an insurance agreement) may be prohibitive. However, their indirect equivalent may be more feasible to create. In particular, it may be possible to establish insurance mechanisms which protect the poor by providing states with the ability and means of extending appropriate social protections, regardless of fluctuations in the demand for these protections.

Existing national social safety nets which can meet increases in demands for social support rapidly and at low marginal costs are likely to continue to be the most effective means of protecting the poor from adverse shocks, whether of national or international origin.[36] A central question is that of how such standing social safety nets should be financed. Large countries may be able to finance such schemes through their internal resources. Because of the scale and internal diversity of such countries, shocks are likely to be localized and there is likely to be scope for self-insurance.[37] In contrast, smaller countries may find it difficult to absorb the increased demand on fiscal resources resulting from the expansion of needs in the wake of an adverse shock. The adverse shock may have a sizable negative effect on aggregate national income and government revenues. Foreseeing this, such countries may believe it is inadvisable or infeasible to put in place domestically financed standing social safety nets, which can meet unpredicted increases in needs rapidly and at low marginal costs. How can this obstacle to the creation of effective standing social safety nets which effectively protect the poor be overcome?

A means of addressing this problem may be to create a global reinsurance fund. A global reinsurance fund would provide insurance to poor countries against the risk of expanded demands for social support resulting from sizable unpredicted shocks of national or international origin. The extent and nature of the insurance provided would be determined bilaterally by negotiation between the global reinsurance fund and each individual country, and would reflect the specifics of the risks judged to be faced in an individual country as well as the nature and extent of the social protections offered by actual or proposed domestic standing social safety nets reinsured by the global fund. Reliable and externally verifiable public statistics on the coverage and disbursements of the social safety nets would be required, and would have to be developed systematically in consultation with the reinsurance fund. The creation of such statistics would also serve as a basis for increased public accountability and program efficiency. The reinsurance fund would enable poor countries to withstand the risks associated with rapid increases in demand for social support from standing social safety nets, and thereby make it more feasible to establish them. Premiums for the reinsurance fund would be shared between poor countries and rich countries, with the degree of the subsidy to each country determined by appropriate considerations. Each rich country's contribution to the cost of these subsidies would reflect its role in creating risks of international origin faced by poor countries, and its commitment to help the poor in these countries.[38] Funding can be provided through voluntary yearly contributions, a permanent cost-sharing agreement between governments (perhaps embodied in a transparent formula established and periodically revised by the governing body of the reinsurance fund) or through earmarked international taxes (such as those which been recently proposed in relation to short-term capital inflows and jet fuel) collected by governments and provided to international institutions including the reinsurance fund for agreed purposes.

A global reinsurance fund of this type would help countries to establish standing social safety nets that offer effective protection to the poor or potentially poor against adverse shocks, whether national or international in origin. It is appropriate that the costs of creating and maintaining such a fund should be shared between poor and rich countries. Such sharing would underline a conception of shared responsibility for eliminating serious disadvantages and recognize the causal role that countries may have played in creating adverse shocks that are experienced elsewhere. It would also create an incentive for developing countries to establish standing systems of social protection by reducing their potential costs.

A global reinsurance fund is only one example of an international mechanism for expanding protections available to the actually or potentially severely disadvantaged. Other possible mechanisms must be envisioned and explored. Practical insight and institutional imagination are required in order better to develop innovations that spread risks more equitably – across societies and persons.

Notes

1 I would like to thank the participants in the workshop Workshop on Pro-Poor Macroeconomics held in Florence on 24–5 February 2005, and Stuart Corbridge, Andy Mold and Giovanni Andrea Cornia for helpful written comments.
2 On the latter, see e.g. the contributions in Dercon (2004).
3 See Dodd (2004), Table 1, for some illustrative evidence of the relation between commodity export prices, GDP, and government revenue for some developing and transition countries.

4   '... between 1990 and 1998, 94 per cent of the world's major disasters and 97 per cent of disaster-related deaths were in developing countries' (IMF 2003). See also Freeman, Keen and Mani (2003a, b).
5   Of course, the consumption basket of the affluent may also be quite import intensive so this is in the end an empirical question. At any event, we are not at pains to show that the poor are more subject to these vicissitudes than the non-poor, but rather to show that they are vulnerable to them in absolute terms. Discuss Indonesia's domestic rice price regime – an effort to come to terms with this problem.
6   Evidence on correlation between government revenues and price shocks.
7   See, for example, Aldy (2004) who shows that heating subsidies diminish deaths of the elderly due to cold weather shocks in the United States.
8   See, for example, Ravallion (1987).
9   Basu and Tzannatos (2003), Carter and Barrett (2005), Dasgupta (2003).
10 See Appendix III in Freeman *et al.* (2003b).
11 In this way, it acts as federal countries do with respect to regions within countries.
12 Given the existence of complete derivatives markets and the assumption that arbitrage opportunities have been exhausted, for any insurance contract that may be offered an equivalent set of state-contingent outcomes can be achieved through the buying and selling of appropriate derivatives products.
13 See Shiller (1993, 2003).
14 For an accessible presentation of the issues, see Dodd (2004).
15 See Barry (2005a,b,c).
16 Ibid.
17 See Oi (1961), and Abel (1983), Friberg and Martensen (2000), Gil (2005), Hartman (1972, 1976), Leahy and Whited (1996).
18 For example, the IMF 'has provided Emergency Assistance for Natural Disasters since 1962, when it agreed to lend Egypt 25 percent of quota to help cover temporary liquidity needs resulting from a major crop failure' (IMF, 2003, p. 23). The IMF's Compensatory Financing Facility (CFF) has provided 'financing for members experiencing balance of payment difficulties resulting from a temporary decline in export earnings or a temporary increase in cereal import costs' (ibid, p. 25). A variety of rules restrict eligibility to temporary shocks of external origin of a sufficiently large magnitude. Use of the CFF was extensive in the 1980s and 1990s but has been limited subsequently, as greater use has since been made of 'augmentation' of general lending arrangements (in particular, the so-called Poverty Reduction and Growth Facility (PRGF)) to meet unanticipated needs, typically during semi-annual reviews. As pointed out by Mold (2005), since January 2000 it has not been used once. It is arguable whether these mechanisms should be considered to be forms of insurance. Insofar as the IMF is a co-operative of member countries with capital paid-in by all members, the IMF mechanisms just surveyed might be viewed as insurance. Of course, contributions of paid-in capital vary according to the member and no explicit insurance 'premia' are paid, as a result of which it may contrarily be argued that these mechanisms constitute safety nets rather than insurance schemes.
19 The rate of interest charged may also be quite high. See, for example, Martin and Bargawi (2004, 15): 'The IMF Compensatory Financing Facility (CFF) is so expensive that it would breach the concessional borrowing ceilings which are standard in African PRGF programmes, with the result that no African low income country has used it recently.'
20 See Bower and Kamel (2003) and Turnell (1998). Keynes built on the ideas presented by Benjamin Graham in his 1937 book *Storage and Stability*.
21 IMF (2003), Mehta and Chavas (2004).
22 Price stability has been an avowed goal (arguably achieved) of successful cartels in industries such as oil and diamonds. Of course, the primary goal of such cartels may be to raise rather than stabilize prices.
23 See the description of the collapse of the International Rubber Agreement in IMF (2003), p. 72.

24 Bower and Kamel (2003) describe concisely the insights of Newbery and Stiglitz (1981) on the dilemmas facing buffer stock schemes, as a result of the stochastic nature of commodity prices: 'Two issues arise: first, that the financing and insurance may be so large that it exceeds the potential benefit of stockpiling even if prices are very volatile. More importantly, even if the benefits justify the costs, there is always a possibility that a very long run of low prices followed by an equally long run of high prices might occur or indeed *vice versa*. This means that, no matter what the starting stock level, there would always be some probability that stocks would be depleted before prices fell or that stocks would grow so large that they exceeded total available storage capacity or finance before prices rose again. For all practical purposes, Newbery and Stiglitz conclude that complete price stabilization in a buffer stock scheme is therefore impossible.'
25 See, for example, Cashin, Liang and McDermott (1999).
26 See Mold (2005).
27 'Over the period 1975–1995, STABEX transfers totaled about €3 billion, and four products (coffee, groundnuts, cotton and cocoa/copra) accounted for 80 per cent of effective transfers' (IMF, 2003, p. 82).
28 'Compensation for Fluctuations in the Export Earnings of ACP Countries', UK. Parliament, Select Committee on European Scrutiny Twenty-First Report.
29 Exchange-traded catastrophe options currently trade on the Chicago Board of trade. The market in weather derivatives is now relatively large, possessing a market value of $4.5 billion in the United States in 2001 (IMF, 2003). So far, catastrophe bonds have been issued primarily by insurance firms. However, Froot (1999) found that there was 'no coverage for the largest, most severe events'.
30 See, for example, Bower and Kamel (2003), Dodd (2004), Gilbert (1996), ITFCRM (1999), Sarris (n.d).
31 See Bower and Kamel (2003).
32 Ibid.
33 See Reddy and Heuty (2005) for more on the concept of peer and partner review.
34 See e.g. Mold (2005).
35 Indeed, the STABEX fund prohibited beneficiary countries from expending the monies received from it for purposes other than to protect the income of firms and persons involved in production of covered exports.
36 The Employment Guarantee Scheme in Maharashtra, India, in which the poor are entitled to demand public employment at the statutory wages, provides an especially successful example of a scheme of this kind. For an elaboration of this general argument see, for example, Cornia and Reddy (2004) and Cornia (2001).
37 The contrast between India's internal response to the Indian Ocean Tsunami disaster of December 2004 as compared to other countries, which relied more greatly on external resources, is illustrative in this regard. The relative ease with which it has handled the crisis is due not only to the smaller number of people affected but, equally importantly, to the manageable magnitude of the demands created by the crisis in relation to available internal resources, including existing provisions for emergencies.
38 In principle, the equivalent of this scheme can be achieved through private reinsurance or through the creation of appropriate derivatives markets. The World Food Programme is presently developing, in conjunction with private reinsurance companies, rainfall based insurance contracts. Premiums would be partially or fully paid by donors and would finance rapid drought-related emergency assistance when required. See 'Radical plan for Ethiopia aid', *Financial Times*, 11 May 2005.

References

Abel, A. 1983. 'Optimal Investment Under Uncertainty'. *American Economic Review*, 73, 228–33.
Aldy, J. E. 2004. *Insurance against Weather and Energy Price Shocks: The Benefits of Energy Subsidies to Low-Income Households*. Job Market Paper, November 2004 draft.

www.people.fas.harvard.edu/~aldy/papers/LIHEAP Paper Nov 04.pdf, accessed on 11 August 2005.
Barry, C. 2005a. *The Contribution Principle: Its Meaning and Significance for Allocating Responsibility to Address Acute Deprivation*, PhD Dissertation, Department of Philosophy, Columbia University.
Barry, C. 2005b. 'Understanding and Evaluating the Contribution Principle', in *Real World Justice: Grounds, Principles, Human Rights and Social Institutions*. Dordrecht: Kluwer.
Barry, C. 2005c. 'Applying the Contribution Principle', in C. Barry and T. Pogge (eds), *Global Institutions and Responsibilities: Achieving Global Justice*. London: Routledge.
Basu, K and Tzannatos, Z. 2003. 'The Global Child Labor Problem: What do We Know and What Can we Do?' *World Bank Economic Review*, 17(2), 147–73.
Bower, J. and N. Kamel. 2003. *Commodity Price Insurance: A Keynesian Idea Revisited*. econwpa.wustl.edu/eps/othr/papers/0504/0504012.pdf, accessed on 11 August 2005.
Carter, M.R., and C.B. Barrett. 2005. *The Economics of Poverty Traps and Persistent Poverty: An Asset-Based Approach*. Paper, Department Applied Economics and Management, Cornell University. http://www.cfnpp.cornell.edu/images/wp178.pdf, accessed on 12 August 2005.
Cashin, P., H. Liang, and C.J. McDermott. 1999. 'Do commodity price shocks last too long for stabilization schemes to work?' *Finance & Development*, 36(3), pp. 40–3.
Cornia G.A. 2001. 'Social Funds in Stabilisation and Adjustment Programmes: A Critique'. *Development and Change*, 32, 1–32.
Cornia G.A and S. Reddy. 2004. 'The Impact of Adjustment-Related Social Funds on Income Distribution and Poverty'. In G.A. Cornia (ed.), *Inequality, Growth and Poverty in an Era of Liberalization and Globalization*. Oxford: Oxford University Press.
Dasgupta, P. 2003. *World Poverty: Causes and Pathways*. Plenary Lecture at Annual Bank Conference on Development Economics, Bangalore, 21–2 May 2003, revised June. http://www.econ.cam.ac.uk/faculty/dasgupta/worldpov.pdf, accessed on 12 August 2005.
Dercon, S. 2004. *Insurance Against Poverty*. Oxford: Oxford University Press.
Dodd, R. 2004. *Protecting Developing Economies from Price Shocks*. Special Policy Brief 18, Financial Policy Forum Derivatives Study Center. http://www.financialpolicy.org/fpfspb18.htm, accessed on 26 January 2005.
Freeman, P. K., M. Keen, and M. Mani. 2003a. 'Being Prepared'. *Finance & Development*, 40(3), 42–5.
Freeman, P. K., M. Keen, and M. Mani. 2003b. *Dealing with Increased Risk of Natural Disasters: Challenges and Options*. Working Paper 03/197, IMF. http://www.imf.org/external/pubs/ft/wp/2003/wp03197.pdf, accessed on 12 August 2005.
Friberg, R. and K. Martensen. 2000. *Variability and Average Profits – Does Oi's Result Generalize?* Working Paper in Economics and Finance No. 402, Stockholm School of Economics. http://swopec.hhs.se/hastef/papers/hastef0402.pdf, accessed on 12 August 2005.
Froot, K. 1999. *The Evolving Market for Catatrophic Event Risk*. NBER Working Paper 7287. Cambridge, MA: National Bureau of Economic Research.
Gil, P.R.M. 2005. *Expected Profitability of Capital Under Uncertainty: A Microeconomic Perspective*. FEP Working Paper 157. Universidade do Porto, Faculdade de Economia do Porto.
Gilbert, C. L. 1996. 'International Commodity Agreements: An Obituary Notice'. *World Development*, 24(1), 1–19.
Guillaumont, P., S. Guillaumont Jeanneney, P. Jacquet, L. Chauvet, and B. Savoye. 2003. *Dampening the Vulnerability to Price Shocks: A Role for Aid*. http://www.uneca.org/eca_resources/major_eca_websites/DebtForum/Dampening%20the%20vulnerability%2012.05.pdf, accessed on 12 August 2005.
Hartman, R. 1972. 'The Effects of Price and Cost Uncertainty on Investment'. *Journal of Economic Theory*, 5, 258–66.
Hartman, R. 1976. 'Factor Demand with Output Price Uncertainty'. *American Economic Review*, 66, 675–81.
International Cocoa Organization. *ICCO Buffer Stock*. http://www.icco.org/buffer.htm, accessed on 5 August 2005.

International Coffee Organization. *International Coffee Organisation – History*. http://www.ico.org/history.asp, accessed on 5 August 2005.

International Monetary Fund Policy Development and Review Department. 2003. *Fund Assistance for Countries Facing Exogenous Shocks*. http://www.imf.org/external/np/pdr/sustain/2003/080803.pdf, accessed on 12 August 2005.

International Task Force on Commodity Risk Management in Developing Countries (ITFCRM). 1999. *Dealing with Commodity Price Volatility in Developing Countries: A Proposal for a Market-Based Approach*. Discussion Paper for the Roundtable on Commodity Risk Management in Developing Countries. http://www.itf-commrisk.org/documents/dsp73.pdf, accessed on 12 August 2005.

Leahy, J.V. and T.M. Whited. 1996. 'The Effect of Uncertainty on Investment: Some Stylized Facts'. *Journal of Money, Credit and Banking*, 28(1), 64–83.

Loser, C.M. 2004. *Counter-Cyclical Financing Mechanism for Developing Countries: Wishful Thinking or Policy Requirement?* G-24 Research Program. http://www.g24.org/lose0904.pdf, accessed on 11 August 2005.

Martin, M., and H. Bargawi. 2004. *Protecting Africa Against Shocks*. Africa Commission Background Paper, Development Finance International. http://www.dri.org.uk/pdfs/DFI_AC_Shocks.pdf, 11 August 2005.

Mehta, A., and J.P. Chavas. 2004. *Responding to the Coffee Crisis: What can we Learn from Price Dynamics?* Staff Paper No. 472, University of Wisconsin-Madison Department of Agricultural & Applied Economics. http://www.aae.wisc.edu/pubs/sps/pdf/stpap472.pdf, accessed on 11 August 2005.

Mold, A., 2005. 'Tackling the Commodity Price Problem – New Proposals and Revisiting Old Solutions'. *Africa Development Perspectives Yearbook 2005*. New Brunswick, NJ: Transaction Publishers.

Newbery, D.M. and J.E. Stiglitz. 1981. *The Theory of Commodity Price Stabilization: A Study in the Economics of Risk*. Oxford: Clarendon Press.

Oi, W.Y. 1961. 'The Desirability of Price Instability Under Perfect Competition'. *Econometrica*, 29(1), 58–64.

Pollner, J. 2001. *Managing Catastrophe Disaster Risk Using Alternative Risk Financing and Pooled Insurance Structures*. Washington DC: World Bank.

Ravallion, M. 1987. *Markets and Famines*. Oxford: Clarendon Press.

Reddy, S.G. and A. Heuty 2005, 'Peer and Partner Review: A Practical Approach to Achieving the MDGs', Columbia University, available on http://www.millenniumdevelopmentgoals.org.

Sarris, A. (n.d.) *Market Based Commodity Price Insurance for Developing Countries: Towards a New Approach*. http://www.gdnet.org/pdf2/online_journals/cerdi/issue1/Sarris_paper1.pdf, accessed on 12 August 2005.

Shiller, R.J. 1993. *Macro Markets: Creating Institutions for Managing Society's Largest Economic Risks*. Oxford: Oxford University Press.

Shiller, R.J. 2003. *The New Financial Order: Risk in the 21st Century*, Princeton, NJ: Princeton University Press.

Turnell, S. 1998. *The Quest for Commodity Price Stability: Australian Economists and Buffer Stocks*. Working Paper, MacQuarie University. Available on http://www.econ.mq.edu.au/research/1998/10-98Turnell.doc.

Part II
Country Case Studies

8
Financial and Trade Reforms and Impact on Poverty and Income Inequality: The Case of Mauritius

Sunil Kumar Bundoo

Introduction

Mauritius' economic performance over the last two decades has been remarkable. During this period, real Gross Domestic Product (GDP) growth rate has averaged 5.4 per cent per year, inflation has declined from over 25 per cent in the early 1980s to less than 5 per cent in 2004 and per capita income has increased over the same period from around $1,166 to nearly $5,000. Social conditions have also improved; life expectancy at birth increased from 61 years in the 1960s to 71 in the 1990s, primary enrolment from 93 to 105 per cent, the Gini coefficient declined from 0.5 to 0.37 and the Human Development Index (HDI) increased from 0.626 in 1980 to 0.772 in 2000.

Mauritius is a small island developing country with limited resources. From a mono-agricultural industry, based on the production of sugar, Mauritius has successfully diversified into other sectors such as manufacturing, tourism, and, recently, into financial services. Earnings from the high price paid on its sugar exports have allowed Mauritius to implement a sustainable development process over the years. From the mid-1970s Mauritius embarked on a diversification process focused on manufacturing sector and tourism. Mauritius set up the Export Processing Zone (EPZ). The manufacturing sector became critical for the country in terms of employment and export earnings. On the other hand, tourism was developed since the early 1970s to become one of the main pillars of the local economy. In 2003, the tourism industry accounted for approximately 6 per cent of GDP. The EPZ sector accounted for about 70 per cent of exports and 23 per cent of GDP, while sugar represented 7 per cent of GDP and 14 per cent of total exports. The government has also taken measures to extend the role of the financial sector. Over the last 10 years this type of activity has increased strongly to account for 15 per cent of GDP. These financial services include banking and offshore activities. Furthermore, Mauritius is positioning itself in the field of Information and Communication Technology (ICT) for software and hardware developments and business process outsourcing.

Though there is no absolute poverty in Mauritius, it is estimated that around 10 per cent of the population live below the poverty line. The common internationally accepted poverty line of $1 per day is not appropriate for Mauritius given the extensive social welfare programmes available such as free health and education for all, non-contributory pension for those over 60 years and subsidized necessities such as basic food, electricity and water.

However, recent social unrest in February 1999 has brought the issue of inequality and poverty to the forefront of the economic and political agenda. Mauritian policy makers are aware that they need to remain vigilant to poverty and exclusion because it has an impact on social cohesion. On the one hand, the country has to implement various macroeconomic policies to try and retain its competitive edge; on the other it has to address the problems of the vulnerable groups. Mauritius is a signatory of the Millennium Declaration and the target is to bring poverty to 5 per cent by 2015.

The process of economic development in Mauritius can be broadly classified into three periods: a period where the economy was under structural adjustment reform, the period 1980–87; the next phase was the move towards financial and trade liberalization, the period from 1987 to late 1990s and the third phase from 1999 onwards, a sustained policy towards economic diversification in light of eroding preferences in our major export markets, viz, the dismantling of the Multi-Fibre Agreement (MFA) in 2005 and the revision of the Sugar Protocol.

The chapter is structured as follows. The next three sections review the economic reforms during the three periods identified above and then analyse the impact on the economic and social indicators during these same periods. Then we consider the targeted approach to poverty alleviation. Later the author presents an econometric analysis of the impact of the financial and trade reforms on relative poverty. The final section draws some policy conclusions about pro-poor growth.

Phase 1: Structural reforms and economic diversification, 1979–87

In the first half of the 1980s, the emphasis of macroeconomic policy was on economic adjustment with a view to re-establishing economic stability after a period of serious economic imbalances linked to external shocks and inclement weather conditions. During the period 1979 to 1983, the emphasis was on macroeconomic stabilization. The economy in the 1970s was principally a mono-crop economy, depending heavily upon sugar production. The Export Processing Zone (EPZ) sector and the tourism industry were still in their infancy. Following the oil price shocks in 1979 and 1981, coupled with economic mismanagement and the fact that severe cyclones hit the country, most of the economic indicators were alarming, with inflation in double digits, unemployment as high as 20 per cent, a high budget deficit and a chronic balance-of-payments (BOP) deficit. Mauritius engaged into several structural adjustment programmes with the International Monetary Fund (IMF) in order to address the major macroeconomic imbalances prevailing at the time.[1] The structural adjustment or supply-side measures concentrated on the three most important productive sectors: sugar, manufacturing and tourism. During the sub-period 1983–87, with the structural reforms in progress and taking advantage of the trade preferences under the Lome Convention and the MFA, an export-led growth strategy was pursued vigorously, with a particular emphasis on textile and clothing. The Convention gives Mauritius a considerable advantage over non-ACP countries, such as Hong Kong and the Republic of Korea, as their exports were subject to a 17 per cent duty on entry into the European Union. The tourism sector was also being strengthened. GDP annual growth rate increased from just under 0.4 per cent in 1983 to nearly 7 per cent in 1987. Around the same period, unemployment has declined from 20 per cent in 1983 to 3.1 per cent in early 1988.

Fiscal policy

The fiscal policy measures were geared towards generous fiscal incentives to promote the EPZ sector and an escalating external tariffs structure to protect local firms engaged in import substitution. The main fiscal incentives given to EPZ firms were: a tax holiday on corporate profits, the free repatriation of profits, no tax on dividend income, investment tax credits (ITC) for investment in plant and machinery, finance at preferential interest rates and import duty exemptions on plant, machinery and raw materials. Companies in the tourism sector were given similar incentives but paying a corporate tax of only 15 per cent.

Moreover, in the late 1970s and early 1980s, revenue-raising efforts shifted from direct taxation to indirect taxation. The corporate tax rate was reduced from 55 to 35 per cent in 1985 and the income tax rate was reduced from 70 to 35 per cent in 1986. The income tax bands were reduced from eight to four. There was also the introduction of the sales tax in 1983 with the initial rate set at 5 per cent.

Foreign direct investment

During this phase, Mauritius had a good record in terms of attracting FDI. This was expected, given the generous fiscal incentives and the cheap labour comparative advantage. This rising trend in FDI continued until early 1991. The average FDI inflow per annum over the period 1981 to 1988 was Rs 462 million and in 1987 it was 3.33 per cent of GNP and peaking to 7.55 per cent of GNP in 1988. After 1991, the inflow of FDI has been much more erratic, as will be seen in the section describing phase 3.

Monetary policy: administered interest rate regime and directed credit programmes

A tight monetary policy was needed to control consumption expenditure, particularly expenditure on imports in order to restore balance-of-payments equilibrium and to contain the already high inflation rate. The government also considered that the key sectors of the economy should have adequate access to bank credit and at reasonable interest rates.

Therefore, the maximum lending rates banks could charge on loans to priority and non-priority sectors were controlled. The practice was to change these rates at fixed intervals in light of developments in the monetary and real sectors. Annual credit ceilings were established for the expansion of bank credit. However, maximum lending rates to priority sectors were removed in 1983. The removal of interest rate controls on deposits came later. The minimum interest rates on time deposits were removed in March 1984. The objective was to encourage domestic savings to finance the rising levels of private investment.

Small farmers and small entrepreneurs would not meet the lending criteria required by commercial banks. Appropriate schemes were set up under the Development Bank of Mauritius to finance such projects, usually at subsidized interest rates. The objective was not only to promote self-employment but also to tap all opportunities to reduce the relatively high rate of unemployment. Today, these enterprises in Mauritius employ a significant minority of the labour force. As at December 1997, employment in small establishments accounted to about one fifth of the labour force and their contribution to GDP was around 14 per cent.

Exchange rate regime

The process of exchange rate determination has also evolved from the Special Drawing Rights (SDR) peg in the late 1970s and early 1980s to a market-determined rate, with occasional government intervention (see Chapter 4). The SDR peg lasted from January 1976 to February 1983. The rationale for pegging the rupee to the SDR was that positive and negative changes in the value of the rupee against the 16 currencies in the SDR basket would lead to a fairly stable exchange rate with the country's trading partners. As it appeared that the SDR peg would lead to an overvaluation of the rupee, a new method of determining the exchange rate was adopted as from March 1983, where the rupee was linked to an undisclosed basket of currencies of major trading partners. This lasted until July 1994.

During this period, foreign exchange allocation was controlled, import permits were required, and a stamp duty of 45 per cent was imposed on capital transfers other than those from inward investments.

Impact of reforms on economic and social indicators

There is much less consensus as to what exactly is pro-poor growth, let alone what it consists of (Ravallion and Chen 2003) (see also Chapter 13). One view is that growth is pro-poor if the accompanying change in income distribution by itself reduces poverty. A broader definition is that growth is pro-poor if the poverty measure of interest falls (Kraay 2004). In addition, in Mauritius there is no established official poverty line. Information obtained from Household Budget Surveys (HBS) give some indication of the extent of income poverty. Low-income households are defined as those households whose income is below the half median income or those earning less than one third the mean income. Therefore the poverty measure of interest[2] that will be used throughout following sections will be the percentage of households earning less than half the median income and the percentage earning less than one third the mean income. Tables 8.1 and 8.2 compare the social indicators in relation to the economic indicators over the period 1981–87.

Table 8.1 Main economic indicators

	1981	1983	1985	1987
Macroeconomic policy inputs				
Nominal interest rate	9.25	12.06	9.46	9.38
Real rate	−17.25	4.56	1.16	8.68
Money supply (M2, Rs million)	3655	5213	6551	11459
Nominal exchange rate (Rs/US$)	8.937	11.706	15.442	12.878
Real exchange rate	88.4	91.2	93.1	95.7
Budget deficit (% of GDP)	15	9.4	5.3	2.3
Macroeconomic outputs as % of GNP				
Current account balance	−21.70	−9.88	−8.86	−2.09
Overall BOP balance	−9.84	−2.71	2.50	11.16
FDI	0.684	2.53	1.39	3.33
Portfolio flows	n.a	n.a	n.a	n.a
Tax revenue	18.49	19.85	18.80	18.73
Public debt:				
Domestic	15.89	15.51	41.40	35.44
External	28.27	34.13	35.31	21.19
Inflation (%)	26.5	7.5	8.3	0.7
Real economy outputs				
GDP growth rate	6.4	0.4	6.5	8.9
Investment rate	21.9	17.73	19.0	22.1
Savings rate	15.0	17.10	20.8	25.7
Openness	0.804	0.726	0.813	0.930
Unemployment rate	18	21	15	10[1]
GDP per capita (US$)	1,166	1,063	1,050	1,714
Population growth rate[2] (%)	n.a	0.76	1.96	0.78

Notes:
1. The rate of unemployment has fallen to 3.1 per cent by the end of 1988.
2. Growth rate over previous year and same in all tables.

Source: Bank of Mauritius, Annual Reports, various issues and author's computations.

Table 8.2 Movements in social indicators

HBS indicators	1975	1980–81	1986–87
Average monthly income (Rs)	740	2,212	3,496
Median monthly income (Rs)	552	1,518	2,663
Gini coefficient	0.420	0.445	0.396
Half median (Rs)	276	759	1,332
One-third mean (Rs)	247	737	1,165
% of total income:			
Lowest quintile	6.2	5.1	6.7
Highest quintile	48	51	45.5
Half Median at constant prices[1]	NA	759	1,062

Note: This is a measure to track the incidence of absolute poverty in constant prices using 1981 as the base period. The poverty line is kept constant in real terms using the half median income for the 1980–81 HBS as the base.

Source: Household Budget Surveys and author's computations.

When we analyze the HBS statistics available during the same period, we can see from Table 8.2 that, overall, there has been a significant improvement in the poverty indicators over the period from the 1970s to late 1980s. In 1975, around 17.5 per cent of households were earning less than half the median income. In 1980/81 around 17 per cent of households were earning less than half the median income. Over the same period, there was deterioration in the Gini coefficient, moving from 0.420 to 0.445. From the HBS of 1986/87, around 15 per cent of households had an income of less than half the median income. In real terms, based on the adjusted half median income, the percentage of households earning less than half median income in 1986/87 was only 11.2 per cent. The Gini coefficient also fell to 0.396. Also when compared with the 'less than one third mean income measure', we see a sizeable reduction in poverty – from 28 per cent down to 11.5 per cent. Our estimates also show the income share of the highest quintile falling from 48 to nearly 45 per cent. Over the same period, real GDP growth rate picked up to 8.9 per cent, unemployment rate felt, inflation and the budget deficit were reduced to less than three per cent of GDP. In fact, from Table 8.1, the consistent improvements in all the major economic indicators stand out. The macroeconomic measures were not only successful in steering the economy out of recession and towards a boom situation, but also significantly improving the standards of living, particularly of the middle- and lower-income groups.

We therefore see a strong correlation between the improvements in the major economic indicators and the reduction in poverty. The whole philosophy during that period was that growth would reduce poverty – a support for the Kuznets hypothesis. A growing and prosperous economy was believed to be the most effective antipoverty policy instrument. When the structural measures were being implemented, initially the poverty situation worsened and then, towards the late 1980s, when the benefits of the macroeconomic policies started to pay off, there was a significant reduction in the levels of poverty and substantial rises in the average standards of living. In parallel, during the same period some social safety net measures were reinforced and others introduced. The two most important ones were the Unemployment Hardship Relief Scheme and the Food Aid Scheme, both introduced in 1983. These are outlined under the next section below.

The recipe for the economic success during that period, besides the trade preferences under the Lome Convention and the MFA, were sound macroeconomic management, a high level of political commitment, a stable democracy, respect for law and order and a ready pool of an educated and relatively cheap labour force. In fact, the political decision of the government in 1976 to declare free secondary education[3] ironically proved to be a fundamental pro-poor growth measure enabling not only the poor but also particularly female labour[4] to be educated. Without the high participation rate of female labour in the EPZ sector, the latter would not have known the rapid growth that it did.

Moreover, Mauritius is an example which lends credibility to the hypothesis that income growth is only effective in reducing poverty and inequality if the initial levels of inequality are not too high (Gini coefficient was under 0.43) and if educational levels are sufficiently high.[5]

The welfare state and pro-poor measures

Mauritius has a strong welfare state with free health and education services and an impressive array of social services and safety nets. The consumer prices of rice, flour, sugar and potatoes are subsidized. There are also price controls on some other commodities such as cement, petroleum products, bread, onions and edible oils.

The state plays a key role in social welfare and security. In fact, expenditure on community and social services attracts the largest share of total government expenditure. The percentage out of total government expenditure spent on health, education, social security and welfare, and housing, over the period 1980 to 1988 averaged 43 per cent and by 1999 was as high as 52.1 per cent. Preferential access to markets in the European Union and the USA has facilitated this strong welfare state.

An Unemployment Hardship Relief scheme was introduced in 1983, paying unemployment benefits only to married couples who are unemployed and not deriving income from other sources and usually at the lower end of the income strata. Among the other important allowances paid are a social aid allowance and a rent allowance. But these allowances are targeted strictly to households meeting some eligibility criteria. However, in September 1982, the subsidies on rice and flour were reduced and a Food Aid allowance was paid to those in the lowest-income bracket.

Health is another area in which significant progress has been made. Its strengths are free public health care for all patients and upgrading and establishing new hospitals catering for the needs of various sections of the population. There has also been a spread of community health centres over the island in order to increase access to public health. To date, Mauritius has also been able to contain the spread of HIV/AIDS. Current estimates show that less than one per cent of the population has the virus.

Providing decent shelter for low-income groups has been another major social priority of the government. In the face of the rising price of rented accommodation, the government initiated projects for the construction of working-class flats in different parts of the country. The National Housing Development Corporation (NHDC) was set up in order to expedite large-scale construction of low-cost housing. House ownership grew from 66 per cent in 1983 to almost 93 per cent in 2001.

The social security system in the country, however, is not targeted enough and many beneficiaries may just be free-riding the system. Allowances in many cases therefore remain low and insufficient. With an ageing population, there is an urgent need to scrutinize the different forms of social security payments and establish the profiles of the recipients. The system of universal coverage is no longer affordable. Politicians are, however, following an over cautious approach as reforms can attract severe political costs.

Table 8.3 House ownership

	1983	1990	2001
House ownership (%)	66	76	92.9
With Piped Water (%)	93	97	99
With Electricity (%)	99	99	>99

Source: IMF Country Reports, various years and HBS 2001/02.

Given the difficult phase of the early years of the structural adjustment period, several pro-poor measures were taken in order to assist the weaker sections of the population. The main ones are:

- Full compensation to workers in the low-income bracket and a rate of compensation exceeding the rate of inflation for old age pensioners and other recipients of social security benefits.
- A National Solidarity Fund (NSF) was set up, with contribution from the government and the private sector to give financial assistance to the unemployed and the needy.
- Subsidization of the price of rice, flour and potatoes.
- The low-income groups are exempted from the payment of income tax. The exempted amount has been progressively increased over the years.
- Staple foods and other basic commodities are exempted from sales tax.
- As indicated earlier, an Unemployment Hardship Relief scheme was introduced in 1983.
- A rent allowance.

Most of the above measures are still in place, except for the subsidies on the price of rice, flour and potatoes, which have been reduced. Also by September 2005, public transport is free for all pensioners and also all full-time students from primary to tertiary level.

Phase 2: enhanced financial and trade liberalization, 1988–98

Towards the end of the 1980s and during the first half of the 1990s, macroeconomic policy was centred on financial and trade liberalization and the management of an economic boom in order to secure sustained growth. The economy was still being propelled by the EPZ export-led growth, the tourism industry and sugar, but with some diversification into the financial services sector with the objective of establishing this sector as another pillar of the Mauritian economy. In fact, between 1992 and 1998, the financial services sector witnessed a rapid growth, with its contribution to GDP averaging 15 to 16 per cent. As from late 1989 an offshore banking sector is also fully operational. The Stock Exchange of Mauritius was set up in July 1989. A Mauritius Freeport was set up in 1992 and the sector gained momentum due to the strategic location of Mauritius. On the social front, however, visible signs of deterioration appeared towards the mid-1990s. There was evidence of growing social inequalities and expanding pockets of poverty mainly in some suburban and coastal regions.

Fiscal policy

The main thrust of fiscal policies during that period was the modernization of the tax system, a move from direct to indirect taxes and significant reforms of the external tariff regime (see Chapter 2). In fact, in the late 1980s and early 1990s the country witnessed several no-tax budgets and towards the end of the 1990s the emphasis on indirect taxes was being reinforced. From Table 8.4 we can see that the share of trade taxes in total tax revenue has decreased from 59 per cent in 1987/88 to around 33 per cent in 1998/99, and the share of indirect taxes has increased from 22 to 45 per cent over the same period. The reform of the indirect tax system is aimed at simplifying the system and eventually reducing effective protection and eliminating reliance by government for budget revenue from import tax. Sales tax was increased to 8 per cent in 1996. In September 1998, the government introduced a Value Added Tax (VAT) as a major step in the reform of the country's indirect tax system. The initial rate set was at 10 per cent. There are limited exemptions for selected foodstuffs and also for goods and services used in education and health activities. The Pay As You Earn (PAYE) system was introduced in 1993 for the payment of income taxes in order to improve tax collection, and the number of tax bands for income tax were reduced from four to three.

The phase of import liberalization and reduction of protection for local firms began in the period 1986–88, with the progressive dismantling of quantitative import restrictions. In 1991, import licensing was eliminated for all except a limited range of products subject to health, sanitary or strategic controls. However, it was only in July 1994 that a major revision of the tariff structure was introduced. In 1994, a three-column tariff consisting of fiscal duty, general customs duty and a preferential duty was consolidated into a one-column import duty and the number of tariff rates reduced from 60 to eight. Maximum customs duty was lowered to 100 per cent and for preferential countries the maximum was set at 80 per cent.

Table 8.4 Share in total tax revenue (per cent)

Year	Share in total tax revenue (%)		
	Income and corporate tax	Taxes on goods and services	Taxes on int. trade
1985/86	10.13	22.17	62.21
1986/87	12.03	22.03	60.36
1987/88	12.76	21.68	58.92
1988/89	14.72	23.77	55.06
1989/90	16.03	23.84	53.06
1990/91	15.33	25.14	51.93
1991/92	16.33	25.11	51.71
1993/94	13.12	29.41	50.51
1994/95	16.23	31.30	45.0
1995/96	17.17	32.30	42.64
1996/97	16.34	36.83	39.78
1997/98	15.36	38.30	39.25
1998/99	15.08	44.72	33.37
1999/00	14.14	45.84	34.04
2000/01	15.05	46.89	31.45
2001/02	16.23	50.29	27.39

Source: Bank of Mauritius, Annual Reports, various issues and IMF Country reports, various issues.

Before June 1994 the maximum customs duty was 600 per cent. Tariffs were lowered on more than 4,000 items in 1994.

It must be noted that the government chose a slower pace of reform of the tariff structure than that advised by the IMF as it considered the negative impact on budget revenue would not only make the budget deficit unsustainable, but would also put at stake important government expenditure on social welfare. But the IMF holds the view that there are still too many high rates and many exemptions, to the extent that the exemptions represent a loss of around 90 per cent of tariff revenue.

Monetary policy

Prior to the 1990s monetary policy was implemented through ceilings on commercial bank credit and administered interest rates. In the 1990s the Bank of Mauritius (BOM) switched from direct to indirect monetary control in line with the general move towards economic liberalization and deregulation. Directed credit programmes were phased out, interest rates were market determined and a series of prudential measures were introduced.

Summary of financial liberalization measures

In July 1988 minimum interest rates on saving deposits were abolished. This was followed four years later by the abolition of the ceiling on bank credit to priority sectors. By July 1993, there was full liberalization of credit, as ceilings on non-priority sectors were also lifted. A Monetary Policy Committee was set up in July 1996 with the view of consolidating the shift to indirect market-based monetary policy. In order to establish a framework to effectively carry out open market operations, there was also the development of a treasury bills market with treasury bills being auctioned from November 1991. A Secondary Market Cell for treasury bills was established in February 1994. Finally, in July 1995, the bank rate was linked to the average Treasury bill rate.

The liberalization of the financial system has also necessitated supplementary measures for reinforcing prudential regulations in order to sustain the stability of the financial system. In accordance with the Basle Capital Accord, minimum risk-weighted capital adequacy ratio was introduced for banks in November 1993 and the minimum capitalization of all banks raised from Rs 25 million to Rs 75 million by January 1998.

Exchange rate policy

It was only when the level of foreign exchange reserves kept rising in the early 1990s and when it became clear that there would not be any excess demand for foreign exchange that imports were fully liberalized and the restrictions on current payments were removed. The sustainability of liberalization was an important objective adopted by policy makers. In September 1993, current account transactions were liberalized.

There was also an important move towards market determination of the exchange rate of the rupee as from mid-July 1994. The rate is now set on the inter-bank

Table 8.5 Current account balance and net reserves

Year	1994	1995	1996	1997	1998	1999	2000	2002
Current account balance (% of GDP)	−2.3	−5.3	−0.6	0.8	−2.9	−1.6	−1.6	5.4
Net int. reserves (Rs million)	15,513	15,007	19,304	21,443	21,349	22,575	25,214	40,551
Net int. reserves (in months of imports)	6.1	5.2	6.3	5.9	5.1	5.0	4.1	5.4

Source: Bank of Mauritius Annual Reports, various issues and author's computations.

market, where the leading commercial banks initially quote the rupee rates at which they would buy and sell the US dollar. The rates are averaged by the Bank of Mauritius to obtain the opening exchange rate of the dollar, which is then used to determine the market cross-rates of other foreign currencies widely used in Mauritius. In August 1994, with the suspension of the Exchange Control Act, capital account transactions were liberalized.

Following the liberalization of external transactions, though the current account has been in deficit, the level of net international reserves has remained satisfactory (see Table 8.5) and there has been no major upward pressure on the exchange rate value of the Mauritian rupee. In fact, there has been more or less, a steady depreciation.[6]

Wage policy and labour productivity

During the early part of the 1980s – that is, the stabilization period – the Mauritian government consciously pursued a policy of ensuring that wage awards were less than the rate of inflation. This policy changed sharply after 1986/87. The declining rate of inflation during the first half of the 1980s has been reversed since 1987, exceeding 10 per cent in the period 1989 to 1991. In fact, the average inflation rate over the period 1989 to 1997 was close to 9 per cent. This had a yo-yo effect on the real interest rate, though as from 1994 onwards, a positive real interest rate was restored (see Table 8.6).

There were three significant wage awards[7] by the Pay Research Bureau for the public sector in 1987/88, 1992/93 and in 1997/98 (Table 8.7). As a result wage increases have exceeded productivity gains, so that unit wages have risen. Towards the end of 1990s, Mauritius has lost its comparative advantage of low-cost labour. Adjustments were falling on the exchange rate.

Compared to the labour cost in some other countries, it can be seen from Table 8.8 that Mauritius no longer has a cheap labour comparative advantage.

From 1995 onwards, the rate of unemployment has gone above 5 per cent and was close to 7 per cent in 1998 and this upward trend has continued and reaching 10 per cent in 2004. Various factors can account for this. First the rising cost of labour, the closure of many EPZ firms, the Voluntary Retirement Scheme (VRS) as

Table 8.6 Trends in inflation and interest rates

	1989	1990	1991	1992	1993	1994	1995	1996	1997	1998
Deposit rate	11.06	12.56	12.31	10.07	8.4	11.04	12.23	10.77	9.08	9.28
Inflation rate	16	10.7	12.8	2.9	8.9	9.4	6.1	5.8	7.9	5.40
Real rate*	−4.96	1.86	−0.49	7.17	−0.50	1.64	6.13	4.97	1.18	3.88

Note:
*Real rate = Deposit rate − inflation rate.
Sources: IMF, *International Financial Statistics*, various issues and Bank of Mauritius, *Annual Reports*, various issues.

Table 8.7 Productivity indicators: annual average growth rate (1995–99)

	Economy	Manufacturing	EPZs
Labour productivity (%)	3.2	2.9	3.5
Average salaries, wages & other benefits (%)	8.5	7.3	7.5
Unit labour cost in Rupee terms (%)	5.2	4.2	3.9
Unit labour cost in US$ terms (%)	−3.6	−4.4	−4.7

Source: Government of Mauritius, 2000.

Table 8.8 Hourly labour cost in US$ terms in the textile industry in 1998

Mauritius	Madagascar	Bangladesh	India	China
1.41	0.41	0.43	0.60	0.62

Source: Werner International in Government of Mauritius, 2000.

part of the strategic plan of the sugar industry and, last, skills mismatch in the labour market.

In fact, one can argue that the BOM, to a certain extent, lost hold of domestic monetary policy during that period, with the generous wage increases, excess liquidity in the banking system and the rise in consumption expenditure. Moreover with the liberalization of the current and capital accounts and the high domestic inflation rates, savers were moving into saving instruments denominated in foreign currencies. As a result, gross domestic savings as a percentage of GDP was falling short of the investment rate by about two to three percentage points over the period 1994–97. In fact, empirical evidence shows that many countries, which liberalized the capital account, witnessed a fall in domestic savings and had an adverse effect on capital formation and Mauritius was no exception.

Foreign investment flows

Mauritius was also attracting the least foreign capital in all of Africa. Whilst FDI soared by 49.5 per cent between 1985 and 1990, it edged up by a mere 13.9 per cent

Table 8.9 FDI inflows (US$ milion)

	1996	1997	1998
Mauritius	37	57	13
Botswana	71	100	168
Uganda	120	175	210
Zimbabwe	81	135	444

Source: World Investment Report, 1999.

in 1991–97. Mean FDI over this period was Rs 482 millions and was negative Rs 37 millions in 1998. The World Investment Report (1997) draws attention to the fact that Mauritius has the lowest record in terms of attracting FDI.

In order to reverse the trend, a Board Of Investment (BOI) was set up in 1999, to act as a one-stop shop for all FDI. But in the years 2000 and 2001, this downward trend was persisting and net FDI was in fact negative.

Public debt

Over the period June 1995 to June 1999, total public debt increased by an annual average rate of 15 per cent, as compared to 7 per cent during the preceding five-year period. As at June 1999, public debt was close Rs 68 billion, representing around 66 per cent of GDP, a threshold that attracts the attention of economic observers and can adversely affect our creditworthiness.

Comparison of economic and social indicators

Tables 8.10 and 8.11 show the evolution of the economic and social indicators from the end of phase 1 to the end of phase 2. Towards the end of the 1990s, the economy was thus marked by a number of adverse developments. The deficiency in domestic savings and investment, high rate of private sector credit expansion, excess liquidity, relatively high rate of inflation and rising unemployment. The economy was characterized by macroeconomic imbalances, reflecting mainly the lagged impact of generous increases in wages and salaries in previous years.

We can see that the deterioration in the macroeconomic indicators (except the growth rate of GDP which was close to 6 per cent) was matched by deterioration in the Gini coefficient and in the percentage of households earning less than half the median income. Poverty and inequality are closely linked to the economic cycle. In Mauritius towards the end of the 1990s, this 'trickle down effect' of growth on poverty was not happening. In fact, this phenomenon of growth losing its antipoverty effectiveness has been observed in many countries.[8]

From the late 1980s to the early 1990s, we can see an improvement in the Gini coefficient, showing a further reduction in the levels of income inequality. However, from the mid-1990s to 1997, there has been deterioration in the Gini coefficient, rising from 0.379 to 0.387, despite a significant improvement in the

Table 8.10 Trends in economic indicators

	1989	1991	1993	1995	1997
Macroeconomic policy inputs					
Nominal interest rate	11.06	12.31	8.4	12.23	9.08
Real rate	−4.94	−0.49	−0.5	6.13	1.18
Money supply (M2)	18460	26767	36380	47859	60359
Nominal exchange rate (Rs/$)	15.250	15.652	17.648	17.386	21.057
Real exchange rate	98.0	100.5	101.2	104.1	106.7
Budget deficit (% of GDP)	3.8	2	2	3.7	4.5
Macroeconomic outputs as % of GNP					
Current account balance	−5.16	−2.1	−2.4	−5.3	0.80
Overall BOP balance	6.05	5.53	−1.61	−1.44	1.82
FDI	4.17	3.15	0.53	0.33	1.11
Portfolio flows	n.a	n.a	n.a	4.37	−1.59
Tax revenue	20.20	20.38	18.13	15.83	15.96
Public debt:					
Domestic	35.96	38.18	29.17	31.02	34.47
External	17.39	13.43	10.09	8.26	11.02
Inflation (%)	16	12.8	8.9	6.1	7.9
Real economy outputs					
GDP growth rate	4.0	4.4	5	5.6	5.6
Investment rate	27.1	28.9	28.4	24.4	27.1
Savings rate	21.5	24.1	24.7	22.9	24.5
Openness	0.979	0.964	0.866	0.873	0.855
Unemployment rate	2.6	2.6	1.8	5.1	6.6
GDP per capita US$	2,019	2,500	3,000	3,490	3,525
Population growth rate (%)	0.77	1.07	1.18	0.85	1.26

Source: Bank of Mauritius, Annual Reports, various issues and author's computations.

Table 8.11 Movements in social indicators

Year	1986/87	1991/92	1996/97
Average monthly income per household (Rs)	3,496	6,503	10,179
Median monthly income (Rs)	2,663	5,300	7,870
Gini coefficient	0.396	0.379	0.387
Half-median (Rs)	1,332	2,650	3,935
One-third mean (Rs)	1,165	2,168	3,393
% of total income:			
Lowest quintile	6.7	6.6	5.9
Highest quintile	45.5	43.75	46.2
Adjusted half-median	1,062	1,395	1,684

Source: Bank of Mauritius Annual Report, various issues, Household Budget Surveys and author's computations.

Table 8.12 Government expenditure on community and social services

Percentage on	1991/92	1992/93	1993/94	1994/95	1995/96	1996/7	1997/98	1998/99
Education	14	13.7	15.8	16.7	15.7	16.6	16.9	15.8
Health	8	9.4	9.1	8.7	8.3	7.7	8.3	8.4
Social security and welfare	15.1	16	16.1	16.2	17.2	18.6	20.6	21.1
Housing	3.9	5.9	6.9	6.7	5.3	5.9	5.9	5.1
% of total govt. exp.	43.8	46.8	49.4	50	48.3	50.5	53.2	52.1

Source: Government Annual Digest of Public Finance, various issues.

average monthly income and the median income. Moreover, in 1991/92, around 14 per cent of households were earning less than half median income and around 8.5 per cent were earning less than one third mean income. In 1996/97, the corresponding figures deteriorated to 14.7 per cent and 11 per cent respectively. There was also a regression in the percentage of income earned by the lowest and highest quintile. However, absolute poverty (based on the adjusted half median-income measure), fell from around 5 per cent in 1991/92 to around 3.7 per cent of households in 1996/97.

With the deterioration in the social indicators, policy makers and other stakeholders considered that poverty needed to be tackled by direct policies designed for this purpose. Various programmes to tackle poverty were set up. These targeted programmes are discussed briefly further in this chapter.

As a result, we observe from Table 8.12 that there has been an increase in government expenditure on community and social services, including social security and welfare during that period, in a way, reinforcing the social safety nets. The government also did not waver regarding its housing policy. In fact, expenditure on housing has doubled compared to the 1980s, where it was around 3 per cent of total government expenditure.

Phase 3: sugar protocol uncertainty, dismantling of trade preferences, AGOA, 1999–2005

In the wake of globalization and trade liberalization, the Mauritian economy is confronted with some serious challenges both on the domestic front and at the international level. The emphasis of macroeconomic policies is therefore directed to economic restructuring in terms of the reorientation of the EPZ sector towards better-quality products, improving productivity by using better technology, improving efficiency of the sugar industry and enhancing economic diversification by promoting the ICT sector,[9] non-sugar agricultural diversification and promoting the fishing industry. Mauritian entrepreneurs are also tapping into investment opportunities in the African region.

It is certain that the price of sugar on the EU market is going to fall in the near future. The local sugar production costs are high. However, the scope for cost reduction in the production of sugar is real and, with appropriate restructuring and re-engineering of this sector, sugar can still play an important role in the development of the country. In 2001, the government of Mauritius, fully conscious of the threats and challenges facing the sugar sector, launched the Sugar Sector Strategic Plan (SSSP) 2001–05, with the participation of all the stakeholders in the sugar industry. The major issues of the plan include more centralization, cost reduction, enhanced productivity, labour force rightsizing using a Voluntary Retirement Scheme (VRS) and mechanization processes, the optimum use of cane sugar resources and the creation of new opportunities. Many aspects of the plan are already being implemented.

The phasing-out of the Multi-Fibre Agreement (MFA) in December 2004 has placed the Mauritian textile sector on a level playing field with its competitors. Cheaper Asian garments and the emergence of cheap labour countries such as Madagascar, Sri Lanka, and China to name a few certainly represent important challenges for Mauritius.

However, the adverse effects of these developments could be offset in part by the Africa Growth and Opportunity Act (AGOA), which provides preferential access for apparel exports to the US market from sub-Saharan Africa, including Mauritius. The AGOA may also act as a further incentive for EPZ companies to accelerate their de-localization process, especially in favour of Madagascar. In fact, quite a number of textile firms have already migrated to Madagascar.

As a result, the grim reality is that the rate of employment in the EPZ sector has fallen by about 17 per cent between 2001 and 2003 (see Table 8.13). Many of these workers are in the low-income group and many of them have spent 15 to 20 years in the textile sector and are finding it difficult to retrain into another sector. Moreover, many of them are in their late 40s and find themselves practically unemployable. The government is providing some assistance to them in terms of vocational training. In this transition process, the low-income group, with their poor ability to cope with risks, is bearing a significant share of the adjustment costs. Suddenly, many of these households find themselves with only one income earner, with direct consequences on their standard of living, on their debt repaying capacity and on the education of their wards.

Table 8.13 Number of firms and employment in the EPZ sector

Year	1995	1996	1997	1998	1999	2000	2001	2002	2003
Firms	477	475	478	485	505	519	524	509	506
Employment	81,823	79,269	81,915	87,057	90,812	90,765	92,966	86,987	77,623

Source: Bank of Mauritius Annual Report, various issues.

The tourism sector has remained buoyant: four new hotels have been constructed recently, and the sector is presently attracting around 700,000 tourists per annum. The Mauritius Tourism Promotion Authority is pursuing a more aggressive marketing campaign in order to project this industry on a higher growth path. Airline access is being liberalized.

Fiscal and monetary policies

Fiscal and monetary policies are aimed to facilitate the restructuring of the sugar and textile sectors and, at the same time, to promote the emerging ICT sector. Government is encouraging vertical integration in the textile sector so that firms can fully exploit AGOA. A special package of fiscal incentives has been devised to promote investment in spinning plants. The scheme includes a special tax credit of up to 60 per cent of the equity invested, spread over a maximum period of six years. At the Development Bank of Mauritius, a Textile Modernisation Loan Scheme has been set up.

The emphasis of fiscal policy during this period has also been on further reforms of the external tariffs regime and increased reliance on indirect taxes for government revenue. In June 2000, tariffs have been removed on an additional 1,300 items. On the other hand, the VAT rate has been increased twice – to 10 per cent in July 2001 and then 15 per cent in July 2002. Though there are exemptions for some basic commodities, there are many commodities bought by the poor, which are not VAT exempt. The fiscal policies, in terms of reduction in personal income tax rates, and income tax bands, have benefited mainly the middle- and high-income groups.

In 2002, trade taxes account for only 27 per cent of tax revenue whereas taxes on goods and services account for 45 per cent (see Table 8.4). In July 2001, the corporate tax rate was further reduced from 35 to 25 per cent and the maximum income tax rate has been lowered from 28 to 25 per cent. In addition, there are only two income tax bands. There are also efforts to improve tax collection and reduce fiscal fraud. The Mauritius Revenue Authority was established in 2004 in order to bring all taxes, internal taxes and custom duties, under a single central administration.

The basic thrust of monetary policy in this period continues to be directed towards the achievement of low inflation and a stable exchange rate of the rupee while allowing a greater interplay of market forces in the determination of interest rates and exchange rates. Special lines of credit are being made available to the sugar industry and the EPZ sector in order to assist them in their modernization process.

Legislation will be amended to provide for a more generalized conduct of repurchase operations (repo) among financial institutions. This will enhance the effectiveness of liquidity management and improve the conduct of monetary policy. The legislative and institutional framework for the financial services sector is also being strengthened.

Debt policy

With a view to containing the rise in public debt, the government has decided to separate debt management from monetary management. Since August 2003, the

BOM has been auctioning Treasury Bills and other government securities solely for meeting government's cash flow requirements. For monetary policy purposes, it is issuing Bank of Mauritius Bills. While these measures will contribute to improve debt management, by themselves they will be insufficient. A durable reduction in the budget deficit will be necessary to achieve long-term debt sustainability. The target is to bring the budget deficit down to 3 per cent of GDP by 2005, but it is unlikely that this target will be achieved.

Exchange rate policy

The exchange rate policy continues to reflect the macroeconomic fundamentals of the country. Intervention by the CB in the currency market is limited to smoothing out seasonal and unwarranted short-term fluctuations in the exchange rate of the rupee. The BOM has consistently signalled to the market that long-run competitiveness of our products on international markets depends essentially on productivity gains rather than exchange rate changes. The CB has made it clear that in a more liberalized financial environment, it is imperative for export-oriented sectors to adjust and be more productive so as to operate without the protective net of exchange rate adjustment.

Foreign investment

As emphasized under phase 2, Mauritius was not doing well in terms of attracting FDI and an urgent need to reverse the situation was felt. As a result, the entire system of issuing permits and licences for investment projects have been reviewed. The system was clogged by red tape. The aim is to reduce waiting time, provide for greater predictability, and fast-track procedures. A time frame has been set for the determination of applications. Legislative changes will be introduced to streamline procedures relating to development permits at local government level. A Permits and Licences Committee will be established in each local authority to interact with the Board of Investment. Net FDI flows have resumed a positive and significant trend as from 2002.

Trends in economic and social indicators

From the period 1996/97 to 2001/02, we can see an improvement in the income distribution, despite the fact that most of the macroeconomic indicators were deteriorating, with the exception of the rate of economic growth, which was still reasonable at 5.6 per cent and the inflation rate, which stood at 4.4 per cent in 2001. From HBS 2001/02, we also note that 13.2 per cent of households were earning less than half the median income and around 9.7 per cent less than one-third the mean income. The corresponding figures in 1996/97 were 14.7 and 11 per cent respectively. Moreover, base on the absolute poverty indicator, the percentage of households below the poverty line is around 2.8 per cent.

The major targeted programmes to alleviate poverty mainly through micro-credit and micro-finance also started as from 1995 and with added vigour in 1999. Possibly these programmes could also have contributed for the improvement in the poverty indicators as they are specifically designed for the poor.

Table 8.14 Economic indicators

	1999	2001	2003	2004
Macroeconomic policy inputs				
Nominal interest rate	10.92	9.78	9.53	6.86
Real rate	3.02	5.38	4.43	2.96
Money supply (M2, Rs million)	80,204	97,753	123,405	141,132
Nominal exchange rate (Rs/$)	25.186	29.129	27.901	28.46
Real exchange rate	107.7	108.5	107.9	n.a
Budget deficit (% of GDP)	3.6	6.7	6.2	5.6
Macroeconomic Outputs as % of GNP				
Current account balance	−1.57	1.67	3.40	1.10
Overall BOP balance	0.65	3.85	5.79	1.86
FDI	1.01	−0.63	1.20	n.a
Portfolio flows	1.04	−0.425	−0.318	n.a
Tax revenue	16.73	15.22	16.49	16.59
Public debt:				
Domestic	38.35	40.26	55.07	48.94
External	9.39	5.41	5.78	4.85
Inflation (%)	7.9	4.4	5.1	3.9
Real economy outputs				
GDP Growth rate	2.3	5.6	4.8	4.5
Investment rate	27.5	22.5	22.7	22.2
Savings rate	23.1	26.7	26.0	26.2
Openness	0.896	0.765	0.762	0.715
Unemployment rate	7.7	9.1	10.2	n.a
GDP per capita US$	3,558	3,767	4,493	5,000[1]
Population growth rate (%)	1.28	1.09	1.04	0.86

Note:
[1] Estimate.
Source: Bank of Mauritius Annual Report, various issues and author's computations.

Table 8.15 Movements in social indicators

HBS indicators	1996/97	2001/02
Average monthly income (Rs)	10,179	14,208
Median monthly income (Rs)	7,870	11,017
Gini coefficient	0.387	0.371
Half-median (Rs)	3,935	5,508
One-third mean (Rs)	3,393	4,736
% of total income:		
Lowest quintile	5.9	6.6
Highest quintile	46.2	44.5
Half-median in constant prices	1,684	1,906

Source: Household Budget Surveys and author's computations.

Targeted approach to poverty alleviation

Overall, over the period 1990 to 2001, one can argue that there has not been a significant impact on reduction of income inequality in Mauritius, with the Gini coefficient moving from 0.379 to 0.371 and only a modest improvement in the relative poverty indicators.[10] An urgent need was therefore felt for a re-dynamized targeted approach to combat poverty in Mauritius.

In fact, Ravallion (2003) argues that growth is not enough as the impact of growth on poverty is heterogeneous and also growth does not spread well to backward regions, those marginally connected to the modern economy. As a result, a targeted approach is also an important ingredient of a pro-poor growth strategy.

There are some regions in the country where there is a compounded concentration of different forms of vulnerabilities. In 1996, the Central Statistical Office came up with a Relative Development Index in order to better assess the regions in the country, which are lagging behind in terms of economic development. 52 regions were identified (see Household Budget Survey 1996/97). 12 variables[11] are used in the computation of the index.

The areas of intervention are mainly in: the provision of housing units, food, social infrastructure, income-generating activities via micro-finance and micro-credit, and education and vocational training support.

In 1995 a plan (called the Marshall Plan) for the development of deprived regions were set up comprising of 60 projects. In 1995/96 a provision of Rs 500 million was made to the Trust Fund for the Social Integration of Vulnerable Groups (TFSIVG) to fight against exclusion. In the context of the 8th European Development Fund, a unit called 'A Nou Diboute Ensam' (ANDE) was set up. The International Fund for Agricultural Diversification (IFAD) is financing rural diversification program to create income-generating activities for the poor particularly in agriculture and fishing.

Overall, these programmes have contributed to poverty alleviation. However, there are doubts whether some of these programmes are reaching the poorest of the poor.

Econometric analysis

In this section we analyze the impact of some important economic variables known to affect income inequality, based on previous research. As mentioned before in the introduction to this chapter, relative poverty is more of an issue in Mauritius than absolute poverty, so our analysis will concentrate on the impact of the reforms on relative inequality. Given that we do not have sufficient observations on half median income, we use the one-third mean income as our measure of relative poverty and as the dependent variable in our regression model. We investigate the impact of the following explanatory variables: the rate of inflation, the rate of unemployment, the budget deficit as a percentage of GDP, a measure of openness, proxied as the sum of exports and imports to GDP and a measure of financial liberalization, proxied as the ratio of M2 to

GDP. The regression model is as follows and all variables are converted in log form:

One-third mean income = $\alpha_0 + \beta_1$ Inflation + β_2 Unemployment + β_3 GNP percapita + β_4 Budget Deficit + β_5 Openness + β_6 Financial Liberalization

We expect high inflation rate, high unemployment rate and high budget deficits to have a negative impact on the one-third mean income and to therefore make the poor worse off. We expect GNP per capita, openness and financial liberalization to have a positive impact on the relative poverty measure.

The results are reported in Table 8.15. The results must be interpreted with caution given the low number of observations, but based on the data set, the reported coefficients are the best estimates of the relationships.

We find that inflation has a negative impact on relative poverty, but is not significant. This could be due to the fact that households in the lowest-income bracket are given full compensation for increases in the cost of living. Unemployment also has a negative impact and is significant at the 5 per cent level. The above result is consistent with Blank and Binder (1986) who concluded that 'unemployment', and not 'inflation' has the strongest bearing on the welfare of the poor. High budget deficits have a negative impact on income inequality, but statistically insignificant. Increases in GNP per capita, proxy for growth, have a significant impact on reducing relative poverty. Openness has a positive effect but surprisingly is not significant. It could be that the effects are already captured by increases in per capita income. We find that financial liberalization is highly significant but had an adverse effect on low-income earners. This is consistent with the findings of Székely (2003). One would expect that low-income earners are high-risk borrowers and are, as a consequence, crowded out of the formal financial market.

Table 8.16 Dependent variable: one-third mean income (relative poverty measure)

Explanatory variables	Coefficient	t-statistic
Constant	−75.98	−4.53*
Inflation	−0.11	−0.248
Unemployment (−2)	−0.96	−2.20**
GDP per capita	6.93	5.00*
Budget Deficit	−0.39	−0.54
Openness	1.46	0.33
Financial liberalization	−22.90	−5.41*
Number of Obs.	22	
F (6, 15)	5.80	
Adj. R-Squared	57.84	

Note: *t-statistic significant at 1% and **at 5% level respectively.

Conclusion

This chapter has analysed the financial, trade and other economic reforms over three time periods in Mauritius and the corresponding impact on poverty and inequality during these same periods. Over the three periods combined, the economic reforms made a significant contribution in fighting absolute poverty and reducing income inequality. Surprisingly, the econometric analysis reveals that the financial reforms made the poor worse off. Moreover, in the mid-1990s, productivity was not keeping pace with the increase in wages in preceding years and there was also a delay in addressing economic restructuring and diversification. Therefore, emphasis is being placed on improving productivity and expanding the economic space. Furthermore, given that the linkage between growth and improvements in the social indicators has become less apparent as from the mid-1990s, in parallel, a more coherent targeted grass-roots approach is being followed to alleviate poverty and reduce social exclusion.

The ingredients of a pro-poor growth strategy would therefore embrace the following:

- sound macroeconomic management
- high levels of political commitment
- political stability
- respect for law and order and functioning institutions to fight corruption
- appropriate policies with respect to health, education, housing and social security
- economic diversification to reduce exposure to external shocks
- a targeted approach

Mauritius is an ethnically diverse society and, as Bleaney and Nishiyama (2004) found in a recent study, that in ethnically diverse countries, wealth is likely to be distributed more equitably in order to maintain political stability. Also where voting behaviour can influence government policy, we usually see a greater commitment to providing social safety nets and reducing inequality.[12] In Mauritius, since the 1980s, every government has been a coalition government, which demonstrates that in order to come to power, votes from all segments of the population must be solicited.

Moreover, the ingredients of a pro-poor growth strategy would be incomplete without taking into account growth rates of the world economy, and the commitments undertaken by developed countries[13] at major international meetings such as in Doha (the Doha Development Agenda) and in Monterrey (the Monterrey Partnership Consensus) to open market access, reduce non-tariff barriers, eliminate subsidies on agriculture, promote technological transfer and increase targeted foreign aid. At the global level, however, 'le constat' is that, the impact of pro-poor growth has yet to assert itself. The stark reality as at 2002, some three billion people (around half of the world's population) live on less than $2 a day and have no access to sanitation; nearly half of these live on less than $1 a day and have no access to clean water; almost two billion people have no access to electricity.[14]

Notes

1. Two devaluations were undertaken, one in October 1979 by 23 per cent and the next one in September 1981 by 16.7 per cent in order to improve the competitiveness of the export sector and to reverse the chronic current account deficit.
2. It must be noted that unfortunately in Mauritius the statistics published on poverty are quite scarce. There is no information available on the headcount ratio, poverty gap, FGT(2), etc.
3. This was given as a political bribe before the general election.
4. In Mauritius, as is common in other developing countries, there was a bias for girls to stay at home when secondary education was fee-paying.
5. For instance, see Janvry and Sadoulet (1999).
6. See Tables 8.9 and 8.13.
7. There was another salary revision award in 2003.
8. For instance, see Haveman and Schwabish (2000).
9. Already renowned international firms engaged in software development, ICT training and call centres are operating in Mauritius.
10. In 1991/92, 14 per cent of households were earning less than half the median income compared to 13.2 per cent in 2001/02. Similarly, 8.5 per cent were earning less than one-third the mean income compared to 9.7 per cent in 2001/02.
11. Among other variables, household physical infrastructure such as electricity, piped water, flush toilet, dwelling with concrete walls, educational attainment such as primary and secondary enrolment ratio, employment rate in the region etc.
12. See Iyigun and Owen (2004).
13. Commitments undertaken by developing countries also, in terms of improved governance, more stable democracy, implementation of structural reforms etc. See International Monetary Fund and World Bank, *Global Monitoring Report 2004: Policies and Actions for Achieving the MDGs and Related Outcomes*, Washington DC: IMF and World Bank, 2004.
14. See Arvin and Barillas (2002).

References

Arvin, B.M. and F. Barillas. 2002. 'Foreign Aid, Poverty Reduction, and Democracy', *Applied Economics*, 34(17), 2151–6.
Bank of Mauritius. Various years. *Annual Reports*. Mauritius.
Blank, R. and A. Binder. 1986. 'Macroeconomics, Income Distribution, and Poverty'. In S.H. Danziger and D.H. Weinberg (eds), *Fighting Poverty: What Works and What Doesn't*. Cambridge, MA: Harvard University Press.
Bleaney, M. and A. Nishiyama. 2004. *Economic Growth, Income Distribution and Poverty: Time-Series and Cross-Country Evidence from the CFA-Zone Countries of sub-Saharan Africa*, Research Paper No 2004/3. Helsinki: WIDER.
Government of Mauritius. Various issues. 'Annual Digest of Public Finance'. Central Statistical Office.
Government of Mauritius. 2000. *The Present State of the Economy*. Ministry of Finance, Mauritius.
Government of Mauritius. 2000. *Housing Census*. Mauritius: Central Statistical Office.
Haveman, R. and J. Schwabish. 2000. 'Has Macroeconomic Performance Regained its Antipoverty Bite?' *Contemporary Economic Policy*, 18(4), 415–27.
Household Budget Surveys (HBS). 1975, 1980/81, 1985/86, 1996/97, 2001/02. Mauritius: Central Statistical Office.
International Monetary Fund (IMF). Various years. *Country Reports on Mauritius*
International Monetary Fund (IMF). Various years. *International Financial Statistics*.

International Monetary Fund and World Bank. 2004. *Global Monitoring Report 2004: Policies and Actions for Achieving the MDGs and Related Outcomes*. Washington DC: IMF and World Bank.

Iyigun, M. and A.L. Owen. 2004. 'Income Inequality, Financial Development And Macroeconomic Fluctuations'. *The Economic Journal*, 114, 352–76.

Janvry, A. and E. Sadoulet. 1999. *Growth Poverty, And Inequality In Latin America: Causal Analysis, 1970–94*. Conference on Social Protection and Poverty. Washington DC: Inter-American Development Bank.

Kraay, A. 2004. *When is Growth, Pro-poor? Cross-Country Evidence*. Working Paper 3225. World Bank Policy Research.

Ravallion, M. 2003. 'The Debate On Globalization, Poverty And Inequality. Why Measurement Matters?' *International Affairs*, 79(4), 739–53.

Ravallion, M. and S. Chen. 2003. 'Measuring Pro-Poor Growth'. *Economic Letters*, 78(1), 93–9.

Székely, M. 2003. 'The 1990s in Latin America: Another Decade of Persistent Inequality, But With Somewhat Lower Poverty'. *Journal of Applied Economics*, 6(2), 317–39.

UNCTAD. 1999. World Investment Report, 1999. Geneva: UNCTAD.

9
Macroeconomic Policy, Growth, Redistribution and Poverty Reduction: the Case of Malaysia

Wee Chong Hui and Jomo K. S.

Malaysia's management of its economy is often seen as being rather unconventional and inconsistent. Even before the controversial September 1998 imposition of capital controls, Malaysia's economic management style was described as unorthodox. After the events of May 1969, the government formulated the New Economic Policy (NEP) to 'eradicate' (reduce) poverty and to 'restructure society' (reduce inter-ethnic economic disparities). Accordingly, the government sector grew with increased expenditure, budgetary deficits and public debt in the 1970s. The government initiated a heavy industrialization drive in the early 1980s, but in the mid-1980s it abruptly opted for a more restrictive fiscal policy and in the mid-1990s it even ran modest budget surpluses. Huge deficits were incurred again after the 1997–98 financial crisis, but these were justified as being pro-recovery, rather than pro-poor (Jomo 2001, 2003).

Although Malaysia has been committed to eliminating poverty since 1970, there is mixed evidence about the efficacy of its poverty eradication programmes. Over the years, NEP expenditure shifted from poverty eradication to 'restructuring society'. However, there has also been a significant decline in poverty, especially during the 1970s. Macroeconomic policy in Malaysia has historically been seen as subordinate to development policy, but the understanding of what constitutes development has also changed radically, especially under Prime Minister Mahathir Mohamad's leadership from 1981 to 2003.

During the last three and a half decades, and especially during the 1970s and early 1980s, Malaysia substantially reduced the incidence of poverty – it decreased from 49.3 per cent in 1970 to 20.7 per cent in 1984, 17.1 per cent in 1990 and 5.1 per cent in 2002 (see Table 9.1).

This chapter suggests that poverty in Malaysia has been significantly reduced, mainly due to growth and structural change, particularly during the 1970s. Hence, although there has been reduced emphasis on poverty reduction since the 1970s, episodes of high growth contributed significantly to poverty reduction. Available evidence also suggests that income inequality declined during the 1970s and slightly during the 1980s, but that it has risen slightly since then. There is some evidence that a greater role for the state has been good for reducing inequality, but the relationships are too complex to test conclusively

Table 9.1 Malaysia: incidence of poverty, 1970–2002 (percentage)

Year	Overall	Rural	Urban
1970[a]	49.3	58.6	24.6
1976[a]	39.6	47.8	17.9
1984	20.7	27.3	8.5
1987	19.3	24.7	8.4
1990	17.1	21.8	7.5
1993	13.5	18.6	5.3
1995	9.6	16.1	4.1
1997	6.8	11.8	2.4
1998	7.6	NA	NA
1999	7.5	12.4	3.4
2002	5.1	10	1.9

Notes:
[a]Consumer Peninsular Malaysia only.
NA = not available.

Sources: Malaysia (1981, 1989, 1991a, 1993, 1995, 1999a, 2001b); Noriyah bt Ahmad (2004).

Macroeconomic regime

Malaysian macroeconomic policy has been summarized as 'optimizing growth subject to restraint on prices and the balance of payments'. Investment is critical, not only as a factor input, but also because technological change, skills upgrading and improved coverage of social and physical infrastructure comes with investment. By influencing the rate and allocation of investment, economic policy makers have also hoped to facilitate desired structural changes. Growth was also considered necessary for achieving the socioeconomic objectives of the NEP (1971–90) and its successors, the National Development Policy (1991–2000) and the National Vision Policy (2001–10). Basically, macroeconomic management has focused on sustaining high growth by raising the rates of productive investment.

The price constraint is built into the growth cum investment targets. The investment rate was targeted to be in line with the country's capacity to 'absorb' investment without incurring bottlenecks and price tensions – for example, increasing wage rates. The balance-of-payments constraint is also built into the growth target. Thus, the investment rate is deemed manageable, given the country's saving rate and expected long-term capital inflows. The savings–investment gap approximated the capital account surplus and, hence, the current account deficit. In this way, the overall balance-of-payments position would be balanced, and the currency reserves and value of the ringgit would remain stable.

External sector

Malaysia has long been an open economy with a relatively liberal trade regime, though it adopted selective protection measures to advance import-substituting industrialization, which have been reduced since the late 1960s since moving to an export-oriented industrialization strategy. In general, tariff rates have been quite low by international standards.

Malaysia has long been keen on attracting long-term capital inflows, particularly in the form of greenfield foreign direct investment (FDI). To maintain investor confidence, Malaysia maintained relatively liberal foreign exchange controls until September 1998, and both residents and non-residents were allowed to freely remit their own funds abroad. In addition, the government concluded investment guarantee agreements that provide for protection against nationalization and expropriation, compensation in the event of nationalization or expropriation, the unlimited repatriation of profits, capital and other fees and payments as well as the settlement of investment disputes in accordance with the Convention on Settlement of Investment Disputes. It has also granted generous tax holidays, investment tax allowances, reinvestment allowances and export allowances to foreign-owned companies in order to encourage them to establish operations in Malaysia[1].

Monetary policy

Macroeconomic management in Malaysia has been led by the real side of the economy. Monetary management has thus been mainly facilitative in nature, and laws largely implemented by managing money supply. Money supply growth is anchored to the gross domestic product (GDP) growth target, which allows for increased monetization and some 'tolerated' inflation. As monetary variables may be quite volatile, the money supply target is only a rough benchmark, and it is not adhered to rigidly as long as GDP growth, prices, exchange rates and so on remain within acceptable bounds.

The central bank has tried to maintain an interest rate policy consistent with inflation management. It thus raises interest rates when inflation is of concern and lowers them when growth is of concern. Government loans have been used to 'mop up' excess liquidity. In contrast, interest rate policy does not play a central role in the control of inflation as other tools are used to manage aggregate demand and prices.

Interest rate policy has also been used to control currency volatility, especially when this is caused by short-term flows into and out of the country. Thus, if there is speculation against the ringgit, causing the currency to weaken against its 'fundamental value', the central bank may buy ringgit; or, if foreign exchange reserves are low, it may increase short-term interest rates to attract funds from abroad. Furthermore, the interest rate policy has primacy over other tools in the central bank's management of foreign reserves.

In contrast, interest rate policy has rarely been used to influence the level of investment, including private investment that has instead been encouraged by tax and other incentives. Not surprisingly, most empirical studies find only a weak relationship between interest rates and investments.

Fiscal policy

Fiscal policy is primarily used to influence the level and direction of public sector investment. Fiscal policy is an integral part of the planning process and the yearly fiscal budget is the valve through which the state (in particular, public sector development programmes) intervenes. Spending authority is approved by Parliament through the annual budget's supply bills.

Overall economic management

The key positive feedback targeted by Malaysian policy makers is between output growth, savings and exports. Output growth in excess of the population growth rate should lead to higher per capita incomes and higher savings. As the rate of growth of consumption is planned to be slower than the rate of output growth, appropriate policies are put in place to encourage savings or restrain consumption. Savings may also be facilitated by enhancing the development of financial markets, for example, by providing a reliable legal and institutional framework, maintaining low rates of inflation or raising the rate of mandatory savings of the Employees' Provident Fund (see Chapter 5 of this volume). Meanwhile, consumption may be restrained by tightening credit and by administrative measures besides raising interest rates. As long as growth supports savings and vice versa, growth itself will sustain investments and thus further growth. Positive feedback between output growth and exports growth has been ensured by focusing on the tradable sectors of the economy so that output growth leads to either rising export earnings or import substitution. In this way, export performance has been a policy-sensitive variable.

Rapid growth may lead to a rapid rise in imports, which may not be fully matched by exports, resulting in a balance-of-payments deficit. If the deficit persists, the country's reserves will decline and the value of the currency with it, with potentially serious results. The balance of payments is thus a very binding constraint. The expected rate of growth of imports must therefore be exceeded by – or at least equal – the target export growth rate.

While Malaysian macroeconomic policy makers treat the balance-of-payments constraint as binding, their method of managing such constraint is unconventional. By ensuring that the investment rate is close to the savings rate, planners try to align the growth target with the balance-of-payments constraint. By focusing on growth in the tradable sector, rapid growth can contribute positively to increasing net export earnings. Finally, detailed policies to involve other components of the balance of payments to improve the situation have been undertaken. For example, large net capital inflows have allowed Malaysia to spread adjustment processes over several years.

Though Malaysia's macroeconomic management has been conventional in several respects, many policy criteria, tools and targets have been 'unconventional' (Ghazali 1990). Growth is the dominant objective, and it has been only rarely deliberately constrained, simply for fear it may be inflationary. Problems leading to 'overheating' were generally treated as being the result of structural reasons requiring long-term solutions and policy makers went to great lengths to sustain growth, even when the economy is 'overheating'. As inflation is seen as due to aggregate demand exceeding aggregate supply, 'balancing' the two sides – by raising aggregate supply, for example, via increased imports, even of labour, rather than reducing aggregate demand – is seen as the appropriate solution. This may involve increasing access to industrial inputs, physical infrastructure, labour and so on. Malaysia also undertakes price management and administrative measures to prevent prices from rising during temporary shortages and to prevent artificial shortages that could arise if monopolies use their market power at the expense of consumers.

The focus on structural factors reflects the longer time perspective typical of development economics and thus entailed more detailed interventions than conventional macroeconomics that merely focuses on counter-cyclical objectives to be reached by means of the fiscal and monetary policies. Policy making in Malaysia is also concerned with mobilizing resources and facilitating investment, managing structural transformation, defining detailed sectoral policies, pursuing trade policies, undertaking public investment, facilitating and guiding private investment, upgrading social and physical infrastructure and planning human resources.

In Malaysia, such policies were all considered to be part of the 'macroeconomic framework'. This framework was revised at regular intervals in the form of plan documents, policies and strategies. Neither monetary nor fiscal policy was independent. The central bank often used monetary policy to stabilize prices or to defend the currency. Fiscal and administrative measures were often used to influence private sector consumption and investment behaviour. These policies addressed short-term concerns, but also involved long-term policies.

Macroeconomic targets

Per capita income and living standards have been projected to rise for the country to reach developed status. Given expected Malaysian population growth of 2–3per cent, a growth rate of 7 per cent to 8 per cent was considered desirable for a steady annual increase in per capita income of between 4.5 per cent and 5.5 per cent.

Inflation used to be deemed acceptable as long as it stayed below 5 per cent per annum, with 4–5 per cent targeted for planning purposes. An investment rate of over 30 per cent of GDP was long considered feasible without causing labour, infrastructure and other implementation constraints. Such an investment rate usually translated into growth of between 6 and 8 per cent, which was regarded as sustainable without being inflationary. To avoid 'balance-of-payments constraints to growth' over the long term, Malaysian planners usually target a current deficit or surplus of 1–2 per cent of gross national product (GNP).

Macroeconomic policies and outcomes in the 1970s

The government adopted a conservative stance in the 1960s, when it focused on low budget deficits. After the racial riots of May 1969, the government formulated the NEP to 'eradicate poverty irrespective of race' and to 'restructure society' – that is, to reduce inter-ethnic economic disparities, especially between the ethnic Malay majority and the ethnic Chinese. Budget deficits grew accordingly in the 1970s (see Table 9.2).

Table 9.2 Malaysia: federal government finance, 1963–2004 (nominal value in RM million)

	Revenue	Operating expenditure	Current balance	Development expenditure	Overall balance
1963–1965	4,188	3,959	229	1,527	−1,298
1966–1970	9,897	9,309	588	3,187	−2,599
1971–1975	18,645	18,026	619	7,371	−6,752
1976–1980	47,189 (23.8%)	38,199 (19.3%)	8,990 (4.5%)	20,659 (10.4%)	−11,669 (−5.9%)
1981–1985	93,025 (26.8%)	82,004 (23.6%)	11,021 (3.2%)	46,571 (13.4%)	−35,550 (−10.2%)
1986–1990	114,422 (24.7%)	109,480 (23.6%)	4,942 (1.1%)	28,738 (6.2%)	−23,796 (−5.1%)
1991–1995	215,394 (25.2%)	164,225 (19.2%)	51,169 (6.0%)	48,429 (5.7%)	2,740 (0.3%)
1996–2000	301,265 (20.6%)	236,360 (16.2%)	64,903 (4.4%)	90,668 (6.2%)	−25,764 (−1.8%)
2001–2004 estimate	355,087 (23.09%)	243,187 (15.8%)	47,769 (3.1%)	117,134 (7.6%)	−69,371 (−4.5%)

Note: Figures in brackets indicate % of GDP.
Source: Ministry of Finance (various issues).

Table 9.3 Malaysia: federal government expenditure by functional classification, 1963–2000 (percentage)

Total expenditure	Social services	Economic projects	Defence & security	Administration	Others (transfers, debt servicing)
1963–1965	27	26	21	9	18
1MP, 1966–1970	28	22	22	9	19
2MP, 1971–1975	30	24	22	8	16
3MP, 1976–1980	28	26	20	8	18
4MP, 1981–1985	27	27	18	6	22
5MP, 1986–1990	27	22	14	9	29
6MP, 1991–1995	30	20	17	10	24
7MP, 1996–2000	33	21	13	11	22
2001–2003	42	18	13	10	19

Notes:
MP = 1st to 7th Malaysia Plan.
Source: Calculated with data from the Ministry of Finance (various issues).

However, government expenditures on social development never exceeded those on economic projects, defence and security (see Table 9.3). Since the latter two serve the status quo or promote business interests, they are not presumed to be progressive except in terms of employment and demand generation and should be ignored in equity analysis (Meerman 1979).

Despite the rhetorical commitment by politicians to poverty eradication, the 1970s saw growing emphasis on the NEP's other pronounced objective to 'restructure society' to abolish the identification of ethnicity with economic function, especially to create, expand and consolidate the ethnic Malay capitalist and middle classes. As officially interpreted, 'restructuring' is not meant to change socioeconomic relations between classes or economic interest groups, but in practice it mainly seeks to increase Bumiputera (indigenous) capital ownership and employment in the more attractive – mainly professional – occupations.

After the NEP's inception, the state's commitment and priorities – as reflected by NEP expenditure allocations – increasingly shifted away from poverty eradication to restructuring (Jomo 1990). More specifically, development allocations for poverty eradication decreased over time (see Table 9.4).

Only a small percentage of Bumiputera benefited significantly from restructuring expenditure and there is considerable evidence that only a fraction of poverty eradication funds actually benefited the poor, considering the huge bureaucracy and other expenses involved and the considerable share of such expenditure received by the non-poor. Since poverty is officially conceived in absolute – rather than relative – terms, if economic growth is sufficiently high, then income inequality can grow even as the poverty rate declines. Therefore, changes in income distribution provide an additional important indication of the welfare implications of economic growth, especially as they affect inter-ethnic, spatial and other aspects of income distribution. However, it should be remembered that under the NEP, there has been no official commitment to reducing overall income inequality, as the emphasis was on reducing economic disparities between ethnic groups, particularly between Bumiputeras and non-Bumiputeras. When inflation reached an exceptionally high 17.4 per cent in 1974, the government increased expenditure to counter the related slowdown in growth (see Table 9.5). Although the rate of increase of expenditure for social services was high, it remained below that of other activities and fluctuated markedly from year to year.

Policy impact and growth performance

In 1968, while the Gini ratio and the Atkinson index for household income distribution after deducting indirect taxes were lower than for the distribution of household income before taxation, the reverse occurred in 1970 and particularly in 1973, suggesting that the incidence of indirect taxes became more regressive between 1968 and 1973 (Ismail 1977).

Following the export boom of 1968–72, the statutory reserve requirement was raised from 3.5 per cent to 5 per cent. Meanwhile, in order to maintain a liberal exchange control regime after the collapse of the Bretton Woods system in 1971, the ringgit was floated in 1973 and regulations on foreign exchange transactions were relaxed. In 1973, the interest rate was increased by 0.2 per cent and long-term loans limited to two years. The minimum liquidity ratio was also increased.

Despite the open economy regime and the oil shock of 1973, Malaysia's real GDP growth averaged 5.2 per cent per annum for the period 1971–81 (see Table 9.6). Nominal per capita income growth was generally well in excess of the

Table 9.4 Malaysia: development and poverty eradication expenditure, 1971–2005

	Total (RM million)	Expenditure on poverty eradication	
		(RM million)	% of total expenditure
2nd Malaysia Plan 1971–1975	7,415.0	2,350.1	31.7
3rd Malaysia Plan 1976–1980	21,202.0	6,373.4	30.1
4th Malaysia Plan 1981–1985	46,329.0	11,238.5	24.3
5th Malaysia Plan 1986–1990	35,300.0	12,970.7	36.7
6th Malaysia Plan 1991–1995	54,705.0	13,900.8	25.4
7th Malaysia Plan 1996–2000	67,500.0	16,084.8	23.8
8th Malaysia Plan 2001–2005	160,000.0	15,025.8	9.4 (estimate)
Total (1971–2005)	392,442.0	78,270.0	19.9

Source: Various Malaysia Plan documents, cited in Chamhuri Siwar (2004).

Table 9.5 Malaysia: changes in total government expenditure and expenditure on social services, 1973–1989 (percentage of nominal value per annum)

	1973	1974	1975	1976	1977	1985	1986	1987	1988	1989
Total	4	39	14	16	29	−4	2	−10	9	20
Social	5	29	17	6	39	4	12	−17	6	19
Education	4	31	11	9	36	NA	NA	−3	7	13
Health	12	22	18	4	33	NA	NA	−8	8	20
Housing	NA	NA	NA	NA	NA	NA	NA	−90	−3	116

Note:
NA = not available.
Source: Ministry of Finance (various issues).

Table 9.6 Malaysia: long-term economic track record, 1971–2003

	1971–1981	1982–1986	1987–1996	1997	1998	1999	2000–2003
GDP growth (% per year)	5.2	3.4	9.5	7.3	−7.4	6.1	3.2
CPI[a] inflation (% per year)	6.7	2.2	3.2	2.7	5.3	2.8	1.5
	1970	1980	1990	1995	1997	1998	2003
Per capita GNP (RM)	1,071	3,734	6,513	10,710	17,027	11,753	12,547
Per capita GNP (US$)	348	1,715	2,414	4,119	4,377	3,093	3,302
Unemployment rate	2.4	5.6	6.0	2.8	2.6	3.4	3.5
RM/US$	3.078	2.218	2.698	2.538	3.89	3.80	3.80
RM/100 yen	0.86	1.09	2.00	2.469	2.992	3.314	3.555

Note:
[a] Consumer Price Index.

Sources: Ministry of Finance (various issues); calculated with data from the Bank Negara Malaysia *Monthly Statistical Bulletin* (various issues).

Table 9.7 Malaysia: savings, investment and FDI, 1970–2003 (percentage of GNP)

	1970	1975	1980	1985	1990	1995	2000	2003
Savings	20.5	20.0	27.6	27.2	35.9	36.5	40.1	36.3
Investment	17.7	25.9	32.3	32.1	33.8	40.1	26.7	28.2
Savings–investment gap	2.8	−5.9	−4.7	−4.9	2.1	−3.6	13.4	12.1
FDI	2.4	3.9	4.0	2.4	5.5	4.3	2.1	1.5
Current account balance	0.2	−4.9	−1.2	−2.1	−2.2	−8.9	10.3	18.7
Overall balance	0.6	0.8	1.9	4.5	4.7	−1.8	−1.2	14.4

Source: Calculated with data from the Ministry of Finance (various issues).

inflation rate, resulting in improvements in the standard of living. Meanwhile, employment grew steadily, so that despite a rapidly expanding population and higher labour force participation, the unemployment rate declined.

Actual growth exceeded its target because investment was higher than expected, largely as a result of a higher inflow of FDIs (see Table 9.7) that came to exceed the domestic investments. Thus, the overall balance of payments did not deteriorate and the ringgit remained stable. FDI-financed investments reflected a domestic savings-investment gap.

As noted, employment grew rapidly. In the pre-crisis boom years, Malaysian workers enjoyed an environment of burgeoning employment and rising wages. Manufacturing industries created most employment opportunities, contributing to the decline in the poverty headcount ratio. It catered to rural migrants in search of higher-paid jobs to improve their standard of living. The decline in urban poverty was faster than for rural poverty in spite of the rural poor migrating to urban centres.

Household income trends by ethnicity and location in Malaysia, especially Peninsular Malaysia, suggest that the rising incomes and poverty reduction in the 1970s may have been accompanied by constant or only slowly declining inter-ethnic income disparities, at least until 1976. Countrywide income distribution trends by location suggests that income inequality declined moderately between 1970 and 1979 (see Table 9.8).

Macroeconomic policies and outcomes in the 1980s

Fiscal stance

During the 1980s, the federal government's overall deficit continued to increase, especially because of the heavy industrialization effort that characterized that period. Even before the recession of the mid-1980s, however, the government embarked on an austerity drive and opted for 'fiscal prudence', thereby reducing its deficits. The growing emphasis on the NEP's other pronounced objective to 'restructure society' continued, as did the decrease in allocations for poverty eradication.

Table 9.8 Malaysia: mean monthly household incomes by ethnic group and stratum, 1970–1999

	Peninsular Malaysia		Malaysia						
	1970	1973	1976	1979	1984	1987	1990	1995	1999
All	423	502	566	669	792	760	1,167	2,020	2,472
Bumiputera (B)	276	335	380	475	616	614	940	1,604	1,984
Chinese (C)	632	739	866	906	1,086	1,012	1,631	2,890	3,456
Indian (I)	478	565	592	730	791	771	1,209	2,140	2,702
Others	1,304	1,798	1,395	1,816	1,775	2,043	955	1,284	1,371
Urban (U)	687	789	913	942	1,114	1,039	1,617	2,589	3,103
Rural (R)	321	374	431	531	596	604	951	1,326	1,718
Disparity ratio (C/B)	2.30	2.21	2.28	1.91	1.76	1.65	1.74	1.80	1.74
Disparity ratio (I/B)	1.73	1.69	1.56	1.54	1.28	1.26	1.29	1.33	1.36
Disparity ratio (U/R)	2.14	2.11	2.12	1.77	1.87	1.72	1.70	1.95	1.81
Gini ratio	0.506	NA	0.529	0.493	0.474	0.458	0.4421	0.4560	0.4431

NA = not available.

Note: Figures for 1970–1987 are constant 1978 prices; figures for 1990–1999 are constant 1990 prices.

Sources: Canadian Policy Alternatives (no date); Malaysia (1981, 1989, 1991b, 1995, 2001a).

Government fiscal response to the recession of the 1980s was less counter-cyclical than in the 1970s (see Table 9.5). Following the economic contraction of 1984, public expenditure was cut, with the expenditure on social development being particularly badly affected. Expenditure on social services was given renewed priority in 1986, was reversed in 1987 and picked up again only in 1988, as part of a general increase in public expenditure, with economic recovery and following the political strife of 1987.

Privatization policy

Public policy from the late colonial period – resulting in the emergence, growth and privatization of state-owned enterprises (SOEs) in Malaysia – involved a combination of development and distribution concerns. By the 1970s, there was considerable evidence that many SOEs had been poorly planned, developed and managed, and that poor accountability and ineffective budget constraints and low incentives to improve performance undermined their performance. The government introduced its SOE privatization policy in 1983, ostensibly to reach higher growth, reduce the financial and administrative burden represented by the SOEs, improve efficiency and productivity and reduce the size of the public sector in the economy.

The complex circumstances surrounding the emergence of SOEs (Jomo 1995) suggest that privatization did not address the problems affecting them. In Malaysia, as elsewhere, the transfer of ownership from public to private hands did not entail reduced consumer prices or enhanced quality of services. Instead, consumer prices generally rose significantly, resulting in net consumer welfare losses (Goh and Jomo 1995). Hence, efficiency gains were not significant, and were exaggerated by the proponents of privatization in Malaysia. And in so far as they have occurred, they are unlikely to have been the result of privatization per se, but have been mainly due to managerial and organizational reforms that do not rely on privatization.

It was also argued that privatization was an important means to enhance Bumiputera stock ownership, but since the early 1980s there has been little increase in the overall Bumiputera share of corporate wealth. Instead, there is now considerable evidence that privatization was an important means of enhancing the private wealth of the politically influential and well connected, and not just among the Bumiputera elite. There is no evidence that this was either necessary or desirable for improving interethnic relations.

Taxation

Guidelines to reduce fiscal deficits or to maintain balanced budgets have meant that planners had to ensure rapid growth and good revenue buoyancy, in addition to controlling the level of public expenditure. Taxation was the main source of government revenue, contributing more than 70 per cent of federal government revenue in the last three decades (see Table 9.9). Major changes in the tax structure were implemented since the mid-1980s, with generally regressive consequences (Asher and Jomo 1987; Wee Chong Hui 2005).

Tax coverage in Malaysia has increased over the years. The number of taxpayers has been growing with rises in income. Indirect taxes on goods and services – such as excise duties as well as taxes on goods and services – have been extended to more items. The coverage of international trade taxes, such as import and export duties, have also been extended, though this was later reduced following Malaysia's entry in the World Trade Organization (WTO).

The statutory rates of direct taxes were reduced, based on the argument that doing so would encourage growth – as low corporate tax rates are supposed to

Table 9.9 Malaysia: sources of federal government revenue, 1963–2000 (percentage)

	Taxes			Others
	Total (%)	Direct taxes (%)	Indirect taxes	
1963	79.6	20.9	58.7	20.5
1970	76.7	28.5	48.1	23.3
1980	86.6 (26.1)	39.5 (10.3)	47.1 (12.3)	13.4 (3.5)
1990	72.0 (24.8)	35.2 (8.7)	36.7 (9.1)	28.0 (7.0)
2004 estimate	72.5 (22.2)	49.0 (10.9)	23.5 (5.2)	27.5 (6.1)

Note: Figures in brackets indicate % of GDP.

Source: Calculated with data from the Ministry of Finance (various issues).

encourage investments, while lower individual income tax rates are supposed to increase labour supply. Some taxes affecting high-income groups – such as estate duty, development tax and excess profit tax – were reduced or abolished. Except for the gradual reduction or abolition of international trade taxes on numerous items, indirect taxes increasingly affected more consumers (see Chapter 2).

The statutory corporate income tax rate in Malaysia was 40 per cent. However, the effective tax rate was lower in view of liberal investment incentives, including the accelerated depreciation allowances introduced after 1977, the generous depreciation allowances introduced after 1980 and the re-investment allowances introduced in 1988. In 1989, the marginal effective tax rate for equity investments – the difference between pre-tax and post-tax rates of return to investments, that is, the tax due – was lower in Malaysia (32.0 per cent) than in all other Association of South East Asian Nations (ASEAN) countries except Singapore (28.4 per cent) and Thailand (24.9 per cent) (Pellechio and Dunn 1989, cited in Wee 1997).

Liberalization policies

The 1959 Pioneer Investment Ordinance sought to attract import-substituting industrial investments, while the Investment Incentives Act of 1968 sought export-oriented industrial investments. In 1985, a major revision to the 1968 Act liberalized the guidelines on FDI to allow foreigners greater equity participation in companies, increasing with the degree of export orientation, level of technological sophistication, positive spin-off effects, capital outlay and added value.

To lower export costs, exchange controls were further loosened on 1 January 1987 (Ariff *et al.* 1997). Formalities, which businesses have to comply with when exporting goods, were also simplified. The move also allowed investors greater access to credit facilities, enabling them to expand their domestic productive capacities.

Rising labour costs due to the strengthening of currencies and labour shortages and the 1988 withdrawal of privileges under the Generalised System of Preferences from the first-tier East Asian newly industrialized economies of Hong Kong, the Republic of Korea, Singapore and Taiwan encouraged the relocation abroad of production facilities from these countries, while selective deregulation as well as new incentives made relocation in Southeast Asia as well as China more attractive. Yet Malaysia's natural wealth and comparatively cheap labour sustained the production for export of agricultural, forest, mineral and, more recently, manufactured products.

Much of the wealth generated was secured by the business elite, who in turn contributed to growth by re-investing in the 'protected' domestic economy, mainly in import-substituting industries, commerce, services, real estate, privatized utilities and infrastructure. Thus, from the late 1980s, the traditional investment- and export-led growth started to be accompanied by rising domestic consumption, construction and property booms, fuelled by financial interests favouring 'short-termist' investments in the non-tradable sector – involving loans with tangible asset collateral.

After the Malaysian banking crisis of the late 1980s, when the share of non-performing loans (NPLs) in the system rose to almost 30 per cent, the authorities significantly strengthened prudential regulation – for example, through the

Banking and Financial Institutions Act of 1989. Although this regulation was subsequently undermined by various liberalization measures, it nevertheless served to protect Malaysia to a greater degree than in the more crisis-hit countries.

While foreign bank borrowings were effectively limited and discouraged by the relatively lower domestic interest rates available in Malaysia, the regulatory authorities did not do much to discourage lending for property and stock market purchases, and such purchases rose rapidly (see Table 9.10). With much more lending for consumption available, the share going to productive investments in manufacturing, agriculture and mining accounted for less than a quarter of total loans.

The current account imbalances that started to emerge during that period were mainly due to the growing proportion of non-tradables (property construction and infrastructure) being produced in Malaysia with imported inputs and equipment. The authorities seemed lulled into a false sense of complacency by their success in 'sterilizing' such inflows in order to control money supply and consumer price inflation. However, the high investment rate, with considerable flows into the property and stock markets, instead fuelled asset price inflation, mainly involving real estate and share prices. High levels of FDI and foreign debt (see Table 9.11) also caused growing investment income outflows (see Table 9.12).

Table 9.10 Malaysia: distribution of bank credit for select purposes, 1970–2004 (percentages share)

	Manufacturing	Agriculture	General commerce	Broad property	Share
1970	15.5	23.0	3.7	13.1	NA
1980	19.9	8.4	18.0	27.6	1.0
1985	6.0	17.5	17.9	34.7	2.2
1990	19.0	4.9	10.1	27.9	2.8
1995	18.8	2.0	8.3	28.4	3.7
2000	15.1	2.6	8.4	28.4	6.7
2004[a]	15.8	2.7	46.2	10.0	4.0

Notes:
[a] end of July.
NA = not available.
Source: Bank Negara Malaysia Monthly Statistical Bulletin (various issues).

Table 9.11 Malaysia: external debt service ratio, 1970–2003 (percentage)

	1970	1975	1980	1985	1990	1995	2000	2003 estimate
Federal Government	2.6 (1.2)	3.4 (1.6)	1.9 (1.1)	6.7 (4.0)	3.6 (2.8)	1.4 (2.3)	1.2 (1.4)	6.6 (6.5)
National	NA	3.4 (1.6)	4.3 (2.6)	13.6 (8.0)	8.3 (6.5)	6.6 (10.8)	5.8 (6.6)	6.2 (6.1)

NA = not available.
Note: Figures in brackets indicate % of GNP.
Source: Ministry of Finance (various issues).

Table 9.12 Malaysia: net services balance, 1965–1999 (RM million)

	1965	1970	1975	1980	1985	1990	1995	1998	1999[a]
Freight & insurance	−162	−304	−621	−1,934	−1,852	−3,837	−9,028	−8,435	−9,731
Other transportation	−16	−21	98	−11	64	−25	737	2,268	2,479
Travel	−80	−105	−105	−521	−1332	632	4143	3,070	5,568
Investment income	−255	−355	−727	−1,954	−5,434	−5,072	−10,338	−14,817	−18,790
Government transactions	225	68	47	36	−31	−3	−23	−215	46
Other services	−53	−145	−402	−792	−1,806	−1,418	−4,720	−4,209	−8,422
Services balance	−341	−862	−1,710	−5,176	−10,391	−9,723	−19,227	−22,338	−28,946
% of GNP	NA	−7.1	−7.9	−10.1	−14.4	−8.5	−7.9	−8.3	−10.4

[a]estimate.
NA = not available.
Source: Bank Negara Malaysia *Quarterly Economic Bulletin* (various issues).

The recession of the 1980s reversed the decade-long decline in the unemployment rate, which reached a peak of 8.3 per cent in 1986, after the government initiated an austerity drive. The decline in urban poverty was slowed by the recession of the mid-1980s. Nonetheless, there is evidence to suggest that inter-ethnic disparities declined (see Table 9.8).

The early and mid-1990s

Guidelines set during the Second Outline Perspective Plan period (1991–2000) included reductions in fiscal deficits to below 3 per cent of GNP, reduction of the debt service ratio to below 7 per cent of exports and reduction of the debt service payments to below 20 per cent of operating expenditure. After the early 1990s, new guidelines called for the achievement of balanced budgets.

Malaysia's trade liberalization has kept pace with trends led by the General Agreement on Tariffs and Trade (GATT) Uruguay Round and its successor, the WTO. Also, the advent of the ASEAN Free Trade Area (AFTA) in 1992 and the Asia Pacific Economic Cooperation (APEC) forum have lowered some import barriers. Trade liberalization has led to an increased propensity to import, though this has been mainly due to greater imports of intermediate and capital goods. Malaysia's trade to GNP ratios (see Table 9.13) have been exaggerated by the high import content of Malaysia's principal manufactured exports in the electric and electronic sector.

Malaysia's central bank had long claimed that the ringgit was pegged to a basket of currencies of its major trading partners. However, for all intents and purposes, it had been virtually pegged to the US dollar for many years. The currency had long been held within a limited band against the greenback – not unlike the other currencies in the region. Malaysia's economic boom since the late 1980s had been helped by the significant depreciation of the ringgit against the yen and the US dollar since late 1985 (see Table 9.6).

As the Malaysian economy continued to grow rapidly, an even more liberal regime emerged to further ease foreign exchange transactions by residents.

Table 9.13 Malaysia: merchandise account, 1970–2003 (percentage of GNP)

	1970	1975	1980	1985	1990	1995	2000	2003
Exports	41.3	41.9	54.5	52.2	67.9	74.2	119.6	146.8
Export growth(%)	−0.6	−9.6	16.4	−2.3	16.1	20.9	16.1	11.3
Of:								
manufactured goods	11.9	21.9	22.4	32.8	58.8	79.6	85.2	79.5
Imports	32.5	38.6	44.3	39.9	61.7	74.1	99.8	117.0
Import growth(%)	13.5	−10.9	32.8	−8.8	19.6	24.5	25.3	−22.0
Of:								
intermediate goods	38.3	42.3	51.6	50.6	51	48.5	47.5 (1998)	
merchandise balance	8.8	3.4	10.2	12.3	6.2	0.1	19.8	29.9

Source: Ministry of Finance (various issues).

Accordingly, exchange controls were further relaxed after December 1994 to reduce costs of compliance, allow greater access to foreign credit facilities for small- and medium-scale industries, enhance efficiency in cross-border transactions by residents and encourage multinational corporations to relocate their operational headquarters in Malaysia (Ariff *et al.* 1997).

Against this trend towards greater liberalization, exchange controls were temporarily tightened in early 1994 when the central bank sought to stem the volatile inflows the economy had already experienced in 1992–93 due to the perception that the ringgit was undervalued because of its 'managed float' against the US dollar. The central bank did so by subjecting funds deposited with banking institutions to statutory reserve and liquidity requirements, imposing limits on net outstanding non-trade-related external liabilities of banking institutions, restricting sales of short-term monetary instruments to non-residents, compelling commercial banks to place the ringgit funds of foreign banking institutions in non-interest-bearing vostro accounts with the central bank and forbidding commercial banks from undertaking non-trade-related swaps and outright forward transactions on the bid side with foreign clients.

These measures were subsequently repealed around August 1994. One explanation is that the pressure from short-term capital inflows had eased by then. Another view is that the controls had so effectively discouraged speculative portfolio inflows that Malaysia was no longer attractive to foreign portfolio investors, unlike the heady days of 1992–93. The controls were probably lifted to encourage foreign investments in the stock market, which had been languishing after the imposition of controls.

The decade-long decline of the US dollar against the yen was reversed after the greenback fell to 79 yen in June 1995. This problem was exacerbated by the failure to 'progress' rapidly towards higher value-added production, mainly due to inadequate or misallocated public investments, and poor incentives for education and training as well as limited internationally competitive indigenous industrial capabilities. The appreciation of the Southeast Asian region's currencies – coupled with labour shortages in Malaysia and Thailand – rendered them even less competitive, adversely affecting exports and growth.

Such managed pegs offered certain advantages, including the semblance of monetary stability so much desired by financial interests. This growing influence of financial sector concerns, often at the expense of the real economy, reflected the political weakness of export manufacturer interests in Malaysia, especially in influencing economic policy making. Most major internationally competitive non-resource based industries are foreign-owned. The 1990 and 1994 devaluations of China's yuan also put greater pressure on emerging second-generation Southeast Asian newly industrializing countries such as Malaysia.

The late 1990s

Changes in policy stance

In the 1990s, Malaysia had a relatively high tax–GDP ratio (about 20 per cent) compared to other Southeast Asian countries (Asher and Heiji 1999). While the government's efforts to cut deficits and spending and the privatization of the 1980s had reduced expenditures on social services, the changes in direct taxation have not been pro-poor and the regressiveness of indirect taxation increased. The statutory corporate income tax rate in Malaysia was reduced from 40 per cent to 35 per cent in 1994, 30 per cent in 1995 and 28 per cent in 1998 – that is, a level lower than in most ASEAN countries. There is also evidence that the distribution of household income after deducting indirect taxes worsened from 1995 to 1999. This change was induced by the reduction in international trade taxes and taxes on domestic goods under the GATT Uruguay Round and its successor, the WTO, as well as other regional agreements such as AFTA.

Though foreign bank borrowings rose rapidly during 1996 and the first half of 1997, exposure to foreign loans was still relatively lower in Malaysia than in the other crisis-affected economies. In fact, foreign borrowings as a proportion of the funds raised by the private sector decreased from 23 per cent for the period 1980–85 to 16 per cent for 1990–97 and 11 per cent for 1998–2003 (Bank Negara Malaysia *Annual Report* various issues). Not only were foreign borrowings restricted in Malaysia, but a higher proportion of them were not short-term in nature despite Malaysia's relatively more open economy and correspondingly greater need for (usually short-term) trade credit.

Meanwhile, equity or portfolio flows became more significant in the early and mid-1990s (see Table 9.14). After speculative attacks on the baht and its subsequent float after 2 July 1997, currency speculators turned their sights on the other economies in the region perceived to have maintained similarly unsustainable US dollar pegs for their currencies. The Malaysian central bank put up a spirited – and expensive (believed to have cost more than 9 billion ringgit, then worth almost $4 billion) – defence of its currency until mid-July.

With the preceding financial liberalization, fund managers had an increasing number of investment options to choose from, and could move their funds much more easily than ever before. The flight of foreign funds could not be easily

Table 9.14 Malaysia: annual capital inflows by major category, 1989–2002 (percentage of GDP)

	1989	1990	1991	1992	1993	1994	1995	2000	2002a
Net capital inflows	3.5	4.2	11.9	15.2	16.8	1.6	8.5	−7.0	−3.3
Official development finance	−2.4	−2.4	−0.5	−1.4	0.6	0.3	2.7	1.2	1.3
FDI	4.4	5.4	8.5	9.0	7.8	6.0	4.7	4.2	2.0
Commercial bank funds	1.1	2.0	2.8	6.3	6.6	−7.0	0.1	−7.3	4.0
Portfolio equity	NA	NA	−1.5	5.6	14.5	5.7	1.2	2.7	3.3

Note:
aestimate.
NA = not available.
Sources: Ong (1998); Bank Negara Malaysia, Annual Report (various issues).

replaced by domestic funds. Difficulties in recovering loans reduced liquidity, constrained the financial system and, eventually, economic activity. Thus, the currency and financial crises, triggered by the collapse of the baht in July 1997, led Malaysia and its Southeast Asian neighbours to economic recession.

The crisis

In late August 1997, the authorities designated the top one hundred indexed Kuala Lumpur Composite Index (KLCI) share counters, that is, requiring actual presentation of script at the moment of transaction – rather than later, as has been the practice – ostensibly to check 'short-selling', which was exacerbating the stock market collapse. After reaching a peak of around 1,300 in February 1997, the decline of the Malaysian stock market index was greatly exacerbated by the currency crisis as well as its repercussions on the banking system. It had fallen by about 80 per cent from its peak in the first quarter of 1997, to reach its nadir of 262 on 2 September 1998. The rapid exit of high-stake foreign portfolio investors from the Malaysian capital market contributed to its collapse. The proportionately very high capitalization of Malaysia's stock market meant that the adverse wealth effect of this collapse was probably greater than experienced elsewhere in the region.

On 3 September 1997, the government announced a special RM60 billion fund for selected Malaysian firms, though the fund was never properly institutionalized. Nevertheless, government-controlled public funds – mainly from the Employees' Provident Fund, Petronas and Khazanah – were used to bail out some of the most politically well-connected and influential corporate interests, popularly referred to as 'cronies'. Many of those who had previously advocated and benefited from privatization urged the government to nationalize their debt and liabilities.

After December 1997, Bank Negara gradually raised its three-month intervention rate from 8.7 per cent in early December 1997 to 11.0 per cent in early February 1998, and redefined the NPLs as loans in arrears for three months, compared to the previous six months (Malaysia 1999b). Banks were also obliged to meet higher statutory requirements. Such pro-cyclical, contractionary measures helped transform the currency crisis into a more general economic crisis. In the wake of the currency crisis, interest rates rose, reflecting tighter liquidity as money supply contracted further due to capital flight in response to the currency devaluation, the reversal of capital inflows – portfolio investments as well as expiring foreign bank lending and tighter central bank monetary policy, as demanded by financial markets and the IMF. Credit growth slowed down and barely rose after September 1998 despite central bank directives to increase it to 8 per cent in both 1998 and 1999. Loan defaults and foreclosures increased, gathering momentum through 1998 until the radical change in monetary policy of September (Malaysia 1999b).

The depreciated ringgit increased the relative magnitude – in Malaysian currency – of the mainly privately held foreign debt as well as the external debt-servicing burden, both of which were typically denominated in US dollars. With a massive devaluation of the ringgit, imported inflation was inevitable, especially in Malaysia's very open economy, where gross exports were equivalent to annual GDP. Over-zealous efforts to check inflation under these circumstances exacerbated deflationary tendencies, as did business failures, growing unemployment and reduced incomes.

Major events – for example, the 1998 Commonwealth Games and the APEC summit in Kuala Lumpur – and other government efforts to prop up the real estate market, especially its residential component, served to delay the inevitable collapse of this asset price bubble. The completion of more construction projects and the new Putrajaya administrative capital exacerbated the glut in the high-class residential, office and commercial segments of the property market. Given the heavy exposure of so many companies, especially among the KLCI's top one hundred counters, to the property sector, such efforts may well have averted greater corporate distress.

Danaharta was established in mid-1998 to 'take out' the NPLs from the portfolio of the worst affected banks and financial institutions. This – together with re-capitalization of de-capitalized banks by a companion agency, Danamodal – served to restore liquidity to the banking system. By early 2000, Danaharta had expended RM45 billion to take over the NPLs from financial institutions at a (substantial) discount, thus enabling them to restore badly needed liquidity to the system.

Although banks became more careful about lending for property purchases, raised quotas for lending for share purchases helped boost the stock market, with positive wealth effects contributing to renewed domestic demand, helped by expansionary fiscal policies. Similarly, consumer credit was officially encouraged, particularly for vehicle purchases and residential property purchases.

Restrictive measures on outflows were introduced again in September 1998 following the massive exodus of funds from the country during the East Asian financial turmoil (see Chapters 4 and 5). These measures did not apply to current account and long-term capital flows. Apart from pegging the ringgit to the US dollar at RM3.80 on 2 September 1998,[2] other measures undertaken included banning offshore ringgit trading, restricting ringgit exports and imports, limiting ringgit loans to non-residents and compelling non-residents to retain their portfolio investments in Malaysia for at least 12 months.

As regional financial markets stabilized and the likelihood of massive capital flight receded, the rules on portfolio investments were amended on 15 February 1999, with the introduction of an exit levy option. Under the new system, foreign portfolio investors were permitted to repatriate the principal sum of their portfolio funds subject to an exit levy that declined over time, that is, the longer the wait, the lower the levy, declining to zero in September 1999. This system was subsequently modified on 21 September 1999, when a flat 10 per cent exit levy was imposed on repatriated profits from portfolio investments. With the 2001 budget, only profits from investments of less than a year would be subject to the levy. The levy was later abolished altogether.

Fiscal response

The government initially responded to the financial crisis of 1997–98 with procyclical contractionary budgets, before reversing policy and increasing spending. Public expenditure thus picked up following the 1997–98 financial crisis, with social expenditure increasing faster than other expenditure types (see Table 9.15) as the government took anti-cyclical measures, avoiding widespread unemployment, extensive impoverishment and a groundswell of social discontent. Nonetheless, the depth of the 1998 recession caused more households to slip into poverty, although income distribution improved slightly as the incomes of many of the non-poor also fell (see Table 9.8). In fact, the post-crisis policy stance can be characterized as pro-growth rather than pro-poor. For example, there were moves to privatize government health services.

As expected, the impact of the financial crisis on employment was most pronounced in the construction and manufacturing sectors, which depended heavily on imported inputs. However, the economy as a whole did not experience much structural change despite the loss of 255,000 jobs in 1998 – 141,000 in manufacturing and 111,000 in construction. The overall inflation rate did not change significantly from March 1997 to March 1998. Of course, the ringgit devaluation also raised the prices of consumer as well as producer imports, particularly during 1998. Food prices were especially adversely affected, reflecting the high import content in the national food bill.

Table 9.15 Malaysia: changes in total government expenditure and expenditure on social services, 1996–2003 (percentage of nominal value per annum)

	1996	1997	1998	1999	2000	2001	2002	2003[a]
Total expenditure	17.9	3.3	3.3	6.9	21.9	17.2	5.7	9.5
Social services:	20.1	6.2	6.2	13.0	26.8	34.6	16.3	−0.7
Education	NA	NA	NA	13.5	30.7	60.4	15.9	4.5
Health	NA	NA	NA	10.3	21.1	15.7	6.5	34.9
Housing	NA	NA	NA	4.5	10.1	29.5	16.7	8.3

Notes:
[a] estimate.
NA = not available.
Source: Ministry of Finance (various issues).

Summary and recommendations

The Malaysian authorities have long been intent on promoting growth, with subsidiary concerns for price stability and a sound balance of payments. With conventional macroeconomic understanding of savings, investments and credit to stimulate growth, they sought to direct investments to desired sectors through incentives and requirements. They have also undertaken administrative measures to control prices, stem capital outflows when deemed necessary and sought to preempt sociopolitical discontent, due to adverse economic conditions and shocks.

Malaysia has generally maintained a relatively open economy with a relatively free trade regime, but has also used protection to promote new economic activities – for example, import-substituting industrialization – and for food security reasons. It has also long encouraged FDI, initially to secure political independence, but also to check the influence of ethnic Chinese business interests and secure access to foreign technology and markets, rather than for attracting capital per se. While long emphasizing its commitment to open and *laissez-faire* economic policies, it has generally been pragmatic in its approach to economic development and macroeconomic policies. Hence, in 1974–75, 1986 and 1998, it intervened counter-cyclically in response to external shocks. Malaysia was almost alone in adopting counter-cyclical monetary policies from September 1998 when it ended ringgit convertibility, temporarily stopped capital outflows and pegged its currency to the US dollar. It has been suggested that the fixed exchange rate and lower interest rates associated with the introduction of capital controls after September 1998 helped Malaysia rebound from the crisis. However, this is difficult to confirm as exchange rates became more stable and interest rates declined throughout the region in East Asia from around the same time after the US Federal Reserve lowered interest rates in response to the Russian crisis and its aftermath on Wall Street in August 1998. All crisis-hit economies in the region recovered after the last quarter of 1998, whereas Malaysian recovery started in the second quarter. And although the Malaysian recovery in 1999–2000 was stronger than in Indonesia and Thailand, the Republic of Korea performed more impressively than Malaysia. And even if Malaysia had performed better than the Republic of Korea, it still has to be demonstrated that this was due to capital controls, which have largely been amended and dropped – except for the dollar peg and related currency controls – since September 1999. Since Malaysia was not affected as badly by the crisis in the first place, compared to the three other economies, meaningful comparisons remain problematic.

Kaplan and Rodrik (2001) suggest that the controls may have averted another crisis 'yet to come', which was developing in mid-1998 as overnight ringgit interest rates in Singapore rose to 40 per cent. Some have challenged this, claiming that this speculative market was too 'thin' to have made much difference, though others dispute this empirical assertion. Currency controls undoubtedly succeeded in killing the offshore ringgit market, thus enabling the authorities to gain greater control over monetary policy. The hard dollar peg introduced in September 1998 helped many enterprises with international exposure to plan better after more than a year of monetary turbulence from July 1997.

State intervention for developmental or industrial policy purposes in Malaysia has been of much poorer quality and less effective than in the Republic of Korea, Singapore and Taiwan. Instead, state intervention has often been motivated by other (non-developmental) considerations (Jomo et al. 1997; Jomo 2003, forthcoming). Such interventions – often cited as evidence of 'crony capitalism' – bear some responsibility for the vulnerability of the second-tier Southeast Asian newly industrialized countries to the factors that precipitated the mid-1997 financial crisis. Even more importantly, such interests influenced policy responses in ways that exacerbated the crisis. In other words, while 'crony capitalism' does not explain the origins of the crisis, it certainly exacerbated it in Malaysia. Indeed, government efforts to bail out influential business interests and otherwise protect or even advance such interests – at the expense of the public purse, workers' forced savings, taxpayers and minority shareholders – exacerbated the crisis by undermining public and foreign confidence.

There has since been considerable doubt as to whether the Malaysian economy will be able to resume its pre-crisis growth trajectory. There has been less FDI as well as domestic private investment despite the subsequent reversals of the temporary policies introduced in 1998. There is also growing regional concern about de-industrialization and jobless growth.

Recent trends suggest that generic manufactured goods not enjoying strong intellectual rights – and the associated protection of monopoly rents – are vulnerable to downward price pressures and that productivity gains have not been translated into commensurate wage gains for workers. The advent of China, India and other lower-cost producers in similar production niches in global commodity chains threatens an intensification of competition among low-cost producers. Much will therefore depend on whether Malaysia will be able to reposition itself to stay ahead of such competition. It is unclear how sustainable short-term successes in particular niches will be in the medium and long term. Growth has become heavily reliant on foreign resources, both capital and labour, while the domestic engines of growth seem unsustainable. Clearly, Malaysia's future economic progress cannot be secured by continued reliance on its earlier economic strategy emphasizing cheap labour and low production costs.

While export-led growth has long been important for the Malaysian economy, trade dependency has rendered it more susceptible to changes in world economic conditions. Declining commodity prices, discrimination and protectionism against Malaysian products, competition from other producing countries and slow global demand growth have adversely affected the Malaysian economy. Endogenous growth, led by domestic demand, can ensure greater resilience, but this cannot be generated overnight in Malaysia's long open economy. Given the inverse relationship between the marginal propensity to consume and income per capita, generating domestic demand from mass consumption is only feasible with an improving distribution of income.

In this regard it is proposed that the government's capacity to intervene countercyclically be strengthened and adapted to the new national and international circumstances, and that the government lead the development process to sustain high growth to ensure full employment and decent work. Better capital account management should also be developed to reduce the economy's vulnerability to fickle capital flows. There is also a need for improved efficiency and governance in public sector management to reduce costs, thereby increasing public and foreign confidence. Taxation will be more acceptable if the state can efficiently provide infrastructure and services. This can stem and reverse the declining progressiveness of direct taxation and the rising regressiveness of indirect taxes, as well as the loss of revenue due to the provision of investment incentives.

The government should prioritize economic equity as in the 1970s. Increasing the incomes of low-income earners will increase their purchasing power and the significance of domestic demand, reducing the historical overdependence on export-led growth, while social protection should be provided on a universal, rather than on a targeted basis, to minimize inter-ethnic and other suspicions and to ensure broad and sustained political support.

Notes

1 One of the first steps taken to attract FDI in export-oriented industries was the creation of free trade zones for factories to manufacture products for export. To date, there are 12 such zones throughout the country. Companies located in the zones are subjected to minimal customs control formalities for the imports of raw materials, parts, machinery and equipment as well as for exports of their finished products. Licensed Manufacturing Warehouses were also established where it is neither practical nor desirable to establish a free trade zone. This facility was first introduced in 1975 and is offered to companies that export at least 80 per cent of their products and import almost all of their raw materials. Other export incentives appeal to both foreign and domestic investors. They include export credit refinancing, double tax deduction for expenses incurred for export promotion and export credit insurance, industrial building allowance for warehousing exports, import duty exemption and drawback of excise and sales taxes paid for imported intermediate goods, sales tax exemption for imports of machinery and equipment and other tax incentives for research and development, training and industrial upgrading to promote efficiency.
2 Bank Negara Malaysia announced that the ringgit was being floated again on the eve of 22 July 2005, thus the peg introduced on 2 September 1998 came to an end after almost seven years.

References

Ariff, M., Z.A. Mahani and E.C. Tan. 1997. *Trade and Investment Policies in Developing Countries: Malaysia Case Study.* Monograph, Economic Development Research Department, Institute of Developing Economies, Tokyo, March.
Asher, M.G. and G. Heiji. 1999. *Southeast Asia's Economic Crisis: Implications for Tax System and Reform Strategy*, Working Paper No. 98/99, Department of Economics, National University of Singapore, Kent Ridge.
Asher, M.G. and K.S. Jomo. 1987. 'Recent Malaysian Tax Policy Initiatives'. In K.S. Jomo, K.H. Ling and S. Ku Ahmad (eds), *Crisis and Response in the Malaysian Economy*. Kuala Lumpur: Malaysian Economic Association.
Bank Negara Malaysia. Various issues. *Monthly Statistical Bulletin*. Kuala Lumpur.
Bank Negara Malaysia. Various issues. *Quarterly Economic Bulletin*. Kuala Lumpur.

Bank Negara Malaysia. Various issues. *Annual Report*. Kuala Lumpur.
Canadian Policy Alternatives. No date. www.policyalternatives.ca/publications/snakes-and-ladders.pdf, accessed on 7 October 2003.
Chamhuri Siwar. 2004. *Keberkesanan Dasar, Strategi dan Program Pembasmian Kemiskinan: Satu Penilaian*. Paper presented at the Seminar Kemiskinan, Yayasan Kemiskinan Sarawak, Holiday Inn Kuching, Sarawak, Malaysia, 25–6 February.
Ghazali, A. 1990. *An Empirical Evaluation of the Effect of Foreign Capital Inflows on the Economy of Malaysia, 1961–1986*. PhD thesis, International Development Centre, University of Manchester, Manchester.
Goh, W. and K.S. Jomo. 1995. 'Efficiency and Consumer Welfare.' In K.S. Jomo (ed.), *Privatizing Malaysia*.
Ismail, M.S. 1977. *Tax Incidence and Income Distribution in West Malaysia*. PhD thesis, University of Illinois, Urbana-Champaign.
Jomo, K.S. 2003. *Malaysia's September 1998 Controls: Background, Contents, Impacts, Comparison, Implications, Lessons*. www.g24.org/ksjomgva.pdf, accessed on 7 May 2005.
Jomo, K.S. 1990. *Growth and Structural Change in the Malaysian Economy*. London: Macmillan.
Jomo, K.S. (ed.) Forthcoming. *Industrial Policy in Malaysia: The Chequered Record of Selective Investment Promotion*. Singapore: Singapore University Press.
Jomo, K.S. (ed.). 2001. *Malaysian Eclipse: Economic Crisis and Recovery*. London: Zed Books.
Jomo, K.S. 1995. *Privatizing Malaysia: Rents, Rhetoric, Realities*. Boulder, CO: Westview Press.
Jomo, K.S. et al. 1997. *Southeast Asia's Misunderstood Miracle: Industrial Policy and Economic Development in Thailand, Malaysia and Indonesia*. Boulder, CO: Westview Press.
Kaplan, E. and D. Rodrik. 2001. *Did the Malaysian Capital Controls Work?* National Bureau of Economic Research Working Paper No. 8142 presented at the NBER meeting on The Malaysian Currency Crisis, Cambridge, MA, 16 February.
Malaysia. 1981. *The Fourth Malaysia Plan, 1981–1985*. Kuala Lumpur: Economic Planning Unit, Prime Minister's Department.
Malaysia. 1989. *The Mid-Term Review of the Fifth Malaysia Plan, 1986–1990*. Kuala Lumpur: Economic Planning Unit, Prime Minister's Department.
Malaysia. 1991a. *The Sixth Malaysia Plan, 1991–1995*. Kuala Lumpur: Economic Planning Unit, Prime Minister's Department.
Malaysia. 1991b. *The Second Outline Perspective Plan, 1991–2000*. Kuala Lumpur: Economic Planning Unit, Prime Minister's Department.
Malaysia. 1993. *The Mid-Term Review of the Sixth Malaysia Plan, 1991–1995*. Kuala Lumpur: Economic Planning Unit, Prime Minister's Department.
Malaysia. 1995. *The Seventh Malaysia Plan, 1996–2000*. Kuala Lumpur: Economic Planning Unit, Prime Minister's Department.
Malaysia. 1999a. *The Mid-Term Review of the Seventh Malaysia Plan, 1996–2000*. Kuala Lumpur: Economic Planning Unit, Prime Minister's Department.
Malaysia. 1999b. *White Paper: Status of the Malaysian Economy*. Kuala Lumpur: Economic Planning Unit, Prime Minister's Department.
Malaysia. 2001a. *The Eighth Malaysia Plan, 2001–2005*. Kuala Lumpur: Economic Planning Unit, Prime Minister's Department.
Malaysia. 2001b. *The Third Outline Perspective Plan, 2001–2010*. Kuala Lumpur: Economic Planning Unit, Prime Minister's Department.
Meerman, J. 1979. *Public Expenditure in Malaysia: Who Benefits and Why*. New York: Oxford University Press.
Ministry of Finance. Various issues. *Economic Report*. Economic Planning Unit, Prime Minister's Department, Kuala Lumpur, Malaysia.
Noriyah bt Ahmad. 2004. *Poverty in Malaysia: General Trends and Strategies*. Paper presented at the Seminar Kemiskinan. Yayasan Kemiskinan Sarawak, Holiday Inn Kuching, Sarawak, Malaysia, 25–6 February.
Ong, H.C. 1998. 'Coping with Capital Flows and the Role of Monetary Policy: The Malaysian Experience, 1990–95.' In C.H. Kwan, D. Vandenbrink and C.S. Yue (eds), *Coping with*

Capital Flows in East Asia. Tokyo: Institute of Southeast Asian Studies, Singapore and Nomura Research Institute.

Wee Chong Hui. 2005. *Fiscal Policy and Equity in Malaysia*. Kuala Lumpur: University of Malaya Press.

Wee, V.E.L. 1997. *An Analysis of Tax Reform in Malaysia*. PhD thesis, University of Bristol.

10
The Search for Macroeconomic Stability and Growth under Persistent Inequality: The Case of Chile

Andrés Solimano and Molly Pollack[1]

Introduction

The Chilean economy is praised in international financial circles for combining an open, market-oriented economy with prudent macroeconomic management. Most of the policies of external opening, liberalization and privatization were undertaken under military rule in the mid-1970s and 1980s. The return to democracy in the early 1990s consolidated the prevailing economic model and placed more emphasis on poverty reduction and social protection. However, the persistence of inequality of income and wealth distribution has remained a stubborn feature of the Chilean model. As Chile faced a presidential and parliamentary election by the end of 2005, the inequalities of income, wealth and opportunities became the centrepiece of national debates on the future of the Chilean economy and society.

This chapter examines the main features of the macroeconomic and social policies and their outcomes in 1990–2004, the period of restoration of democracy in Chile after 17 years of military rule. Economic policies during this period have been dominated by an overriding concern to maintain macro and financial stability: low inflation, fiscal solvency and a lower reliance in external savings. Fiscal policy has been oriented to achieve fiscal *surpluses*, sending a strong signal to the international financial community and the internal private sector that a centre-left coalition comprising the centre and the traditional left parties – without the communists – was also able to run sound macro-financial policies. In 2000, the administration of President Ricardo Lagos put in place a fiscal rule of a 'structural' fiscal surplus of one per cent of gross domestic product (GDP), which is an institutional innovation in fiscal policy. At the same time, the extent to which fiscal policy helped to shorten, or maintain, the long cycle of sluggish growth in 1998–2003 is a matter of controversy. Another point of debate is the investment of fiscal surpluses in certain assets, such as retiring public external debt, in a country with persistent social needs and potential projects with high social rates of return. Fiscal austerity has been combined with an active concern for achieving low inflation supported by an independent central bank whose main purpose is to maintain low and stable inflation, along with normal internal and external payments (it has no full employment objectives).

Albeit sharing general, common objectives, the macro policy regimes adopted by the Aylwin, Frei and Lagos governments differed considerably. The Aylwin and Frei administrations did not have an explicit fiscal rule: there was an exchange rate system of exchange bands (until mid-1999) and a tax on short-term capital inflows. In contrast, the Lagos administration used the fiscal policy rule of structural surpluses, eliminated the tax on short capital flows and operated a flexible exchange rate regime with minimal intervention by the central bank.

These policies led to declining inflation, approaching the levels of developed countries. Economic growth was significant but with cycles – a rapid boom in 1990–1997 followed by a protracted period of sluggish growth between 1998 and 2003 and a new acceleration of growth in 2004–2005 helped by favourable copper prices. In spite of almost three decades of reform, growth in Chile continues to be closely linked to the cycles of the global economy.

Weak points have been the persistence of unemployment – near 10 per cent for more than half a decade since 1998 – and nominal and real exchange rates that have exhibited large fluctuations.

In the social area, the priorities of the *Concertación* governments, in power since 1990, have been poverty reduction and social protection of low-income groups. The objective of redistribution of income and wealth, apparently, was *not* an explicit policy goal in 1990–2004. Although new theories of economic growth view inequality as having a dominant *negative* effect on efficiency and growth, Chilean policies did not aim at a strategy leading to lower inequality that would have supported rapid growth and more effective poverty reduction. The core of social policies post-1990 was a reliance on transfers to the poor in addition to sustained increases in public spending in education and health. Other dimensions, such as explicit attention to the middle class and empowerment of workers, consumers and excluded groups, have not been an explicit goal of the policy agenda post-1990.

There are two reasons why income distribution was left off the policy agenda in 1990–2004. First, the transition to democracy started from a delicate political economy balance between the forces of the old military regime and the new emerging democratic forces that relegated potentially controversial issues, such as income distribution, to a lesser policy priority. Second, the collective memory of experiments in the late 1960s and early 1970s, when redistributive policies were accompanied by social conflict, economic crisis and, ultimately, the collapse of democracy, contributed to separating both income and wealth distribution issues from policy discussions. This chapter is organized in two parts. The first part analyses the macro and growth policies followed since 1990 and the second part discusses related poverty, inequality and social policies. It concludes with an interpretation of policies and outcomes in 1990–2004 and the persistence of inequality in Chile.

The Chilean economy in the last 40 years: a brief overview

The last 40 years in Chile have been a scenario of various experiments trying to transform its economy and society. In the 1960s, there were strong pressures to reform the economy and to move to a more participative democracy. The prevailing economic model of import substitution, dating from the 1930s, although achieving a degree of economic and social modernization, was showing signs of exhaustion. The symptoms were moderate growth (see Figure 10.1), recurrent fiscal and external imbalances, chronic inflation and persistent inequality. The conservative Alessandri administration (1958–1964) largely focused on managing several macroeconomic crises of varying intensity, but without articulating a clear agenda of structural change of the prevailing development model. The Christian Democratic administration of President Frei Montalva (1964–1970) started a programme of reforms of the economy along with a more progressive social agenda. The trade regime was partially reformed to make it more export oriented, a vast educational reform was launched, housing construction was expanded and the modernization of the agricultural sector was sought through a combination of more inclusive credit policies and agrarian reform. This was also a period of growing social organization of urban dwellers and peasants. The average rate of economic growth in the period 1960–1969 was 4.4 per cent per year (2 per cent in per capita terms). Inflation remained stubborn at around 26 per cent per year and the country lived with chronic external and fiscal imbalances.[2] In 1970, the left-wing coalition of President Salvador Allende and *Unidad Popular* (Popular Unity) won the national elections on an economic and social programme of transition to socialism with a strong redistributive component. On the structural front, copper mines under foreign ownership were nationalized and a sector of state-owned enterprises (*el area social*) was created through the expropriation of large industrial firms, banks and other financial institutions. Moreover, the agrarian reforms started by Alessandri and Frei were deepened and accelerated with the aim of eliminating the *Latifundio* system (large and generally unproductive states) to change proprietary relationships in the countryside. Politically, the agrarian reform was expected to align peasants (and small landowners) on the side of the government programme. The 'Chilean way to socialism' attempted to combine economic and political transformations in a socialist direction, but they were conducted under the institutional framework of Chilean democracy.

On the economic front, the Allende government undertook expansionary fiscal and wage policies coupled with price controls. The growing fiscal deficit was financed by money creation and, in 1972, repressed inflation and shortages became pervasive, starting to alienate the middle class against the government. Inflation became very high and apparent in 1973. Acute internal political conflict, (covert) external intervention by the United States and a severe internal economic crisis led to a military coup in September 1973 that ousted the Allende government and inaugurated 17 years of military rule under General Augusto Pinochet. In the economic area, the first year and a half of the military regime was devoted to

Table 10.1 Chile: selected macroeconomic indicators, 1960–2004

		Averages					
	1960–2004	1990–2004	1960–1969	1970–1979	1980–1989	1990–1999	2000–2004
(1) GDP[a]							
(1a) Rate of growth (%)	4.4	5.6	4.4	2.5	4.4	6.4	4.0
(1b) Index (1960 = 100)	265.6	466.3	122.5	158.0	215.3	414.0	570.9
(2) GDP per capita[a]							
(2a) Rate of growth (%)	2.6	4.0	2.0	0.8	2.7	4.9	2.4
(2b) Index (1960 = 100)	161.3	241.8	109.6	117.4	136.4	223.0	279.3
(3) Inflation rate (%)[b]	51.8	8.1	24.9	175.2	20.7	10.8	2.7
(4) Unemployment rate (%)[c]	10.2[k]	7.8	ND	12.9	12.1	7.3	8.9
(5) Fiscal balance (% of GDP)[d]	−0.6[l]	0.9	ND	−3.3	−0.1	1.3	0.0
(6) Real wages[e]							
(6a) Rate of growth (%)	2.1	3.1	ND	ND	0.5	3.8	1.6
(6b) Index (1980 = 100)	122.5	137.6	ND	ND	99.9	128.3	156.1
(7) Current account balance (% of GDP)[f]	−3.7	−2.3	−2.3	−3.7	−7.3	−3.1	−0.7
(8) Real exchange rate (1986 = 100)[g]	86.8	93.5	ND	65.1	83.2	92.0	96.4
(9) Terms of trade (January 1995 = 100)[h]	121.3	96.4	179.1	132.5	89.5	99.2	90.7
(10) International reserves (millions of US$)[g]	5,523.2	13,851.1	62.0	451.7	3,564.1	13,103.8	15,345.7
(11) Gross national saving (% of GDP)[i]	15.3	21.8	12.3	12.0	11.8	22.2	21.1
(12) Foreign saving (% of GDP)[i]	3.5	2.2	2.6	2.8	7.1	2.9	0.7
(13) Gross fixed capital formation (% of GDP)[i]	18.8	24.0	14.9	14.8	18.9	25.1	21.9
(14) Exports of goods, fob (% of GDP)[e]	19.3	25.2	11.8	16.0	21.4	23.3	28.9
(15) Real exports of goods, growth rate (%)[e]	7.8	9.8	3.3	8.3	8.4	11.4	6.5
(16) External debt (% of GDP)[j]							
(16a) Public	26.9	15.4	14.8	28.8	53.5	17.4	10.2
(16b) Private	19.7	32.0	7.9	7.9	26.2	26.2	46.7
(16c) Total = public + private	46.7	47.4	22.6	36.7	79.7	43.6	56.9

Notes and sources:

ND = no data.

[a] World Development Indicators (WDI) for 1960–1989; central bank of Chile for 1990–2004.
[b] Central bank of Chile and National Bureau of Statistics.
[c] Solimano and Larraín (2002) for 1974–1975; central bank of Chile for 1976–2003.
[d] Larraín and Selowsky (1991) for 1970–1986; El Directorio de Prestadores de Servicios and authors' calculations for 1987–2004.
[e] Economic Commission for Latin America and the Caribbean (ECLAC).
[f] Authors' analysis based on the central bank of Chile data and WDI for 1960–1969; ECLAC for 1970–2001; central bank of Chile for 2002–2004.
[g] Central bank of Chile.
[h] Authors' analysis based on ECLAC information for 1960–1964; Bennett and Valdés (2001) for 1965–2000; authors' analysis based on central bank of Chile data for 2000–2004.
[i] Bennett et al. (1999) for 1960–1984; central bank of Chile for 1985–2003.
[j] Central bank of Chile.
[k] Available data from 1974.

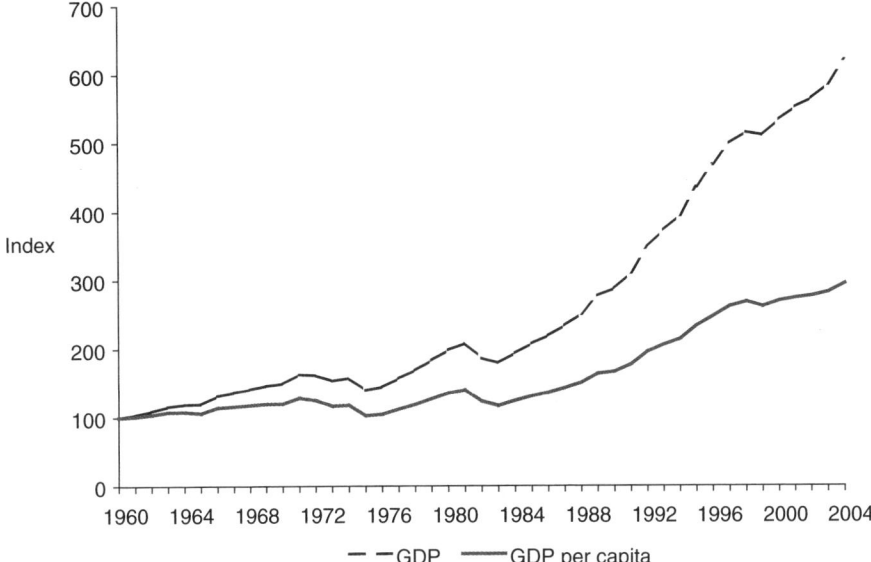

Figure 10.1 Chile: GDP and GDP per capita levels, 1960–2004 (Index 100 = 1960)
Note: The rate of growth of GDP for 2004 corresponds to the IMACEC index, central bank of Chile.
Source: Authors' analysis based on data from WDI and the central bank of Chile.

stabilizing inflation, reinstating property to former owners and securing external credits. The persistently high inflation levels led in 1975 (see Figure 10.2) to the adoption of 'shock therapy' policies entailing money-based stabilization complemented by a drastic fiscal adjustment programme in which nearly 100,000 public employees left the state sector in one year. Although, historically, the Chilean military were traditionalists in economic matters, the Pinochet regime, helped by a team of neoliberal economists trained at the University of Chicago, adopted free market economic policies within a highly authoritarian political system. Trade liberalization, privatization, fiscal adjustment and other market liberalization policies dominated the second half of the 1970s. An exchange rate-based stabilization programme was used between 1978 and 1982 to reduce inflation, although in 1982 the experiment resulted in a severe economic and financial crisis.[3] The economy suffered a sharp decline in GDP and a jump in unemployment and bankruptcies, accompanied by a crisis in the banking sector, recurrent currency devaluation and serious external debt-servicing problems. The crises in the financial and real sectors were tackled with the technical and financial support from the international financial institutions – International Monetary Fund, World Bank and Inter-American Development Bank – that complemented internal crisis management policies, including bail-outs in the financial and corporate sectors, a real depreciation of the currency that restored profitability in tradable goods activities and a cut in domestic absorption. The social consequences of the crises were dire. Unemployment climbed

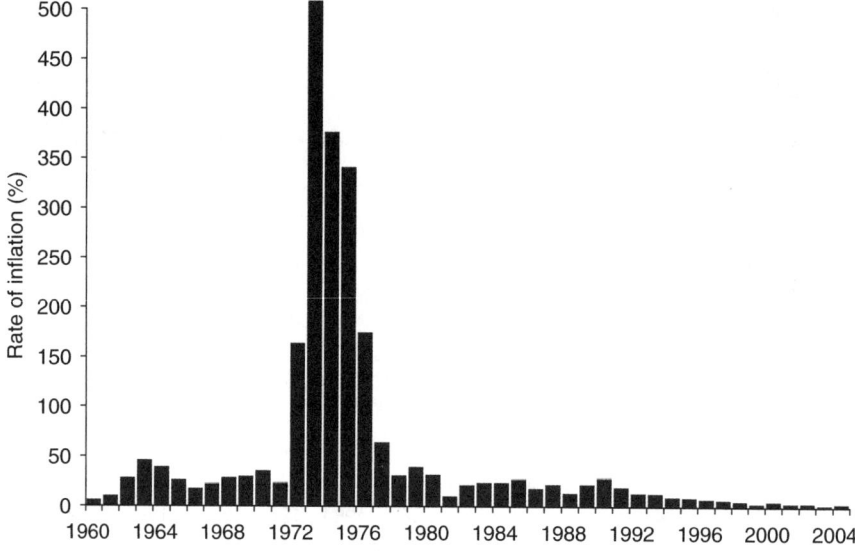

Figure 10.2 Chile: inflation rate, 1960–2004 (percentage per year)
Source: National Bureau of Statistics, Chile.

to near 30 per cent in 1983, real wages fell and many small and medium-sized firms drowned in debt or went bankrupt with the ensuing destruction of organizational capital and jobs.

The Chilean economy once again recovered and started to grow in the second half of the 1980s. The recovery was supported by a more competitive real exchange rate, the financial rehabilitation of firms, tax cuts, easier credit and higher internal demand. However, by the end of the 1980s, the economic recovery was incubating inflationary pressures and external imbalances that the new Aylwin administration – the first democratic government elected after Pinochet – had to tackle. The Aylwin government raised taxes to fund social programmes to revert the social deterioration of the previous years in terms of minimum wages, reduced monetary subsidies to the poor and the chronic underfunding of the public health and education systems. Additionally, fiscal resources were needed to start revamping public infrastructure such as ports, roads and highways that had deteriorated after years of little public investment. Macroeconomic policies in the 1990s accommodated higher social spending, while reducing inflation, avoiding short-term capital inflows and reducing public external debt. These policies were further deepened during the Frei and Lagos administrations – particularly the latter, which followed conservative fiscal policies (adopting the explicit rule of one per cent fiscal surplus), achieved further reduction inflation, suspended a tax on short-term capital inflows and deepened a floating exchange rate regime. Macroeconomic stability was consolidated in 2000–2004, but this period delivered lower growth than previous years and sluggish increases in real wages.

Macroeconomic policies in 1990–2004

The macroeconomic policies followed by the *Concertación* governments in the 1990s were influenced by recent history. The fiscal and inflationary crises of the 1970s and the currency and financial crises of the early 1980s created a consensus on the need to ensure macroeconomic stability for development. In a way, Chile still lived under the ghost of the economic (and political) traumas of the recent past. Thus, the *Concertación* administration – including the Christian Democratic Party, Socialist Party and other left-wing parties, but not the Communist Party[4] – was keen to avert any hint that it would repeat the economic policies of the left in the past, chiefly the economic policies under Allende. Historically, the leftist economic policies stressed attaining distributive economic and social goals more than the maintenance of macroeconomic and financial stability. This ranking of policy priorities was reversed post-1990. Also, it is worth noting that the macro policies of the 1990s were gradualist in the anti-inflationary front and pragmatic in other areas such as the use of taxes to deter short-term capital inflows (see Chapters 4 and 5). Gradualism did not preclude, however, the use of shock treatment in 1998 in the aftermath of the Asian crises by the central bank. As a consequence of the monetary crunch, interest rates soared, cooling down expenditure – particularly investment – and increasing the cost of debt servicing by consumers and firms. In retrospect, it is apparent that the policy of very high interest rates made the sector of small and medium-sized enterprises, which were in debt and faced sluggish internal demand since 1998, particularly vulnerable. This policy also led to a delayed and sluggish recovery in output and employment in subsequent years since it weakened a labour-intensive sector, generating adverse effects on expectations, consumption and employment. We turn now to a more detailed analysis of the nature of fiscal, exchange rate and monetary policies that were followed in 1990–2004.

Fiscal policy

In the fiscal area, the three governments in 1990–2004 pursued either an implicit or explicit policy of fiscal surpluses, although this policy was not complied with every year. For example, in 1999, 2001, 2002 and 2003 there were fiscal deficits associated with slower growth and reduced fiscal revenues,[5] and in 2000 the Lagos administration formalized a *fiscal rule* in which the government was to run a *structural* fiscal surplus of one per cent of GDP – the structural budget is calculated using medium-run projections of the main sources of fiscal revenues such as the price of copper and the level and rate of growth of GDP. This rule is consistent to some degree with counter-cyclical fiscal policy as it allows the government to run deficits in years when GDP is below the full capacity level and financed, in principle, by surpluses accumulated in good years. It is an open question as to the extent that aggregate demand polices in 2000–2004 were counter-cyclical in spite of favourable conditions to accelerate a recovery of growth and employment because there was low inflation, existing unused capacity and access to external borrowing at a low cost. On the other hand, fiscal policies in 1990–2004 focused on reducing the stock of foreign public debt, which declined from 39 per cent of GDP in 1990 to 13 per cent in 2004. Under these conditions, more expansive demand management policies could have been undertaken to shorten this cycle of sluggish growth and slow employment creation in 1998–2003 that was created by a combination of adverse external shocks and the policies of credit crunch cum reduced exchange rate flexibility of the central bank in 1998.

Summarizing, the fiscal policy stance of the *Concertación* governments aimed to put public finances on a solvency path and reduce public debt to make fiscal policy less vulnerable to external shocks. The absence of explicit redistributive goals released public finances[6] from the extra pressure beyond that of poverty reduction and social protection of lower-income groups in Chilean society. In the medium term, a policy of fiscal restraint helps to reduce inflationary pressures, maintain external balance and release pressures on interest rates that facilitate private investment and growth-generating fiscal resources to finance social policies. Further issues are what should be the optimal macro fiscal policy, the level of fiscal budgets and the investment and debt policy of the state in a country with accumulated social debts and potential profitable investment opportunities in education, health and other sectors.

Exchange rate policy

A main shift in exchange rate policy in the last five years has been the abandonment of an 'intermediate regime' – for example, an exchange rate band regime – for a system of free floating with minimal intervention by the monetary authorities[7] (see Chapter 4 of this volume). In September 1999, the exchange rate band regime was abandoned. The management of the adjustable band regime was not simple as persistent capital inflows during most of the 1990s, mainly until 1997, exerted a 'downward' pressure on the exchange rate (to appreciate), moving the market exchange rate to the floor of the band, and leading the central bank to engage in expensive sterilization operations to counteract the monetary effect of massive purchases of foreign exchange. In 1998–1999, a tight monetary policy was complemented by a policy of *reduced* exchange rate flexibility, which *narrowed* the band and reduced the distance between the floor and the ceiling, in the face of adverse terms of trade shocks and a reduction in capital inflows. In general, adjustments to adverse external shocks that are not fully financed require *more* (not less) exchange rate flexibility. In recent years, under the flexible exchange rate regime, the central bank has intervened in the foreign exchange market on only a few occasions: (i) in 2001 associated with the instability created by 11 September and the crisis of the Argentinean currency board; and (ii) in 2002, after turbulence linked to the Brazilian elections. The free-floating exchange rate regime has been associated with significant fluctuations in the nominal exchange rates (see Figure 10.3); this volatility can be highlighted as a problem of the free-floating regime adopted since 1999 and adds to an already volatile path of the real exchange rate observed since the 1970s in Chile (see Figure 10.4). On the positive side, the free-floating regime has benefited from: (i) the decline in 'pass-through' coefficients between exchange rate and prices that reduces the inflationary effect

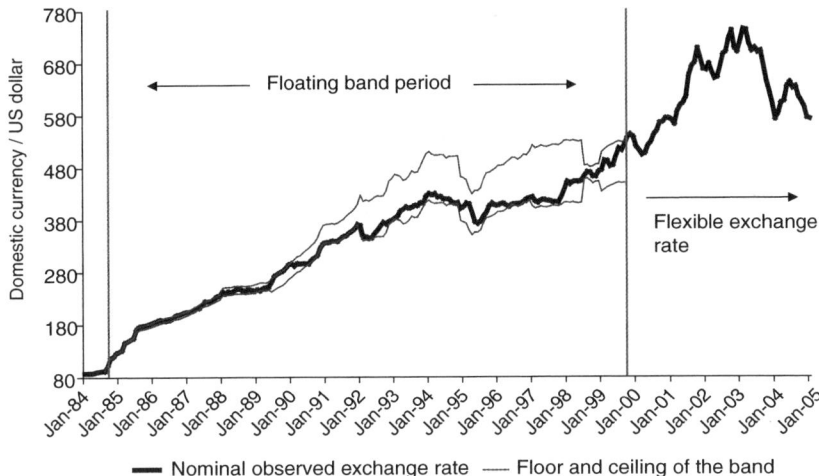

Figure 10.3 Chile: exchange rate regimes – Floating band and flexible exchange rate systems periods, 1984–2005

Source: Authors' analysis based on data from the central bank of Chile.

Figure 10.4 Chile: real exchange rate, 1977–2004 (Index 100 = 1986)

Notes: An increase in the index indicates depreciation and a decline is an appreciation. The value of 2004 corresponds to the average until November of that year.

Source: Authors' analysis based on data from the central bank of Chile.

of currency depreciations; (ii) the small liability-dollarization in the banking system although the increase in external indebtedness of the corporate sector reduces this effect; and (iii) the development of more sophisticated financial instruments to deal with exchange fluctuations.[8]

Disinflation and monetary policy

An important policy accomplishment in the period 1990–2004 has been the decline in inflation from 27.3 per cent in 1990 to 2.4 per cent in 2004 (see Figure 10.5). However, this is also part of a general shift to a low-inflation regime in the world economy, a trend shared by the Chilean economy. Moreover, there was a further decline in inflation in 2000–2004 – averaging 2.7 per cent per year, a level that is very close to the average inflation rate of Organization for Economic Co-operation and Development economies. Chile instituted an independent central bank in the late 1980s with a mandate to ensure low and stable inflation and normalcy in internal and external payments (the charter of the central bank of Chile, unlike that of other central banks of developed economies, excludes any objective of growth or full employment in its mission).[9] The strong anti-inflationary mandate of the central bank also stipulates that it must contribute to lowering inflation. However, the policy actions of the central bank also affect output and employment. The 1998–1999 *credit crunch* of the central bank and *reduced* exchange rate flexibility probably *amplified* the real effects on domestic output and employment of the external shocks associated with the global turbulence of

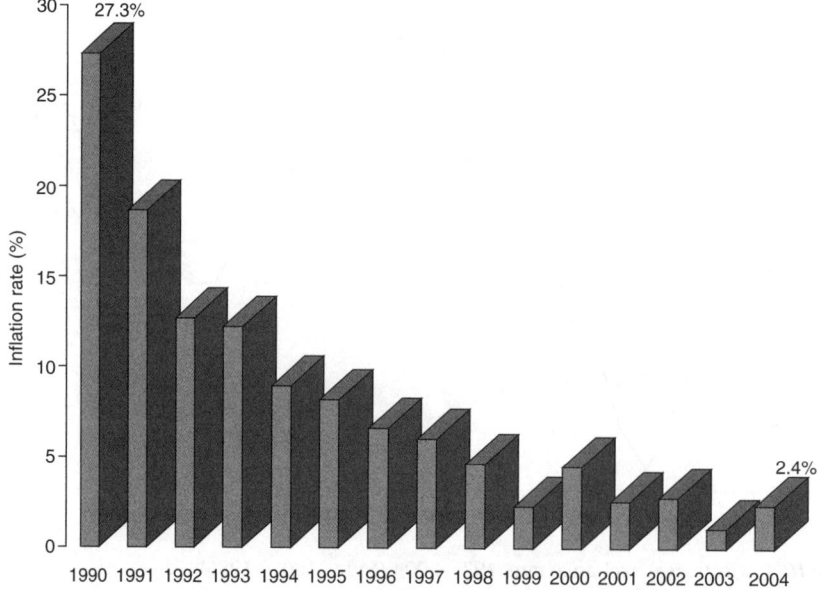

Figure 10.5 Chile: inflation rate, 1990–2004 (percentage per year)
Source: Central bank of Chile.

1997–1999. Monetary policy in recent years has operated using an inflation target, which as of 2004–2005 is in the range of 2 per cent to 4 per cent with a mean value of 3 per cent annual inflation. Monetary policy has regained more autonomy with the floating exchange rate regime, although, as addressed later, this has taken place in a context of large fluctuations in nominal exchange rates.

The current account, terms of trade and external debt

The performance of the Chilean economy in the period 1990–2004 was also influenced by the cycles of the international economy, the behaviour of terms of trade, international interest rates, capital flows and demand for exports. The terms of trade experienced several swings through the period with a decline in 1991–1993 followed by a boom in 1994–1997 and then a decline in 1998–2003 to recover again in 2004 (see Figure 10.6). It is worth noting that economic activity, except in the early 1990s, closely followed the behaviour of the terms of trade.

The average current deficit in 1990–2004 was 2.3 per cent of GDP (see Table 10.1), a moderate number by the standards of developing countries that are in the phase of the development process where foreign savings are needed to complement national savings to support economic growth. The levels of current account deficits were higher in 1990–1997 than in 1998–2004 due to rapid growth of the Chilean economy and the return of capital inflows to Latin America in those years. The concern of Chilean policy makers in maintaining a sustainable level of absorption of capital flows was complemented by the objective of discouraging short-term capital inflows. For that purpose, a tax on short-term capital was in effect until March 2000. There is some controversy whether the low level of short-term

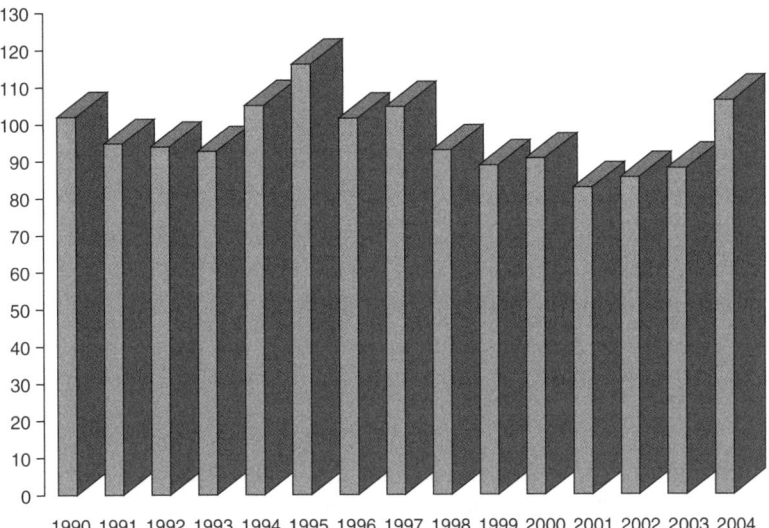

Figure 10.6 Chile: terms of trade, 1990–2004 (January 1977 = 100)

Source: Authors' analysis based on data from Bennett and Valdés (2001) and the central bank of Chile.

Table 10.2 Chile: ratio of total external debt to GDP (percentage)

	Argentina	Brazil	Chile	Mexico
2000	51.5	39.2	49.2	25.6
2001	52.2	44.5	58.0	23.2
2002	131.5	49.4	60.4	21.6
2003	112.2	47.8	59.9	22.4

Source: ECLAC (2003, 2004).

inflows was due to this tax, to the effect of other 'macroeconomic fundamentals' or to a combination of both sets of variables.

Chilean total external debt was near 60 per cent of GDP in 2003, up from 57.5 per cent in 1990, not a small amount if compared with other developing countries. As shown in Table 10.2, the ratio of total external debt to GDP in 2003 in Chile is below the level of Argentina, but is above the levels of both Brazil and Mexico. However, the cost of servicing that debt is much lower in Chile as it can borrow at lower interest rates in international markets due to a reduced sovereign risk premium, well below that of Argentina and Brazil as well as Mexico.

Although the total level of external debt has not changed much over the period 1990–2004, there has been a substantial change in its composition between public and private debt. The democratic governments followed an active policy of reducing public external debt both in absolute terms and as a share of GDP. In fact, the ratio of public external debt to GDP declined by nearly 26 percentage points between 1990 and 2004. In contrast, private external debt increased substantially in this period. Private external debt was $5.633 million in 1990 (19 per cent of GDP) and climbed to $34.079 million in 2004 (47 per cent of GDP). Much of the attention has been focused so far on public debt and comparatively little on the evolution of private external debt. We know from past experience that when debt-servicing difficulties arise there is a need of costly macroeconomic adjustment, even though the debt was contracted by the private sector, which was the case prior to the crises of 1982–1983 in Chile. Clearly, the Chilean economy is much more robust today than it was in the early 1980s; however, monitoring of the evolution of private external debt is still necessary.

Growth and macro performance in 1990–2004

The rate of economic growth in Chile in 1990–2004 was higher than in previous decades[10] and stood above the Latin American average, but below that of other dynamic economies (see Table 10.3). Rapid growth has also been accompanied by volatility and growth cycles of long duration[11] (see Figure 10.7). A sharp turning point in the growth process took place in 1997–1998, associated with the Asian and Russian crises. In fact, annual GDP growth decreased from 7.7 per cent in 1990–1997 to 3 per cent in 1998–2004.

In 2004, as a consequence of a boom in copper prices, the main export product of Chile, and other export commodities as well as a policy of low interest rates, the

Table 10.3 Chile: GDP growth rates of selected countries, 1990–2004

	Chile[a]	China[b]	Hong Kong[b]	Ireland[b]	Mauritius[b]	Singapore[b]	Uganda[b]	Latin America and the Caribbean[c]
1990–2004	5.5	9.3	4.1	6.7	5.1	6.4	6.4	2.5
1990–1999	6.4	9.7	3.8	7.1	5.4	7.6	6.9	2.7
2000–2004	3.9	8.4	4.8	6.0	4.5	4.0	5.4	2.2

Sources:
[a] Central bank of Chile.
[b] WDI for 1990–2003; EIU estimates for 2004.
[c] ECLAC, on the basis of official figures converted into US$ at constant 1995 prices.

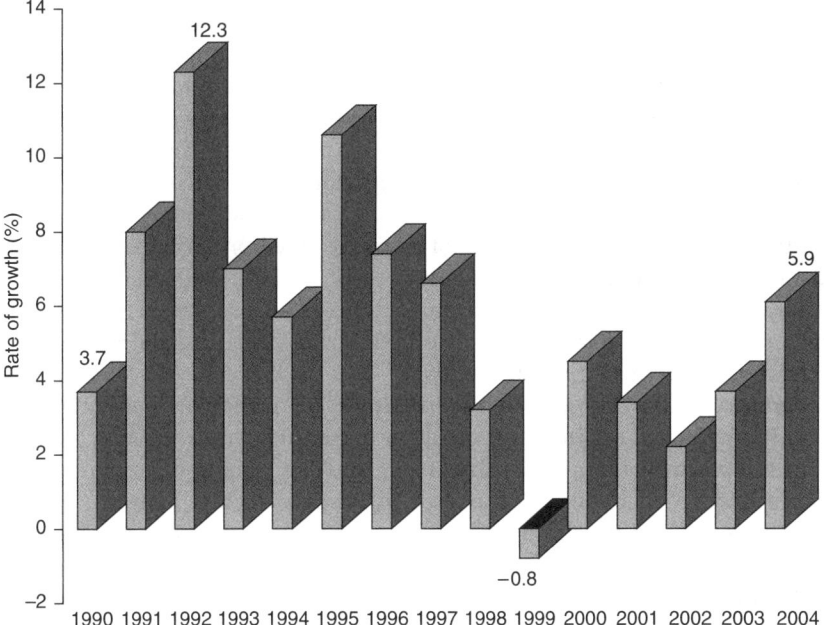

Figure 10.7 Chile: rate of growth of GDP, 1990–2004 (percentage per year)
Note: [a] averages correspond to 1990–1993.
Source: Central Bank of Chile; Authors' calculations.

Chilean economy grew to nearly 6 per cent a year, approaching the levels of the golden years of growth of 1986–1997. A look at the underlying factors of the boom of 1990–1997[12] shows that growth was supported by an increase in national savings and in the ratio of investment to GDP, the latter over 27 per cent of GDP in 1996–1997 – the ratio of investment to GDP was the highest ratio of the last 40 years. There is controversy about the causality between savings and investment. Do

230 *Country Case Studies*

national savings precede GDP growth or, conversely, does the savings ratio follow acceleration in GDP growth?[13] In addition, Chilean growth has been accompanied by rising exports to GDP ratios in an export-led growth fashion.

In retrospect, the golden age of rapid growth from the mid- to late 1980s to the mid- to late 1990s has proved difficult to replicate. The Chilean economy turned vulnerable to the spell of global instability triggered by the Asian and Russian crises of 1997–1998 that led to a decline in terms of trade for Chile and a reduction in capital inflows. Although domestic financial stability and lower inflation have been maintained in the aftermath of those shocks, the economy entered into a cycle of slow growth that lasted for more than half a decade (until 2003). In addition, it is unlikely that a rapid return to growth at 7 per cent per year, which characterized the last growth boom, will occur. The policy mix of the post-1998 cycle combined tight money by the central bank in 1998–99 with more expansive fiscal policies as the economic authorities of the Frei government apparently sought to moderate the effects on aggregate demand of the credit crunch of the central bank – the fiscal balance turned from a surplus to a deficit of 1.4 per cent of GDP in 1999. In any case, a recession took place and GDP fell by 0.8 percentage points in 1999. The Lagos government that took office in early 2000 reversed the course of fiscal policy adopted in the later years of the Frei government and adopted a more restrictive fiscal stance that perhaps deprived the economy of an additional impulse coming from internal demand. The strategy of recovery relied on an increase in exports and a recovery of private and public investment. In 2003–2004, monetary policy became expansionary, with successive reductions in interest rates set by the central bank that, given their lagged effects on aggregate demand, contributed to the acceleration of economic growth in 2004.[14]

In terms of funding for growth, the banking system is active in providing credit for consumption and housing, but with a low degree of intermediation in productive credits to the small and medium-sized firms, the main source of employment creation in Chile. Other sources of investment finance such as venture capital are underdeveloped and the funding of innovation is a complex task for risk-taking, innovation-oriented entrepreneurs.

Comparing the macroeconomic and growth performance of the Aylwin, Frei and Lagos administrations, there are differences in outcomes (see Table 10.4). Economic growth was highest during the Aylwin administration (1990–1994) with average GDP growth of 7.8 per cent per year and lowest during the Lagos administration (2000–2004) with average GDP growth of 3.7 per cent per year.[15] In contrast, inflation was the highest under Aylwin (average 17.7 per cent annual) and the lowest under Lagos (2.4 per cent annual). The macro performance of the Frei administration lies between Aylwin and Lagos in terms of growth and inflation. Of course, initial economic conditions and the international economy affected the growth record of each administration. For example, a complicated international scenario associated with the occurrence of the Asian and Russian crises hit the Frei government in 1997–1998 and also affected, to some extent, the Lagos government (until 2003). Although fiscal policy has been austere in the three governments, the lowest fiscal deficits are observed during the Lagos administration, which implemented an explicit rule of a structural fiscal surplus. At the same time, fiscal policy has been only mildly counter-cyclical in this period. Regarding labour market indicators, unemployment has been higher and real wages have grown more slowly in the Lagos administration compared to those of Frei and Aylwin. In contrast, lower current account deficits are experienced in the Lagos administration, which seems to have been the most orthodox in macroeconomic policy of the three *Concertación* governments.

Table 10.4a provides a summary of the regimes' exchange rate, monetary, fiscal and capital account policies across the three administrations from 1990 to 2004.

Table 10.4 Chile: economic performance by administration, 1990–2004

	Aylwin administration 1990–March 1994[a]	Frei administration 1994–1999	Lagos administration 2000–2004
Rate of growth of GDP (%)			
Total	7.8	5.5	3.7
Per capita	5.9	4.1	2.4
Rate of inflation (%)	17.7	6.1	2.7
Real wages (rate of change, %)	3.7	3.8	1.6
Unemployment (%)	7.3	7.3	8.9
Fiscal balance (% of GDP)	1.6	1.1	0.0
Terms of trade (1997 5 100)	95.8	101.5	90.7
Current account (% of GDP)	22.5	23.5	20.7

Note:
[a] averages correspond to 1990–1993.
Source: Authors' calculations.

Table 10.4a Chile: macroeconomic policy matrix by administration, 1990–2004

	Aylwin administration 1990–March 1994	Frei administration 1994–1999	Lagos administration 2000–2005
Exchange rate policy	Exchange rate band	Exchange rate band	Flotation
Monetary policy	Eclectic	Eclectic	Inflation goals
Fiscal policy	Austere without fiscal rule	Moderately austere without fiscal rule	Rule of structural fiscal superavit (1% of GDP)
Taxes to short-term capital flows	Yes	Yes	Yes

Source: Authors' analysis.

Poverty, income distribution and social policies

This section focuses on the social dimension of the Chilean model. Chile has been successful in decreasing the proportion of the population below the poverty line, but unsuccessful in improving income distribution, which remains unequal by international standards.

There is a growing economic literature that indicates that inequality of income – closely related to inequality of opportunities – is problematic both on ethical grounds as well as for instrumental reasons.[16] Inequality can harm growth for various reasons; it can generate social polarization and political instability and invite higher taxation, which is detrimental to investment. In addition, in unequal societies there is an economic loss since many talented individuals and excluded social groups cannot realize their initiative and productive potential due to a lack of credit and social contacts, limited information about opportunities and reduced access to political power.[17]

The following diagnoses the dimension, characteristics and evolution of poverty in Chile during the 1990s and early 2000s and analyses the worrying trends in income distribution before and after transfer showing the persistence of inequality in Chile.[18] The social policies of the *Concertación* governments relied on four principles: (i) growth-led poverty reduction; (ii) increasing the level and better targeting of monetary transfers to the poor; (iii) increasing public spending in education, health, housing and pensions; and (iv) initial attempts of reform of systems of private provision of social services, such as the health system. Missing components, in our view, of a more comprehensive social policy have been: (i) lack of an explicit concern for inequality of income and wealth; (ii) absence of explicit consideration of the middle class as a valid recipient of social policy; (iii) excessive emphasis on targeting that generates unintended exclusions of benefits for border-line groups; (iv) lack of policies to rebalance the bargaining power of workers severely debilitated after the Pinochet regime; and (v) absence of an explicit concern for the concentration of ownership in a few economic groups including the banking sector and pension funds management companies.[19]

As shown in Table 10.4b, social policy did not establish explicit redistributive goals – neither are they explicit in the UN Millennium Development Goals – although, in practice there was an implicit redistribution by increasing subsidies to the poor and increasing direct and indirect taxes. The social concern of the democratic governments has been a very active one; however, in retrospect it should be noted that it did not include areas related to assets distribution and concentration (private property). Neither is it evident that one of the priorities has been to strengthen the negotiating capacity of workers. This would have led to a more equitable distribution of increases of productivity between labour and capital during period of rapid economic growth. This issue of organization and information capacity is also relevant for consumers and other non-favoured groups of the economic system.

Table 10.4b Chile: economic behaviour matrix and social policy/public policy by administration, 1990–2004

	Aylwin administration 1990–March 1994	*Frei administration 1994–1999*	*Lagos administration 2000–2004*
Poverty	Decreases	Decreases	Decreases
Inequality(Gini coefficient)	Remains stable	Remains stable	Remains stable
Increase and focalization of subsidies	Yes	Yes	Yes
Minimum wage	Real increase	Real increase	Real increase
Education: expenditure reforms	Increase Program P-900 (poor schools), Program MECE (quality of education)	Increase School day extension, teachers' evaluation	Increase Compulsory 12 years of education, digital alphabetization
Health: expenditure reforms	Increase Strengthening of public hospitals, coverage extension	Increase Strengthening of public hospitals, coverage extension	Increase Plan Auge, modification in law about Isapres
Goals of less inequality made explicit	No	No	No
De-concentration of property policy	No	No	No
Strengthening of trade unions and social organizations	Light	Light	Light
Policy of consumer defense			Creation of a board of free competition, modification of the consumer law
Democratization of the access to credit[1]	Partial	Partial	Partial/increases

Note: [1]See Pollack and García (2004) for a discussion on the role of the financing sector in equity and competitiveness in Chile.
Source: Authors' analysis.

Solimano (2005) compares Latin American and Scandinavian social policies and enumerates the various difficulties faced by 'focalization in the poorest', which do not incorporate the middle class. This approach has been in practice in the Latin American region through the Washington Consensus policies, and Chile has not been an exception. These difficulties can be summarized as: (i) problems related to identifying and implementing mechanisms to effectively reach the poorest population groups; (ii) the exclusion of potential beneficiaries who are close to the poverty line; (iii) an emphasis on the redistributive character of the social policy

Table 10.5 Chile: households and population below the poverty and indigence line (percentage)

Year	Poverty line		Indigence line	
	Households	Population	Households	Population
1990	33.3	38.6	10.6	12.9
1996	19.7	23.2	4.9	5.7
2000	16.6	20.6	4.6	5.7
2003	15.4	18.8	3.9	4.7

Source: ECLAC (2004).

by separating groups paying taxes to finance social policies, which include the middle class as well as higher income groups, from the beneficiaries of social policies; and (iv) the fragmentation and weakening of the middle class that, historically, has been the most stable socially and politically. Policies dealing with consumer protection and their rights were more strongly developed during the Lagos administration, when the Consumers Law was modified and the Free Competition Court was created (see Table 10.4b). The increasing complexity of the delivery of services such as health, insurance and credits require informed consumers in order to avoid redistribution of income from consumers to suppliers.

Poverty

Between 1990 and 2003, the proportion of the Chilean population below the poverty line decreased from 38.6 per cent to 18.8 per cent. At the same time, extreme poverty or indigence experienced a reduction from 12.9 per cent to 4.7 per cent as shown in Table 10.5.[20] Interestingly, when growth was rapid (1990–1997), poverty declined quickly, yet these gains were not eroded when growth slowed down (1998–2003).

Regional distribution of poverty

Poverty is not uniformly distributed across the different regions of Chile. The *largest number* of indigent and poor households is concentrated in the Metropolitan Region, the most populated region of the country and which includes the capital city of Santiago; but the *incidence* of poverty in this region is not among the highest in the country. The incidence of poverty is much higher in the Region of Araucanía and Bío-Bío, in the south of the country, where almost 30 per cent of households are under the poverty or indigence line. On the other hand, Magallanes and Antofagasta, followed by the Metropolitan Region, have the lowest incidence of poverty. This dimension of the regional distribution of poverty must be considered in formulating policies to alleviate it. Macroeconomic policies affect the different regions with different intensities and in distinct ways, according to their production profiles.

Table 10.6 Chile: sociodemographic profile and labour market indicators by poverty strata, 2000 (average)

Variables	Indigent	Poor no indigent	No poor	Total
Number of household members	4.8	4.8	3.7	3.9
Dependency demographic rate[a]	75.9	70.2	50.4	54.3
Proportion of inactive population	52.1	48.9	37.9	40.1
Unemployment rate	42.4	21.2	7.3	10.2
Proportion of employed household members:				
less than 8 years of education	44.4	35.3	18.8	21.1
less than 10 years of education	69.2	58.9	31.6	35.3
less than 12 years of education	83.1	74.4	42.1	46.3
Proportion working in low productivity sectors	47.4	42.3	32.6	33.9

Note:
[a] Defined as the ratio between the population less than 15 years old and older than 65 and the total population.
Source: Authors' analysis of data from ECLAC (2003).

Family characteristics and employment patterns of the poor

The main sociodemographic and labour market characteristics of Chilean households of different income strata for 2000 are presented in Table 10.6, revealing several important features:

- poor families are larger than non-poor families and have higher dependency ratios;
- poor families (indigent and poor non-indigents) have a high incidence of unemployed and inactive members;
- the incidence of unemployment among the poor is closely related to their education level, which is much lower among the poor income strata; and
- workers from indigent and poor households tend to work in lower productivity sectors.

Informality and segmentation in the labour market

The Chilean labour market is characterized by segmentation (significant differences of labour productivity and income earnings among the employed population). Two classifications are often used for segmentation in goods and labour markets: (i) the duality between formal and informal sectors (Infante and Sunkel 2004); and (ii) the dichotomy of low-productivity and high-productivity sectors (ECLAC 2004).

The traditional characterization of the 'formal sector' in goods and labour markets assumes that it is composed of firms of higher capital and technology intensity and reflected in higher labour productivity, compared to informal sector activities. In turn, formal firms often pay taxes, have more formal labour relations – labour contracts and social benefits – and provide more training and better salaries to their workers.[21] In contrast, the 'informal sector' is characterized by lower-productivity firms and more flexible entrance and exit of workers under less formalized labour relations. Often, workers in the informal sector earn lower salaries than workers in the formal sector, enjoy fewer social benefits and have a lower educational level (Infante and Sunkel 2004).

According to Infante and Sunkel (2004), there are six main differences between the formal and the informal sector in Chile:

- The average product of formal workers is almost four times greater than of informal workers, explaining the differences between average labour income and wages between the two sectors.
- There are important differences between both sectors in the degree of social protection and labour relations: while 87 per cent of formal workers have a labour contract, only 50 per cent of informal workers have one; 84 per cent of formal workers have social security benefits, only 35 per cent of informal workers have them.
- Working conditions are worse in the informal than in the formal sector: longer working hours and less safety at the workplace.
- Informal workers are less educated (on average 9.6 years of education) than formal workers (on average 12.2 years).
- Poverty is higher among informal workers than among formal workers.
- Women are concentrated in the informal sector and receive lower salaries than men: 20 per cent lower in the formal sector and 45 per cent lower in the informal sector.

In Chile, a trend toward certain formalization of employment was observed during the boom of growth in 1990–1997, but this trend was abruptly reversed after the Asian crisis. Since 1998, most new jobs have been generated in the informal sector; at the end of the 1990s it was at the same level as in 1990.

Table 10.7 shows the pattern of labour market segmentation among different income groups. While 36 per cent of workers from the poorest group (1st quintile) work in the informal sector, only 3.2 per cent of the richest workers (5th quintile) work in that sector.

Table 10.7 Chile: population working in the informal sector by income level, 2000 (per cent)

	Income quintile					
	1	2	3	4	5	Total
Informal	36	28.8	16.7	13.1	3.2	16.4
Formal	64	71.2	83.3	86.9	96.8	83.6
Total	100	100	100	100	100	100

Source: Infante and Sunkel (2004).

Low-productivity sectors, demographics and women's participation

Using an alternative definition of productive sectors provided by ECLAC, Table 10.8 shows the distribution of Chilean workers in low-productivity sectors in the period 1990–2003. The proportion of workers in low-productivity sectors diminished from 38.8 per cent in 1990 to 31.9 per cent in 2003, suggesting a shift to higher-productivity sectors. During the years of adjustment and lower growth after 1998, relatively more low-productivity jobs were created. Another variable influencing income distribution is the participation rate of working age population. While the participation rates of the total working age population remained more or less constant around 73 per cent during the whole period, female participation experienced a significant increase – from 36 per cent to 45 per cent. Even more significant is that women of reproductive age experienced the highest increase in labour market participation, from 47 per cent to 61 per cent. Although women have increased their participation rates in the labour market, the data on unemployment for women (higher than for men) suggest a gender bias with female workers facing more difficulties than men in accessing the labour market. In fact, women's unemployment rate increased from 8.7 per cent in 1990 to 10.2 per cent in 2003.

The persistence of unequal income distribution

In spite of the progress in achieving more macro stability and the reduction in absolute poverty levels and indigence, the unequal income distribution constitutes a significant unsolved problem on the road to effective economic development in Chile.[22]

Table 10.8 Chile: urban population employed in low-productivity sectors of the labour market, 1990–2003 (percentage of employed urban population)

			Microenterprises wage or salary earners				Unskilled self-employed		
Year	Total (1)	Employers (2)	Total (3)	Professional and technical (4)	Non-professional, non-technical (5)	Domestic employment (6)	Total (7)	Industry and construction (8)	Commerce and services (9)
1990	38.8	0.8	10.3	0.9	9.4	7.0	20.7	5.7	14.0
1994	34.6	1.8	9.4	0.8	8.6	6.1	17.3	5.4	11.2
1996	34.3	2.0	10.1	1.0	9.1	6.1	16.1	4.2	10.7
1998	34.4	2.6	10.7	1.0	9.7	5.9	15.2	4.1	10.2
2000	32.5	2.4	9.0	1.0	8.0	6.2	14.9	4.3	9.6
2003	31.9	2.4	8.0	0.8	7.2	6.5	15.0	4.9	9.2

Notes:
(1) = (2) + (3) + (6) + (7)
(3) = (4) + (5)
(7) = (8) + (9) + employment in agriculture, forestry, fishing and hunting.

Source: ECLAC (2004).

Table 10.9 Chile: household total income distribution, 1990–2003 (percentage)

	Share of total income of:					Ratio of average per capita income	
Year	Average income	Poorest 40%	Next 30%	20% below the richest 10%	Richest 10%	D10/D (1 to 4)	Q5/Q1
1990	9.4	13.2	20.8	25.4	40.7	18.2	18.4
1996	12.9	13.1	20.5	26.2	40.2	18.3	18.6
2000	13.6	13.8	20.8	25.1	40.3	18.7	19.0
2003	13.5	13.8	20.8	25.7	39.7	18.6	18.3

Source: ECLAC (2003).

Table 10.9 presents data on total household income distribution for selected years. The data show that households in the first four income deciles of the distribution (the poorest 40 per cent) received about 14 per cent of total income in 2003, an increase in income share of 0.6 percentage points since 1990. The richest 10 per cent of households received around 40 per cent of total income on average during the whole period (declining slightly in 2003). These numbers show an unequal pattern of income distribution that remained basically unchanged throughout the period 1990–2003. Other ratios confirm these trends. For example, the average income of the richest decile is more than 18.6 times the share of the four poorest deciles (40 per cent), while the average income of the richest quintile is equivalent to 18.3 times that of the poorest quintile. Households in the fifth, sixth and seventh deciles (the 'Next 30%' column) received around 21 per cent of total income. This segment can be considered as the *middle class* with an income share that remained stable and relatively independent of GDP growth during the whole period.[23] The Gini coefficient confirms that the degree of concentration of income distribution between 1990 and 2003 has basically remained constant.

Income distribution before and after transfers

Social policy, and in particular transfers, affects income distribution. Thus, it is important to compare personal income distribution based on the percentage of total income received by households and individuals *before* transfers that are ranked in ascending order according to per capita income with income distribution after transfers. The evolution of income before transfers distribution is also a helpful concept and measurement of inequality since it shows the extent that the economic system – the market, its institutions and the growth process – generates, endogenously, unequalizing or equalizing trends in income distribution.

We turn now to the concept of income distribution, which considers not only income derived from work or the ownership of assets, to the extent that they are declared in the CASEN (national socioeconomic) surveys, but also income received from subsidies and transfers from government to people and/or households

Table 10.10 Chile: income distribution considering pre-transfers per capita income from households by deciles, 1990–2000

Deciles	1990	1992	1994	1996	1998	2000
20/20	20.8	20.1	20.8	22.3	24.3	24.6
20/40	6.6	6.5	6.6	6.9	7.3	7.3
10/9	3.0	3.1	3.0	3.0	3.0	3.1

Source: Infante and Sunkel (2004).

Table 10.11 Chile: income distribution considering total per capita income from households by deciles, 1990–2000

Deciles	1990	1992	1994	1996	1998	2000
Top20/bottom 20	17.2	16.8	17.1	17.8	18.8	16.1
Top20/bottom 40	5.9	5.9	5.8	6.1	6.3	5.9
Top10/bottom 9	2.9	3.1	2.9	2.9	2.9	3.0

Source: Infante and Sunkel (2004).

(referred to as 'total income distribution'). This concept is only partially accurate since it does not provide a monetary value for social expenditure in education, health and other areas that may increase the future capacity of individuals to generate income.

Table 10.10 shows pre-transfers income distribution and Table 10.11 shows total income distribution (including transfers) between 1990 and 2000 by income deciles.

Table 10.11 shows that according to various indicators the pre-transfers income distribution did not improve and actually worsened for the poorest deciles in the 1990s. In the pre-transfers income distribution of households, the ratio between the incomes of the top to the bottom quintile (ratio 20/20) increased from 20.8 in 1990 to 24.6 in 2000, while the ratio 20/40 increased from 6.6 in 1990 to 7.3 in 2000. This situation changes, but only slightly, if total income instead of pre-transfers income is considered in the calculations. If total income is considered to calculate income distribution, the ratio top to bottom 20/20, *decreases* from 17.2 in 1990 to 16.1 in 2000, and the ratio 20/40 remains constant around 5.9 between both years.

Thus, the distribution of income generated by the market and the growth process actually worsened during the 1990s. These unequalizing trends were dampened by transfers, although they have not changed in a significant way the overall income distribution,[24] which remains unequal.

Targeting of social subsidies

Monetary transfers have played a significant role in dampening the effects of inequality of the poor. Thus, it is worth noting that the policy has been to increase the degree of targeting of subsidies toward the poorest segments of the population (see Table 10.12). In 1987, the poorest quintile of households received 33.6 per cent

Table 10.12 Chile: distribution of monetary household subsidies by autonomous per capita income (percentage)

Income quintile	1987	1990	1992	1994	1996	1998	2000
I	33.6	33.7	36.4	38.7	36.1	46.3	45.3
II	22.3	23.9	26.2	26.2	27.8	26.4	27.7
III	17.9	18.4	17.9	17.3	20.6	16.0	16.0
IV	14.9	13.9	12.0	12.1	11.5	8.4	8.3
V	11.3	10.1	7.4	7.4	4.0	2.9	2.7
Total	100.0	100.0	100.0	100.0	100.0	100.0	100.0

Source: Arellano (2004).

Table 10.13 Chile: structure of total income households by quintile, 2003 (percentage)

	Quintile of national autonomous income				
Type of income	I	II	III	IV	V
Autonomous income	88.3	96.7	98.6	99.5	99.9
Income from work	74.0	83.0	82.3	83.4	87.0
Retirement income	9.8	10.4	12.6	10.8	5.6
Capital income	0.6	0.9	1.5	2.9	5.8
Other autonomous income	3.8	2.3	2.2	2.3	1.5
Monetary subsidies	11.7	3.3	1.4	0.5	0.1
Unemployment subsidy	0.1	0.0	0.0	0.0	0.0
Family subsidy	1.9	1.2	0.6	0.2	0.0
PASIS[a]	6.8	1.5	0.6	0.2	0.0
Unique family subsidy	2.1	0.3	0.1	0.0	0.0
Others	78.0	0.2	0.1	0.0	0.0
Monetary income	100.0	100.0	100.0	100.0	100.0

Note: In-house domestic service is excluded.
[a]Disability allowance (Pensión Asistencial de Invalidéz).
Source: Ministry of Planning (2004).

of total subsidies, and 45.3 per cent in 2000. When including the 1st and 2nd quintiles, more than 70 per cent of subsidies are concentrated in the poorest 40 per cent of the population.[25]

However, the middle class – defined as households in the 3rd and 4th quintiles – was the main loser in this regard as their share in total subsidies decreased from 32.8 per cent in 1987 to 24.3 per cent in 2000. The composition of total income of households by quintile for 2003 is presented in Table 10.13.

In all households groups, income from work is the most important component of total income, fluctuating between 74 per cent and 87 per cent. Monetary subsidies represent almost 12 per cent of total household income in the poorest quintile and diminish by income quintile, reaching near zero for the 5th quintile in 2003.

Table 10.14 Chile: social expenditures, 1990–2000 (percentage)

	Annual growth rate	Accumulated growth rate
Total social expenditures	8.0	214
Health	9.4	247
Housing	5.1	164
Social Security	6.1	181
Education	10.6	274
Subsidies	5.9	177
	13.3	346

Source: Foxley (2004).

Social policies

Since 1990, the social strategy of the democratic governments relied on a combination of poverty reduction led by GDP growth, complemented by increased and more targeted transfers, and a recovery of the real value of the minimum wage and an increase in pensions. In addition, policies have focused on a significant increase in public spending on education, health, housing and social security (see Table 10.14). In the early 1990s, the Aylwin government sought to ensure a minimum income for poorer families – minimum wage increased by 17 per cent in real terms between 1989 and 1991. Family allowances and various subsidies for disadvantaged families, for people with disabilities and for the unemployed as well as pensions were also increased.[26] The emphasis on monetary transfers was complemented by a policy of expanding social expenditures in public health, housing for the poor and education. Between 1990 and 2000, there was a significant increase in public expenditures in health and education, which increased by 247 per cent and 274 per cent respectively (see Table 10.14).

Programmes dealing with poverty alleviation

In the democratic period, various social programmes have been put in place to reduce poverty. For example, in the early 1990s, an experimental programme that allowed community-based organizations to apply for public funds to develop projects to improve neighbourhood infrastructure or start micro-enterprises was coordinated by the new Solidarity and Social Investment Fund, essentially a social emergency fund. These programmes were implemented in other Latin American countries during the late 1980s and the 1990s to cope with the social consequences of structural adjustment programmes and/or economic crises.

At least three main operational difficulties emerged during the implementation of these programmes: (i) co-ordinating all executing agencies involved; (ii) reaching the poorest populations; and (iii) lack of resources. These weaknesses have also characterized similar initiatives in most Latin American countries.

In 1994, in an attempt to overcome these limitations, the National Program of Poverty Eradication was launched in 80 municipal districts with high poverty ratios. The municipalities were then asked to co-ordinate the effort to reach the poorest families. The programme had some limited success, but once again the difficulty of coordinating ministries and agencies and the availability of resources proved to be pervasive problems.

In 2002, a new approach, Chile Solidario, was launched to target indigent individuals and families through a decentralized system designed to ensure that poor families have effective access to income-support subsidies and public services. Chile Solidario also has an employment-support component to help find jobs and training for the head of households.

Social outcomes and the persistence of inequality in Chile: the role of macro and structural factors

The persistence of high inequality in Chile, a phenomenon with historical roots, is an important issue that deserves further analysis. Some possible explanations for the situation, which require further empirical study, follow.

Factors associated with macroeconomic policies

Several changes in macro policies affected poverty and inequality post-1990. The reduction of inflation is expected to help those who earn fixed incomes, such as workers and public sector employees, although specific salary adjustment rules also matter for minimum wages and public sector salaries. The effects of changes in real exchange rates and interest rates have various effects on wages and the value of debts and it is unclear if their net effects were pro-poor or not. The effects of cycles of economic activity and unemployment levels are also relevant. The 1990–1997 boom increased employment and real wages and led to rapid poverty reduction. The slow growth period of 1998–2003 increased unemployment and slowed down real wages increases, but apparently did not lead to increases in poverty of a serious magnitude, in part due to social policies.

Factors associated with the pattern of economic growth and globalization

The Chilean economy accelerated its rate of economic growth in the period 1990–2004, but faster growth per se did not correct income inequalities, although rapid growth did lead to reduced poverty. The demand for labour in the traditional traded goods sector (copper) is very capital intensive and the new tradable sectors (wine, fruits, timber, fish products and others) apparently are not very labour intensive. In addition, the demand for labour in the sectors linked to international trade is biased toward skilled labour and technical change saves unskilled labour, a trend that widened wage inequality. Another trend was globalization, which paid a premium to people with higher education levels and entrepreneurial capacities who were able to capture the opportunities opened by globalization, but who also coped with its risks.

Concentration on the ownership of productive assets

A recent study in Chile by Molina (2005) documents a tendency for the concentration of property in the stock market, banking, administration of pension funds and private companies that provide health services. The study shows that the five largest economic groups in Chile own close to 50 per cent of the shares of Chilean companies traded on the stock market. There is a concentration in the banking sector, with the three largest private banks owing 60 per cent of lending of the banking system. The three biggest pension funds management companies accounted for 70 per cent of the stock of pension savings by the end of 2004 (around $61 million). Concentration in service provision by a few of the private health care companies is also high.

Unequal and restricted access to credit

There is unequal and restricted access to credit by small-, medium- and micro-enterprises, workshops, young entrepreneurs without a credit history and others that prevents the realization of potentially profitable projects by non-rich individuals.

Weak labour unions and lack of consumers' organization

An important factor driving income distribution is the appropriation of productivity gains by labour, capital and other contributing factors. This depends, among other things, on the relative power of bargaining and access to information and capacities by the different actors in the production process. Labour unions in both the private sector and the central government administration are relatively weak. There is a weak tradition of consumer associations that protect the rights of consumers against monopolistic practices that lead to income redistributions from consumers to traders and producers.

Conclusion

In 1990–2004, Chile made significant progress in shifting to a more permanent regime of low inflation and established a fiscal rule of structural surplus to avoid fiscal pressures and reduce public external debt. Growth accelerated, but is still subject to ample fluctuations and cycles of long durations, driven mainly by changes in the international economy. Currently, Chile combines a fiscal rule with a flexible exchange rate system with virtually no intervention by the central bank. The volatility of nominal and real exchange rates is high and another macro challenge on the road to stability. In addition, the domestic capital market is segmented and the lack of credit is a serious problem for small and medium producers as well as for innovators.

The combination of more accelerated average growth and more aggressive social policies since 1990 led to rapid decline in poverty from the high levels of the late 1980s at the end of the Pinochet regime, although sizeable low-income groups still live close to the poverty line and are vulnerable to adverse shocks. In fact, the poor still have a limited capacity to generate sustained income without support from the state. On the other hand, inequality of income has proved resilient to spells of prosperity and to more active, targeted social policies of the democratic administrations since 1990. Inequality seems to be reproducing a combination of strongly differentiated access by income levels and geographical location to education, health, credit and other wealth-creating assets. Moreover, the concentration in ownership (and/or management) of productive assets in industry and commerce, banking and pension funds is also a factor that can explain income concentration in income distribution. In addition, the weak bargaining power of organized labour has reduced the share of productivity gains of the working class. We have documented that the Chilean poor have relatively large families, high dependency ratios, lower education levels and suffer a higher incidence of unemployment. As recent economic literature shows, a more progressive (egalitarian) income distribution is not only desirable on moral grounds, but can also lead to efficiency gains and broader-based growth that allows productive initiatives, projects and efforts by traditionally excluded social groups and individuals.

Our results show that the market-generated income distribution – the so-called distribution of autonomous income – has worsened for the lowest income quintile between 1990 and 2003, although the increased level and targeting of monetary transfers has ameliorated this trend. Income distribution, which has been historically regressive in Chile, has remained relatively constant in spite of the significant rise in per capita income of the Chilean economy. On average, Chilean citizens are economically better off than they were 15 years ago, but the fruits of progress are unevenly distributed. Although changes in income distribution take a long time to implement, the Chileans can gain in terms of efficiency, growth and social inclusion by seeking a more equitable income distribution.

Notes

1 The views expressed in this chapter are those of the authors and do not necessarily represent the views of the institutions to which they belong. The authors are grateful to Giovanni Andrea Cornia and other participants in the United Nations Research Institute for Social Development workshop on Pro-Poor Macroeconomics at the University of Florence on 24–5 February 2005 for the comments provided on an earlier version of this chapter.
2 See Ffrench-Davis (1973) for a complete reference of economic policies in 1950–1970. Analyses of the Allende experience include Bitar (1979), Larraín and Meller (1990) and Vuskovic (1993).
3 References for this period include Corbo and Solimano (1991), Edwards and Edwards (1987), Solimano (1993, 1999), Foxley (1983) and Meller (1997).
4 The Communist Party was, along with the Socialist Party and other parties, a member of *Unidad Popular*, the coalition that backed the Allende government of 1970–73.
5 Arellano and Pablo (2005) provides a thorough discussion of fiscal policies in Chile, stating that, correcting for trend, there was no fiscal deficit in 1999–2003.
6 See Arellano and Pablo (2004) and Foxley (2004) for insightful analyses of the social policies in 1990–2004. Interestingly, they made no mention that income or wealth redistribution were an explicit social objective of the *Concertación* governments.
7 See Cornia (2005) and Williamson (2000) for analyses of intermediate exchange-rate regimes.
8 See De Gregorio and Tokman (2004).
9 Of course, monetary authorities cannot be completely oblivious to the real cycles of the economy and the effects of their own policies on the intensity and timing of these cycles. Also, as part of the accountability mechanisms, the authorities of the central bank must present a yearly report to Congress on the march of the economy.

10 The average annual rate of growth of Chile in 1990–2004 was 5.6 per cent, 1.2 percentage points per year higher than the average rate of growth over the last 40 years (4.4 per cent, see Table 10.1).
11 See Solimano (2005).
12 See Solimano (1999).
13 See Schmidt-Hebbel, Servén and Solimano (1996) for a survey on savings, investment and growth for developing countries.
14 An easy monetary policy does not necessarily imply more bank credit for the productive sector, particularly for small- and medium-size firms. In contrast, in Chile there seems to be an abundance of and easy access to credit to finance consumption, and to some extent for housing, but not for productive endeavours, except for well-established large firms.
15 This number will probably increase when 2005 is included if the forecast of near 6 per cent growth is achieved.
16 See Solimano (1998) for a discussion on theories of inequality. On the links between distributive justice and Economic Development, see Solimano et al. (2000).
17 See the World Bank (2005) World Development Report 2005/06 devoted to equity and development, which stresses the multidimensional nature of inequality encompassing economic, institutional and political determinants.
18 See Pollack and Uthoff (1989) for poverty evolution during the 1970s and 1980s.
19 See Pollack and García (2004) for a discussion on the role of the financing sector in equity and competitiveness in Chile.
20 The proportion of households below the poverty line diminished from 33.3 per cent to 15.4 per cent during the same period, while the proportion of households below the indigence line diminished from 10.6 per cent to 3.9 per cent (see Table 10.5).
21 People working in the formal sector are identified with wage employees, employers in small, medium-sized and large enterprises in the public and private sectors and professionals and technicians (Infante and Sunkel 2004).
22 See Marcel and Solimano (1994) for an analysis of income distribution in Chile from the 1960s to the early 1990s.
23 See Solimano (2004) for an analysis of how the 'middle class' has been a forgotten segment in the design of social policies under the Washington Consensus in various Latin American countries.
24 The share of the 1st quintile within total income increased from 3 per cent (share of autonomous income before subsidies) to 3.5 per cent (share of income after subsidies) in 1990, and from 2.6 per cent to 3.8 per cent in 2000. As a result of social transfers to the poorest groups, autonomous income increased to 17 per cent during the years of economic expansion (1990–1996) and to 46 per cent during the economic contraction (1998–2000). In other words, social expenditure meant an average increase in autonomous income of households belonging to the 1st quintile during the decade.
25 In 1987, around 11 per cent of total subsidies were allocated to the 5th quintile, decreasing to 2.7 per cent in 2000.
26 For an analysis of social policies over the last 30 years in Chile, see Ffrench-Davis (2002, chapter 9).

References

Arellano, M. and J. Pablo. 2004. *Políticas sociales para el crecimiento con equidad, Chile 1990–2002*. Mimeo, Santiago.
Arellano, M. and J. Pablo. 2005. *Del déficit al superávit fiscal: Razones para una transformación estructural en Chile*. Mimeo, Santiago.
Bennett, H. and R. Valdés. 2001. *Series de términos de intercambio de frecuencia mensual para la economía chilena: 1965–1999*. Documentos de trabajo No. 98, Banco Central de Chile, May.

Bennett, H., K. Schmidt-Hebbel and C. Soto. 1999. *Serie de ahorro e ingreso por agente económico en Chile: 1960–1997*. Documentos de trabajo No. 53, Banco Central de Chile, December.
Bitar, S. 1979. *Transición, socialismo y democracia*. Mexico City: Editorial Siglo XXI.
Corbo, V. and A. Solimano. 1991. 'Chile's Experience with Stabilization Revisited.' In M. Bruno *et al.* (eds), *Lesson of Economic Stabilization and Its Aftermath*. Cambridge, MA: Massachusetts Institute of Technology Press.
Cornia, G.A. 2005. *On Intermediate Exchange Rate Regimes*. University of Florence, Italy.
De Gregorio, J. and A. Tokman. 2004. *Overcoming Fear of Floating: Exchange Rate Policies in Chile*. Working Papers No. 302, Central Bank of Chile, Santiago.
Economic Commission for Latin America and the Caribbean (ECLAC). 2003. *Social Panorama of Latin America 2003*. Santiago: ECLAC.
Economic Commission for Latin America and the Caribbean (ECLAC). 2004. *Social Panorama of Latin America 2004*. Santiago: ECLAC.
Edwards, S. and A. Edwards. 1987. *Monetarism and Liberalism: The Chilean Experiment*. Boston, MA: Ballinger.
Ffrench-Davis, R. 1973. *Políticas económicas en Chile 1950–1970*. Santiago: Ediciones Nueva Universidad.
Ffrench-Davis, R. 2002. *Economic Reforms in Chile: From Dictatorship to Democracy*. Development and Inequality in the Market Economy Series. Ann Arbor: University of Michigan Press.
Foxley, A. 1983. *Latin American Experiments in Neo-conservative Economics*. Berkeley, CA: University of California Press.
Foxley, A. 2004. *Successes and Failures in Poverty Eradication: Chile*. Prepared for the Scaling Up Poverty Reduction: A Global Learning Process and Conference, Shanghai, 25–7 May.
Infante, R. and G. Sunkel. 2004. *Chile trabajo decente y calidad de vida familiar, 1990–2000*. Santiago: Organización Internacional del Trabajo.
Larraín, F. and P. Meller. 1990. *La experiencia socialista-populista Chilena: La Unidad Popular, 1970–1973*. Santiago: Colección de estudios, CIEPLAN.
Larraín, F. and M. Selowsky. 1991. *The Public Sector and the Latin American Crisis*. San Francisco: International Center for Economic Growth.
Marcel, M. and A. Solimano. 1994. 'The Distribution of Income and Economic Adjustment'. In B. Bosworth, R. Dornbusch and R. Labán (eds), *The Chilean Economy: Policy Lessons and Challenges*. Washington, DC: The Brookings Institution.
Meller, P. 1997. *Un siglo de economía política Chilena: 1890–1990*. Santiago: Andrés Bello.
Ministry of Planning (MIDEPLAN). 2004. *Encuesta de caracterización socioeconómica nacional 2003*. Santiago. MIDEPLAN.
Molina, S. 2005. *Es el tiempo de la equidad*. Academia Chilena de Ciencias Sociales, Políticas y Morales, Instituto de Chile y Banco del Desarrollo, Santiago.
Pollack, M. and A. Uthoff. 1989. 'Poverty and the Labour Market: Greater Santiago 1969–1985'. In G. Rodgers (ed.), *Urban Poverty and the Labor Market: Access to Jobs and Incomes in Asian and Latin American Cities*. Geneva: PREALC, International Labour Organization.
Pollack, M. and A. García. 2004. *Crecimiento, competitividad y equidad: Rol del sector financiero*. Serie financiamiento del desarrollo No. 147. Santiago: ECLAC, July.
Schmidt-Hebbel, K., L. Servén and A. Solimano. 1996. 'Saving, Investment, and Growth in Developing Countries: An Overview'. In A. Solimano (ed.), *Road-Maps to Prosperity: Essays on Growth and Development*. Ann Arbor: Michigan University Press.
Solimano, A. 1993. 'Chile'. In L. Taylor (ed.), *The Rocky Road to Reform: Adjustment, Income Distribution and Growth in the Developing World*. Cambridge, MA: Massachusetts Institute of Technology Press.
Solimano, A. 1999. 'The Chilean Economy in the 1990s on a "Golden Age" and Beyond'. In L. Taylor (ed.), *After Neoliberalism: What Next for Latin America?* Development and Inequality in the Market Economy Series. Ann Arbor: University of Michigan Press.

Solimano, A. 2004. *Reassessing Social Policies in Latin America: From the Washington Consensus to Rights-Based Development*. Paper presented at the ECLAC IDB Seminar on Social Rights and Inequality, Santiago, 9–10 December.

Solimano, A. 2005. 'Hacia nuevas políticas sociales en América Latina: Crecimiento, clases medias y derechos sociales'. Revista de la CEPAL, Santiago, December.

Solimano, A. (ed.). 2005. *Vanishing Growth in Latin America: The Experience of Late XX Century*. London: Edward Elgar Publishers.

Solimano, A. (ed.). 1998. *Social Inequality: Values Growth and the State*. Development and Inequality in the Market Economy Series. Ann Arbor: University of Michigan Press.

Solimano, A. and G. Larraín. 2002. *From Economic Miracle to Sluggish Performance: Employment, Unemployment and Growth in the Chilean Economy*. Mimeo, Santiago.

Solimano, A., E. Aninat and N. Birdsall (eds). 2000. *Distributive Justice and Economic Development: The Case of Chile and Other Developing Countries*. Development and Inequality in the Market Economy Series. Ann Arbor: University of Michigan Press.

Vuskovic, P. 1993. 'Obras escogidas sobre Chile 1964–1992'. In R. Maldonado (ed.), *Colección Chile en el siglo XX*. Santiago: Ediciones Centro de Estudios Políticos Latinoamericanos, Simón Bolívar.

Williamson, J. 2000. *Exchange Rate Regimes for Emerging Markets: Reviving the Intermediate Option*. Policy Analyses in International Economics 60. Washington, DC: Institute of International Economics.

World Bank. 2005. *Equity and Development: World Development Report 2005/06*. Washington, DC: World Bank.

11
Macroeconomic Policy, Inequality and Poverty Reduction in Fast-Growing India and China

C. P. Chandrasekhar and Jayati Ghosh

It is now commonplace to regard China and India as the two economies in the developing world that are the 'success stories' of globalization, emerging as economic giants of the twenty-first century. The success is defined by the high and sustained rates of growth of aggregate and per capita national income; the absence of major financial crises that have characterized a number of other emerging markets; and substantial reductions in income poverty. These results in turn are viewed as the consequences of a combination of a 'prudent', yet extensive programme of global economic integration and domestic deregulation, as well as sound macroeconomic management. Consequently, the presumed success of these two countries has been used to argue the case for globalization and to indicate the potential benefits that other developing countries can reap, provided they also follow 'sensible' macroeconomic policies. The importance of these two countries also spills over into discussions of international inequality.[1] This makes a comparison of the nature of macroeconomic policies in India and China, and the extent to which these have been 'pro-poor', of particular current relevance. In this chapter, we attempt such an examination, assessing growth performance and its impact on poverty and inequality, and also specifically addressing the question of how the macro policies have contributed to observed outcomes.

It is important to note that in analysing China and India we are not actually comparing fundamentally similar economies. Although they share some superficial attributes, such as large populations covering substantial geographical areas, regional diversity, relatively high rates of growth over the recent period and so on, the institutional conditions in the two economies have been and remain very different. Since Independence India has been a traditional 'mixed' developing economy with significant private sector participation, and even during the period of the 'dirigiste' regime the emphasis was primarily on the regulation of private capital rather than actual determination of levels of production by the state. The neoliberal reforms undertaken in the phase of globalization have, however, substantially expanded the scope for private activity and reduced regulation. Essentially, macroeconomic policies in India have been designed and implemented in contexts similar to those existing in other capitalist economies, where involuntary unemployment is rampant and fiscal and monetary measures have to be used to stimulate effective demand.

China, by contrast, has had a very different institutional structure throughout most of this period, where the basic elements of a command economy have been much more in evidence. Even after the wide-ranging economic reforms that have taken place since 1979, state control and influence, including in the determination of macroeconomic outcomes, remains substantial. But that control is not always exercised through what are seen as standard fiscal and monetary macropolicy instruments such as fiscal and monetary contraction or changes in interest rates. Because of the significance of state-owned enterprises in the level of total production and of state agencies in total investment, the ability to influence aggregate demand has not depended only upon fiscal policy in terms of purely budgetary measures, since many 'off-budget' expenditures can be increased or reduced. Further, monetary policy, as it is generally understood in capitalist economies, has very little meaning in China where private financial activity is limited and state-owned banks still dominate overwhelmingly in the provision of credit.

This means that for most of the period under discussion, macroeconomic policies in China were necessarily very different and had very dissimilar implications, from those pursued in developing capitalist economies. In particular, macroeconomic adjustment in China takes the form of 'administrative measures', which typically involve direct restraints on investment and expenditure by regional and provincial governments and public and private corporations ensured through administrative fiat rather than the use of specific economic levers. We will argue in this chapter that the Chinese economy is currently in a phase of transition into one where more traditional 'capitalist macroeconomics' may be applicable in future. But China's periodic macroeconomic imbalances and its ability to quickly ensure macroeconomic correction when it is seen to be required are related to the fact that advances in this direction are still limited and the process already reflects its own tensions and challenges.

In this chapter, we deal with the Indian and Chinese experiences in separate sections. This is followed by a comparative assessment and the drawing of some relevant policy conclusions.

Economic growth, poverty and macroeconomic policies in India

It is now accepted that after a period of deceleration in industrial growth during the late 1960s and 1970s, widely considered to be a period of 'stagnation', India moved from a path characterized by a slow 3 per cent 'Hindu rate of growth' to a rather more creditable growth trajectory involving GDP growth of around 5–6 per cent per annum from the early 1980s. That is, the recovery from a period when growth decelerated sharply starting in the mid-1960s began not with the 'economic reform' of 1991, but rather a decade earlier. However, there were a number of weaknesses characteristic of this otherwise creditable rate of growth. First, growth was far less pronounced in the commodity-producing sectors than in the services sector. In fact, during the 1990s, the rate of growth of per capita food production in the country stood at its lowest level for decades.

Secondly, there were signs that this growth was accompanied by increased vulnerability inasmuch as it exploited the benefits for developing countries associated with the rise of international finance. Especially during the 1980s, growth was driven by debt-financed public expenditure, which was supported by debt-creating inflows from the international system. This resulted in a doubling of India's external debt to GDP ratio and led to a crisis in 1991 when a loss of investor confidence resulted in a freeze in such flows. During the 1990s non-debt-creating inflows and remittances from migrant Indian workers abroad (particularly in the Gulf countries) helped shore up the balance of payments in a relatively stable way, yet financial liberalization has encouraged volatile capital flows that imply that vulnerability is still a problem. This vulnerability is not immediately visible because of the large inflows on the current account of remittances from non-resident workers and earnings from software and IT-enabled services exports. Further, the response of the central bank to the substantial inflows of portfolio capital involves purchasing foreign exchange to prevent excessive appreciation of the rupee, creating large holdings of foreign exchange reserves.

Finally, very recent trends in the economy suggest that performance has been far below potential. This is illustrated by the extremely poor performance of agriculture and allied sectors and the increased volatility of industrial growth over the recent period. Indeed, only the services sector shows sustained high growth rates.

Table 11.1 presents decadal compound rates of growth since the early 1950s, for Gross Domestic Product (GDP) and per capita Net National Product at constant 1993–94 prices. It is evident that real GDP growth rates increased to a higher level in the last two decades. Increases in per capita income were even more marked because of the fall in the rate of population growth.

As Table 11.2 shows, this has been associated with some amount of structural change, although perhaps not as much as might be expected. Investment rates have increased over time, which is only to be expected in a developing economy

Table 11.1 Annual rates of growth of national income (percentage)

Period (year starting April)	Gross domestic product	Per capita net national products
1950–52 to 1960–62	3.9	1.8
1960–62 to 1970–72	3.5	1.2
1970–72 to 1980–82	3.5	1
1980–82 to 1990–92	5.6	2.9
1990–92 to 2000–02	5.6	3.5

Notes:
1. Both GDP and NNP are measured in constant 1993–94 prices.
2. Rates of growth are compound annual rates for the three-year averages.

Source: CSO, *National Accounts Statistics*, various issues.

Table 11.2 Structural change in the Indian economy (percentage of GDP)

Period (year starting April)	Investment rate	Primary	Secondary	Tertiary
1950–52	15.5	59	13.4	27.6
1960–62	19.4	53.1	17.3	29.6
1970–72	23.8	46.6	20.4	33.0
1980–82	22.0	41.3	21.8	36.9
1990–92	26.0	34.4	24	41.6
2000–02	26.2	26.1	24.7	49.2

Source: CSO, National Accounts Statistics, various issues.

Table 11.3 Growth rates of employment (percentage change per annum)

	Rural	Urban
1983 to 1987–88	1.36	2.77
1987–88 to 1993–94	2.03	3.39
1993–94 to 1999–2000	0.58	2.27

Note: Employment here refers to all workers, Principal Status plus Subsidiary Status.

Source: Based on NSS employment rates and Census population figures.

achieving higher rates of per capita income, but the rate of increase actually slowed down, and the last decade shows almost no change in the investment rate. Meanwhile, the share of agriculture in GDP has fallen along predictable lines in the course of development, but there has been little increase in the share of the secondary sector, which has not changed since the early 1990s. Rather, the share of the tertiary sector has increased dramatically, to the point where it now accounts for around half of national income.

Such changes in output shares were not accompanied by commensurate changes in the distribution of the workforce? The proportion of all workers engaged in agriculture as the main occupation has remained stubbornly above 60 per cent, despite the collapse in agricultural employment generation of the most recent decade and the fall in agriculture's share of national income. It is also intriguing that the higher rates of investment of the last two decades have not generated more expansion of industry, but have instead been associated with an apparent explosion in services, that 'catch-all' sector of varying components.

The economic recovery of the 1980s and 1990s

In the 1980s, the escape from the growth impasse of the earlier period was enabled by the adoption of an expansionary macroeconomic policy. Public expenditure rose rapidly, more as a result of an expansion in the current expenditure of the government rather than in capital formation. Increases in government employment and the per capita earnings of government employees was an important element contributing to the increase in the government's current expenditure.

This increase in expenditure was not accompanied by an increase in resource mobilization by the government, resulting in three tendencies: first, a rise in the fiscal deficit to GDP ratio, especially at the centre; secondly, an increase in the revenue deficit which explained a growing share of the fiscal deficit; and, thirdly, a rise in the current account deficit in the balance of payments. The significance of the third of these needs noting. While a fiscal deficit *per se* is not inflationary, it can have inflationary consequences if there are major supply-side bottlenecks in the economy. Such bottlenecks were indeed a reality in India, especially in the agricultural wage goods sector. However, inasmuch as the government was in a position to import commodities and ensure domestic supplies in excess of domestic production in these areas, inflation was avoided but the trade and current account deficit tended to rise.

In addition, from the mid-1980s, the Indian government began a process of liberalization of imports of capital goods, intermediates and components. These imports, together with imported technology, permitted production of a range of goods targeted at the more affluent sections of the population. They also contributed to a widening of the trade and current account deficits that were financed by external commercial borrowing.

Thus, the fiscal stimulus to the economy provided by government spending and the growth of import-intensive consumption were financed increasingly by external commercial borrowing. One reason why the model of public sector-led expansion inherited from the 1950s and 1960s could continue for some more time without generating higher inflation was, of course, the liberalization of imports. However, despite the import liberalization from the middle of the 1980s, throughout the decade of the 1980s the capital account of the balance of payments was quite strictly controlled and the exchange rate of the rupee, rather than being market-determined, was administered to maintain some degree of stability with respect to a basket of currencies reflecting India's trade pattern.

Some role in avoiding inflation in this period was also played by the intersectoral terms of trade, as indicated in Figure 11.1. The first half of the 1970s marked a peak in terms of the relative price of agricultural goods, but after 1977, and through to about 1985, such a tendency was effectively contained and the domestic terms of trade were generally favourable for industrial expansion. In turn, this pattern of the terms of trade can be partly explained by the fact that world agricultural prices were declining over the 1980s. But what was more significant was that after 1980 growth in the Indian economy generated much less employment than before, as indicated in Table 11.3, and therefore implied much less demand for food than would have been the case with more employment-intensive expansion.

Thereafter, while intersectoral terms of trade for agriculture remained low compared to the early 1970s, from the mid-1980s onwards for about a decade Indian agriculturalists were relatively protected from the international movement of terms of trade against primary products. The liberalization of imported

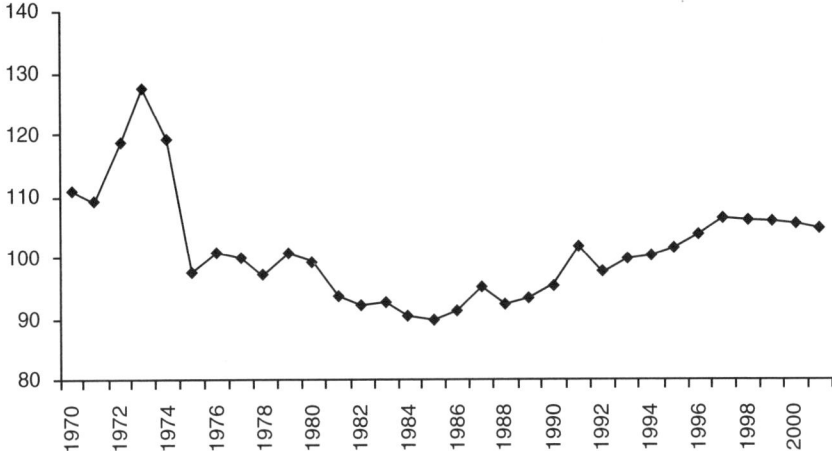

Figure 11.1 Terms of trade (by GDP price deflators)
Source: CSO, *National Accounts Statistics*, various issues.

manufactured goods that started from the 1980s also played a role in ensuring that terms of trade improved to some extent for agriculture. The domestic relative prices for agriculture worsened again in the late 1990s, when trade liberalization exposed farmers to declining world prices (see Chapter 1).

The 1980s experience suggests that over this period, notwithstanding the limited liberalization, Indian economic growth still depended upon the fiscal stimulus provided by government expenditure, rather than on an expansion of exports. Since such government expenditure was not accompanied by tax and related measures aimed at mobilizing additional resources, but was financed through borrowing, the excess demand in the system was bound to spill over in the form of either inflation or a current account deficit. Keeping inflation under control through imports enabled by trade liberalization in turn required more external borrowing to finance the growing current account deficit.

This strategy could be continued only as long as India had access to capital inflows. To the extent that such access tapered off, the economy would be faced with a crisis involving both inflation and balance-of-payments stringency. In the short run dealing with such a crisis would require severe import contraction and resort to conditional borrowing, which would be recessionary and have extremely adverse implications for the level of poverty incidence and the pace of poverty reduction. To avoid this, the government would have had to mobilize through taxation the resources necessary to finance its expenditures. Needless to say, such taxation if it is to be pro-poor in character must consist of direct taxes on the rich and/or indirect taxes on non-essential consumption (see Chapter 2). Overall, a reliance on foreign finance as a substitute for domestic resource mobilization, especially in a context of low and even declining tax–GDP ratios, cannot be part of a pro-poor growth strategy.

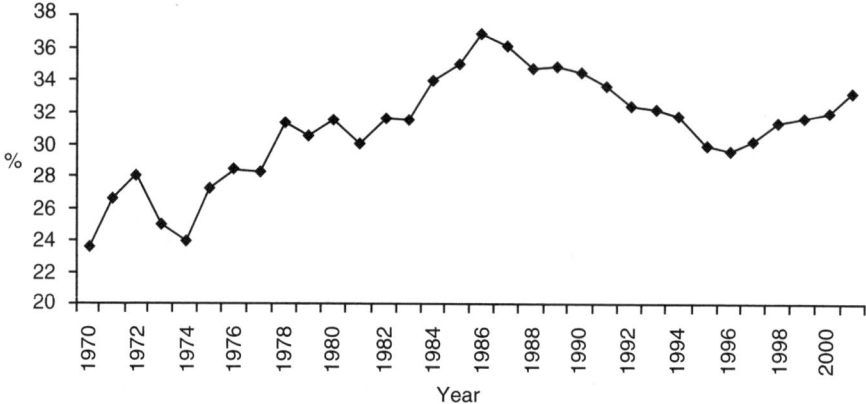

Figure 11.2 Total government expenditure as a percentage of GDP

Sources: Ministry of Finance, *Public Finance Statistics of India*; and CSO, *National Accounts Statistics*, various issues.

Does this imply that the macroeconomic stance of the 1980s, while stimulating growth in the short run, was not effective from the point of view of poverty reduction? It does not, inasmuch as public expenditure generated employment and incomes that helped reduce poverty. Figure 11.2 indicates that the period 1975 to 1986 was one characterized by very large increases in the share relative to GDP of total government expenditure (minus interest payments from which it is assumed that the marginal propensity to consume is low).[2] This was clearly the basis for the high growth rates observed in the 1980s, since the positive effects of such expenditure operate immediately as well as with a time lag.

The effects of state expenditure were particularly marked in rural India in the second half of the 1980s. This was a period when, along with a rapid increase in all sorts of subsidies and transfers to households from government, there was a very large increase in expenditure on the rural sector by both state and central governments. This flow of resources involved an expansion of 'rural development' schemes with an explicit redistributive concern, as well as the greater accessibility of the rural elites to the varied benefits of aggregate government expenditure. While the various rural development programmes did not always reach target groups, they still represented a fairly massive net transfer to rural areas. This was instrumental in causing the rural employment diversification of that period as well as allowing for a greater spread of economic growth in the country than has been achieved subsequently.

Figure 11.2 suggests that this positive fiscal stimulus declined after 1986. During the 1990s, the proportion of state expenditure to GDP decreased. But since economic liberalization measures such as reduced import tariffs and domestic duty rates caused the total tax–GDP ratio to decline (see Figure 11.3), the ratio of the fiscal deficit to GDP still remained high despite the lower absolute fiscal stimulus. Further, in the early 1990s, financial liberalization measures significantly increased the cost of government borrowing, such that total interest payments of

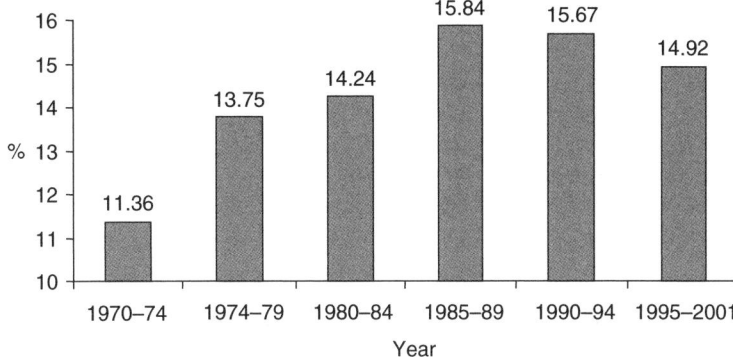

Figure 11.3 Total taxes–GDP ratios
Sources: Ministry of Finance, *Public Finance Statistics of India*; and CSO, *National Accounts Statistics*, various issues.

central and state governments became ever more significant, accounting for as much 7.3 per cent of GDP on average by the turn of the decade.

In sum, while during the 1980s the macroeconomic situation was characterized by an expansionary fiscal stance of the government facilitated by foreign borrowing to finance larger deficits, the 1990s saw a transition to a deflationary fiscal stance, even if in some years the fiscal deficit appeared to be high relative to GDP. This had significant implications for poverty reduction. It implied that the flow of investment funds to rural areas declined, that the emphasis on employment generation programmes in rural areas was reduced and that social expenditures and subsidies had to bear a part of the burden of adjustment involving reduced revenue generation because of tariff reductions and tax concessions aimed at stimulating private investment.

The question that arises is: what allowed the rate of growth in the period after the mid-1980s to be maintained despite the apparent decline in the fiscal impetus after 1986? First, while fiscal expansionism was checked, government expenditure was still quite significant – above 26 per cent of GDP – until around 1993. Thereafter, there was a brief period in the mid-1990s when high growth was partly the result of the 'once-for-all' spurt provided by import liberalization, as indicated by the spurt in private investment in the mid-1990s (see Figure 11.4). Private investment as a share of GDP reached a peak in 1995, and thereafter stabilized at around 16 per cent of GDP. Meanwhile, the fiscal stimulus, which had been falling continuously, started increasing again around 1998, although it still remained below the levels of the early 1980s. The tapering off of growth in the latter part of the 1990s (from a compound rate of 5.8 per cent per annum in the period 1989–91 to 1995–97 to a lower compound rate of 4.6 per cent in the period 1995–97 to 2000–02) should be seen in this context. What this essentially shows is that the Indian economy remains critically dependent upon state expenditure to ensure growth, despite the periodic stimuli provided by liberalization, exports and so on.

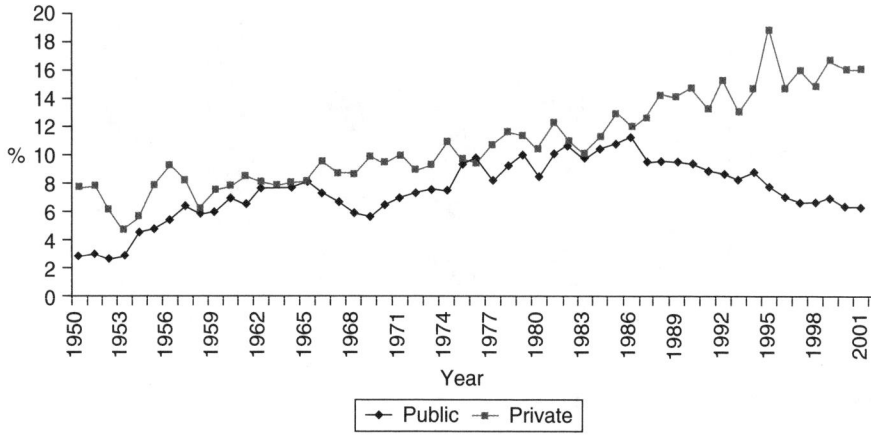

Figure 11.4 Investment as percentage of GDP
Source: CSO, National Accounts Statistics, various issues.

Economic reforms in the 1990s

The explicit aims of the neoliberal economic reform process adopted from 1991 onwards were: (i) to do away with or substantially reduce controls on capacity creation, production and prices, and let market forces influence the investment and operational decisions of domestic and foreign economic agents within the domestic tariff area; (ii) to allow international competition and therefore international relative prices to influence economic decisions; (iii) to reduce the presence of state agencies in production and trade; and (iv) to liberalize the financial sector by reducing controls on the banking system, allowing for the proliferation of financial institutions and instruments and permitting foreign entry into the financial sector. These were all based on the notion that greater freedom given to private agents and market functioning would ensure more efficient and more dynamic outcomes. The government's aim was also to restructure production towards areas of international 'comparative advantage' (defined in static rather than dynamic terms). These areas were seen as inherently more labour-intensive, which led to the further prediction that, after an initial brief period of net job loss, such a strategy of trade liberalization would actually create more employment over time in more sustainable ways.

These aims translated into successive changes in the pattern of regulation in different sectors as well as in aggregate macroeconomic policies. By the early years of the current century, therefore, the Indian economy had undergone the following policy changes:

- a reduction in direct state control in terms of administered prices and regulation of economic activity;
- the privatization of state assets, often in controversial circumstances;
- the rationalization and reduction of direct and indirect tax rates, which became associated with declining tax–GDP ratios;

- attempts to reduce fiscal deficits which usually involved reducing on public productive investment as well as certain types of social expenditure, reducing subsidies to farmers and increasing user charges for public services and utilities;
- trade liberalization, involving shifts from quantitative restrictions to tariffs and typically sharp reductions in the average rate of tariff protection, as well as withdrawal of export subsidies;
- financial liberalization involving reductions in directed credit, freeing of interest rate ceilings and other measures which raised the real cost of borrowing, including for the government;
- shift to market-determined exchange rates and liberalization of current account transactions;
- some capital account liberalization, including the easing of rules for foreign direct investment, permission for non-residents to hold domestic financial assets, easier access to foreign commercial borrowing by domestic firms, and, later, even freedom for domestic residents to hold limited foreign assets.

There was one area in which the reforms in India during most of the period were more cautious when compared with many other developing countries: capital account liberalization (see Chapter 5 of this volume). While there were certainly some changes in this area – primarily in terms of easing the rules for foreign direct investment (FDI) and allowing foreign portfolio investment – external financial liberalization was still relatively limited, and this meant that the Indian economy was not subject to sharp and potentially destabilizing flows of capital, either inflows or outflows, over this period. Further, the Indian economy was not really chosen to be a favourite of international financial markets until the very recent period from 2002. Meanwhile, greater stability was imparted to the balance of payments by the substantial inflows of workers' remittances from temporary migrant workers in the Gulf and other regions, which amounted to more than all forms of capital inflow put together and ensured that the current account was characterized by either low deficits or even surpluses in most years.

It has already been observed that the transition to a higher economic growth trajectory was associated in the 1980s with the fiscal stimulus provided by the state in a context of import liberalization. In the 1990s, this fiscal stimulus was much weaker, declining in the first part of the decade and only increasing somewhat from 1997 onwards (see Figure 11.2). The growth performance was more uneven, with deceleration in agricultural output growth and fluctuating performance in manufacturing. Since the 1990s liberalization was not accompanied by any new dynamism in the commodity-producing sectors of the economy, the expansion of services proved to be crucial over this later period.

Despite the weakened fiscal stimulus, both in terms of public investment and aggregate expenditure, the role of the state remained crucial, since it was the state that determined the contours of tax reductions, deregulation and other policies that allowed for economic growth based on the demands of a relatively small and dominantly urban section of the population. The explosion in the consumption of the upper quintile of the population (discussed below and shown in Figure 11.5)

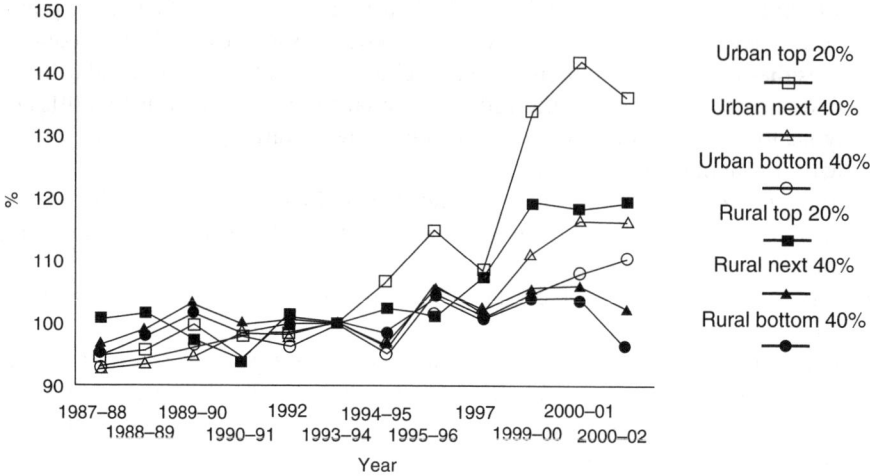

Figure 11.5 Indices of real per capita income by fractile groups
Source: Sen and Himanshu (2005).

that fed this growth that involved increased inequality, both across regions of India and within regions across different economic and social categories. There was also a widening gap between incomes in agriculture and non-agriculture, such that the ratio of per worker domestic product in non-agriculture to that in agriculture increased from about 2 in the 1950s to well over 4 in the 1990s.

Trends in income inequality and poverty in India

One consequence of the pattern of growth during the 1990s was a very low rate of employment generation. Rural employment in the period 1993–94 to 1999–2000 grew at the very low annual rate of less than 0.6 per cent per annum, well below the rate of growth of rural population. Urban employment growth, at 2.3 per cent per annum, was also well below that recorded in earlier periods, and formal employment stagnated. There was a dramatic deceleration in employment defined in terms of the number of main workers, with greater increases in the number of 'marginal workers' (that is, those having employment for less than 183 days in the year). Further, the quality of employment deteriorated, with increases in casual and part-time work rather than regular, as well as greater fragility of contracts.

Agricultural employment showed the sharpest deceleration of all, with absolute declines in the number of people usually employed in agriculture over the 1990s. Part of this was due to technological and cropping pattern changes that reduced labour demand in agriculture. In addition, the growing land alienation by the peasantry (as cultivation became less viable given the squeeze on the peasantry because of rising input costs and falling or stagnant crop prices) also had an impact, since peasants using family labour tend to use labour more intensively than farmers using hired labour.

For urban India, the deceleration and even decline in organized sector employment was one of the more disturbing features of the period after 1990, especially given that industrial output increased manifold and the service sector (in which much organized employment was based) was the most dynamic element in national income growth.[3] This was due to the decline in public sector employment, which was not compensated by the increase in private organized sector employment. Further, several 'economic reform' measures – such as trade liberalization, the reduction of credit allocation to the priority sector and the removal of various forms of support – worked against the interests of most small producers, who accounted for not only the most labour-intensive forms of urban production but also the dominant part of urban manufacturing employment.

Inadequate employment growth obviously implies that the process could not have been pro-poor in practice. There is a lively debate among economists about whether or not income and consumption inequalities have increased in India in the post-reform period. Most studies have used various rounds of NSS consumption expenditure survey statistics for calculating per capita incomes and Gini coefficients. As regards inequality, it is well known that the NSS surveys with a relatively low lower bound for its highest expenditure range, does not capture upper-income group consumption adequately. With regard to poverty estimates, there is a well-known problem about the lack of comparability of NSS statistics between the quinquennial large-sample consumption survey for 1999–2000 (55th Round) and the earlier ones.[4] According to Sen and Himanshu (2005), this has lowered the measured rural poverty in India by almost 50 million. As a consequence, rural inequality measures have also been affected.

Revised estimates of rural inequality have been calculated by Deaton and Dreze (2002), Sundaram and Tendulkar (2003a, b) and Sen and Himanshu (2005). The general observation of these studies is that although unadjusted data show inequality has reduced between rounds 50 and 55, if one uses the adjusted (comparable) data, then it shows that rural inequality has in fact risen in India between 1993–94 (50th Round) and 1999–2000 (55th Round). Striking evidence about increased inequality in India in the post-reform period comes from Sen and Himanshu (2005). Based on indices of real mean per capita expenditure (MPCE) on uniform reference period (URP) basis by fractile groups, they show that whereas the consumption level of the upper tail of the population, including the top 20 per cent of the rural population, has risen remarkably during the 1990s, the bottom 80 per cent of the rural population have suffered during this period (see Figure 11.5). This graph clearly shows that the income/consumption disparity between the rich and poor and between urban and rural India has increased during the 1990s.[5]

Deaton and Dreze (2002) find both increased rural–urban inequality in per capita expenditure at an all-India level and greater rural–urban inequalities within states between 1993–94 and 1999–2000. Sen and Himanshu (2005) also find that statewise rural and urban Gini coefficients, adjusted for changes in estimates, increased for a majority of states between 1993–94 and 1999–2000. For all-India, the rural Gini increased from 25.8 to 26.3 and the urban Gini increased from 31.9 to 34.8.

Estimates of the extent of poverty are similarly affected by attempts to make the various NSS surveys compatible. Table 11.4 indicates the differences in estimates that can result from using even slightly different methodologies to interpret the

Table 11.4 Trends in poverty (percentage of population below poverty line)

	Urban			Rural		
	Planning commission estimate	Method 1	Method 2	Planning commission estimate	Method 1	Method 2
1977–78	45.2	45.2		53.1	53.1	
1983	40.8	40.8		45.7	45.6	
1987–88	38.2	38.2		39.1	39.1	
1993–94	32.4	32.6	27.9	37.3	37	31.6
1999–2000	23.6		24.8	27.1		28.4

Note: Method 1 refers to the earlier pattern of questioning with 30-day and 365-day reference periods, while Method 2 refers to the new pattern with 7-day questions also added, as well as different reference periods for particular commodities.

Source: Economic Survey, GOI and Abhijit Sen and Himanshu (2005).

same survey data. However, it does also suggest that while the incidence of headcount poverty had been declining from the mid-1970s to 1990, subsequently that decline has been slowed or halted. This suggests that greater inequality is clearly one major reason why India has not made more progress in reducing poverty.

Agricultural growth, non-agricultural activity and poverty

The proximate role of inequality in worsening poverty or limiting gains in terms of poverty reduction has conventionally been situated in arguments that point to a complex combination of influences on rural poverty in particular. The early literature focussed on two kinds of variables: movements in agricultural production or productivity, and movements in prices (such as of food) that may impact, either directly or indirectly, on real income and poverty. Even though movements in agricultural production would obviously impact on poverty, the significance of that impact would depend upon whether agricultural growth is accompanied by an increase in inequality or whether there is a simultaneous increase in sources of non-agricultural income in the rural areas.

As for prices, the relevant variable is not the nominal price level of food, but the relative price of food and the rate of increase of nominal food prices. A faster rate of increase of agricultural prices can have two contradictory effects on poverty. First, to the extent that agricultural growth is stimulated by a shift in terms of trade in favour of agriculture, and assuming that inequality does not increase, the rise in agricultural prices would contribute to some extent to a reduction in rural poverty. Secondly, since a large part of the rural population consists of agricultural labourers, small farmers and non-farm workers, who are all net purchasers of food, a sharp increase in the price of food would squeeze real incomes and worsen poverty.

If inequality is increasing, we should expect that the effect of any increase in per capita agricultural output on poverty would be weaker. However, there have been a number of experiences to the contrary. In India, for example, the Green Revolution of the 1970s and 1980s, while leading to some increases in agricultural output per capita, was characterized by some increase in concentration of operated area and marketed surpluses, as well as a substantial increases in regional inequalities in agricultural production. Yet the incidence of poverty during these years was declining significantly, forcing researchers to look to other factors that could explain the decline in rural income poverty.

This decline was all the more surprising because evidence indicated that the output increases during the Green Revolution years and later were accompanied by a decline in the output elasticity of the demand for labour in agriculture. There seemed to be one factor that was neutralizing the effect of these trends, viz. a rise in agricultural wages, which was then seen as an important influence on poverty. But why were real agricultural wages rising if employment in agriculture was inadequately responsive to agricultural growth? The empirical answer seemed to lie substantially in an increase in rural non-agricultural employment. Over the 15-year period from 1972–73 and 1987–88, the share of rural male non-agricultural employment in total rural male employment rose by 9 percentage points and that of female non-agricultural employment in total rural female employment by 5 percentage points. This seemed to make the growth of rural non-farm activities and rural non-farm employment an important cause for reduction in rural poverty – a conclusion supported by experience in other countries, especially China. Further, the subsequent deceleration of poverty reduction, especially in rural India, in the later period, can be related to the stagnation of rural employment opportunities in the 1990s.

There are some important inferences that can be drawn from this brief survey of the literature. It is clear that in India, macro policies have not contributed to a substantial reduction in poverty in the recent past, because of the negative effects of such policies upon relative prices of food and employment generation. Poverty reduction has been predicated on the following: (i) a relatively egalitarian path of growth; (ii) increases in agricultural productivity that help to raise wages and keep food prices under control; (iii) the expansion of non-agricultural employment, including in rural areas; and (iv) direct public action in the form of poverty eradication programmes aimed at generating productive employment for the poor. The process of fairly continuous poverty reduction from the late 1970s to the early 1990s hinged upon a combination of a certain pattern growth with expansion in rural non-agricultural employment led by public expenditure increases. The subsequent slowdown in the pace of poverty reduction has been associated with macro policies that have adversely affected employment generation, especially rural employment generation, possibly worsened inequality in consumption and contributed to an increase in the relative price of food. However, since policies of reform did not go far enough to embroil India in the financial crises of the late 1990s, the slow pace of poverty reduction was not capped by a sharp increase in the incidence of poverty over a relatively short span during a crisis, as did occur in many East Asian countries.

Economic growth, poverty and macroeconomic policies in China

Macroeconomic policy discussions rarely incorporate any recognition that the institutional structure of the system influences economic outcomes. This is partly because conventional macroeconomic discussions are principally concerned with market economies, which, from a Keynesian, structuralist or Marxist point of view, are demand-constrained systems. This obviously renders discussions of macroeconomic policy in centrally planned economies, which in ideal form are supply-constrained systems, *sui generis*. This is substantially true of China, prior to the launch of economic reforms in 1978. Even after 1978, macroeconomic mechanisms differed substantially from those in predominantly market-driven economies. These differences relate to the availability of monetary or fiscal levers of the kind available in market economies, the nature of the institutionally determined transmission mechanisms and the outcomes of what appear to be similar policies.

Because of the nature of state control over monetary institutions and the use of non-fiscal levers to manage the economy, a role for autonomous macroeconomic tendencies in China is relatively recent. Before the 1978 reforms, the financial system of China was vastly different from that in most countries. From 1951, banks and other financial institutions had been taken over by the state and assimilated into a system dominated by the People's Bank of China (PBC).[6] Until 1984 this system essentially implemented the cash and credit plans formulated by the central authorities, which supported the physical plan for the mobilization, allocation and utilization of real resources. All public sector transactions, including those between various levels of government and the state enterprises, were through transfers on their accounts with the PBC. These account transfers at the PBC accounted for an overwhelming share (of up to 95 per cent) of all transactions.

Moreover, cash (to serve the needs of households and non-state-owned enterprises) was printed and issued by the PBC on demand by the central government and allocated according to instructions issued. The main elements of money in circulation were wage payments to workers and staff, the purchase of agricultural products by the government, other purchases of goods in the rural sector, and the withdrawing of savings deposits by individuals. The banking system was not responsible for provision of resources for fixed asset investments by the state-owned enterprises (SOEs) and for much of their working capital requirements, which were made available free of charge by the Ministry of Finance. The banking system was merely responsible for providing additional working capital and some loans, for accepting deposits from households and other non-government entities and for settlement of transactions.

So there was little role for monetary policy prior to reform. Credit provision was centralized and strictly controlled, with enterprises and other economic entities receiving grants and loans directly from the PBC. Bank branches had to merely meet credit targets. And lower-level banking entities had to hand over deposits that exceeded their credit provision targets to higher-level units. If the government felt the need for restricting economic activity, it did so directly through administrative means rather than using levers of monetary policy. To manage the supply of cash and its utilization, the central authorities could adjust (administered) prices relative to money wages (using a turnover tax if necessary). However, since the objective was to keep prices mostly stable, excess cash in circulation was absorbed through rationing, when commodity supplies fell short of demand, and by encouraging savings.

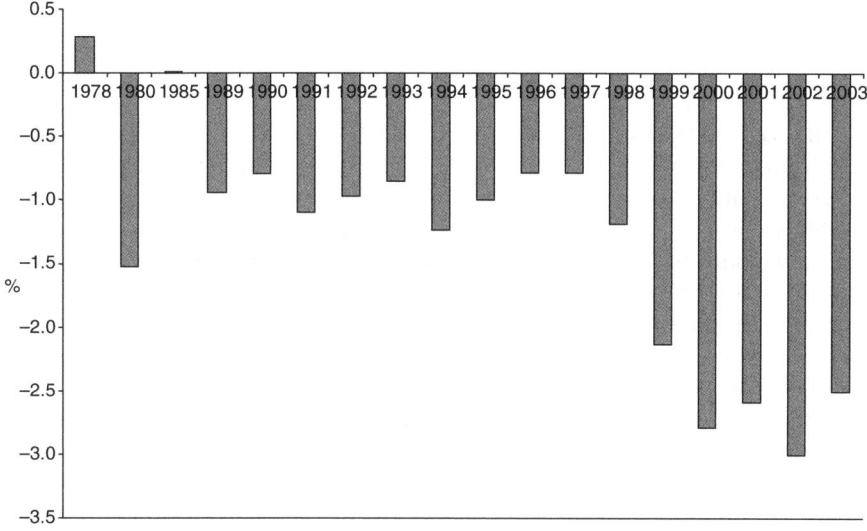

Figure 11.6 Budget surplus/deficit to GDP ratio
Source: *China Statistical Yearbook, 2000* and *2004*. Beijing: China Statistical Press.

Despite the government's complete control over the creation of money, fiscal policy, in the sense of using deficit-financed expenditures to prime the economy, does not appear to have been a major thrust of the government. As Figure 11.6 shows, even though deficits have been recorded on the budget in the early reform years, until the late 1980s these have rarely exceeded one per cent of GDP. It is only in recent years that the government has started resorting to expansionary fiscal policies to stimulate recovery or growth.

Finally, with both prices and imports controlled by the government, any excess of demand over supply did not spill over in the form of inflation or a current account deficit, but was dealt with through rationing. This implied the enforced realization of a certain level of household financial savings in keeping with the physical plan. On the other hand, any excess of supply over demand in particular sectors resulted in the accumulation of inventories the holding of which was financed by the government and the banking system.

The effects of reform

The process of reform has resulted in a gradual change in all elements of this system. To begin with, financial reform has created a situation in which banks, financial institutions and enterprises at provincial and local levels have more flexibility in providing and accessing loans, so the ability of the government to control sharp increases in investment and consumption has been to an extent reduced. Second, faced with the inadequacy of monetary levers, the government has quite recently attempted to use counter-cyclical fiscal policy to correct for recessionary or inflationary tendencies. Third, price reform has meant that a growing number of commodities have been removed from the administered price category, so that excess demand can lead to inflation. Fourth, trade policy reform has meant that excess demand can spill over onto the balance of payments in the form of a reduced current account surplus or a current account deficit.

In the early phases of the economic reforms, along with price reform, certain significant changes were also made in the financial field. In 1979, the government declared its intention to reduce the share of investment funds for enterprises granted exclusively from the cost-free state budget, and to gradually replace budgetary grants with bank loans which were subject to interest charges. This did result in major changes in the financing of investment. The share of budgetary appropriations in financing capital construction declined dramatically and that of loans and self-raised funds increased quite significantly (see Table 11.5).

A two-tiered banking system was established in 1984 by the conversion of the PBC into the country's central bank and getting the specialized banks to undertake the commercial banking business. Furthermore, in 1986, reform of the non-bank financial sector resulted in the creation of a number of trust and investment companies, and financial intermediaries such as leasing companies, pension funds and insurance companies. Subsequently, foreign banks were allowed to undertake business for the first time. However, even under the new arrangement it was in

Table 11.5 Investment in capital construction by source of funds and administrative relationship (percentage)

Year	By source of funds					By administrative relationship	
	State budgetary appropriations	Domestic loans	Foreign investment	Fund-raising	Others	Central Government projects	Local projects
1978	77.7		5.6	16.7		53.2	46.8
1980	53.7	7.4	9.6	29.3	0.0	52.4	47.6
1985	35.5	17.5	6.8	31.6	8.5	53.5	46.5
1989	20.8	18.9	14.3	31.9	14.1	54.0	46.0
1990	21.3	22.2	13.2	31.1	12.2	53.9	46.1
1991	16.5	24.9	11.3	35.3	12.0	50.1	49.9
1992	10.2	27.6	11.1	41.3	9.8	44.5	55.5
1993	9.2	23.8	9.7	42.4	14.9	39.8	60.2
1994	6.8	24.9	14.3	44.3	9.7	37.8	62.2
1995	6.8	22.7	14.6	43.1	12.9	40.1	59.9
1996	6.1	22.7	14.5	44.2	12.5	39.2	60.8
1997	5.9	23.1	13.9	45.6	11.4	38.9	61.1
1998	8.8	24.2	12.4	41.9	12.6	34.6	65.4
1999	12.5	25.1	9.0	41.0	12.4	32.5	67.5
2000	12.6	28.3	6.7	41.3	11.0	32.0	68.0
2001	14.4	25.5	6.3	43.7	10.1	29.7	70.3
2002	14.7	25.6	6.0	44.5	9.2	25.6	74.4
2003	9.2	26.9	5.4	49.3	9.1	18.1	81.9

Source: China Statistical Yearbook, 2000 and 2004. Beijing: China Statistical Press.

principle possible for the PBC to rein in overdrafts being run by these banks and to prevent them from exceeding loan limits or quotas. In addition, the PBC could now control the terms of its lending by charging lower rates of interest for loans within the credit plan and penalizing unauthorized borrowing. Thus the ability of the PBC to realize its credit plan was strengthened by the reform.

However, with a greater degree of decentralization of financial activity and the ability of local officials to influence provincial and local appointments in the banks, it was possible for provincial and local government to easily obtain finance for special projects, thereby adding another element to the investment hunger determined by soft budget constraints in the SOE sector. Over time this problem has only worsened, with an increase in number of financial entities, a change in property rights in the financial sector and a far greater degree of functional autonomy. In the process the capacity of the central bank to use monetary levers to control investment expenditures has been weakened.

Macroeconomic trends since the reform

China's spectacular growth performance – an annual trend rate of growth of GDP of 9.8 per cent during the quarter century ending 2003 – is shown in Figure 11.7. This is most fundamentally a reflection of the high investment rates that have characterized the economy during this period. As Figure 11.8 shows, capital formation as a share of GDP has been very high by international standards, varying between 32 per cent and 44 per cent of GDP. Rates of growth of GDP have been strongly associated with investment rates, which is only to be expected, but there has also been substantial volatility in both of these indicators, around an increasing trend.

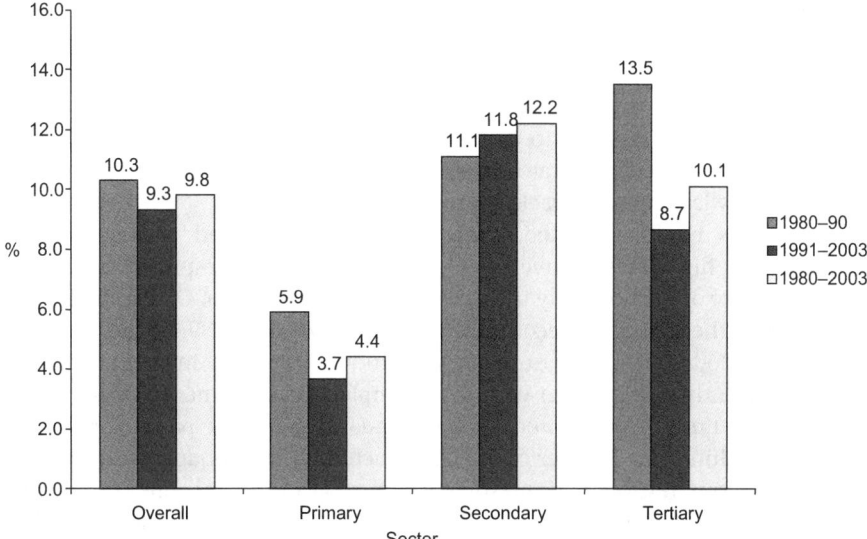

Figure 11.7 Trend rates of growth of GDP: sub-periods
Source: *China Statistical Yearbook, 2000* and *2004*. Beijing: China Statistical Press.

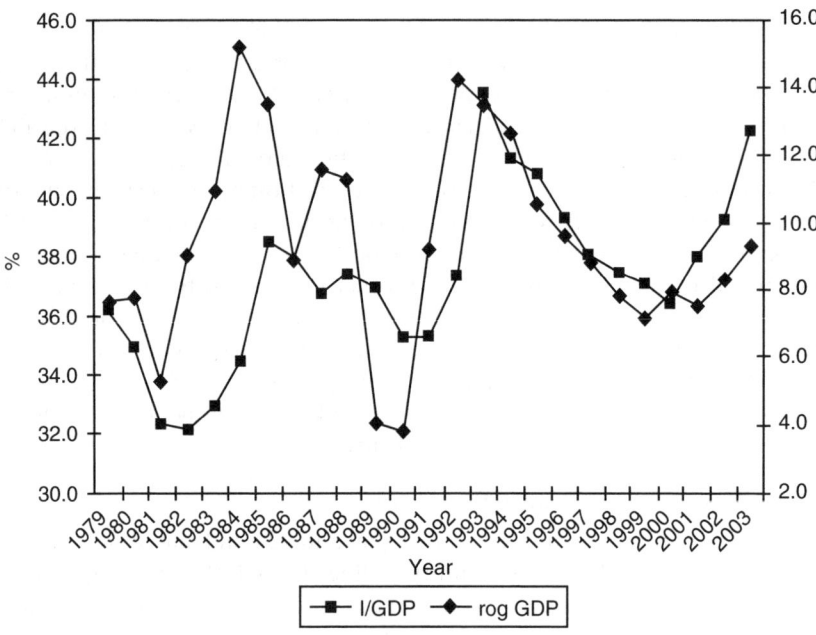

Figure 11.8 Investment rate and rate of growth of GDP
Source: *China Statistical Yearbook, 2000* and *2004*. Beijing: China Statistical Press.

The question then becomes, what explains this pattern of volatile but generally high rates of investment? It is evident that the stop–go cycles that characterize investment reflect the broader macroeconomic policy of adjusting domestic investment (and indeed consumption demand) to price changes. Macroeconomic policy generally – and therefore aggregate investment, which continued to be substantially influenced by government decisions given the nature of the economy – appears to have been strongly responsive to the inflation rate. Figure 11.9 indicates the extent to which higher investment rates have caused high inflation in the subsequent period, thereby leading to cutbacks in investment.

However, as has been noted, these fluctuations occurred in a context of generally very high rates of investment. It is notable that, despite volatility, the investment rate of the economy increased from 34.5 per cent of GDP for the three-year period at the start of the 'economic reforms' (1979–81) to 39.8 per cent for the three-year period 2001–03. Most recent data indicate that the investment rate in China is currently above 40 per cent. These imply rates of domestic saving which are exceptional not only by international standards, but more particularly for an economy at China's level of per capita GDP. Such high rates of domestic saving in turn imply a suppression of domestic consumption out of incremental income, which reflects a combination of the sheer rapidity of the growth itself, as well as evident spatial inequalities.

It may be argued that domestic savings has been less significant than foreign savings, and in particular FDI, in allowing for such high rates of investment

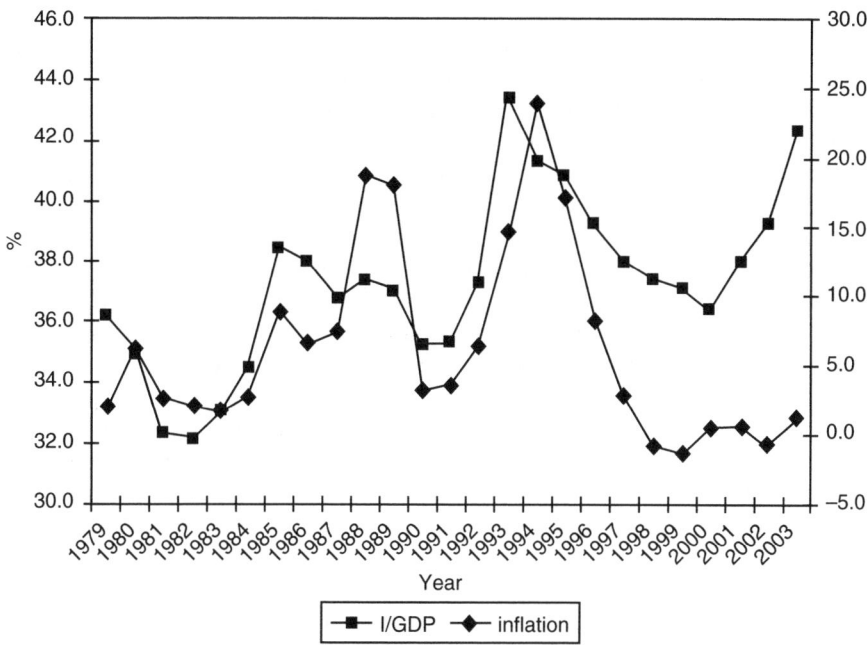

Figure 11.9 Investment rate and inflation rate

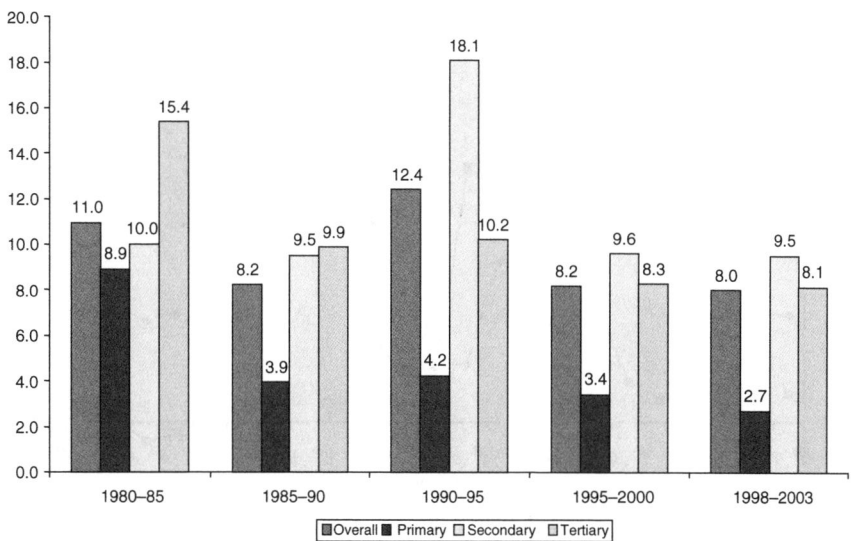

Figure 11.10 Trend rates of growth of GDP: sub-periods
Source: *China Statistical Yearbook, 2000* and *2004*. Beijing: China Statistical Press.

(see Chapter 6). This is particularly so because of the emergence of China as the second largest recipient (and the largest in the developing world) of FDI, which has increased from near zero in the early 1980s to more than $50 billion in recent years on average. However, in fact China's dependence upon external capital for financing investment has been relatively low, especially when compared to other developing countries. At its peak, the ratio of foreign capital inflow to GDP was 8 per cent in 1994, and thereafter has hovered around 5 per cent. Furthermore, the large inflows of the past few years have not contributed to domestic investment, macroeconomically speaking, since they have been associated with even higher domestic savings rates and the consequent build-up of foreign exchange reserves.

There has been some noticeable deceleration of growth in the primary sector during the periods 1980–1990 and 1991–2003 (see Figure 11.10), and also to some extent in the services sector (see Table 11.9). The secondary sector, in particular industrial production, has been crucial to the consistently good growth performance. This structure of growth is of relevance because, despite the overall high trend rate of growth, discussions on the need to manage bouts of deflation or 'overheating' recur periodically in Chinese economic discussions. As evident from Figure 11.11, since 1979, the Chinese economy has been through a series of cycles defined by movements in retail prices and output.

Monetary policy, though important, was limited in its role in mediating these cycles. In the increasingly liberalized financial environment, the PBC encountered difficulties in enforcing quantitative credit controls, leading to signs of 'overheating' and accelerated inflation when demand was buoyant. Though occasionally in the

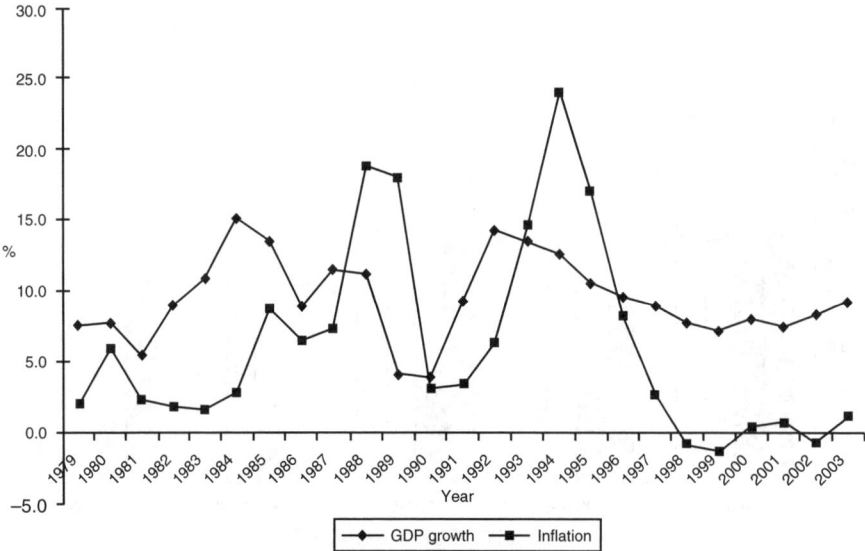

Figure 11.11 Annual rates of GDP growth and inflation
Source: *China Statistical Yearbook, 2000* and *2004*. Beijing: China Statistical Press.

1980s and once in the 1990s, the exchange rate was devalued, this instrument was also used rather sparingly. Thus elements of monetary policy were combined with a range of 'administrative measures'. For example, in the middle of 1993, policy measures to deal with inflation involved the recall of unauthorized loans extended by specialized banks to enterprises and non-bank financial institutions. Interest rates were raised and the returns on long-term deposits were pegged to inflation to encourage the public to hold more illiquid savings deposits. Administrative orders were also issued to restrain construction works and investment in real estate and property development.

However, around 1997 the Chinese government did change course, shifting to an expansionary monetary environment. This involved: eliminating ceilings on commercial bank lending; reducing excess reserve requirements; and reducing interest rates on central bank refinance to commercial banks, on deposits with commercial banks and on loans provided by commercial banks. However, the evidence seemed to be that this was inadequate to stimulate the economy. This was partly because the earlier process of stabilization merged with the recession induced by the East Asian currency crisis in 1997, which saw a collapse in export growth, capital flows and some currencies. Hence, 1998 proved to be one of the most difficult years of the 1990s. Due to the global recession, China's export growth fell in late 1997 and it deteriorated further in 1998. In the event China experienced a tendency it had not encountered before: that of deflation.

By this time, China was grappling with another problem: the dramatic upsurge of foreign exchange inflows fuelled a strong expansion of reserve money. This, combined with the continuous expansion of domestic credit, made control of the money supply extremely difficult. The ineffectiveness of monetary policy during the late 1990s downturn can be attributed to a number of changes in the financial and monetary sphere. First, with capital flows being autonomous and export growth becoming a crucial component of the growth process, foreign reserves are 'autonomously' determined, making it difficult for the central bank to control money supply. While the PBC initially attempted to deal with the problem through sterilization involving the sale of government securities, that became increasingly unviable as the central banks' holding of securities declined.

The second cause for the breakdown of monetary policy is that deregulation and the decentralization of banking control have meant that provincial and local governments are able to easily influence banks to provide them with credit based on their own deposits. Higher interest rates do not affect these borrowers, because they do not face conventional budget constraints. On the reverse side, in times of deflation, it is extremely difficult to get banks to lend to SOEs in difficulty. Chinese banks have accumulated a huge amount of non-performing loans (NPLs), and the government has tightened the regulation and supervision of their lending activities. Heavy penalties are being imposed on bank managers who are responsible for the creation of new NPLs. As a result, commercial banks have become much more concerned about loan safety than profitability. Banks are very reluctant to lend to most enterprises, because of the risks.

Firms are also reluctant to take on debt during a downturn. Owing to structural problems, such as low profitability, lack of exit mechanisms and high debt–equity ratios, enterprises are not responsive to the easier access to bank credits and lower interest rates offered during a deflation. Thus, the relaxation in monetary policy after 1997 failed in some areas to lead to increases in investment demand. Instead, the capital market tended to absorb the increased liquidity.

In China, the transition from a controlled to a more decentralized monetary system has implied a relatively lax monetary policy. This has resulted in a situation where local government functionaries, who influence the appointment of banking and other functionaries at the local level, are easily able to access funds for their projects. More recently, the decision to maintain a pegged exchange rate while liberalizing the capital flows into and out of the country, has forced the central bank to buy dollars by selling yuan (RMB) so as to pre-empt any appreciation of the currency. The increase in the foreign exchange assets of the central bank this implies is not easily sterilized, since the government has almost exhausted its holding of government securities because of past sales aimed at sterilizing the capital flows that lead to reserve accumulation. As a result, the high-powered money base of the central bank has expanded and the Chinese economy has been characterized by an easy money situation that makes available the funds that finance sometimes unwarranted capital construction projects.

With growing evidence that monetary policy was proving increasingly ineffective because of changes in financial structures, the government turned to fiscal policy as a means of macroeconomic control that accompanied the so-called 'administrative measures'. During the 1980s and up to the first half of the 1990s, the role of the government budget in macroeconomic management was very limited, because of the dramatic fall in the proportion of GDP which comprised the government's budget, and because of other institutional constraints. For example, implementation of the enterprise contract responsibility system in the 1980s virtually deprived the government of any flexibility to use expenditure and taxes to influence macroeconomic activities. Consequently, monetary policy assumed a dominant role in macroeconomic management in China during this period. However, since the middle of 1998, due to the impotence of monetary policy, fiscal policy has replaced monetary policy as a more active instrument in China's macroeconomic management, aimed at getting rid of deflation.

The Chinese government also retained very substantial control over trade policy despite the various measures towards trade liberalization undertaken from the early 1990s. A substantial proportion of trade volumes remained under administrative authority, either through trade restrictions, including quota controls and fairly high tariffs, or indirectly because SOE accounted for more than half of all trade. The asymmetric liberalization not only allowed the Chinese government to retain control over macroeconomic processes more systematically than was possible in India, but also had implications for employment and therefore poverty. Unlike India (and many other developing countries over the same period), where the employment benefits of export expansion were outweighed by the

Table 11.6 Composition of fixed assets formation

	2002	2003
Capital construction	40.6	41.2
Innovation	15.5	15.5
Real estate development	17.9	18.3
Others	26.0	25.0

Source: *China Statistical Yearbook, 2000* and *2004*. Beijing: China Statistical Press.

employment losses in import-competing activities, in China almost all of the increases in export employment were net increases in employment until the turn of the century. The mercantilist emphasis on net export expansion therefore allowed for more employment generation than would have been possible otherwise.

However, the crucial role of the government in spurring expansionary bouts and contractionary spells in the process of sustaining a high trend rate of growth is explained in part by the composition of fixed assets formation. As Table 11.6 shows, productive investment captured by the components 'capital construction' and 'innovation' account for significant shares of fixed assets formation. (Capital construction refers to the new construction projects or extension projects of enterprises, institutions or administrative units mainly for the purpose of expanding production capacity or improving project efficiency. Innovation refers in general to the technological improvement of original facilities, including renewal of fixed assets, by the enterprises and institutions.)

However, what is interesting is the high share of real estate development in the total.[7] This item includes real estate development by central and local government bodies as well as investment in residential construction. The former includes investment by local government bodies in economic development zones and what have come to be referred to as 'image projects' launched by local leaders to enhance their public stature. The latter includes a substantial amount of private residential construction that is underway, especially in urban China, in the wake of relaxation of laws governing residential property ownership. The relaxation of residential property ownership rules resulted in the conversion of savings accumulated in the past into investment in residential property. This spurt, together with the high degree of volatility of local government development expenditures, has made real estate development the most volatile part of fixed assets formation.[8]

This kind of volatility is partly facilitated by the manner in which capital formation is financed in China. Budgetary appropriations and foreign investment account for small shares of between 4.4 and 7 per cent of total fixed assets formation in 2002 and 2003. The major finance comes from three sources, all of which involve a substantial degree of borrowing. Domestic loans refer to loans of various forms borrowed by investing units from banks and non-bank financial institutions. 'Raised' funds refer to extra-budgetary funds for investment in fixed assets received by investing units from central government ministries, local governments, enterprises and institutions. And 'other funds' refers to funds for investment in fixed assets received from sources other than those listed above, including capital raised through issuing bonds by enterprises or financial institutions, funds raised from individuals, and funds transferred from other units. All of these involve some degree of direct or off-budget borrowing.

The importance of expenditures of this kind financed in this fashion becomes clear when we realize that the fiscal stimulus for growth in China is limited. Fiscal revenues in 2000 stood at just 15 per cent of GDP, and it is the growing desire of the centre to control expenditures that is seeing an increase in that ratio to 20 per cent by 2004. But even of these expenditures a considerable share goes to current expenditures rather than capital formation. This is illustrated by the priorities for fiscal policy set by the government for 2004, which include expenditures that support the rural sector; education, health and science and technology; transfers to poor provinces; tax reforms; and wages and salary expenditures of government.

Hence, expenditures financed through other means account dominantly for the spurt in fixed asset formation (see Table 11.7). Clearly then it is the flexibility to acquire funds that enables different entities to undertake such investment expenditure that raises the investment income ratio and sustains high levels of growth. And, given the observed volatility of these expenditures, it must be true that finances to undertake such expenditures are easily available 'on demand'. If the government is to control volatility, it must use a range of administrative measures, including restrictions on the use of land, to influence expenditures and outcomes.

The problem is that when growth is triggered with such expenditures, it propels further such expenditures and the resulting expansion soon runs into bottlenecks of various kinds, especially bottlenecks in the power, steel and other infrastructural areas. Inevitably, inflation ensues. The Chinese government has to manage the inflation that results in such circumstances of 'overheating'. There is no evidence that the kind of investment expenditure being spoken of is interest rate sensitive, and in any case interest rates increases could create various problems, such as lead to a spurt in capital inflows into the economy, thereby worsening the exchange rate management problem, or adversely affecting the viability of the already weakened SOEs.

Table 11.7 Sources of finance for fixed asset formation

	2002	2003
State budgetary appropriation	7.0	4.6
Domestic loans	19.7	20.5
Foreign investment	4.6	4.4
Fund-raising	50.6	53.7
Others	18.0	16.8

Source: China Statistical Yearbook, 2000 and 2004. Beijing: China Statistical Press.

Hence the Chinese government still uses administrative measures, including the use of central 'commands' and guidelines to hold back runaway rates of investment. The difficulty is that once such commands and guidelines are carried down to decision makers at lower levels in what is still politically a centralized system, they remain in place till the government retracts these guidelines and works to ensure that the message reaches down to where it matters. In the meantime a bout of deflation is a possibility. And if this occurs in a context of the kind created by the East Asian crisis, that adversely affected China's exports, such deflation can indeed be prolonged. 'Stop–go' around a high trend therefore seems to be an inevitable feature of the current conjuncture.

The essential point, however, is that thus far the reform has not adversely affected the high rates of saving and investment that sustain the high trend rate of growth of the economy. Further, since this high rate of saving is supported by large increments in income it has not resulted in a squeeze in consumption that can neutralize the effects of growth on poverty reduction. The 'unconventional' demand management policies used by the Chinese government to regulate economic cycles – which have been possible only because of the particular institutional conditions prevailing in China – have also ensured that despite the oscillations, there have been no serious or prolonged contractions and growth has remained at a very high level.

Implications for poverty reduction

How has this evolving macroeconomic scenario affected inequality and poverty? The evidence relating to the early years of reform suggest worsening inequality in China. China's economic reforms seem to have led to an increase in regional inequality. Official statistics indicate that the income ratio of urban residents to rural increased from 2.4 in 1978 to 2.8 in 2000. Other analysts corroborate this observation.[9] Before the start of reforms in 1978, the ratio of urban to rural income had declined to 2.36 from 3.48 in 1977. Price and production reform in agriculture ensured that this trend continued till 1985. However, after 1985, the ratio began to rise again and stood at 2.61 in 1994. Further, within rural and urban areas the Gini coefficient of income distribution rose from 0.31 and 0.19 respectively to 0.41 and 0.37 between 1986 and 1994 (see Table 11.8). This worsening of income distribution may have reduced some of the significant benefits in terms of poverty reduction ensured by the rapid rates of growth in aggregate income China has managed to ensure since the beginning of the reform.

One reason for this inequality was the priority given to coastal development from the early 1980s to the late 1990s. In order to attract investment to the coastal regions, the government provided a range of incentives, though these regions were already more advanced than the rest of China. In the event, the slow and inadequate development of the central and western regions, where much of China's poverty is concentrated, became an obstacle to reducing poverty in these provinces.

The Chinese and Indian cases both illustrate the crucial importance of growth in agricultural incomes for poverty reduction. The relation between poverty

Table 11.8 Estimates of inequality, 1984–2000

| | Kanbur and Zhang | | | | Chen and Wang | | |
| | | | GE (Theil) | | | | |
	Gini (%)	GE (%)	Rural-Urban	Inland-Coast	Rural	(Gini) Urban	National*
1984	25.6	10.9	6.3	0.4			
1985	25.8	11.1	6.6	0.5			
1986	26.8	11.9	6.9	0.5			
1987	27.0	12.0	6.8	0.6			
1988	28.2	13.1	7.7	0.8			
1989	29.7	14.4	9.3	1.0			
1990	30.1	14.9	9.5	1.0	29.87	23.42	33.34
1991	30.3	14.9	9.9	1.2			
1992	31.4	16.0	10.2	1.5	32.03	24.18	37.23
1993	32.2	16.8	10.9	1.7	33.70	27.18	40.18
1994	32.6	17.2	10.8	2.0	34.00	29.22	41.46
1995	33.0	17.7	11.5	2.3	33.98	28.27	39.84
1996	33.4	18.2	11.7	2.6	32.98	28.52	38.16
1997	33.9	18.9	11.7	2.7	33.12	29.35	38.21
1998	34.4	19.6	12.2	2.9	33.07	29.94	38.70
1999	36.3	23.4	12.8	3.2	33.91	29.71	39.97
2000	37.2	24.8	13.9	3.8			

Source: Kanbur and Zhang (2003); Chen and Wang (2000).

reduction and growth has varied over time, being strong at the beginning of the period, that is in the period 1979–82, and much weaker afterwards, especially in the late 1990s.[10] This change had much to do with the nature of the growth, which began by being centred on agriculture and the rural economy where most of the poor live, and then shifted towards the coastal cities where the poor are less evident.

What is striking about the post-reform Chinese experience with growth and its effects on poverty reduction is that while Chinese growth was consistently high across time, poverty reduction was concentrated in particular periods. Thus, while the early Chinese record in terms of the reduction in the absolute number of poor is impressive, the reduction was concentrated in two relatively brief periods: the first five years of the reform period, 1979–1984; and the middle three years of the 1990s. The first period, corresponding to the beginning of the era of reform and transition, was when reform focused on the countryside. Over these years the rural people's communes were dismantled, land was parcelled out to households on an essentially egalitarian basis, farmers were encouraged to abandon the previous 'grain first' policy and to diversify production, and farm prices were raised 30 per cent. In addition, chemical fertilizer supplies increased rapidly.

The second period of sharp decline in rural poverty occurred in the middle years of the 1990s. In the first third of the decade the rural poverty rate according to this line was running at over 40 per cent of the population; it dropped to about 24 per cent by 1996. The Poverty Reduction Plan (1994–2000) brought the number of absolute poor down from 80 million to below 30 million by the end of 2001. The main operative factor in explaining this steep fall is an equally steep rise in farm purchase prices, especially of food grain, which doubled in the middle of the decade. This increase in income benefited middle-income families who were reliant on agricultural returns (Chen and Wang, 2001). The real per capita income of rural Chinese increased by 21 per cent in the three years from 1993 to 1996.[11] Thus, poverty reduction proved to be highly income elastic: a 21 per cent increase in rural income was accompanied by a 40 per cent decrease in rural poverty.

However, it has been argued (Hu Angang, Hu Linlin and Chang Zhixiao 2004) that despite China's substantial improvement in poverty reduction since 1978, the pace of poverty reduction has slowed recently and new forms of poverty have arisen. The annual decrease in the poverty population has reduced by half with the number of poor decreasing only by eight million annually; the average growth rate of farmers' consumption per year was only 2.5 per cent; the average growth rate of farmers' per capita net income was only 3 per cent. This is explained by the authors in terms of two factors: the deteriorating quality of growth and an increase in the degree of inequality. Trends in poverty have also been closely linked with the trends in employment and social sector expenditure. In the rural areas, slow growth in the agricultural sector resulted in almost stagnant rural employment after the mid-1990s. Rising unemployment was a major driver of urban poverty in the post-1985 phase, a scenario further strengthened by migrant population from rural areas.

It is known that reforms in China impacted adversely on urban poverty by generating unemployment through the restructuring of the state-owned sector in a context where the social security system was weak or absent. Bouche *et al.* (2004) argue that urban poverty is closely associated with inability to work, and that the increase in urban unemployment as a result of market-oriented reforms and withdrawal of financial support for ailing state enterprises, had been a prime cause of the increase in urban poverty. Prior to the restructuring of the SOEs, there was no great variation in urban poverty among regions due to guaranteed employment and the ubiquitous urban welfare system. This regional pattern changed when market-oriented reforms restructured the SOEs and weakened the social welfare system. Changes in the regional distribution of urban poverty were highly correlated with the original structure of industry and with regional economic growth. Poverty was higher in regions where the heavy industries set up during the era of central planning were concentrated.

Moreover, financial stringency also limited the poverty reduction effort. In China, most poverty reduction programmes financed by the central government and by international donors required counterpart funds from local governments, but most local governments in poor counties faced severe budgetary constraints. As a result a report by the State Auditing Bureau indicated that 370 out of 592 poor counties had not provided any counterpart funds from 1997 to 1999. The problem was similar in urban areas, since many city and town governments lacked the fiscal resources to provide counterpart funds for financing the new unemployment, pension and medical insurance systems.

Despite high growth, the most important and urgent economic problem China has been facing is unemployment. Every year a labour force totalling 10 million is thrown into the job market. In addition, there are more than five million redundant workers from former SOEs waiting for re-employment. Finally, there are hundreds of millions of migrant farmers constantly moving around the country seeking jobs. As a result, even the high rate of growth in China, if not accompanied by special structural features, cannot meet the pressure for job creation. In 2003, with a 9.1 per cent growth rate, eight million jobs were created, but even this was inadequate given the continuously growing 'backlog' of increase in the labour force and reduced demand for labour in many traditional activities including agriculture.

Recent work by Khan and Riskin (2005) reporting on a national sample survey of household expenditure conducted by the Chinese Academy of Social Sciences (CASS) with an independent international group of economists in 1988, 1995 and 2002, is particularly interesting in this light. These surveys suggest that income inequality rose sharply in China between 1988 and 1995, due to increases in interregional inequality; slow and inequalizing rural income growth; regressive transfers to households and reduced transfer from rich to poor provinces; slow growth in employment and inadequate social protection for retrenched workers; and restrictions on migration along with discriminatory treatment of migrants.

After 1995, while these trends still continued, a number of developments including greater rural–urban migration and policy changes aimed at reducing regional inequality by promoting investment in western and interior provinces, ensuring the spread of wage employment in rural areas and provision of better social security benefits, appear to have reversed the tendency towards an increase in inequality. Between 1995 and 2002, income inequality in both rural and urban China declined as a result of a decline in regional inequality, improvement in the distribution of both farm and wage incomes, housing reform and the reform of public finance. But the Gini coefficient for China as a whole did not change between the two years because of a rise in the already high gap between average urban and rural incomes. In fact, the increase in the rural–urban income gap would have been even larger, but for a substantial decline in rural population after 1995, when the absolute size of the rural population peaked.

While income poverty in rural areas has been reduced by rural–urban migration, in the urban areas most of the poor are recent migrants, who tend to be much worse off than other urban residents. Migrant workers typically have high turnover of employment, and also suffer from the disadvantages of being excluded from the formal labour market, public housing and access to health services and schooling for children at low cost that urban residents are entitled to. In the early 1980s the urban poverty rate was about 2 per cent and the absolute amount of the urban poverty population was four million. This decreased to only about one million in 1989 according to official estimates. There is evidence that the decline in urban poverty has slowed or even been reversed in the 1990s. The most recent government estimate of the number of urban poor is as high as 12 million people. This can only be because of the increase in urban income inequalities coming from the gap in incomes and benefits accruing to migrant and full status urban residents.

This study suggests that poverty reduction in China has been more strongly related to declines in inequality than to GDP growth *per se*. If so, China's ability to sustain the pace of poverty reduction will depend on its ability to keep in place recent policies aimed at reducing inequality. This is also in keeping with lessons derived from the pre-reform experience. China was served well by a combination of egalitarian land distribution and experience with commune and cooperative forms of organization, which ensured a degree of income equality and helped release and pool labour resources for undertaking non-agricultural activities that were jointly managed with state support. To the extent that economic reform undermines such egalitarianism and adversely affects the growth of the township and village enterprises (TVEs), it would set back the poverty reduction effort as well.

Conclusion

The implications of all this evidence need to be drawn out. To start with, it should be clear that the egalitarianism that the Chinese revolution ensured and the control state could promote because of the persistence of substantial state ownership of and investment in capital assets as well as the continuance of the earlier financial structure and system, meant that the process of global economic integration was carried out under fundamentally different premises from that which occurred in India. To a significant extent, some of the basic development issues, including ensuring adequate food supplies and universal primary education, were already dealt with. The domestic market for consumption goods was also significantly larger than proved to be the case in India. More significantly for our current purposes, the control retained by the Chinese state over financial institutions and the activities of the SOEs allowed it to sustain high levels of investment and deal with volatility, to prevent undesired levels of inflation from persisting beyond relatively short periods. In the event, the state could ensure that cyclical fluctuations occurred around a high overall trend rate of income growth. The early phase of opening up, which essentially involved increasing remuneration to farmers, operated substantially to reduce poverty and deprivation. Subsequently, the heavy emphasis on infrastructure development, combined with some amount of 'controlled' trade and investment liberalization, created much greater possibilities for export-oriented employment generation, which became the next engine of growth. Because this occurred in a context of still heavily regulated and monitored imports, it ensured that export employment was a net addition to aggregate manufacturing employment, rather than having to balance for losses in employment in other domestic sectors, since these were not really having to face import competition on a par with other countries that underwent trade liberalization in that period. When import liberalization accelerated, a drastic devaluation of the yuan was resorted to in 1994, which meant that import competition was still limited.

The transition to a market-driven system in China, while indeed delivering growth, proved to be inequalizing beyond a point. But measures by the state aimed at preventing such tendencies and the migration-mediated process of 'trickle down' have helped to partially reverse these inequalizing outcomes (see Figure 11.12). However, in as much as the current pattern of economic expansion is predicated on high rates of saving and investment as well as loosening of the earlier credit and cash planning system, the dangers of volatile growth and inadequate reductions in unemployment and poverty persist, necessitating appropriate macroeconomic corrections as well as supportive policies.

In comparison, India, with its market-driven and demand-constrained system, which has greater space for conventional macroeconomic levers, has not only failed to deliver the same growth success but has also been far less successful on the poverty reduction front. The implication is that macroeconomic flexibility in a market-driven environment is not the best recipe either for growth and stability or for poverty reduction. India's growth experience, while more stable than for many other developing countries, was still nowhere near the rapid growth experienced by China and other East and Southeast Asian economies. This was strongly related to the reduced public expenditure by the Indian state in the period of reform, most significantly the substantial reduction in central capital expenditure (mainly on infrastructure) as a share of GDP, but also public spending directed towards the rural areas generally. In addition, central government policies in various ways created resource problems for the state governments, forcing them to cut back on crucial developmental expenditure. This meant that first, rates of aggregate income growth were well below those which could have been achieved; and second, that employment growth was well below the rate of GDP growth. These problems were compounded by the effects that trade liberalization had on small scale production in some manufacturing sectors. Agrarian distress and inadequate employment generation have therefore emerged as the most significant macroeconomic problems at the current time.

Of course, it is true that the Indian experience has allowed for greater financial and macroeconomic stability than experienced by many other 'emerging markets' over this period, primarily because until relatively recently liberalization of the capital account was limited and India was not 'chosen' as an attractive destination for finance capital. With changes occurring on both these fronts, the country is currently experiencing a surge in capital inflows that exert an upward pressure on the exchange rate as well as reduce macroeconomic flexibility.

There is an overarching conclusion, of wider relevance, that can be drawn from this comparative analysis of the experiences of macroeconomic management in China and India over the past twenty years. Discussions on macroeconomic policy counterpose the policies adopted in the *dirigiste* period, ostensibly characterized by financial repression, with the framework increasingly in vogue in emerging market economies characterized by a reduced role for fiscal policy and state expenditures and a greater role for a liberalized financial sector in mobilizing and channelling investment. The Chinese experience makes it clear that such either–or dichotomies are not inevitable and that a pro-poor macroeconomic framework must provide a role for state policies pursued within an area of control ensured with state regulation. On the other hand, India's experience suggests that

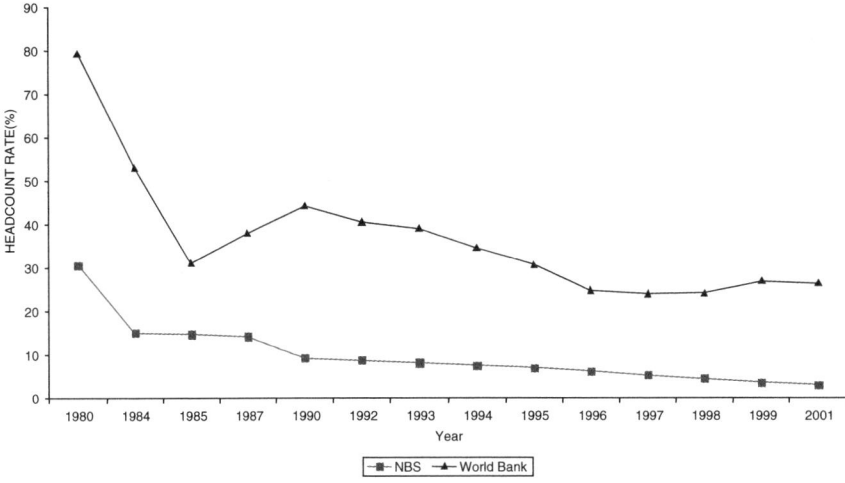

Figure 11.12 Poverty in rural China

relentlessly pursuing the transition to a marketist macroeconomic framework makes it difficult to sustain investment and growth and to translate the benefits of that growth into better outcomes with regard to employment and poverty reduction. In fact, India seems to have avoided the volatility that has characterized countries that were even more successful on the growth front by limiting liberalization with respect to capital flows. Country-specific choices of a consistent set of policies derived from the rich experience with macroeconomic world-wide, rather than easy choices from either–or options seems to be the route that any appropriate and pro-poor macroeconomic policy should take.

Notes

1 Almost all of the studies which have found that global inequalities have reduced in the period of globalization (Dollar and Kraay (2002) and Bhalla (2003) among others) rely very substantially on the increase in per capita GDP in China and India – which together account for around one-third of the world's population – to arrive at their conclusion. Conversely, those who have been more sceptical of the impact of global economic integration on inequality have tended to look at patterns of inequality within these countries in particular (Cornia 2004; Milanovic 2004; and so on) to find that there has been an increase in economic differentiation (including increased rural–urban inequalities) and probably more vulnerable conditions for the poor in these countries (hidden by the per capita GDP figures), which change the conclusions with respect to global inequalities.
2 There are several reasons for believing that increases in interest payments by government are likely to have lower multiplier effects. Most government securities are held by economic agents whose marginal propensity to consume is very low. In India, a significant proportion is held by banks, whose increased returns from such investment do not tend to translate into greater spending by the system as a whole.

3 The only positive feature in employment patterns was the increase in opportunities for the educated groups, largely related to the expansion of IT-enabled services in metropolitan and other urban areas. However, while this feature, along with that of software development, received much international attention, it still remained too insignificant in the aggregate economy to make much of a dent in overall employment.
4 As Sen (2002) points out, the reference periods in the Consumer Expenditure Survey of the 55th Round of NSS survey were changed from the uniform 30 day recall used till then to both 7 and 30 day questions for items of food and intoxicants and only 365 day questions for items of clothing, footwear, education, institutional medical expense and durable goods.
5 These findings are based on NSS 'thin sample' surveys, conducted annually since 1986. These surveys are not as comprehensive as the NSS comprehensive rounds or the 'thick sample' surveys but provide sufficiently good estimates at the national level. Also, these thin samples results are comparable across successive surveys as they use a common form of questionnaire.
6 For a discussion of the evolution of China's financial system, see Xu (1998).
7 This category includes the investment by real estate development companies, commercial building construction companies and other real estate development units of varied ownership, in the construction of residential buildings, factory buildings, warehouses, hotels, guesthouses, holiday villages, office buildings, and the complementary service facilities and land development projects, such as roads, water supply, water drainage, power supply, heating, telecommunications, land levelling and other projects of an infrastructural kind. It excludes simple land transactions.
8 During the early 1990s, the growth rate of investment in real estate varied between 11.7 and −1.2 per cent.
9 See, for example, Kanbur and Zhang (2003), Chen and Wang (2001), Khan and Riskin (2005).
10 A similar argument is made by Bouche *et al.* (2004).
11 Zhongguo Tongji Zhaiyao (1998), p. 78.

References

Bhalla, S.S. 2003. 'Recounting the Poor: Poverty in India, 1983–99'. *Economic and Political Weekly*, 25–31 January.
Bouche, N. et al. 2004. *The Macroeconomics of Poverty Reduction: The Case of China*. Beijing: UNDP.
Chen, S. and Y. Wang. 2001. *China's Growth and Poverty Reduction: Trends Between 1990 and 1999*. Washington DC: World Bank Development Research Group Poverty and World Bank Institute Economic Policy and Poverty Reduction Division.
Cornia, G.A. 2004. *Inequality, Growth and Poverty in an Era of Liberalisation and Globalisation*. Oxford: Oxford University Press.
Deaton, A. and J. Dreze. 2002. 'Poverty and Inequality in India: A Re-examination'. *Economic and Political Weekly*, 7 September.
Dollar, D. and A. Kraay. 2002. 'Growth is Good for the Poor'. *Journal of Economic Growth*, 7(3), 195–225.
Hu, A., L. Hu and C. Zhixiao. 2004. *China's Economic Growth and Poverty Reduction*.
Kanbur, R. and X. Zhang. 2003. *Fifty Years of Regional Inequality in China: A Journey Through Central Planning, Reform and Openness*. Paper prepared for the UNU/WIDER Project Conference on Spatial Inequality in Asia, Tokyo.
Khan, A. Rahman and C. Riskin. 2005. 'China's Household Income and its Distribution, 1995 and 2002'. *China Quarterly* 182, 356–84.
Milanovic, B. 2004. *Half a World: Regional Inequality in Five Great Federations*. Washington DC: World Bank and Carnegie Endowment for International Peace.

Sen, A. 2002. 'Agriculture, Employment and Poverty: Recent Trends in Rural India'. In V.K. Ramachandran and Madhura Swaminathan (eds), *Agrarian Studies*. New Delhi: Tulika Books.
Sen, A. and Himanshu. 2005. 'Poverty and Inequality in India: Getting Closer to the Truth'. www.macroscan.org and *Economic and Political Weekly*, January.
Sundaram, K. and S.D Tendulkar. 2003a. 'Poverty Has Declined in the 1990s: A Resolution of Comparability Problems in NSS Consumer Expenditure Data', *Economic and Political Weekly*, 25–31 January.
Sundaram, K. and S.D Tendulkar. 2003b. 'Poverty in India in the 1990s: Revised Results for All-India and 15 Major States for 1993–94'. *Economic and Political Weekly*, 15–22 November.
Xu, X. 1998. *China's Financial System under Transition*. London: Macmillan.
Zhongguo Tongji Zhaiyao (Statistical Abstract of China) 1998. Beijing.

12
Heterodox Macroeconomic Policies, Inequality and Poverty in Uzbekistan

Giovanni Andrea Cornia[1]

Introduction: transition in Central Asia and the 'special case' of Uzbekistan

The Central Asian Republics (CARs) offer an interesting comparative study in reform paths of formerly centrally planned economies. While the CARs share a considerable geographical, religious and cultural unity, and while they initiated the transition to the market economy from fairly similar conditions, they pursued different policies following the demise of the Soviet Union in December 1991. The Kyrgyz Republic has been most committed to the introduction of Washington Consensus-type reforms. Turkmenistan has been the least committed, with a regime concerned more with the distribution of oil rents than with creating a market-oriented economy. In turn, both Kazakhstan and Uzbekistan have made some progress with economic reforms, with the former increasingly following an orthodox approach, while the latter adopted a more controlled reform process. The specificity of the Uzbek approach has been evident throughout the heterodox macroeconomic stabilization of 1991–1995, the import-substitution-led recovery of 1996–2002/03, and the new and more liberal regime that started emerging in 2002–2003. This home-grown approach to policy making has been and remains the object of considerable controversy, and many predicted that it would have led sooner or later to a growth collapse.

On becoming independent in 1991, all CARs experienced a severe and prolonged transformational recession. Output fell markedly (see Table 12.1), inflation soared, the distribution of income and wealth became more unequal and poverty reached previously unknown levels. Interestingly, Uzbekistan – the Central Asian country that chose a gradual approach to the transition – experienced the smallest decline in gross domestic product (GDP) during 1991–1995, has sustained an acceptable growth of GDP since then, exceeded its pre-transition level of GDP per capita in 2001 (see Table 12.1) and was comparatively successful in controlling hyperinflation. However, between 1996 and 2003 growth was perceptibly lower than in the other CARs, raising the issue of whether the Uzbek approach to

Table 12.1   GDP index (1989 = 100) in the Central Asian transitional economies, 1990–2004

	1990	1992	1994	1995	1995-1989	1997	1999	2000	2001	2002	2003	2003-1995	2004-2003
Kazakhstan	100	84	67	61	61	63	60	66	75	80	87	142	109
Kirghizistan	103	79	53	50	50	59	60	63	66	68	73	143	105
Tagikistan	98	65	47	41	41	40	44	48	52	56	62	151	108
Turkmenistan	102	92	66	63	51	51	63	74	82	94	101	160	107
Uzbekistan	102	90	85	84	84	87	93	97	101	104	106	126	107

Source: EBRD (2005).

stabilization generated long-term efficiency costs that more than offset the comparative advantage recorded during the initial phase of the transition.

The macroeconomic stabilization of 1991–1995

Initial conditions

Uzbekistan started out the transition in conditions that were neither particularly favourable nor unfavourable. It produced items for export – such as gold and cotton – that could be easily redirected to the international markets. It also could count on unexploited oil and natural gas reserves and smaller deposits of silver, copper and coal. It also had a well-educated population and a large supply of semi-skilled and skilled workers. In addition, it could count on an industrial structure that was far more developed than that of other CARs (Pomfret 2001). At the same time, the Uzbek economy was dependent on the imports of price-inelastic items such as food and oil and suffered from considerable isolation from the international markets.

Exogenous shocks

As elsewhere in the region, during the initial reform period transition policy in Uzbekistan had to deal with the severe exogenous shocks that resulted from the change of the economic system or from the break-up of the Soviet Union (Griffin 1996). To start with, the country was hit by a devastating loss of Soviet budgetary support equivalent to 21 per cent of the republic's 1991 GDP. A second shock was caused by the disruption of international trade following the collapse of Comecon and the sudden decline in inter-republican trade that in 1990 accounted for 40 per cent of its GDP. Third, the country was hit by a sharp deterioration in external terms of trade caused by the rise to the world level in the price of oil that in the past was supplied by Russia at a low price. Fourth, these changes in international terms of trade and domestic liberalization caused large shifts in relative prices – for example, the prices of inputs versus those of output – that rendered unprofitable those enterprises consuming large amounts of inputs that were underpriced during the socialist era. Finally, in 1991–1993, 300,000 Russian and Ukrainian professionals left the country, making the restructuring of the national economy more problematic.

Policy stance

The Uzbek approach to macroeconomic stabilization differed markedly from the orthodox model that demands rapid price liberalization, the removal of all consumer and producer subsidies, budgetary austerity, tight money, trade and capital account liberalization and privatization.

Among the measures introduced as part of this heterodox approach, a gradual price liberalization played a key role. Instead of removing all price restraints at once, price controls and administrative rationing were abandoned gradually and price liberalization was completed only in 1995. Even then, a few key prices remained at levels below world prices. Energy prices were aligned to world prices in 1996. Wheat and cotton price controls remained in place for much longer. With privatization progressing slowly, the government retained an active role in large enterprises. While consumption subsidies were cancelled quickly, with the exception of those on flour, sugar and edible oil, subsidies to state enterprises were kept in place through direct budget support, cheap credit, access to low-cost foreign exchange and state orders.

In turn, fiscal policy followed an accommodating approach. During the initial phase of 1991–1994 and the crisis year of 1996, when the cotton harvest fell by 15 per cent, fiscal policy was deliberately expansionary, and the government monetized large budget deficits to sustain public expenditure and aggregate demand. But as early as 1995 revenue collection had returned to a hefty 34.6 per cent of GDP that enabled the government to finance substantial income transfers to compensate for the rises in the prices of essentials, expand the coverage of existing social programmes – for example, child allowances – introduce unemployment compensation and poor relief programmes and pursue an ambitious investment programme, while incurring a limited budget deficit (see Table 12.2).

For much of the stabilization period, the Uzbek authorities were unable to pursue an independent monetary policy, as the country initially remained in the rouble zone. In November 1993 did the country leave the rouble zone, introducing a temporary currency, the soum-coupon, but it was only on 1 July 1994 that the soum was introduced. During this period, monetary policy was accommodating and interest rates remained negative in real terms (see Table 12.3) so as to reduce the cost of credit to the protected sector. Credit was rationed and was mainly allocated to state enterprises on an administrative basis.

While the growth of broad money was high in both 1994 and 1995, the GDP price deflator grew significantly more rapidly, suggesting a tight monetary policy,

Table 12.2 Government expenditure, revenue and budget balance (percentage of GDP)

	1991	1992	1993	1994	1995	1996	1997	1998	1999	2000	2001	2002	2003	2004
Government expenditure	52.7	49.7	46.4	35.3	38.7	41.6	32.5	33.1	32.0	29.8	27.0	25.8	24.6	22.9
Government revenue	49.1	31.4	36.0	29.2	34.6	34.3	30.1	30.1	29.2	28.6	26.0	25.2	24.2	22.5
Budget balance	−3.6	−18.3	−10.4	−6.1	−4.1	−7.3	−2.4	−3.0	−2.8	−1.2	−1.0	−0.6	−0.4	−0.4

Sources: Kotz (2003a); CEEP (2004, 2005).

Table 12.3 Money and interest rates

	1994	1995	1997	1999	2000	2001	2002	2003	2004
Broad money growth rate[a]	725.9	144.3	45.6	32.1	37.1	54.3	29.7	27.2	21.7
GDP deflator growth rate	1,239.2	371.0	71.0	39.0	47.3	45.2	45.5	26.7	15.0
Refinancing rate (%)	NA	84.0	48.0	36.0	32.3	26.8	34.5	27.1	18.8
Bank loan rate (%)	100.0	105.0	28.0	30.0	25.7	28.0	32.2	28.1	21.2
Consumer price index	1,065.9	304.6	58.8	29.2	24.9	27.4	27.6	10.3	1.6

Note:
NA = not available.
[a]M3, end-year, percentage change.
Sources: Kotz (2003a); CEEP (2004, 2005); IMF (2005); EIU (2005); EBRD (2005).

as real money supply fell (see Table 12.3). Inflation continued to increase due to a rapidly rising velocity, suggesting an inertial inflationary process. Monetary policy did, however, exert a downward pressure on inflation, which declined sharply in 1995, therefore facilitating macroeconomic stabilization.

As there was a concern that free trade could displace domestic producers not used to international competition, trade liberalization was limited and restrictive trade and foreign exchange policies were kept in place throughout the entire stabilization period. In the mid-1990s, tariffs were simplified and reduced but remained comparatively high. Privatization proceeded slowly, due in part to the lack of buyers. In the absence of a competition law – that was promulgated only toward the end of the 1990s, it would have created private monopolies, with a negative impact on employment and value-added creation.

Uzbekistan attracted a limited amount of foreign direct investment, mostly because of the strong regulation of the economy and, until 2003, the non-convertibility of the soum for current account transactions. In turn, the foreign debt policy was characterized by sharp changes but was – altogether – fairly prudent. Large loans were obtained in the initial years from the World Bank, the European Bank for Construction and Development (EBRD) and the Asian Development Bank to stabilize the economy. Foreign debt continued rising until 1999, but has stabilized since then, mainly due to the improvement of the trade balance (see Table 12.4).

As noted, the soum was introduced only in 1994. It is difficult to establish if the initial soum–dollar parity was competitive. In any case, the soum steadily depreciated over time against the dollar (see Table 12.5) as an inevitable result of high domestic inflation. Since the beginning, however, the parallel exchange rate, in soums per dollar, was higher than the official rate, and the real exchange rate appreciated.

This overall approach to policy making was the object of sharp criticism. In 1993, for instance, the World Bank (1993) noted that in the absence of comprehensive reform, the few scattered and partial reforms that the government had implemented would have no major impact. This muddle-through scenario would imply that none of the sectors was restructured significantly. This failure to adjust

Table 12.4 International transactions of Uzbekistan (US$ millions)

	1993	1994	1995	1997	1999	2000	2001	2002	2003	2004[a]
Merchandise exports	2,877	2,940	3,475	3,695	2,790	2,935	2,740	2,510	3,240	4,050
Merchandise imports	3,255	2,727	3,238	3,767	2,587	2,441	2,554	2,186	2,404	3,020
Trade balance	−378	213	237	−72	203	494	186	324	836	1,030
Current account balance	−429	119	−21	−583	−163	218	−113	122	883	922
Foreign direct investment[b]	48	73	−24	167	121	75	83	65	70	NA
External debt[c]	NA	1,107	1,771	2,594	4,805	4,418	4,279	4,260	4,149	3,884
External debt/total exports (%)	NA	35.9	47.1	64.0	155.4	131.4	133.7	142.7	110.9	84.9
Debt service/total exports (%)	NA	10.5	17.0	9.0	17.8	25.5	26.2	24.6	22.2	17.7

Notes:
NA = not available.
[a] estimates.
[b] net inflows.
[c] value in current US$.

Sources: For 1993–2000: Kotz (2003a), based on the sources cited therein; for 2001–2004: CEEP (2004, 2005); EBRD (2005); World Bank (2003); WDI (2005); EIU (2005).

Table 12.5 Exchange rates of the soum

	1994	1995	1997	1999	2000	2001	2002	2003	2004
Official exchange rate (soum/$)[a]	10.2	29.9	66.4	124.6	236.6	422.9	769.0	971.3	1,019.2
Market exchange rate (soum/$)[a]	NA	40.2	146.6	513.2	782.6	1,095.0	1,321.7	1,064.2	1,058.0
Market to official exchange rate ratio	NA	1.3	2.2	3.7	2.4	1.6	1.4	1.1	1.0
Real index of $/soum	100	220	235	265	185	185	NA	NA	NA

NA = not available.
[a] average of period.

Sources: For 1994–2000: Kotz (2003a) based on the sources cited therein; for 2001–2004: CEEP (2004, 2005); EBRD (2005); EIU (2005).

would lead to a supply-led contraction of the level of economic activity, reduction in savings and investment, and unnecessary hardship on the population in the medium term represented by a decline in consumption per capita of no less than 30 per cent by 1997.

Stabilization outcomes

Despite this and similar predictions, there is no indication that the Uzbek approach to macroeconomic stabilization caused major losses of output or led to some kind of 'macroeconomic populism' (see Chapter 1). Though GDP declined by some 18 per cent between 1991 and 1995, the recession recorded in Uzbekistan was substantially less pronounced than that experienced in the other CARs (see Table 12.1). GDP began to recover in 1996 and continued expanding at an acceptable rate. Heterodox stabilization, therefore, allowed containment of the costs of a transformational recession that turned out to be the shortest and least pronounced of the entire former Soviet Union. In addition, by 1995 macroeconomic balance was almost re-established (see Tables 12.2 and 12.4). The fiscal deficit had declined to a bearable 4.1 per cent and the current account deficit was under

Table 12.6 Energy balance of Uzbekistan (thousand tons)

	1993	1994	1995	1996	1997	1998
Domestic crude oil extraction	3,944	5,517	7,586	7,621	7,891	8,104
Oil and oil product imports	4,762	3,153	250	11	0	0
Domestic consumption of oil products	8,201	7,368	6,961	6,547	6,520	6,934
Net oil and oil product imports	4,258	2,009	−500	−939	−1,190	−948

Note: Domestic consumption of oil and oil products declined by 15 per cent in 1993–1995, which contributed to attaining oil self-sufficiency.

Source: IMF (2000).

control, in part because of the successful efforts at improving oil and wheat self-sufficiency (see Table 12.6). Oil self-sufficiency was achieved in three years by developing, without any foreign direct investment, oil resources that had lain undeveloped in the Soviet era. The programme to increase wheat production was equally successful. From 1.91 million tons in 1991, wheat production rose to 3.22 million tons in 1995 without causing a corresponding decline in the output of other crops. Only inflation remained high despite widespread recourse to price repression. However, while stabilization was broadly achieved, the exchange rate and the interest rate remained perceptibly misaligned while credit was rationed, thus causing a misallocation of resources.

Another undisputable success of Uzbekistan during this period was that fiscal balance was achieved without squeezing pro-poor or pro-growth public expenditures that in 1995 absorbed a remarkable 22.4 per cent of GDP (see Chapter 2). The composition of public outlays reflected a clear concern for alleviating the impact of the transition on the poor and keeping the state machinery running. Such fiscal policy was made possible by the rapid introduction of a new tax regime and tax administration that by the mid-1990s had collected more than 40 per cent of GDP in taxes and social security contributions, compared to 25 per cent to 28 per cent in the rest of the region.

Evaluation of macroeconomic policy

Opinions differ about the factors that explain the success of Uzbekistan in containing the impact of the transitional recession and restarting growth. Three main hypotheses have been put forward to explain such success.

The first hypothesis emphasizes the supposedly favourable initial conditions enjoyed by Uzbekistan at the beginning of the transition. According to this viewpoint – which is based on the results of a regression model developed by the World Bank for 26 transition economies (Zettelmeyer 1999) – the comparatively better performance of Uzbekistan can be attributed to its lower degree of industrialization in relation to other economies in transition, that is, the famous Gershenkron's 'advantage of backwardness', the availability of easily reorientable exports, gold and cotton in particular, and the achievement of self-sufficiency in the energy sector that lessened the balance-of payments-constraint.

The above explanation suffers, however, from a few problems. The first concerns the specification of the above regression model in which a higher liberalization index leads by itself to faster growth. This conclusion is not generally accepted in the empirical and theoretical literature (see for example, Cornia and Popov 2001). Indeed, not only is the construction of such an index highly subjective, but also the relation between such an index and growth is not always positive, depends on the countries and variables included in the analysis, and loses significance when structural factors, wars, revenue generation and other variables are included in the regression. A paper by Alam and Banerji (no date) comparing the transition in Uzbekistan and Kazakhstan from 1991 to 1999 confirms this finding. It shows that while Kazakhstan introduced more radical reforms in the fields of price liberalization and privatization, Uzbekistan did better in terms of GDP growth, the revenue–GDP ratio and the fiscal and current account deficits. In addition, the supposed advantage of Uzbekistan in terms of greater endowment of exportables may explain why Uzbekistan did better than resource-starved Kyrgystan, but not why countries better endowed with exportables, such as Russia or Kazakhstan – both of which followed a more liberal approach – performed worse during the initial part of the transition. Another concern, the supposed 'advantage of backwardness' of Uzbekistan, is ambiguous. While in 1991 the country was less industrialized than Russia or Ukraine, it was more industrialized than all of the other CARs (Pomfret 2001).

A second explanation of the Uzbek success, promoted in the government circles in the early days, is that the comparatively better performance of the country was due to high levels of public investment, particularly in the oil, gas and grains sectors (Kotz 2003b). As shown in Table 12.7, from 1993 to 1995 investment was the most dynamic component of aggregate demand. While, as noted above, investment in energy and grains was highly successful in increasing output and reducing import dependence, this explanation is partial as the period analysed does not cover 1991–1992, the years when output declined less than in the rest of the region while investment stagnated. In addition, the near stabilization of output during the period 1993–1995 was also due to a rapid growth in exports. And, finally, the medium-term effect of such investments varied substantially from sector to sector, depending on their rate of utilization.

The third, and most plausible, explanation focuses on the deliberate policy adopted in an attempt to limit supply shocks. Most macroeconomic policies

Table 12.7 Growth rates of GDP and its components (average annual % rate of change)

	GDP	Consumption	Investment	Government purchases	Exports of goods and services	Imports of goods and services
1993–1995	−2.8	−14.8	24.6	−1.2	16.8	13.9
1996–2001	4.0	7.5	2.4	0.7	−2.2	1.4
2002–2004	5.4	NA	4.5	NA	16.4	8.2

Note:
NA = not available.

Sources: derived from Kotz (2003a); 2002–2004 data derived from CEEP (2002, 2005).

followed during this period – especially fiscal, monetary, subsidies and price control policies – were clearly 'second best' and were in most cases abandoned at a later stage. Yet, under the difficult circumstances of 1991–1995 these unorthodox policies helped contain the impact of 'supply shocks' and subsequent 'demand shocks' that hit other transition economies.

Indeed, during difficult years, 'first best' orthodox policies can generate adverse supply effects leading to what Blanchard and Kremer (1997) call 'disorganization'. First of all, the collapse of Comecon negatively affected those firms depending on inputs from other former socialist countries for their production. While this problem could hardly be avoided, domestic policies supporting, if only temporarily, bilateral supplier–buyer agreements and subsidizing part of the losses incurred by firms helped moderate the impact of the breakdown of socialist trade. Second, rapid shifts in relative prices following comprehensive price liberalization bankrupted some firms without giving them the time to adjust to the new price structures. Lack of gradualism turned out to be a problem for the firms directly affected, as well as for those relying on their inputs for their production processes. This 'domino effect' was particularly acute in the former socialist countries where there were fewer suppliers in each industry than in the West, and where recourse to foreign trade to substitute for domestic supplies was not immediately practicable for lack of foreign exchange and contacts. Third, as noted by Blanchard and Kremer (1997), disorganization may also occur because of the inefficiency of the bargaining process between suppliers and buyers. Under central planning, supplier–buyer relations were highly specific-bilateral rather than competitive-multilateral.

Market liberalization offered suppliers the option to switch between buyers. In the presence of informational asymmetries about the outside options of the suppliers, buyers may not have paid a price that prevented the supplier from switching to new buyers, thus disrupting the old supply chain, a fact that could not be remedied by other suppliers as their number was very limited. For all of these reasons, 'big-bang' liberalization leads to massive shortages of inputs that cause otherwise sound companies to exit the market, and a leftward shift in the aggregate supply curve (see Figure 12.1). These effects have been verified empirically in 10 transition countries. Supply-side disruptions were particularly pronounced in sectors characterized by a complex production process and depending on a large number of suppliers (Blanchard and Kremer 1997; Konings and Walsh 1998). Thus, while orthodox policies may have led rapidly to transparent market prices, a more efficient allocation of resources and property rights regimes in greater consonance with a market system, and while the gradual policies followed in Uzbekistan may have caused allocative inefficiencies and bureaucratic waste, in economies with incomplete markets, asymmetric information and inefficient institutions, rapid liberalization leads to growing disorganization, recessions and macroeconomic imbalances.

Furthermore, it must be noted that a policy that limits supply shocks has the advantage of preventing large falls in aggregate demand for private consumption that takes place if supply shocks are allowed to work through all of their effects. If this is the case, the fall in wages in firms affected by supplier–buyer problems

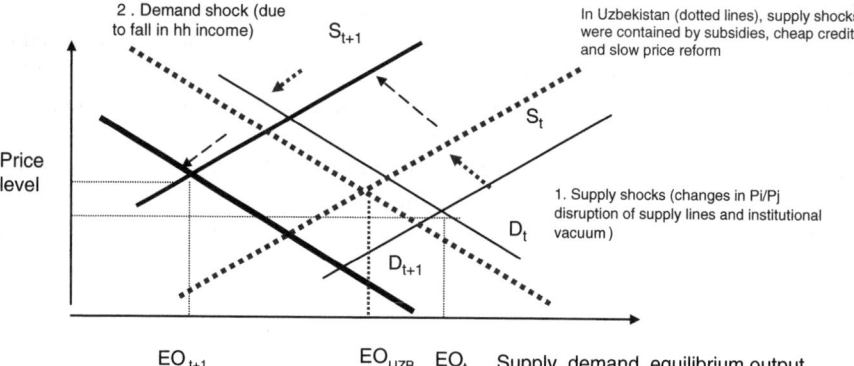

Figure 12.1 Impact of uncontrolled shocks on aggregate supply and demand: general case (solid lines) and case of Uzbekistan (dotted lines)

inevitably causes serious 'demand shocks' (see Figure 12.1), with the final effect of depressing not only the demand for the goods produced by inefficient enterprises, but also the goods produced by efficient ones. In graphical terms, this can be represented by an inward shift in the aggregate demand curve and the determination of lower equilibrium output level EO_{t+1}. The approach to price and trade liberalization and production subsides followed by Uzbekistan thus permitted containing both supply and demand shock and moderating the decline of equilibrium output from EO_t to EO_{UZB}.

Inequality changes during the stabilization phase of 1991–1995

The shocks experienced between 1991 and 1995 led to a severe recession and high levels of inflation that required the introduction of painful, but unavoidable stabilization measures which reduced household income and raised wage and income concentration. In turn, price liberalization led to very high inflation that affected relative prices, wages and incomes in an un-equalizing manner. As a result of these changes, between 1991 and 1995 the overall Gini coefficient rose from 0.26 to 0.31. The decile ratio rose less – from 8.5 to 9.3 – as the budgetary priority assigned to transfers to the poor and the creation in 1994 of a decentralized social assistance system based on *mahallas* (neighbourhood associations) permitted sustaining the income share of the poorest decile. In contrast, the income share of the second through the seventh decile dropped markedly, while that of the top three deciles rose. Thus, the reforms sheltered in part the very poor, rewarded in relative terms a middle-upper class of skilled workers and earners of capital incomes and placed most of the adjustment burden on the middle-lower class. Yet, as the average money income declined during this period by 45.7 per cent, absolute incomes fell for all except the top few percentiles.

Poverty trends during the stabilization phase

The impact of the recession and hyperinflation on the poor was extremely pronounced. Despite Uzbekistan's comparatively smaller contraction of GDP and the introduction of comparatively well-funded social protection measures, the poverty headcount ratio (PHR) rose sharply, as underlined by the results of the first Household Budget Survey (HBS) of 1994–5, which found that 44.5 per cent of the population had an income below the minimum wage, a level close to the poverty line that was subsequently adopted. The sharp rise in poverty experienced during this period was mainly driven by the fall in GDP and a sharp rise in inflation and less by a worsening of income distribution that during this period reached a level similar to that of the market economies.

The import-substitution industrialization of 1996–2002/03

Once the macroeconomic crisis of 1992–95 had been stabilized, more attention was given to the choice of a long-term development strategy. Towards the end of the stabilization phase, the government appeared to consider a shift towards a fairly liberal approach. An International Monetary Fund (IMF) stand-by arrangement was signed in 1994, trade and foreign exchange were partially liberalized in 1995, current account convertibility was planned for 1996 and large loans were obtained from the international financial institutions.

Yet, in 1996, both internal and external conditions deteriorated. Cotton production declined by 15 per cent. At the same time, the world price of cotton fell by 15 per cent. As cotton exports represented half of Uzbekistan's foreign exchange earnings, these two shocks imparted a severe blow to the Uzbek economy. This crisis was instrumental in advising the adoption of a development strategy that prioritized the diversification of the economy through a process of domestic industrialization led by large enterprises on which the government exerted some influence. This approach was possibly encouraged by the success of the earlier import-substitution programme in energy and wheat. In practice, the government responded to the crisis by making a large loan to the cotton sector and changing course on its economic policy. In January 1997, the government formally introduced a multiple exchange rate system along with tighter controls on trade that were intended to support a strategy of import substitution, aimed at reducing its dependence on cotton. The choice of this inward-looking and state-centred approach was also influenced by the preference for what was perceived as a less risky 'muddle-through' approach, combined with a strong preference for a familiar command economy approach, and the desire to retain control over the allocation of resources and, ultimately, political power. Be this as it may, the IMF responded to the shift away from liberalization by suspending its stand-by facility. Large-scale lending by the EBRD and the World Bank were also cancelled. Relations with the IMF were basically put on hold – a situation that lasted until 2004.

External conditions and policy stance

Also during this period, policy making was influenced by a number of exogenous shocks, though these were generally less violent than during 1991–1995. Besides the 1996 cotton crisis mentioned above, the country was also hit by the 'contagion' of the Russian financial crisis of August 1998 and the ensuing 100 per cent devaluation of the rouble, a bad cotton harvest in 1998–1999 and a 25 per cent deterioration in international terms of trade between 1995 and 1999.

The macroeconomic stance was characterized by an effort to attain low budget and current account deficits, low inflation and low debt–GDP ratio through a mixture of orthodox and heterodox measures, including price repression, import controls and licensing. For instance, the government followed an unorthodox policy of gradual money tightening – except for the crisis periods – to avoid weakening the exchange rate, while a low fiscal deficit was achieved through an orthodox tax policy of sustained revenue collection and expenditure cuts. In turn, external balance was achieved mainly through import controls and rationing of foreign exchange, while external indebtedness remained low due to limited borrowing and the de facto closure of the capital account. Altogether, the policy stance was more orthodox than during the prior period.

In contrast, development policy differed substantially from the Washington Consensus model, which assigns a dominant role to a market-led allocation of resources and external integration based on comparative advantages. In the Uzbek's import-substitution industrialization strategy, the state retained a major control on the intersectoral allocation of resources,[2] the domestic market played a main role in absorbing the domestic output and the imports of investment and intermediate goods needed for the modernization of industry were financed by the exports of cotton, gold and other commodities with which the country is richly endowed.

Consistent with this goal, the government adopted the following policies. As noted, in an attempt to offset the cotton shock of 1996, fiscal policy turned sharply expansionary and the budget deficit widened from 4.1 per cent to 7.3 per cent of GDP. However, during the period 1997–1999 the deficit was reduced to a sustainable 2.5 per cent to 3.0 per cent of GDP. After 1999, the fiscal stance became even tighter as the deficit fell to 1 per cent of GDP, and in 2002–2003 it almost reached zero (see Table 12.2). Meanwhile, in an attempt to stimulate economic activity, the tax–GDP ratio was steadily reduced, entailing in this way a reduction of public expenditure on public investments and social transfers.

Likewise, in the aftermath of the 1996 cotton crisis monetary policy became very expansionary (see Table 12.3), as the growth rate of money supply in 1996 exceeded inflation and the ratio of money to GDP soared. This policy was quickly reversed and in subsequent years the government adopted a tight monetary policy, and real money supply trended downwards. Such policy aimed at avoiding putting pressure on the exchange rate, the 'policy tool of choice' for the achievement of the import-substitution industrialization objectives. Yet this policy occasionally resulted in liquidity shortages, leading in some cases to labour unrest and exchange problems. Meanwhile, the previous huge gap between nominal interest rates and inflation rates was reduced, though real interest rates remained negative. Credit policy continued to direct resources to the preferred sectors through the National Bank of Uzbekistan (NBU) and state-controlled commercial banks and so bypassed most small and medium-sized enterprises.

In early 1997, a multiple exchange rate regime was introduced by which currency proceeds from centralized exports of gold and cotton, as well as a 30 per cent to 50 per cent from non-centralized exports, were to be surrendered to the NBU at an official (overvalued) exchange rate. Access to foreign exchange at the (highly favourable) administratively-set official rate was ensured for selected enterprises that import essential inputs and for the servicing of foreign loans guaranteed by the government, while non-priority firms had to compete for limited supplies of foreign exchange at the bank rate – some 12 per cent to 15 per cent less favourable than the official rate – or at the open market rate, which was 1.3 times (in 1997) to 3.7 times (in 1999) more expensive than the official rate (see Table 12.5). The spread between the official and open market rate stabilized in 2000, and in 2002 the spread had fallen to 1.4. Estimates of the real exchange rate of the soum against the US dollar show a constant appreciation through 1999, followed by a decline starting in 2002–2003.

Thus, the exchange rate policy from 1997 to 2002 caused a huge resource transfer from the exporters of gold, cotton and other non-centralized exports to priority importers of capital and intermediate goods and entities that had to service international loans with government guarantees that were authorized to buy dollars at the official or commercial rate. The value of such transfer rose in line with the spread between official, commercial and curb market rate and the foreign exchange surrendering requirements (Rosenberg and de Zeeuw 2000). In addition, by causing an overdevaluation of the curb market rate well beyond the equilibrium level, such a system also caused a transfer of resources from the informal importers to the informal exporters. In 1999, the cotton sector transferred an estimated 6.7 per cent of GDP to the import sector, while gold transferred 5.2 per cent of GDP and decentralized exports 4.4 per cent (see Table 12.8). In addition, assuming a third of the transactions took place on the curb market, in 1999 the transfer from informal importers to informal exporters reached some 8 per cent of GDP (see Chapters 1 and 4 of this volume).

In principle, one can support the idea of using primary product earnings to finance the diversification of the economy, and that a system of direct control over foreign exchange may be the only concrete way to do so. While transparent taxes and subsidies are in theory superior, in practice it might be impossible to tax the exporters and transfer the revenue so obtained to the protected sector. Yet, such system of multiple exchange rates – as well as the overvaluation of the official rate – generated work disincentives in the export sector, a loss of efficiency in the overly protected import sector and a massive transfer of resources from the labour-intensive cooperatives (*shirkats*) and smallholder export agriculture, that is, sectors where over 70 per cent of the poor were located, towards a small, mostly urban-based, capital-intensive sector where poverty rates were low.

In addition, while most prices were freed by 1995, the prices paid by state agencies for the compulsory procurement of wheat and cotton remained well below world prices. From 1995 to 1999, the price paid for state orders of cotton averaged 54 per cent of the world price if the comparison is based on the official exchange rate, or 21 per cent if the comparison is based on the curb market rate (IMF 2000).

Table 12.8 Implicit taxes and subsidies on foreign trade due to multiple exchange rate regime (in percentage of GDP, unless otherwise stated)

	1997	1998	1999
Foreign exchange inflows (implicit taxes)	6.0	10.7	16.2
Centralized exports	5.2	8.1	11.8
Cotton	3.4	5.4	6.7
Gold	1.8	2.7	5.2
Decentralized exports	0.9	2.6	4.4
Foreign exchange outflows (implicit subsidies)	8.5	10.4	15.1
Centralized imports	7.0	6.3	7.1
Other imports	1.5	4.1	8.0
Implicit subsidy provided by the NBU	2.5	−0.3	−1.1
Memo items:			
Surrender requirement on non-centralized exports	30	30	50
Official exchange rate (sum/dollar)	67	95	125
Commercial bank's exchange rate (sum/dollar)	75	105	163
Curb market exchange rate (sum/dollar)	150	270	540
Indicative equilibrium exchange rate[a]	90	151	285

Note:
[a] weighted average of the three exchange rates listed above; the weights are the estimated shares of currency transactions in each of these three markets.

Source: adapted from Rosenberg and de Zeuw (2001).

Thus, pricing policies combined with exchange rate policies to transfer resources out of agriculture and toward the capital-intensive industrial sector – that is, the automotive, chemical and some mechanical industries – which was further protected from foreign competition by means of tariff and non-tariff barriers.

In turn, the foreign debt policy remained prudent. While rising above the 25 per cent alarm threshold in 2000 and 2001 – because of poor export performance and the bunching of short-term borrowings coming due in 2000 and 2001 – the debt servicing ratio remained at an acceptable level (see Table 12.4), in part because of the limited new external debt contracted. In contrast, the reform of the domestic banking and credit sector lagged behind. Though a few private banks were created, the majority of large banks remained in state hands.

Finally, expenditure on social transfers declined from 4 per cent to 2 per cent of GDP between 1996 and 2002. Child allowances suffered the biggest decline, as they were under-indexed for inflation and were targeted only on very poor families. Meanwhile, the funds assigned to social assistance dropped by half relative to GDP.

Macroeconomic and growth performance

Aggregate performance was mixed. On the one side, macroeconomic balance further improved (see Tables 12.2, 12.3 and 12.4). The twin deficits fell to levels lower than those of most industrialized countries, the foreign debt service remained sustainable and in 2002 the NBU started accumulating sizeable reserves (see Table 12.4). Inflation fell further, though it remained above that of the other CARs. All this meant that the import-substitution strategy followed by Uzbekistan since 1997 was not characterized by the 'macroeconomic populism' that featured prominently in other unorthodox policy experiments.

In contrast, while approaching an acceptable 4 per cent a year, aggregate growth during 1996–2003 was systematically lower than the 6 per cent to 7 per cent recorded in the other CARs during the same period. What were the causes of such comparatively slower growth? As noted, the substitution of imported oil and wheat with domestic production was very successful and quickly reduced the country's dependence on price-inelastic imports (see Table 12.6). In both cases, government control over the collective farms and the oil industry enabled it to quickly focus investments and technical assistance on these sectors, and to achieve self-sufficiency. Given the features of Uzbek agriculture, the weakness of its input and credit markets and the large indivisible investments required in the oil sector, it is unlikely that self-sufficiency could have been achieved so quickly had a market-led approach been followed.

In contrast, the import substitution in the industrial sector was – on the whole – less successful and implied a considerable misallocation of foreign exchange, credit and other resources that could have been assigned to the small and medium enterprise sector and agriculture. In addition, in view of the high capital intensity of the protected sector, the price paid in terms of lower employment was substantial (see below). As for microeconomic efficiency, data on capacity utilization, production and exports in the protected sector point to an uneven situation. Utilization rates were high in the oil, chemical and raw material complex, but mediocre or low in most others. For instance, capacity utilization oscillated between 19 per cent and 35 per cent in the automotive sector, and 10 per cent and 30 per cent in the engineering sector.

Inequality trends during the import-substitution-led recovery

Official data suggest that the Gini coefficient of the distribution of gross income rose from 0.31 in 1995 to 0.42 in 1997 and subsequently decreased to 0.39 in 2000. However, a closer look at the data suggests that – as in other economies in transition – rents, interests, property and entrepreneurial incomes are massively underreported and that, therefore, the Gini coefficient of overall inequality is likely to have reached 0.45–0.48 in the early 2000s. This means that inequality rose at a faster pace during the growth years of 1996–2002 than during the recessionary years of 1991–1995.

What explains this rapid inequality increase? To answer this question, the rise in total inequality is decomposed in the change in the degree of inequality of each income component – that is, wages, transfers, sales of agricultural products and capital incomes – and in the increase–decrease in the share of each income component in total income.[3] With this approach, the changes in macroeconomic policies can be more easily linked to the changes in income shares and concentration coefficients.

A first factor leading to higher income disparity was a shift in the structure of household incomes. Indeed, the low-inequality components of total income – that

Table 12.9 Percentage structure of the monetary income of the population, 1991–2004

	1991	1995	1997	1999	2000	2001	2002	2003	2004[a]
Wages and salaries	57.0	44.2	39.4	32.3	28.3	30.4	28.4	28.6	29.6
Social transfers	25.2	16.7	14.8	13.8	14.9	15.5	16.2	15.7	15.8
Income from the sale of agricultural products	9.7	19.2	20.4	25.9	26.1	16.6	18.6	18.0	17.4
Other (interests, rents, profits, mixed entrepreneurial incomes)	8.1	19.9	25.4	28.0	30.7	37.5	36.8	37.7	37.2

Note:
[a] January–November 2004.
Sources: Ministry of Macroeconomics and Statistics (Tashkent); CEEP (2004).

is, social transfers and wages – fell and the high-inequality ones – profits, rents, mixed entrepreneurial incomes and incomes from the sale of agricultural products – rose. The most dramatic shift concerned the collapse of the wage economy and social transfers (see Table 12.9). Meanwhile, the privatization of state assets, the removal of restrictions on private enterprises and the spread of commercial and speculative activities made it possible for those counting on assets, credit and information to start new businesses and acquire considerable profits and rents. All this raised the share of mixed incomes, profits, rents and other capital income that are distributed in a comparatively unequal way.[4] One peculiar aspect of liberalization in Uzbekistan was the rise of incomes from the sale of agricultural products, though this benefited families with access to land, inputs, credits and markets but not those living in remote areas with limited amounts of good quality land and lacking access to credit, inputs and technical assistance.

How about changes in the concentration of the main income components? Information in this field is available only for wages and transfers. While during the stabilization phase of 1991–1995 the Gini coefficient of the wage distribution rose from 0.263 to 0.343, during the subsequent six years it climbed by another eight points to 0.421 (see Table 12.10).[5] During the first period the increase was mainly due to the (somehow unavoidable) fall in the wage share of unskilled workers belonging to the bottom quintile and a symmetric rise in the share of the top quintile following the liberalization of wage formation and a severe recession that increased unemployment, especially among unskilled workers (see Table 12.10). The Gini rise observed between 1995 and 2001 resulted, in contrast, from a gradual but steady erosion of the wage share of the three central quintiles (see Table 12.10).

A common explanation of such increases in wage dispersion is that wage liberalization raised the demand for and wages of people with high human capital and new skills – for example, computer specialists, accountants, highly skilled industrial workers and bankers – who were in short supply. However, more than by skill level, wage inequality increased across industries.[6] The sectors that gained were energy, petrochemicals, mining, metallurgy, construction, automotive, transport and finance. On the other hand, wages in state sectors, such as health, education

Table 12.10 Changes in the distribution of money wages, 1989–2001

	1991	1995	1996	1997	1998	1999	2000	2001
Wage share by quintiles	100	100	100	100	100	100	100	100
First 20%	11.2	6.9	6.5	6.1	6.0	6.5	6.5	6.1
Second 20%	11.8	11.1	10.9	10.6	10.5	9.3	9.3	9.2
Third 20%	15.7	15.4	15.0	14.4	14.3	13.8	13.8	13.8
Fourth 20%	22.7	22.5	21.4	21.6	22.1	21.2	21.4	22.3
Fifth 20%	38.6	44.1	46.2	47.3	47.1	49.1	49.0	48.7
Quintile ratio (5th/1st)	3.4	6.4	7.1	7.8	7.9	7.5	7.6	8.0
Gini coefficient	0.263	0.343	0.360	0.374	0.375	0.420	0.418	0.421

Source: UNICEF (2002).

and culture, declined faster than average due to the wage restraint imposed by the drive to fiscal balance. But the most dramatic decline concerned agricultural wages that by 2000 had fallen by almost two-thirds in real terms compared to 1991. Increasing wage inequality is thus explained by the highly capital-intensive pattern of the import-substitution industrialization that employed comparatively few, relatively highly skilled workers in the protected industrial and energy sector, the compression of agricultural wages in *shirkats* via the dual exchange rate mechanism and various forms of taxation of agriculture. In addition, the concentration of credit on the import-substitution industrialization sector led to a rapid rise in the number of people employed in the capital- and credit-starved informal sector where low wages and unstable labour relations were prevalent.

Changes in the volume and targeting of social transfers – that is, child allowances, unemployment compensation, pensions and other less important benefits – may also have contributed to the rising levels of inequality. The bulk of social assistance expenditures consisted of financial aid to needy families, families with children and subsidies to social services – in other words, expenditures that are well targeted on the poor. However, the increasingly tight fiscal policy that has been followed since 1997 led to a fall in the share of such expenditures in total expenditure and GDP, though their progressively more precise targeting moderated the negative impact of the decline in their volume on income inequality. Outlays on unemployment insurance and active labor market policies remained, in turn, insignificant.[7] In contrast, the country's universal pension system,[8] which provides less equalizing transfers, was less affected and pensions broadly maintained their position in relation to wages. Thus, a decline in highly progressive expenditures and the relative stability of pensions are other factors, though likely not a central ones, that contributed to the rise in income inequality observed since 1995.

Poverty[9] outcomes

With the recovery of 1996–1997, the PHR began to decline. Though data problems do not allow reaching clear-cut conclusions, it appears that the PHR fell from 44.5 per cent in 1994–1995 – a difficult biennium characterized by hyperinflation (see Table 12.3) – to an official rate of 16 per cent in 2000–01. This value was computed on the basis of the HBS, and a poverty line computed according to the methodology developed by the Center for Economic Research based in Tashkent (CER 1997). Such a poverty line, however, is unrealistically low and underestimates the PHR. An assessment based on a common-practice poverty line leads to an estimate of 25 per cent. In turn, the World Bank (2002), which also used a poverty line different from the CER one, projected the 2000–01 PHR at 27.5 per cent.

There is also evidence that this less than satisfactory decline in the PHR fluctuated in line with the yearly changes in income inequality (see Figure 12.2) that, as just noted, followed an upward trend during this period. Indeed, given a constant poverty line (z), the changes over time in the poverty headcount ratio (ΔPHR) can be decomposed into a percentage change in mean income per capita, ($\Delta GDP/c$), a percentage change in its distribution ($\Delta Gini$) and an interaction term (IT):

$$\Delta PHR = -\Delta GDP/c + \Delta Gini + IT$$

Such a relation – in which ΔPHR and $\Delta Gini$ co-variate – is verified in Uzbekistan during the 1996–2002 period (see Figure 12.2) and confirms that any policy aiming at reducing poverty requires that inequality declines or, at least, does not increase.

The pattern of poverty that emerged during this period is linked to the macroeconomic policies that were followed. Indeed, unlike in many developing countries, poverty in Uzbekistan was not closely related to demographic and educational factors, but depended on employment status, activity levels, sector of employment, rural location and access to land, credit and inputs – that is, factors whose allocation was affected by the macroeconomic policies adopted during this

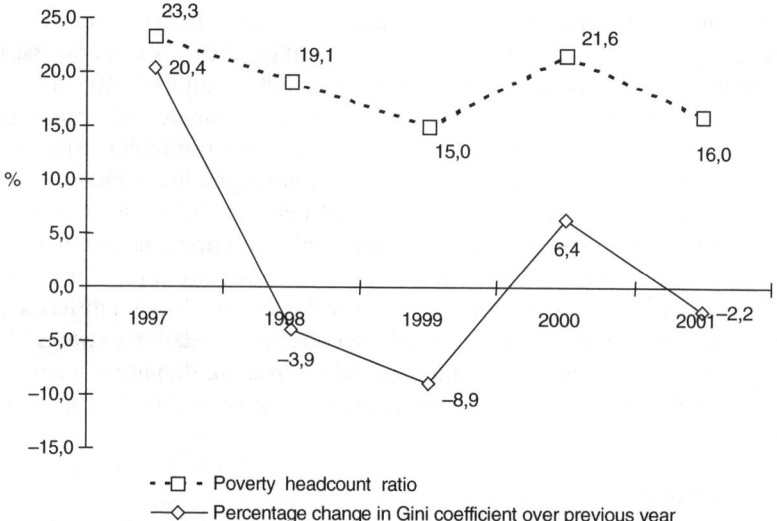

Figure 12.2 Percentage changes in the Gini coefficient and the PHR
Source: CER (1997); World Bank (2002).

Table 12.11 Incidence of poverty by location, employment status and level of education, 2001

Characteristic	Incidence of poverty	Incidence of extreme poverty	Share of population	Share of the poor	Share of extreme poor
Education of household head					
0–4 years	34.0	NA	8.4	10.4	NA
5–9 years	32.4	NA	13.3	15.7	NA
Secondary	31.3	NA	47.4	53.9	NA
Higher education	16.6	NA	14.7	8.9	NA
Location					
Urban	22.5	7.1	37.4	30.6	27.4
Rural	30.5	11.2	62.6	69.4	72.3
National	27.5	9.7	100.0	100.0	100.0

Note:
NA = not available.
Source: World Bank (2002).

period. For instance, while in many developing countries, the level of education of the head of the household is the main predictor of poverty, this was not the case in Uzbekistan, where – as shown in Table 12.11 – families where the head of the household has completed secondary school have a risk of poverty that does not significantly differ from that of families where the head of the household has a lower education. Only families where the head of the household has a university education experienced lower levels of poverty.

Likewise, household size was not significantly greater among the poor than the non-poor (Cornia *et al.* 2003). The same applies to disability, the share of elderly and children in the total number of household members (in the rural sector) and dependence on minimum pensions. However, poor households had three or more children per family and lower activity rates in both rural and urban areas. For instance, while poor rural households had 5.4 dependents for each person with a regular income, for the non-poor the ratio falls to 2.9 (Cornia *et al.* 2003), meaning that poverty was associated to inactivity, part-time employment or underemployment among active adults (see Table 12.12). The unemployment rate (International Labour Organization definition) was only 4 per cent. Under-employment and low wages posed a bigger problem (Cornia *et al.* 2003). Underemployment took the form of part-time work, full-time work at low intensity and productivity, full-time employment with low productivity because of a lack of imported inputs or investments (as in small and medium enterprises), high-intensity jobs that produce goods that fetch artificially low prices or whose wages are paid with long arrears (as in agriculture, in the *shirkats* in particular) or in case of intense competition among job-seekers for few available jobs (as in the informal sector). Much underemployment of one kind or another was in agriculture, where low wages depended on the bad terms of trade of agriculture and low investment and productivity. The problems of underemployment and job

Table 12.12 Employment and incomes of the poor and non-poor

	Rural			Urban		
	All	Poor	Non-poor	All	Poor	Non-poor
Share of able bodied head of household who are:						
employed in the formal sector	46.1	35.6	48.4	52.3	33.7	55.4
employed at wage < 2*minimum wage	38.4	65.1	34.2	14.2	42.3	11.5
employed but affected by wage arrears	23.8	34.0	22.2	7.2	17.4	6.2
with only one job	98.8	99.1	98.8	98.7	99.4	98.6
with more than one job	1.2	0.9	1.2	1.3	0.6	1.4
un/underemployed (working < 10 hours/week)	12.4	15.4	11.9	7.4	11.9	7.0
employed in agriculture	39.7	49.3	38.2	NA	NA	NA

Note:
NA = not available.
Source: Cornia *et al.* (2003) based on HBS 2001 data.

informality were compounded by the low (0.3–0.4) employment elasticity of growth in the capital-intensive sectors.

A dominant feature of Uzbekistan was – and still is – that rural poverty was significantly higher than urban poverty (see Table 12.12). Indeed, some 70 per cent of the poor and 72 per cent of the extreme poor are located in rural areas. The growing 'urban bias' of public policy, which led to the allocation of a disproportionate share of public expenditure, credit, foreign exchange, investment and other scarce resources to urban centres, has aggravated this trend in recent years. And so have the foreign exchange regime and state compulsory procurement in agriculture (see Table 12.8). While not all of the people in rural areas depended on agriculture, some two-thirds of them were engaged in farming. The available evidence (Cornia *et al.* 2003; World Bank 2002) suggests that in 2000–2001 much rural poverty was constituted by *shirkat* workers with low-paying jobs and owning small amounts of land that were not fully used for market production, either for its low quality or because of lack of credit and inputs.

The emergence of a more liberal policy regime since 2002–2003?

There are increasing, if contradictory, signs that the policy package that has evolved since 1996 is being gradually overhauled. No major changes have been reported in the field of macroeconomic balance, which continued to be characterized by low deficits and fairly low inflation and could, in fact, now be characterized as too deflationary. Fiscal and monetary policy (see Tables 12.3 and 12.4) permitted the reduction in the growth in consumer prices to 1.6 per cent in 2004, achieved fiscal balance and generated a huge surplus (13 per cent of GDP) in the current account balance (see Table 12.4).

The main sign of change in policy regime comes from the abandonment of the 'cornerstone policy' of multiple exchange rates and overvaluation of the nominal rate (see Chapter 4). Already in 2002, the official exchange rate was brought closer to the curb market rate (see Table 12.5). In October 2003, it was further devalued and unified at 975 soums per US$, while convertibility for current account transactions was introduced. Since then, the nominal exchange rate has been allowed to depreciate at a rate of 0.5 per cent per month, principally leaving the real exchange rate unchanged. The demand for foreign exchange is, however, indirectly restrained through border controls, import restrictions and a tight money supply – that is, through a high real interest rate and restriction of cash in circulation – that reduce the demand for dollars, so as to avoid putting pressure on the exchange rate and preserving currency reserves. Despite a huge trade surplus – estimated in 2004 at 13 per cent of GDP, import compression remained common (see Table 12.4). Meanwhile, the external debt situation poses no problem, especially in view of the rapid accumulation of reserves. Not all macroeconomic problems have disappeared, however, and major reforms are still needed in the fields of banking, credit and money supply. In particular, real borrowing rates are too high, loans are difficult to obtain and there is a shortage of cash in circulation.

While it is too soon to assess the impact of the recent policy changes, it appears that the unification and devaluation of the nominal exchange rate and the introduction of current account convertibility have generated – *ceteris paribus* – favourable equity and efficiency effects, as they improved the terms of trade of agriculture and enhanced the incentives to expand the domestic output of import substitutes and the production of labour-intensive exports that emerged as the most dynamic component of aggregate demand from 2002 to 2004 (see Table 12.7) and a key source of growth (see Table 12.1).

The positive poverty and inequality effect of the changes in the exchange rate area have, however, been partially offset by structural reforms. For instance, tax policy continued to aim at further reducing the tax–GDP ratio, though this likely had adverse equity effects as it entailed a reduction of highly equalizing social transfers. But the reform that had the greatest impact on poverty concerns was the land privatization programme. Beginning with the Presidential Decree of October 2003, poorly performing *shirkats* were converted into private farms, with the aim of distributing the land of 1,020 *shirkats* – out of a total of 1,840 – to private commercial farms by the end of 2006.[10] By 2005, it had become clear that this process was accelerating, and that the conversion of *shirkats* into private farms will be completed by 2007. The emerging agrarian structure is being characterized by some 200,000 private farms with a modal size of 20–30 hectares claiming some 85 per cent of the sown area, and four million small family plots (*dehkans*) producing high-value foods, including fruits, vegetables and livestock, with an average size of 0.12 hectares, encompassing the entire rural population – and part of the urban one – and claiming 12 per cent of the sown area.

As suggested by Khan (2005), this approach is leading to a situation in which only one out of 14 rural households will receive enough land for private farming, thus exacerbating the already high level of assets and income concentration. This pattern of land distribution is responsible for the reduction in farm employment and the stagnation in rural poverty – despite an increase in agricultural exports – recorded since the implementation of these reforms. Ministry of Labour data suggest that employment per hectare in private farms is about 36 per cent lower than in *shirkats*. In addition, many private farms moved from cotton to wheat production, which is less labour intensive, causing a further reduction in employment of almost 7 per cent. As a result, between 2002 and 2005, many *shirkats* workers were made redundant,[11] contributing to a rise in rural unemployment and a decline in agricultural wages. Most of the people made redundant depend upon casual work, have fallen back on household production using small plots or have migrated under distress to the daily labour market of Tashkent or to Russia or Kazakhstan.

Tentative conclusions

The policies pursued in Uzbekistan since 1995 represent an interesting policy experiment that produced appreciable results – such as a stable macroeconomy, moderate but steady growth, an acceptable capital accumulation, some initial export diversification and so on. Together with the successful heterodox stabilization of 1991–1995, the Uzbek policy model represents an original 'second best' approach that is well suited to the specific conditions of an economy in transition lacking markets and institutions and prone to external shocks. At the same time, this approach has become increasingly suboptimal as it does not permit maximizing output growth and poverty reduction under the present, relatively favourable, circumstances. The exchange rate policy adopted until 2002–2003 imposed excessive distributive and efficiency costs on agriculture and the small and medium enterprise sector, and its abandonment generated perceptible gains. Likewise, the credit and banking policies have penalized small and medium enterprises and the farm sector. As a result, such policies skewed the distribution of income and thus reduced the poverty alleviation elasticity of growth. Indeed, the distributive distortions caused by these policies more than offset the redistributive effects of declining but still comparatively generous, minimum pensions, child allowances and *mahallas*-administered social assistance. Finally, some of the macroeconomic changes introduced since 2002–2003 in part corrected these problems but need to be expanded, while the land privatization programme launched in recent years generated considerable unemployment, worsened the distribution of assets and income and pushed rural poverty upward.

This criticism does not entail a wholesale abandonment of the import-substitution industrialization experiment initiated in 1996 or of the land privatization programme started in 2003. But it requires a revision of the sectors and instruments of the import-substitution policy, a shift to a strategy that combines protection of some domestically-oriented infant industries with the promotion of exports in sectors with considerable potential, as well as a more equitable distribution of land.

Notes

1 The author would like to thank Uktam Abdurakhmanov, Bahkodur Eshonov, Sheila Marnie, Ulugbek Olimov, C.P. Chandrashekar and participants in the United Nations Research Institute for Social Development meeting on 'Pro-poor Macroeconomics' in

Florence on 24–5 February 2005 for providing comments or helping to obtain the data included in this study. The usual caveats apply.
2   The government retained significant control over many enterprises, whether public or privatized, and over cotton and grain production. In all of these cases, the government developed 'indicative plans' that in many instances served as output targets.
3   At any point in time, the Gini coefficient can be decomposed as follows:

$$G_t = \sum s_{it} C_{it}$$

where C_{it} is the concentration coefficient of the i-th income component and s_i its share in total income – the concentration coefficient C_{it} is similar to the Gini index except that the ranking of individuals is by the total income and not the i-th income components. As a result, C_{it} can rank between 1 and -1). Changes over time in Gini coefficient can therefore be decomposed: $\Delta G = G_{t+n} - G_t = \sum \Delta s_i C_i + \sum \Delta C_i s_i + \sum \Delta s_i \Delta C_i$ where Δs_i and ΔC_i refer to changes of the income shares and concentration coefficients over the period $t - t + n$. In practice, this decomposition of the overall increase in income inequality requires knowledge of the shares of each type of income and the concentration coefficients for both the initial and final year.
4   To give an idea of the different degree of inequality of the distribution of the various income components, it suffices to note that in 2000 the concentration coefficient (or 'quasi-Gini') of their distributions ranked by total household income per capita was -0.028 for poor relief and aid to families with children administered by the *mahallas*, 0.208 for income in kind from food self-consumption, 0.367 for pensions, 0.386 for wages and salaries, 0.449 for entrepreneurial (mixed) income, 0.523 for income from the sale of farm products, 0.546 for private transfers and 0.548 for property and other incomes.
5   A Gini coefficient of the wage distribution of 0.42 is rather high and denotes an inadequate functioning of the labour market. For instance, in the transition economies of Central Europe the Gini coefficient of the wage distribution ranged between 0.28 and 0.30 in 1995. Only Russia and Ukraine had coefficients in the 0.44–0.46 region (Cornia 1996).
6   The ratio of the *maximum* to *minimum* wage by sector rose from 2.76 in 1995 to 4.36 in 2001.
7   In 2000, there were only 42,000 registered unemployed (or 0.4 per cent of the labour force). The reason for such a low rate is that the value of the unemployment subsidy is insignificant, while the related transaction costs are high.
8   Men retire at 60 and women at 55. Pensions are paid by a pension fund, which has an independent status from the national budget that, however, covers its shortfall in case of deficit.
9   Prior to 1994, the country did not conduct an HBS based on a random sample. Income inequality and poverty were estimated on the basis of a (non-representative) Soviet-style HBS of 4,000 households drawn from the employed population of different sectors. This type of survey, which does not include those employed in the growing informal sector or who opted for voluntary inactivity, have continued to be undertaken. In addition, in 1994, 20,000 randomly selected families were surveyed by the State Statistical Commission. In turn, in 2000–2001 and 2003, HBSs were carried out with the technical assistance of the World Bank. The 2003 data, however, are not yet available.

The country does not have an officially sanctioned poverty line. In 1997, a poverty line equal to the per capita cost of a basic food basket ensuring an energy level of 2,100 calories and a few basic non-food consumption items was established by CER (CER 1997). Such an approach takes into account the fact that most families own the house where they live and have almost free access to education and primary medical services. In 2001, this unofficial poverty line was equal to 2,917 soums or almost $7 per person per month, based on the official exchange rate of 423 soums to the US$.
10 This period also witnessed a reduction in state procurement quotas for cotton and wheat and the abolition of all other products.
11 For instance, 75,000 agricultural workers were made redundant in Kashkadaria, one of Uzbekistan's 14 regions.

References

Alam, A. and A. Banerji. No date. *Uzbekistan and Kazakhstan: A Tale of Two Transition Paths?* Unpublished manuscript. Washington DC: World Bank.

Blanchard, O. and M. Kremer. 1997. 'Disorganisation'. *The Quarterly Journal of Economics*, 112(4) (November), 1091–1126.

Center for Effective Economic Policy (CEEP). 2002, 2004, 2005. 'Uzbekistan Economy'. *Statistical and Analytical Review*, Annual Issue. Tashkent: CEEP.

Centre for Economic Research (CER). 1997. *Methodological Approaches to Determination of Poverty Threshold in Uzbekistan*. Tashkent: CER.

Cornia, G.A. 1996. 'Transition and Income Distribution: Theory, Evidence and Initial Interpretation'. *WIDER Research in Progress*, No. 1. Helsinki: UNU/WIDER.

Cornia, G.A. and V. Popov. 2001. *Transition and Institutions: The Experience of the Gradual and Late Reformers*. Oxford: Oxford University Press.

Cornia, G.A., N. Zavikhulla, A. Tuktarov and Y. Abduganieva. 2003. 'Trends in Poverty, Inequality and Human Deprivation'. In United Nations Development Programme (ed.), *Linking Macroeconomic Policies to Poverty Reduction*. Tashkent: UNDP.

Economist Intelligence Unit (EIU). 2005. *Country Report: Uzbekistan*. London: EIU, February.

European Bank for Construction and Development (EBRD). 2005. *Strategy for Uzbekistan*. London: EBRD.

Griffin, K. 1996. *Poverty in Uzbekistan*. Tashkent: United Nations Development Programme.

International Monetary Final (IMF). 2000. *Republic of Uzbekistan: Recent Economic Development*. IMF, Washington, DC.

International Monetary Fund (IMF). 2005. *Republic of Uzbekistan: Interim Poverty Reduction Strategy Paper*. Country Report No. 05/160. Washington, DC: IMF, May.

Khan, A.R. 2005. *Land System, Agriculture and Poverty in Uzbekistan*. Mimeo. Tashkent: Centre for Economic Research.

Konings, J. and P.P. Walsh. 1998. *Disorganisation in the Transition Process: Firm Level Evidence from the Ukraine*. LICOS Discussion Paper NO. 71/1998. Leuven: LICOS Centre for Transition Economics, Katholieke Universiteit Leuven.

Kotz, D.M. 2003a. 'The Record of Economic Transition in Uzbekistan'. Chapter 1, United Nations Development Programme report *Macroeconomics and Poverty in Uzbekistan*. Tashkent: UNDP.

Kotz, D. M. 2003b. 'Sources and Features of the "Uzbek Growth Puzzle". Chapter 2, United Nations Development Programme report *Macroeconomics and Poverty in Uzbekistan*. Tashkent: UNDP.

Pomfret, R. 2001. 'Reform Paths in Central Asian Transition Economies'. In G.A. Cornia and V. Popov (eds), *Transition and Institutions: The Experience of the Late and Gradualist Countries*. Oxford: Oxford University Press.

Rosenberg, C.B. and M. de Zeeuw. 2000. *Welfare Effects of Uzbekistan's Foreign Exchange Regime*. International Monetary Fund Policy Working Paper WP/00/61. Washington, DC: IMF.

United Nations Children's Programme (UNICEF). 2002. *The Regional Transition Report*. State Department of Statistics of the Republic of Uzbekistan. Florence: Innocenti Research Centre.

World Bank. 1993. *Uzbekistan: An Agenda for Economic Reform*. Washington, DC: World Bank.

World Bank. 2002. *Living Standards Assessment in Uzbekistan*. Tashkent: World Bank.

World Bank. 2003. *Uzbekistan Country Economic Memorandum*. Report No. 25625-UZ, Tashkent: World Bank.

Zettelmeyer, J. 1999. *The Uzbek Growth Puzzle*. International Monetary Fund staff papers, 46 (3) Washington, DC: IMF.

13
Macroeconomic Policy and Pro-Poor Growth in a Dualistic Economy: The Case of Bolivia

Stephan Klasen[1]

Introduction

With the adoption of the Millenium Development Goals, poverty reduction has been placed at the centre of international policy debates on economic development. The ability to achieve rapid poverty reduction critically depends upon the extent of economic growth and on its impact on poverty. This, in turn, depends on initial inequality and changes in inequality during the growth process (Klasen 2005). As can be shown analytically, the highest poverty impact will occur in an environment of low initial inequality and pro-poor distributional changes (World Bank 2000; Bourguignon 2003). As a result of these findings, the term 'pro-poor growth' (PPG) has been coined to describe growth that achieves high rates of poverty reduction (Klasen 2004; AfD *et al.* 2005).

The policy implications of aiming for PPG have been discussed for some time (see Klasen 2004) and are the subject of a recently concluded 14-country case study project called Operationalising Pro-Poor Growth co-ordinated by several bilateral donors and the World Bank (AfD *et al.* 2005). While many policies are likely to affect the ability of a country to achieve PPG, the focus of this chapter is narrower. It investigates the ability of macroeconomic policy to foster or hinder PPG. After a general discussion, the chapter focuses on Bolivia to illustrate in which ways macroeconomic policies adopted in that country have affected PPG in this country over the past 20 years. In this sense, the analysis draws on selected findings from the study on Bolivia prepared for the Operationalising Pro-Poor Growth project (see Klasen *et al.* 2004 for more details), but also places this in a larger context of the debates on PPG.

The chapter is organized as follows. The first section discusses the concept of PPG and the findings of the recent debate about the potential impact of macro policy. The next section then discusses the recent trends in growth and poverty reduction in Bolivia. The following sections discuss macro policies and link them to the results of a Computable General Equilibrium (CGE) analysis on the impact of macroeconomic policies on PPG, both to understand the past record of the link as well as to analyse forward-looking policy options. The last section summarizes the main results and suggests policy conclusions for the scope of macro policy to promote PPG in Bolivia and elsewhere.

PPG and macro policy: concepts and evidence

Before discussing the role of macro policy in PPG, it is useful to briefly discuss the concept of PPG. This is a large topic, which will only be summarized briefly here.[2] While some authors see PPG as growth that is accompanied with inequality reduction (see Kakwani and Pernia 2000), others (Ravallion and Chen 2003) talk of PPG when aggregate growth yields some positive benefits to the poor, independently of what happens to inequality. While these are significant differences on a very serious issue, the two positions can be reconciled from a policy perspective if PPG is considered as a rate rather than as a state, that is, if the aim is to maximize income growth of the poor (see Klasen 2005; AfD et al. 2005). If this position is taken, it is clear that high average growth as well as pro-poor distributional change could both contribute to raising income growth of the poor. Also, this way of framing the issue clarifies that there can be trade-offs or win–win situations between growth and changes in inequality that will affect the income growth of the poor. As is shown below, there can indeed be win–win situations as well as trade-offs when examining particular macro policies and their impact on PPG.

There is a very large literature that has examined the impact of macro policy on growth or distributional change, much of which was generated from the debates about structural adjustment and its ability to foster growth and poverty reduction. While some of the findings of this literature remain contentious, Klasen (2004) attempted to summarize what we have learned from these debates about macroeconomic policy and its effects on PPG and argued that a core policy consensus has emerged on a number of macro issues, while there are also intense remaining debates and/or insufficient research on particular aspects. Table 13.1 presents the results of this consensus as well as the areas of debate as they pertain to macroeconomic policy (see also Chapter 1). This general debate sets the stage for an analysis of macroeconomic policy issues in Bolivia, a subject to which this chapter now turns.

Macroeconomic developments, structural reforms and PPG in Bolivia

Bolivia is a large land-locked country with low population density, difficult terrain and a poorly developed transport and communications infrastructure. It is characterized by great economic and social inequalities with deep historical roots. Apart from a Spanish-speaking minority consisting of people of Spanish and mixed descent that has dominated political and social affairs since its independence was achieved in the early nineteenth century, the majority is constituted of a heterogeneous indigenous population living in different parts of the country.

Table 13.1 Macroeconomic policies to promote PPG: research findings, consensus policies and remaining debates

Policy issue	Research finding	Agreed policy implication	Areas of debate
Macro-economic stability	Macroeconomic stability is a critical (though not sufficient) condition for PPG; the poor are hurt particularly hard by high inflation and high macroeconomic volatility.	Monetary and exchange rate policy should aim for low inflation and competitive exchange rates; fiscal policy should aim for low budget deficits.	Should exchange rate policy principally be used to fight inflation? How quickly should stabilization occur in order to avoid a recession?
Monetary and exchange rate policy	Overvalued exchange rates and high black market premia hurt economic growth and tend to be anti-poor.	A competitive and possibly undervalued exchange rate is a critical ingredient to ensure macro stability; government intervention necessary to manage capital inflows.	Fixed or floating rates? What is the role of capital controls to manage inflows and outflows during crises? Should undervaluation be a goal?
Fiscal stance	Large budget deficits hurt growth and are unsustainable. Rapid expenditure cuts can often undermine delivery and quality of critical services such as health and education and thus hurt the poor.	Governments should aim for moderate budget deficits through broadening of the tax base and, if necessary, a refocusing of expenditures (especially cuts in subsidies to state-owned enterprises and unproductive sectors). During crises, cutting expenditures rapidly is neither feasible nor desirable.	Mix of tax increases, tax broadening and expenditure cuts?
Financial sector	Severe financial repression hurts savings and promotes capital flight. Poorly sequenced financial sector reforms can be counter-productive and destabilizing.	Capital account and financial sector reform should be phased in slowly, be implemented only if macro stability has been achieved and be accompanied by tight regulation, competition policies, and policies to improve access of the poor.	Should the state allocate credit to priority sectors? Should the state be involved in providing credit for the poor? What policies should be adopted to mobilize domestic savings?
Trade policy	An anti-export bias hurts growth and the poor; import liberalization can be anti-poor and not sufficient to generate supply response. Diversification is essential for long-term growth.	Focus should be on removal of anti-export bias (for example, competitive exchange rate and duty draw-back schemes); should provide of infrastructure to assist exports, especially for export diversification.	Is more activist state intervention – for example, export subsidies and subsidized credit for exporters – needed to boost non-traditional exports?

Source: Adapted from Klasen (2004).

Until the revolutionary government of Victor Paz Estenssoro was installed in 1952, most indigenous people lived in serf-like arrangements in rural areas. The agrarian reform in 1953 freed the peasants in the highlands and gave them access to land. Since then, population pressure has led to increasingly smaller landholdings and growing landlessness. In other parts of the country, particularly the lowlands, large estates dedicated to commercial farming predominate. As a result, the Gini coefficient of land inequality stood at 0.768 in 1989, indicating, as in other Latin American countries, a high degree of land concentration (Deininger and Squire 1998). The other main sources of income in the highlands, tin and silver mining, became progressively less lucrative and were sharply curtailed in the 1980s. Instead, the production and exports of coca leaves became a major source of income in some highlands and valley areas and the ebb and flow of coca eradication efforts have played a significant role in the income sources of poor rural households in these areas. In contrast, the previously largely unpopulated lowlands surrounding Santa Cruz have become the focus of settlement and growth in recent decades, fuelled by large-scale farming and the discovery of important oil and gas deposits.

Politically, Bolivia oscillated between military dictatorships and civilian rule between the 1950s and the early 1980s when the latest military government was replaced with a democratic one, and democracy has persisted ever since. But Bolivia's democracy remains fragile with, until recently, little indigenous representation, and a significant extra-parliamentary opposition that has ousted two governments in the last three years.

Regarding economic policies, Bolivia had pursued a state-led import-substitution policy until the 1980s, which was largely financed through the export of tin and silver. The first democratic government under Hernán Siles-Zuazo (1982–1985) faced a very difficult internal (drought, social unrest) and external environment (debt crisis, global recession and collapse of tin prices in 1985) and allowed hyperinflation to develop, which led to a collapse of the government in 1985. Paz Estenssoro took over and first undertook a strict stabilization plan, which ended hyperinflation and brought back internal and external stability (Sachs and Larraín 1998).

In addition, the Paz Estenssoro government began implementing a Nueva Política Económica comprising a wide range of World Bank and International Monetary Fund (IMF)-supported structural reforms. These reforms were continued by most successive governments so that Bolivia stands out as having undertaken more structural reforms inspired by the so-called 'Washington Consensus' than most other developing countries (Rodrik 2003; Lora 2001). These reforms included product market deregulation, domestic and external capital market deregulation, fiscal reforms involving the simplification and broadening of the tax structure, expenditure cuts on the public service and parastatals, while expanding social sector spending, trade liberalization, liberalization of the foreign direct investment (FDI) regime and the restructuring, closure and 'capitalization' of the large state-owned companies.[3] In contrast, labour market reforms were minor and consisted only of reducing government intervention in wage setting and cutting wages and benefits for public sector employees.

In several respects, Bolivia's structural reforms produced positive outcomes. Macroeconomic stability was achieved and low inflation, low fiscal deficits and a relatively stable exchange rate were maintained throughout this period. The fiscal reforms, combined with the reform of the public sector, ensured that the fiscal situation improved dramatically during the 1990s (see Table 13.2). Exports and economic performance also improved and Bolivia grew at around 4 per cent per year from 1990 to 1998, though in per capita terms output grew at only 1.5 per cent. This relatively positive performance was aided by a favourable external environment characterized by a high rate of growth among Bolivia's main trading partners, the expansion of natural resource exports and a surge in FDI that accompanied the capitalization process. The memories of the 1985 hyperinflation, an open capital account and the

Table 13.2 Basic economic indicators for Bolivia

	1985–1989	1989–1994	1994–1999	1999–2002
Economic indicators				
Real GDP growth	1.62	4.08	3.93	2.18
Agriculture excluding mining	0.33	4.10	2.08	2.38
Mining	−0.16	4.07	2.36	2.80
Services excluding public administration	1.21	4.94	6.93	1.47
Public administration	−0.98	1.88	3.93	2.44
Industry/manufacturing	2.02	4.40	3.80	1.94
Export growth (goods and services)	15.56	4.08	1.54	0.02
Export growth (merchandise)	5.04	5.89	−0.89	0.09
Export growth (mineral and hydrocarbon)	−0.81	−2.49	−2.81	0.18
Average share of mineral and hydrocarbon exports to GDP	13.68	10.17	7.57	7.65
Average share of agricultural exports to GDP	2.14	3.87	5.16	5.28
Current account deficit	−5.28	−3.53	−6.05	−4.38
Budget balance	−0.38	−1.92	−2.33	−5.06
Inflation	2,414.35	13.41	7.43	3.10
Savings rate (domestic)	10.91	9.05	10.53	7.52
Investment rate	14.42	15.15	18.70	15.09

Source: World Bank (2003); UDAPE (various issues); INE (various issues).

uncertainty typical of a small open economy led to an increasing dollarization of the economy, which permeates the financial system and significantly limits the possibility of conducting an active monetary and exchange rate policy. There were few attempts to combat dollarization, which remains extremely high, as 77 per cent of deposits and 97 per cent of loans are denominated in dollars (Schweickert *et al.* 2005). In fact, Bolivia is probably the most dollarized economy among those countries that stopped short of adopting the US dollar as legal tender (IMF 2003).

In addition, a range of structural weaknesses remain, including a high reliance on the exports of primary commodities such as minerals, hydrocarbons and cash crops, weak institutions (weak protection of property rights, high corruption, contraband economy, high regulatory burden for start-ups, high informality of the economy) (Kaufman *et al.* 2003; World Bank 2004b) and a persistently low domestic savings rate (see Table 13.2), which makes Bolivia heavily dependent on capital inflows to finance investment.

Since 1998, growth decelerated to an average of only about 1.5 per cent per year and became negative in per capita terms. The main causes for this slowdown were a series of external shocks, including the strong devaluations and recessions in Argentina and Brazil in 1999 and 2002. This led to a sharp real appreciation of the Boliviano that was fixed to the US dollar. The monetary authorities did little to combat such phenomenon due to the risks entailed by devaluation in a dollarized economy, and instead stuck to their policy of allowing only small devaluations against the dollar, by some 8 per cent in 2001, falling to 4 per cent in 2002. As a result, the economy slowed down considerably, credit contracted sharply as the financial sector experienced a build-up of non-performing loans. As a result of this recession and of costly amendments to the pension reforms, the budget deficit soared to an unsustainable level, making even more uncertain an already explosive political and social situation (World Bank 2004a). The financing of this soaring budget deficit through domestic and international borrowing has placed Bolivia in an increasingly vulnerable situation where a rising share of government spending must be allocated to debt-service payments, thereby wiping out some of the gains realized with the heavily indebted poor countries (HIPC) debt relief programme (World Bank 2004a).

The most important results regarding poverty and inequality are summarized in Table 13.3. There is a steep gradient in poverty levels between capital cities, towns and rural areas, with poverty being much higher in the latter. As far as the poverty rate is concerned, the differential between capital cities and rural areas grew over time – from about 25 percentage points in 1989 to nearly 29 in 2002. This is not true, however, when we consider the poverty gap, for which the differences

Table 13.3 Poverty and inequality trends using the moderate poverty line[a]

	1989		1994		1999		2002
	Observed	Simulated	Observed	Simulated	Observed	Simulated	Observed
Poverty headcount ratio							
Capital cities[b]	67.2	64.8	59.5	57.4	51.1	48.1	55.1
Towns	ND[c]	81.1	ND	75.1	69.1	64.2	67.7
Rural areas	ND	89.7	ND	89.6	83.4	79.1	83.8
Total	ND	76.9	ND	72.4	65.2	60.3	67.2
Poverty gap							
Capital cities[b]	32.9	32.9	25.7	25.3	21.0	21.3	24.4
Towns	ND	51.3	ND	44.7	34.7	33.6	32.9
Rural areas	ND	58.3	ND	60.9	47.7	43.1	44.9
Total	ND	45.5	ND	41.9	32.5	30.1	32.9
Gini Coefficient							
Capital cities[b]	0.505	0.497	0.481	0.455	0.480	0.488	0.540
Towns	ND	0.547	ND	0.537	0.455	0.500	0.452
Rural areas	ND	0.475	ND	0.497	0.423	0.443	0.421
Total	ND	0.555	ND	0.555	0.525	0.531	0.551

Notes:
[a]The moderate poverty line is, in line with standard practice in Bolivia, applied to income in urban areas and consumption in rural areas (as income data are considered not to be reliable there and consumption data are not available for the urban household surveys prior to 1997). While the extreme poverty line in Bolivia is only based on ensuring adequate nutrition, the moderate poverty line also makes allowance for some non-food expenditures. The moderate poverty line stood at about $40 per capita per month, the extreme poverty line at about $20. For details about the poverty lines and the incidence of extreme poverty line, see Klasen et al. (2004).
[b]Capital cities refer to the nine departmental capitals and El Alto (the city adjacent to La Paz).
[c]ND = no data. Due to the absence of nationally representative and comparable household surveys prior to 1999, the results for the years before 1999 are based on a data-matching exercise between urban household surveys and nationally representative Demographic and Health Surveys (Klasen et al. 2004).

Source: Author's calculations.

between capital cities, towns and rural areas has somewhat narrowed. This suggests that the very poor were able to make some gains in the 1990s while rural dwellers close to the poverty line did not benefit as much. Third, there is a clear poverty trend in capital cities, which closely mirrors macroeconomic conditions. Thus, poverty declines considerably between 1989 and 1999 and increases again between 1999 and 2002. In contrast, in towns and rural areas the poverty dynamics is not as closely related to macroeconomic developments. In particular, there is no poverty reduction at all in rural areas between 1989 and 1994, then poverty fell considerably between 1994 and 1999, while between 1999 and 2002 the poverty headcount ratio stagnated and the poverty gap recorded a slight reduction. Sensitivity analyses (not shown, see Klasen *et al.* 2004) generally confirm this picture, but suggest that poverty reduction in rural areas was even lower.

The trends in income inequality closely follow that of poverty, but with some additional features. In particular, the sharp increase in inequality in capital cities between 1999 and 2002 is noteworthy. In other areas, inequality seems to have fallen, thereby somewhat offsetting the dramatic worsening of inequality in capital cities. Overall, the Gini in 2002 is similar to 1989. In contrast, the much poorer rural poor have been more insulated from changes in the overall economic environment and their poverty trends have followed another logic.

A way to examine the linkages between growth, inequality and poverty is the Ravallion measure of Pro-poor Growth, which calculates the average growth rates of the population quantiles that were poor in the initial period (Ravallion and Chen 2003). The growth incidence curve derived from this analysis is shown for the period 1989–2002 (see Figure 13.1), while data for sub-periods are available in Klasen *et al.* (2004).

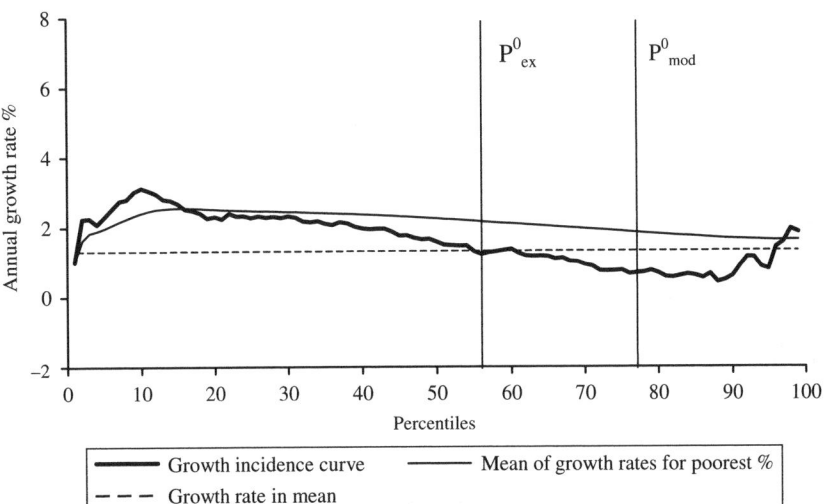

Figure 13.1 Growth incidence curve for Bolivia, 1989–2002
Source: Ravallion and Chen (2003).

Figure 13.1 shows that, for the entire country and period, quantile growth rates were positive for all groups, and moderately downward sloping from the 10th to the 90th percentile suggesting that, on the whole, the poor gained proportionately more from growth than the rich. This is not true below the 10th percentile and above the 90th percentile suggesting that the extremely poor did not benefit as much and that the very rich benefited more from growth.[4] Matters are different when different parts of the country are considered. In departmental capitals and in El Alto, growth over the period was anti-poor with the poor gaining less than the rich – particularly because of the influence of the 1999–2002 period – while it was strongly pro-poor in towns and moderately pro-poor in rural areas.

Table 13.4 presents for different sub-periods the annual rates of PPG provided for the entire 1989–2002 period in Figure 13.1. Overall, there was PPG of 1.9 per cent to 2.2 per cent per year between 1989 and 2002, which was mostly due to high PPG in towns and some PPG in rural areas, while the rate of PPG in capital cities was negligible.

Table 13.4 Annual growth rates per capita

	1989–2002	1989–1999	1999–2002
		Total Bolivia	
Growth rate in the mean	1.41	2.23	−1.29
Mean of growth rates for:			
Extremely poor	2.16	3.39	−0.88
Moderately poor	1.85	3.21	−2.22
All	1.67	2.98	−2.56
		Departmental capitals	
Growth rate in the mean	1.19	2.01	−1.51
Mean of growth rates for:			
Extremely poor	0.44	2.56	−6.30
Moderately poor	0.48	2.58	−6.44
All	0.69	2.50	−5.01
		Other urban areas	
Growth rate in the mean	1.76	2.89	−1.90
Mean of growth rates for:			
Extremely poor	4.70	6.23	0.48
Moderately poor	4.22	5.80	−0.22
All	3.75	5.25	−1.03
		Rural areas	
Growth rate in the mean	0.87	0.94	0.59
Mean of growth rates for:			
Extremely poor	2.07	2.31	1.86
Moderately poor	1.86	2.18	0.99
All	1.73	1.99	0.86

Notes: Growth rates use the actually observed levels of income/expenditure where available (in capital cities throughout and elsewhere from 1999 onwards). For a sensitivity analysis of such results, see Klasen *et al.* (2004), which mainly shows that growth and PPG in rural areas was smaller.

Source: Author's calculations.

It is useful to consider sub-periods. Between 1989 and 1999, there was a considerable amount of PPG in total Bolivia, in other urban areas and in rural areas regardless of the poverty line. In addition, the rate of PPG exceeded the growth rate in the mean, suggesting that growth was accompanied by falling inequality. The particularly high growth rate across Bolivia as a whole (2.23 per cent) was due to growth in the three areas plus a shift in the composition of the population from the poorer rural areas to the richer urban areas. In contrast, between 1999 and 2002 there was a strongly anti-poor contraction in capital cities, wiping out most of the gains the urban poor had made in the previous 10 years. In the other urban areas, the contraction was not particularly anti-poor so that the poor had roughly stagnant incomes. In rural areas, incomes continued to rise, although slowly, and growth continued to be somewhat higher for the poor than the non-poor. Given that the rural poor predominate among the poor, overall growth was only slightly anti-poor between 1999 and 2002, and this finding is sensitive to the choice of the poverty line.

With the exception of the strongly anti-poor growth in capital cities in recent years, it appears that growth has been quite pro-poor throughout most of the last 15 years, and particularly so in towns and moderately so in rural areas. While these results appear inconsistent with the low poverty reduction in rural areas shown in Table 13.3, they are entirely consistent when it is noted that the depth of poverty in rural areas is so large that even considerable PPG does not lift many of the poor above the poverty line, though it does reduce the poverty gap, as indeed happened particularly between 1994 and 1999. Thus, the problem of Bolivia's poverty is not so much that growth in the 1990s has been biased against the poor, but that overall growth has not been very high and that the initial inequality was so large that the poor remained poor despite some improvements in incomes. It would probably have taken another decade of such growth to make serious inroads into poverty, particularly in rural areas. Unfortunately, that did not happen. Thus, with the type of growth experienced since 1999, rural poverty will not change much in the future, while urban poverty would sharply increase.

Before discussing the determinants of PPG, it is useful to briefly discuss the structure of gross domestic product (GDP) and the sources of overall growth in Bolivia during the past 15 years. In 2002, agriculture made up about 14 per cent of GDP, half of which is subsistence agriculture where many of the rural poor live. Another 10 per cent is generated by mining, oil, and gas and only about 16 per cent by manufacturing. Most of this manufacturing consists of food and raw materials processing, with hardly any light or heavy industry present in the country. The remainder of GDP consists of services of various kinds. In contrast to its low contribution to GDP, agriculture employs 60 per cent of the workforce, sales employs another 10 per cent, while manufacturing, oil and gas and high-value services employ only a small fraction of the workforce. Thus, Bolivia is a highly dualistic economy with most employment in low value-added agriculture and the small-scale service sector and little employment in manufacturing and the modern resource sector.

Overall growth between 1989 and 1999 was mainly driven by rapid growth in commercial agriculture, oil and gas production – and associated construction and production in the electricity, gas and water sector, some small-scale food processing industries and some services. In contrast, subsistence agriculture, mining, hotels and restaurants and public administration grew less than proportionately. Between 1999 and 2002, virtually all sectors grew at a slower rate, with the exception of oil and gas, which expanded production due to enhanced exports to Brazil. It should also be noted that the oil, gas and mineral sectors only account for about 10 per cent of Bolivia's GDP and less than one per cent of its employment, but more than 40 per cent of Bolivia's exports, so that the importance of these sectors for Bolivia's external position is much larger than its GDP share. Thus, Bolivia has a highly dualistic economy, with the most dynamic sectors being the oil and gas sector, industrial agriculture – concentrated in the lowlands – and some high-value service sectors, which are also highly capital-intensive with few linkages to the poor.

Clearly, Bolivia's economy suffers from considerable segmentation, with the poor being largely excluded from the income-generating and growth processes. This segmentation primarily reflects a significant urban–rural divide, an ethnic divide and a segmentation of the economy into a subsistence agriculture in the highlands and a resource-based economy in the valleys and lowlands. The urban–rural divide is largely due to a strong educational inequality, an uneven population distribution, poor infrastructure and a highly segmented urban formal labour market with few opportunities for outsiders. The ethnic divide overlaps considerably with the urban–rural divide, but further discriminates the indigenous populations who have fewer opportunities in the education system and labour market.

These divisions would be less important if it had been possible to ensure that productivity in highlands agriculture, the mainstay of incomes for many of the poor, had improved in past decades. But here, success has proved elusive for most producers. Given the importance of highland agriculture for employment and incomes, the failure to improve productivity there is critical (see Eastwood and Lipton 2000; Timmer 1997; Klasen 2004).[5]

The poverty impact of macro policies

Bolivia's macro and public expenditure approach to poverty reduction has closely followed the World Bank's 1990 blueprint (World Bank 1990), which focused on a growth-oriented strategy and investments in human capital of the poor aimed at enhancing their participation in the growth process. For those who were left behind, safety nets – such as the Bolivian Social Fund and public works programmes – were supposed to try to address this problem. While this approach worked as long as growth generated increasing resources available for expanding social spending, it failed to sufficiently promote the productive activities of the poor and to address the large equity problems permeating Bolivia's society.

The macro policy agenda mainly focused on stabilization and liberalization. One particular objective was to ensure low and stable inflation and this was achieved over the last 20 years (see Table 13.2). Given that inflation tends to hurt disproportionately the poor, this policy is likely to have supported poverty reduction. In addition, the external capital account was liberalized and a friendly foreign investment regime was established. While this allowed a significant increase in FDI throughout the 1990s (Schweicker *et al.* 2003; World Bank 2004a) the liberalization of the external capital account contributed to a further dollarization of the economy, with the result of severely limiting the room of manoeuvre of exchange rate policy. While being neither pro-poor nor anti-poor, dollarization increases the vulnerability of the economy to exchange rate shocks – such as the appreciation of the US dollar, or the sharp devaluation of the Argentinian and Brazilian currencies in 1998 and 2002 – which hit the poor most as they are unable to shield themselves against such shocks. It also prevents Bolivia from using devaluation to kick-start export-based growth, as has been done in many other developing countries (Rodrik 2003).[6] In addition, while improving the allocative efficiency of Bolivia's economy, the strong trade liberalization that was pursued further undermined the ability of Bolivia to manage its external environment in ways to support poor producers, particularly in an environment of sharp fluctuation in the exchange rates of its trading partners.

In the fiscal and public expenditure area, the pro-growth agenda initially dominated policy making and fiscal policy aimed at low budget deficits, which was achieved through tax reforms, prudent expenditure policies and divestiture from loss-making state-owned enterprises. Tax reforms largely focused on broadening the tax base through a value added tax and a transactions tax, which together made up some 60 per cent of tax revenues in 2002. A hydrocarbons tax is the only other significant tax, generating about 18 per cent of revenues (Servicio de Impuestos Internos 2003). As a result, the tax system is less progressive, an objective that could have been achieved by imposing an income tax on those employed in the formal sector, a serious tax on large land-holdings or other real estate or surcharges for particular items mainly consumed by the non-poor.[7]

As long as growth was relatively high in the 1990s, and tax revenues continued to rise, the government was able to maintain a relatively low budget deficit, while at the same time ensuring rising expenditures for priority social sectors, such as health and education. Public social expenditures as a share of GDP rose sharply in the 1990s, and public capital expenditure was also high by international standards (World Bank 2004a). Indeed, excluding social security, Bolivia now devotes the second-highest share of its GDP to public social expenditures in Latin America and was consequently able to sharply improve average health and education indicators in the 1990s (World Bank 2004c). This approach was supported by generous aid flows and complemented by funds made available by HIPC I and II, with the latter being channelled entirely to the municipalities to fund priority investments, mostly in the social sectors and infrastructure.

Public social expenditure reaches the poor to varying degrees (World Bank 2004a, 2004c). It is proportional in health, slightly pro-poor in primary education, but anti-poor for higher levels of education, infrastructure spending and strongly anti-poor as far as public pension expenditure is concerned.

The ability to combine fiscal discipline with rising social expenditures collapsed in the late 1990s and led to ever-rising and now unsustainable budget deficits that reached 9 per cent of GDP in 2002. Three factors account for this deterioration (World Bank 2004a). First, tax revenues plummeted in line with the economic slowdown that began in 1999, while expenditures continued to rise. Second, a mismanaged pension reform led to much higher than anticipated outlays and now absorbs 5 per cent of GDP, while providing benefits to only two per cent of the population, most of them non-poor formal sector retirees in urban areas. Third, due to Bolivia's decentralization programme and the allocation of the HIPC funds to the municipalities, there is little central control or even information over expenditures at subnational levels, thereby weakening the ability of the central government to maintain fiscal discipline.

Thus, the Washington Consensus-type policies that maintained economic growth and social stability in the 1990s became unstuck. In a situation where inequality, social and ethnic tension are high, such an approach proved unsustainable and extremely fragile. It has contributed to great opposition to the government and calls for populist reforms and thrown wide open the debate about the appropriate economic model that the constitutional assembly should now adopt.

Simulation of past and future macro policy changes using a dynamic CGE model

To formally assess the impact of shocks and policies on PPG, this section makes use of a dynamic CGE model. The model has an overall neoclassical structure but with important structuralist features, particularly relating to a segmented labour market, credit rationing in the capital market and the limited mobility of factors between sectors and household types.[8] While this section focuses on the simulation of forward-looking policies and on the ability of such policies to reduce poverty and inequality, it will also comment on the extent to which the model is able to explain past performance in the fields of growth, inequality and poverty reduction. While assessing its results, two central characteristics of the model have to be kept in mind. First, growth is determined by changes in the endowments of factors of production such as capital and labour, as well as by the efficiency with which these are used. As for the latter, the model assumes an exogenously given rate of total factor productivity (TFP) growth of 2 per cent per year.[9] Thus, all simulated changes will depend on changes in the stocks of capital and labour. The major driving forces of labour dynamics are population change, migration, the rate of labour productivity growth and the change in human capital. Of these, the model takes into account only population changes, which are kept constant over simulations, and migration. The driving forces of capital accumulation are domestic savings and foreign capital inflows as well as relative returns on financial – domestic and foreign – and physical assets. Since net capital inflows are exogenously given in most simulations,[10] differences in growth rates across simulations are the result of changes in total domestic savings.[11] Second, the model assumes full employment for all types of labour and capital categories in each period of the simulation horizon. Hence, unlike other models for Bolivia that analyse short-run issues (see Jemio 2001; Jemio and Wiebelt 2003; Thiele and Wiebelt 2004), this model neglects Keynesian multiplier effects that might result from changes in consumption and investment expenditures. These two characteristics imply that the model cannot be viewed as a short-run projections model, and is not intended for that purpose. It is better suited to explain medium- to long-term trends and structural responses to changes in external conditions and development policy. But the problems facing PPG are inherently longer-run problems, and the model thus naturally places an emphasis on the long run rather than on the short run, growth rather than stabilization and trends rather than cyclical fluctuations.[12]

A scenario that describes how the Bolivian economy might evolve in the absence of shocks and policy changes serves as a benchmark against which all alternative developments will be evaluated. In this scenario, the economy exhibits smooth economic growth of about 4.7 per cent on average over a 10-year period (see Table 13.5), where economic growth is driven by capital accumulation, an exogenously given growth of the labour force and an exogenously given growth of 2 per cent of TFP. This not only describes an optimistic forward-looking scenario, but also effectively describes the record of the 1990s. The growth process is associated with roughly constant domestic savings and investment ratios, which implies that the large savings gap is not closed over time. The continuing savings gap corresponds to a persistent current account deficit, and both are reflected in a fairly stable real exchange rate.

While total value added by sector barely changes over time, more pronounced shifts are taking place within sectors. Within agriculture, for example, the more productive export-oriented segment gains at the expense of the traditional subsistence sector. The same pattern prevails in services, where higher productivity growth and a higher income elasticity of demand raise the provision of formal relative to informal services.

Table 13.5 The impact of shocks and policies on growth and poverty

	Average growth (%)	National headcount[a]	Urban headcount[a]	Rural headcount[a]
Baseline scenario	4.7	55.3	38.9	82.8
Terms-of-trade shock	4.7	55.6	39.1	83.3
El Niño	4.4	56.3	39.7	84.1
Declining capital inflows	4.4	56.3	40.3	83.3
Nominal devaluation	4.5	56.7	40.4	83.9
Real devaluation (restrictive monetary policy)	4.7	54.8	38.1	82.9
Labour market reform	5.0	54.4	37.4	82.8
Tax reform (revenue-neutral)	5.0	53.9	37.0	82.4

Note:
[a]Ratio at the end of the 10-year simulation period; the initial poverty headcounts are: 63.6 per cent national, 49.7 per cent urban, and 86.9 per cent rural.

Source: Klasen et al. (2004).

The baseline scenario suggests that without further policy reforms and without external shocks the rise in urban inequality observed during the 1990s will continue, and that the rural–urban income gap will widen. In addition, inequality within rural areas will also increase. In both urban and rural areas inequality is already high, which is why aggregate growth in Bolivia barely reduces poverty. As the following data indicate, this holds in particular for rural areas. Indeed, in the course of the simulated 10-year period, the national poverty headcount ratio merely declines from 63.6 per cent to 55.3 per cent. The moderate reduction in poverty is a consequence of a decrease in the urban headcount from 49.7 per cent to 38.9 per cent, and a reduction in rural poverty of only four percentage points from 86.9 per cent to 82.8 per cent. Even under this optimistic scenario, Bolivia would just manage to reach its revised and rather modest national poverty reduction target. Poverty reduction in rural areas falls short of the reduction projected in the Poverty Reduction Strategy Papers (PRSP), while urban poverty declines faster.

The next scenarios consider, more realistically, the effect of recurrent output shocks due to El Niño, terms of trade and capital flows (see Table 13.5). The simulations show that El Niño lowers growth, increases poverty in rural areas directly and raises urban poverty indirectly. It also leads to higher inequality in both areas. Terms of trade shocks, such as the 10 per cent decrease in world market prices for agricultural and mineral products, differ from supply shocks, such as El Niño, in that they do not impair production capacities and thus do not lead to major output losses as long as the economy operates at or near full employment. They nevertheless increase rural poverty, particularly in modern agriculture, and indirectly affect urban poverty. A FDI fall by almost a third, as observed in 2000, causes only about half of the immediate output losses of El Niño, but the impact turns out to be much more persistent. Even after 10 years, growth has not fully recovered and poverty has increased substantially, particularly in urban areas.

All in all, a realistic baseline scenario for Bolivia's medium-run development prospects would have to acknowledge that under the current policy framework average growth rates are unlikely to lie markedly above 4 per cent. Compared to the optimistic scenario, this implies worse prospects for poverty reduction. These simulations also help explain Bolivia's record in the 1990s, where both favourable and unfavourable shocks of the type investigated here explain well the growth and poverty performance recorded then.

The discussion now turns to simulations involving macroeconomic policies, the main focus of this analysis. One of Bolivia's biggest achievements since the beginning of reforms in 1985 has been the containment of inflation by means of prudent monetary, fiscal and exchange rate policies. It might be argued that, with an internal equilibrium that is firmly established, the exchange rate could be devalued to improve external competitiveness and income distribution (Schweickert *et al.* 2003).

Yet a higher yearly devaluation of the Boliviano within the present crawling peg regime causes an almost complete exchange rate pass-through to domestic prices, which will rise by nearly the same amount as the nominal devaluation, as the country's ability to respond to higher import prices with an increase in competitive import-substituting domestic production is limited.

The resulting real devaluation is therefore too small to provide the incentives for a significant reallocation of resources and have a discernible effect on aggregate performance. Real effects, however, are felt on the financial side of the economy. Indeed, in the highly dollarized Bolivian economy the value of most assets and liabilities is indexed to the dollar exchange rate. As a consequence, the net wealth position of net creditors in the financial system improves, while that of net debtors worsens. Since the economy as a whole – in particular, the government – is a strong net foreign debtor, the overall wealth effect of the devaluation is negative. The deterioration of the domestic wealth position leads to a drop in aggregate real investment and a fall in the growth rate, which accelerates over time due to the compound interest rate effect. Meanwhile, the two richest household groups – that is, employers and employees – are net creditors and thus benefit from the revaluation of assets caused by the devaluation that in this way reinforces existing wealth disparities. All other household groups are adversely affected by the decline in growth. Unskilled workers and urban informal workers are hurt most severely because many of them are employed in the construction sector where production slows down due to lower real investment demand. As a consequence, urban inequality increases and urban poverty rises somewhat more than rural poverty. Thus, in the present environment of near complete pass-through to domestic prices, high dollarization and large foreign debt, a real devaluation would be counter-productive and poverty-increasing. Conversely, removing any one of these three constraints would change the impact of devaluation considerably. In fact, follow-up work with the CGE model (Schweickert *et al.* 2005) shows that – in the absence of dollarization – the ability to effect a real depreciation through a nominal devaluation is much enhanced, thus allowing Bolivia to offset the impact of external shocks and actually use devaluation as a policy to stimulate GDP growth, as done in many other developing countries (Rodrik 2003).

In the current dollarized environment, a real devaluation can be achieved only if the central bank conducts a restrictive monetary policy. By constraining the ability of banks to supply credit, such policy temporarily lowers real investment demand and thereby exerts downward pressure on the domestic price level. The drop in real investment, in turn, causes a temporary economic slowdown. While the investment slowdown makes non-agricultural workers, in particular construction workers, less well off, the real depreciation entails minor losses for urban informal sector workers and minor gains for rural households. After the short-run adjustments, the economy soon shifts back to the old growth path, and household incomes evolve largely as in the base run. All in all, the negative impact on poor households often attributed to real devaluations is unlikely to occur in Bolivia, but clearly such a policy does little to promote PPG, thereby highlighting the bind Bolivia is in regarding its ability to use monetary and exchange rate policies to further PPG.

By Latin American standards, Bolivia has also made remarkable progress in the area of structural reforms (Lora 2001). The main exception is labour market reform, where Bolivia lags behind most other Latin American countries. Among the labour market distortions that still prevail, the segmentation of the urban labour market stands out. The tax system is another area where further reforms may be warranted. In particular, the question arises of whether the income tax, which hitherto has been of only marginal importance, should become a major source of government revenues.

If the government makes it easier for urban informals to be employed as unskilled workers in the formal labour market, for example, by lowering the costs of dismissal or by granting more options for temporary work, the obvious direct effect is that average real wages fall for unskilled formal workers and rise for urban informals. Better earning opportunities in the urban informal sector, in turn, induce a sizeable rural–urban migration, which moderately increases the incomes of those who remain in traditional agriculture. At the macro level, the efficiency gains achieved by reducing labour market segmentation – the wage differential between informal labour and unskilled labour is roughly halved – translate into an acceleration in the average growth rate of 0.3 percentage points in relation to the base run (see Table 13.5). Urban poverty decreases because of higher growth, but it takes several periods for the positive growth effect to materialize. The rural income distribution changes somewhat in favour of poorer groups due to the gains experienced by smallholders. This change and a slight increase in rural growth do not show up in the poverty headcount, but the rural poverty gap falls moderately (see Klasen *et al.* 2004 for details).

Next, the switch to a more progressive income tax regime is considered. If higher income taxes are combined with lower indirect taxes so as to arrive at a revenue-neutral tax reform, the economy-wide outcome is quite positive. Lower indirect tax rates cause an expansion of capital-intensive industries – oil and gas, mining, intermediate goods – on which the indirect tax burden is highest, and so boost investment and growth. Overall, given the current tax structure, a revenue-neutral tax reform can be expected to improve Bolivia's growth performance. As for household incomes, the decrease in indirect taxes raises private consumption expenditures, thereby offsetting the negative demand effect that higher income taxes have on smallholders and urban informals. The main beneficiaries of the reform are non-agricultural workers, many of whom work in the mining and intermediate goods sector, as well as in construction, which benefits from higher investment demand. The expansion of the construction sector additionally favours urban informals so that on balance their incomes rise significantly in relation to the base run. The gains of these two groups reduce the urban headcount ratio by up to two percentage points, and even rural poverty falls a little due to the growth effect (see Table 13.5).

To summarize the findings of the policy simulations, it is worth noting that the evolution of poverty and growth in urban areas followed the external shocks in the 1990s. Rural development was more dependent on climatic conditions and the lack of private and public investments. The failure to implement labour market reforms appears to have held back growth and urban poverty reduction. A deregulation of the urban labour market would also have had a positive, if limited, impact on rural incomes by providing an incentive for additional rural–urban migration.[13]

As for the future, some conclusions can be drawn about the policy options for PPG as well as the constraints of Bolivia's economy that the model analysis has served to highlight. Turning to the former issue, the main conclusion is that, currently, the opportunities for achieving PPG are much better in urban than in rural areas. Given the available policy choices, Bolivia could clearly exceed the targets for urban poverty reduction set in the revised PRSP. Rural poverty reduction, by contrast, risks falling short of the targets due to a combination of recurrent external shocks and limited policy options.

Turning to the constraints, the analysis has shown that accelerating PPG in Bolivia requires reducing the country's significant structural weaknesses. A critical weakness is the low domestic savings rate that forces Bolivia to rely on foreign capital inflows, which in turn leads to a high degree of dollarization, foreign debt, vulnerability to external shocks and inability to manage the external trade and monetary environment to support PPG. A second weakness is Bolivia's high dependence on natural resources whose exploitation has few linkages to the poor, but can have significant anti-poor effects.[14] Third, Bolivia's economy exhibits such a high degree of dualism that even well-managed growth policies do not reach the poor in rural areas or have little impact on their poverty. Last, Bolivia's high initial inequality militates against success in poverty reduction, particularly in rural areas. While the policy packages discussed above can help with PPG, only success in tackling these four deep-seated issues will enable Bolivia to enter a sustainable path toward higher growth and poverty reduction.

Conclusion and policy implications

The following key lessons emerge from the above discussion. First, macro stability has been a prerequisite for PPG.[15] The stabilization of hyperinflation in 1985 and the structural reforms that ensured low inflation and low fiscal deficits since the late 1980s have been critical in setting the stage for the sustained growth of the 1990s. Second, the reforms of the trade and investment regime, privatization and financial sector reform also helped to sustain growth in the 1990s. At the same time, they did little to address Bolivia's main structural weaknesses. Also, the structural reforms further increased the vulnerability to external shocks, which are the key driver of growth in the last 20 years. In particular, the open trade regime, dollarization and open capital account were critical elements in increasing the external vulnerability of the economy. While a favourable external environment boosted growth and FDI in the 1990s, the growth slowdown of the late 1990s was largely driven by external events. Third, this approach to policy making has severely circumscribed the options for active macro management in the area of exchange rate and monetary policy (see Chapter 4). In particular, dollarization and open capital account prevent the adoption of a monetary policy to counteract external shocks or kick-start an export-led growth process.

Fourth, the growth associated with these structural reforms did little to address the large inequalities in Bolivia while the recent slowdown has hurt the poor, particularly the urban poor, considerably. Thus, this approach to macro policy making proved to be insufficient for achieving sustained PPG. Fifth, an approach to policy making combining Washington consensus policies in the macro area with an expansion in social investments leads to PPG only if the macro policies deliver sustained long-term growth. Due to the external vulnerability of that growth, this was not possible in Bolivia and thus the approach to address poverty and inequality through social spending is no longer a viable option. This calls into question the policy package proposed by the World Bank in 1990 which promoted such a policy package all over the developing world.

While it is fairly easy to identify the short-comings of this macro policy approach, it is considerably harder to come up with a policy package that would avoid these shortcomings. In particular, many of the constraints to developing a PPG agenda cannot be addressed by macro policy. This is so for several reasons. First, the deep-seated inequalities in the economic, political, and social sphere cannot wait for positive distributional consequences of better macro policies that might materialize over the long term. In fact, in the current political environment, it is very hard to have a frank discussion about medium- to long-term PPG strategies at all. In such a discussion, the issues of land reform, tax reform, and conditional transfer programmes for the poor must now receive high priority (Klasen et al. 2004). Similarly, further political, constitutional, and governance reform might be necessary. Second, PPG is often less constrained by policies, than by their insufficient and distorted implementation. As discussed in Klasen et al. (2004) and Kaufman et al. (2003), severe governance problems often undermined otherwise well-intentioned pro-poor policy approaches such as decentralization, the national dialogue and PRSP process, and the implementation of agrarian reform. Third, Bolivia's unfavourable initial conditions reduce its options for pro-poor policy making. Being a small landlocked economy with a poor infrastructure and an uneven population distribution is likely to reduce the returns to any PPG agenda considerably.

Nevertheless, it is useful to point to a few macro policy issues that ought to be considered as part of a pro-poor policy agenda. First, at the international level the question should be re-opened whether debt relief in the case of Bolivia was deep enough. After several years of low growth, the foreign debt burden is high, putting pressure on the fiscal side and sharply curtailing any room for devaluations to improve the country's competitiveness. Fortunately, Bolivia looks set to benefit from the new round of debt relief agreed by Group of 8 leaders recently.

Second, measures to raise domestic savings should be strengthened (see Chapter 5). These should focus on the institutional strengthening of the financial sector by establishing reliable savings institutions in small towns and rural areas, expanding the coverage of the new fully-funded pension system – which, at the moment, covers only 10 per cent of workers (World Bank 2004c), shielding savings from the risk of inflation through indexed products and a complete indexation of the economy, and promoting public savings by limiting transfers to the pension system, saving part of the proceeds from the gas project, obtaining further debt relief or increasing share of grant aid. Third, measures to reduce dollarization should be pursued more vigorously so as to increase the ability of monetary authorities to adopt pro-poor monetary policies. The results presented in this chapter and in Schweickert *et al*. (2005) show that such a policy could enable the government to manage its exchange rate in support of a PPG agenda. Given the long record of low inflation, it should be in the interest of the government to begin pushing back the dollarization of its economy. This could be done by introducing a tax levied only on dollar-denominated transactions and differential reserve requirements for dollar versus Boliviano deposits, and by popularizing inflation-indexed securities as the main form of new government debt.

Once dollarization and the associated external vulnerability are reduced, a much more active management of the exchange rate would become possible, and a one-off devaluation to promote international competitiveness and boost outward-oriented growth ought to be seriously considered. To maintain this flexibility, controls on capital inflows might be needed to ensure that they do not destabilize the currency and financial markets. Last, to achieve sustained PPG, Bolivia will need to diversify its export base. To do this, a more active export promotion strategy would be needed to develop high-value niche exports. The currently considered *cadenas productivas* initiative is a good start, but should be strengthened by providing strategic incentives to promote non-traditional exports.

Notes

1 I would like to thank Giovanni Andrea Cornia and the participants in the United Nations Research Institute for Social Development workshop on Pro-Poor Macroeconomics at the University of Florence on 24–5 February 2005 for helpful comments and discussions. I specifically thank Rainer Thiele and Manfred Wiebelt for their work on the CGE model and for helpful comments and discussions on a broader version of this chapter. Part of this work is based on a larger case study on PPG (Klasen *et al*. 2004). Funding from the BMZ Bank via KfW Development Bank for this larger case study is gratefully acknowledged.
2 Interested readers are referred to Ravallion and Chen (2003), Klasen (2004, 2005) and AfD *et al*. (2005) for detailed discussions on this issue.
3 This refers to a scheme where public companies sell a 50 per cent stake to strategic investors (where the proceeds remain with the companies to finance a pre-specified investment programme). The proceeds from the remaining shares are used to finance an annual old age pension (the Bonosol) for all citizens over the age of 65. This way, electricity, railway, telecommunications, mining, the national airline and the national hydrocarbon company were transferred to (mostly foreign) strategic investors who took management control of these companies.
4 It should be noted that measurement error might have a considerable influence at the two tails of the distribution so that these results should be treated with some caution.
5 Given these divisions, the generally pro-poor nature of growth – including in rural areas – seems surprising and is probably due to favourable weather conditions, the coca economy and some migration and remittance linkages. See Klasen *et al*. (2004) for more details.
6 Similarly, it was not possible to affect the distribution of income via a real depreciation that would favour poor export- and import-competing producers at the expense of wealthier consumers of imports (Klasen 2004).

7 Such taxes could, however, face compliance problems in an economy where contraband is widely available and tax evasion is considerable (Delgadillo 2000). In 2003, a few taxes were changed to increase tax revenues, but they did not seriously affect the progressivity of the tax system.
8 See Wiebelt (2004) for a detailed discussion of the model.
9 Two comments are in order. First, while a TFP growth of 2 per cent is slightly higher than in the 1990s, it appears realistic for an 'optimistic' baseline scenario. Second, it can be speculated that some of the simulated policies will have a favourable impact on TFP growth via knock-on effects.
10 Exceptions are the simulations of declining capital inflows, where capital inflows are changed exogenously, and of a devaluation, which changes the domestic currency value of capital inflows.
11 Domestic savings are the sum of savings by households, firms and government. Households are assumed to have a constant marginal propensity to save. For firms and banks, savings are determined residually as the difference between their revenues and costs. For the state, savings are determined residually, with revenues depending on the tax base and expenditures being based on fixed real consumption expenditures and investment related to GDP growth.
12 This feature of the model explains the rather small effects that are identified, as the model is not intended to capture short-run demand-related changes in productivity and capacity utilization as well as structural shifts of the economy, both of which would probably lead to larger effects.
13 There are indications that the model underestimates the response of migration to changes in wage differentials. Additional research is needed to see whether the modeling of migration replicates the adjustment patterns actually observed in Bolivia.
14 In Klasen et al. (2004) an expansion of natural gas exports is also investigated as a potential means to higher growth, particularly if combined with labour market and tax reforms and if the proceeds were channelled into investment rather than consumption. But due to Dutch disease effects and their capital-intensive and enclave nature, such an expansion would bypass rural areas and significantly increase inequality. Only a coordinated policy package combining higher gas exports with targeted transfer programmes and other pro-poor interventions would allow Bolivia to achieve higher PPG and allow significant poverty reduction also in rural areas.
15 For an investigation of the impact of macro stability on PPG, see Lopez (2005).

References

AfD, BMZ, DFID, GTZ, KfW and World Bank. 2005. *Pro Poor Growth in the 1990s: Lessons and Insights from 14 Countries*. Washington, DC: World Bank.

Bourguignon, F. 2003. 'The Growth Elasticity of Poverty Reduction'. In T. Eicher and S. Turnovsky (eds), *Inequality and Growth*. Cambridge, MA: MIT Press.

Deininger, K. and L. Squire. 1998. 'New Ways of Looking at Old Issues: Inequality and Growth'. *Journal of Development Economics*, 57(2), 259–87.

Delgadillo, M. 2000. *¿Es bueno el sistema tributario en Bolivia?* La Paz: Unidad de Análisis de Políticas Sociales y Económicas.

Eastwood R. and M. Lipton. 2000. 'Pro-poor Growth and Pro-Growth Poverty Reduction: Meaning, Evidence, and Policy Implications'. *Asian Development Review*, 18(2), 22–58.

International Monetary Fund (IMF). 2003. *Bolivia – Selected Issues and Statistical Appendix*. Country Report No. 03/258. Washington, DC: IMF.

Instituto Nacional de Estadística (INE). Various issues. *Información Estadística*. Online database. http://www.ine.gov.bo, accessed on 16 June 2004.

Jemio, L.C. 2001. *Debt, Crisis and Reform in Bolivia: Biting the Bullet*. Basingstoke: Palgrave Macmillan in association with the Institute of Social Studies.

Jemio, L.C. and M. Wiebelt. 2003. '¿Existe espacio para políticas anti-shocks en Bolivia? Lecciones de un análisis basado en un Modelo de Equilibrio General Computable (with L.C. Jemio)'. *Revista Latino Americana de Desarrollo Económico*, 1(1), 37–68.
Kakwani, N. and E.M. Pernia. 2000. 'What is Pro-Poor Growth?' *Asian Development Review*, 18(1), 1–16.
Kaufmann, D., M. Mastruzzi and D. Zavaleta. 2003. 'Sustained Macroeconomic Reforms, Tepid Growth: A Governance Puzzle for Bolivia?' In D. Rodrik (ed.), *In Search for Prosperity*. Princeton, NJ: Princeton University Press.
Klasen, S. 2004. 'In Search of the Holy Grail: How to Achieve Pro-poor Growth.' In B. Tungodden, N. Stern and I. Kolstad (eds), *Towards Pro-poor Policies: Aid, Institutions, and Globalization*. Oxford New York: University Press.
Klasen, S. 2005. *Economic Growth and Poverty Reduction*. Development Centre Working Paper No. 246. Paris: OECD.
Klasen, S., M. Grosse, J. Lay, J. Spatz, R. Thiele and M. Wiebelt. 2004. *Operationalizing Pro-Poor Growth: Country Case Study Bolivia*. Discussion Paper No. 101. Göttingen: Ibero-America Institute for Economic Research.
Lopez H. 2005. *Pro-Poor Growth: How Important is Macroeconomic Stability?* Mimeo. Washington, DC: World Bank.
Lora, E. 2001. *Structural Reforms in Latin America: What Has Been Reformed and How to Measure it*. Research Department Working Paper 466. Washington, DC: Inter-American Development Bank.
Ravallion, M. and S. Chen. 2003. 'Measuring Pro-Poor Growth'. *Economics Letters*, 78(1), 93–9.
Rodrik, D. 2003. *Growth Strategies*. Working Paper 10050. Cambridge, MA: National Bureau of Economic Research.
Sachs, J.D. and F.B. Larraín. 1998. 'Bolivia 1985–1992: Reforms, Results, and Challenges'. In H. Costin and H. Vanolli (eds), *Economic Reform in Latin America*. Orlando, FL: The Dryden Press.
Schweickert, R., R. Thiele and M. Wiebelt. 2003. *Makroökonomische Reformen und Armutsbekämpfung in Bolivien: Ebnet die HIPC-Initiative den Weg zu sozialverträglicher Anpassung?* Kiel Discussion Papers 398, Institute for World Economics, Kiel.
Schweickert, R., R. Thiele and M. Wiebelt. 2005. *Exchange Rate Policy in a Dollarized Economy: A CGE Analysis for Bolivia*. Paper presented at the Conference on Poverty, Inequality, and Policy in Latin America, Göttingen, 14–16 July.
Servicio de Impuestos Internos. 2003. *Recaudación renta interna por tipo de impuestos*. La Paz.
Thiele, R. and M. Wiebelt. 2004. 'Growth, Poverty, and Income Distribution in Bolivia: A Regional and Sectoral Perspective (with R. Thiele)'. In M. Krakowski (ed.), *Attacking Poverty: What Makes Growth Pro-Poor?* HWWA Studies 75. Baden-Baden: Nomos.
Timmer, P. 1997. 'The Agricultural Transformation'. In H. Chenery and T.N. Srinivasan (eds), *Handbook of Development Economics, Volume 1*. Amsterdam: North-Holland.
Unidad de Análisis de Políticas Sociales y Económicas (UDAPE). Various issues. *Dossier de Estadísticas Sociales y Económicas de Bolivia*. La Paz: UDAPE.
Wiebelt, M. 2004. *GEMPIA: A Dynamic Real-Financial General Equilibrium Model for Poverty Impact Analysis*. Kiel Working Papers (in print). Kiel: Institute for World Economics.
World Bank. 1990. *World Development Report*. Washington, DC: World Bank.
World Bank. 2000. *World Development Report*. Washington, DC: World Bank.
World Bank. 2003. *World Development Indicators*, CD-ROM. Washington, DC: World Bank.
World Bank. 2004a. *Bolivia: Public Expenditure Management for Fiscal Sustainability and Equitable and Efficient Public Services*. Report 28519-Bo. Washington, DC: World Bank.
World Bank. 2004b. *Bolivia Poverty Assessment: Establishing the Basis for More Pro-Poor Growth*. Report No. 28068-Bo. Washington, DC: World Bank.
World Bank. 2004c. *Social Expenditure and its Relation to Poverty and Equity in Bolivia*. Poverty and Social Impact Analysis. La Paz: World Bank.

14
Has Macroeconomic Policy Been Pro-Poor in Brazil?

Jorge Saba Arbache[1]

Introduction

Over the last 25 years, Brazil has experienced profound economic changes. Following the international economic instability of the late 1970s and the debt crisis of the early 1980s, Brazil launched structural adjustment programmes with the intention of solving external account imbalances and controlling high inflation rates. In 1990, Brazil undertook a major break from a century-long era of import-substitution strategy (ISI) that left its economy essentially closed towards the end of the 1980s, and introduced economic reforms involving trade and capital account liberalization, the privatization of state companies, the deregulation of markets and a successful stabilization plan. These reforms have been reshaping the economy very rapidly and are giving rise to economic transformations. Table 14.1 shows, however, that the pre-reform per capita output growth rate is significantly higher than that of the post-reform period (1990–2004). The social indicators are also disappointing. Poverty is at a very high level for a middle-income country and has been reduced only very slowly, while income inequality is not only at a very high level, but has also increased over time. To the extent that structural reforms are widely understood to be conducive to growth and be pro-poor, these statistics suggest that something went wrong.

Brazil is a country that is particularly well suited to grasping a better understanding of whether macroeconomic policies in general and structural reforms in particular favour the poor. Its economy ranks among the highest globally in terms of gross domestic product (GDP), and has experienced one of the highest average growth rates of the last century. However, it remains thoroughly rooted in the developing world. Socioeconomic inequality involves subtle forms of residential, educational and workplace discrimination that tends to segregate members of distinct socioeconomic strata, so that they live, work and circulate in different settings. The poor have limited – and at times no – access to government services such as health, education and sanitation and limited participation in the formal labour market. Consequently, they are generally not covered by labour legislation or by most social protection schemes. Poverty is widespread in urban and rural

Table 14.1 Per capita output growth and social indicators – Brazil

Period	Per capita output growth rate (%)	Percentage of population below poverty line	Gini coefficient
1970s	5.9	40.0	0.561
1980s	0.98	43.0	0.592
1990s–2004	0.58	35.5[a]	0.600[a]

Note: [a]refers to 1990–2002.
Sources: Hoffmann (1995); Brazil population census; Ipeadata, www.ipeadata.gov.br/ipeaweb.dl/ipeadata?365018906.

areas, reaching the highest levels in rural parts of the northeast region. Various forms of deprivation, growth of *favelas* (shanty towns), urban violence, street children and epidemics of diseases have been common not only in large, but also in medium-sized and small cities all over the country. The pervasiveness of high levels of poverty and inequality, along with the high concentration of land and property and low growth rates, have created tensions in rural and urban areas in the last few years. Pillaging and seizures of unused private land and urban properties fuelled conflicts in various parts of the country, especially in the poorest regions, as the numbers of landless workers increased. The rising social problems and the limited effectiveness of governmental policies to tackle the huge social problems raised concerns and uncertainties and a call for urgent policies to promote growth and create jobs.

This chapter reviews the recent economic policies and their impacts on the poor, and examines macro policies required to allow poverty reduction. I begin by presenting the economic policies of the following periods and their impacts on growth and the poor: 1980–89, 1990–2002 and 2003–04. The split between the first and second periods is due to the major break of policy orientation from 1990 onwards. The last period seeks to examine whether the economic policy of President Lula da Silva favours the poor as compared to his predecessors. This is followed by a discussion of macroeconomic policy alternatives that can lead Brazil towards a faster and more equitable growth and rapid poverty reduction. The chapter concludes with some final remarks and the lessons drawn from Brazil's case.

The 1980–1989 period

The economic policy

A brief description of the economic policy orientation in previous decades is helpful as they set the starting conditions for the 1980s. The closure of international markets to Latin American goods during the Great Depression encouraged a shift from export-oriented to domestic-oriented economies. In Brazil, it encouraged a drive towards industrialization, which was already underway, and towards a greater role of the state in the economy. Although the shift in economic orientation was a response to market closures, it soon developed ideological components, both political and economic.

Credit was provided at subsidized rates and the financial sector was repressed. The relative abundance of credit, along with an overvalued exchange rate, encouraged importing inputs to develop capital-intensive industries. This allowed for considerable industrialization in Brazil and for the decline of agricultural output as a percentage of GDP. The 'infant' industries were protected through a host of measures such as import licenses, tariffs and subsidized interest rates. Unlike the rapidly growing Asian economies, protected industries were not forced to compete in international markets, which had not created an incentive for higher productivity. The ISI favoured high employment and the domestic industry, but at the cost of low levels of efficiency.

Despite the rapid growth of world trade following the Second World War, Brazil was preoccupied with domestic markets. Brazil began to consider exports only in the 1960s. However, the dynamic of the economy was still inward-oriented and institutional incentives allowed the survival of firms that would have been uncompetitive in international markets. The size of Brazil's internal market, the possibility of limited competition and changes in US banking laws encouraged foreign investment. By the 1970s, foreign lending became critical to Brazilian development strategies, which explicitly accepted moderately high levels of inflation – 15 per cent to 30 per cent – and increased indebtedness as a fundamental part of the development process. Viewing the oil shocks of the 1970s as short-term disturbances, the government refused to slow down the economy or to correct inflationary distortions and fiscal deficits.

After the second international oil shock, however, policy makers moved from the ISI to a pragmatic economic policy seeking to solve the balance-of-payments and the accelerating inflation problems. In practice, the government alternated measures based on the restriction of demand with expansionist policies. The lack of clear macroeconomic targets is seen as a source of increasing economic instability (see Table 14.2, which should be referred to for most economic variables addressed in the text).

The debt crisis that followed the Mexican default of 1982 exposed the inconsistencies of the fiscal regime. The sudden halt in international financing of the balance-of-payments deficits called for fiscal adjustment, which, in fact, did not happen. As a consequence, the fiscal and balance-of-payments deficits fuelled inflation and caused widespread demand for indexation, thus accelerating inflation very rapidly in the first half of the 1980s. The re-democratization process in 1985 was followed by expansionist fiscal policies that brought even more inflationary pressures.

The main outcome of the accelerating inflation was an increasing economic instability, which had an impact on economic growth, investments and income inequality. Several desperate stabilization attempts based on price and wage freezes were undertaken between 1986 and 1991, but all failed mainly due to the lack of fiscal adjustment.

Table 14.2 Brazil's economic and social indicators, 1980–2004

Year	GDP growth rate	Per capita output growth rate	Investment to GDP ratio	Inflation (IGPDI)	Real exchange rate index (2004 = 100)	Average effective tariff (%)	Trade to GDP ratio	Trade balance (US$ million)	Current account (US$ million)	Capital and financial account (US$ million)	FDI (net, US$ million)	Portfolio capital (US$ million)	External debt (US$ million)	Selic annual interest rate (%)
1980	9.20	6.70	0.24	110.23	244.77	NA	0.181	−2,822.77	−12,739.19	9,610.14	1,910.20	350.80	64,259	NAP
1981	−4.25	−6.35	0.24	95.20	205.91	NA	0.176	1,202.46	−11,705.87	12,745.74	2,521.90	0.70	73,963	NAP
1982	0.83	−1.33	0.23	99.73	203.55	NA	0.146	780.07	−16,273.20	12,100.73	3,115.20	1.80	85,487	NAP
1983	−2.93	−4.96	0.20	211.02	257.32	NA	0.197	6,470.39	−6,773.03	7,418.76	1,326.10	−278.90	93,745	NAP
1984	5.40	3.27	0.19	223.81	254.82	NA	0.216	13,089.52	94.91	6,529.19	1,501.20	−267.50	10,2127	NAP
1985	7.85	5.74	0.18	235.13	264.50	NA	0.184	12,485.52	−248.34	196.56	1,418.40	−228.00	105,171	NAP
1986	7.49	5.46	0.20	65.04	239.52	NA	0.141	8,304.30	−5,323.26	1,431.54	317.15	−475.70	111,203	NAP
1987	3.53	1.65	0.23	415.95	213.39	67.76	0.146	11,173.10	−1,437.92	3,258.62	1,169.10	−428.20	121,188	NAP
1988	−0.06	−1.81	0.24	1,037.53	182.73	46.79	0.158	19,184.11	4,179.77	−2,098.33	2,805.00	−497.90	113,511	NAP
1989	3.16	1.42	0.27	1,782.85	136.85	38.82	0.127	16,119.19	1,031.89	629.08	1,129.90	−391.40	115,506.10	NAP
1990	−4.35	−5.90	0.21	1,476.71	116.03	36.95	0.111	10,752.39	−3,783.72	4,592.49	988.80	578.87	123,438.50	NAP
1991	1.03	−0.54	0.18	480.23	136.13	28.60	0.130	10,579.97	−1,407.46	163.01	1,102.20	3,808.03	123,910.40	NAP
1992	−0.54	−2.05	0.18	1157.84	138.92	17.74	0.145	15,238.89	6,108.83	9,947.32	2,061.00	14,465.60	135,948.80	NAP
1993	4.92	3.37	0.19	2708.17	124.98	15.19	0.149	13,298.77	−675.88	10,495.24	1,290.90	12,929.10	145,725.90	NAP
1994	5.85	4.33	0.21	1093.85	97.79	12.34	0.141	10,466.47	−1,811.23	8,692.21	2,149.90	54,046.80	148,295.20	NAP
1995	4.22	2.76	0.21	14.77	83.12	15.59	0.137	−3,465.62	−18,383.71	29,095.45	4,405.12	10,372.17	159,256.20	43.36
1996	2.66	1.24	0.19	9.33	82.04	16.08	0.130	−5,599.04	−23,502.08	33,968.07	10,791.69	22,021.67	179,934.50	24.47
1997	3.27	1.87	0.20	7.48	81.59	18.64	0.140	−6,752.89	−30,452.26	25,800.34	18,992.93	10,907.94	199,997.50	22.36
1998	0.13	−1.21	0.20	1.71	84.54	18.13	0.138	−6,574.50	−33,415.90	29,701.65	28,855.61	18,582.21	241,644.07	25.58
1999	0.79	−0.55	0.19	19.99	118.80	17.26	0.181	−1,198.87	−25,334.78	17,319.14	28,578.43	3,542.37	241,468.16	23.02
2000	4.36	2.99	0.19	9.80	105.21	NA	0.184	−697.75	−24,224.53	19,325.80	32,779.24	8,650.78	236,156.35	16.18
2001	1.31	−0.01	0.19	10.40	122.58	NA	0.223	2,650.47	−23,214.53	27,052.10	22,457.35	872.12	226,067.25	16.08
2002	1.93	−0.39	0.18	26.41	134.14	NA	0.234	13,121.30	−7,636.63	8,004.43	16,590.20	−4,797.43	227,689.39	17.67
2003	0.54	−0.91	0.18	7.66	115.10	NA	0.246	24,793.92	4,177.29	5,110.94	10,143.52	5,128.76	235,414.13	21.17
2004	5.18	3.68	0.20	12.13	100.00	NA	0.263	33,669.57	11,645.02	−7,362.34	18,165.69	−3,995.57	220,182.31	15.15

Continued

Table 14.2 Continued

Domestic public debt to GDP ratio	PSBR to GDP ratio – operational concept	PSBR to GDP ratio – primary concept	PSBR – interest payment to GDP ratio	Taxation to GDP ratio	Population under poverty line (%)	Gini index	Income share of 1% richest	Income share of 50% poorest	Family consumption to GDP ratio	Unemployment	Labour income growth rate	Informal labour as share of labour force
NA	NA	ND	ND	NA	NA	NA	13.2	13	0.691	NA	NA	NA
NA	6.31	ND	ND	NA	40.84	0.584	12.7	13.1	0.664	NA	NA	NA
NA	6.89	ND	ND	NA	41.01	0.591	13	12.7	0.677	NA	NA	0.376
NA	3.15	ND	ND	NA	48.79	0.596	13.5	12.5	0.687	NA	NA	0.384
NA	2.88	ND	ND	NA	48.39	0.589	13.2	13	0.669	NA	NA	0.399
NA	4.42	−2.61	7.03	NA	42.07	0.598	13.6	12.5	0.637	7.80	−11.63	0.387
NA	3.58	−1.59	5.17	NA	26.45	0.588	13.8	13	0.662	6.11	−13.42	0.370
NA	5.63	0.99	4.64	NA	38.77	0.601	14.1	12.2	0.608	6.09	2.19	0.367
NA	4.87	−0.91	5.78	NA	43.64	0.616	14.4	11.5	0.567	7.03	23.94	0.370
NA	7.09	1.03	6.07	NA	41.41	0.636	16.5	10.6	0.542	6.59	4.06	0.363
NA	−1.32	−4.69	3.36	29.60	41.99	0.614	14.2	11.5	0.593	7.21	4.43	0.376
15.93	0.19	−2.71	2.90	24.43	ND	ND	13.7	12.3	0.616	7.92	−12.66	0.409
15.60	1.74	−1.58	3.32	24.96	42.17	0.583	13.2	13.1	0.615	9.13	−17.92	0.430
17.02	0.80	−2.18	2.98	25.30	43.04	0.604	15.1	12.3	0.601	8.68	−5.71	0.439
21.76	−1.57	−5.64	4.07	27.90	ND	ND	14.5	12.4	0.596	8.93	9.94	0.454
22.72	5.00	−0.26	5.26	28.44	35.08	0.601	13.8	12.4	0.599	8.95	16.52	0.460
26.13	3.40	0.10	3.30	28.63	34.72	0.602	13.5	12.1	0.625	9.93	18.39	0.476
29.29	4.31	0.96	3.35	28.58	35.18	0.602	13.8	12.1	0.627	10.16	7.21	0.481
34.14	7.40	−0.02	7.42	29.33	33.97	0.600	13.9	12.3	0.619	11.68	1.18	0.486
39.38	3.41	−3.23	6.64	31.07	35.26	0.594	13.2	12.7	0.623	12.06	0.17	0.499
39.41	1.17	−3.47	4.64	31.61	ND	ND	13.6	12.7	0.609	11.02	−5.48	0.509
41.64	1.40	−3.64	5.04	33.40	35.13	0.596	13.9	12.6	0.605	11.18	−1.34	0.497
44.13	−0.01	−3.89	3.88	34.88	31.27	0.589	13.4	13	0.580	12.12	−3.27	0.500
43.97	0.88	−4.25	5.14	34.01	NA	NA	NA	NA	0.567	12.72	−2.53	NA
45.04	−2.07	−4.61	2.54	NA	NA	NA	NA	NA	NA	11.76	NA	NA

Notes: (1) Real exchange rate index (R$/US$), 2004 = 100. Deflator: IGP–DI. (2) Average effective tariffs are weighted by the value added (source: Kume *et al.* 2004). (3) Selic is the basic interest rate of the economy set by the Central Bank. (4) The poverty line is constructed on basis of the families' financial capacity to provide a minimum number of calories per capita per day in accordance with the Food and Agriculture Organization's standard. (5) Portfolio capital refers to foreign investments in shares, bonds, notes and other Brazilian financial papers. (6) Unemployment refers to the metropolitan region of São Paulo. (7) Labour income refers to main job income in metropolitan regions. Deflator: IPCA. No data for 2003–2004 due to methodological change of series. (8) Informal labour refers to informal labour contract and self-employed as a share of labour force in metropolitan regions. No data for 2003–2004 due to methodological change of series. (9) PSBR stands for Public Sector Borrowing Requirements.

Sources: Central Bank of Brazil; Ipeadata; Instituto Brasileiro de Geografia e Estatística.

NA = not available
NAP = not applicable
ND = no data

The impact of economic policy on growth

After decades of rapid growth, there was an abrupt slowdown in the 1980s and the average per capita output growth rate fell to one per cent, compared to 5.9 per cent in the 1970s. The monthly inflation rate series seems to be a mirror image of the quarterly real GDP growth rates series. In other words, it seems that inflation has hindered economic growth.

Bugarin *et al.* (2002) show that the de-trended per working age output dropped 26.5 per cent below the 1992 trend, as compared with 1980, which characterizes economic depression. A sharp drop in output followed the Mexican crisis and, after some recovery, a much stronger drop followed during the period of heterodox stabilization plans. Bugarin *et al.* (2002) show that the main cause of this output drop was the relative price of investment goods. They argue that the increasing macroeconomic instability caused by the price and wage freezes and fiscal deterioration encouraged economic agents to seek protection for their savings, fuelling the demand for real estate. As a consequence, the price level of the construction sector, which accounts for the largest share of total investments in Brazil, grew much faster than the price level of the economy and gross investment fell from 23.6 per cent in 1980 to 14 per cent in 1992.

Pinheiro (2003) presents a similar story. He conducted a growth accounting decomposition and shows that capital accumulation drops from 4.5 per cent in 1964–80 to 1.3 per cent in 1981–93, accounting for half of the average output growth fall of 6.2 per cent. Total factor productivity (TFP) also fell significantly, from 1.7 per cent to -0.7 per cent. Capital accumulation, together with TFP, explains 90 per cent of the output growth collapse.

The impact of economic policy on poverty and inequality

After decades of very strong state tutelage, there was an emergence of a new labour union movement in the late 1970s. With the slow re-emergence of democracy in the late 1970s and early 1980s, unions gained political power and an increasing role in wage determination. As a reaction to accelerating inflation, unions started to act strategically trying to over-index wages, which intensified an already very unsynchronized wage bargaining process and contributed to the breakdown in the coordination of wage determination.

The different levels of monopolistic product market power, the highly protected and regulated economy, the dominance of state-owned companies in a variety of sectors and the huge informal labour market, which buffers the costs of displacement, provided little incentives for unions to discipline and moderate wage demands. This environment was conducive to the growth of considerable insider power in wage determination, allowing powerful groups of industrial, formal sector workers to secure a share of product market rents through the wage bargaining process and, as a consequence, driving the economy to an increasing income inequality. Yet Arbache (1999) shows that unions are a key variable in explaining wage inequality in Brazil, a result that is at odds with the role they are supposed to play.

The inability of the government to impose fiscal equilibrium, and the deterioration of the economic and political environments, gave scope for strong, self-interested pressure groups acting in a free-rider manner demanding wages, prices and public subsidies in an unco-ordinated way according to their market and political powers. This process would quickly collaborate to a steady acceleration of inflation and further deterioration of fiscal accounts. These developments had potential impacts on the poor, not only because of their inability to secure indexation to inflation, but also because of their higher dependency on the state expenditures and social policies.

The 1981–83 recession that followed the external debt crisis seems to have impacted on poverty. Unemployment rates rose and were accompanied by social disturbances, sacks and pillages. The Plano Cruzado in 1986 gave an immediate gain to the poor due to the income effect observed in the aftermath of freezing prices programmes, and wages and minimum wages were frozen 8 per cent and 16 per cent above their averages, respectively. This measure would not last long, as it reinforced the distributive conflicts that followed the stabilization, eventually bringing the inflation back.

Ferreira and Litchfield (1999) show that the increase in inflation in the 1980s helps to explain the rising poverty and inequality. The modesty of the social policies in place and the lack of safety nets made things even harder for the poor. Family consumption remained relatively stable from 1980 to 1986, but there was a substantial drop thereafter. Despite the poverty and inequality indicators, the unemployment rate was relatively low by the end of the 1980s, which resulted from at least three factors: (i) the role of the informal sector in accommodating the unemployed; (ii) the ISI regime, which secured the domestic market for the local firms; and (iii) the populist fiscal policies, which kept public expenditures at high levels.

The 1980s became known as the 'lost decade' because of the combination of GDP stagnation, hyperinflation, increasing income inequality and raising poverty. Its severe economic problems would spill over into the 1990s.

The 1990–2002 period

The economic policy

Trade liberalization

Prior to 1990, the Brazilian economy was highly protected and regulated by virtue of the ISI strategy. Some modest tariff reduction and the lifting of redundant barriers started in 1988. However, the major break with the ISI era began in 1990 under the Collor administration, when efforts to contain inflation were combined with drastic trade liberalization. By the middle of 1993, most of the complex and bureaucratic non-tariff barriers had been removed and a new tariff structure was imposed, which substantially reduced the degree of protectionism. On the export side, subsidies were eliminated and tax incentives were drastically reduced. Although the new tariffs were still relatively high by international standards, the removal of non-tariff barriers shifted the pattern of protection, and signalled that the long period of protectionism was at an end.

Coupled with the appreciation of the exchange rate, trade liberalization led to a significant importation of consumer goods, enhancing the competition in domestic markets and consequently pushing the local firms to improve competitiveness.

The trade flow rose steadily, with imports increasing by 257 per cent and exports by 151 per cent between 1990 and 1996. By 1996, the quantum of imports had increased almost three times. In 1994, the combination of further pragmatic liberalizing measures seeking to discipline domestic prices in the aftermath of the Plano Real and increasing appreciation of the exchange rate affected the trade accounts in such a way that the trade balance started to face growing deficits.

Privatization

Facing imminent hyperinflation and a virtually bankrupt public sector, plans for privatizing public enterprises were launched by the Collor administration in conjunction with a stabilization attempt. Although much of the rhetoric used by advocates of privatization at the time emphasized economic efficiency and competitiveness, privatization is better understood as a desperate response to the deterioration of public finance and the rapid worsening of macroeconomic indicators. Its ultimate aim was to generate fiscal revenues to reduce the public debt and consolidate price stability.

Privatization gained momentum under the first Cardoso administration. The constitutional amendments necessary for privatizing the public monopolies and infrastructure were possible mainly because of the initial success of the Plano Real, which gave the government sufficient power and public support to push for the changes. The government regarded privatization as a key measure for raising revenues and achieving the fiscal discipline needed to maintain the Plano Real, and vital for a sustainable growth.

Between 1990 and 2002, more than 130 state and federal companies were sold, rendering US$105.5 billion in total revenues, which made it one of the largest privatization programmes in the world. These funds played a substantial role in preventing a worsening of the current account deficit and public debt. According to Pinheiro *et al.* (2001), the ratio between foreign direct investment (FDI) inflows associated with privatization and current account deficit averaged 25 per cent in 1997–2000. Macedo (2000) argues that privatization had a 'macroeconomic cost' as the enormous proceeds made the government less inclined to pursue fiscal and current accounts adjustments in 1995–98, postponing the needed measures and inflating the costs of the adjustment later. Despite the huge amounts involved, the privatization programme was not sufficient to balance the public accounts, as the increase in the debt surpassed the revenue obtained from privatization.

Deregulation of markets

Major moves towards the deregulation of markets were introduced in 1990. Restrictive rules and laws that had prevented contest in many sectors began to be removed, and price controls and restrictions to entry were eliminated to stimulate competition. Over the following years, the anti-trust legislation was strengthened and modernized, a consumer protection bill was passed, a new legislation on the protection of intellectual property rights was approved in line with the Trade-Related Aspects of Intellectual Property Rights–World Trade Organization and measures in several areas were modernized, including remittances of royalties, technology transfers, patents and partnerships. Constitutional amendments were approved, eliminating discrimination against foreign capital in various businesses and discontinuing public monopolies.

With regard to the labour market, some changes were introduced aimed at increasing flexibility of labour relations. In 1994, a bill was passed allowing firms to hire workers through co-operatives. The co-operatives in turn were not obliged to comply with certain labour costs, which in practice meant that employers were allowed to bypass some provisions of the Labour Code. In 1998, a bill was passed allowing part-time labour contracts to be issued.

Stabilization, monetary and exchange rate policies

The Plano Real was introduced during particularly favourable conditions. On the one hand, there was large international financial liquidity, which reduced the external sector constraints. On the other hand, trade and capital account liberalization, privatization and other market reforms were in place, which helped to discipline price formation, attract foreign capital and provide extra revenues for the state. There was recognition that fiscal discipline was critical for the success of stabilization. Indeed, in a low inflationary environment, fiscal disequilibrium soon becomes apparent, and only a new fiscal regime could sustain the Plano Real. Major fiscal reforms were desperately needed, which required constitutional amendments and strong political support. Reforms in areas such as public pension system, social security funding, transfers of funds and division of spending among federal and state authorities, among others, were bringing about the collapse in public finance.

In spite of authorities' commitment to fiscal discipline and to the implementation of reforms, the fiscal accounts went from an operational surplus of 1.57 per cent of GDP in 1994 to a deficit of 5 per cent in 1995. The deterioration of public accounts continued, reaching a deficit of 7.4 per cent in 1998. Amann and Baer (2000) argue that the government's 'soft' approach to fiscal discipline resulted, on the one hand, from the failure of President Fernando Henrique Cardoso to secure the fiscal reforms in the Congress, reflecting the lack of political will in his political coalition to cut spending and, on the other hand, from the outcome of the president's relentless pursuit of the constitutional amendment to allow his re-election in 1998. This amendment demanded such intense political negotiations and bargaining that it eventually changed the political agenda, thus delaying fiscal reforms.

In view of the worsening of fiscal accounts, the Plano Real became largely contingent on the role of the exchange rate for maintaining price stability. The interest rates (Selic) were increasingly used to attract foreign capital aimed at keeping the exchange rate anchor. Of course, this regime was unsustainable, especially because the high interest rates were having negative effects on the fiscal accounts, causing severe fiscal disequilibria. The public sector's interest payments jumped from 3 per cent of GDP in 1993 to 5.3 per cent in 1995.

In the external sector, there was a substantial deterioration in the current account resulting from various factors. First, the use of the exchange rate as an anchor to keep inflation down, along with high foreign capital inflows, appreciated the *real* and caused trade balance disequilibrium. Second, there was a substantial increase in interest and dividend payments between 1994 and 1998, reaching 4 per cent of GDP in 1997. Third, after decades of strong protection, the rapid trade liberalization led to high growth in imports. At the same time, post-stabilization consumption, investment booms and the expansionist fiscal policy stimulated the growth of imports even further. As a result, the current account increased from a deficit of US$1.8 billion in 1994 to a deficit of US$18.4 billion in 1995. The deficit worsened from then on, reaching US$33.4 billion in 1998.

Indeed, the Plano Real was being sustained at the expense of increasing deterioration of the fiscal and external accounts, compounding what later would bring very serious difficulties to output growth and social indicators. The gradualist policy adopted to tackle the growing macroeconomic imbalances can be explained by the easy access to portfolio capital and increasing FDI inflow. The net FDI-to-current account ratio in 1995 was 18 per cent and reached 78 per cent in 1998. Of course, this strategy could not last long as the increasing dependency on foreign capital to finance the explosive current account deficits made the economy highly vulnerable to external shocks and eventually to speculative attacks.

The Mexican crisis in March 1995 began to bring up uncertainties about the sustainability of the Plano Real. In order to protect the *real*, the government adopted a tight monetary policy. In the aftermath of the Asian crisis in October 1997, the annualized interest rate reached 42 per cent. In view of the widespread concerns over the macroeconomic indicators and increasing fears of the devaluation of the *real*, the government was forced to take action with regard to the fiscal deficit and the appreciated exchange rate. Public spending was cut in 1998, generating some improvement in the primary result, while the exchange rate was depreciated.

The Russian crisis in August 1998 forcefully exposed the contradictions of the Plano Real and made the situation unsustainable. The government substantially raised interest rates in a dramatic attempt to maintain the exchange anchor in place, but the measure was useless as investors increasingly believed that a strong devaluation of the *real* was inevitable. As a result, they started withdrawing funds in large quantities from the country. Between August and September 1998, Brazil lost about US$30 billion in international reserves. The desperate increases in interest rates to save the *real* in 1997 and 1998 profoundly affected the public accounts, causing public sector interest payments to reach an astonishing 7.4 per cent of GDP in 1998.

In view of the increasing risk of collapse of the economy, the International Monetary Fund (IMF), the World Bank and the US government announced a large emergency loan of US$41.5 billion to Brazil. In October 1998, just after the re-election of Cardoso, the government proposed major fiscal reforms to the Congress in a desperate attempt to avoid economic collapse. By December, the Congress had approved only part of the proposed reforms, raising expectations of an imminent default. Capital outflows accelerated, depleting international reserves at about US$1 billion a day during the first days of January 1999. In a dramatic and desperate move, the government was forced to allow the exchange rate to float freely in mid-January. This caused the *real* to overshoot, jumping from 1.21 *real* per dollar before devaluation to 2.06 by February 1999. The devaluation brought immediate changes to the external accounts. Current account deficit diminished rapidly as a result of major cuts in imports and profit remittances and a drastic drop in international travel.

Stringent fiscal measures were taken in 1999. The Congress approved a significant tax raise, an inflation target system was introduced and the interest rate was kept high. By the end of the year, the budget surplus attained was larger than that required by the IMF agreement. Further fiscal measures were introduced over the next years, giving rise to a rapid reduction of the deficit.

Between 2000 and 2002, a series of external factors adversely affected the economic performance of Brazil. Concerns and speculations on the prospects of recovery were renewed. First, the moratorium and deepening of Argentina's crisis – one of Brazil's main trade partners – heavily affected exports. Second, the downturn of the US economy had an adverse impact on the world economy. Third, there were major declines in FDI inflows. Fourth, an unprecedented energy crisis developed because of draught and the paucity of investments, resulting in severe rationing of electricity.

The weak performance of the economy in 2001, the poor post-devaluation export growth and the falling inflow of foreign capital increased anxiety that Brazil, similar to Argentina, might default. As a consequence, there was a substantial reduction in international financing, which led to strong exchange rate depreciations and increased volatility. The exchange rate volatility and the high interest rates affected both the long-term private investments and fiscal accounts, as a substantial amount of the public debt was dollar denominated. The macroeconomic deterioration led to further interest rate hikes, thus reducing the chances of an eventual economic recovery.

In 2002, the prospects that the leftist candidate in the upcoming presidential elections, Lula da Silva, could win soared uncertainties once again. The concerns of a socialist regime and unsound policies led the country-risk ratings to soar to unprecedented levels, bringing additional difficulties to companies and public accounts.

Financial and capital liberalization

In 1991, a series of initiatives towards the liberalization of the capital account were taken, including the opening of the domestic capital market to foreign portfolio investment, the permission given to Brazilian companies to issue different types of securities and bonds abroad and the adoption of tax relief over the issuing of bonds in the international markets as well as over profit remittances and royalties by multinational companies (see Chapters 4 and 5). An additional feature of the financial liberalization includes the increased participation of foreign banks in the domestic market and privatization of state banks. In 1994, some opening to capital outflows was also adopted in view of the massive capital inflow.

As a result of the opening of the capital account, the participation of foreign investors in the volume of transactions in the stock market increased from 6 per cent in 1991 to 30 per cent in 1995. The portfolio investment increased dramatically, going from an average of minus US$221 million per year in the 1980s to US$12 billion per year in 1990–2002. Foreign investors were granted the right to participate in privatization, and by 2002 their share in the total privatization proceeds reached 48 per cent, amounting to about US$50 billion. This was a substantial change in view of the long-established position among influent politicians and business leaders who maintained that the greater participation of foreign capital could end up denationalizing the economy. The government varied the degree of controls over external borrowing and investment in bonds for macroeconomic management purposes, and taxation and maturity have been used to control capital flows.

The capital account liberalization, privatization of major utility sectors and the foundation of Mercosur in 1991 played a substantial role in attracting FDI to Brazil, as many multinational companies made the country the regional export base for Mercosur. From 1990 to 1995, the net inflow of FDI was, on average, US$1.5 billion per year. From 1996 to 1999, it jumped to an average of US$21.8 billion per year and reached US$32.8 billion in 2000. Since then, FDI inflows have reduced as a consequence of the slowdown of the privatization programme and the economic and political crisis.

It has to be stressed that the capital account liberalization was implemented before the major liberalization of the trade account and the price stabilization, which does not fit the classical order of sequencing and timing of reforms that calls for stabilization coming first and the opening of trade and capital accounts last.

The impacts of economic policy on growth

The delay of fiscal adjustment and conflicts over policy reforms created an atmosphere of unsustainable macroeconomic deterioration that could not last long. The rising uncertainties about the sustainability of the Plano Real had stringent effects on the prospects of growth. Since the end of 1997, the investment-to-GDP ratio triggered a period of contraction and was one immediate cause of vulnerability of the *real*. After the collapse of the *real* in early 1999, the rising costs of investment and input goods, the very high interest rates, the implementation of an enormous fiscal adjustment and the unfinished regulatory system for utilities and infrastructure added to the main causes of investment stagnation.

It seems that the disappointing post-reform output growth is explained by the sequencing of policy reform issues, political economy constraints and the timing when the reforms were introduced. One critical sequencing issue is the fact that the stabilization-cum-exchange rate nominal anchor was introduced *after*, and not before, trade liberalization, hence in opposition to the long-established consensus of policy literature (Edwards 1994; Krueger 1981). The appreciation of the exchange rate prior to stabilization made the anti-export bias created by the nominal anchor larger than it would have been otherwise. It was subsequently reinforced by the long period of appreciation after Plano Real. The sizeable FDI and portfolio capital inflow favoured by capital account liberalization and privatization in the aftermath of Plano Real also contributed to keeping the *real* appreciated. As productivity increases take time to materialize and the reallocation of resources is a slow and long process, especially in a country such as Brazil that had been long protected from imports, the trade-off between the exchange rate used to steer inflation down and to guide the reallocation of resources was counter-productive for improving exports. The obvious outcome was a rapid worsening of the current accounts, which ultimately constrained the output growth potential. Unfortunately, Brazil repeated the earlier policy mistakes made by other Latin American countries in their stabilization attempts, but with the aggravated implications of inducing a stagnant economic cycle and exposing the economy to speculative attacks in a liberalized financial market framework.

Another critical issue for growth is related to fiscal accounts. Serious fiscal adjustment was left until *after* stabilization. Thus, the fiscal adjustment required in the aftermath of the Plano Real was huge and difficult to implement. It appears that the government overestimated its capacity to control fiscal accounts and to have the Congress pass fiscal reforms in such a short time. Instead of surpluses, the post-Plano Real period witnessed explosive operational public deficits, revealing the inconsistency of fiscal budgets in the inflationary era. The rise in interest rates to finance balance-of-payment deficits with portfolio capital affected public accounts and aggravated the fiscal disequilibria. The unwillingness of politicians to adopt the measures necessary to achieve fiscal discipline delayed the essential reforms and added to the costs of adjustment. At the time, the 'way out' for fiscal adjustment was not to rely on inflation tax, as had been done in previous decades, but to take advantage of the success of Plano Real to resort to obtain funding from both local and foreign financial markets, at the cost of worsening fiscal and current accounts.

Trade liberalization and deregulation of capital seem to have had some impacts on productivity and efficiency. Technology transfers and diffusion from abroad rose from 0.04 per cent of GDP in 1990 to 0.35 per cent in 1999. New methods of production and management were introduced, which led to an increase in a variety of goods and improvements in quality. Ferreira and Rossi (2003) find evidence that the fall of tariffs and import penetration increased TFP growth in manufacturing. Hay (2001) analyses a set of large manufacturing firms and finds substantial productivity growth after openness and evidence of a fall in profits and market shares. Muendler (2004) investigates TFP change and finds that the removal of tariffs and import penetration induced firms to rationalize and forced less competitive firms to exit the market, thus leading to the rise in TFP. If, on the one hand, the opening facilitated the access to capital and new technologies, on the other hand, it imposed a heavy cost to the least advanced firms, as a significant share of them went bankrupt in the early years after the Plano Real.

Anuatti-Neto *et al.* (2003) assess the impacts of privatization on efficiency and output of former state-owned enterprises and find indications of increased profitability and reduced operating costs. Danni (2004) shows that the provision of utilities and services grew after privatization. Carvalho (2001) observes that the privatization programme improved the managerial practices and efficiency, reduced public debt – albeit much less than anticipated earlier, reorganized the public finances of the federative states and reduced the public debt interest payments in the short and long run, versus the levels they would have been in the absence of privatization.

Despite the modernization of the economy, the average growth rate of the post-reform period (1990–2002) was 1.97 per cent, lower than the 1980–89 figure of 3.02 per cent, and far below the historical rate of 5.34 per cent (1947–2002). A decomposition of the output growth shows that if TFP growth had not increased, the economy would have experienced a sharp depression in the post-reform period. The investment-to-GDP ratio remained at around 19 per cent. The stagnation in investments is somewhat puzzling, as openness, privatization, stabilization and deregulation of markets are often assumed to reduce the prices of investment goods and create business opportunities, the elements needed to encourage capital accumulation. In fact, the evidence for Brazil suggests that structural reforms seem to be conducive to growth, but do not cause growth.

The impact of economic policy on poverty and inequality

The labour market indicators experienced substantial changes in 1990–2002. By 2002, more than half of the labour force was employed in the informal sector, unemployment was at a very high level, about 12 per cent; and real average wage had lost 15 per cent of its purchasing power compared with 1997. The causes of such deterioration are certainly associated with the country's mediocre economic growth.

A significant drop in poverty occurred just after the Plano Real in mid-1994, and since then the indigence and poverty lines have remained stable. Income inequality Gini index remained very high and stable, at around 0.6. In the aftermath of the Plano Real, consumption experienced an unprecedented boom. From the second quarter of 1994 to the second quarter of 1995, family consumption rose by 3 per cent of GDP, mainly a reflection of the purchasing-power gains of the lower income groups. As they had no or very limited access to mechanisms to protect their consumption from inflation, stabilization gave them a one-time real income raise. Workers at the lowest income decile experienced a 100 per cent rise in income in the first year of the Plano Real, while workers at the second lowest decile enjoyed a 46 per cent rise (Rocha 2000). The euphoria of post-Plano Real, accompanied by expansionary fiscal policies, fuelled the average growth rate during 1994 and 1995 to 5 per cent. As a result, the proportion of people below the poverty line fell from 43 per cent in 1993 to 35 per cent in 1995, remaining at this level thereafter.

Empirical literature shows that wages in the traded sector were substantially harmed by openness (Arbache *et al.* 2004). This is consistent with the evidence that the reforms raised the degree of competition in the traded industries and thereby reduced bargaining power of workers and rent sharing. Green *et al.* (2001) find evidence of skill-biased technical change as a result of trade openness, and that it prevented reduction in wage inequality. Maia and Arbache (2001) investigate the sources of employment changes and find that imports accounted for the destruction of 1.97 million jobs, while technological changes eliminated 4.9 million jobs between 1985 and 1995, most of them unskilled jobs. Overall, the empirical evidence suggests that trade and capital liberalization benefited skilled workers and was not conducive to income inequality reduction, as one could expect based on the Stolper–Samuelson theorem. As the compression of margins tends to reflect increased competition in the domestic market, the above results can be explained by the introduction of new technology, rationalization of production, better management, outsourcing and turnover. The exit of the least competitive firms and the high interest rates in the Plano Real era may have imposed an asymmetric distribution of the burden on unskilled workers and on small manufacturing businesses, as they tend to be employed in such firms.

Mota (2003) runs a cost–benefit analysis to evaluate the impacts of privatization of the electricity supply and finds that most efficiency gains from privatization went to the benefit of the producers. Danni (2004) finds that privatization of communications and energy increased the provision of fixed phone lines and distribution of energy and that the poor were the main beneficiaries. Thus, it seems that increased coverage after privatization played a role in improving the well-being of the poor.

Fiani (2002) shows that the residential energy cost was subjected to a 40 per cent rise above the consumer price index between 1995 and 2002, while the industry energy cost dropped 60 per cent below the industrial price index. The fixed billing charge for energy distribution and fixed residential telephone connections also increased sharply after privatization, imposing a regressive cost on the poor. As a result, the share of utilities in the budget of the poor may have risen after privatization. These results suggest that privatization had both positive and negative effects on poverty.

The 2003–2004 period

The economic policy

The incoming government decided to maintain the orthodox economic policy orientation that was in place. This was perhaps a reaction to the very harsh economic conditions and to the suspicion of the investors that the Labor Party could follow a heterodox economic agenda. As a matter of fact, the primary fiscal surplus target set by the previous government was elevated significantly, and the central bank was given some independence to guide the monetary policy. The novelty brought by the new government was the intention to combine fiscal discipline with a social agenda.

The high interest rates used as a means to control the inflation pressures have had at least two side effects: an impact on public debt and on the exchange rate. It is estimated that for every one per cent rise of the Selic, the annual debt service increases by about R$6.7 billion. On the external side, the high real interest rates attracted portfolio investment, thus appreciating the exchange rate and harming the competitiveness of exports. Yet the average nominal exchange rate fell from R$3.08 in 2003 to R$2.92 in 2004. In January 2005 it was R$2.69, and in late April 2006 it was about R$2.08. The Lula da Silva administration seems to be replicating the mistakes of the previous government in regard to interest and exchange rates. While it may be somehow effective to control inflation in the short run, in the medium term it potentially affects the fiscal and the external accounts, thus compromising growth and poverty reduction.

Despite the appreciation of the *real*, the exports have boomed, partly due to the very favourable prices of agricultural, live stock and mineral commodities, and of some semi-manufactured goods such as steel and cellulose. From 2002 to 2004, the total exports rose by 60 per cent, contributing to significant surpluses in the current accounts and alleviating the always troublesome balance-of-payments situation.

The social security has been an important source of fiscal concerns, as it has presented growing deficits. This was caused by various reasons, including the huge informal sector, the demographic transition, the establishment of social benefits and retirement rights for rural workers, elderly people and disabled people (who have never contributed) and the increasing disequilibria in the public sector pension system. According to Portela *et al.* (2004), in the last few years the nominal deficit of the social security has amounted to more than 4 per cent of GDP, and the estimated implicit deficit for the next few years is expected to reach 7 per cent of GDP, thus combining the debt service with the main fiscal constraints.

With regard to the social agenda, Lula da Silva established the Bolsa Família, a combination of social projects intended to tackle starvation and misery, and also to bring the poor to the markets through credit to informal workers, small urban entrepreneurs and family farming, training programmes, *bolsa-escola* and compensatory programmes, among other measures.

One way to fund a social agenda is through tax increases. However, during recent years the tax burden increased immensely, going from 29 per cent in 1998 to 34 per cent in 2004, which is seen as a response to the public accounts disequilibria. In 2003, the total deficit was about 3.7 per cent of GDP, and in 2004 it was estimated to be 3.5 per cent. Thus, the tax burden plus the nominal deficit amounted to about 38.5 per cent of GDP. In view of the fiscal constraints and the firm decision of the government to keep inflation at low levels, funding an ambitious pro-poor programme was the highest challenge of the government.

The impact of the economic policy on growth, poverty and inequality

The GDP growth of 2003 was 0.54 per cent, a consequence of the economic crisis of the previous year and the tough fiscal and monetary policies in place. The GDP growth of 2004 was 4.9 per cent, a quite high figure if compared to the rates observed in the previous two decades. It has often been questioned whether the economy is able to keep growing at similar figures because of the low investment rates and the severe bottlenecks in infrastructure.

In regard to social indicators, there is some sign of improvements. Although unemployment remained high, it dropped from 12.7 per cent in 2003 to 11.8 per cent in 2004, and the proportion of people living below the poverty line fell significantly from 2003 to 2004 reaching the lowest figure since 1992 (Neri 2005). Neri (2005) credits this result to economic growth and the Bolsa Família.

Policy alternatives

This section discusses micro and macro policy alternatives that pursue policies protective of the poor.

Output growth and poverty

In view of the developments of the social indicators presented above, it is hard to say that poverty is a hot policy issue in Brazil. One obvious reason for the poor social indicators is the low growth rates observed over the last two decades. Figure 14.1 shows the per capita output growth rate, and the dotted line is a third-order polynomial trend. The instantaneous rate of growth of the per capita output during the whole period was 2.84 per cent. In 1947–79, it was 4.2 per cent; it then declined sharply to 0.7 per cent in 1980–2004; and, finally, it reached a disappointing 0.5 per cent in the post-Plano Real period. The macro policies implemented since the 1980s were not able to reverse the long-term trend of declining output growth. The lack of a clear focus and the inability to follow the sequencing of reforms as discussed above is perhaps responsible for the stops-and-goes and the lack of coherent economic policies.

Figure 14.2 presents the fitted and actual logarithm of the per capita output. The fitted line can be interpreted as the (linear) long-term trend of the per capita output. Two points seem to emerge. First, taking the fitted line as a reference, Brazil has experienced long economic cycles over the last several decades. Second, after a strong boom, the economy has entered in a stagnant period since 1980, and the fitted–actual gap has been increasing since 1990, thus suggesting an economic depression. Certainly, policies intended to seriously tackle poverty and inequality are more difficult to gather political support in such a stagnant economy. In such an environment, fiscal policies may be needed to resume economic growth, reduce growth volatility and, above all, protect the very poor and the least skilled from economic downturns, as they seem to have been disproportionately affected by the economic reforms. In view of the fiscal constraints, however, additional measures to boost growth have to be considered, and export promotion is perhaps among the best alternatives.

Figure 14.3 depicts the real GDP per capita and the share of population under the poverty line. There seems to be a strong relationship between the two variables

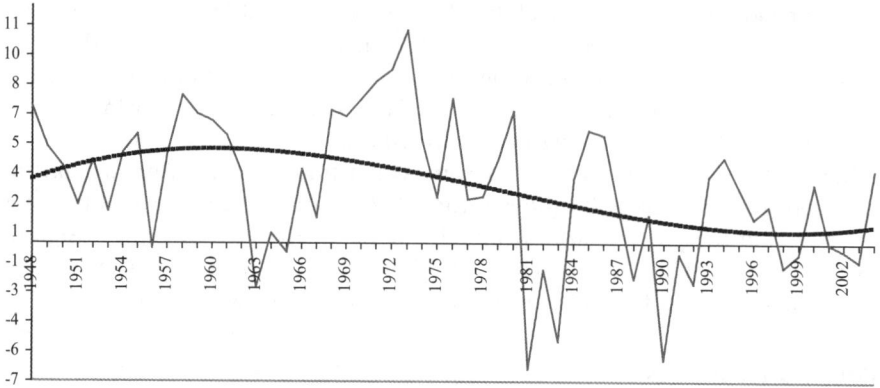

Figure 14.1 Per capita output growth rate
Source: Ipeadata, http://www.ipeadata.gov.br/ipeaweb.dll/ipeadata?494065500.

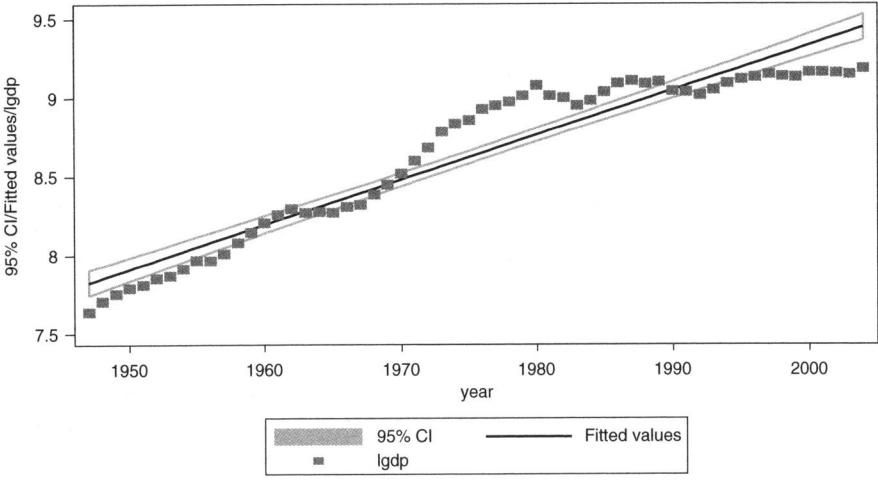

Figure 14.2 Ln per capita output
Source: Author's calculations.

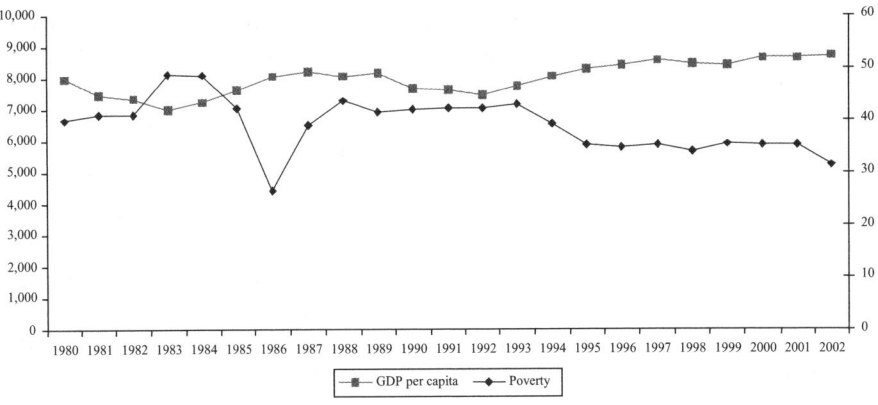

Figure 14.3 Population under poverty line and GDP
Source: Ipeadata, http://www.ipeadata.gov.br/ipeaweb.dll/ipeadata?494065500.

(the correlation coefficient is −0.79). Thus, policies that boost growth seem to be good for the poor. However, as poverty indicators remained relatively stable over growing periods, growth should be viewed as a necessary, although not a sufficient condition to tackle poverty.

Income distribution and poverty

It has been found that income inequality is one of the main causes of poverty in Brazil. Barros *et al.* (2001) find that if it were possible to identify all the extremely poor and poor people, extreme poverty could be significantly reduced at the cost of only about R$6 billion a year, thus revealing the low cost of eradicating misery; and that poverty levels are much more sensitive to changes in the degree of inequality than to changes in economic growth. So, if poverty were not so responsive to inequality, the correlation between output growth and poverty would perhaps be stronger.

Menezes-Filho and Vasconcelos (2004) estimate the growth elasticity of poverty in Brazilian states as −0.9. When they control for inequality, the growth coefficient goes to −1.0 and the inequality coefficient is 2.3. If initial conditions of income and inequality by state are controlled for, then the growth elasticity of poverty rises to −1.8, while the inequality coefficient is 2.6, meaning that the poverty reduction effect of growth is much higher when the initial level of income is high and lower when initial inequality is high. These results support those of Barros *et al.* (2001) that poverty is more responsive to inequality changes than to growth changes. An implication of this result is that growth may be positively correlated with inequality. Accordingly, Menezes-Filho and Vasconcelos (2004) estimate regressions of Gini and other variables on output growth and find that inequality is positively correlated to growth. These results are illustrative of the pattern of growth developed in Brazil and calls for changes of the growth model.

Barros *et al.* (2000) estimate the unemployment elasticity of poverty using monthly data from six metropolitan areas for the period 1982–98. The measure of poverty is the average income gap. The coefficient of unemployment estimated is 1.47. Barros *et al.* also estimate a series of local regressions using a 36-month observation. The average coefficient of unemployment for 1984–89 – one of increasing inflation – is 1.3. During 1990–92, a period marked by recession and increasing inflation, the mean coefficient scaled to 1.6. From early 1993 until mid-1996, a period of strong decline of inflation and rising growth rates, the mean coefficient dropped steadily, averaging 0. This result may capture the income effect of the Plano Real, and the relatively low unemployment rates of the period. Thereafter, the local coefficients increased monotonically and very rapidly, possibly reflecting the rising unemployment rates and the economic stagnation.

These results suggest that fighting poverty based solely on economic growth may produce slow changes in social indicators, especially in view of the low per capita growth observed in the last few decades. The implications are important, as they suggest that actions aimed at eradicating poverty must include strategies to reduce inequality. Some of the distributional policy alternatives are minimum wage rise, progressive income taxation, increasing opportunities for human capital formation and the improvement of sectors that absorb proportionately more unskilled labour.

Fiscal accounts, stabilization, interest rate and exchange rate

The fiscal disequilibria have been the key economic characteristic of the last few decades in Brazil, and are among the main causes of the country's persistent inflation and economic instability. In the post-Plano Real, the increasing deterioration of the fiscal accounts has constrained growth through the crowding-out effect on interest rates and investment. As a side effect, the high interest rate has attracted portfolio capital, thus appreciating the exchange rate and harming growth.

Economists have been arguing that solving the fiscal disequilibria is fundamental for cutting interest rates and attracting long-term investments, and the way out most often proposed is cutting government expenditures. If, on the one hand, it is healthy for long-term growth, on the other hand, demand compression and public expenditures cuts disproportionately harm the poor. Thus, the issue is one of how to conciliate the short-term versus long-term policy targets.

In the last few years, the inflation rate has remained relatively high and above the ambitious inflation targets set by the central bank. As a result, a very orthodox monetary policy has been put in place to contain inflation. Yet Brazil has had one of the highest real interest rates in the world. An inflation target policy will be effective if prices are sensitive to interest and to demand reduction and the credit is rationed. These outcomes have not been the case, however, as low-interest credit has increased dramatically for pensioners and civil servants – the pension and salary are used as a collateral – and several key prices, such as privatized utilities and public services, are highly indexed.

Franco (2004) finds that the interest rate set by the central bank is strongly sensitive to inflation. He shows that for every percentage point of inflation, interest raises by 1.77 per cent. The output gap coefficient, however, is -0.72, suggesting that the central bank's policy is not only unresponsive of unemployment, but is also not counter-cyclical as one could expect from a pro-poor macro policy. Franco (2004) also shows that the interest rate policy is guided by the deviation of the expected inflation to the inflation target. Certainly, in the presence of an opened capital account, a tough monetary policy can cause deleterious impacts on growth and fiscal accounts and expose the economy to speculative attacks and shocks. On the one hand, the high interest rates increase the public debt, thus pushing the debt service up. On the other hand, the high interest rate attracts portfolio capital. Thus, the monetary and fiscal policies seem to reinforce the fiscal disequilibria and the exchange rate appreciation, driving the country into a low-growth trap.

Policies aimed at breaking the low-growth trap have to consider generating, in the short run, considerable fiscal primary surpluses, additional policies to containing inflation apart from interest rate rises and exchange rate appreciation, and consolidating the trade account surpluses as a way to reduce the external shocks and the foreign capital dependency. In such an unequal society with its lack of social cohesion, the political economy challenges are how to promote fiscal cuts without imposing extra burdens onto the poor and on policies directed to increasing long-term productivity and competitiveness.

Integrating the poor to the markets

According to what has been discussed above, the eradication of poverty should not rely solely on growth. Moreover, the extent to which growth favours the poor depends heavily upon the level of markets integration and on their imperfections. In less integrated or segmented markets, the benefits of growth may not be shared by all, or are unevenly shared. Some obvious examples are labour market discrimination and restrictions to credit and market access. Certainly, in such environment sound macroeconomic policies alone may not be enough to successfully reduce poverty. A promising approach to tackle poverty is integrating and coordinating macro with micro policies that challenge the structural determinants of poverty, engage the poor into the markets in permanent basis, facilitate their access to technologies and remove imperfections of markets functioning (see Chapter 1).

Market integration is essential for the poor to be able to develop their businesses, get contracts, enhance the value of their assets and, above all, benefit from the economic growth. Empirical evidence, however, shows that the markets in which the poor are found in Brazil are not fully integrated into the rest of the economy. One piece of evidence refers to the long time that the poverty and inequality indices have remained stable. This stability could be a consequence of the isolation of the poor people from the credit, education, raw materials, goods and services markets. If this isolation raises the costs of obtaining, say, education, then the accumulation of human capital can become economically infeasible. But this isolation can also result from the lack of infrastructure, transport, communications and electrical energy, among other public services, which isolate the poor in their regions and keep them away from new technologies. This would be the case in rural areas and in the small towns spread throughout the country, and can be seen as one reason for the failure of many settlements set up under the umbrella of agrarian reform that have become economically unviable.

The main obstacle that prevents the poor having access to the markets and the one that makes it more difficult for them to benefit from economic growth in Brazil is perhaps the low level of qualification and schooling. Brazil has one of the highest adult illiteracy rates in Latin America, and one of the lowest average schooling rates among middle-income countries – 4.5 years in 2000. Education improves productivity, opens up opportunities for access to good jobs and increases income. Education is found to be the most important factor to explain wage and income inequality in Brazil – it explains 48 per cent of wage inequality and 26 per cent of income inequality (Barros and Mendonça 1995) – and the return rate for each additional year of schooling is about 16 per cent, one of the highest in the world. The main way to overcome this obstacle is to distribute education better. The distribution of education is not transferable, is reproducible and can, for this reason, contribute towards reducing inequalities and poverty at large. The problem of using education as a tool to fight poverty, however, is that it is a long-term approach to affecting poverty and inequality and does not solve the problem of poverty and misery, which requires short-term measures.

Final remarks

This chapter examined the economic policies implemented in Brazil in the last 25 years and commented on their failures, weaknesses and impacts on the poor. After a long period of inward-oriented strategy and a series of policy mistakes, the economy ended up in external debt crisis, hyperinflation, slowdown of growth, high poverty levels and increasing inequality. Brazil then undertook structural reforms in line with the Washington Consensus aimed at promoting growth and fighting poverty. If the standard market-oriented reforms had been adequate to boost growth and social conditions, Brazil would have grown at higher rates and improved social indicators. Therefore, it can be said that structural reforms are not a panacea. They may contribute to growth and fight poverty, but only if supported by macro- and microeconomic policies tailor made to address the country's characteristics and needs, and if they are biased toward the poor.

Some points seem to emerge from the Brazilian case: (i) growth is necessary but not sufficient to reduce poverty; (ii) fighting income inequality seems to be essential for reducing poverty; (iii) sound fiscal and monetary policies are essential to growth; and (iv) policies aimed at engaging the poor into the markets seem to be promising for reducing poverty on a permanent basis and enabling them to benefit from growth. Therefore, in order to make growth more pro-poor, it is important that growth be achieved with a decline in income inequality and with more and better opportunities for the poor to benefit from economic growth.

Note

1 I would like to thank, without implicating them, the comments on a previous version of this chapter by Giovanni Andrea Cornia, Stephan Klasen, Christian Weller, Ricardo Bielschowsky and the participants in the United Nations Research Institute for Social Development workshop on Pro-Poor Macroeconomics at the University of Florence on 24–5 February 2005.

References

Amann, E. and W. Baer. 2000. 'The Illusion of Stability: The Brazilian Economy under Cardoso'. *World Development*, 28(10), 1805–19.
Anuatti-Neto, F., M. Barossi-Filho, A.G. Carvalho and R. Macedo. 2003. *Costs and Benefits of Privatization: Evidence from Brazil*. Latin American Research Network Working Paper No. R455. Washington, DC: Inter-American Development Bank.
Arbache, J.S. 1999. 'Do Unions Always Decrease Wage Dispersion? The Case of Brazilian Manufacturing'. *Journal of Labor Research*, 20(3), 425–36.
Arbache, J.S., A. Dickerson and F. Green. 2004. 'Trade Liberalisation and Wages in Developing Countries'. *Economic Journal*, 114, F73–F96.
Barros, R.P. and R. Mendonça. 1995. *Os Determinantes da Desigualdade no Brasil*. Texto para Discussão No. 377. Rio de Janeiro: Institute for Applied Economic Research.
Barros, R.P., R. Henriques and R. Mendonça. 2001. *A Estabilidade Inaceitável: Desigualdade e Pobreza no Brasil*. Texto para Discussão No. 800. Rio de Janeiro: Institute for Applied Economic Research.
Barros, R.P., C.H. Corseuil, R. Mendonça and M.C. Reis. 2000. *Poverty, Inequality and Macroeconomic Instability*. Texto para Discussão No. 750. Rio de Janeiro: Institute for Applied Economic Research.
Bugarin, M.S., R. Ellery Jr., V. Gomes and A. Teixeira. 2002. *The Brazilian Depression in the 1980s and 1990s*. Paper presented at the 2003 Brazilian Econometric Society Meeting, Porto Seguro, Bahia, 10–12 December.
Carvalho, M.A.S. 2001. *Privatização, Divida e Déficit Público no Brasil*. Texto para Discussão No. 847. Rio de Janeiro: Institute for Applied Economic Research.
Danni, L.S. 2004. Análise do Efeito Distributivo das Reformas Regulatórias e Privatização dos Serviços Públicos no Brasil. Dissertacao de Mestrado, Universidade de Brasilia, Brasília.
Edwards, S. 1994. *Macroeconomic Stabilization in Latin America: Recent Experience and Some Sequencing Issues*. Working Paper No. 4697. Cambridge, MA: National Bureau of Economic Research.

Ferreira, F.H.G. and J.A. Litchfield. 1999. *Education or Inflation? The Roles of Structural Factors and Macroeconomic Instability in Explaining Brazilian Inequality in the 1980s*. DP-DARP No. 41. London: STICERD-LSE.

Ferreira, P.C. and J.L. Rossi. 2003. 'New Evidence from Brazil on Trade Liberalization and Productivity Growth'. *International Economic Review*, 44(4), 1383–405.

Fiani, R. 2002. *Os desafios da estrutura tarifária*. Rio de Janeiro: GESEL-IE-UFRJ.

Franco, J. 2004. *Política Monetária, Estrutura a Termo da Taxa de Juros, Dívida Pública e Prêmio de Risco*. Tese de Doutorado, Universidade de Brasilia, Brasilia.

Green, F., A. Dickerson and J.S. Arbache. 2001. 'A Picture of Wage Inequality and the Allocation of Labour Through a Period of Trade Liberalization: The Case of Brazil'. *World Development*, 29(11), 1923–39.

Hay, D. 2001. 'The Post-1990 Brazilian Trade Liberalization and the Performance of Large Manufacturing Firms: Productivity, Market Share and Profits'. *Economic Journal*, 111(473), 620–41.

Hoffmann, R. 1995. 'Desigualdade e Pobreza no Brasil no Período 1979–90'. *Revista Brasileira de Economia*, 49, 277–94.

Krueger, A.O. 1981. 'Interaction Between Inflation and Trade Regime Objectives in Stabilization Programs'. In W. Cline and S. Weintraub (eds), *Economic Stabilization in Developing Countries*. Washington, DC: Brookings Institution.

Kume, H., G. Piani and C.F. Souza. 2003. 'A política brasileira de importação no período 1987–98: Descrição e Avaliação'. In C.H. Corseuil and H. Kume (eds), *A Abertura Comercial nos Anos 1990 – Impactos Sobre emprego e Salários*. Brasilia: Ministério do Trabalho e Emprego and IPEA.

Macedo, R. 2000. *Privatization and Distribution of Assets and Income in Brazil*. Working Paper No. 14. Washington, DC: Carnegie Endowment for International Peace.

Maia, K. and J.S. Arbache. 2001. *O Impacto do Comércio Internacional e da Tecnologia na Estrutura de Emprego no Brasil*. Mercado de Trabalho–Conjuntura e Análise No. 16. Rio de Janeiro: Institute for Applied Economic Research.

Menezes-Filho, N. and L. Vasconcellos. 2004. *Has Economic Growth been Pro-poor in Brazil? Why?* Mimeo, University of São Paulo, São Paulo.

Mota, R.L. 2003. *The Restructuring and Privatization of Electricity Distribution and Supply Businesses in Brazil: A Social Cost–Benefit Analysis*. Mimeo, University of Cambridge, Cambridge.

Muendler, M.A. 2004. *Trade, Technology, and Productivity: A Study of the Brazilian Manufacturers, 1986–1998*. Mimeo, University of California, San Diego.

Neri, M. 2005. *Miseria em Queda: Mensuracao, Monitoramento e Metas*. Centro de Politicas Sociais, Fundacao Getulio Vargas, Rio de Janeiro.

Pinheiro, A.C. 2003. *Uma Agenda Pós-liberal de Desenvolvimento para o Brasil*. Texto para Discussão No. 847. Rio de Janeiro: Institute for Applied Economic Research.

Pinheiro, A.C., F. Giambiagi and M.M. Moreira. 2001. *Brazil in the 1990s: A Successful Transition?*, Texto para Discussão No. 91. Rio de Janeiro: Banco Nacional de Desenvolvimento Econômico e Social.

Portela, A., H. Zylberstajn and L. Afonso 2004. *O Sistema Previdenciário Brasileiro: Diagnóstico e Impactos Fiscais das Recentes Reformas*. Mimeo, Universidade de São Paulo, São Paulo.

Rocha, S. 2000. *Pobreza e Desigualdade no Brasil: O Esgotamento dos Efeitos Distributivos do Plano Real*, Texto para Discussão No. 721. Rio de Janeiro: Institute for Applied Economic Research.

Index

adequacy 146–50
  minimal 153–4
advantage of backwardness 287, 288
adverse shocks 144–6
Africa Growth and Opportunity Act 184
aggregate budget restraint 65
aggregate income 160
antirural bias 12
Argentina 5
  Austral Plan 6
  capital account adjustment 62
  FDI 128
  public expenditure 36
  tax revenue 114
Asia 99
Asian Development Bank 285
asset losses 89
Association of South East Asian Nations (ASEAN) 204, 206
Atkinson index 199
Austral Plan 6

balance of payments 89
Bangladesh, tax buoyancy 44
bankruptcies 89
baseline modification mechanisms 147
Bhutan, tax buoyancy 44
Bolivia 24, 305–25
  devaluation 319
  dynamic CGE model 316–21
  economic growth 312
    effect of shocks and policies 317
  economic indicators 309
  GDP 313
  growth incidence curve 311
  income inequality 310
  macroeconomic policies 306–14
    poverty impact 314–15
  poverty 310
    effect of shocks and policies 317
  Poverty Reduction Strategy Papers 318
  tax revenue 114
  tax structure 320
Brazil 24, 326–48
  capital account adjustment 62
  capital account liberalization 336–7
  Cruzado Plan 6
  economic growth 331
  economic indicators 329–30
  economic policy 327–30
    effect on growth 331, 337–9
    effect on poverty and inequality 331–2, 339–40
  economic stabilization 334–6
  exchange rate 334–7, 344–5
  FDI 128
  financial liberalization 336–7
  financial stability 344–5
  fiscal accounts 344–5
  Gini coefficient 327
  income distribution 343–4
  income inequality 331–2, 339–40
  interest rate 344–5
  market deregulation 333–4
  market integration 346
  output growth 327, 342–3
  Plano Real 334, 335
  poverty 331–2, 339–40
    and income distribution 343–4
    and output growth 342–3
  privatization 333
  social indicators 327, 329
  tax revenue 114
  trade liberalization 332–3
Bulgaria
  FDI 128
  IMF programmes 62
Burkina Faso, tax buoyancy 44
Burundi, tax buoyancy 44

Cameroon
  public expenditure 36
  tax buoyancy 44
capital account 3, 4, 7–11, 13
  effects of devaluation 86–7
capital account liberalization 9–10, 75–6
  Brazil 336–7
capital controls 108–10
capital inflow
  controlling 14–15
  sectoral allocation 14–15
capital outflow 209
catastrophe bonds 158
Central Asian Republics 282
  GDP index 283
Chad, tax buoyancy 44

349

Chile 16, 21, 24, 217–47
  credit access 243
  current account, terms of trade and
      external debt 227–8
  disinflation and monetary policy 226–7
  economic growth 228–31, 242
  economy 219–22
  employment patterns 235
  exchange rate policy 224–5
  FDI 128
  fiscal policy 223–4
  gross domestic product 221
  income distribution 232–43, 237–9
  inflation 222
  macroeconomic indicators 222
  macroeconomic policies 223–31, 242
  poverty 232–43
    regional distribution 234–5
  poverty alleviation 241–2
  public expenditure 36
  segmentation of labour market 235–6
  social policies 241
  social subsidies 239–41
  sociodemographic profile 235
  stabilization funds 40, 41
  tax revenue 114
  unremunerated reserve requirement 109
  women's participation 237
China 4, 24, 97, 113, 261–77
  budget surplus/deficit to GDP ratio 263
  economic growth 25, 229
  economic reform 263–5
  fixed assets formation 271, 272
  foreign investment 14
  GDP 267, 268
  Gini coefficient 273
  income inequality 274
  inflation 267, 268
  investment 266, 267
  macroeconomic trends 265–73
  non-performing loans 269
  poverty 279
  poverty alleviation 273–7
  Poverty Reduction Plan 274–5
  tax–GDP ratios 31
civil liberties 110
Colombia 15
  public expenditure 36
  tax revenue 114
Commodity Price Insurance 158
Commonwealth and Small States Disaster
    Management Scheme 156
Comoros, tax buoyancy 44
Compensatory Financing Facility 17
Congo, tax buoyancy 44

consumer goods, price of 91
consumption instability 12
contingency rules 16–17
Costa Rica, tax revenue 114
Côte d'Ivoire, tax buoyancy 44
credibility 89–90
credit availability 91–2
crisis management 28
  insulation of poor from crises 30–5
  pro-poor mode 18–23
crisis prevention 13–18
  controlling capital inflows and harnessing
      sectoral allocation 14–15
  international safety nets 17–18
  limitation of foreign debts 13–14
  mobilization of savings 13–14
  pro-poor exchange rate regime 15–16
  stabilization funds and contingency rules
      16–17
Croatia, FDI 128
crony capitalism 213
Cruzado Plan 6
current account 227–8
current account balance 63
Czech Republic, FDI 128
Czechoslovakia, IMF programmes 62

deficit reduction 19–20
  how to achieve 20–1
deficit size 19–20
devaluation 18–19, 84–7
  Bolivia 319
  capital account effects 86–7
  impact on growth 86
  poverty impact matrix 93
  structural effects 85–6
developing countries
  FDI 127–32
  fiscal policy 28
  lack of financial depth 29
  pro-poor deficit finance policy 41–5
  pro-poor expenditure reform 37–8
  pro-poor tax reforms 35–41
  public expenditure reform 36–7
  tax policy 31–5
development policies 150
development strategy approach 82–4
distributional effects 53–4
Doha Development Agenda 190
domestic credit market 112
domestic institutions 121–2
domestic safety nets 21
Dominican Republic
  public expenditure 36
  tax revenue 114

East Asian crisis 49
economic growth 85–6, 148
  Bolivia 312
    effect of shocks and policies 317
  Brazil 331
  Chile 228–31, 242
  China 25, 229
  and FDI 124–7, 134–6
  impact of devaluation on 86
  India 251
  instability 12
  literature analysis 138–9
  Malaysia 199–201
  and portfolio flows 100–1
  and poverty 101
  Uzbekistan 285
economic indicators
  Bolivia 309
  Brazil 329–30
  Mauritius 172–4, 181–3, 186–7
economic performance, and exchange rate 84
economic reform
  China 263–5
  India 256–8
economic stabilization
  Brazil 334–6
  emerging economies 110–11
  monetary approaches to 49–74
  overkill 8–9
  pro-poor 67–9
  and self-insurance 151–2
  space of 22
  Uzbekistan 286–7
Ecuador, tax revenue 114
efficiency seeking 121
Egypt
  public expenditure 36
  tax–GDP ratios 31
El Salvador, tax revenue 114
emerging economies, stabilization of 110–11
employment 11–12
  Chile 235
  India 251
  Uzbekistan 300
Estonia, FDI 128
Ethopia, tax buoyancy 44
European Bank for Construction and Development 285
exchange rate 20, 75–96
  adjustment 18–19
  Brazil 334–7, 344–5
  Chile 224–5
  development strategy approach 82–4

distributive effects 92–4
and economic performance 84
and income distribution 90–4
Mauritius 172, 178–9, 196
nominal 87–8
nominal anchor approach 80–1
post-1991 de jure and de facto 75–8
pro-poor 15–16
  crisis situations 84–90
  normal conditions 80–4
real targets approach 81–2
Uzbekistan 286
expenditure 65–7
expenditure cuts 21–2
expenditure reform, pro-poor 37–8
Export Processing Zone 169, 170, 183, 184
exports 89
external debt 227–8
external finance 29

FDI *see* foreign direct investment
financial crises, and portfolio flows 103–6
financial liberalization 100
  Brazil 336–7
  Malaysia 204–6
  Mauritius 176–83
  Uzbekistan 300–2
financial programming model 58–60
financial repression 5
fiscal deficit 29–30
fiscal policy 19–20
  Chile 223–4
  developing countries 28
  Malaysia 195–6, 201–2
  Mauritius 171, 176–8, 185
  pro-poor institutional reform 40–1
fiscal space 21
fixed nominal exchange rate 5
FLEX fund 17, 157
foreign aid 20
foreign direct investment 8, 29, 98
  developed and developing countries 127–32
  and economic growth 124–7
  effects on growth and inequality 119–43
  growth and income inequality 134–6
  India 257
  literature analysis 138–9
  Malaysia 128, 201
  Mauritius 171, 180–1, 186
foreign exchange regimes 78–80
  free floats 80
  intermediate regimes 79
  pegged regimes 78–9

foreign public debt 20, 21
  limitation of 13–14
foreign trade, exclusion from 89–90
France, FDI 128
free floats 80

Gambia, tax buoyancy 44
GDP 5, 29, 88, 169
  Bolivia 313
  Central Asian Republics 283
  Chile 221
  China 267, 268
  Uzbekistan 288
General Agreement on Tariffs and Trade (GATT), Uruguay Round 206
Germany, FDI 128
Ghana 90
  tax buoyancy 44
  tax reforms 34
Gini coefficient 199
  Brazil 327
  China 273
  Mauritius 174
  Uzbekistan 295, 298
Global Commodity Insurer 158
global contingency fund 159
global reinsurance fund 160–1
globalization 97, 242
globalized economy 27–48
gross domestic investment 64
gross domestic product *see* GDP
Guatemala, tax revenue 114
Guinea, tax buoyancy 44
Guinea-Bissau, tax buoyancy 44

Haiti, tax buoyancy 44
headcount ratio 50–1
  sources of change 51–2
Honduras, tax revenue 114
Hong Kong, economic growth 229
Hungary
  FDI 128
  IMF programmes 62

IMF 4, 43, 291, 335
  World Economic Outlook projections 99
IMF monetary model
  123PRSP model 60
  financial programming approach 58–60
  Polak version 55–8
IMF programmes 62
  current account balance 63
  gross domestic investment 64
impossible trinity debate 10, 80, 81, 83

income distribution 90–4
  Brazil 343–4
  Chile 237–9
  Uzbekistan 297
income fluctuations 145
income inequality 132–4
  Brazil 331–2, 339–40
  China 274
  and FDI 134–6
  India 258–60
  Uzbekistan 290
incomplete institutions 9
index numbers 153
India 4, 15, 29, 106–8, 113, 248–61
  capital inflows and foreign exchange 107
  economic growth 251
  economic recovery 251–6
  economic reforms 256–8
  employment growth 251
  Employment Guarantee Scheme 38, 163
  FDI 257
  income growth rate 250
  investment 256
  per capita income 258
  poverty
    and agricultural growth 260–1
    and income inequality 258–60
    and non-agricultural activity 260–1
  public expenditure 36
  tax–GDP ratio 255
  tax buoyancy 44
  tax reforms 35
  terms of trade 253
  total government expenditure 254
Indonesia
  capital account adjustment 62
  FDI 128
  poverty ratio 49
  public expenditure 36
  tax buoyancy 44
inflation
  Chile 222, 226–7
  China 267, 268
  devaluation-induced 86
  Mauritius 180
  and poverty 84–5, 88–9
  targeting 22–3
insurance 154–5
insurance equivalence 153
insurance policies 151–3
insurance schemes 155–7
interest rates 88
  Brazil 344–5

interest rates – *continued*
  Mauritius   180
  Uzbekistan   285
intermediate currency regimes   79
intermediate macroeconomic regimes   6–8
International Cocoa Agreement   156
International Coffee Agreement   156
International Fund for Agricultural Diversification   188
International Monetary Fund *see* IMF
International Natural Rubber Agreement   156
international safety nets   17–18
International Tin Agreement   156
Inti Plan   6
investment
  China   266, 267
  India   256
  Malaysia   201
Ireland, economic growth   229
Israel   7
Italy, FDI   128

Kazakhstan   282
Kenya, tax buoyancy   44
Keynes, John Maynard   156
Keynesian approach   88
Korea
  capital account adjustment   62
  FDI   128
Kuala Lumpur Composite Index   209
Kuznets hypothesis   174

labour market   91
Latin America   4, 27
  economic growth   229
Latvia, FDI   128
least developed countries   126
Lesotho, tax buoyancy   44
liberal macroeconomics   8–13
  financial liberalization and antirural bias   12
  frequent crises   13
  growth and consumption instability   12
  incomplete institutions   9
  loss of domestic policy making   9–10
  policy instruments vs policy reversals   10–11
  sequencing problems   9
  stabilization overkill   8–9
  trade and financial globalization   11–12
Liberia, tax buoyancy   44
Lithuania, FDI   128

Lome Convention   17, 156, 171, 174
Lorenz curve   53, 71

macroeconomics   3
macroeconomic indicators   222
macroeconomic policies
  Bolivia   306–14
  Chile   223–31, 242
  Malaysia   194–201
  Uzbekistan   284–6
macroeconomic populism   6
Madagascar
  tax buoyancy   44
  tax reforms   34
Malawi, tax buoyancy   44
Malaysia   14, 15, 24, 193–216
  capital outflows   209
  crisis   209–11
    fiscal response to   211
  Employees' Provident Fund   196
  exchange rate adjustment   18
  external debt service ratio   205
  external sector   194–5
  FDI   128, 201
  federal government finance   198
  financial liberalization   204–6
  fiscal policy   195–6, 201–2
  household income   202
  macroeconomic policies   194–201
  macroeconomic targets   197
  merchandise account   207
  monetary policy   195
  net services balance   206
  New Economic Policy   193
  overall economic management   196–7
  policy impact and growth performance   199–201
  poverty   194
  poverty eradication expenditure   200
  privatization policy   202–3
  public expenditure   36
  savings and investment   201
  tax–GDP ratios   31
  taxation   203–4
Mali, tax buoyancy   44
marginal workers   258
market integration   346
market seeking   121
Marshall–Lerner conditions   85
Mauritania, tax buoyancy   44
Mauritius   7, 14, 24, 169–92
  debt policy   185–6
  dismantling of trade preferences   183–8
  econometric analysis   188–9

354 *Index*

Mauritius – *continued*
  economic growth   229
  economic indicators   172–4, 181–3, 186–7
  exchange rate regime   172, 178–9, 196
  Export Processing Zone   169, 170, 183, 184
  FDI   171, 180–1, 186
  financial and trade liberalization   176–83
  fiscal policy   171, 176–8, 185
  Gini coefficient   174
  inflation and interest rates   180
  Mauritius Tourism Promotion Authority   185
  monetary policy   178, 185
  National Housing Development Corporation   175
  poverty alleviation   188
  public debt   181
  social indicators   173, 181–3, 186–7
  Special Drawing Rights peg   172
  structural reforms and economic diversification   170–6
  sugar protocol uncertainty   183–8
  tax revenue   177
  Unemployment Hardship Relief scheme   175
  wage policy and labour productivity   179–80
  welfare state and pro-poor measures   175–6
Menchini, Leonardo   95
mergers and acquisitions   120, 122, 123, 128–9, 136, 137
Mexico   99
  capital account adjustment   62
  FDI   128
  poverty ratio   49
  Progresa 21–2, 45
  tax revenue   114
Middle East   4
Milesi-Ferretti, Gian Maria   95
Millennium Development Goals   3, 232, 305
monetary policy   22–3
  Chile   226–7
  Malaysia   195
  Mauritius   178, 185
money-based adjustment   18–19
Monterrey Partnership Consensus   190
moral hazard   89, 152
moral reasoning   153–4
Morocco, FDI   128
multinational banks   103
mutual insurance   152–3
Myanmar, tax buoyancy   44

national public debt   20, 21
Nepal, tax buoyancy   44
net capital flows   98
net income   52–3
Nicaragua   45
  tax buoyancy   44
  tax revenue   114
Nigeria, tax buoyancy   44
nominal anchor approach   80–1
nominal exchange rate   87–8
non-performing loans   269
non-tax revenue   20
non-traded sector   90
North Africa   4
Norway   16

Organization for Economic Co-operation and Development   111, 131
output contraction   88

Pacific Economic Cooperation forum   206
Pakistan
  tax buoyancy   44
  tax reforms   35
Panama, tax revenue   114
Papua New Guinea, tax reforms   34–5
Paraguay, tax revenue   114
Pareto income distribution   54, 70–1
pegged currency regimes   78–9
People's Bank of China   262
Peru   90
  Inti Plan   6
  tax revenue   114
Polak model   55–8
Poland
  FDI   128
  IMF programmes   62
policy framework   28–9
policy options   150–4
policy space   6–7
poor countries   144–6
populist macroeconomic policies   4–6
portfolio flows
  and domestic credit market   112
  and economic growth   100–1
  and economic performance   102
  and financial crises   103–6
  and income inequality   103
  poverty alleviation   100–1
    arguments against   101–6
  short-term   97
  trends in   98–100

poverty
  Bolivia 310
    effect of shocks and policies 317
  Brazil 331–2, 339–40
    and income distribution 343–4
    and output growth 342–3
  Chile 232–43
    regional distribution 234–5
  China 279
  and economic growth 101
  India
    and agricultural growth 260–1
    and income inequality 258–60
    and non-agricultural activity 260–1
  and inflation 84–5, 88–9
  Malaysia 194
  Mexico 49
  Uzbekistan 290–1, 299
poverty alleviation
  Chile 241–2
  China 273–7
  Mauritius 188
  Uzbekistan 297–300
poverty indicator 55–61
poverty line 52–3
  attending to 54–5
poverty ratio 49–74
Poverty Reduction and Growth Facility 17
primary public expenditure 20
privatization
  Brazil 333
  Malaysia 202–3
pro-poor growth 3, 305
  and macro policy 306
pro-poor macroeconomics 4, 21
  elements of 13–23
  123PRSP model 60
    Get-Real component 61
    Trivariate Var component 61
public expenditure reform 36–7

real targets approach 81–2
Relative Development Index 188
reserve funds 151–2
resource seeking 121
risk 146–50
risk modification mechanisms 147
risk reduction policies 150–1, 155–7
risk-sharing 152–3
Romania
  FDI 128
  IMF programmes 62
Russia 99
  capital account adjustment 62

Russian Federation 5
Rwanda, tax buoyancy 44

safety nets 21, 144–65, 314
savings
  Malaysia 201
  mobilization of 13–14, 111–14
Securities Exchange Board of India 106
self-insurance 151–2, 160
Senegal, tax buoyancy 44
sequencing 9
Sierra Leone, tax buoyancy 44
Singapore 15
  economic growth 229
Slovakia, FDI 128
Slovenia, FDI 128
small and medium-sized enterprises 5, 12, 103
social indicators
  Brazil 327, 329–30
  Mauritius 173, 181–3, 186–7
Solomon Islands, tax buoyancy 44
South Africa 29
  public expenditure 36
  tax reforms 35
  tax–GDP ratios 31
Spain, FDI 128
spillover effects 124
Sri Lanka 39, 132
  public expenditure 36
STABEX fund 17, 156, 163
stabilization funds 16–17, 40, 41
strategic asset seeking 121
sub-Saharan Africa 4
subsidy reform 39–40
SYSMIN fund 157

Taiwan 15
targeting 38–9
tax buoyancy 43, 44
tax elasticity 43
tax reforms 31–5
  pro-poor 35–41
tax revenue 113, 114
tax–GDP ratio 31, 32
  Chile 31
  India 255
taxation 20
  Malaysia 203–4
technology transfer 124
terms of trade
  Chile 227–8
  India 253

Thailand 132
　capital account adjustment 62
　FDI 128
　public expenditure 36
　tax–GDP ratios 31
Tobin taxes 109–10, 157
Togo, tax buoyancy 44
traded sector 90
Tunisia, FDI 128
Turkey 7
　capital account adjustment 62
　FDI 128
Turkmenistan 5, 282

Uganda
　economic growth 229
　tax buoyancy 44
　tax reforms 34
United Kingdom, FDI 128
United States, FDI 129, 130
unsustainable macroeconomic policies 4–6
Uruguay
　capital account adjustment 62
　tax revenue 114
Uzbekistan 5, 7, 282–304
　demand shocks 290
　economic growth 285, 294–5
　economic stabilization 286–7
　employment and incomes 300
　energy balance 287
　exchange rates 286
　exogenous shocks 283
　financial liberalization 300–2
　foreign trade subsidies 294
　GDP growth rate 288

Gini coefficient 295, 298
government expenditure, revenue and
　　budget balance 284
implicit taxes 294
import-substitution industrialization
　291–300
income distribution 297
income inequality 290, 295–7
interest rates 285
international transactions 286
macroeconomic policies 284–6
macroeconomic stabilization 283–91
poverty 290–1, 299
poverty alleviation 297–300

value added tax 33
Venezuela 16
　stabilization funds 40, 41
　tax revenue 114
Viet Nam 4, 113
　tax buoyancy 44
volatility 154–5

wage goods 85, 91
Washington Consensus 308
World Bank 23, 285

Yemen,
　tax buoyancy 44

Zambia 27
　tax buoyancy 44
Zimbabwe 27
　public expenditure 36
　tax buoyancy 44